MAKING TRANSNATIONAL LAW WORK IN THE GLOBAL ECONOMY

This tribute to Professor Detlev Vagts of the Harvard Law School brings together his colleagues at Harvard and the American Society of International Law, as well as academics, judges and practitioners, many of them his former students. Their contributions span the entire spectrum of modern transnational law: international law in general; transnational economic law; and transnational lawyering and dispute resolution. The contributors evaluate established fields of transnational law, such as the protection of property and investment, and explore new areas of law which are in the process of detaching themselves from the nation-state, such as global administrative law and the regulation of cross-border lawyering. The implications of decentralised norm-making, the proliferation of dispute settlement mechanisms and the rising backlash against global legal interdependence in the form of demands for preserving State legal autonomy are also examined.

The editors of this volume represent three generations of Professor Detlev Vagts' Harvard students: RUDOLF DOLZER (LLM 1972, SJD 1979), PIETER H. F. BEKKER (LLM 1991) and MICHAEL WAIBEL (LLM 2008). Vagts' profound impact on academics and practitioners worldwide is evidenced by the background and geographical breadth of the contributors, twenty-three of whom have studied at Harvard Law School.

Professor Detlev Vagts

MAKING TRANSNATIONAL LAW WORK IN THE GLOBAL ECONOMY

Essays in Honour of Detlev Vagts

Edited by

PIETER H. F. BEKKER,
RUDOLF DOLZER
and
MICHAEL WAIBEL

CAMBRIDGE
UNIVERSITY PRESS

CAMBRIDGE UNIVERSITY PRESS
Cambridge, New York, Melbourne, Madrid, Cape Town, Singapore,
São Paulo, Delhi, Dubai, Tokyo, Mexico City

Cambridge University Press
The Edinburgh Building, Cambridge CB2 8RU, UK

Published in the United States of America by Cambridge University Press, New York

www.cambridge.org
Information on this title: www.cambridge.org/9780521192521

© Cambridge University Press 2010

First published 2010

Printed in the United Kingdom at the University Press, Cambridge

A catalogue record for this publication is available from the British Library

Library of Congress Cataloguing in Publication data
Making transnational law work in the global economy : essays in honour of Detlev
Vagts / edited by Pieter Bekker, Rudolf Dolzer and Michael Waibel.
p.   cm.
Includes bibliographical references and index.
ISBN 978-0-521-19252-1 (hardback)
1. Law.   2. International and municipal law.   3. International law.
I. Bekker, Pieter H. F.   II. Dolzer, Rudolf.   III. Waibel, Michael
IV. Vagts, Detlev F.   V. Title.
K561.M295   2010
341–dc22
2010027669

ISBN 978-0-521-19252-1 Hardback

CONTENTS

CONTRIBUTORS

WILLIAM P. ALFORD
Henry L. Stimson Professor of Law, Vice-Dean for the Graduate Program and International Legal Studies, Director of East Asian Legal Studies, Harvard Law School

ANTONY ANGHIE
Samuel D. Thurman Professor of Law, S.J. Quinney College of Law, University of Utah

PIETER H. F. BEKKER
Member of the Bar of New York; Adjunct professor in international investment law and arbitration, Columbia Law School, New York

ANDREA BIANCHI
Professor of International Law, Graduate Institute of International and Development Studies, Geneva

CHARLES N. BROWER
Judge, Iran–United States Claims Tribunal, The Hague; Member, 20 Essex Street Chambers, London. Formerly Acting Legal Adviser of the United States Department of State and Deputy Special Counsellor to the President of the United States

JAN H. DALHUISEN
Professor of Law, School of Law, King's College London; Miranda Chair in Transnational Financial Law, Catholic University Lisbon

JOST DELBRÜCK
Professor of Law Emeritus, Kiel University

OLIVIER DE SCHUTTER
Professor of Law, University of Louvain and College of Europe; UN Special Rapporteur on the right to food

WILLIAM S. DODGE
Professor of Law, University of California, Hastings College of the Law

RUDOLF DOLZER
Professor of Law and Director, Institut für Völkerrecht, Bonn University

JEAN NICOLAS DRUEY
Professor of Law, St. Gallen University

WERNER F. EBKE
Professor of Law and Director, Institut für deutsches und europäisches Gesellschafts- und Wirtschaftsrecht, University of Heidelberg

BARDO FASSBENDER
Professor of International Law, Bundeswehr University, Munich

DANIEL KALDERIMIS
Principal, Chapman Tripp, Wellington

JULIANE KOKOTT
Advocate General, European Court of Justice, Luxembourg; Professor of Law, St. Gallen University

BARTON LEGUM
Partner and Head of Investment Treaty Arbitration, Salans LLP, Paris

CALINE MOUAWAD
Counsel, King & Spalding, New York

PETER L. MURRAY
Robert Braucher Visiting Professor of Law from Practice, Harvard Law School

GEORGE C. NNONA
Professor of Law, Roger Williams University School of Law, Bristol, Rhode Island

WILLIAM W. PARK
Professor of Law, Boston University; President, London Court of International Arbitration

ANDREAS L. PAULUS
Professor of Public and International Law, Georg-August-University, Göttingen; Judge, German Federal Constitutional Court

HERNÁN PÉREZ LOOSE
Partner, Coronel y Pérez, Guayaquil

ANNE PETERS
Professor of International Law and Constitutional Law, Basel University

JULIA YA QIN
Professor of Law, Wayne State University Law School, Detroit

CATHERINE A. ROGERS
Professor of Law, Penn State University, University Park, Pennsylvania; Università Commerciale Luigi Bocconi, Milan

JESWALD W. SALACUSE
Henry J. Braker Professor of Law, Fletcher School of Law and Diplomacy, Tufts University, Medford

STEPHAN W. SCHILL
Senior Research Fellow, Max Planck Institute for Comparative Public Law and International Law, Heidelberg

HENRY J. STEINER
Jeremiah Smith, Jr. Professor of Law, Emeritus, Harvard Law School

MICHAEL WAIBEL
British Academy Postdoctoral Fellow, Lauterpacht Centre for International Law and Downing College, University of Cambridge

DAVID A. WESTBROOK
Floyd H. and Hilda L. Hurst Faculty Scholar, Professor of Law, State University of New York at Buffalo

SIEGFRIED WIESSNER
Professor of Law, Director of the Graduate Program in Intercultural Human Rights, St. Thomas University School of Law, Miami

JAN WOUTERS
Professor of International Law and International Organisations, Jean Monnet
Chair *ad Personam* The European Union and Global Governance,
Director of the Leuven Centre for Global Governance Studies and
Institute for International Law, Catholic University of Leuven

ANDREAS ZIMMERMANN
Professor of International Law, Director of the Potsdam Center of
Human Rights, University of Potsdam

FOREWORD: THE TRANSNATIONALISM OF DETLEV VAGTS

HAROLD HONGJU KOH*

Before meeting in person, scholars often meet in print. And so it was that, more than three decades ago, I met Detlev Vagts, Harvard's Bemis Professor of International Law, in the pages of *Transnational Legal Problems*, a book we later came to co-author.[1] I had seen him from a distance long before, when I was a Harvard law student. Although I never took his class, I often saw him sitting in his office deep in the stacks of the Langdell Library, usually with his door open, absorbed in a book he had pulled from the shelves. Someone told me that he was the son of a German scholar who had fled Nazi Germany. I heard from another that he was a man of great moral fiber, who would occasionally preach at Harvard's Memorial Church or speak with passion at contentious faculty meetings.

But I did not come to know Vagts' mind until I had graduated from law school, and started teaching International Business Transactions at night as an instructor at George Washington University Law School. As a young international lawyer in Washington in the 1980s, one day I found myself spending my whole day with Vagts the scholar: conducting research during the day as a Justice Department lawyer leafing through the *American Journal of International Law (AJIL)*, for which he wrote and later served as Co-Editor-in-Chief; ducking out of work at lunchtime to attend a public session of the American Law Institute regarding the *Restatement (Third) of the Foreign Relations Law of the United States*,[2] of which Vagts was Associate Reporter; then teaching at night from the 2nd edition of *Transnational Legal Problems* by Steiner and Vagts.[3] I came to appreciate the startling breadth of

---

* Legal Adviser, US Department of State (2009–); US Assistant Secretary of State for Democracy, Human Rights and Labor (1998–2001); Martin R. Flug '55 Professor of International Law (on leave) and former Dean (2004–9), Yale Law School.
[1] See D. F. Vagts, H. J. Steiner and H. H. Koh, *Transnational Legal Problems*, 4th edn. (Westbury, NY: Foundation Press, 1994); D. F. Vagts, W. S. Dodge, and H. H. Koh. *Transnational Business Problems*, 4th edn. (Westbury, NY: Foundation Press, 2008).
[2] *Restatement (Third) of the Foreign Relations Law of the United States* (1990).
[3] H. J. Steiner and D. F. Vagts, *Transnational Legal Problems*, 2nd edn. (Westbury, NY: Foundation Press, 1976).

Vagts' knowledge of law, spanning public and private international law, international dispute resolution, comparative law, military law, the law of development, professional responsibility, securities regulation, and corporate law. He seemed the complete transnationalist legal scholar.

When I began to teach from *Transnational Legal Problems*, a totally revised version of the Harvard casebook first developed by Milton Katz and Kingman Brewster,[4] I began to realize that Vagts' view was revolutionary. Instead of accepting the formalistic divide that created a 2×2 matrix between public and private, domestic, and international law, his casebook "exploded the matrix": it cut across issue areas ranging from international human rights to trade, environment, international business transactions, and the law of US foreign policy. All transnational legal issues, he and his co-author Henry Steiner reasoned, "occupy different positions on a spectrum between the extremes of 'national' and 'international' law, or on one between 'private' and 'public' law."[5] Just before I started teaching full-time, I was asked to write a book review of *Transnational Legal Problems*.[6] A few months later, to my amazement, I received a letter from Detlev Vagts, saying that he had read the book review and wondering whether I might join the authors as their junior member.

When I finally met Detlev Vagts in the flesh, he struck me – from the start, and ever since – as a supremely gentle, wise, and gracious man. He revealed a wry sense of humor and an unshakeable sense of decency. Over annual lunches at the American Society of International Law Meetings, we would discuss each round of revisions. In between, I learned from both his humanity and his work ethic, which led him, like clockwork, to send me drafts of each of his chapters long before my own had been revised.

During the same time, in my own scholarly work, I began more fully to appreciate what Detlev Vagts had brought to international legal theory. Vagts and Steiner inaugurated what I have since called the study of "transnational legal process": the theory and practice of how public and private actors interact in a variety of public and private, domestic and international fora to make, interpret, internalize, and enforce rules of transnational law.[7] Transnational legal process focuses on the

---

[4] See M. Katz and K. Brewster, Jr., *Law of International Transactions and Relations* (London: Stevens & Sons, 1960).

[5] Steiner and Vagts, *Transnational Legal Problems*, *supra* n. 3, xvii.

[6] H. H. Koh, Book Review of H. J. Steiner and D. F. Vagts, *Transnational Legal Problems*, 3rd edn. (Westbury, NY: Foundation Press, 1986) and D. F. Vagts, *Transnational Business Problems* (Westbury, NY: Foundation Press, 1986), *International Lawyer*, 20 (1986), 1417–24.

[7] H. H. Koh, "Transnational Legal Process," *Nebraska Law Review*, 75 (1996), 181–207.

transnational, normative, and constitutive character of global legal process: *transnational*, in the sense of cutting across historical private–
public, domestic–international dichotomies; *normative*, in the sense of
illustrating how legal rules generated by interactions among transnational actors shape and guide future transnational interactions; and
constitutive, in the sense of dynamically mutating from public to private,
domestic to international and back again in a way that reconstitutes
national interests.[8]

After September 11, 2001, Vagts' scholarship reaffirmed his unwavering
commitment to the rule of international law. He challenged expedient resort
to a military paradigm in a time of terror,[9] and reminded us of the role of
international lawyers as guardians of ethical professional behavior in international dispute resolution.[10] From my current post, I am particularly
moved by Vagts' depiction of the role of international lawyers in Nazi
Germany, an object lesson for any government legal adviser.[11]

This sweeping *Festschrift*, edited by Detlev Vagts' devoted former students and friends Pieter Bekker, Rudolf Dolzer, and Michael Waibel, unites
the varied subject matters of Vagts' life's work under the title of *Making
Transnational Law Work in the Global Economy*. The editors bring together
works by many of Vagts' most illustrious colleagues and students under
three headings: International Law in General; Transnational Economic Law;
and Transnational Lawyering and Dispute Resolution. The chapters in this
collection highlight the key leitmotifs of Vagts' career: the critical role of the
transnational lawyer, the function of transnational law in the global economy, and transnational law and institutions as tools for the peaceful resolution of disputes. Although the chapters that follow are varied, they grow out
of a common inspiration: the admirable accomplishments of a student of
legal process, a mentor of integrity and principle, and a seminal scholar of
transnationalism.

---

[8] H. H. Koh, "Why Do Nations Obey International Law?," *Yale Law Journal*, 106 (1997),
2599–2659.

[9] D. F. Vagts, "Military Commissions. The Forgotten Reconstruction Chapter," *American
University International Law Review*, 23 (2008), 231–74; D. F. Vagts, "Military
Commissions. A Concise History," *AJIL*, 101 (2007), 35–48; D. F. Vagts, "Which
Courts Should Try Persons Accused of Terrorism?," *EJIL*, 14 (2003), 313–26.

[10] D. F. Vagts, "Professional Responsibility in Transborder Practice. Conflict and Resolution,"
Georgetown Journal of Legal Ethics, 13 (2000), 677–98; D. F. Vagts, "The Impact of
Globalization on the Legal Profession," *European Journal of Law Reform*, 2 (2000),
403–14; D. F. Vagts, "The International Legal Profession. A Need for More
Governance?," *AJIL*, 90 (1996), 250–62.

[11] D. F. Vagts, "International Law in the Third Reich," *AJIL*, 84 (1990), 661–704.

CASES CITED

Commission *v.* Sweden (Case C-249/06) [2009]

Commission *v.* United Kingdom (Case C-146/89) ECR I-3533 [1991]

Commission *v.* United Kingdom (Case C-246/89) [1991] ECR I-4585

Commission v. United Kingdom (Case 382/92) [1994] ECR I-2435

Committee of United States Citizens Living in Nicaragua [CUSCLIN] *v.* Reagan 859 F.2d 929 (1988)

Commonwealth Coatings Corp. *v.* Continental Casualty Co. 393 US 145 (1968)

Commune de Mesquer (Case C-188/07) [2008] ECR I-4501

Compagnie nouvelle de gaz de Deville-lès Rouen *v.* Deville-les Rouen 1902

Compagnie Générale des Eaux de Caracas (Belgium *v.* Venezuela) 9 *RIAA* 329 (1903)

Compagnie nouvelle du gaz de Déville-lès-Rouen *v.* Déville-lès-Rouen, Sirey 1902, III, 563

Connelly *v.* RTZ Corp. plc and Others [1997] UKHL 30; [1998] AC 854; [1997] 4 All ER 335; [1997] 3 WLR 373

Consortium RFCC *v.* Kingdom of Morocco 2003

Consorzio Groupement LESI–DIPENTA *v.* People's Democratic Republic Algeria ICSID Case No. ARB/03/8 (2005)

Container Corp. of America *v.* Franchise Tax Bd 463 US 159 (1983)

Corfu Channel (UK *v.* Albania) 1949 ICJ Rep. 4

Costa *v.* ENEL (Case 6/64) [1964] ECR 585

Cunard SS Co. *v.* Mellon 262 US 100 (1923)

Dearle *v.* Hall 3 Russ. 1 (1828)

Debenture Holders of the San Marcos & Pinos Co. (UK *v.* Mexico) 5 191 (1931)

Demirel (Case 12/86) [1987] ECR 3719

Deutsche Bank AG *v.* Democratic Socialist Republic of Sri Lanka ICSID Case No. ARB/09/2 (2009)

Dickson Car Wheel Company (USA) v. United Mexican States 4 *RIAA* (2002)

Didier Mayeur *v.* Associations Promotion d'Information Messine (APIM) (Case C-175/99) [2000] ECR I-7755

Dispute Regarding Navigational and Related Matters (Costa Rica *v.* Nicaragua) 2009 ICJ Rep.

Doe *v.* Unocal 27 F.Supp. 2d 1174 (1998)

Dr. Bonham's Case 77 Eng. Rep. 646 (1610)

Dred Scott *v.* Sandford 60 US 393 (1856)

Duke Energy *v.* Perú 2006

Dyestuffs, Imperial Chemical Industries *v.* Commission (Case 48/69) [1972] ECR 619

EEA Agreement I [1991] ECR I-6079

Elettronica Sicula SpA (ELSI) (United States of America *v.* Italy) 1989 ICJ Rep. 15

Ella Wyman FCSC Claim Nos. CZ-4347–4348 (1960)

Elmar Gundel *v.* Fédération internationale d'équitation [ATF] 119 (1993)

El-Yassini *v.* Secretary of State for Home Department (Case C-416/96) [1999] ECR I-1209

Emil Bohadlo Claim No. CZ-1734 (1962)

Emma Brunner Docket Y-1281 1954

Handyside v. United Kingdom ser. A No. 24 §62 (1976)

Hanson v. Deckel 357 US 235 (1958)

Harper v. Virginia State Bd of Elections 383 US 663 (1996)

Hartford Fire Ins. Co. v. California 509 US 764 (1993)

Hauptzollamt Mainz v. Kupferberg (Case 104/81) [1982] ECR I-3641

Head Money Cases 112 US 580 (1884)

Heald v. District of Columbia 259 US 114 (1922)

Hepburn and Dundas v. Ellzey 6 US (2 Cranch) 445 (1805)

Hewlett v. Minister of Finance and Another 1982 (1) SA 490 (ZSC)

Hill v. Tupper [1863] 2 Hurlst. 7 C 121

Horst Ziemann v. Ziemann Sicherheit GmbH and Horst Bohn Sicherheitsdienst [1998]
    ECR I-8237

Hrvatska Elektroprivreda d.d.[HEP] v. The Republic of Slovenia ICSID Case No. ARB/
    05/24 (2008)

Hughes de Lasteyrie du Saillant v. Ministère de L'Économie, des Finances et de
    l'Industrie (Case C-9/02) [2004] ECR I-2409

IATA and ELFAA (Case C-344/04) [2006] ECR I-403

Imperial Chemical Industries Ltd v. Commission (Case 48/69) [1972] ECR 619

Impregilo v. Pakistan ICSID Case No. ARB/03/3 12 *ICSID Reports* 245 2005

Ina M. Hofmann and Dulce H. Steinhardt v. The Republic of Turkey American–
    Turkish Claims Commission (1937)

In re Agent Orange Product Liability Litigation 373 F.Supp. 2d 598 (2000)

In re Medicaments & Related Classes of Goods (No. 2) [2001] 1 WLR 700 (CA)

In re The Owners of the Steamship Catalina & The Owners of the Motor Vessel Norma
    Lloyd's Rep. 61 (1938)

In the Case of James and Others 8 EIIRR 123 (1986)

Interfoto Picture Library Ltd v. Stiletto Visual Pictures Ltd [1989] 1 QB 433

International Agreement on Natural Rubber [1979] ECR

International Fruit Company and Others (Cases 21/72 to 24/72) [1972] ECR 1219

International Shoe v. Washington 326 US 310 (1945)

International Thunderbird Gaming v. The United Mexican States UNCITRAL
    NAFTA 2006

Internationale Handelsgesellschaft (Case 11/70) [1970] ECR

Intertanko (Case C-308/06) [2008] ECR I-4057

Ireland v. United Kingdom (Case 5310/7) (1978) ECtHR

Irene Bogiatzi, married name Ventouras v. Deutsches Luftpool, Luxaire SA, European
    Communities, State of the Grand Duchy of Luxembourg, Foyer Assurances SA
    (Case C-301/08) [2009]

Ivcher Bronstein Case (Baruch Ivcher Bronstein v. Peru) Inter-American Court of
    Human Rights 6 February 2001

James and Others v. The United Kingdom Application No. 8793/79
    ECHR

ABBREVIATIONS AND ACRONYMS

Selected journals and archive collections

AFDI	*L'Annuaire français de droit international*
AJIL	*American Journal of International Law*
AVR	*Archiv des Völkerrechts*
BSK	*Basler Kommentar*
BYBIL	*British Year Book of International Law*
CJTL	*Columbia Journal of Transnational Law*
CMLR	*Common Market Law Reports*
EJIL	*European Journal of International Law*
EuR	*Europarecht*
GYIL	*German Yearbook of International Law*
HILJ	*Harvard International Law Journal*
ICLQ	*International & Comparative Law Quarterly*
ILDC	*International Law in Domestic Courts*
ILM	*International Legal Materials*
ILR	*International Law Reports*
IP	*Internationale Politik*
Iprax	*Praxis des Internationalen Privat- und Verfahrensrechts*
Iran–US CTR	*Iran–US Claims Tribunal Reports*
JR	*Juristische Rundschau*
JZ	*Juristen Zeitung*
NJW	*Neue Juristische Wochenschrift*
RabelsZ	*Rabels Zeitschrift*
RADIC	*African Journal of International and Comparative Law*
RdC	*Recueil des Cours*
RGDIP	*Revue générale de droit international public*
RIAA	*Reports of International Arbitral Awards*
RIW	*Recht der Internationalen Wirtschaft*
SJZ	*Schweizerische Juristenzeitung*
YJIL	*Yale Journal of International Law*
ZaöRV	*Zeitschrift für ausländisches öffentliches Recht und Völkerrecht*

General abbreviations and acronyms

AAA	American Arbitration Association
ABA	American Bar Association
ADR	alternative dispute resolution
APEC	Asia–Pacific Economic Cooperation
ASEAN	Association of Southeast Asian Nations
ASIL	American Society of International Law
ATCA	Alien Tort Claims Act
BEPA	Bureau of European Policy Advisers
BIA	Bilateral Immunity Agreement
BIT	bilateral investment treaty
CAMA	Companies and Allied Matters Act (Nigeria)
CAS	Court of Arbitration for Sport
CBA	cost-benefit analysis
CCBE	Council of the Bars and Law Societies of Europe
CCP	Common Commercial Policy
CDPC	European Committee on Crime Problems
CEO	chief executive officer
CFI	Court of First Instance
CITES	Convention on International Trade in Endangered Species
DFCR	Draft Common Frame of Reference
DSU	Dispute Settlement Understanding
DSU	Understanding on Rules and Procedures Governing the Settlement of Disputes
EC	European Community
ECB	European Central Bank
ECHR	European Convention for the Protection of Human Rights and Fundamental Freedoms
ECJ	European Court of Justice
ECR	Court of Justice of the European Union; Reports of cases before the Court of Justice and the Court of First Instance
EDC	European Defence Community
EEA	European Economic Area
EEC	European Economic Community
EFTA	European Free Trade Association
EMU	European Monetary Union
ERTA	European Agreement on Road Transport
EU	European Union
FCC	Foreign Compensation Commission (UK)
FCSC	Foreign Claims Settlement Commission (US)
FDI	foreign direct investment

FINRA	Financial Industry Regulatory Authority
FTA	free trade area
FTAIA	Foreign Trade Antitrust Improvements Act
FTC	Free Trade Commission (NAFTA)
GAAP	Generally Accepted Accounting Principles (US)
GATT	General Agreement on Tariffs and Trade
GATS	General Agreement on Trade in Services
HIL	hegemonic international law
IBA	International Bar Association
IBRD	International Bank for Reconstruction and Development (World Bank)
ICC	International Chamber of Commerce
ICC	International Criminal Court
ICCPR	International Covenant on Civil and Political Rights
ICESCR	International Covenant on Economic, Social and Cultural Rights
ICJ	International Court of Justice
ICM	idealised cognitive model
ICSID	International Centre on Settlement of Investment Disputes
ICT	International Criminal Tribunal
ICTR	International Criminal Tribunal for Rwanda
ICTY	International Criminal Tribunal for the Former Yugoslavia
IFI	International Financial Institution
IHL	international human rights law
IHL	international humanitarian law
IIA	International Investment Agreement
ILA	International Law Association
ILC	International Law Commission
ILO	International Labour Organization
ILSA	International Law Students Association
IMF	International Monetary Fund
Incoterms	international sales terms (ICC)
INE	National Institute of Ecology (Mexico)
IOC	International Olympic Committee
IOSCO	International Organisation of Securities Commissions
IRS	Internal Revenue services (US)
ISA	Investment and Securities Act
ISO	International Standardisation Organisation
ITLOS	International Tribunal for the Law of the Sea
LCIA	London Court of International Arbitration
MAI	Multilateral Agreement on Investment
MDGs	Millennium Development Goals
MFN	Most Favoured Nation
MIA	Multilateral Investment Agreement
MNC	multinational corporation

MNE	multinational enterprise
MTA	Multilateral Trade Agreements
NAFTA	North American Free Trade Agreement
NAM	Non-Aligned Movement
NASD	National Association of Securities Dealers
NGO	non-governmental organisation
NIEO	New International Economic Order
NSDAP	German Nazi Party
NYSE	New York Stock Exchange
OAS	Organization of American States
OECD	Organisation for Economic Cooperation and Development
OSCE	Organisation for Security and Cooperation in Europe
PCA	Permanent Court of Arbitration
PCIJ	Permanent Court of International Justice
PPI	Producer Price Index (US)
RTA	regional trade agreement
SCSL	Special Court for Sierra Leone
SEA	Single European Act
SEC	Securities and Exchange Commission (US)
SFR	Socialist Federal Republic (of Yugoslavia)
SI	Statutory Instrument
SPE	European Private Company
TAS	Tribunal Arbitral du Sport
TEU	Treaty on European Union
TFEU	Treaty on the Functioning of the European Union (Lisbon Treaty)
TNC	transnational corporation
TRIMS	Agreement on Trade-Related Investment Measures
TRIPS	Agreement on Trade-Related Aspects of Intellectual Property Rights
UBS	Union Bank of Switzerland
UCC	Uniform Commercial Code
UCP	Uniform Customs and Practice for Documentary Credits
UMA	Uniform Mediation Act (US)
UNCITRAL	UN Commission on International Trade Law
UNCLOS	UN Convention on the Law of the Sea
UNDP	UN Development Programme
UNFCCC	UN Framework Convention on Climate Change
UNMIK	UN Interim Administration in Kosovo
UNTAET	UN Transitional Administration in East Timor
VCLT	Vienna Convention on the Law of Treaties
WHO	World Health Organization
WIPO	World Intellectual Property Organisation
WTO	World Trade Organization

Introduction: a *Festschrift* to celebrate Detlev Vagts' contributions to transnational law

PIETER H. F. BEKKER, RUDOLF DOLZER AND
MICHAEL WAIBEL

This *Festschrift* honours Professor Detlev Vagts and celebrates his profound scholarly contributions to and influence on the study and practice of transnational law over the last half-century.

On the occasion of his recent retirement from the Harvard Law School faculty and his eightieth birthday, the book brings together a wide range of leading scholars and practitioners from around the globe with a personal connection to the honouree: his colleagues at Harvard Law School and the American Society of International Law (ASIL, especially its Journal), as well as academics, judges and practitioners, many of them former students of Detlev Vagts, with whom his rich life and career have intersected. The book spans the entire spectrum of modern transnational law.

Soon after graduating from law school, Detlev Vagts realised that in the new reality of international relations, law may more readily be understood as extending beyond the classical State system. Philip Jessup, in his famous Storrs Lectures at Yale in 1956, labelled this phenomenon 'transnational law', which he defined as 'all law which regulates actions or events that transcend national frontiers. Both public and private international law are included, as are other rules which do not wholly fit into such standard categories.'[1] The increasing mobility of people, capital and goods required an expansion of the legal horizon beyond classical public international law and a State-centred view of norm-making. Since then, transnational law has moved to the centre of the law curriculum everywhere. For decades, it has been central to law practice in major world centres.

---

[1] P. C. Jessup, *Transnational Law* (New Haven, CT: Yale University Press, 1956).

1

Detlev Vagts became one of the founders of transnational law, along-side other legal giants such as Philip Jessup and Myres McDougal, and he played a central role in the transnational legal revolution, as described in the tribute by his Harvard colleague and contemporary Henry Steiner (chapter 2). Harvard Law School recruited Detlev Vagts in the old-fashioned way: seemingly out of the blue, he received a telephone call one day from Dean Erwin Griswold inviting him to join the Harvard faculty. In 1959, he became an assistant professor of law at his *alma mater*, eight years after graduating with his LLB in the class of 1951. He received tenure in 1962.

In 1984, having been the Eli Goldston Professor of Law for four years, Detlev Vagts was appointed Bemis Professor of International Law, the first chair of international law at Harvard Law School. George Bemis (1816–78), a prominent Boston lawyer, had endowed the Bemis profes-sorship at the end of the nineteenth century. Bemis prescribed that the holder of the chair shall 'aid the popular and professional understanding [of that special department of study and practice that is international law]. In that sense I should desire him to be not merely a professor of the science but a practicable co-operator in the work of advancing knowl-edge and good-will among nations and governments . . .. [T]he incum-bent should have had some official connection with public or diplomatic life, or at least have had an opportunity by foreign travel or residence to look at the United States from a foreign point of view, and so to estimate it as only one of the family of nations.'

Detlev Vagts' predecessors in the Bemis chair were the first Bemis professor, Edward H. Strobel (1897–1908), Jens I. Westengard (1915–18), Manley O. Hudson (1923–54) and Louis B. Sohn (1961–81). As the fifth Bemis Professor of International Law (1984–2005), Detlev Vagts played a central role in broadening the notion and understanding of international law and redefined its centre of gravity. He pioneered a comprehensive view, including not only classic interstate relations, but also the varied forms of non-governmental actors and institutions which emerged over the course of his academic career. The tribute by William Alford in this volume (chapter 1) highlights Detlev Vagts' many contributions to Harvard.

The first edition of his classic casebook entitled *Transnational Legal Problems* appeared in 1968 (with Henry Steiner; 2nd edn. 1976; 3rd edn. 1986; 4th edn. 1994, adding Yale's Harold Hongju Koh as co-editor). In its current edition, the book stands for a happy cooperation between Harvard and Yale. This cooperation is characteristic of the open and all-inclusive approach for which Detlev Vagts has stood throughout his life.

The first edition of *Transnational Business Problems* followed in 1986 (with William Dodge and Harold Koh as co-authors, 2nd edn. 1998; 3rd edn. 2003; 4th edn. 2008).

In the 1990s, Detlev Vagts served with distinction as Co-Editor-in-Chief of the *American Journal of International Law (AJIL)*, which is widely considered to be the world's leading scholarly journal devoted to public international law. In that capacity, he worked closely with his Co-Editor-in-Chief, Theodor Meron.

The influence of the transnational law school on the academy has been profound and lasting. Today, a number of scholarly student-run journals which are devoted to international and comparative law feature the word 'transnational' in their title. Examples include the *Columbia Journal of Transnational Law* (published by New York's Columbia Law School since 1961), the *Vanderbilt Journal of Transnational Law* (published by Vanderbilt University School of Law in Nashville since 1971,[2] after having appeared as *The Vanderbilt International* between 1967 and 1971), *The Transnational Lawyer* (published by California's University of the Pacific McGeorge School of Law since 1988), *Transnational Law & Contemporary Problems* (a journal of The University of Iowa College of Law first published in 1991) and the *Journal of Transnational Law & Policy* (published by the Florida State University College of Law since 1992). As these journals demonstrate, 'transnational' has come to replace 'international' or 'public international law' in US academic parlance.

This collection of transnational law essays is published at a time when the very concept of transnational law has been challenged in certain corners of the world. Just how controversial transnational law can be in the twenty-first century was demonstrated in connection with the confirmation hearings of Yale Law School Dean Harold Hongju Koh for the post of Legal Adviser to the US Department of State in 2009. The Legal Adviser is the highest-ranking international lawyer in the United States, advising the US Secretary of State on national security law, human rights law and the legal aspects of international engagements and representing the United States before international bodies and tribunals. Soon after Dean Koh was nominated by US President Barack Obama in March

---

[2] The first re-named edition aptly featured a lead article by Philip Jessup. P. C. Jessup, 'The Development of a United States Approach Toward the International Court of Justice', *Vanderbilt Journal of International Law*, 5 (1971–2), 1–46. For a transnational law perspective on the role of the International Court of Justice, see Pieter Bekker's chapter 23 in this volume.

2009, he faced heavy criticism from some American groups and politicians in the US Senate for his transnational approach to the law. Indeed, Koh's nomination provoked hysteria in some circles. 'Transnationalist' became a fighting word. Notwithstanding the efforts of these groups to derail Koh's appointment during four months of attacks and wrangling over his thinking on transnational law, the US Senate voted 62–35 (60 votes being necessary) to confirm him on 25 June 2009. We are grateful to Harold Koh for having agreed to write the foreword for this book honouring his co-author and friend.

At a time when the transnational law concept is under attack and international law scholarship on both sides of the Atlantic appears to be drifting further apart than ever, Detlev Vagts remains one of the few able and willing to bridge that gap. As a formidable generalist across the range of international legal problems, from international business transactions to human rights to classic public international law, he is a firm believer in an international rule of law which applies equally to all international law actors. He represents the finest American tradition of seeking legal solutions to transborder problems in public and private law, or indeed in new bodies of law, regardless of the old conceptual distinctions between private and public international law.

Early in his career, Detlev Vagts' personal background (his father Alfred, a prominent German history professor, moved his family to the United States in political protest against the rise of the Third Reich in Germany) and his immediate familiarity with both the Common law and the Civil law systems, together with his keen knowledge of the political and social context on both sides of the Atlantic, helped him develop a comparative and transnational perspective.

The overall theme of this book is the regulation of the global economy, whether of interstate relationships setting economic and monetary policy or of individual conduct of an economic nature, through a transnational law approach. Globalisation has transformed the study and practice of transnational law, just as transnational law has changed the approach to the regulation of cross-border dealings between the various subjects of international law. It has broken down the last remaining barriers of compartmentalised legal thinking. Yet, there has been a surprising dearth of recent works devoted to general transnational law, aside from specialist areas such as foreign investment law. As a result, the growing legal complexity resulting from a patchwork of jurisdictions is often ill understood. The time has come to take stock, and assess the potential and prospects of transnational law in the age of globalisation. Besides honouring one of the finest transnational lawyers of his generation, this is the primary aim of the book.

This book covers the core subjects of transnational law, which have been divided into three broad areas: (I) International Law in General; (II) Transnational Economic Law; and (III) Transnational Lawyering and Dispute Resolution. As the Bibliography of Detlev Vagts at the end of this volume demonstrates, our honouree has made important contributions in each of these areas, and continues to do so even at the age of eighty.[3]

The individual contributions in this book re-evaluate established fields of transnational law, such as the protection of property and investment. At the same time, the book explores new areas of law which are in the process of detaching themselves from the nation-state, such as global administrative law and the regulation of cross-border lawyering; it examines the implications of decentralised norm-making and diffusion and the proliferation of dispute settlement mechanisms on the international plane; and it analyses the rising backlash against global legal interdependence in the form of demands for preserving State legal autonomy.

The primary audience of this book is scholars and specialists in international law. We hope, however, that this book will be of interest to a wide array of scholars with a comparative and interdisciplinary outlook, including international relations theorists and social scientists, and that it will foster further study of transnational law in all its aspects.

What is perhaps the most remarkable feature of the project underlying this book is that it has brought together more than thirty lawyers from different legal systems and nationalities. Their common bond is a personal connection with and affection for the honouree. Detlev Vagts' life intersected with their careers in various ways, whether as young students/scholars[4] or as seasoned colleagues from academia and practice. A glance at their names, backgrounds and accomplishments in the list of contributors (p. xi) gives but a small indication of the influence which Detlev Vagts has had on the legal profession, and on fellow lawyers, the world over.

One such lawyer was the late Thomas W. Wälde (1949–2008), a German jurist and world-renowned scholar in international energy law

---

[3] See D. F. Vagts, 'The Financial Meltdown and its International Implications', *AJIL*, 103 (2009), 684–91.

[4] At least twenty-three of the thirty-five authors who have contributed to this book have earned one or more law degrees from Harvard Law School.

who had studied with Detlev Vagts at Harvard (LLM 1973). In April 2008, after securing Detlev Vagts' blessing, Thomas Wälde approached fellow European Pieter Bekker, one of the editors of this volume, about paying the ultimate tribute to their academic mentor and long-time friend in true German fashion: publishing a collection of essays honouring Detlev Vagts' contributions as a scholar and teacher in the form of a *Festschrift*, also known as a *liber amicorum*. At a meeting in New York City in August 2008, Bekker and Wälde quickly agreed on the title for the book and embarked on an ambitious project which would bring together friends and admirers of Detlev Vagts from around the world, especially Europe and the United States, the two continents which are the most closely associated with the honouree. It was agreed to assign priority to 'new voices' – 'the next generation' of scholars and scholarly practitioners – most of whom Detlev Vagts taught personally, at Harvard and elsewhere. It is this generation of lawyers which has profited the most from his teaching and writings.

This project would not have got off the ground were it not for Thomas Wälde's characteristic energy and drive. After his untimely death in October 2008, Rudolf Dolzer and Michael Waibel agreed to take his place and see this project through to completion. The editors of this volume represent three generations of Detlev Vagts' Harvard students – Rudolf Dolzer (LLM 1972, SJD 1979), Pieter Bekker (LLM 1991) and Michael Waibel (LLM 2008). The editors have arranged for all royalty proceeds from this book to be paid to The Energy, Petroleum, Mineral and Natural Resources Law & Policy Education Trust, an educational fund established in Thomas Wälde's memory at the University of Dundee (Scotland), where he occupied his Chair.[5]

The editors wish to thank Cambridge University Press and its dedicated staff, especially Finola O'Sullivan, for publishing this special collection of essays in honour of Detlev Vagts – a gentle giant of the law to whom the editors and contributors, and indeed the international legal profession at large, will forever be indebted.

---

[5] Those interested in contributing directly to the Fund are advised to contact the Fund's Administrator, Christine Hulbert, at The Centre for Energy, Petroleum and Mineral Law and Policy, University of Dundee, Carnegie Building, Dundee DD1 4HN, Scotland.

1

Detlev Vagts and the Harvard Law School

WILLIAM P. ALFORD

When we think of people who form the foundation of august educational institutions, such as Harvard Law School, our attention, understandably, turns first to official leadership and others very much in the public eye. That ought not to obscure the immense and varied contribution that Detlev Vagts, notwithstanding his characteristic and heartfelt modesty, has made to the life of his law school over the past half-century.

From his initial appointment to the Harvard Law School faculty in 1959 through his two-decade-long tenure (1984–2005) as holder of the Bemis Professorship (Harvard's earliest in international law and a position in which he took great pride), Detlev has been someone who instinctively and imaginatively cut across existing boundaries – disciplinary, national and other – long before that became as fashionable as it now is. That willingness to defy convention, albeit in a mannered fashion, took many forms, but perhaps the most noteworthy involved the development and launching of several courses that greatly enriched the Harvard curriculum and helped cement the School's reputation for innovation in international legal studies during the second half of the twentieth century. Two, in particular, stand out.

Together with his friend and colleague Henry Steiner, Detlev in the late 1960s seized upon the challenge posed by Philip Jessup in his celebrated 1956 Storrs Lectures to devise a pioneering course that they entitled 'Transnational Legal Problems', which both discerned patterns of legal interaction across jurisdictional lines that did not fit neatly into the existing fields of public and private international law, and that engaged learning from beyond the law itself to illuminate these patterns. (For more on the transnational legal problems project, please see Steiner's chapter 2 in this volume.) By the 1970s, it had become a hallmark for Harvard's legions of students interested in the larger world and a national resource via a casebook by the same name that was widely adopted throughout the United States (and that for its fourth edition added as co-author Harold Hongju Koh, subsequently US Assistant Secretary of State for Democracy, Human Rights and Labor; Dean of Yale Law School, and now Legal Adviser, US Department of State).

A second major contribution of Detlev to the Harvard curriculum has concerned the role of the legal profession in a global setting. At a time when international law courses did not address professional responsibility issues, and professional responsibility courses did not address international issues, Detlev, with customary foresight, understood how vital and how vexing this area would be. The result was a prescient course on the legal profession in a transborder setting and a set of course materials drawn from multiple jurisdictions and informed by his keen understanding of the businesses, governments and people with whom lawyers work.

Nor were these his only innovative contributions to the Harvard Law School curriculum. As early as 1962, Detlev was teaching a seminar entitled 'International Aspects of the Corporation', and even as he moved toward retirement in the early years of the twenty-first century, he continued to offer a course on 'Transnational Business Problems' that eventuated in the well-regarded casebook by the same name, co-authored with William Dodge and Harold Koh.

Detlev's crossing of boundaries took a variety of other forms – again to the great benefit of his School. As several other chapters in this volume will demonstrate, through the reach of his scholarship internationally, his editorship of the *AJIL*, his service as Counselor on international law in the US Department of State and his role as lecturer and arbitrator across the world, Detlev enhanced Harvard's reputation immeasurably. Closer to home, along with Arthur von Mehren and Peter Murray, he was central to the Law School's engagement with Germany, both through his thoughtful scholarship and through his many links to academics in his father's native land. And yet closer to home, for years, Detlev served as the Law School's bridge to a world some denizens of the 02138 zip code might describe as even more foreign – namely, the Harvard Business School.

His accomplishments on these broader stages and the concomitant demands on his time notwithstanding, Detlev has always been and still is unqualifiedly generous with his time for colleagues (senior and junior alike), students and visitors, particularly from abroad. To this day, Detlev remains my most faithful informant about China, my principal area of specialisation, at least weekly sending me clippings from a wide range of publications, such as *Science* and *Scientific American*, lest I miss an important new development. He remains a regular and valuable participant in faculty workshops, routinely finding constructive ways in which to offer younger colleagues wise advice. When a gap arose in the leadership of the Law School's International Tax Program following the retirement of its extraordinary leader, Oliver Oldman, Detlev unselfishly stepped in to head it for two years, rather than leave its fellows, most from developing nations, in the lurch. As busy as he was, he always found time for the large numbers of students he guided through doctoral dissertations, LLM theses and other papers (several of whom have achieved positions of prominence themselves) and to advise the *Harvard International Law Journal* and other student activities concerning matters international. It is no surprise that he retains the gratitude of so many students, not only for his immense learning but his genuine kindness, and that invitations to participate in this *Festschrift* were so readily accepted.

The Law School and its students are fortunate for Detlev Vagts' presence for so many years and I congratulate him on this volume in his honour, in which it has been a privilege to participate.

2

Constructing and developing transnational law: the contribution of Detlev Vagts

HENRY J. STEINER

During the fifteen years following the Second World War, 'transnational' (activities, enterprises, organisations, networks, movements, processes, law) had not yet become a household word – even in academic households. But the times were propitious for its coinage and rapid evolution as a commonly used descriptive term with ever-broadening references. With its distinctive form of stability among major States imposed by the Cold War, this period and the following decades witnessed dramatic recovery from the war's massive devastation. It gave birth to many intergovernmental organisations and multinational companies, as well as to new practices and rules for international finance, international trade and investment, peacekeeping and human rights. These years generated heightened international flows of goods and capital and new types of international intercourse. Traditional classifications of the many bodies of law and kinds of transactions germane to international life bowed to the new circumstances and to a fresh vocabulary. The term 'transnational' emerged as a winner.

Such was the period of Detlev Vagts' university education, military service and brief but instructive career as a practising lawyer involved with international corporate and financial transactions, all a prelude to his almost fifty years of professorial engagement with this new and volatile world. Much of Detlev's teaching and scholarship fell comfortably within the developing idea or category of the transnational. His work transcended the boundaries of any one of the component fields included in the concept of transnational law. It increasingly embraced several of these components, emphasising their interconnections within an increasingly complex web of transactions and norms. In the process, Detlev's published writing clarified and enriched the idea of the transnational.

The term gained notoriety principally through the publication in 1956 of Columbia Law School Professor Philip Jessup's *Transnational Law*. This influential book offered what remains a classic if terse definition of that body of law: 'all law which regulates actions or events that transcend national frontiers. Both public and private international law are included, as are other rules which do not wholly fit into such standard categories.'[1]

This definition was attractive and congenial to both Detlev and myself when we combined forces as co-authors and co-editors of *Transnational Legal Problems*, a 1968 coursebook consisting of our text and edited legal materials that eventually went through four editions. Like others of our generation who taught and wrote on transnational topics, we would have self-identified as liberal internationalists – scholars who found hope for peace and prosperity in the construction of a decolonised and more closely interrelated system of States benefiting from regulation and facilitation by an innovative network of international organisations. That network embraced political, economic, human rights and other types of organisation that, its creators hoped, would move the world from mutually destructive behaviour among States toward a safer and more humane future. The stark and tragic lessons from a global depression and the Second World War were much in mind.

As spelled out in our coursebook's preface (similar in all editions), several themes were at work in our usage of 'the word'. It came to be employed by scholars at American universities to accommodate the world's new structures and aspirations. Departing from earlier methods of doctrinal and conceptual formalism and positivism that had characterised much of the preceding study of the international legal system, the new term challenged scholarly boundaries and uprooted definitions. The curriculum of academic institutions had largely observed those boundaries and definitions. Courses examined 'international' or 'national' matters, 'private' transactions among multinational companies or 'public' international law. Discussion within that older curriculum and methodology had little place for explicitly political analysis or for analysis of policy choices that were the context for or were closely related to legal change. Hybrid classifications were not encouraged. Autonomous bodies of law had little to do with economics, politics and formulation of or choice among policies.

---

[1] P. C. Jessup, *Transnational Law* (New Haven, CT: Yale University Press, 1956), 2.

The academic courses of the earlier period generally held to paradig-matically legal materials: judicial opinions, legislation, treaties and so on. They rarely brought into discussion writing on closely related but dis-tinct disciplines, like international relations, or the economics of trade and finance, or theories of socio-economic or political development. Over the coming decades, such legal autonomy gradually bowed to the ongoing interpenetration of fields and disciplines, in the spirit of legal (and political) realism that had swept across much of the American legal academy by the 1950s. The policies informing this internationalised and 'transnationalised' world order became explicit and formative compo-nents of this enlarged conception of law.

The concept of the 'transnational', as developed by Vagts and similar-minded scholars, embodies three significant elements of change. First, matters that 'transcend' national frontiers can reach deeply into (or indeed be first formulated deeply within) national legal systems, and in this sense depart significantly from the earlier discrete categories of international and national law. Three examples suffice. The foreign relations law of a country constitutes part of interactive transnational process – the powers of an executive or legislative branch of government with respect to matters such as making or annulling or implementing treaties. Important fields of national law, sometimes consisting of legis-lation that was required and shaped by treaty obligations, regulate non-governmental business organisations with respect to transnational and often extraterritorial activities: domestic legislation on trade, finance, antitrust, intellectual property, labour and other vital matters. The inter-national human rights movement starting in the late 1940s brought about deep interpenetration of the international and national systems, with respect to norm generation, implementation and enforcement. Today that movement rests on myriad interconnections and comple-mentarities between national and international law, the two bodies of law being intricately intertwined. Hardly a path to clearer understanding of such fields of law, efforts to keep national and international law discrete analytically and conceptually could only obscure the essential character of this movement.

Secondly, consider Jessup's reference to the public and private – the traditional distinction separating public international law between States, and private international law applicable to non-governmental actors in transactions involving more than one State. The 'private' side inquired into matters like which State law should be selected as the applicable law (the so-called 'conflict of laws' within the federal United

States), but it reached more broadly. As Detlev's work illustrates, the two fields have important overlaps and similarities in character and are often informed by closely related or identical policies – comity in private and public international law, for example.

Consider, for example, national regulatory law posing questions of the extraterritorial reach to non-State actors of antitrust, tax, labour, criminal or antidiscrimination legislation. Consider typical business transactions, perhaps involving multinational production, trade, licensing, or investments, that involve non-State entities and agreements. Two or more bodies of national law, regional or universal intergovernmental organisations and aspects of international law add further regulatory complexity. Even the 'private' world of contract or corporate law and its application to agreements between non-State entities are now broadly understood to be informed by public, regulatory policies of legislatures and courts. The easy distinction between the private and public hearken back to an earlier age.

A third effect of the shift to the notion of the 'transnational' was to weaken a further landmark of the pre-war years. Positivist criteria of what constituted international law fastened on factors of recognition such as the 'sources' of international law that Art. 38 of the Statute of the International Court of Justice (ICJ) carried over from the pre-war years (in slightly changed form). But the post-war years blurred, expanded and complicated the earlier typology of sources. To some extent, the change in approach occurred within the terms of the older typology; custom, for example, became more open-textured, less exacting in its formal criteria (which were themselves very flexible). Moreover, new phenomena such as resolutions voted within international organisations, or decisions of organs of those organisations, assumed greater prominence with respect to 'making' international law, while the requirement of State practice weakened.

Consideration of what norms 'international' law declared reached out to embrace the so-called 'soft' law that stood well outside the traditional sources, and that at best in an earlier period could have been considered an element of law-in-the-making, *de lege feranda*. Consider, for example, the diverse positions taken on novel questions by international law scholars and advocates for multinational corporations (MNCs). One major question concerned international human rights obligations (with respect to labour practices) of such corporations, which were clearly non-State business entities. Guidelines, recommendations, debates and agreements among non-State entities and related practices now figured in argument about international law. So did resolutions and drafts of proposed norms of organs of international organisations that had been given by treaty only recommendatory powers.[2] Moreover, scholars and advocates today tend to draw on a range of other disciplines – economics, political theory, international relations and so on – that are viewed as complexly intertwined with legal materials – indeed, as an essential element of legal analysis and theory.

To sum up, three related phenomena can be associated with the evolving concept of 'transnational' law: the larger scope of the term contrasted with the earlier compartmentalisation of bodies of law and types of transactions that are now associated with the 'transnational'; the erosion of boundaries between national/international, public/private and law/politics as well as the perceived interpenetration of these 'opposites', so that each term in a polarity contained aspects of the other; and the trend toward greater attention to an interdisciplinary approach to the understanding and analysis of transnational law and problems.

When Detlev started a new venture – the coursebook entitled *Transnational Business Problems*, now in its fourth edition (2008, with co-authors/editors William Dodge and Harold Koh) – such phenomena were evident in the book. The preface to that edition referred to transnational business as a field 'broad and complex, potentially including almost any legal materials anywhere in the world' (2008: iii). As if to bear out that observation, the table of contents included: distinctive aspects of transnational lawyering; different forms of dispute resolution; international financial and trade institutions; typical corporate agreements for transnational operations such as licensing of distributorship arrangements; joint ventures; distinctive aspects of corporate actors within transnational business environments; and bodies of law including national and international law (each of which were said to penetrate and influence the other) and public and private law.

Detlev has written prolifically in the broad field that he has helped to shape. I have selected a few characteristic illustrations for the purposes of this comment. His 1970 article on multinational enterprises (MNEs),[3] a classic in its systematic description and analysis of a relatively new institution of ever-great power and significance, described such

---

[2] For an early discussion of such issues, see D. F. Vagts, 'The UN Norms for Transnational Corporations', *Leiden Journal of International Law*, 16 (2003), 795–802.

[3] D. F. Vagts, 'The Multinational Enterprise. A New Challenge for Transnational Law', *Harvard Law Review*, 83 (1970), 739–92.

enterprises as a new challenge for transnational law. They exhibited national and international aspects, private and public aspects, legal and political aspects. Detlev's analysis drew on legal, political and economic analysis to describe the operating environment. Similarities between State power and the power of these enterprises emerge forcefully from this early and prescient article.

The 1987 article on alternative dispute resolution[4] showed several of the same characteristics. It concentrated on disputes between governments and foreign non-governmental actors, and it looked at the field 'from a private and then a public point of view'.[5] The subject was dispute resolution's new complexity and possibilities in a 'transnational context'. Detlev's particular strength in the comparative dimension of corporate law with respect to litigation and dispute resolution enriched this article, which traced the consequences of cultural differences among States for the character of their dispute resolution institutions.

Two articles on the effects of globalisation on the legal profession and the responsibility of the profession in transborder practice[6] reflected the author's detailed and comprehensive knowledge of the matters under discussion as well as sensitivity to the implications for transnational life of different types of national ordering and policy. The developing global context for the work of lawyers required a degree of harmonisation of differing State rules in the quickly changing transnational environment, as a path toward resolution of conflicts in the regulation of the profession to which bodies of public and private law were relevant.

The interconnectedness of States and regions stands as a major feature of these decades of ascent of the transnational in global affairs. Consider the current global financial crisis, a subject on which Detlev wrote in 2009.[7] In describing the transnational implications of action taken by governmental and non-governmental entities in the United States to overcome the crisis, the text interweaves actions and decisions by several States, by international organisations, by international networks of non-governmental parties, and of course by numerous non-governmental

---

[4] D. F. Vagts, 'Dispute-Resolution Mechanisms in International Business', *RdC*, 203 (1987-III), 1–94, 13 *et seq.*

[5] *Ibid.*, 21.

[6] D. F. Vagts, 'Professional Responsibility in Transborder Practice. Conflict and Resolution', *Georgetown Journal of Legal Ethics*, 13 (2000), 677–98; D. F. Vagts, 'The Impact of Globalization on the Legal Profession', *EJIL*, 2 (2000), 403–14.

[7] D. F. Vagts, 'The Financial Meltdown and its International Implications', *AJIL*, 103 (2009), 684–91.

business entities. The point of canvassing such a range of participants in transnational economic life was to sketch the many ways in which freedom of action by the US government is seriously curbed not only by formal international rules, but also by non-governmental networks (such as the International Organisation of Securities Commissions, IOSCO), and by pressure from foreign governments.

In a volume of essays meant to honour the work and contribution of Detlev Vagts, it is not out of place to note that his contribution far exceeded the scholarship itself, as important as it has been. For decades, Detlev's presence on the Harvard Law School faculty added considerably to its distinction in matters international. His persistent engagement with learned societies such as the ASIL, partly by holding important and time-consuming positions within them, brought credit to that faculty. I should also note the illuminating historian's perspective that he brought to much of his work. We his friends and colleagues have much to be thankful about when we think of Detlev's long association with the School, and with us.

PART I

International law in general

3

'Hegemonic international law' in retrospect

ANTONY ANGHIE

Introduction

My first encounter with Professor Detlev Vagts took place far from Cambridge, Massachusetts. I was browsing through the foreign law section in the library at Monash University, in distant Melbourne, Australia, when I came across his article in the *Harvard Law Review* on a topic that interested me a great deal at the time – the status of multinational corporations (MNCs). These entities, which have now acquired such enormous significance, were presented by Professor Vagts in a more benevolent light than I – an undergraduate law student who had been inspired by the ideals of the New International Economic Order – would care to see them. It was hard to imagine that a few years later I would have the great privilege of being a student in his class, Transnational Legal Problems, at Harvard Law School. This class addressed, in particular, the relationship between US constitutional law and international law, a field that I now know as 'Foreign Relations Law'. For a few of us who saw ourselves as determinedly cosmopolitan – my close colleagues in that class included Pieter Bekker and Andrea Bianchi – this emphasis on domestic law was somewhat disturbing, particularly when it was further asserted that domestic law had precedence in the event of a conflict between these two systems. But that course, despite the discomfiture it generated, proved very significant and even in some ways prescient. I still rely on what I learned in that course to teach both my international law course and international business transactions course at the University of Utah; and foreign relations law acquired a significance, post-9/11, that few international law scholars could have predicted.

But I found Vagts' classes interesting for an entirely different reason that had nothing to do with international law. I was quite mesmerised by his way of speaking. His circumlocution, his ability to construct ornate sentences that combined the powers of both suggestion and indirection, occasionally reminded me of the late style, that had completely defeated me, of a particularly gifted Harvard Law School drop-out, Henry James. I had come to the class expecting to learn from an expert in transnational law and international business transactions. And that Professor Vagts was such a person was obvious – another of his major fields was corporate law. But what I gradually grew to appreciate was the formidable range of his learning. Although my research interests had far more to do with human rights and the history of international law than with business transactions, I found that he could shed important light on virtually anything relating to international law that I wanted to discuss with him.

Vagts has written with insight and expertise on most of the fundamental issues of international law: on custom, on treaties, on the work of the International Court of Justice (ICJ),[1] on State succession – and he has written in addition on more specialised themes such as the legal status of multinational corporations. A few simple and abiding themes have featured in his work – chief among them the binding character of international law and also, less prominently but still powerfully, the question of the challenges of following the vocation of international law. Thus he has had an ongoing concern to monitor and analyse US attitudes towards international law. Even while he regarded the ICJ's treatment of the United States in the 1980s *Nicaragua Case* as unsatisfactory, for instance, he also describes various US unilateral manoeuvres to dissociate itself from different international regimes as 'troubling'.[2] The question is explicitly addressed again in his 1998 editorial comment, 'Taking Treaties Less Seriously', in the *American Journal of International Law (AJIL)*. This piece, written in what seems in retrospect to be a far simpler and innocent time, focuses, again presciently, on the way in which developments in American constitutional law were limiting the application of international law.[3]

As a consequence of his achievements in all these other fields – his expertise in international transactions and the broader field of transnational law, and international economic law,[4] Vagts is not often thought of

---

[1] D. F. Vagts, 'Going to Court, Internationally', *Michigan Law Review*, 87 (1989), 1712–17, 1717.

[2] D. F. Vagts, 'Going to Court', *supra* n. 1, 1717.

[3] D. F. Vagts, 'Editorial Comment. Taking Treaties Less Seriously', *AJIL*, 92 (1998), 458–62.

[4] D. F. Vagts, 'International Economic Law and the American Journal of International Law', *AJIL*, 100 (2006), 769–82.

as a historian of international law. And yet, I would argue, in this chapter, all his work is imbued with a historical sensibility; it is the character of this sensibility that I try to sketch here, this in order to better understand his approach to what he has termed, in a very influential article, 'hegemonic international law'.

The historical dimension of Vagts' scholarship is evident in a number of respects. Even his articles that adopt what might be termed a doctrinal approach outline the history of the doctrine, the political events that shaped it and the scholars who developed it.[5] He adopts a more explicitly historical approach when examining the history of the concept of the balance of power in a learned survey of the relationship between international law and a particular system of politics that maintained relative order in Europe for the long nineteenth century. The broader and ever-enduring question raised by this article was the ongoing puzzle of the relationship between law and politics.[6]

It is also clear that Vagts' expertise in German international law scholarship had made him very familiar with the ambitious and powerful historical works of Wilhelm Grewe and Carl Schmitt. There is now taking place something of a resurgence of interest in the field of the history of international law.[7] Long before this occurred, however, and long before Grewe and Schmitt had been translated into English and had become such well-known and discussed figures, Vagts had studied and written about their work. Equally importantly, he was more aware than some recent commentators of the backgrounds of these authors who were now enjoying a sudden resurgence, of the particular legal and political settings in which they had produced their works and the alarming uses to which they were put.[8] The relationship between publicists and power, and the manner in which scholars and lawyers respond in times of crisis, might be seen as another of his enduring interests.

But there is a more personal and pressing aspect to the historical dimension of Vagts' work. Perhaps it is inevitably the case that all

---

[5] D. F. Vagts, 'State Succession. The Codifier's View', *Virginia Journal of International Law*, 33 (1993), 275–97.

[6] A. Vagts and D. F. Vagts, 'The Balance of Power in International Law. A History of an Idea', *AJIL*, 73 (1979), 555–80.

[7] For a more recent overview of this phenomenon, see I. De La Rasilla Del Moral, 'Review Essay. International Law in the Historical Present Tense', *Leiden Journal of International Law*, 22 (2009), 629–49.

[8] D. F. Vagts, 'Carl Schmitt in Context. Reflections on a Symposium', *Cardozo Law Review*, 23 (2002), 2157–63.

international lawyers bring their own histories to bear, more or less explicitly, on their understanding of and approach to the discipline. In the case of Vagts, his writings strongly suggest that the experiences of Germany have profoundly shaped his vision of international law and institutions. Vagts' acquaintance with German history, the Nazis and the Second World War was, of course, more than academic. His father was Professor Alfred Vagts, a prominent German historian who fled Nazi Germany and immigrated to the United States in the 1930s.

His article on 'International Law in the Third Reich',[9] in particular, can be seen as a product of this personal history. The express concern of this article is to examine a history that, for reasons of sensitivity and embarrassment, perhaps, had not been closely examined at the time of its writing even by the German legal community itself.[10] Vagts appeared concerned that its themes may be too particular to be of general interest, and it commences with a question: 'What justifies asking American readers to take time in 1990 to review German international law during the Third Reich, which ended in 1945?'[11] Several answers present themselves. It is a 'dramatic story'; and the 'peculiarities of the period enable one to develop hypotheses about the interactions in the law among people, institutions, ideas and policies'.[12] It seems to me that it is precisely because this article adopts such a wide-ranging approach, one that even encompasses the existential and psychological dilemmas confronting the German international lawyers of the time, that it is in many ways his most powerful, personal and searching work of scholarship.

The article provides a vivid picture of how a State could set about the task of formulating a framework that would 'justify' such an expansionary and aggressive regime. The elements of the framework can be broadly summarised. Firstly, international law was not binding on the German State; the *Volk* was the 'highest and finest institution of common life'; as such, 'there was nothing higher than the foreign relations law of the *Volk*, those rules which served its interests and which might from time to time coincide with generally accepted practices of States. But where they diverged, the rule of the *Volk* would predominate.'[13] Secondly, a wide range of justifications was developed for disregarding treaties.[14] Thirdly, international organisations were an object of concerted attack,

---

[9] D. F. Vagts, 'International Law in the Third Reich', *AJIL*, 84 (1990), 661–704.
[10] Vagts, 'International Law', *supra* n. 9, 661–2.   [11] *Ibid.*, 661.   [12] *Ibid.*, 661.
[13] *Ibid.*, 691.   [14] *Ibid.*, 692.

and dismissed as 'Jewish, pacifist internationalism'.[15] Fourthly, the laws of war did not apply, for instance, to the Reich's war on the Eastern front because such a war was so entirely different from the wars that had been envisaged by the authors of the Hague and Geneva Conventions.[16] Fifthly, the rules of occupation were disregarded – through deportations and forced labour, for instance – and prisoners were subjected to grave mistreatment.[17] No real legal justification was given for these abuses. Sixthly, more broadly, the overall international law jurisprudence of the legitimisers of the Third Reich led to the inexorable conclusion that 'there could be no international law but only German foreign relations law'.[18]

Equally compellingly, the article presents a penetrating and wide-ranging portrait of the individuals – many of them brilliant – who acted as counsel for the Nazis and their counterpoints who bravely resisted, and who often paid a very high price for doing so. In addition to learning about Nazi practices and the relationship between those practices and international law, then, Vagts points to the human and professional dilemmas faced by German international lawyers of that period: and he points to a challenge confronted by many lawyers who 'may find themselves in governmental positions where they are asked to do or say things that run against their conscientious views even though the State overall is not undemocratic'.[19]

Too much might be made of the impact of an individual's personal history in assessing and interpreting their scholarship. And yet, it seems to me that this article is crucial in understanding some of Vagts' major intellectual and professional concerns. It illuminates the respect that many distinguished scholars of his generation had for international law; it helps us understand his scrupulous monitoring of US treaty practice and his concern about ensuring that the most fundamental principle of international law, *pacta sunt servanda*, was upheld.

History and hegemony

What might be termed a 'sense of history' is a major and animating presence in Vagts' article 'Hegemonic International Law'. The emergence of the United States as single global superpower which was historically rivalled only by Rome had already, by the beginning of the new millennium, generated a considerable scholarship on the relationship between

---

[15] *Ibid.*, 693.   [16] *Ibid.*, 696.   [17] *Ibid.*, 697.   [18] *Ibid.*, 700.   [19] *Ibid.*, 701.

hegemony and international law – and, in particular, on the effect of US hegemony on the international legal order.[20]

Hegemony, in many respects, is a concept that is especially useful in linking the concerns of international law and international relations. It offers an entire analytic framework for examining one of the major preoccupations of international lawyers – what roles do rules play in a system of international relations that appears to be driven by power and the competition among States for survival and supremacy?

More 'realist' international relations scholars have argued that hegemony is essential for international order; and that, for instance, stability and economic expansion in the nineteenth century was achieved because of the predominance of the British Empire which in effect acted as underwriter of the entire system. Correspondingly, international law scholars have argued that it is only inevitable that formal inequality is entrenched in the system of international law despite the fundamental premise of the international system that all sovereign States are equal.[21] Approached more historically, it can be seen that hegemons have always been provided with special rights in the international system.[22] But international law has also been seen, traditionally, as a check to the ambitions of hegemony. Nico Krisch, for example, has asserted that '[i]nternational law … occupies an always precarious but eventually secure position between the demands of the powerful and the ideals of justice held in international society'.[23] More recently and less traditionally, scholarship has focused on the relevance to international law of Gramsci's idea of hegemony.[24]

Vagts' article, too, draws on broader ideas about the relationship between hegemony and international law, but in order to address a more specific question that was presented to a number of distinguished

---

[20] D. F. Vagts, 'Hegemonic International Law', *AJIL*, 95 (2001). See, e.g., M. Byers and G. Nolte (eds.), *United States Hegemony and the Foundations of International Law* (Cambridge University Press, 2003). As the editors note, while this work was published in 2003, the project on which it was based pre-dated 9/11.

[21] E. Benvenisti, 'The US and the Use of Force. Double-Edged Hegemony and the Management of Global Emergencies', *EJIL*, 15 (2004), 677–700.

[22] G. Simpson, *Great Powers and Outlaw States* (Cambridge University Press, 2004).

[23] N. Krisch, 'International Law in Times of Hegemony. Unequal Power and the Shaping of the International Legal Order', *EJIL*, 16 (2005), 369–408, 369.

[24] S. Buckel and A. Fischer-Lescano, 'Gramsci Reconsidered. Hegemony in Global Law', *Leiden Journal of International Law*, 22 (2009), 437–545. The broad argument here is that 'hegemonic law' is not the law of any superpower, but an asymmetric consensus which relies on a climate of world-society-recognition. *Ibid.*, 437.

international lawyers – how was the United States to respond to the tragedy of 9/11:

> The terrible blows of September 11, 2001, raise the question whether the United States can or will act as a hegemon in a drastic way, that is, in Krauthammer's terms, whether it can carry out 'unapologetic and implacable demonstrations of will'.[25]

The article then goes on to elaborate the characteristics of hegemonic international law (HIL) – its normative impact on the foundational principle of sovereign equality; its endorsement of intervention; and its approach to the sources of international law, in particular treaties and customary international law, for the purpose of demonstrating, usually, that they do not create any binding obligations.

It is clear, in all these respects, in terms of both broader theories and particular legal strategies, that Vagts' model of hegemonic international law is drawn from his study of international law in the Third Reich. Indeed, his article on hegemony makes numerous references, once again, to his earlier article,[26] and in particular to Schmitt's work. HIL resists and repudiates the ideas that all States are equal.[27] It favours unilateral intervention – just as Germany did in the 1930s.[28] It finds various justifications for avoiding treaties, and can depart more readily from international custom on the basis that it is being 'creative'.[29] More broadly, HIL was an attempt to ensure that international law reflected the realities of power; more powerful States, within this scheme, had greater freedom under the law, and indeed could change the law to serve their own purposes.

The historical dimension of the article makes explicit connections with the great German theorists of hegemony, Triepel, Schmitt and Grewe. Schmitt himself had drawn on American precedents, such as the Monroe doctrine, to justify German expansionism. An examination of Vagts' article on Nazism reveals further techniques used by these theorists – including the argument that treaties did not apply in changed

---

[25] Vagts, 'Hegemonic International Law', *supra*, n. 20, 843–8; the reference is to the writings of a major proponent of American hegemony, Charles Krauthammer. It is interesting to note how many advocates of empire focus on the phenomenon of 'will' and the proper exercise of it. Another such advocate, Conrad's Mr Kurtz, asserted that '[b]y the simple exercise of our will we can exert a power for good practically unbounded'. J. Conrad, 'Heart of Darkness', in M. Dauwen Zabel (ed.), *The Portable Conrad*, rev. edn. (New York: Penguin Books, 1976), 561.

[26] Vagts, 'Hegemonic International Law', *supra* n. 20.

[27] *Ibid.*, 845.   [28] *Ibid.*, 846.   [29] *Ibid.*, 847.

circumstances (the *rebus sic stantibus* rule); and the argument that constitutional law – national law – prevailed as against international law.

Vagts asserts that the article he authors (note how he distances himself here from his own writings) 'does not take a position as to whether the US is or should be a hegemon'.[30] But now, more than nine years after the writing of that article, it is possible to make some sort of assessment of what followed. It is now surely clear that the response of the Bush administration in its launch of a 'war on terror' was very much an attempted exercise in hegemonic international law. And, further, somewhat disconcertingly, that the legal strategies followed by the Bush administration conformed very closely to the model of hegemonic international law that Vagts had outlined. A vast literature now exists on how the United States departed from the strictures of international humanitarian law – regarding, for example, the treatment of prisoners and renditions.[31] What of course was especially disconcerting was that lawyers, through their controversial interpretations of human rights and international humanitarian law conventions, were endorsing practices that were abusive and injurious.[32]

More particularly, Vagts argued that 'the historical record shows that it can be convenient for the hegemon to have a body of law to work with, provided it can be suitably adapted'.[33] While the attempts of the Bush administration to free itself of the fetters of international humanitarian law and international human rights law are good examples of 'HIL', perhaps the most dramatic effort to achieve what might be seen as hegemonic goals through the suitable adaptation of international rules is provided by the administration's articulation of a right to pre-emptive self-defence. The Bush doctrine, as it has come to be known, asserted in effect that the United States had a right to use force against 'emerging threats'. The administration argued, among other things, that such a right was provided by scholars such as Grotius and Vattel. It was a clear and explicit exercise in 'hegemonic law', not only because it enabled the United States to wage wars against other States perceived as threats almost at will – a classic behaviour of the hegemon, war being the ultimate

---

[30] *Ibid.*, 843.
[31] E.g. J.J. Paust, *Beyond the Law. The Bush Administration's Unlawful Responses in the 'War' on Terror* (Cambridge University Press, 2007).
[32] E.g. M.C. Bassiouni, 'The Institutionalization of Torture Under the Bush Administration', *Case Western Journal of International Law*, 37 (2006), 389–425.
[33] Vagts, 'Hegemonic International Law', *supra* n. 20, 845.

action available to it – but because it was so clearly a right that could only be exercised by powerful States. The doctrine of sovereign equality would hold that if the United States enjoyed a right to pre-emption, then this was a right available to all other States. Smaller States could follow the United States in their disregard for international human rights law or international humanitarian law (IHL) – especially in relation to ongoing civil conflicts. With pre-emption, however, small States would find themselves clearly disadvantaged. They would be in no position to exercise any such ostensible right as they risked potentially catastrophic retaliation by larger States. In this sense, the right was carefully calibrated with power and completely negated the idea of sovereign equality. As Eyal Benvenisti points out, '[t]he US claim is essentially an assertion of the right to review the policies adopted by the other government and to override them whenever the US finds it necessary'.[34]

While many recent studies cited have closely examined the impact of hegemons on international law and the techniques they use to transform international law – or else disregard it completely – less emphasis has been given to the question of how other States respond to these actions – both politically and legally. Several States endorsed the idea of pre-emption when it was first asserted; it was revealing, however, that many of these were allies of the United States, and included the United Kingdom, Israel, Australia and Japan.[35] Overall, however, the clear consequences of the doctrine were apparent to many States. The widespread adoption of the doctrine of pre-emption could have created a system of international relations that was comparable to the nineteenth century, when it was legal to go to war, and when a precarious peace was maintained only by the political system – the balance of power – precisely the system studied much earlier by Vagts. The fragile nature of that balance was, of course, demonstrated by the First World War.

Kofi Annan, the then-Secretary-General of the United Nations, pointed to the gravity of pre-emption and its impact on international law when he asserted that it would alter the basis of international order that had existed since the creation of the Charter itself.[36] The United Nations then acted by appointing a High-Level Panel to examine the question of whether

---

[34] Benvenisti, 'The US and the Use of Force', *supra* n. 21, 691.

[35] J. T. Gathii, 'Assessing Claims of a New Doctrine of Pre-Emptive War under the Doctrine of Sources', *Osgoode Hall Law Journal*, 43 (2005), 67–103.

[36] Kofi Annan, Address to the UN General Assembly, 23 September 2003, Press Release SG/SM/8891, www.un.org/News/Press/docs/2003/sgsm8891.doc.htm.

international law could address the new threats it was confronting. The Panel, unsurprisingly, reported that existing international law could meet the security challenges of the time.[37] The established law of the United Nations Charter was asserted in this way against this radical doctrine. All this tends to confirm Krisch's argument that international law could serve to both further and inhibit the ambitions of the hegemon. Perhaps even more significantly, the Iraq war, which was widely perceived as an example of pre-emption in action, as a result of the Bush administration justifying it to the public as necessitated by Saddam Hussein's possession of weapons of mass destruction, did not prove to be the triumph that its architects and proponents had predicted and promised. All these factors have contributed to the receding of pre-emption from current analysis. The further irony here is that many States would have had additional incentives to arm themselves precisely because of the Bush doctrine. The Obama administration has not attempted to reassert the doctrine of pre-emption. However, the ongoing complications surrounding Iran's nuclear programme could very well result in a return to the question.[38]

What was most surprising about this particular exercise of hegemony, however, was the extent to which it resulted in a divide between the long-standing and traditional allies, the United States and Europe. Robert Kagan was most emphatic in positing this division, between American realism and misplaced European idealism.[39]

Equally, American scholars developed a whole series of arguments to suggest, for instance, that the United States was fundamentally different from Europe. Thus Europe's preoccupation with rules of international law and the Kantian vision of a system governed by a higher law was understandable on the basis that this was a different form of constitutionalism from that which existed in the United States. The United States had a constitutional tradition which required that the Constitution took precedence over international law, even if this meant violating the latter.

Simultaneous with this argument, which located supreme authority in the US Constitution, however, was the argument that, in times of

---

[37] Report of the High-Level Panel on Threats, Challenges, and Change, *A More Secure World. Our Shared Responsibility*, UN Doc. A/59/565 (1 December 2004).

[38] US President Barack Obama, in his Nobel prize speech, asserted that '[t]hose who care for their own security cannot ignore the danger of an arms race in the Middle East or East Asia. Those who seek peace cannot stand idly by as nations arm themselves for nuclear war.' President Barack Obama, Nobel Peace Prize speech, *New York Times*, December 11, 2009.

[39] R. Kagan, *Of Paradise and Power. America and Europe in the New World Order* (New York: Vintage Books, 2004).

emergency, under the Constitution, it was the President who had expansive authority to deal with whatever emergencies were confronted. These were exceptional circumstances that required the suspension of legal regimes designed to deal with everyday problems.

It was also clear that much of Europe and many European international law scholars regarded America with some alarm: the first panel of the inaugural Conference of the European Society of International Law in Florence in 2004 bore the title 'International Law in the Shadow of Empire'. And there was little doubt as to who the Empire was in this situation.

Hegemonic international law in retrospect

Putting aside for the moment the question of whether HIL is good or bad, it is surely an occasion for wonder that a State which was hailed, nine years ago, as a force more powerful than Rome or Britain at the height of their imperial might, could now find itself in such a parlous state, its formidable military stretched and weakened, its finances undermined, its moral stature still, despite recent signs of renewal, deeply compromised and questioned. Traditionally, the hegemon is seen as the one indispensable nation which must act to resolve international crises in distant places. It is a measure of the dramatic change that has occurred since 2000 that the global financial crisis that began in 2008 originated in the United States itself, and that President Bush, the fervent and unapologetic unilateralist, was compelled to call for international cooperation to address the massive problems that resulted.

The last nine years have also witnessed the decisive emergence of China. The power shift that this represents, and the implications of these changes for international law – if we are to remain consistent with the view that the international legal structure in some way reflects power realities in the international system – are yet to be assessed. What is especially notable, however, is the completely different approach to the international system and international law that appears to have guided China over the years. The principles underlying this approach and deriving from the Bandung Conference in 1955, include: (1) mutual respect for sovereignty and territorial integrity; (2) mutual non-aggression; (3) non-interference in each other's internal affairs; (4) equality and mutual benefit; and (5) peaceful coexistence.[40] This approach disavows a system

---

[40] See Z. Cui, 'The Bush Doctrine and Neoconservatism. A Chinese Perspective', *HILJ*, 46 (2005), 403–10, 410.

based on distinguishing between 'friends' and 'enemies' depending on social systems and values.

China, like the Non-Aligned Movement (NAM) more broadly, has consistently maintained that any global responses to terror must be based on the law of the United Nations Charter. The interesting question here is whether these principles – which appear so clearly respectful of sovereignty and the formal notion of sovereign equality – will prevent the emergence of a different type of hegemony. We also now know that hegemony does not necessarily need to depart from the law to assert itself. Gerry Simpson's pioneering work – which traces many of the themes covered in Vagts' article on the Balance of Power – points out that hegemons create international structures and institutions that entrench and further their own power.[41] Indeed, as José Alvarez, expressly elaborating on the theme of HIL, points out, it is precisely through existing mechanisms of international law, such as the Security Council, that HIL can manifest itself.[42] The far-reaching Security Council resolutions that deal with counter-terrorism, including the Sanctions Committee created by resolution 1267, reveal the Council working in 'legislative mode', and can be further seen as manifestations of this species of hegemonic international law.[43] A vision of international relations that is based emphatically on respect for sovereignty and territorial integrity could exist in tension with an alternative vision that stressed human rights and the responsibility to protect. However, if the proclamations of human rights are used to justify initiatives that plausibly appear to be hypocritical or ineffective – or, even worse, destructive and destabilising even when sincere – then it is the vision based on the classic idea of respect for sovereignty that might seem attractive – as it always has been – to sovereigns themselves, and even to the people they might rule. This vision, of course, does not preclude the emergence of hegemonic power. The resulting hegemony could be exercised in new ways that may not involve the explicit adaptation of hegemonic international law – and it will be all the more effective, perhaps, as a consequence. This is merely to reiterate what Vagts points out, that hegemony can take many different forms; it seems to follow that it can be exercised through very different legal arrangements.[44]

[41] Simpson, *Great Powers and Outlaw States*, *supra* n. 22.
[42] J. E. Alvarez, 'Hegemonic International Law Revisited', *AJIL*, 87 (2003), 873–88.
[43] Alvarez, 'Hegemonic International Law Revisited', *supra* n. 42, 874.
[44] Vagts, 'Hegemonic International Law', *supra* n. 20, 848.

While American power is in a state of relative decline, it would be far too premature to pronounce its end. Nevertheless, the reasons why such a decline in power has occurred have yet to be properly addressed – and it is probably the case that this large task cannot be undertaken without the perspective that only the lapse of time provides. One suspects, somehow, that America's military/security and financial crises are connected by some common and deeper malaise, and that similar political, institutional and intellectual failures are responsible for both, whatever the massive differences in the disciplinary fields involved. A provisional analysis of decline would, however, suggest a great irony: it is, arguably, precisely by asserting its sovereignty despite international law, despite the discomfort of the international community and, more particularly, its long-standing allies, that the United States has proceeded to elaborately and insistently play out its own drama of descent. It is by acting hegemonically in disregard of international norms that the United States has dissipated its power, both morally and militarily. It is commonplace to describe 9/11 as a tragedy without dwelling too closely on what the term 'tragedy' meant to the great dramatists who were preoccupied by this question. Greek tragedy involved an internecine violence that would continue inexorably, reproducing itself, for generations. By the time we arrive at Shakespeare, tragedy could be simplistically and yet usefully thought of as the fall of a great man as a result of a fundamental weakness. We might see the years since 9/11, then, as embodying both these themes. Hundreds of civilian deaths have occurred as a result of the massive violence that the United States has launched in various countries and this is surely likely to create a resentment and sense of injustice that will last for the foreseeable future. Proclamations that all this is being done to further peace, security and human rights may not suffice. And the disturbing and yet inevitable lurch and stumble towards war in Iraq, perhaps even an action desired by Al Qaeda, and certainly one urged by many neo-conservative commentators, has some resemblance to Macbeth succumbing to the goading of Lady Macbeth, or Othello being enmeshed in the wiles of Iago, his nobility and warrior prowess proving to be of little protection against his crucial weaknesses. 'Who is it that can tell me who I am?' demands that other deeply injured sovereign, King Lear, shocked to discover a previously inconceivable vulnerability and presenting more a challenge than a question.

This turn to hegemony, which has had such varied and imponderable consequences, did not occur in a vacuum. It occurred within an intellectual framework constructed by bold and confident scholars and policy-makers who presented themselves as having the answers to these profoundly difficult questions of world order, and as willing to take the firm and decisive action that the international system was too timid, vacillating and cowardly to engage in. It is in this context that Vagts' article on HIL seems so remarkable. It is remarkable not only because of its acute and prescient analysis of the character of HIL, but because of the position it adopted in that particular political context. Given the shocking events of 9/11 it would have been natural to respond, as many did, with a call to arms, a declaration that world order was being fatally undermined and that decisive and world-transforming action was required. 9/11 generated new theories – of history, of global policy, of international law and relations. Many of these grand theories were impressively erudite, thorough and wide-ranging in reference and yet, somehow, glib and superficial. Much that was proclaimed to be new and radical would have been revealed, on closer scrutiny, to be quite old and indeed, even, discarded. Vagts' work stands in stark contrast.

Vagts states at the beginning of his article on HIL that he takes no position on whether the United States is or should be a hegemon. His posture initially appears to be that of the detached but curious observer. And yet he does take sides, and his own position is made quite clear, not only by his pointed reference to Ozymandias but, more particularly, in the conclusion of his article, where he quietly and powerfully suggests the dangers, for States, and for world order, of imperial overreach – this by simply citing the last verses of 'Recessional', the warning issued by that ardent champion of Empire, Rudyard Kipling himself. Vagts' approach and tone – concise, ironic, quizzical, even diffident – contrast markedly with the scholars who urged the United States to embrace their imperial role[45] and who proclaimed their theories and histories in the grand manner and soaring rhetoric. Where others advocated shock and awe, he subtly pointed to the phenomenon that has played such a prominent role in both Greek tragedy and imperial histories – hubris.

I have suggested that Vagts' vision of international law is infused by a profound sense of history which in turn has shaped his understanding of the relationship between law and violence and of our vocation as international lawyers.[46] This combination has created, not merely an expertise

---

[45] M. Boot, *The Savage Wars of Peace* (New York: Basic Books, 2002), for instance, directly invokes Kipling's clarion call to the United States to take up the white man's burden.

[46] R. Bilder and D. F. Vagts, 'Speaking Law to Power. Lawyers and Torture', *AJIL*, 98 (2004), 689–95.

but what can only be termed, for want of a better term, a wisdom about international law in the world. It is a modestly presented, understated and sometimes underappreciated wisdom; but it has also a wisdom that is hard won, painfully acquired; it is a wisdom that has proven to be powerful and prophetic and one that we would do well to heed.

4

Textual interpretation and (international) law reading: the myth of (in)determinacy and the genealogy of meaning

ANDREA BIANCHI*

Introduction

Lawyers find certainties very appealing. Perhaps this is the case because they regard the law as stable and predictable. Law's fundamental certainties lie in its rules. The certainties of lawyers are also found there. Rules are called upon to perform the reassuring function of making us believe that what the law-maker considered to be right or wrong is clearly expressed in them. If there is doubt or ambiguity, objective canons of interpretation can readily be used to solve them. The law can thus regain its stabilising function. Reflections about law and its interpretation, which depart from the practitioner's task of saying what the law is, are often looked down upon and strictly relegated to the narrow boundaries of the academic discourse. To be fair, legal philosophers have long engaged in a debate about what interpretation is and how it works,[1] but the discourse within particular legal disciplines is usually confined to the rules and techniques (rules under the guise of technical tools) that

* The author would like to express his gratitude to Fouad Zarbiev for his inspiring suggestions for the drafting of this chapter.

[1] See, among others, J. Raz, *Between Authority and Interpretation. On the Theory of Law and Practical Reason* (Oxford University Press, 2009); M. H. Kramer, *Objectivity and the Rule of Law* (Cambridge University Press, 2007); A. Marmor, *Interpretation and Legal Theory*, 2nd edn., (Oxford and Portland, OR: Hart, 2005); A. Marmor (ed.), *Law and Interpretation. Essays in Legal Philosophy* (Oxford: Clarendon Press, 1997); P. Amselek (ed.), *Interprétation et droit* (Brussels: Bruylant, 1995); N. D. McCormick and R. S. Summers, 'Interpretation and Justification', in N. D. McCormick and R. S. Summers (eds.), *Interpreting Statutes. A Comparative Study* (Dartmouth: Aldershot, 1991), 511–44; R. Dworkin, *Law's Empire* (Cambridge, MA: Harvard University Press, 1986); R. Dworkin, *A Matter of Principle* (Cambridge, MA: Harvard University Press, 1985).

lawyers must follow while interpreting legal provisions.[2] Lately, a certain interest has arisen within the community of international lawyers about interpretation, partly due to its potential use for coping with the phenomenon of fragmentation. Interestingly enough, interpretation is regarded as both the problem, given the increasing number of epistemic communities within the discipline, and the solution, for its potential harmonising effect.[3]

Be that as it may, the official interpretive discourse remains strictly focused on the rules of interpretation and most of the current literature, thriving on a long-established tradition,[4] is almost obsessed with the primacy of the text and the need to use rules of interpretation to secure legal certainty. The current reflection of mainstream international legal scholarship remains imbued with traditional rule-based approaches to legal interpretation and lags far behind other disciplines, in which interpretive issues are analysed in depth and from different perspectives. The fact that the official discourse about interpretation in international law is impermeable to new approaches makes the theory of textual determinacy still the prevailing paradigm. At the opposite pole of the spectrum lie theories that maintain the indeterminate character of any textual interpretation. Although such theories, primarily developed in other fields, have so far failed to substantially affect mainstream thinking about interpretive issues, their consideration seems appropriate, given the steady advance of critical legal studies in international law. This chapter contends that both textual determinacy and indeterminacy are but myths and that the interpretive process, far from being merely the produce of linguistic analysis, is deeply embedded in a societal context where different actors interact with one another. Any serious attempt to

[2] See, e.g., R. Gardiner, *Treaty Interpretation* (Oxford University Press, 2008); A. Orakhelashvili, *The Interpretation of Acts and Rules in Public International Law* (Oxford University Press, 2008); U. Linderfalk, *On the Interpretation of Treaties* (Dordrecht: Springer, 2007); R. Kolb, *Interpretation et création du droit international. Esquisse d'une herméneutique juridique moderne pour le droit international public* (Brussels: Bruylant, 2006).

[3] *Fragmentation of International Law. Difficulties Arising from the Diversification and Expansion of International Law*, Report of the Study Group of the International Law Commission, A/CN.4/L.682 (13 April 2006) and the *Addendum on Draft Conclusions of the Work of the Study Group*, Finalised by Martti Koskenniemi, A/CN.4/L.682/Add. 1, 2 May 2006.

[4] See, for instance, Sir Gerald Fitzmaurice's well-known statement that 'texts must be interpreted as they stand, and, prima facie, without reference to extraneous factors', Sir G. Fitzmaurice, 'The Law and Procedure of the International Court of Justice. Treaty Interpretation and Other Treaty Points', *BYBIL*, 33 (1957), 203–93, 212.

investigate the genealogy of meaning cannot overlook this fundamental characteristic of the interpretive process. This should be a cause for shifting the focus of analysis from the alleged inherent properties of the text to the interpretive communities whose strategies ultimately determine what a text means.

This chapter explores the ways in which (international) lawyers deal with textual interpretation. Such expressions as 'plain meaning' or 'ordinary meaning' seem to reflect the determinacy of the text and the objective character of interpretation. An attempt will be made to demonstrate that language as such conveys no clear and objective meaning and that only by resorting to context and/or other extra-linguistic elements may 'meaning' be considered clear. By the same token, there is no such thing as an absolute indeterminacy of a legal text. Postulating an infinite regress of legal interpretation and, therefore, its indeterminate character fails to consider that the problem of 'meaning' in law poses a practical challenge, as decisions must be taken on the basis of what a certain interpretive community perceives to be the law. While deconstructing the myths of determinacy and indeterminacy of textual interpretation, the chapter ultimately attempts to show that meaning originates in a social community and that legal interpretation is constrained by factors and circumstances that are often overlooked by international legal scholarship.

'Plain meaning' and the linguistic paradigm

The discourse about legal interpretation primarily revolves around the linguistic paradigm. The linguistic properties of a rule or other legal prescription are regarded as determinant in establishing the rule's plain meaning or ambiguity. In international law, Art. 31 of the Vienna Convention on the Law of Treaties endorses this approach by giving priority to literal interpretation. The ordinary meaning to be attributed to the terms of a treaty is considered a primary interpretive tool. The idea that words have a 'plain meaning' is widely shared among international lawyers. It suffices to cast a quick glance at international case-law to realise that international tribunals fairly frequently resort to language dictionaries. If recourse by the International Court of Justice (ICJ) to *The Oxford English Dictionary* to determine the ordinary meaning of the word 'commerce' has remained an isolated instance,[5] its frequent use

---

[5] *Oil Platforms (Islamic Republic of Iran v. United States of America)*, Judgment on Preliminary Objection, ICJ Rep. 1996 818, para. 45.

by the WTO Dispute Settlement Body caused one of its former members to speak of *The Shorter Oxford Dictionary* as 'one of the covered agreements'.[6] It would be misleading to think that the 'plain meaning' as evidenced by a language dictionary is used to shed light only on such prosaic terms as the ones that may appear in a trade agreement. Sir Gerald Fitzmaurice, deeply committed to the 'correct handling of language', made use of dictionaries to prove that the five interrogation techniques used by the United Kingdom against IRA terrorist suspects could not be reasonably defined as 'inhuman treatment' under Art. 3 of the European Convention on Human Rights.[7]

As is well known, the interpretive techniques of textual reference and plain meaning were instrumental for the Office of the Legal Counsel at the US Department of Justice to provide a definition of torture which would allow US officials to use highly coercive techniques of interrogation *vis-à-vis* terrorist suspects. In the notorious 'Bybee Memo',[8] which interpreted the notion of torture under the 1984 UN Convention as implemented by Section 2340 and 2340A of title 18 of the United States Code, the drafter expressly stated that the text of the statute 'must be the starting point'. Since torture is defined in the statute as an act that causes 'severe physical or mental pain or suffering', the question arose of how to construe the term 'severe' in accordance with 'its ordinary and natural meaning'. Having first resorted to a number of dictionaries, including the 1935 (*sic!*) version of *Webster's New International Edition*, the focus shifted from dictionaries to statutory sources without apparent reason, but always with the goal of spotting the natural and ordinary meaning of the expression 'severe pain'.

---

[6] C.-D. Ehlermann, 'Six Years on the Bench of the "World Trade Court", Some Personal Experiences as Member of the Appellate Body of the World Trade Organization', *Journal of World Trade*, 36 (2002), 605–39, 616.

[7] ECtHR, *Ireland* v. *United Kingdom*, Case No. 5310/71 (1978), Judgment of 18 January 1978, Separate Opinion of Judge Sir Gerald Fitzmaurice, §§22 and 25, footnote 16: 'The principal dictionaries I have consulted are the Shorter Oxford ("shorter" only than the full Oxford in several volumes, and itself running to 2,500 pages); the superlative American Random House Dictionary of the English Language – probably the best one-volume English Dictionary extant; Webster's Third International; and, in the popular category, Professor Garmonsway's excellent Penguin English Dictionary.'

[8] See Memorandum for John Rizzo, Acting General Counsel for the Central Intelligence Agency, from Jay S. Bybee, Assistant Attorney General. Re: Standards of conduct for Interrogation under 18 USC §§2340–2340A, 1 August 2002. A substantially similar argument is developed also in Memorandum for William J. Haines, II, General Counsel of the Department of Defense, from John Yoo, Deputy Assistant Attorney General. Re: Military Interrogation of Alien Unlawful Combatants Held Outside the US, March 14, 2003, esp. 38 ff.

In particular, the memorandum examined those other US statutes in which the notion appeared. Eventually reference was made to those statutes which define an emergency medical condition, where the expression 'severe' refers to damage that rises 'to the level of death, organ failure, or the permanent impairment of a significant body function'. The plain meaning of 'severe pain' was thus equated to death, organ failure, or permanent impairment of a significant body function, short of which there *plainly* cannot be torture.

The 'plain meaning' doctrine is widely supported in both national and international law. Such eminent specialists in semiotics as Umberto Eco provide further support to the doctrine by advocating the existence, within any given language, of a literal meaning of lexical terms, which represents a constraint to any further effort at interpretation.[9] Although it is not easy to free legal interpretation from the shackles of linguistics and propose alternative readings, it may nonetheless be worth questioning whether 'the search for the power of words is to be carried out within the words themselves'.[10]

A few illustrations from actual practice may help shed light on the limits of 'plain meaning' and provide its most fervent followers with some food for thought. In a case which has been made well known by critics of the doctrine of plain meaning,[11] a US district court had to pass judgment in a suit concerning the sale of chicken by an American retailer to a Swiss company.[12] The latter complained that the kind of chicken delivered to it was not what it expected. In particular, the Swiss company maintained that according to commercial usages the word 'chicken' had

---

[9] U. Eco, *The Limits of Interpretation* (Bloomington and Indianapolis, IN: University of Indiana Press, 1994), 5–6: 'within the boundaries of a given language, there is a literal meaning of lexical items and that is the one listed first by dictionaries as well as the one that Everyman would first define when requested to say what a given word means ... No reader-oriented theory can avoid such a constraint. Any act of freedom on the part of the reader can come *after*, not *before*, the acceptance of that constraint' (emphasis in original).

[10] The concept of 'chercher le pouvoir des mots dans les mots' is borrowed from P. Bourdieu, *Ce que parler veut dire. L'économie des échanges linguistiques* (Paris: Fayard, 1982), 103. See the English translation of the relevant passage: 'As soon as one treats language as an autonomous object ... one is condemned to looking within words for the power of words, that is, looking for it where it is not to be found' (P. Bourdieu, *Language and Symbolic Power* (Cambridge, MA: Harvard University Press, 1999), 108).

[11] See A. L. Corbin, 'The Interpretation of Words and the Parole Evidence Rule', *Cornell Law Quarterly*, 50 (1965), 161 n. 190, esp. 164–70, and W. Benn Michaels, 'Against Formalism. The Autonomous Text in Legal and Literary Interpretation', *Poetics Today*, 1 (1979), 23–34, esp. 25–7.

[12] See *Frigaliment Importing Co. v. BNS International Sales Corp.*, 190 F. Supp. 116 (SDNY 1960).

a precise meaning (fryers and roasters) which did not correspond to what it had actually got (stewing chicken or fowl). The American company, in turn, argued that its interpretation of the word 'chicken', as it appeared in the contract, could also cover the animals it had actually delivered. The judge then famously asked the question 'What is chicken?', and, acknowledging that standing alone the term is ambiguous, resorted to the expert testimony of the operator of a chicken-eviscerating plant in New Jersey, who declared: 'Chicken is everything except a goose, a duck, and a turkey. Everything is a chicken but then you have to say, you have to specify which category you want or that you are talking about.'[13]

If the word 'chicken' hardly conveys a plain meaning for the purpose of a simple commercial sale, let us imagine a more complex setting in which the use of arms and criminal law are at stake. In the case of *Smith* v. *US*,[14] the Supreme Court was sharply divided on the issue of whether the bartering of a firearm for drugs constitutes 'use of a firearm' within the meaning of 18 USC §924(c)(1). The relevant criminal law provision provides that 'whoever, during and in relation to any crime of violence or drug trafficking crime . . . uses or carries a firearm, shall, in addition to the punishment for such a crime of violence or drug trafficking crime, be sentenced to imprisonment for five years'. The fact that the defendant had traded in his firearm for drugs made the meaning of the expression 'uses or carries a firearm' less plain than it ought to have been, with the Justices arguing vehemently over how the statutory construction canon of plain meaning should be properly applied to the case.[15]

---

[13] As quoted by Benn Michaels, *supra* n. 11, 26.   [14] 508 US 223 (1993).

[15] See, by way of example, Justice Scalia's dissent: 'When someone asks "Do you use a cane?" he is not inquiring whether you have your grandfather's silver handled walking stick on display in the hall; he wants to know whether you *walk* with a cane. Similarly, to speak of "using a firearm" is to speak of using it for its distinctive purpose, i.e., as a weapon. To be sure, "one can use a firearm in a number of ways,". . . including as an article of exchange, just as one can "use" a cane as a hall decoration – but that is not the ordinary meaning of "using" the one or the other. [footnote omitted] The Court does not appear to grasp the distinction between how a word *can be* used and how it *ordinarily is* used. It would, indeed, be "both reasonable and normal to say that petitioner 'used' his MAC-10 in his drug trafficking offense by trading it for cocaine." . . . It would also be reasonable and normal to say that he "used" it to scratch his head. When one wishes to describe the action of employing the instrument of a firearm for such unusual purposes, "use" is assuredly a verb one could select. But that says nothing about whether the *ordinary* meaning of the phrase "uses a firearm" embraces such extraordinary employments. It is unquestionably *not* reasonable and normal, I think, to say simply "do not use firearms" when one means to prohibit selling or scratching with them' (emphasis in the original).

International lawyers, too, have used similar examples to caution against excessive reliance on plain meaning. Lord McNair, in his famous treatise on the law of treaties, reports of a case concerning the will of a man who had left everything he possessed to 'mother'.[16] Indeed, he wrote unambiguously in his will: 'All for mother.' Interestingly enough, the whole heritage was attributed to the man's widow, who was referred to by all her family members, including her husband, as 'mother'.

Even silence can be deemed to have a plain meaning. For instance, the US Supreme Court in the 1992 *Alvarez Machain* case,[17] relying on the plain meaning of the bilateral US–Mexico Extradition Treaty, upheld the legality of Alvarez Machain's kidnapping from Mexico by US officials. According to the Supreme Court, the silence of the treaty could have no other meaning than that of allowing conduct which was neither expressly nor deliberately prohibited in its text. Along similar lines, the absence in domestic State immunity statutes of an explicit exception concerning torture has been a cause for US[18] and UK[19] courts to uphold the general rule of immunity to the benefit of foreign States.[20]

These examples are interesting as they show that words as such (or even their absence) are neither clear nor ambiguous. After all, such words as 'chicken' and 'mother' hardly present any lexical ambiguity. As McNair put it, '[n]o term could be "plainer" than "mother", for a man can only have one mother'.[21] In fact, what makes the meaning of a word 'plain', 'clear', or 'unambiguous' is not any linguistic property the word may have but rather the context in which it is used and the code used for communication in a particular situation by a certain community. In

---

[16] A. McNair, *The Law of Treaties* (Oxford: Clarendon Press, 1961), 367.

[17] *US v. Alvarez Machain*, 504 US 655 (1993), reproduced in *ILM* 31 (1992) 902.

[18] *Saudi Arabia v. Nelson*, 507 US 349 (1993), relying on its previous interpretation of the Foreign Sovereign Immunities Act in *Argentine Republic v. Amerada Hess Shipping Corp. et al.*, 488 US 428 (1989), esp. 435–6.

[19] In *Al-Adsani v. Government of Kuwait (No. 2) ILR* 107 (1996), 536, Ward, LJ said (549) 'the Act is as plain as plain can be'. This approach was confirmed by the House of Lords in *Jones v. Ministry of Interior Al-Mamlaka Al-Arabiya AS Saudiya (The Kingdom of Saudi Arabia) and others* (per Lord Bingham of Cornhill), Judgment of 14 June 2006, para. 13.

[20] On the interpretive issues underlying the question of state immunity for human rights violations, see A. Bianchi, 'Denying State Immunity to Violators of Human Rights', *Austrian Journal of Public and International Law*, 46 (1994), 195–229; A. Bianchi, 'L'immunité des Etats et les violations graves des droits de l'homme. La fonction de l'interprète dans la détermination du droit international', *Revue générale de droit international public*, 108 (2004), 63–101.

[21] A. McNair, *The Law of Treaties, supra* n. 16, 367.

other words – as Chaïm Perelman once put it – a text is clear not so much because its meaning is uncontroversial. It is clear because the text is uncontested.[22]

The relevance of context

The above remarks notwithstanding, the fact that any given text may have a clear or ordinary meaning or a meaning that goes without saying cannot be ruled out. What is called into question is the proposition that this comes from some intrinsic linguistic properties of the text itself. In fact, plain meaning is not the product of linguistic analysis but rather of context, broadly understood. Context includes not only a set of circumstances that are external to the interpreter. It also includes what could be termed as the interpreter's internal context – namely, her past experience, the knowledge she has of the domain to which the text belongs, her presuppositions and so on and so forth. This internal context creates a communicational structure which allows the interpreter to dispel the ambiguities surrounding the text – or, even, not to notice them at all.

An apt illustration of the importance of context, both external and internal, is given by Garrett, who uses as an example the statement: 'The boy chased a dog with a car.'[23] In interpreting this statement, we presuppose that the boy makes use of the car to chase the dog. It is highly unlikely for anyone of us to think that the dog, which the boy is chasing, has a car. And yet nothing in the grammatical structure of the phrase compels this conclusion. We think that the boy rather than the dog has a car because of our experience and knowledge of the empirical world. By the same token, if the statement to be interpreted were: 'The boy chased the dog with a bone', we would presuppose that the dog rather than the boy has the bone. Our conclusion is mandated not so much by the plain meaning of words but by what we know about dogs (and boys).

If you are addressed in a written statement in which the words 'You have been negligent' appear, the precise meaning as well as the consequences of these words may well vary depending on who issued the statement and on the context and circumstances in which you have

---

[22] C. Perelman, *Logique juridique. Nouvelle rhétorique* (Paris: Dalloz, 1990), 36.
[23] M. F. Garrett, 'Does Ambiguity Complicate the Perception of Sentences?', in G. B. Flores d'Arcais and W. J. M. Levelt (eds.), *Advances in Psycholinguistics* (Amsterdam: North-Holland, 1970), 51–2.

received it. You may be in the classroom and receive it from your teacher who wants to formally reproach you (and to let your parents know) that you have not done your homework properly, which may imply that you get a bad mark and possibly something else once you go back home. Or, you may read these words in a legal summons and soon find yourself in a courtroom before a judge, in which case the consequences may depend on which legal rules and prescriptions you have violated by your negligent conduct. Finally, you may read these very words in a registered letter sent from your boss, who is not happy with your work performance and you may soon need to find another job. 'You have been negligent' has therefore no plain meaning outside of its context.

To insist on this particular point seems all the more necessary, as most of the time the 'plain meaning' of a text presents itself as self-evident. As such, it seems to require no interpretation.[24] If the literal or plain meaning of a text is so readily comprehensible to us, regardless of its context, this is so because the interpretive act that we carry out is so deeply embedded in the societal and contextual setting that we do not perceive of it as an interpretive act at all.[25] In other words, the context is so 'deeply assumed' that it becomes 'invisible to the observer'.[26]

Categories, rules and idealised cognitive models

An interesting strand of investigation is the one that traces the relative clarity of a text to its correspondence to idealised cognitive models that

---

[24] 'We are never not in a situation. Because we are never not in a situation, we are never not in the act of interpreting. Because we are never not in the act of interpreting, there is no possibility of reaching a level of meaning beyond or below interpretation.' (Stanley Fish, 'Normal Circumstances, Literal Language, Direct Speech Acts, the Ordinary, the Everyday, the Obvious, What Goes without Saying, and Other Special Cases', in S. Fish, *Is There a Text in This Class? The Authority of Interpretive Communities* (Cambridge, MA: Harvard University Press, 1980), 276–7.

[25] *Ibid.*, 276: 'Every literal meaning comes to us with that claim, but it is a claim that seems supportable only because an interpretive act is already in force but is so embedded in the situation . . . that it doesn't seem to be an act at all.'

[26] S. Fish, 'Consequences', in S. Fish, *Doing What Comes Naturally. Change, Rhetoric, and the Practice of Theory in Literary and Legal Studies* (Bloomington and Indianapolis, IN: Duke University Press, 1989), 320–1: 'To be sure, there are sentences which, when presented, seem to be intelligible in isolation, independently of any contextual setting. This simply means, however, that the context is so established, so deeply assumed that it is invisible to the observer – he does not realize that what appears to him to be immediately obvious and readable is a function of its being in place.'

are based on knowledge and experience. In order to understand the functioning of this theory, inspiration can be drawn from the works of Georges Lakoff,[27] Charles Fillmore[28] and Steven Winter.[29] Their respective studies of 'categories' is particularly enlightening as categories are fundamental to legal thinking.

According to the traditional view, categories have fixed boundaries and their content is predetermined. They are not supposed to be influenced by teleological considerations and operate by the logic of necessary and sufficient conditions. If any given object meets a certain number of predetermined properties, the object can be deemed to belong to the category. If it does not, it cannot belong to that particular category. *Tertium non datur*. This mode of thinking, however, is flawed and hardly explains how things happen in the real world. If one takes the noun 'bachelor', often used as an example in logic, the word is immediately associated with the condition of an unmarried man. But if we were to provide an example of a bachelor, most likely James Bond will do better than Tarzan or the Pope.[30] Why should it be so? Tarzan and the Pope are bachelors, just as James Bond is. According to formal logic, neither Tarzan nor the Pope can be at the same time bachelors and non-bachelors.

The answer to this puzzling question lies in the fact that a category is not created *ex nihilo*, nor does it operate in a vacuum. As explained by Charles Fillmore, categories are inconceivable outside the background of knowledge and experience that originated their creation and justify their existence. We cannot infer whether a certain person can be categorised as

[27] G. Lakoff, *Women, Fire, and Dangerous Things. What Categories Reveal about the Mind* (University of Chicago Press, 1990); G. Lakoff and M. Johnson, *Metaphors We Live By* (University of Chicago Press, 2003).

[28] See, in particular, the following works by Charles Fillmore: 'Frame Semantics and the Nature of Language', in S. Harnad, H. D. Steklis and J. Lancaster (eds.), *Origins and Evolution of Language and Speech*, Annals of the New York Academy of Sciences, 280 (1976), 20–32; 'Scenes-and-Frames Semantics', in A. Zampolli (ed.), *Linguistic Structure Processing* (Amsterdam: North-Holland, 1977), 55 n. 82; 'Frame Semantics', in Linguistic Society of Korea (ed.), *Linguistics in the Morning Calm* (Seoul: Hanshin Publishing Co., 1982), 111–37; 'Towards a Descriptive Framework for Spatial Deixis', in R. J. Jarvella and Wolfgang Klein (eds.), *Speech, Place and Action. Studies in Deixis and Related Topics* (New York: John Wiley, 1982), 31–59.

[29] S. L. Winter, *A Clearing in the Forest. Law, Life, and Mind* (University of Chicago Press, 2001).

[30] *Ibid.*, 86.

a 'bachelor' unless we know the reasons that prompted a linguistic community to forge this particular category.[31]

The idea that the functioning of categories is not governed by formal logic is further attested by another example provided by Georges Lakoff and Mark Johnson, which clearly shows that the categories we use are never rigidly predetermined in terms of the inherent properties of the objects belonging to them. To establish whether something belongs to a given category depends on the use that we make of such categories. If a friend asks you to bring along four additional chairs for tonight's discussion group and you turn up with a hardback chair, a rocking chair, a beanbag chair and a hassock, reporting back to your friend that you brought the four chairs he wanted, your statement can be regarded as true and your friend will be grateful to you. But if you had brought those four chairs to a friend who had asked for four additional chairs for a formal dinner, your statement that you brought the four chairs that he wanted could be considered as false or misleading and most likely your friend will not be happy about it, since the chairs you brought are not proper chairs for a formal dinner.[32]

A correct understanding of how categories function is all the more important in law. Legal rules are as flexible and context-sensitive as the categories from which the above-mentioned examples are borrowed. Formalists find it hard to accept that this is the case. An eminent representative of legal formalism, Frederic Schauer asks whether a rule that prohibits bringing animals on the bus should be applicable to somebody who brings a goldfish on to a bus in a little plastic bag.[33] To Schauer the answer is in the affirmative, as the fish, however small, is 'literally' an animal. Winter objects, however, arguing that in this case 'a literal approach to the rule is literally impossible'.[34] Schauer's perspective

---

[31] This point is well made by Charles Fillmore in 'Towards a Descriptive Framework for Spatial Deixis', *supra* n. 28, 34: 'The noun bachelor can be defined as an unmarried adult man, but the noun clearly exists as a motivated device for categorizing people only in the context of a human society in which certain expectations about marriage and marriageable age obtain. Male participants in modern long-term unmarried couplings would not ordinarily be described as bachelors; a boy abandoned in the jungle and grown to maturity away from contact with human society would not be called a bachelor; John Paul II is not properly thought of as a bachelor . . . The assumption that a word is being properly used brings with it the assumption that the conditions obtain within which the existence of the category is motivated.'

[32] G. Lakoff and M. Johnson, *Metaphors We Live By*, *supra* n. 27, 164.

[33] F. Schauer, 'Formalism', *Yale Law Journal*, 97 (1988), 509–48, 533.

[34] Winter, *A Clearing in the Forest*, *supra* n. 29, 102.

presupposes that legal rules (like categories) have boundaries that are fixed once and for all and can never vary in content depending on context and purpose. This approach may lead to fairly absurd results. For instance, the way in which Schauer uses the adverb 'literally' to say that a fish is an animal, could be used also to say that man is 'literally' an animal. Should one infer that men are prevented from taking buses? How about some paramecia (protozoan) for medical experiments brought on to the bus? Would they be covered by the prohibition as well?[35]

If formalism can lead to such absurd results, the reason lies in its misunderstanding of how legal categories, like any other type of categories, function. The category 'animal' is not to be taken in isolation. In the context we analysed it has to be defined in relation to the category 'bus'. Our understanding of the function that a bus performs allows us to say that human beings do not fall within the scope of the prohibition. Along similar lines, our knowledge of the problems that may be caused to passengers by animals in the bus can lead us to conclude that neither the little goldfish nor the paramecia should be concerned by the rule.[36]

The understanding of categories and rules presupposes an idealised cognitive model (ICM). This concept, elaborated by Georges Lakoff, is instrumental to realising how our understanding of a category always relies on an idealised model created by our knowledge and experience, which creates cognitive expectations. The clear character of a case or of a rule depends on how easily it relates to making an almost automatic association with such an idealised cognitive model. For instance, the use of such words as 'to sell' or 'to buy' elicits the cognitive model of a commercial transaction which sets in motion such other words associated with it by our experience as 'good', 'property' and 'money'. By the same token, the category of bachelor functions in accordance with an idealised cognitive model which implies the existence of human society, presupposes as a rule heterosexual marriage, a certain age for getting married, the absence of reasons which might make marriage impossible and so on and so forth. If a person is not yet married and most of the above-mentioned conditions are met, as with James Bond, there would be something distinct about his way of living, which could justify the existence of the category of 'bachelor'.[37] The use of the same category

---

[35] *Ibid.*   [36] *Ibid.*, 102–3.
[37] *Ibid.*, 86–7; see also C. Fillmore, 'Scenes-and-Frames Semantics', *supra* n. 28, 69.

would be justified neither for Tarzan living alone in the jungle, outside human society, nor for the Pope who, as a Catholic clergyman, is prevented from getting married. Similarly, the category 'widow' would not be applied to every single woman whose husband is dead. It would be difficult to refer to a woman who has killed her husband as a widow or use the word to refer to a woman who has lost two out of her three husbands. Here the cognitive model implies that one can be married only to one person at the time, that life is irremediably disrupted by the loss of the husband and so on.[38] Categories function on the basis of idealised cognitive models against which background concrete cases are evaluated.

Such idealised cognitive models are at work any time that we are called upon to interpret and give meaning to a legal text in different contexts. To take just one example, reference to proportionality may be made in numerous areas of international law. Depending on whether proportionality is invoked in relation to the use of force,[39] to the law of counter-measures,[40] to international humanitarian or human rights law,[41] or to trade disputes,[42] its connotations as well as its practical application may vary. Mention of the proportionality principle in any such areas connects the interpreter with a set of specific standards, past decisions and ad hoc rationales that permit us to characterise the content and scope of application of the principle in the particular context in which it is invoked. Similarly, the frequent use by international lawyers of such adjectives as 'fair and equitable', whose meaning would be considered by many as clear as it can be, may denote the existence and applicability of profoundly different legal regimes. Fair and equitable treatment of foreign investment[43] has little to do with the fair and equitable sharing of the

---

[38] *Ibid.*, 69–70.

[39] See J. Gardam, *Necessity, Proportionality and the Use of Force by States* (Cambridge University Press, 2004).

[40] For an overview, see T. Franck, 'On Proportionality of Countermeasures in International Law', *AJIL*, 102 (2009), 715–67. See also E. Cannizzaro, 'The Role of Proportionality in the Law of International Countermeasures', *EJIL*, 12 (2001), 889–916.

[41] See A. Gross, 'Human Proportions. Are Human Rights the Emperor's New Clothes of the International Law of Occupation?', *EJIL*, 18 (2007), 1–35.

[42] See A. D. Mitchell, 'Proportionality and Remedies in WTO Disputes', *EJIL*, 17 (2006), 985–1008.

[43] See I. Tudor, *The Fair and Equitable Treatment Standard in International Foreign Investment Law* (Oxford University Press, 2008).

benefits arising out of the utilisation of genetic resources,[44] let alone with the equitable use of international watercourses.[45]

The relevance of the ICM theory to interpretation is further attested by the fairly rare situations in which cognitive models do not match. A striking example of diverging cognitive models hampering the comprehension of a text is the well-known case of the 1840 Treaty of Waitangi, between the British Crown and the Maori population, still regarded today as a constitutional moment in the history of New Zealand.[46] The treaty as interpreted by the British Crown conferred sovereignty over the territory occupied by the aboriginal population to the Queen. The word used in the Maori version, *Kawanatanga*, did not really have a meaning in the Maori language and was a transliteration from English of the word 'governorship'. The Maori, most likely convinced to have given away to the British Crown limited control over the new settlers, were reassured that *Rangatiratanga* (chieftainship) was left to them according to Article 2 of the Treaty, as the word meant to them control and authority over all things Maori. By the same token, the British conception of property (in the English text) was left with the Maori chiefs and hardly corresponded to the Maori's broader conception of valued possessions (*Taonga*). Evidence of this latter discrepancy is the controversy attested to by recent domestic litigation in New Zealand about the Maori notion of *Taonga* as including both culture and language as opposed to the narrower Western notion of property.[47] A further difficulty was that oral communication was far more important to the Maori than written language: most likely they paid more attention to what the Queen's representatives actually said in their dealings with them than to what they later signed.[48]

---

[44] See Art. 1 of the 1992 UN Convention on Biological Diversity and the 2002 Bonn Guidelines on Access to Genetic Resources and Fair and Equitable Sharing of the Benefits Arising Out of their Utilization.

[45] See the 1997 UN Convention on the Non-Navigational Uses of International Watercourses, esp. Arts. 5 and 6.

[46] See, among others, C. Orange, *The Treaty of Waitangi* (Wellington: Allen & Unwin and Port Nicholson Press, 1987); P. McHugh, *The Maori Magna Charta* (Oxford University Press, 1991); Douglas Graham, *Trick or Treaty?* (Wellington: Institute of Policy Studies, 1997).

[47] See A. Sharpe, *Justice and the Maori. The Philosophy and Practice of Maori Claims in New Zealand* (Oxford University Press, 1997).

[48] Interesting insights on this and other aspects related to the Treaty of Waitangi are provided in D. F. McKenzie, *Bibliography and the Sociology of Texts* (Cambridge University Press, 1999).

Indeterminacy and its limits

Even though textual indeterminacy has not been overtly advocated in international law, the growing importance of critical approaches to the discipline makes its introduction into the disciplinary discourse more than a mere eventuality.[49] What are the implications of such an approach to legal interpretation? Clearly, the most obvious consequence is that the criteria to which rules of interpretation refer cannot themselves be exempted from interpretation. It is not sufficient to define what context is or to identify the preparatory works of a treaty. They are still to be interpreted because a text is not 'available' or 'readable' independently of interpretation.[50] Sir Percy Spencer warned against this risk in his individual opinion attached to the ICJ judgment in the case concerning the *Application of the Convention of 1902 Governing the Guardianship of Infants (Netherlands v. Sweden)*, when he said that one would tend to interpret the preparatory works and carry the interpretation over to the convention, which should be 'the sole object of interpretation'.[51] In the *LaGrand Case* the ICJ blatantly disregarded such a warning, by relying on the preparatory works of its Statute to establish the binding nature of interim measures.[52] Incidentally, those that unfavourably viewed giving binding force to such measures had used the very same preparatory works to reach the opposite conclusion.[53]

The fundamental idea behind indeterminacy theories is that one can never stop interpreting. Derrida once put it as follows, 'il n'y a pas de hors-texte': one can go as far as one might wish; jumping from one signifier to another, as there is no transcendental signifier. The most compelling counterargument of all, however, is that law does not operate in the world of absolutes. It works in concrete situations where decisions

---

[49] See the seminal works of D. Kennedy, *International Legal Structures* (Baden-Baden: Nomos, 1987), and M. Koskenniemi, *From Apology to Utopia. The Structure of International Legal Argument* (Helsinki: Lakimiesliiton Kustannus, 1989, reprinted by Cambridge University Press, 2005).

[50] See S. Fish, 'Fish v. Fiss', *Stanford Law Review*, 36 (1984), 1325–47.

[51] ICJ Reports 1958, 129–30: 'there is always the danger that, instead of interpreting the relevant treaty or convention, one will find oneself tending to interpret the preparatory work and then transferring that interpretation across to the treaty or convention which is the sole subject of interpretation'.

[52] See *LaGrand Case (Germany v. United States of America)*, Judgment of 27 June 2001, 2001 ICJ Rep. 466 ff., 503–6 (paras. 104–9).

[53] See, among others, M. Hudson, *La Cour permanente de justice internationale* (Paris: Pedone, 1936), 486.

must be taken and disputes must be settled. This is why recourse is made to a certain number of criteria which emerge from practice. As Rorty aptly put it 'a criterion *is* a criterion because some particular social practice needs to block the road of inquiry, halt the regress of interpretations, in order to get something done'.[54]

Another variant of the indeterminacy doctrine emphasises the incapacity of language to constrain the actors. In the famous example given by D'Amato, Professor Hart attempts to enter a public park with his book, *The Concept of Law*, tucked under his arm. The guard on duty stops him and refuses to let him in, pointing to the sign that says: 'No vehicle in the park.' Hart is stunned and replies that he is carrying a book, which is not a vehicle, as it does not have a motor, does not consume petrol and one cannot travel in it. The guard apologetically says that he has no discretion in the matter and that he has to go by the exact definition of 'vehicle', with which statement Hart cannot but agree. At this point, the guard takes out of his pocket a slip of paper and says: 'Well, here it is. I copied it from the dictionary. It says that a book is a vehicle for ideas.'[55] However funny, the example does not prove much. As noted earlier, neither meaning nor interpretation can be meaningfully and productively addressed, let alone solved, by linguistic analysis. Incidentally, those who foster the idea that communication cannot be but indeterminate are at odds with a reality in which social communication, with all its limits and shortcomings, regularly takes place on a day-to-day basis. Moreover, they also fall into a self-referential inconsistency, as the works in which they advance their intellectual stances are effectively communicated and understood.

Finally, it is important to mention the theories of indeterminacy that underscore the contingent character of law. This is the approach of the critical legal studies movement which denies some of the foundational tenets of the law, in particular its alleged coherence and predictability. The critique consists of denying such fundamental characteristics by stressing that the law works solely on the basis of contingencies. At closer scrutiny, to say that law is contingent simply means that it cannot impose itself by its very nature and by its own essence and that it is the produce of the interaction of different actors in a certain context under certain

---

[54] R. Rorty, *Consequences of Pragmatism (Essays: 1972–1980)* (Minneapolis, MN: University of Minnesota Press, 1986), xii (emphasis in the original).

[55] A. D'Amato, 'Can Legislatures Constrain Judicial Interpretation of Statutes?', *Virginia Law Review*, 75 (1989), 596–7.

circumstances. This by no means undermines the reality of meaning. To take contingency to mean that another interpretation or another argument can always be found does not necessarily jeopardise the coherence of law, either. As Alexander Nehamas argues, albeit in a different context, 'the reason for looking for new interpretations is always that they will be better than the readings ... we have produced so far, and not simply the fact that they are new'.[56] In other words, 'this challenge is serious only if a better alternative is *in fact* devised, and in most cases this is not at all a simple task. The new alternative must be, according to some set of criteria, at least as satisfactory as the view it challenges.'[57]

A powerful counterargument to indeterminacy theories is to acknowledge that doubt and scepticism cannot be advanced just for their own sake. As Wittgenstein aptly noted, we do not doubt simply 'because it is possible for us to *imagine* a doubt'. The fact that I can 'easily imagine someone always doubting before opening his front door whether an abyss did not yawn behind it ... does not make me doubt in the same case'.[58] Just as well, since doubting has its own characteristic manifestations, it is not at all sure that we would call doubting the attitude of someone who 'said that he doubted the existence of his hands [and] kept looking at them from all sides'.[59]

Furthermore, the burden of proving the indeterminacy of law and of its interpretation lies with the proponents of such a radical stance. After all, interpretations of the law leading to all sorts of decisions are taken on a day-to-day basis in both domestic and international law. There is certainly no need to prove that law is capable of discharging its basic regulating functions. It may do so in an unjust, unsatisfactory, inefficient, or whatever else manner, but no one would dare argue that legal indeterminacy and the impossibility of providing an interpretation of a statutory provision or a treaty rule hamper the functioning of the legal system. By shifting the burden of proof on to the others, supporters of the indeterminacy theory try to escape what might be an insurmountable obstacle to them, namely to prove that law does not and cannot work.

Overall, the indeterminacy thesis may be true in the absolute. But a certain proposition needs to conform to the discursive policies set up by

---

[56] A. Nehamas, *Nietzsche. Life as Literature* (Cambridge, MA: Harvard University Press, 2002), 63.

[57] *Ibid.* (emphasis in the original).

[58] L. Wittgenstein, *Philosophical Investigations* (Oxford: Blackwell, 1953), n. 84 (emphasis in the original).

[59] L. Wittgenstein, *On Certainty* (Oxford: Blackwell, 1969), n. 255.

each discipline as a form of control. In other words, 'a proposition must fulfill some onerous and complex conditions before it can be admitted within a discipline'.[60] It cannot be spoken 'dans l'espace d'une extériorité sauvage'.[61] Before being recognised as true or false, the proposition must be 'within the truth'('dans le vrai').[62] In many ways, this is certainly not the case for the theory of indeterminacy at the present time. The discourse about indeterminacy could become truly disruptive if it were to leave the terrain of the absolute, enter the constraints of the discipline and turn into a 'political' project.

Meaning as social construct

At this point, having dispelled the opposite myths of textual determinacy and indeterminacy, one wonders how the formation of meaning may be explained. In fact, at the origin of meaning there is always a social community. Only within a community is communication possible and acts come to acquire a certain shared meaning. This fundamental contention, developed by different philosophers, must be the starting point for any attempt to investigate the origin of meaning, even in law. The continuous interaction of a social group in any given societal context determines the background against which meaning is formed. The idea that any act of interpretation, of whatever nature, is embedded in a complex web of social relations is reminiscent of Wittgenstein's notion of 'forms of life'. Although never neatly defined by its creator, the notion of 'forms of life' is crucial to understanding the way in which Wittgenstein deals with meaning. By that expression, Wittgenstein refers to the regularities of attitudes, behaviour and reactions that make up the complex web of societal interactions in which we carry out our existence.[63] According to him our acts, gestures and words acquire their

---

[60] M. Foucault, L'ordre du discours (Paris: Gallimard, 1971), 37, trans. into English by R. Swyer as Orders of Discourse, Social Science Information, 10/2 (April 1977), 16.

[61] Ibid., 17.   [62] Ibid.

[63] Hanna Pitkin explains Wittgenstein's concept of 'forms of life' in the following terms: 'human life as we live and observe it is not just a random, continuous flow, but displays recurrent patterns, regularities, characteristic ways of doing and being, of feeling and acting, of speaking and interacting. Because they are patterns, regularities, configurations, Wittgenstein calls them forms; and because they are patterns in the fabric of human existence and activity on earth, he calls them forms of life' (see H. F. Pitkin, Wittgenstein and Justice. On the Significance of Ludwig Wittgenstein for Social and Political Thought (Berkeley and Los Angeles, CA, University of California Press, 1972), 132).

meaning only against the background of the form of life in which we are set. [64]

To emphasise the communitarian dimension of the interpretive process is no novelty. Some distinguished philosophers such as Royce and Peirce put forward this contention long ago. Royce developed it in his work on Christian religion,[65] arguing that the real world cannot be conceived outside the interpretive community that provides it with a meaning which is common to the members of the community.[66] Along the same lines Peirce maintained that the concept of reality 'essentially involves the notion of community' and that 'the opinion which is fated to be ultimately agreed to by all who investigate is what we mean by the truth, and the object represented in this opinion is the real'.[67] According to Umberto Eco, in Peirce's theory the community transcends the intention of the single interpreter and 'from the moment in which the community is pulled to agree with a given interpretation, there is, if not an objective, at least an intersubjective meaning which acquires a privilege over any other possible interpretation spelled out without the agreement of the community'.[68]

The very notion of 'interpretive community' has been elaborated in great detail by Stanley Fish in the field of law and literary studies.[69] As is well known, Fish used the concept of interpretive community to solve the riddle of the authority of textual interpretation.[70] By shifting the focus from the text as the source of authority to the social dynamic of the community of interpreters, Fish dramatically changes the fundamental paradigms of traditional legal interpretation theories and breaks new grounds for the investigation of the origin of meaning. According to Fish, 'Interpretive communities are made up of those who share interpretive

---

[64] For a scholarly comment on Wittgenstein's concept of 'forms of life', see also G. P. Baker and P. M. S. Hacker, *Wittgenstein. Rules, Grammar and Necessity. An Analytical Commentary on the Philosophical Investigations* (Oxford: Blackwell, 1985), vol. II, 238–43.

[65] J. Royce, *The Problems of Christianity*, 2 vols. (New York: Macmillan, 1914).

[66] *Ibid.*, vol. I, 72. According to Royce a stable community generates mental artefacts such as languages, religions, customs and beliefs that no individual member could ever produce autonomously.

[67] See *Collected Papers of Charles Sanders Peirce* (Cambridge, MA: Harvard University Press, 1960), vol. V, para. 5.311.

[68] U. Eco, *The Limits of Interpretation, supra* n. 9, 40.

[69] The foundations of the theory were laid down by S. Fish in 'Interpreting the Variorum', in Fish, *Is There a Text in This Class?*, *supra* n. 24, 147–73.

[70] See S. Fish, 'Change', in *Doing What Comes Naturally, supra* n. 26, 141.

strategies not for reading (in the conventional sense) but for writing texts, for constituting their properties and assigning their intentions. In other words, these strategies exist prior to the act of reading and therefore determine the shape of what is read'.[71] The fact that interpretive communities may have different interpretive strategies explains why there may be no agreement on the interpretation of any given text.

Detlev Vagts immediately realised the importance of the interpretative community and its potential for being applied to international law and treaty interpretation. In his essay on 'Treaty Interpretation and the New American Ways of Law Reading',[72] he expressly uses the concept of interpretive community to set out on the fascinating journey of explaining how the interpretation of treaties forms itself through the interplay of the various actors, both domestic and international, that make up the interpretive community.[73] It is indeed a pity that this strand of investigation has not been pursued much further by international lawyers[74] and that the shackles of both formalism and radical critical approaches have scleroticised the debate by focusing on opposite, yet equally sterile, stances that refuse to take duly into account the more sociological aspects of interpretive processes.

To attempt to provide an interpretation of texts, including legal ones, on the basis of the notion of 'interpretive community' is not tantamount to denying the authority of interpretation. It simply shifts the focus from the text itself to the actors concerned with its interpretation. This process does not imply at all that any interpretation is admissible. It certainly is not an instrument to foster some sort of interpretive 'anything goes', as there may well be interpretations that are utterly inadmissible. Such inadmissibility, however, would no longer be drawn from some intrinsic textual elements but rather from the fact that, at a given time and in a

---

[71] S. Fish, *Is There a Text in This Class?, supra* n. 24, 171.

[72] D. F. Vagts, 'Treaty Interpretation and the New American Ways of Law Reading', *EJIL*, 4 (1993), 472–505, 480 ff.

[73] Vagts provides an operational definition of interpretive community, by underscoring the following prerequisites: '(1) generic or background consensus – sharing of a language and concerns and participation in the same "form of life"; (2) agreement as to the boundaries of the practice community members share; (3) common recognition of propositions as to what the practice requires as "truth" within the practice; (4) minimal consensus as to the existence of a text and a reading of it that is needed to provide a working distinction between interpretation and invention' (*ibid.*, 480).

[74] But see F. Zarbiev, *Le discours interprétatif en droit international: une approche critique et généalogique* (Geneva: Graduate Institute of International and Development Studies, PhD thesis, 2009), 98 ff.

given social context, shared interpretive strategies within the relevant interpretive community do not provide support to a particular interpretation of the text.[75]

In this respect, it is worth underscoring that the interpretive community theory provides no epistemological foundation for a theory of meaning. It is not a theory that aims to explain what a text means. Its main value lies rather in providing a sociological explanation of how different readings of a text emerge and by what process they become eligible for being considered as the correct interpretation of a text.[76] By departing from the foundationalist approach that presupposes the perfect independence of the object of investigation from the subject of knowledge and aims at getting an objective description of reality, independently of any subjective perspective, this theory focuses on the complex dynamic of social agents in charge of interpretation. This dynamic is such that interpretive communities constantly interact and strive to impose their different interpretive strategies. This causes the process of interpretation to move constantly and there is no guarantee that the prevailing interpretive community at any given time will succeed in preserving its pre-eminence forever. In a way, the interpretive community theory, with its strong social underpinnings, is flexible enough to allow for interpretation to adjust to changing societal needs.

Conclusion

The demystification of myths of dubious foundation lies not only within the intellectual's prerogatives but may also benefit the reflecting practitioner. Law and its interpretation are neither determinate nor indeterminate in absolute terms. To a-critically adhere to one of the two opposite poles of the spectrum is tantamount to ignoring what lies in between. To resist the sirens' song of plain meaning is not necessarily conducive to subscribing to indeterminacy. Law remains a pragmatic project, taken up with regulating social relations of all kinds. Interpretation is instrumental in shaping legal outcomes at all levels, from the decision-making process to adjudication and enforcement. To

---

[75] See S. Fish, 'What Makes an Interpretation Acceptable?', in Fish, *Is There a Text in This Class?*, *supra* n. 24, 345.

[76] S. Fish, 'One More Time', in G. A. Olson and L. Worsham (eds.), *Postmodern Sophistry. Stanley Fish and the Critical Enterprise* (Albany, NY: State University of New York Press, 2004), 277.

know that this is no neutral exercise and that considerations of context and purpose by the actors concerned are always relevant to producing outcomes does not take anything away from the legitimate regulatory function of the law. It may simply help us better understand how law functions in practice. If this process of understanding implies looking at such sociological notions as that of 'interpretive community', this is the fair tribute one has to pay to the complexity of social life and to the impossibility of finding all the answers one needs within the law itself.

Descartes was highly criticised because in the *Meditationes* he instilled doubts about the existence of God, albeit with the aim of dispelling them later through rational argumentation.[77] His defence was that his work was written in Latin and that therefore only an erudite public, perfectly capable of discerning the subtlety of his arguments, would have access to it. (Un)fortunately the book was soon thereafter translated into French and reached out to a much wider public, not necessarily so sophisticated as to understand Descartes' goals and the nuances of his method. History shows that rationalism has survived the critique and that people continue to believe in God.

---

[77] R. Descartes, *Meditationes de prima philosophia*, 1641. See the Trilingual HTML Edition, D. B. Manley and C. S. Taylor (eds.), including the 1647 French translation by the Duc de Luyan and the 1901 English translation by John Veitch (www.wright.edu/cola/descartes/).

5

The changing role of the State in the globalising world economy

JOST DELBRÜCK

Introduction

In the present worldwide financial crisis with its various disastrous impacts on the world economy, we can observe a renewed interest in the role of the State as a regulating actor in the world economy. Put more precisely, the question is whether we are facing a movement toward a State-centred protectionism. There is already a handy catchword around for this alleged movement – i.e. 'de-globalisation'.[1] If this concept is to be understood as a plea for the reinstatement of the State as the main regulatory actor in the world economy which should and could play the dominant role in the struggle to overcome the consequences of the present worldwide financial crisis, the question must be answered whether today's States actually are still in a position to live up to this gigantic task on their own.

In other words, the question must be answered as to whether present-day States still fit the criteria of the traditional concept of the sovereign territorial nation-state as such criteria had been defined in international law and political theory in the early twentieth century.[2] Only if this would be the case could we then consider 'de-globalisation' to be a possibly viable concept for solving the present economic and financial crisis, and potential future ones. The following considerations will proceed in three steps: a short look at the historic role of States in the regulation of their economies will be followed by an analysis of how

---

[1] See, e.g., H. James, 'Entglobalisierung: Vorwärts im Rückwärtsgang (Forward in Reverse Gear)', *IP*, 64(6) (2009), 10 *et seq*.

[2] See Art. 1, Montevideo Convention on Rights and Duties of States of 26 December 1933; see also G. Jellinek, *Allgemeine Staatslehre*, 3rd edn. (Berlin: O. Häring, 1914), 136–83, 394–504.

the means and institutions of the State that fulfil public tasks have changed because of the impact of globalisation. A final section will set out what the role and functions of the State are in the globalising world economy.

The role of classic territorial States in the economic environment of their time

Seventeenth- and eighteenth-century political philosophers defined the provision of internal and external security as well as the promotion of the general welfare as the core public tasks of the State.[3] In the early days of the unfolding modern territorial State, the implementation of these tasks was attributed to the monarchs and princes in the sense that they were a part of their paternal care. But with the stabilisation of the territorial State in the course of the late seventeenth and the beginning of the eighteenth century, the notion of a deliberate policy of directing economic transactions emerged. Although such policy did not yet aim at realising profit, it aimed at securing the necessary means for the implementation of the State's obligation to provide security and foster the general welfare. This approach has become known as the 'mercantilist system'.

When in the second half of the eighteenth century economic policies shifted toward promoting trade and commerce with the aim of realising profit, the question of the role of the State in the economic environment again became the object of debate. While in the mercantilist system State manufactures were the main economic factors, this system was challenged by the concept of the freedom of trade and commerce.

A most prominent expression of the emerging change of the economic paradigms is Adam Smith's famous book on the Wealth of Nations,[4] where he – for the first time – systematically and in a scientific manner calls for the abolition of all economic restrictions. However, contrary to allegations by Smith's critics of his economic liberalism that it was nothing but capitalism let loose, he emphasised ethical limitations within which free trade and commerce were to be carried out. He clearly stated

---

[3] See, e.g., C. Thomasius, *Fundamenta Juris Naturae et Gentium Excensu Communi Deducta* (Halle, 1705), para. 121 *et seq.*

[4] A. Smith, 'An Inquiry into the Nature and Causes of the Wealth of Nations', in R. H Campbell, A. S. Skinner and W.B Todd (eds.), *The Glasgow Edition of the Works and Correspondence of Adam Smith* (Oxford University Press, 1976), vol. 2.

that '[a]ll systems either of preference or of restraint, therefore, being thus completely taken away, the obvious and simple system of natural liberty establishes itself of its own accord. Every man, as long as he does *not violate the laws of justice* is perfectly free.'[5]

In the nineteenth century the relationship between the State and the economy is characterised by a certain ambivalence. On the one hand, there were the socialist and communist critics of Adam Smith's economic liberalism which they considered to be responsible for the social misery. On the other hand, there were the conservative and liberal-conservatives who did favour the concept of free trade and commerce, but who at the same time rejected Smith's liberalism because they associated it with the political liberalism and its emancipatory effects. This ambivalence *vis-à-vis* the concept of economic liberalism shaped the role of the State toward the economy. Internally, the freedoms of trade and commerce were held in high esteem, but they also were subject to strict State supervision.[6] Externally, international free trade and commerce were supported, indeed, but at the same time the States reserved the sovereign right to exercise control over transborder trade. Thus, for instance, many multilateral treaties on the various modes of transborder communication (e.g. postal services, railway traffic, telecommunications, etc.), which are essential for well-functioning markets, provided for strict national control rights. Yet the States – conscious of their right to control – in actual practice followed a rather liberal path. Thus, the potentially strong role of the States remained somewhat abstract. It is not surprising that the late nineteenth century was called the 'happy era of free trade'.[7]

The first half of the twentieth century saw a renaissance of the strong role of the State in the world economy. Under the impact of the economic crisis caused, first, by the widespread inflation immediately after the end of the First World War and later by the disastrous social consequences of the Great Depression of 1929–33, two major models of economic systems emerged. On the one hand, communist dictatorships relied on strong State intervention that became known as the 'central State planning system'. On the other hand, democratic States displayed a variety of

---

[5] Smith, 'An Inquiry', *supra* n. 4, 687 (emphasis added).

[6] A striking example of this ambivalent approach is the German Trade and Commerce Regulation Act of 1869, which introduced the freedom of trade and commerce but at the same time subjected the exercise of respective professions to State direction and restrictions.

[7] See A. Nußbaum, *Geschichte des Völkerrechts* (Munich: C. H. Beck, 1960), 226.

models that oscillated between acceptance of a liberal market economy, in principle, but relying on State interventions by far-reaching nationalisations and/or interventions aimed either at stimulating economic growth or at providing social justice.

After the Second World War, free trade and commerce played a greater role which resulted in the concept of the 'social market economy'. In this system it is the State's responsibility not only to protect free competition against overpowering monopolies, but also to intervene in the cause of social justice. Internationally, more liberal approaches led to the adoption of the General Agreement on Tariffs and Trade (GATT), the forerunner of the World Trade Organization (WTO) in 1994. Except for the GATT, all of the approaches to the appropriate regulation of the world and national economies that are sketched here are characterised by an exclusively State-centred perception: i.e. it is the State and the State alone that has – and must have – the sovereign power to regulate the economy. Whether it does so or not has up to now depended on the socio-political conditions at a particular point in time. In the forthcoming analysis it will be shown that, under the impact of globalisation and its accompanying effects, changes have occurred that have led to a lasting change in the role and status of the State in the economic field.

The institutional changes in the implementation of public tasks under the impact of globalisation

In order to assess the changes of the role of the State in the world economy that are caused by the process of globalisation, it is necessary to define the notion of 'globalisation' in some detail. This is not an easy task, because a host of definitions have been developed in political science, sociology and jurisprudence.[8] First of all, it is necessary to state what globalisation is not: it is not just another name for internationalisation. The latter denotes a State-dominated or rather State-centred interstate cooperation that is mostly institutionalised and serves as a supplement to the increasingly insufficient capabilities of States to live up to their responsibilities *vis-à-vis* their people – i.e. to provide for national security and welfare on their

---

[8] On definitions of the notion of globalisation see, e.g., D. Held, A. MacGrew, D. Goldblatt and J. Perraton, *Global Transformations. Politics, Economics and Culture* (Stanford University Press, 1999), 37; J. Delbrück, 'Structural Changes in the International System and Its Legal Order. International Law in the Era of Globalization', *Swiss Review of International and European Law*, 1 (2001), 1–36, 13 *et seq.*

own. Globalisation, for its part, denotes the implementation of public tasks in the transnational realm by non-State actors in cooperation with States, and sometimes even against the latter. Global acting is not State-centred but is transcending States.

More concretely, globalisation denotes a process of denationalisation (*Entstaatlichung*) of clusters of politics, markets and law, and of the producers of public goods (*öffentliche Güter*), such as non-State actors (international organisations, non-governmental organisations (NGOs) and multinational enterprises (MNEs)) that are increasingly taking over the implementation of public tasks. Globalisation also leads to the dissociation of the congruence of the State and its national society, because the latter's activities transgress the national borders and because of the ensuing worldwide interconnectedness of private individuals due to the modern means of telecommunication. In addition, globalisation leads to the partial de-territorialisation of the exercise of public authority.

This definition of globalisation is not at all comprehensive, but it expresses the core elements of globalisation more clearly than definitions by those who define it merely as an economic phenomenon or as a result of the revolution of telecommunications technology, or even ironically describe globalisation simply as the 'cocacolonisation' of the world.[9] The assumption that globalisation is a process of the partial denationalisation of the State, internally as well as externally, needs to be explained in some detail.

First, it should be noted that, for quite some time, States have withdrawn from fulfilling tasks within the domestic sphere and on the international level which hitherto were regarded as genuinely public tasks. Within the domestic sphere, this withdrawal from public tasks is implemented by shifting such tasks to private actors who are not only private entities in terms of their legal status, but are also clearly part of the private sector in substance. In part, however, the implementation of public responsibilities is also transferred to public–private partnerships – as, for example, in the case of the privatisation of prisons. On the international level, the withdrawal of States from fulfilling public tasks is

---

[9] This term was used in the public debate over the influence of the massive import of light entertainment shows and movies from the United States into England in the early 1980s, where fears were expressed that British lifestyles could be changed; the citation is from S. Buschschlüter, 'BBC-ITV. Versuch einer Bilanz nach 25 Jahren', *Media Perspektiven*, 10 (1980), 678, 683. In similar vein, B. R. Barber spoke of globalisation as culturally and economically resulting in a 'McWorld.' B. R. Barber, 'Global Democracy or Global Law. Which Comes First?', *Indiana Journal of Global Legal Studies*, 1 (1993), 121.

implemented by transferring the 'production of public goods' to non-State entities vested with public authority, such as supranational organisations and to some extent also international organisations where the Member States participate in the organisation's decision-making process. However, the decisions taken are those of the organs of the supranational and international institutions.

Secondly, one has to remember that due to the revolution of telecommunications technology, States are, to some extent, losing their 'steering capacity'. State control over financial markets – and, for example, over radical right-wing or racist internet communications that run counter to the principles and values of the rule of law and democracy-oriented societies – has become difficult, to put it mildly. To compensate for this loss of State control and steering capacity, States increasingly have turned to the extraterritorial exercise of public authority. However, this de-territorialisation of State-based government, in turn, contributes to the further erosion of the classical model of the territorial nation-state.

Finally, it has to be noted that in a variety of contexts non-State organisations and groups have expanded their activities into areas that have become open to them by the withdrawal of the State, on the one hand, and by the new opportunities of transborder communication, on the other. Examples of this process are the growing 'legislative function' of non-State institutions in the area of technical standardisation such as the International Standardisation Organisation (ISO), and of NGOs such as Greenpeace and Amnesty International in their role as (self-appointed) 'advocates of the public interest'. One can add that MNEs have more than ever before assumed a political role as actors in the transnational realm.

What do these developments mean with regard to the structure of the international system and the role of the State within this system? The answer is that the monopoly of the State as an actor in the international system is definitely a matter of the past. Aside from international inter-governmental and supranational organisations, NGOs and MNEs, as well as groups such as indigenous peoples and minorities, and last but not least individuals, are participating in international transactions within the international system today.[10] In the present context, however,

---

[10] See G. Dahm, J. Delbrück and R. Wolfrum, *Völkerrecht*, 2nd edn. (Berlin: W. de Gruyter, 2002), vol. I/2, chapters 17–19; R. Hofmann (ed.), *Non-State Actors as New Subjects of International Law* (Berlin: Duncker & Humblot, 1999), including contributions by R. Wedgwood, D. Thürer, T. M. Franck and S. Hobe; J. Delbrück, 'Prospects for a "World (Internal) Law?". Legal Developments in a Changing International System', *Indiana Journal of Global Legal Studies*, 9 (2002), 401, 411 *et seq.*

the focus has to be on the impact of the membership of States in international and supranational organisations, and the impact of globalisation, particularly in the world economy.

The transfer of State tasks to international and supranational organisations

Today, the vast majority of States is bound by a dense network of about 300 international, and in part supranational, organisations. Of course, most of these organisations are still State-centred – i.e. they are conceived as purely intergovernmental fora of cooperation dealing with very limited subject matters. However, it is those organisations that are dealing with particularly important subject matters like the economy, environment protection and telecommunication, to which essential public tasks have been transferred. In addition, these organisations are vested with regulatory, executive and judicial powers that have limited and changed the status of the hitherto sovereign Member States, normatively and *de facto*.

This is particularly true with regard to the legal order of the European Union (EU)/European Community (EC). Although one could argue that the transfer of parts of the public authority to the EC means the loss of the powers transferred on the part of the Member States, the 'transfer' is interpreted to mean that it establishes, indeed, the creation of a corresponding public authority for the EC, but that the exercise of the powers transferred by the Member States is only suspended and not definitely taken away from them. This means that their public authority, which used to be understood as indivisible, remains with the Member States, although it is now shared with the EC. Be that as it may, the fact is that the Member States are, normatively and *de facto*, clearly limited in the exercise of their capacity to act. Thus, for instance, in subject matters that have been transferred to the EC, Member States lose their domestic regulatory power, including their capacity to enter into international treaties.[11]

In addition, it should be pointed out that the European Court of Justice (ECJ) has persistently ruled 'that the law stemming from the Treaty, an independent source of law, could not, because of its special and original nature, be overridden by domestic legal provisions, however framed, without being deprived of its character as Community law and without

---

[11] See Case 22/70 *AETR* [1971] ECR 263.

the legal basis of the Community itself being called into question'.[12] In plain words: Community law takes precedence over domestic law, including domestic constitutional law. Considering that Community law in part has direct effect within the Member States, leading to a dualism of the supranational and national public authority within them, we now face a situation that is hardly compatible with the classic status of the sovereign State and its exclusive public authority over the State territory.[13] Furthermore, the effect of this dualism is being reinforced by the obligatory jurisdiction of the ECJ over the Member States as well as over the individual citizens who are participating in the European market. However, one must not overlook that the Member States not only participate in the work of the organs of the EC but that, through their national organs, they also partake in the implementation of EC law domestically. In sum, we can see a vertical interlocking of supranational and national levels.[14]

Compared with the extent of the transfer of public tasks to the supranational organisations, such a transfer to international organisations is less intensive. However, these transfers have major effects on the Member States as well. This is particularly true with regard to the Member States' discretionary powers as legislators in the fields of economic and administrative substantive and procedural law, as well as with regard to the protection of fundamental rights. It is impossible here to discuss in detail these effects of membership in all international organisations dealing with relevant economic matters.

By way of an example, the analysis will be confined to the effects of membership in the WTO, as the WTO can be seen as a driving force in the process of economic globalisation, and because the WTO regime contains regulations that underscore most clearly the effects of membership in international organisations on the State. The WTO, which was founded in 1994 as the result of the so-called Uruguay Round (1986–94),[15] pursues a policy of worldwide liberalisation of trade and commerce, but it is not limited to implementing the goal of free trade. The WTO is also committed to principles such as improving living standards, employment,

---

[12] See Case 6/64 *Costa* v. *ENEL* [1964] ECR 585.

[13] See C. Tietje, *Internationalisiertes Verwaltungshandeln* (Berlin: Duncker & Humblot, 2001), 174 *et seq.*

[14] For a detailed analysis of this process, see A. Peters, *Elemente einer Theorie der Verfassung Europas* (Berlin: Duncker & Humblot, 2001), 187 *et seq.*

[15] Text of the Agreement Establishing the World Trade Organization, 15 April 1994, *ILM*, 32 (1994), 1144–1272.

equality of income and sustainable development, as well as environment protection.[16] The WTO's vision of free trade and commerce is thus closer to Adam Smith's approach than to the *laissez faire* liberalism of the late nineteenth century.[17]

WTO membership entails a number of impacts on the Member States that change their traditional role as sovereign actors. First of all, it should be pointed out that the parties to the WTO treaty become *ipso iure* parties to the so-called Multilateral Trade Agreements (MTAs) (Art. II:2 WTO Treaty) – i.e. the GATT (GATT 1994),[18] the General Agreement on Trade in Services (GATS),[19] the Agreement on Trade-Related Aspects of Intellectual Property Rights (TRIPS)[20] and the Understanding on Rules and Procedures Governing the Settlement of Disputes (DSU).[21] Because of this 'single-undertaking approach' States must decide whether they would rather abstain from joining the WTO (the latter, for some reason being a desirable step to take) or wish to accept – lock, stock and barrel – the complete set of treaties that make up the WTO regime, a few exceptions notwithstanding.

What is unusual for classical international law, but typical for the process of the constitutionalisation of international law,[22] is that in case of a conflict between the WTO Treaty and the MTAs, the former prevails to the extent of the conflict (Art. XVI:3). More important in the present context is the obligation of WTO parties to harmonise their laws, other regulations and administrative procedures with their obligations under the annexed MTAs (Art. XVI:4). In order to prevent these obligations from remaining empty appeals, Art. X GATT 1994 and Art. VI GATS provide for comprehensive obligations of the Member States to publish their trade regulations in force as well as the decisions of general importance of the courts and administrative agencies and limitations to both imports and exports.[23]

These comprehensive obligations result in a considerable limitation of the Member States' national legislative powers. However, carrying out

---

[16] For a detailed analysis of the WTO approach, see C. Tietje, '§3 WTO und Recht des Weltwarenhandels', in C. Tietje (ed.), *Internationales Wirtschaftsrecht* (Berlin: W. de Gruyter, 2009), 145 *et seq.*

[17] Cf. P. Stoll, 'World Trade Organization', in R. Bernhardt *et al.* (eds.), *Encyclopedia of Public International Law* (Amsterdam: Elsevier, 2000), vol. IV, 1529, 1532 *et seq.*

[18] Text in *ILM*, 33 (1994), 1154–66.   [19] Text in *ibid.*, 1167–96.

[20] Text in *ibid.*, 1197–1225.   [21] Text in *ibid.*, 1226–47.

[22] Seminal is J. A. Frowein, *Berichte der Deutschen Gesellschaft für Völkerrecht*, 39 (2000), 427 *et seq.*

[23] See P. Stoll, *supra* n. 17, 1533.

these obligations clearly and in detail has a positive effect for the Member States as well, since they not only set limitations for the legislative powers of the States, but they also determine clearly the scope of the areas where the States do have freedom to act.[24] Major impacts are also provided by the WTO regime on the executive branch of the Member States. One prominent example is Art. VI GATS, which provides for detailed substantive and procedural requirements for licensing services by the domestic authorities. Member States must make sure that their domestic regulations or decisions concerning the trade in services are adequate, objective and impartially administered. Similarly, Member States are obliged to establish the necessary administrative and judicial organs that decide on licences to offer services. However, in contrast to the EC/EU regime, WTO Member States are not obliged to establish such organs or procedures if these are incompatible with their constitutions and legal order – a clear indication of the lower intensity of the impact that international organisations have on their Member States compared with supranational organisations. Another difference between international organisations and supranational organisations is that WTO regulations lack direct effect in the Member States, unlike EC/EU laws that do have such effect.

Although such effect of WTO law has increasingly been deemed desirable, it has not been possible to realise proposals to this effect. However, although the lack of direct effect of WTO law seems to preserve the exclusive competence of the Member States to transform and apply WTO law within the national legal order, this competence is actually restricted by the DSU mechanism, which is vested with the power to secure the enforcement of WTO law. Art. 3.2 DSU characterises the DSU as a 'central element in providing security and predictability to the multilateral trading system'. Furthermore, the DSU clearly rejects unilateral trade sanctions (Art. 23 DSU) which frequently occurred under the GATT after 1947.

Acceptance of the DSU by the WTO Member States is enhanced by the provision that States are obliged to engage in a cooperative settlement of their conflicts before they can have recourse to the DSU mechanism. The effectiveness of the mechanism is further enhanced by the provision that decisions handed down in an appellate procedure are strictly binding, and by the competence of the Dispute Settlement Body to authorise Member States affected by a violation of WTO law to apply adequate sanctions against the violator State. Finally, a major advantage of the DSU

---

[24] For further details see Tietje, '§3 WTO', *supra* n. 16, §1, marginal nos. 98 *et seq.*

mechanism is that Art. 25 DSU allows the disputing parties to engage in an arbitration procedure of their own choice in order to reach a speedy settlement of their dispute that is essential for their business transactions. It is important to note that the dispute settlement procedures – of whatever form – are wholly separate from the domestic judiciary. This is in line with a widely observable trend of international and transnational business actors settling trade disputes on the transnational level – a clear indication of the partial denationalisation process affected by globalisation.

Beyond the impact of WTO membership on the traditional status of the State, there is another development having a strong impact on the domestic legal order and thereby on the State's status and role. Some international organisations have been charged with subject matters not directly but indirectly related to the economic sector – i.e. the environment and health protection. In discharging the ensuing responsibilities, these organisations have become increasingly involved in what could be called 'legislative activities'. These are realised by way of so-called 'framework conventions' that set out the general aims or policies. The concrete obligations of the parties and the detailed regulations are left to be formulated by amending protocols or, in cases of highly technical regulations, are delegated to expert committees of technical institutions.[25] The reason for this procedure is that framework conventions, particularly in the area of international environmental law, require a high degree of scientific expertise for the elaboration of detailed regulations and more often than not need to be amended because of the rapid progress of science. Doctrinally, the amending protocols constitute treaty amendments that frequently enter into force through a simplified procedure – i.e. by majority vote of the parties to the framework convention that is then binding upon all parties, including the opposing minority. Such protocols sometimes also allow opposing parties to exempt themselves from the protocol by opting out, albeit within a relatively short term. This procedure too reflects the 'legislative' character of the law-making process.

[25] Generally on the technique of law-making by framework conventions, see Delbrück, 'Prospects', *supra* n. 10, 418 *et seq.*; A Chayes and A. Handler Chayes, *The New Sovereignty – Compliance with International Regulatory Agreements* (Cambridge, MA: Harvard University Press, 1995), 225 *et seq.*; W. Lang, 'Die Abwehr weiträumiger Umweltgefahren, insbesondere durch internationale Organisationen', *Berichte der Deutschen Gesellschaft für Völkerrecht*, 32 (1992), 57, 64 *et seq.*; C. Tietje, 'The Changing Legal Structure of International Treaties as an Aspect of an Emerging Global Governance Architecture', *GYIL*, 42 (1999), 26, 36 *et seq.*

It is also worth noting that the organs responsible for filling in the framework conventions through detailed regulations usually include expert administrators recruited from national government agencies. This leads to a shifting of the law-making process to the executive branch of governments. This, in turn, has major implications for the role of national parliaments in the law-making procedure: their role is significantly reduced. Since in many cases these expert committees also include experts from international organisations, the result is a vertical interplay of international and domestic administrations and an internationalisation of domestic administrative agencies. In sum, the developments just described obviously have a substantial impact on the traditional State, be it in terms of the limitations on its legislative and judicial powers, or in terms of the vertical integration of domestic and international administrative agencies.

The de-territorialisation of the exercise of public authority and of the law

In medieval times, territory was not a legal constituent of the feudal order. Rather, territory served as the *de facto* basis on which the feudal order existed. It was only after the emergence of modern forms of government, including well-organised public administrations and standing armies, that territory acquired a legal or normative dimension. Defending the integrity of the territory along well-marked borders became part of the *raison d'être* of the early modern States. Consequently, the territorial integrity of the State became an essential principle of international law. Recognition of a clearly defined territory was of essential importance for the self-conception of the young States not only in terms of the defence of the State against external threats to its territorial integrity. The recognition of legally defined borders also limited the exercise of public authority by the State to these borders and at the same time excluded any unauthorised exercise of foreign public authority on the State's territory.

However, from the beginning State practice featured numerous exceptions to the principle of territorial integrity. Criminal law, antitrust law and conflict-of-laws law allow for deviations from the strict application of the principle of territorial integrity in favour of the still-recognised principle of personal authority over citizens abroad.[26] Furthermore, due to the growing interdependence of States, modes of cross-frontier

---

[26] See Dahm, Delbrück and Wolfrum, *Völkerrecht, supra* n. 10, vol. I/1, 321.

cooperation increasingly were developed which resulted in the exercise of public authority beyond State borders in a way that is not in line with the traditional dogma of exclusive territorial authority. Thus, the question arises as to whether globalisation actually has added anything to the process of the de-territorialisation of the exercise of public authority already going on before the notion of globalisation became the object of scholarly and political interest.

A number of examples of the increasing de-territorialisation of the exercise of public authority have been given before – i.e. the transfer of the implementation of public tasks to non-governmental international and supranational organisations. A closer look at the reasons for this de-territorialisation of public tasks reveals that the tasks transferred are by their very nature transborder – indeed, global tasks – that transcend the capabilities of individual States to cope with them. To name but a few, the environment and climate protection are tasks that transcend the capabilities of individual States, and problems caused by the revolution of the telecommunication technologies by their nature are transcending national borders as well. In addition, increasingly so-called 'international public interests' (*Staatengemeinschaftsinteressen*) are recognised in international law, which cannot be carried out by individual States, but need enforcement by the international community of States.[27]

In other words, because of these developments the territorial States have lost their steering capacities and thus are depending not only on international cooperation – an intrinsically State-centred internationalisation – for the implementation of their tasks, but need to have them fulfilled on a meta-State level. The ensuing denationalisation of the implementation of public tasks, from this point of view, means the partial de-territorialisation of the exercise of public authority and of the law.

Conclusion

A first conclusion deriving from the foregoing is that the implementation of public tasks solely by sovereign States has given way to a system in which the implementation of public tasks is achieved on several

---

[27] On the notion of international public interests, see J. Delbrück, 'Laws in the Public Interest – Some Observations on the Foundation and Identification of *erga omnes* Norms in International Law', in V. Götz, P. Selmer and R. Wolfrum (eds.), *Liber Amicorum Günther Jaenicke on the occasion of his 85th birthday* (Berlin: Springer, 1998), 17 *et seq.*

levels – i.e. on a sub-State level, on the State level and on the international or supranational level. This is particularly true in the economic realm and related matters. The State is caught up in a multi-layered system of governance, with partly competing and partly cooperating entities vested with public authority and decision-making power that is hardly compatible with the traditional concept of the sovereign State. Particularly because of economic integration, the State has had to open up to the outside world with the result that it has had to expose itself to the ensuing normative and *de facto* impacts on its domestic sphere.

In detail, this means that the State has lost its omni-competence and exclusive authority over its territory, which were the core attributes of the traditional sovereign State. This does not mean, however, that the State as a form of political organisation of social groups has come to an end, as some people fear. Rather, this development means not that the State as such has become outmoded, but that its responsibilities and public tasks have changed to a considerable extent. In compensation, so to speak, the State has gained a new role and new functions within the emerging multi-layered system of global governance. This new role may be graphically described as that of a 'transmission or connecting shaft' within the vertically integrating international system.

That this is not pure fiction can presently be seen with regard to the approach of the international community to the, indeed, gigantic task to overcome the worldwide economic crisis. With the exception of some States that tended to cope with the crisis unilaterally, it is not exaggerated to say that a large majority of States have rather immediately turned to institutionalised as well as ad hoc international and supranational fora to formulate strategies to overcome the crisis. The temptation to fall back on protectionist measures has not got the upper hand, so far at least. Of course, there still is disagreement on details – and it would be greatly surprising if there were no dissenting voices. However, one can safely say that there is a growing consensus with regard to the need for a global legal economic order.

It is for the world's political leaders to implement their respective responsibilities – i.e. to formulate the necessary global codices for the conduct of economic transactions, whether on the global or on the supranational level, and then to see to it that these are ultimately implemented on the regional and domestic level. Having said this, it is evident that the States, indeed, have lost a good deal of their national powers, so that they are unable to deal with economic disasters on their own. But they still have a strong role to play, albeit not as lonely sovereign players – as Abram Chayes and Antonia Handler Chayes have so aptly observed: 'It is that, for all but a few self-isolated nations, sovereignty no longer consists in the freedom of States to act independently, in their perceived self-interest, but in membership in reasonable good standing in the regimes that make up the substance of international life.'[28]

---

[28] Chayes and Handler Chayes, *The New Sovereignty, supra* n. 25, 27.

6

Sources of human rights obligations binding the UN Security Council

BARDO FASSBENDER

Introduction

Since the collapse of the Soviet Union and the end of the Cold War, the Security Council of the United Nations has intensified its work in a way unimaginable in the long period of bipolar stalemate that had begun only a few years after the founding of the United Nations and lasted for some forty years. Lifted up by a wave of post-Cold War enthusiasm, the Council both greatly increased its efforts in its 'traditional' area of responsibility – the maintenance of inter-state peace and security – and expanded its mandate to new fields and issues, among them the fight against global terrorism, democratisation and the protection of human rights.[1] In the meantime, the enthusiasm of the 1990s with its perhaps exaggerated hopes subsided, but the new powers claimed by the Council in the last fifteen years have not been called into question. On the contrary, and somewhat astonishingly, these powers have been generally accepted by the members of the international community, and are awaiting new situations in which the Council will use them.[2]

As a consequence of the sharply growing activities of the Council, a discussion has arisen regarding the scope, and possible sources, of the

---

[1] For a very good overview, see D. M. Malone (ed.), *The UN Security Council. From the Cold War to the 21st Century* (Boulder, CO and London: Lynne Rienner, 2004).

[2] See, e.g., E. de Wet, 'The Governance of Kosovo. Security Council Resolution 1244 and the Establishment and Functioning of EULEX', *AJIL*, 103 (2009), 83–96, 87: 'By now the Security Council is widely acknowledged to have the power to establish a civil administration under the auspices of the United Nations on the basis of its implied powers under Chapter VII of the Charter . . . Second, the Security Council also has the power under Chapter VII of the Charter to authorize individual States to implement a civil administration . . . Furthermore, the Charter enables the Security Council to authorize regional organizations to administer a territory.'

Council's international legal obligations. Is the Council, when discharging its responsibility under the UN Charter, bound by rules of international law, and if so, by which rules exactly? In particular, the issue of the Council's human rights commitments has attracted a great deal of interest. While intuitively most people – and certainly most lawyers – agree that the Council is obliged to observe international rules concerning the protection of human rights, it is not so easy to substantiate this belief on the basis of positive international law.

When the UN Charter was drafted, human rights were at the international level still merely moral postulates and political principles. But even if the founders of the United Nations could have made, through respective Charter provisions, human rights directly binding on the Organisation as a whole or on particular organs, they did not find it necessary. As regards the Security Council, they apparently never entertained the thought that action taken by the Council under Chapter VII of the Charter could violate the human rights of individuals. On the contrary, they believed that the maintenance and – if necessary – restoration of international peace and security entrusted to the Council directly served the 'four essential human freedoms' proclaimed by President Franklin D. Roosevelt in 1941.[3] Accordingly, international peace ('to save succeeding generations from the scourge of war') and the protection of fundamental human rights appear together right at the beginning of the preamble of the UN Charter among the principal aims of the peoples of the United Nations, without the slightest hint of a possible conflict.

In more general terms, one can say that the founders did not expect the United Nations to exercise power or authority in a way that would directly affect rights and freedoms of individual persons. But in the meantime, 'the screen which originally separated the United Nations

---

[3] See F. D. Roosevelt, Address to Congress, 6 January 1941 ('Four Freedoms Speech'), reprinted in R. Hofstadter and B. K. Hofstadter (eds.), *Great Issues in American History. From Reconstruction to the Present Day, 1864–1981* (New York: Vintage Books, 1982), 386–91. The four freedoms proclaimed by the US President were the freedom of speech and expression, the 'freedom of every person to worship God in his own way', the 'freedom from want' and the 'freedom from fear'. See also the Atlantic Charter of 14 August 1941, *ibid.*, 399–401, in which the President and British Prime Minister Winston Churchill announced, *inter alia*, that 'after the final destruction of the Nazi tyranny, they hope to see established a peace which will afford to all nations the means of dwelling in safety within their own boundaries, and which will afford assurance that all the men in all the lands may live out their lives in freedom from fear and want'.

from the man and the woman on the street progressively disappeared'.[4] Increasingly, the United Nations has been entrusted with tasks of global governance that go beyond its traditional purposes and functions.[5] A number of developments, in particular in the context of peacekeeping operations and the international interim administration of territories (such as East Timor and Kosovo), have made it a possibility that violations of human rights and international humanitarian law that are attributable to the United Nations may occur.[6] Accordingly, 'the temporary exercise of governmental or quasi-governmental authority by an international organisation over private persons and enterprises ... give[s] rise to claims that the acts performed by the organisation under that authority are illegal'.[7]

In the case of Chapter VII sanctions of the Security Council targeting individuals and private 'entities',[8] those sanctions do have a direct impact on the rights and freedoms of individuals. In the first place, the existing 'targeted sanctions' affect the right to property, which is protected by regional human rights treaties and today possibly also by customary international law, the freedom of movement and the freedom of association. Sanctions may also affect the right to respect for family and private life and the right to seek and to enjoy in other countries asylum from persecution. Further, the right to reputation is affected, which is a (civil) right within the meaning of Art. 14(1) of the International Covenant on Civil and Political Rights (ICCPR) and

---

[4] See C. Tomuschat, *Human Rights. Between Idealism and Realism*, 2nd edn. (Oxford University Press, 2008), p. 101.

[5] A. Reinisch, 'Governance Without Accountability?', *GYIL*, 44 (2001), 270–306, 270, identifies 'a global trend of shifting governance tasks from States (including their subentities) to non-State actors', i.e. private entities, on the one hand, and international or supranational entities, on the other hand.

[6] See, e.g., F. Mégret and F. Hoffmann, 'The UN as a Human Rights Violator? Some Reflections on the United Nations Changing Human Rights Responsibilities', *Human Rights Quarterly*, 25 (2003), 314–42, 325 *et seq.*

[7] See K. Wellens, *Remedies against International Organisations* (Cambridge University Press, 2002), p. 89.

[8] Of the various sanctions regimes, the one established against individuals and entities belonging to, or associated with, Al Qaeda and/or the Taliban (Security Council resolution 1267 of 15 October 1999 and following resolutions) has gained particular importance because of the relatively large number of individuals and entities listed. This sanctions regime also differs from the others in that, after the Taliban were removed from power in Afghanistan, there has been no special link between the targeted individuals and entities and a specific country. For an overview of the work and procedure of the 1267 Committee of the Security Council, see E. Rosand, 'The Security Council's Efforts to Monitor the Implementation of Al Qaida/Taliban Sanctions', *AJIL*, 98 (2004), 745–63.

Art. 6(1) of the European Convention for the Protection of Human Rights and Fundamental Freedoms (ECHR).

It is true that it is still the Member States which must implement the resolutions of the Council by first enacting rules in accordance with the requirements of their domestic (constitutional) law, and then enforcing those rules by imposing specific measures upon the individuals and entities concerned. As a matter of principle, Security Council resolutions are not self-executing in the domestic legal order of most Member States, and the United Nations does not have at its disposal its own means and mechanisms of enforcement. However, Member States do not possess any discretionary rights – i.e. rights to decide or act according to their own judgment or choice – with regard to the implementation of sanctions determined by the Security Council under Chapter VII of the UN Charter. Instead, they must comply with the terms of the Council resolutions as they stand.[9] In particular, Member States have no authority to review the names of individuals and entities specified by the responsible committee of the Security Council, with the aim of ascertaining whether the persons and entities indeed fall under the categories defined by the respective Council resolution. The obligations of Member States under the UN Charter prevail over any obligation arising from other international agreements or customary international law (Art. 103 of the UN Charter), and in its relationship to the United Nations a Member State may not invoke the provisions of its internal law, including its constitutional law, as a justification for its failure to implement a binding resolution of the Security Council.

In this chapter, I wish to examine the various possible sources of human rights obligations of the Security Council – i.e. treaty and customary

---

[9] Thus, the EU Council and EC Commission in the *Yusuf* and *Kadi* cases correctly described the law, the Court of First Instance (CFI) agreeing: 'As their principal argument, the Council and the Commission, referring in particular to Articles 24(1), 25, 41, 48 (2) and 103 of the Charter of the United Nations, submit, first, that the Community, like the Member States of the United Nations, is bound by international law to give effect, within its spheres of competence, to resolutions of the Security Council, especially those adopted under Chapter VII of the Charter of the United Nations; second, that the powers of the Community institutions in this area are limited and that they have no autonomous discretion in any form; third, that they cannot therefore alter the content of those resolutions or set up mechanisms capable of giving rise to any alteration in their content and, fourth, that any other international agreement or domestic rule of law liable to hinder such implementation must be disregarded.' See Judgments of the Court of First Instance of 21 September 2005, Case T-306/01 *Ahmed Ali Yusuf and Al Barakaat International Foundation* v. *Council of the EU and Commission of the EC* [2005] ECR II-3533, para. 206, and Case T-315/01 *Yassin Abdullah Kadi* v. *Council of the EU and Commission of the EC* [2005] ECR II-3649, para. 153.

international law (including *jus cogens*), general principles of law, constitutional values and traditions common to UN Member States, and the UN Charter. I conclude that the principal source of human rights obligations of the Council is the Charter as the Constitution of the United Nations.

Human rights treaty law

After the Second World War, the proclamation of the Universal Declaration of Human Rights by the UN General Assembly on 10 December 1948[10] set in motion a process of codifying and developing human rights by international treaty-making which is still going on. On a global level, a lasting success was achieved with the adoption of the two international human rights covenants in 1966. Accordingly, one almost naturally turns first to human rights treaty law when trying to identify human rights standards by which the Security Council might possibly be bound.

However, the United Nations, as an international organisation and a subject of international law,[11] is not a party to any of the universal or regional treaties and conventions for the protection of human rights and fundamental freedoms. Accordingly, the United Nations is not directly bound by the respective provisions. The treaties and conventions were drafted only with a view to the performance of States, not of other subjects of international law. For instance, in Art. 2(1) ICCPR it is stated that '[e]ach State Party to the present Covenant undertakes to respect and to ensure to all individuals within its territory and subject to its jurisdiction the rights recognized in the present Covenant'. According to Art. 1 ECHR, '[t]he High Contracting Parties shall secure to everyone within their jurisdiction the rights and freedoms defined in Section I of this Convention'.

The United Nations also could not become a party to the treaties and conventions in question as they stand today, because they are only open to accession by States (see, e.g., Art. 48 ICCPR, Art. 59 ECHR, Art. 74 of the American Convention on Human Rights).

The reason for this restrictive approach of human rights treaties in defining the respective duty-bearers is that traditionally States (i.e. their governmental, administrative, legislative and judicial organs) have been

---

[10] UN General Assembly res. 217 A (III), *United Nations Year Book* (1948–9), 535.
[11] See *Reparation for Injuries Suffered in the Service of the United Nations*, International Court of Justice, Advisory Opinion, 1949 ICJ 174, 179.

regarded as the main potential violators of human rights. '[The] "international" protection of human rights denotes an ensemble of procedures and mechanisms which ... are primarily designed to protect human beings against their own State. Protection is generally needed at home. Human rights have been brought into being as a supplementary line of defence in case national systems should prove to be of no avail. Although the State is on the one hand reckoned with as the indispensable guarantor of human rights, historical experience has also made clear that the State ... may use the sovereign powers at its disposal to commit violations of human rights.'[12] As regards, in particular, the United Nations, it is certainly true that 'until recently, the UN had never thought of itself as actually capable of violating human rights'.[13] Accordingly, the UN Charter requires the United Nations to 'promot[e] and encourag[e] respect for human rights' (Art. 1(3)), and to 'assist' Member States 'in the realization of human rights' (Art. 13(1b)).

It does not follow from the fact alone that UN Member States, or even an overwhelming majority of Member States, ratified certain human rights instruments that a corresponding obligation of the Organisation has come into existence.[14] The concept of international person, or subject of international law, is based on a distinction between particular subjects and their particular rights, duties, or powers.[15] As the International Court of Justice (ICJ) has held, '[t]he subjects of law in any legal system are not necessarily identical in their nature or in the extent of their rights, and their nature depends upon the needs of the community'.[16] Accordingly, the rights and duties of intergovernmental organisations, as autonomous subjects of international law, on the one hand, and of their Member States, on the other hand, must be distinguished.[17] In its advisory opinion in response to a

---

[12] See Tomuschat, *Human Rights*, *supra* n. 4, 97.

[13] See Mégret and Hoffmann, 'The UN as a Human Rights Violator?', *supra* n. 6, 314.

[14] But see A. Reinisch, 'Securing the Accountability of International Organizations', *Global Governance*, 7 (2001), 131–49, 137 *et seq*. and 141–3, arguing that the UN is bound 'transitively' by international human rights standards as a result and to the extent that its members are bound ('functional treaty succession by international organizations to the position of their Member States').

[15] See R. Y. Jennings and A. D. Watts (eds.), *Oppenheim's International Law*, 9th edn., 2 vols. (London and New York: Longman, 1992), vol. I, part 1, 119 *et seq*.; H. G. Schermers and N. M. Blokker, *International Institutional Law*, 3rd edn. (The Hague: Martinus Nijhoff, 1995), 976 *et seq*.

[16] *Reparation for Injuries* case, *supra* n. 11, 178.

[17] See, in general, N. Blokker, 'International Organizations and Their Members', *International Organizations Law Review*, 1 (2004), 139–61, 152 *et seq*.

request by the World Health Organization (WHO), the ICJ explained in 1996 that it is the object of constituent instruments of international organisations 'to create new subjects of law endowed with a certain autonomy'.[18] With regard to the United Nations, the Court had already stated in 1949 that 'the Organization . . . occupies a position in certain respects in detachment from its Members'.[19] The Court also ruled that 'international organizations are subjects of international law and, as such, are bound by any obligations *incumbent upon them* under general rules of international law, under *their constitutions* or under international agreements to which *they are parties*'.[20]

But this traditional picture has been modified by the emergence of 'supranational' organisations such as the European Community (EC). The EC has recognised both human rights treaty obligations of EC Member States as well as 'constitutional traditions common to the Member States' as sources of Community law from which direct obligations of the EC itself arise. The Community thus has developed a legal technique through which the constitutional traditions and international obligations of Member States are integrated into the legal order of the organisation itself. Notwithstanding the special character of the EC which – first supplemented and then increasingly absorbed by the European Union (EU) – is approaching a federal State-like existence, there is reason to expect that the law of other international organisations, including the United Nations, will be influenced by the European example as they, too, begin to engage in 'supranational' law-making with a direct effect on individuals.

According to Art. 2 of the Treaty on European Union (TEU, or EU Treaty),[21] the EU is founded on the values of respect for human dignity, freedom, democracy, equality, the rule of law and respect for human rights. Art. 6(3) says that 'fundamental rights, as guaranteed by the European Convention for the Protection of Human Rights and Fundamental Freedoms [ECHR], and as they result from the constitutional traditions common to the Member States, shall constitute general principles of the Union's law'.[22] By this provision, the terms of an

---

[18] *Legality of the Use by a State of Nuclear Weapons in Armed Conflict*, International Court of Justice, Advisory Opinion, 1996 ICJ 66, 75.

[19] *Reparation for Injuries* case, *supra* n. 11, 179.

[20] *Interpretation of the Agreement of 25 March 1951 between the WHO and Egypt*, International Court of Justice, Advisory Opinion, 1980 ICJ 73, 89–90 (emphasis added).

[21] See Treaty on European Union of 7 February 1992, as amended by the Treaty of Lisbon of 13 December 2007; Official Journal of the EU C 83, 30 March 2010.

[22] Further, the 'Charter of Fundamental Rights of the European Union' of 7 December 2000 (as amended on 12 December 2007) was recognised as a binding part of EU law; see Art. 6(1) of the Treaty.

international agreement concluded by EU Member States with the purpose of securing 'to everyone in their jurisdiction' certain rights and freedoms (Art. 1 ECHR) were made binding on the EU itself. In addition, 'fundamental rights . . . as they result from the constitutional traditions common to the Member States' – i.e. rules belonging to the domestic legal order of Member States – were transferred to the level of the EU in the form of general principles of community law.

Art. 6(3) EU Treaty is an expression of the high degree of integration achieved between EC/EU law and national law, which is typical of the EU and as yet unparalleled in the law of other international organisations. Also, the recognition of common constitutional traditions as a source of EU law is based on the fact that the EU Member States share certain principles of legal and political order. A similar degree of cohesion was already expressed by the States agreeing to the ECHR in 1950. In the Convention's preamble, they described themselves as 'European countries which are likeminded and have a common heritage of political traditions, ideals, freedom and the rule of law'. Art. 4 of the Constitutive Act of the African Union of 2000 also mentions, among the principles in accordance with which the African Union shall function, 'respect for democratic principles, human rights, the rule of law and good governance', the 'promotion of social justice' and 'respect for the sanctity of human life' (Art. 4, lit. m, n and o).

Although the UN Charter includes similar statements of values, in particular in its preamble and Art. 1, for a long time the political divisions of the world prevented UN Member States from agreeing on their substance. However, since the antagonism of the former bloc systems has been overcome, more and more such agreement can be found, as is apparent from many resolutions of the General Assembly in regard to human rights, democracy, the rule of law and good governance. Thus, there is an increasingly broader basis for referring to the constitutional traditions and values common to the Member States of the United Nations as a source of UN law. Compared to the state of EC/EU law, these are only cautious beginnings. But it is a development with a significant growth potential, as today the bold proclamation of the Universal Declaration of Human Rights that 'recognition of the inherent dignity and of the equal and inalienable rights of all members of the human family is the foundation of freedom, justice and peace in the world' (preamble, para. 1) really has been universally accepted.

As UN law stands today, the organs of the United Nations are already prevented from simply ignoring either the constitutional traditions and values common to Member States in the field of human rights or the human rights treaty obligations shared by an overwhelming majority of Member States. To put it differently, such traditions, values and treaty obligations must already be taken into account by UN organs when they exercise functions *vis-à-vis* individual persons. Following the wording of Art. 6(3) EU Treaty, it is therefore possible to say that, as a matter of principle, the United Nations shall respect fundamental rights, as guaranteed by the universal human rights treaties, and as they result from the constitutional traditions common to the Member States, as general principles of UN law.

Customary international law and general principles of law

There is today broad agreement among governments and international lawyers that many of the rules enunciated in the Universal Declaration of Human Rights have crystallised as customary international law, in particular the right to life, the prohibition of torture (as the reverse side of a right to physical integrity), the protection of personal freedom and the prohibition of discrimination on racial grounds.[23]

It has been argued that the respective customary obligations are also binding on international organisations, as subjects of international law, to the extent that the organisations engage in activities which are likely to affect the mentioned rights of individuals.[24] However, as was noted before, international human rights law was primarily designed to protect human beings against their own State. In general, it was not considered necessary to secure protection against acts of 'governmental' power with a direct impact on individuals issued by organs of international organisations, as there virtually were no such acts. Accordingly, there was little room for the development of rules of customary international law concerning the obligation of international organisations to comply with particular human rights standards. By way of example, due process rights may be mentioned.[25] The right to a fair and public hearing by an independent and impartial tribunal (Art. 10 of the Universal Declaration) and other due process rights may today be a part of customary international law, as far as States are the addressees of those

---

[23] See Tomuschat, *Human Rights*, *supra* n. 4, 37–8, with further references.

[24] See Reinisch, 'Governance', *supra* n. 5, 281 *et seq.*, with further references.

[25] I have dealt with this issue in great detail in a study commissioned in 2005 by the Under-Secretary-General for Legal Affairs and Legal Counsel of the United Nations. See B. Fassbender, 'Targeted Sanctions Imposed by the UN Security Council and Due Process Rights: A Study Commissioned by the UN Office of Legal Affairs and Follow-Up Action by the United Nations', *International Organizations Law Review*, 3 (2006), 437–85.

obligations.[26] But because of a lack of relevant practice and *opinio juris*, the same cannot presently be said for international organisations in general, or the United Nations in particular.[27]

In the *Yusuf* case, the Court of First Instance of the European Communities held in 2005 that 'the Court is empowered to check, indirectly, the lawfulness of the resolutions of the Security Council . . . with regard to *jus cogens*, understood as a body of higher rules of public international law binding on all subjects of international law, including the bodies of the United Nations, and from which no derogation is possible'.[28] The Court further said 'that there exists one limit to the principle that resolutions of the Security Council have binding effect: namely, that they must observe the fundamental peremptory provisions of *jus cogens*. If they fail to do so, however improbable that may be, they would bind neither the Member States of the United Nations nor, in consequence, the [European] Community.'[29]

While the Court rightly concluded that the human rights protected by *jus cogens* rules must be observed by the Security Council, the Court's reasoning does not appear to be correct. Due to the lack of a relevant practice and *opinio juris*, peremptory norms of international law (which constitute a sub-category of customary international law) as such are no more binding on the United Nations, or the Security Council, than is customary human rights law. Rather, the respective obligations of the Council follow from the UN Charter, and they extend way beyond human rights specifically covered by *jus cogens* to all human rights recognised as part of the 'international bill of rights'.[30]

Nevertheless, a trend can be perceived widening the scope of customary international law to include direct 'governmental' action of international organisations *vis-à-vis* individuals. To this development, the law of the EC/EU has strongly contributed. As is well known, the EU has been

---

[26] Certain due process rights, like the right to be heard, may also belong to *jus cogens* – i.e. rules from which no derogation is permitted – because they are 'core rights directly related to human existence' (for this expression, see Tomuschat, *Human Rights*, *supra* n. 4, 38).

[27] See Reinisch, 'Governance', *supra* n. 5, 282–6, concluding that '[t]he problem of redress mechanisms in case of unlawful UN action remains an unsolved one'.

[28] Case T-306/01 *Ahmed Ali Yusuf* and *Al Barakaat International Foundation* v. *Council of the European Union* and *Commission of the European Communities* [2005] ECR-II-3533, Judgment of the Court of First Instance, 21 September 2005, para. 277.

[29] *Ibid.*, para. 281.

[30] See *infra*, 'The UN Charter as the principal source of UN human rights obligations'.

endowed with far-reaching powers over the whole breadth of the tasks it is mandated to perform.[31] According to Art. 288 TFEU, the Union can make regulations, issue directives and take decisions. All of these acts produce binding effects for their individual addressees. Consequently, a system of judicial protection against EU acts was established which is by and large equivalent to the protection offered in EU Member States at a national level. A person who is of the opinion that her rights have been breached by an act of Union power can either challenge that act directly by instituting proceedings before the Court of Justice of the European Communities (ECJ) (Art. 263(4) TFEU), or can contest national acts taken on the basis of European legislation before national tribunals which must then, under certain conditions, refer the case to the ECJ.

Since the direct effect of EU law is still a unique feature unparalleled in the law of other international organisations, in particular universal organisations, it is currently not possible to deduce general rules of customary international law from the law and practice of the EC/EU alone. But considering the degree to which the EC/EU has been a model for other regional international organisations, particularly in Latin America and in Africa, it is justified to say that EC/EU law can be regarded as a precedent which in the future will serve as a guide or pattern in analogous cases of direct 'governmental' action taken by international organisations vis-à-vis individuals.

To the extent that certain human rights standards are concurrently recognised in the domestic (constitutional) law of a great number of States of all regions of the world, they have become rules of international law in the form of general principles of law as meant in Art. 38(1)(c) ICJ Statute. Although the standards in question describe obligations of governments vis-à-vis their citizens (and foreigners under their jurisdiction) in the sphere of domestic law, the general principles of international law which have arisen on the basis of those widely recognised standards are also applicable to international organisations as subjects of international law when those organisations exercise 'governmental' authority over individuals.[32] However, if the constituent treaty of an international organisation provides for specific rules, these rules prevail in accordance with the concept

---

[31] For this and the following, see Tomuschat, *Human Rights*, *supra* n. 4, 98.

[32] See D. Sarooshi, *International Organizations and Their Exercise of Sovereign Powers* (Oxford University Press, 2005), 16: 'A domestic public or administrative law principle is arguably only applicable to the exercise by an international organization of governmental power where this principle can be identified as applying to the particular power within the domestic public and administrative law systems of a number of member

of *lex specialis derogat legi generali.*[33] If possible, an effort must be made to interpret the rules of the constituent treaty in accordance with the substance of the respective general principles of international law.

The idea of estoppel

Already in Roman law it was established that no one is allowed to act contrary to his or her prior action or behaviour: *venire contra factum proprium (nemini licet).*[34] Otherwise, she loses the protection of the law. In other words, by adopting a certain position, attitude, or course of conduct one raises certain expectations, and not living up to those expectations may lead to negative legal consequences. The maxim is a general principle of law as defined by Art. 38(1)(c) ICJ Statute. In international law, the 'legal technique whereby States deemed to have consented to a state of affairs cannot afterwards alter their position' is often referred to as estoppel.[35]

In accordance with that concept, it may be said that the development of international human rights law since 1945, to which the work of the United Nations has decisively contributed, has given grounds for legitimate expectations that the United Nations itself, when its action has a direct impact on the rights and freedoms of an individual, strictly observes human rights and fundamental freedoms.[36] As Judge Simma has remarked, 'wherever the future of its human rights work may lead to,

States, since only then can it be considered as a general principle of law and thus a formal source of law applicable to international organizations.' For the applicability of general principles of law in the law of international organisations, see generally Schermers and Blokker, *International Institutional Law, supra* n. 15, 984 *et seq.*

[33] See also C. Tomuschat, 'International Law. Ensuring the Survival of Mankind on the Eve of a New Century', *RdC*, 281 (1999), 9–438, 335: 'They [the general principles of law] provide a residual framework of general precepts for instances where treaty and custom are silent on how to resolve a specific legal issue.'

[34] See D. Liebs, *Lateinische Rechtsregeln und Rechtssprichwörter*, 3rd edn. (Munich: C. H. Beck, 1983), 216. In another version, the rule reads *Nemo contra factum suam venire potest* (No man can contravene or contradict his own deed). See *Black's Law Dictionary*, 6th edn. (St. Paul, MN: West Publishing, 1990), 1037.

[35] See M. N. Shaw, *International Law*, 5th edn. (Cambridge University Press, 2003), 439. For the relationship between the maxim *Venire contra factum proprium* and the concept of estoppel, see R. Kolb, *La bonne foi en droit international public. Contribution à l'étude des principes généraux de droit* (Paris: Presses Universitaires de France, 2000), 357 *et seq.*

[36] See also A. Reinisch, 'Developing Human Rights and Humanitarian Law Accountability of the Security Council for the Imposition of Economic Sanctions', *AJIL*, 95 (2001), 851–72, 869: 'When the United Nations – the major promoter of human rights in the international arena – takes enforcement action, it can be legitimately held to show respect for human rights in an exemplary fashion.'

the further realization of the promise of the United Nations Charter to promote and encourage respect for human rights for all will be one of the decisive tests of the legitimacy of the world organization'.[37] The United Nations would contradict itself if, on the one hand, it constantly admonished its Member States to respect human rights and, on the other hand, it refused to respect the same rights when relevant to its own action. As another author has pointed out, 'it is self-evident that the Organization is obliged to pursue and try to realize its own purpose'.[38]

To a considerable extent, today's international human rights law is a result of the constant endeavours of the United Nations which began with the adoption of the UN Charter and the Universal Declaration of Human Rights.[39] In the preamble of the Charter, human rights appear right after the prevention of war among the principal goals of the United Nations. As Hannum has noted, 'in perhaps no other area has the United Nations been so prolific or, some would argue, so successful as it has been in the adoption of new international norms for the protection of human rights'.[40] When establishing the Human Rights Council, the UN General Assembly acknowledged once more 'that peace and security, development and human rights are the pillars of the United Nations system and the foundations for collective security and well-being'.[41] In its declaration on the sixtieth anniversary of the Universal Declaration of Human Rights, the General Assembly observed that 'we all have the duty to step up our efforts to promote and protect all human rights and to prevent, stop and redress all human rights violations'.[42] This 'we all' includes action taken by the Member States through the organs of the Organisation.

This finding is also in line with essential notions of the concept of international personality. As the ICJ has ruled, 'the rights *and duties* of

[37] See B. Simma, 'Human Rights' in C. Tomuschat (ed.), *The United Nations at Age Fifty. A Legal Perspective* (The Hague, London and Boston: Kluwer Law International, 1995), 263–80, 280.

[38] See Z. Stavrinides, 'Human Rights Obligations under the United Nations Charter', *International Journal of Human Rights*, 3 (1999), 38–48, 40. See also Mégret and Hoffmann, 'The UN as a Human Rights Violator?', *supra* n. 6, 317 *et seq.*

[39] Of the extensive literature, I mention only P. Alston (ed.), *The United Nations and Human Rights* (Oxford: Clarendon Press, 1992); T. J. Farer and F. Gaer, 'The UN and Human Rights. At the End of the Beginning' in A. Roberts and B. Kingsbury (eds.), *United Nations, Divided World. The UN's Roles in International Relations*, 2nd edn. (Oxford: Clarendon Press, 1993), 240–96; H. Hannum, 'Human Rights' in O. Schachter and C. C. Joyner (eds.), *United Nations Legal Order*, 2 vols. (Cambridge University Press, 1995), vol. 1, 319–48; and B. Simma, 'Human Rights', *supra* n. 37.

[40] See Hannum, 'Human Rights', *supra* n. 39, 319.

[41] See General Assembly res. 60/251 of 15 March 2006, preambular para. 6.

[42] See General Assembly res. 63/116 of 10 December 2008, para. 5.

an entity such as the [United Nations] Organization must depend upon its purposes and functions as specified or implied in its constituent documents and developed in practice'.[43] The application of the doctrine of implied powers in the law of international organisations must lead to a recognition not only of implied rights but also of implied duties or obligations. This means that if the recognised practice of an organisation develops in such a way that it includes an exercise of direct authority over individuals, a corresponding duty of that organisation to observe human rights arises under international law.

It may be added here that, foresightedly, the drafters of the 1948 Universal Declaration of Human Rights anticipated that the respect for and observance of human rights and fundamental freedoms called for by the Declaration would not only be demanded from States but also from other bodies and institutions exercising 'elements of governmental authority',[44] including international organisations.

The language of the Universal Declaration is indeed broad enough to cover also official acts of international organisations, such as the United Nations. For instance, the preamble of the Declaration states that 'human rights should be protected by the rule of law', and that the Declaration represents 'a common standard of achievement for all peoples and all nations' to be kept in mind by 'every individual and every organ of society'. By 'progressive measures, national and international', the 'universal and effective recognition and observance' of human rights and freedoms shall be secured. According to Art. 2 of the Declaration, 'everyone is entitled to all the rights and freedoms set forth in this Declaration', and 'no distinction shall be made on the basis of the political, jurisdictional or international status of the country to which a person belongs, whether it be independent, trust, non-self-governing or under any other limitation of sovereignty'. In Art. 28 it is declared that 'everyone is entitled to a social *and international order* in which the rights and freedoms set forth in this Declaration can be fully realized'.[45] Further, the individual rights proclaimed in the Declaration are formulated in a way to make it clear that every body or institution exercising governmental authority *vis-à-vis* individuals, or elements thereof, shall be bound by

---

[43] *Reparation for Injuries Case, supra* n. 11, 180 (emphasis added).
[44] This expression is taken from the International Law Commission's Articles on Responsibility of States for Internationally Wrongful Acts (Annex to UN General Assembly res. 56/83 of 12 December 2001), Arts. 5, 6, 7, 9.
[45] Emphasis added.

them. Arts. 3 and 6 of the Declaration, for instance, say that 'everyone has the right to life, liberty and the security of person' and 'the right to recognition everywhere as a person before the law'.

The above reading of the Universal Declaration has been confirmed by many resolutions of the UN General Assembly, as well as the Vienna Declaration adopted by the World Conference on Human Rights on 25 June 1993.[46] The World Conference declared, *inter alia*, 'that the promotion and protection of human rights is a matter of priority for the international community'. It further expressed the view that 'the promotion and protection of all human rights and fundamental freedoms must be considered as a priority objective of the United Nations in accordance with its purposes and principles', and that 'the promotion and protection of all human rights is a legitimate concern of the international community' (para. 4). Para. 13 of the Vienna Declaration opens with the following statement: 'There is a need for States *and international organizations*, in cooperation with non-governmental organizations, *to create favourable conditions at the* national, regional and *international levels to ensure the full and effective enjoyment of human rights.*'[47]

The UN Charter as the principal source of UN human rights obligations

Notwithstanding the growing legal importance, for the United Nations, of human rights treaty law, on the one hand, and constitutional values and traditions common to UN Member States, on the other hand, and a trend widening the scope of customary human rights law to include direct 'governmental' action of international organizations *vis-à-vis* individuals, the principal source of human rights obligations of the United Nations is the UN Charter as the Organisation's constitution.[48] The

---

[46] UN Doc. A/CONF.157/23 of 12 July 1993.   [47] Emphasis added.

[48] For a recent summary of my work describing the UN Charter as a constitution, see B. Fassbender, *The United Nations Charter as the Constitution of the International Community* (Leiden and Boston: Martinus Nijhoff, 2009). For other constitutional approaches in international law, see, in particular, R. St. J. Macdonald and D. M. Johnston (eds.), *Towards World Constitutionalism. Issues in the Legal Ordering of the World Community* (Leiden and Boston: Martinus Nijhoff, 2005); M. Loughlin and N. Walker (eds.), *The Paradox of Constitutionalism. Constituent Power and Constitutional Form* (Oxford University Press, 2007); and J. L. Dunoff and J. P. Trachtman (eds.), *Ruling the World? Constitutionalism, International Law, and Global Governance* (Cambridge University Press, 2009). See further the special issue of the *Leiden Journal of International Law* (vol. 19 (2006), 3), with contributions by A. Peters, E. de Wet and E. U. Petersmann.

United Nations is an organisation based on the concept of the rule of law. The organs of the Organisation are bound to comply with the rules of the UN Charter, which has a dual constitutional function – it is both the Constitution of the United Nations as an organisation and the constitution of the international community 'as a whole'.[49]

In the preamble of the UN Charter, the peoples of the United Nations have declared their determination 'to reaffirm faith in fundamental human rights, in the dignity and worth of the human person, in the equal rights of men and women'. Art. 1(3) of the Charter defines one of the purposes of the United Nations as 'to achieve international co-operation . . . in promoting and encouraging respect for human rights and for fundamental freedoms for all without distinction as to race, sex, language, or religion'. According to Art. 1(4) of the Charter, the United Nations shall be 'a centre for harmonizing the actions of nations in the attainment of these common ends'.[50]

For the reasons set out above,[51] the UN Charter of 1945 did not explicitly define the human rights obligations of the United Nations itself. But as a constitution, the UN Charter is a 'living instrument'.[52] Early after the San Francisco Conference, an eminent international lawyer, Professor J. L. Brierly of Oxford University, wrote about the Charter that 'constitutions always have to be interpreted and applied, and in the process they are overlaid with precedents and conventions which change them after a time into something very different from what anyone, with only the original text before him, could possibly have foreseen'.[53] More recently, the United Nations was called 'an entire system which is in constant movement, not unlike a national constitution whose original texture will be unavoidably modified by thick layers of political practice and jurisprudence'.[54] By way of example, one can mention as such changes caused by practice and new insight the Uniting for Peace resolution of 1950, the codification and development of Charter principles and rules by the General Assembly, the 'invention'

---

[49] See Fassbender, *The United Nations Charter, supra* n. 48, 116.

[50] For further references of the UN Charter to human rights, see Arts. 13(1b), 55(c), 62(2), 76(c).

[51] See *supra* text accompanying n. 3.

[52] For this notion, originally developed by American legal realism, see Fassbender, *The United Nations Charter, supra* n. 48, 21, 130–1.

[53] See J. L. Brierly, 'The Covenant and the Charter', *BYBIL*, 23 (1946), 83–94.

[54] See C. Tomuschat, 'Obligations Arising for States Without or Against Their Will', *RdC*, 241 (1993), 195–374, 251 *et seq.*

of UN peacekeeping operations and the expansion of the concept of international peace and security in the practice of the Security Council.

Following the adoption of the Charter, human rights have become legal obligations of States under international treaty and customary law. This is essentially due to the incessant work of the organs of the United Nations, in particular the General Assembly and the Commission on Human Rights. The Universal Declaration of Human Rights, the Convention on the Prevention and Punishment of Genocide of 1948, the Convention on the Elimination of Racial Discrimination of 1965 and the two Human Rights Covenants of 1966 have become part of the constitutional foundation of the international community. In the pre-amble of the International Covenant on Civil and Political Rights (ICCPR), the States Parties to the Covenant declared, *inter alia*, that '*in accordance with the principles proclaimed in the Charter of the United Nations*, recognition of the inherent dignity and of the equal and inalienable rights of all members of the human family is the foundation of freedom, justice and peace in the world'.[55]

As mentioned above, another process has led the United Nations to exercise governmental or quasi-governmental authority over private persons and enterprises – in particular, in the context of peacekeeping operations and the temporary administration of territories. Sanctions imposed by the Security Council also have a direct impact on the rights and freedoms of individuals.

In consequence of this dual progress – the coming into existence of a firmly recognised body of human rights in international law, promoted by the United Nations, and the expansion of functions of the Organisation into new areas resulting in acts with a direct impact on the rights of individuals – the references of the UN Charter to human rights have developed into rules embodying direct human rights obligations on the part of the organs of the Organisation. Today, the Charter obliges the organs of the United Nations, when exercising the functions assigned to them, to respect human rights and fundamental freedoms of individuals to the greatest possible extent.[56] The United Nations cannot attain its purpose of achieving 'international co-operation . . . in promoting and encouraging respect for human rights and fundamental freedoms for all' (Art. 1(3) of the UN Charter) if it disregards these rights and

---

[55] Emphasis added.

[56] For discussion, with special emphasis on the Security Council, see Reinisch, 'Developing Human Rights', *supra* n. 36, 853 *et seq.*

freedoms when exercising jurisdiction over individuals. This author agrees with Professor Ian Brownlie, who has written as follows: 'Even if the political organs [of the United Nations] have a wide margin of appreciation in determining that they have competence by virtue of Chapter VI or Chapter VII, and further, in making dispositions to maintain or restore international peace and security, it does not follow that the selection of the modalities of implementation is unconstrained by legality. *Indeed when the rights of individuals are involved, the application of human rights standards is a legal necessity.* Human rights now form part of the concept of the international public order.'[57]

In the absence of a specification of such rights and freedoms in the UN Charter itself, the Universal Declaration of Human Rights and the ICCPR serve, first and foremost, as relevant standards. When the Third Committee of the General Assembly considered the draft of the Universal Declaration in the Fall and Winter of 1948, the French delegate Professor René Cassin described the Declaration as 'an authoritative interpretation of the Charter of the United Nations' ('une explication autorisée de la Charte des Nations Unies').[58] The representative of Chile, Mr Santa Cruz, remarked that the Declaration 'merely stated, explicitly, rights granted by the Charter'. Violation by any State of the rights enumerated in the Declaration would mean violation of the principles of the United Nations.[59] A similar opinion was expressed by the representative of the Republic of China, Mr Chang, who said that the UN Charter committed all Member States to the observance of human rights, and that the Declaration stated those rights explicitly.[60] The Australian delegation also held that the Declaration represented a considerable advance towards a satisfactory definition of the 'fundamental human rights' referred to in the Charter.[61] The delegate of Lebanon, Mr Azkoul, stated that no State could violate the principles of the Declaration without also violating the terms of the Charter. There already existed a place

---

[57] See I. Brownlie, 'The Decisions of Political Organs of the United Nations and the Rule of Law' in R. St. J. Macdonald (ed.), *Essays in Honour of Wang Tieya* (Dordrecht: Martinus Nijhoff, 1993), 91–102, 102.

[58] See United Nations, Official Records of the Third Session of the General Assembly, Part I, Third Committee, Summary Records of Meetings, 21 September–8 December 1948, 61. See also *ibid.*, 34: 'The French representative . . . considered the declaration of human rights to be a complement to the Charter of the United Nations which could not be included in it because of the lengthy preparation it required, a clarification of the Charter, and an organic act of the United Nations having all the legal validity of such an act.'

[59] *Ibid.*, 50.   [60] *Ibid.*, 47 *et seq.*   [61] *Ibid.*, 55 (Mr Watt speaking for Australia).

in the Charter for a declaration of human rights. The implicit agreement concerning human rights, which was reflected in the Charter, was stated clearly in the Declaration.[62]

Speaking for Lebanon before the plenary of the General Assembly on 9 December 1948, Mr Charles Malik, who as a member of the Human Rights Commission had been particularly influential in drafting the Universal Declaration, recalled that the members of the United Nations had already solemnly pledged themselves, under the Charter, to promote respect for human rights and fundamental freedoms, but that it was the first time that those rights and freedoms had been set forth in detail. A convention could subsequently be prepared, but it would rest on the rights laid down in that declaration.[63] Professor Cassin explained that the Declaration was a development of the Charter which had brought human rights within the scope of positive international law.[64] The delegate of Iceland, Mr Thors, said that his delegation regarded the Universal Declaration 'as a preamble to a future world constitution'.[65]

As regards the present legal status of the Universal Declaration, it is important to note that the General Assembly expressly approved of it as one of the standards of the 'universal periodic review' mechanism of the Human Rights Council. Under the heading 'basis of the review', the Declaration is listed right behind the UN Charter and before 'human rights instruments to which a State is party'.[66]

Accordingly, the Universal Declaration of Human Rights may well be counted among the 'constitutional by-laws' of the international community,[67] because it complements, and implements objectives of, the UN Charter.

In the practice of the United Nations, human rights obligations have been expressly recognised in two important areas. With regard to UN peace-keeping operations, the UN Secretary-General in 1999 promulgated 'fundamental principles and rules of international humanitarian law applicable to United Nations forces conducting operations under United Nations

---

[62] *Ibid.*, 51.

[63] See United Nations, Official Records of the Third Session of the General Assembly, Part I, Plenary Meetings of the General Assembly, Summary Records of Meetings 21 September–12 December 1948, 857 *et seq.*, 860.

[64] *Ibid.*, 864 *et seq.*, 866.   [65] *Ibid.*, 877 *et seq.*

[66] See General Assembly res. 62/219 of 22 December 2007, endorsing Human Rights Council res. 5/1 of 18 June 2007 (with Annex 'United Nations Human Rights Council: Institution-Building, [Part] I: Universal Periodic Review Mechanism').

[67] For this notion, see Fassbender, *The United Nations Charter, supra* n. 48, 122 *et seq.*

command and control'.[68] In East Timor and Kosovo, respectively, the UN Transitional Administration in East Timor (UNTAET) and the UN Interim Administration in Kosovo (UNMIK) proclaimed the 'applicability' of human rights standards by stipulating that 'in exercising their functions, all persons undertaking public duties or holding public office [in the respective territories] shall observe internationally recognized human rights standards'.[69]

The need for determining human rights standards to be observed by the Security Council depending on the circumstances of the case

From the foregoing it can be concluded that the UN Charter requires the Security Council, as indeed all organs of the United Nations, to observe 'human rights and fundamental freedoms' (Art. 1(3) of the Charter) as defined, in particular, in the Universal Declaration of Human Rights and the two International Covenants on Human Rights of 1966, when taking action which has a direct impact on individuals. However, this general finding is only the first step towards an effective compliance of the Council with its human rights obligations. The principle of a commitment to human rights must be translated into concrete terms – that is, applied to the circumstances of a particular case. First of all, it must be established which, and whose, human rights exactly could be negatively affected by an act or measure contemplated by the Council. Next, it is necessary to find out whether consideration of the various human rights at stake, and of the different groups of people being entitled to those rights, suggests one and the same course of action to be taken by the Council, or whether that consideration leads to contradictory

---

[68] See 'Observance by United Nations forces of international humanitarian law', Secretary-General's Bulletin, UN doc. ST/SGB/1999/13 of 6 August 1999, reprinted in *ILM*, 38 (1999), 1656–9. Cf. D. Shraga, 'UN Peacekeeping Operations. Applicability of International Humanitarian Law and Responsibility for Operations-Related Damage', *AJIL*, 94 (2000), 406–12; and Wellens, *Remedies, supra* n. 7, 162–6. For an overview of the previous debate over the applicability of international humanitarian law to UN operations, see D. Shraga, 'The United Nations as an Actor Bound by International Humanitarian Law' in L. Condorelli *et al.* (eds.), *Les Nations Unies et le droit international humanitaire – The United Nations and International Humanitarian Law* (Paris: Editions Pédone, 1996), 317–38.

[69] See UNTAET, Reg. No. 1999/1, 'On the Authority of the Transitional Administration in East Timor', Doc. UNTAET/REG/1999/1 of 27 November 1999; UNMIK, Reg. No. 1999/1, 'On the Authority of the Interim Administration in Kosovo', Doc. UNMIK/REG/1999/1 of 25 July 1999. Cf. Mégret and Hoffmann, 'The UN as a Human Rights Violator?', *supra* n. 6, 333 *et seq.*

approaches. In the latter case, the Security Council needs to decide whether, in the particular circumstances, the protection of one particular human right is more important than that of another right. In other words, the Council must balance one human right against another, and possibly also the interests of one particular group of people against those of another group, an exercise with which national and regional human rights courts are familiar.

The Security Council must also weigh its human rights commitments against its Charter responsibility to maintain and restore international peace and security. That responsibility, with the express authority to use armed force to give effect to its decisions (Art. 42 of the Charter), entails, for instance, that the Council may refrain from observing the right to life or the right to physical integrity. The Council may also, for example, discriminate against persons on the grounds of their nationality when it imposes economic sanctions on a particular country and its citizens. When imposing sanctions on individuals in accordance with Chapter VII of the UN Charter, the Security Council must strive to discharge its principal duty to maintain or restore international peace and security while, at the same time, respecting the human rights and fundamental freedoms of targeted individuals to the greatest extent possible. There is a duty of the Council duly to balance the general and particular interests which are at stake. Every measure having a negative impact on human rights and freedoms of a particular group or category of persons must be necessary and proportionate to the aim the measure is meant to achieve.

To mention the example of due process rights of individuals directly affected by acts of the United Nations, the exact scope and intensity of those rights is not generally predefined. Depending on the circumstances of a particular situation, appropriate standards must be determined, suited to that situation, paying due regard to the nature of the affected rights and freedoms and the extent to which action taken by the United Nations is likely adversely to affect those rights and freedoms.[70] In the first place, such a determination of standards is the responsibility of the organ the action of which is directly affecting the rights and freedoms of individuals.

Occasionally it has been remarked that the Security Council is a political organ, and not a court. This is certainly true, but this qualification does not

---

[70] For a proposal on elements of due process rights of addressees of sanctions imposed on individuals under Chapter VII of the UN Charter, see Fassbender, 'Targeted Sanctions', *supra* n. 25, 476 *et seq*. See also Security Council res. 1904 of 17 December 2009 (establishing an Office of the Ombudsperson as a part of the Al Qaeda/Taliban sanctions regime).

exempt the Council from its human rights obligations which arise from the UN Charter. The governments of Member States are also political organs, but no one would deny that they are nevertheless obliged to respect the international human rights commitments accepted by their States. In the same way as governments, the members of the Security Council can seek legal advice. However, an aspect which must be taken into consideration is that, in certain circumstances, the Council must act very swiftly in order to carry out its mandate as defined by the UN Charter. If rapid action is necessary – for instance, to ward off an imminent act of aggression – one cannot expect the Council to be as circumspect and attentive to possible adverse human rights consequences – as, for example, in the case of legislative acts, the drafting of which takes many months.

There can be no doubt about the outstanding importance of human rights in the contemporary international legal order, and about the necessity of a Security Council strictly adhering to those rights. But it would be a mistake to create the impression of a general contradiction between the protection of human rights and effective action by the Security Council, as this could jeopardise the role the Council has come to play in world affairs in the last two decades. The world still requires an exercise of more, not less authority on a global level; and international lawyers should encourage this development rather than warn against it.[71]

---

[71] See B. Fassbender, 'Quis judicabit? The Security Council, Its Powers and Its Legal Control', *EJIL*, 11 (2000), 219–32, 220.

7

Is transnational law eclipsing international law?

DANIEL KALDERIMIS*

Introduction

I recall first studying international law at law school in the mid-1990s. The course I took was taught by a disciple, and former student, of Judge Rosalyn Higgins. As well as to educate, the course's basic objective was to convince young lawyers of the relevance and importance of international law, despite the apparent vagaries and shortcomings of the international legal system.

We are all familiar with the standard critique such an approach sought to address: the critique led by legal positivists such as John Austin that laws properly so called are a species of commands which flow from a determinate source and are enforced by effective sanctions: as in developed domestic legal systems. On this analysis, international law was not law at all, but a mere elaboration of the international morality of State conduct. And even this morality was of limited effect; as States do not, in practice, invoke international law save in the service of their own interests. On this view, international law is merely a tool used in the course of international diplomacy.

We are all also familiar with the standard 'policy-science' riposte, championed by such luminaries as Professor Louis Henkin and Judge Higgins herself. This was that legal positivists ask themselves the wrong questions. What matters is not whether the international legal system has analogues to domestic legal systems of legislative, judicial, or executive branches, but whether international law is reflected in the policies of nations and in relations between nations. The question is not whether and how international law is enforced, but whether it governs or

---

* This chapter is an edited version of an address with the same title given to the 2009 International Law Association (ILA) (British Branch) Annual Conference held in London.

influences behaviour and whether international behaviour reflects stability and order. Higgins famously wrote '[i]nternational law is not rules. It
is a normative system.'[1] International law is 'the entire decision-making
process'; and references to 'rules' can never avoid the element of choice,
nor can they provide guidance to the preferable decision.[2] Despite this
zone of uncertainty and the absence of effective sanctions,[3] the international law process is real and produces legal norms with 'core
predictability'.[4]

The textbook that I studied from, the late Professor Ian Brownlie's
Principles of Public International Law, covered the classical areas of
interest. To use Brownlie's text (6th edn., 2003) as an example, one can
see that its substantive scope covers international legal personality and
recognition (largely of States), territorial sovereignty, State jurisdiction,
attribution and responsibility, succession, the use of common resources
and the use of force. The only specific areas covered are the law of the sea,
the protection of aliens, human rights law and international criminal law.
There is nothing of international trade, monetary, or environmental law
and only a few lines dedicated to the role of bilateral investment treaties
(BITs). There is no reference to rules on intellectual property, securities,
banking, antitrust, or accounting regulations.

Throughout the text one can discern a conception of the international
legal system as consisting fundamentally of custom, leavened with specific instances of treaties. Thus, the section on treaties as a 'formal source
of law' excludes treaties binding only a few States and is apologetically
introduced with the words: '[i]t may seem untidy to depart from discussion of the "formal" sources, of which custom is the most important'.[5]

This view, that most treaties were essentially private contracts between
States and custom was the glue that held the whole system together, was
once very fashionable.[6] It was often difficult to reconcile with practice,

---

[1] R. Higgins, *Problems and Process. International Law and How We Use It* (Oxford
University Press, 1995), 1.
[2] *Ibid.*, 4–5.   [3] *Ibid.*, 16.   [4] *Ibid.*, 8.
[5] I. Brownlie, *Principles of Public International Law*, 6th edn. (Oxford University Press, 2003),
12. Professor Brownlie's view is that only treaties binding a majority of States (which he calls
'general international law') are of interest in this regard as these can produce a 'strong law-
making effect at least as great as the general practice sufficient to support a customary rule'
(13). However, even here, general treaties are discussed together with the conclusions of
international conferences, General Assembly resolutions and ILA drafts. The law of particular
treaties is addressed only in chapter 27 of Brownlie's book.
[6] See, e.g., G. Fitzmaurice, 'Some Problems Regarding the Formal Sources of International
Law' in *Symbolae Verzijl* (The Hague: Martinus Nÿhoff, 1958), 153, 157–8.

however, and became more so following the codification efforts of the 1960s and the gradual emergence of institutional treaties relating to specific issues, such as the United Nations Convention on the Law of the Sea.

My thesis – and it is not a very novel one – is that times have moved on further still. It is now inaccurate to describe the international legal system as being primarily based on custom supplemented with instances of treaty law. Nor is it necessary in many contexts to defend the apparent toothlessness of the international legal system by viewing public international law as a process and not an enforceable body of rules.

Rather, public international law is evolving from a unitary, primitive and normative system to a decentralised system of specific, enforceable obligations created through separate treaty-regimes. This evolution is a phenomenon which Detlev Vagts has acutely observed and recorded in his writings over the last forty years. In many of today's treaty-regimes, not only is the treaty text paramount and the role of custom of limited relevance, but the role of accruing case-law from international tribunals is rapidly gaining in significance.

In this way, public international law is following the same path of development previously trodden by most domestic legal systems. The development of the English legal system has seen the customary or Common law gradually displaced in favour of detailed legislation and court decisions interpreting that legislation. These legal changes were, in turn, caused by Britain's economic and political development; in particular by the changes wrought by the industrial revolution. So it is with international law, which has been forced to mature by the forces of globalisation.

The 'third wave' of globalisation

Globalisation is fundamentally about mobility across frontiers – of goods and commodities, capital and investment, information and communications, services and people.[7] Although not all scholars agree on the

---

[7] K. Robins, 'Encountering Globalization' in D. Held and A. McGrew (eds.), *The Global Transformations Reader. An Introduction to the Globalization Debate*, 2nd edn., (Cambridge: Polity, 2003), 239. David Held has defined globalisation as 'first and foremost, a stretching of social, political and economic activities across frontiers such that events, decisions and activities in one region of the world can come to have significance for individuals in distant regions of the globe': D. Held, 'Rethinking Globalization' in Held and McGrew, *The Global Transformations Reader*, 67.

terminology, there is relatively broad consensus that the periods of recent globalisation – including measures to open barriers and facilitate increased contact between nation-states – translate roughly to the three waves of democratisation classified by Samuel Huntingdon in his well-known book (*The Third Wave*, 1991).[8] The lengthy First Wave took place in the century prior to the 1920s and effectively ended with the Great Depression; the Second Wave took place after the Second World War and ended in the early 1960s; and the third began in the 1970s–1980s. The beginnings of the Third Wave, in the context of the Cold War and international tensions caused by the unwinding of colonisation, were slow to take root.[9] In face of rising commodity prices and oil shocks, however, many countries deregulated their economies as the world struggled to stave off a global recession. By the time of the collapse of the Soviet Union in 1991, a new era of global political and economic interactivity had been borne. This was intensified by advances in modern technology, which greatly increased the opportunities for international contact – be they through global trade, investment, crime, or terrorism. We may now be moving into a Fourth Wave in which climate change issues begin to dominate the agenda.

Each of these waves of globalisation has been accompanied by changes in the international legal architecture. The First Wave created the League of Nations, the Permanent Court of Arbitration and many treaties of friendship, commerce and navigation. The Second Wave created the United Nations, the International Court of Justice (ICJ), the General Agreement on Tariffs and Trade (GATT) and the Bretton Woods institutions. The Third Wave was triggered, in part, by the collapse of the gold standard in 1971 and the subsequent removal of foreign exchange controls by the early 1980s,[10] leading to the increased movement of capital. The modern proliferation of BITs accordingly began in earnest in the 1970s and increased exponentially in the 1990s.[11] The most decisive legal change wrought by the Third Wave was the metamorphosis of the 1944 GATT into the World Trade Organization (WTO) in the 1993 Uruguay Round of negotiations. Vagts famously tracked this sweep

---

[8] S. P. Huntingdon, *The Third Wave. Democratization in the Late Twentieth Century* (Norman, OH: University of Oklahoma Press, 1991).

[9] See, e.g., R. Robertson, 'Globalization is Not Made in the West', *Yale Global Online*, 13 April 2005.

[10] The United Kingdom, for instance, abolished its foreign exchange controls in 1979.

[11] Though the first BIT was signed between the Federal Republic of Germany and Pakistan in 1959.

of international economic regulation in his Centennial Essay in Honour of the 100th Anniversary of the *American Journal of International Law* (*AJIL*) and the American Society of International Law (ASIL).[12]

The modern phenomenon of globalisation, as we are now experiencing it, is characterised by an increased global interconnectedness of local activities and fuelled by technological advances, such as high-speed travel, satellite communications systems, worldwide telecoms cables, digitalisation of information and the ubiquity of the internet.

Above all, globalisation has resulted in an increased economic interconnectedness arising out of what Anthony Giddens calls the 'world capitalist economy'[13] or what Susan Strange called the 'market–authority nexus', reflecting the significant power gained by the global market relative to States since the 1970s.[14] Key features of the global economy include powerful multinational corporations (MNCs) (from both developed and developing countries),[15] the creation of international capital, debt, currency and commodities markets and the increasing integration of global financial systems. The Asian, Russian and Argentinean financial crises in the late 1990s and the 2007–9 global financial crisis underline the extent of modern economic integration.

These changes created the need for new forms of international regulation. Classical public international law – the law of custom and *opinio juris* – was not equipped to provide necessary certainty, predictability and specificity. Much of the necessary regulation has been economic. However, because 'intensive economic interdependence affects social and environmental interdependence',[16] many other forms of regulation have also been needed. Legal responses to non-economic forms of globalisation include the 1989 Montreal Protocol on Substances that Deplete the Ozone Layer against CFCs, the 1997 Kyoto Protocol to the UN Framework Convention on Climate Change (UNFCCC) and the

---

[12] D. F. Vagts, 'International Economic Law and the American Journal of International Law', *AJIL*, 100 (2006), 769 82. Here, Vagts argued that international economic law is not yet a century old; prior to 1914, global economic flows were both unregulated and largely obscure to most practising lawyers.

[13] A. Giddens, 'The Globalizing of Modernity' in Held and McGrew, *The Global Transformations Reader*, supra n. 7, 60–7, 67.

[14] S. Strange, *The Retreat of the State. The Diffusion of Power in the World Economy* (Cambridge University Press, 1996).

[15] D. F. Vagts, 'The Multinational Enterprise. A New Challenge for Transnational Law', *Harvard Law Review*, 83 (1970), 739–92.

[16] R. O. Keohane and J. S. Nye, Jr., 'What's New? What's Not (And So What?)' in Held and McGrew, *The Global Transformations Reader*, supra n. 7, 75–83, 78.

range of UN and other initiatives to combat cross-border crimes and terrorism.[17]

Contrary to some predictions, 'transnational law' has played so far only a comparatively modest role. A few short definitions may assist in explaining why this is so. In its purest form 'transnational law' can be defined as privatised law: that is, rules which arise not as a result of national laws, nor as a result of international laws, but as a result of the private actions of individuals. An example of this is the use of the UNIDROIT Principles, purely between international merchants, to define their contractual obligations; or the Equator Principles, purely between financial institutions, to promote sustainable project finance practices. These rules are gaining in profile, but few would argue they have shaped today's world.

A less pure definition of transnational law is the rules that exist in areas of global activity which are not only, or not strictly, governed by any one national or international law. One can see incipient signs of this type of transnational law in the fields of antitrust, securities regulation and banking law where debates over the extraterritorial reach of domestic statutes, the adoption of voluntary codes of conduct and the need for actors to comply simultaneously with different rules has led to forms of synergy and integration. Vagts has written prominently in this area.[18] Again, the impact can be seen but is not yet pronounced.

An even less pure definition of transnational law is that proposed by Philip Jessup in 1956, in his lectures delivered at Yale Law School, in which he proposed that the doctrinal boundaries of both private and public international law should give way to a broader concept of 'transnational law', which would include 'all law which regulates actions or events which transcend national frontiers'.[19] Jessup's proposal was startlingly clairvoyant and his insights in those lectures are still highly relevant. As he predicted, global conduct is now regulated by a range of rules, customs and codes arising from many different sources.

---

[17] As to cross-border crime, see the 1961 Single Convention on Narcotic Drugs, the 1988 Convention against the Illicit Traffic in Narcotic Drugs and Psychotropic Substances and the 2003 UN Conventions against Corruption and Transnational Organized Crime. See, generally, www.unodc.org/. As to international terrorism, there are more than a dozen treaties designed to prevent terrorist acts, including treaties directed at suppressing aircraft and nuclear terrorism, preventing the taking of hostages and preventing terrorist financing. Currently UN Member States are seeking to negotiate a Draft Comprehensive Convention on International Terrorism. See, generally, www.un.org/terrorism/instruments.shtml.

[18] See, e.g., D. F. Vagts, 'Extraterritoriality and the Corporate Governance Law', *AJIL*, 97 (2003), 289–94.

[19] P. C. Jessup, *Transnational Law* (New Haven, CT: Yale University Press, 1956), 106 and 136.

However, I will not adopt Jessup's definition, for two reasons. First, it would reduce any discussion of whether transnational law was eclipsing international law to mere semantics: because his definition of transnational law *includes* public international law, the former is necessarily eclipsing (or rather subsuming) the latter. More importantly, Jessup's definition serves to avoid the critical question of *which* rules or norms exert the greatest influence. In due course, it may be that States and treaties are no more relevant to the rules governing international interactions than non-State action and codes of conduct. But, we are not there yet. In today's world, a different legal institutional structure has been taking shape.

International treaty-based regimes

That institutional structure is the increasing maturity of treaty-regimes. By 'treaty-regime', I mean the international institutions and treaties that govern an issue area.[20] An issue area is simply a discrete subject matter area. The concept comes from international relations theory and was traditionally used to direct analysis away from a domestic–international dichotomy towards consideration of substantively related issues (such as trade or the environment).[21] Applied to international law, it is very much where Jessup's thinking was headed: that the best way to think about international law was not to focus on the source of the obligation (international law, domestic law, soft law), but on the cluster of obligations which directly or indirectly affect different issue areas.

Globalisation has resulted in some issue areas being relatively lightly regulated and others being much more heavily regulated. The key difference between the two categories is whether a treaty-regime (usually supplemented by satellite institutions and rules existing independently of the treaty itself) is in place. The contemporary debate about the intersection between international trade (a highly regulated regime) and international climate change (a nascent regime) regulation highlights this tension. And it may be that international agreement leads to the latter issue area being much more tightly regulated in future.

---

[20] D. Leebron, 'Linkages', *AJIL*, 96 (2002), 5–27, 10; A. Lang, 'Reflecting on Linkage. Cognitive and Institutional Change in the International Trading System', *Modern Law Review*, 70(4) (2007), 523–49 and D. Kalderimis, 'Problems of WTO Harmonization and the Virtues of Shields Over Swords', *Minnesota Journal of Global Trade*, 13 (2004), 305–52.

[21] D. Leebron, 'Linkages', *supra* n. 20, 7. See, generally, J. G. Ruggie, 'International Regimes, Transactions, and Change. Embedded Liberalism and the Post-War Economic Order', *International Organization*, 36 (1982), 379–415.

In my view, treaty-regimes have played the most fundamental role in responding to the challenges of globalisation. One can see this most clearly in the different issue areas comprising international economic law: an emerging discipline which barely existed fifteen years ago, but which has arisen as a response to increased economic integration. These regimes include:

- *International trade*: where the systemic ground-rules are governed by the WTO and a host of regional and bilateral trade agreements, such as NAFTA;[22] individual transactions are increasingly being resolved by international commercial arbitration made effective by the 1958 New York Convention on the Recognition and Enforcement of Foreign Arbitral Awards (New York Convention); and a body of international sales law and practice has developed, supported by UNCITRAL's[23] prolific outputs.
- *Foreign direct investment (FDI)*: primarily governed by the web of BITs signed between capital-exporting and capital-importing countries (resulting in a highly decentralised, but nevertheless effective, regime), often in conjunction with the 1965 International Convention on the Settlement of Investment Disputes between States and Nationals of other States (ICSID Convention) (and to a lesser extent WTO Agreements such as the General Agreement on Trade in Services (GATS) and the Agreement on Trade-Related Investment Measures (TRIMs)); and supported by domestic laws, codes of conduct and providers of political risk insurance.
- *International capital*: where a partial institutional structure is provided by the International Monetary Fund (IMF) and the World Bank (IBRD), supported by a host of regional development banks and institutions, cross-border banking regulations (such as the Basel Committee on Banking Supervision and the Basel II Framework on capital adequacy) and soft-law instruments, such as the OECD[24] Code of Liberalisation of Capital Movements.
- *Intellectual property*: governed through the World Intellectual Property Organisation (WIPO, which administers twenty-three international treaties[25] and has a binding arbitral dispute resolution system for domain name disputes[26]), as well as through the WTO and, increasingly, BITs.

---

[22] North American Free Trade Agreement between the United States, Canada and Mexico, entered into force on 1 January 1994.

[23] United Nations Commission on International Trade Law, established by the UN General Assembly in 1966.

[24] Organisation for Economic Cooperation and Development.

[25] See www.wipo.int/treaties/en/.

[26] Through the WIPO Arbitration and Mediation Center, see www.wipo.int/amc/en/domains/.

Other issue areas now heavily controlled by treaty-regimes are:

- *International criminal law*: For war crimes and crimes against humanity, this is now anchored by the International Criminal Court (ICC) created by the 1998 Rome Statute and has developed through the jurisprudence of the ad hoc international criminal tribunals established by the Security Council for the former Yugoslavia[27] and Rwanda[28] (and, to a lesser extent, the special tribunals for Sierra Leone, Cambodia and Lebanon[29]); and supplemented by concepts such as universal jurisdiction enforced through domestic courts and domestic laws on extradition. For other crimes, international law is being developed through international treaties on cross-border crime and international terrorism.[30]

- *International law of commons areas*: such as the *deep sea* (eventually agreed through the 1982 UN Convention on the Law of the Sea (UNCLOS), which also creates a complex dispute settlement system), *air space* (through the 1944 Chicago Convention on International Civil Aviation and the International Civil Aviation Organisation); *outer space* (through the United Nations Committee on the Peaceful Uses of Outer Space and four UN treaties on non-military use of outer space, including the Outer Space Treaty,[31] the Rescue Agreement,[32] the Liability Convention[33] and the Registration Convention[34]); and the *South Pole* (through the 1959 Antarctic Treaty and its associated treaty system).

Some important issue areas are strongly influenced, but not yet controlled, by treaty-regimes. These include:

- *International environmental law*: Progress has been made in the Montreal Protocol and the Kyoto Protocol. The question as to whether a binding and effective successor agreement to the latter instrument can be agreed has still not been answered at the time of writing. There has been some progress in other specific instruments, however,

---

[27] See Security Council resolution 827, 25 May 1993.
[28] See Security Council resolution 995, 8 November 1994.
[29] See, generally, www.globalpolicy.org/intljustice/tribindx.htm. [30] See *supra* n. 17.
[31] Treaty on Principles Governing the Activities of States, Including the Moon and Other Celestial Bodies (1967), *AJIL*, 61, (1967), 644–9.
[32] Agreement on the Rescue of Astronauts, the Return of Astronauts and the Return of Objects Launched into Outer Space (1972), *AJIL*, 63, (1969), 382–5.
[33] Convention on Liability for Damage Caused by Objects Launched into Outer Space (1972), *AJIL*, 66, (1972), 702–9.
[34] Convention on Registration of Objects Launched into Outer Space (1974), 28 *UST* 695.

including CITES (prohibiting trading in endangered species),[35] the 1989 Basel Convention on the Movement of Hazardous Wastes and the 1992 Convention on Biological Diversity. So far (and climate change negotiations may defy this trend), multilateral environmental agreements tend to be framework agreements or aspirational. This issue area thus remains reliant on soft law, such as the principles underlying sustainable development enshrined in the non-binding declarations made in Rio de Janeiro and Johannesburg.

- *International labour law*: this is largely regulated by international labour standards established in over 180 conventions overseen by the International Labour Organization (ILO)[36] but which (despite the possibility of complaints to ILO supervisory bodies) are largely unenforceable in practice.

- *International human rights law*: the basic principles are stated in the International Bill of Rights – the 1948 UN Declaration, the 1966 International Covenant on Civil and Political Rights (ICCPR) and the 1966 International Covenant on Economic, Social and Cultural Rights (ICESCR) – as well as a suite of more specific human rights treaties which are overseen by the UN Human Rights Council[37] (for the ICCPR, by the Human Rights Committee) as well as various regional bodies. With the (arguable) exception of the European Court of Human Rights, these bodies cannot issue binding and enforceable decisions against States.

- *International law of armed conflict*: the main rules of this are stated in the four 1949 Geneva Conventions (on wounded and sick armed personnel on land and sea, prisoners of war and the protection of civilians) and the Hague Conventions of 1899 and 1907 (on the law of land and maritime warfare), as well as the various Protocols to those Conventions.[38] As the world has recently seen, not all of them have been clearly or resolutely applied to modern conflicts involving non-State actors and threats of terrorism.

---

[35] Convention on International Trade in Endangered Species of Wild Flora and Fauna (1973), *ILM*, 12 (1973), 1055.

[36] E.g. Conventions on Freedom of Association (1948), Collective Bargaining (1949), Forced Labour (1930, 1957), Minimum Age (1973), Child Labour (1999), Equal Remuneration (1951) and Discrimination (1958). See also the ILO's Declaration on Fundamental Principles and Rights at Work (1998), www.ilo.org/ilolex/english/convdisp1.htm.

[37] Established by General Assembly resolution A/RES/60/251, 3 April 2006.

[38] Including the Geneva Protocols of 1925 (prohibiting biological or chemical warfare), 1977 (relating, respectively, to the protection of victims of international and non-international armed conflicts) and 2005 (relating to the adoption of a distinctive international emblem).

The main advantage of treaty-regimes is their binding and enforceable character for resolving disputes. This provides a form of certainty and leverage which classic public international law (and the 'law as process' explanation) could not provide.

A good example is the WTO case *Antigua and Barbuda* v. *United States* (US-Gambling) filed against the United States concerning the latter's policies on internet gambling services. Antigua brought its WTO claim in March 2003, alleging that the US prohibition of cross-border gambling services offered by Antiguan operators to consumers in the United States constituted a breach of US commitments in the GATS. Antigua won its Panel decision in March 2004, which was upheld by the Appellate Body in April 2005. The United States was given a year to comply and failed to do so. Antigua obtained a ruling from a WTO Compliance Panel ruling that the United States was in default and entitling Antigua to impose trade sanctions. Antigua then applied for the right to impose retaliatory cross-sanctions by suspending intellectual property rights with respect to American copyrighted and trademarked products under the WTO Agreement on Trade-Related Aspects of Intellectual Property Rights (TRIPs). In December 2007, Antigua was given the right to do so (though to a significantly lesser level than it had requested).[39] The fact that Antigua did not ultimately elect to pursue this option does not detract from the importance of the option being available.

My simple point is that these treaty-regimes have not arisen by accident. They have arisen because globalised conduct, such as the offering of international online gambling services, requires clear and enforceable rules. Merchants and international actors wanted precisely what Higgins thought international law could not offer, which was an analogue to dispute resolution procedures of domestic law, producing binding and enforceable decisions. Thus, a new paradigm has emerged.

Marginalisation of classical public international law

In my view, this new paradigm is here to stay. International law, having moved through an era of codification of customary law to the present era of treaty-regimes, will not return to the days where custom was

---

[39] With respect to other WTO 'cross-retaliation' cases, see also *United States – Measures Affecting the Cross-Border Supply of Gambling and Betting Services*, WT/DS285/ARB, 21 December 2007 and *United States – Upland Cotton (Article 22.6 arbitration)*, WT/DS267/ARB/1, 1 August 2008.

paramount. Moreover, the increasing power of non-State actors in international conduct will demand increasing legal certainty and enforcement of individual rights. The future trend will likely involve more private law instruments and industry self-regulation in specific issue areas.

Looking back, it is possible to see some of the ways in which classical public international law failed to provide the certainty globalised actors demanded. One good example is the interminable process of drafting the International Law Commission (ILC) Articles on State Responsibility, which the ILC was requested by the General Assembly to begin in 1953, but which was not completed until 2001 and still has no formally binding force.[40] This can be compared to the fast and prolific output of UNCITRAL which, for example, produced the Model Law on International Commercial Arbitration in three years (between 1982 and 1985), forms of which have been enacted into domestic legislation by fifty-six countries.[41]

Another example is the increasingly creaky UN system. Under the Bush administration, the United States more than once[42] publicly declared its lack of confidence in the United Nations and its (ultimately unratified) 2005 appointment of John Bolton as ambassador to the United Nations sent a clear signal. For the public, the failure to gain a Security Council resolution authorising the Second Iraq War – and the casuistic debate which followed the invasion – seemed to confirm the view of Austinian positivists: even the primary rule in the UN Charter prohibiting the use of force could be flouted by the architects of that Charter choosing to assemble a coalition of the willing. Mr Blair's recent statement that he would have invaded Iraq even without evidence of weapons of mass destruction[43] is further grist to the same mill.

Another way of testing this theory is to look at the relative power of the International Court of Justice (ICJ), which is a symbol of the old, largely consensual, order. An article by Eric Posner demonstrates that the influence of the ICJ is steadily decreasing.[44] More anecdotally, one

---

[40] See generally D. D. Caron, 'The ILC Articles on State Responsibility: The Paradoxical Relationship Between Form and Authority', *AJIL*, 96 (2002), 857–73, 868.

[41] See www.uncitral.org/uncitral/en/uncitral_texts/arbitration/1985Model_arbitration.html. The Model Law text was last amended in 2006.

[42] See R. Perle, Chairman of Defence Policy Board (and advisory panel to the Pentagon), 'Thank God for the Death of the UN', *The Guardian*, 21 March 2003.

[43] 'Unashamed Blair Confronts his Critics' Claims on Iraq', *BBC News*, 12 December 2009, http://news.bbc.co.uk/2/hi/8409596.stm.

[44] E. A. Posner, 'The Decline of the International Court of Justice', Olin Working Paper, No. 233/Public Law Working Paper, No. 81, University of Chicago, December 2004, see

can already see that cases which would once have been tried before the ICJ – such as the 1970 *Barcelona Traction* case (in which Belgium sought to espouse a claim of Belgian shareholders of a Canadian utilities company allegedly expropriated in Spain in the 1960s) – are now being tried before other tribunals, such as BIT tribunals. And the BIT tribunals have reached a different result, now giving shareholder companies rights under BITs and international law.[45] The ICJ's docket is dominated by cases involving border disputes, diplomatic relations, aerial incidents and the use of force. Aside from possibly the last category, where the decisions of the ICJ are but one element in a larger international relations puzzle, these are not issues at the very forefront of globalisation.

Where the ICJ has sought to raise its voice – such as in *Mexico v. United States* (the *Avena* case) – it has been publicly ignored. In that 2004 decision, the ICJ required the United States to provide further 'review and reconsideration' of the convictions of fifty-two Mexican nationals on death row, due to the US failure to accord consular rights to those nationals under the Optional Protocol to the 1963 Vienna Convention on Consular Relations. In March 2008, the US Supreme Court held 6:3 that the UN Charter, the ICJ Statute and the Vienna Convention were not binding federal law – despite Art. VI(2) of the Constitution providing that 'all treaties made, or which shall be made, under the Authority of the United States, shall be the supreme law of the land; and the Judges in every State shall be bound thereby'. Therefore (absent an implementing statute), the ICJ decision was not enforceable by US federal courts against Texas – where the relevant petitioner was being held. Similarly

www.ssrn.com/. Key conclusions reached include the following: (a) there were thirty-six filings during the ICJ's first twenty years (1946–65): there were fifty-three filings during the ICJ's last twenty years (1985–2004) (including ten filings emerging from essentially the same event, the intervention in Kosovo). But the number of UN Member States increased by more than three times during this period (from fifty-five in 1946 to 191 in 2004). Thus, the number of filings per State dropped quite substantially; (b) the fraction of States that are subject to compulsory jurisdiction dropped from about two-thirds to about one-third; (c) the fraction of permanent members of the Security Council that are subject to compulsory jurisdiction dropped from four-fifths to one-fifth (the United Kingdom); and (d) during the ICJ's first twenty years, States entered treaties that provided for ICJ jurisdiction at a rate of almost ten per year; today the rate is less than two per year.

45 *CMS Gas Transmission Company* v. *Argentina*, Decision on Objections to Jurisdiction, 17 July 2003 (ICSID Case No. ARB/01/8); *Ronald S. Lauder* v. *Czech Republic*, Final Award, 3 September 2001, 9 *ICSID Reports* 62 (UNCITRAL, 2001). See generally C. McLachlan, L. Shore and M. Weiniger, *International Investment Arbitration* (Oxford University Press, 2007), 124–5.

unenforceable was a 2005 memorandum from President Bush stating his intention to enforce *Avena*. Although the US Congress is free to enact legislation to give effect to *Avena*, it has not done so.

In 1998 Detlev Vagts wrote with concern about a trend he perceived in the United States of failing to accord due weight to treaty obligations.[46] His conclusion was that '[a] reputation for playing fast and loose with treaty commitments can only do harm to [the US] capacity to be a leader in the post-Cold War world'.[47] I agree that there is evidence for the premise. But my conclusion is slightly different. The *Avena* case does not diminish only the United States' international standing; it further diminishes the normative force of classical international law. This incident, and others like it, are likely to further fuel the development of treaty-regimes with their own, workable, enforcement mechanisms.

Today's most important global challenge is, of course, tackling climate change. Here, whether meaningful progress can be made will be defined by whether a viable treaty-regime, with some form of reciprocal enforcement (or at least measurement) mechanism, emerges. It is quite clear to all that the problem of global warming, like most of the other problems of the modern globalised world, is simply not susceptible to solution by classical public international law.

Role of classical public international law

So, where does this leave classical public international law? Looking ahead, I think there are three potential roles.

First, treaty-regimes do not and will never precisely and exhaustively settle every issue. Thus, the law of treaties will still be needed to help interpret the regimes and customary international law will remain necessary to fill gaps.[48]

Secondly, there remains a need for rules (just as for corporations) relating to the constitutive nature of States and their attributes and powers (issues such as personality and recognition, jurisdiction,

---

[46] D. F. Vagts, 'Editorial Comment. Taking Treaties Less Seriously', *AJIL*, 92 (1998), 458–62.

[47] *Ibid.*, 462.

[48] As Vagts has written, treaty law has not rendered customary international law otiose: D. F. Vagts, 'International Relations Looks at Customary International Law. A Traditionalist's Defence', *EJIL*, 15 (2004), 1031–40. Moreover, the ICJ will also remain the default tribunal for disputes under the thousands of individual treaties for which there is no dispute resolution procedure provided – provided the disputing State parties agree to voluntary jurisdiction under Art. 36(1) of the Statute.

privileges and immunities and rules of attribution) and to deal with uniquely State-to-State issues such as territorial and boundary disputes.

Thirdly, there is also a need for rules and processes which provide legitimacy to the treaty-regimes and other governing norms. Thus, there may still be a role for classical international law as the meta- or constitutional law of the entire international system. In particular, many commentators have already considered the problem of how the treaty-regimes will be linked to each other and to more nascent issue areas so as to achieve a coherent, just and balanced world order. This overarching theory will never be provided by a world constitution. If it is to come from anywhere, it will be from the principles of public international law, as understood and applied by international tribunals, domestic judges, academics and practitioners.

The potential for regime conflict is enormous. Consider the importance of ensuring that the WTO regime does not overwhelm climate change, biodiversity and other environmental agendas; that the international criminal process takes account of both human rights and national security concerns; or that the international investment regime is consonant with sustainable development. It may be that there will never be a centralised solution to these potential issue conflicts; and that linkages between different regimes and issue areas will develop organically. But public international law, and public international lawyers, could do worse than reflect on whether it is possible to fashion workable conflicts of laws rules for public, as well as private, international law.

To conclude, as Vagts predicted as early as 1970,[49] globalisation has changed the world we live in and the international laws we need. Contrary to many predictions, the result is not that transnational law has eclipsed public international law; but that public international law has evolved into a decentralised system largely controlled by treaty-regimes. The days of the generalist public international lawyer are fast disappearing.[50] But the days of the modern, specialised, public international lawyer are only just beginning.

---

[49] Vagts, 'The Multinational Enterprise', *supra* n. 15.

[50] The beginning of this trend was noticed by Vagts almost thirty years ago: D. F. Vagts, 'Are There No International Lawyers Anymore?', *AJIL*, 75, (1981), 134–7, 135 ('Evidently it is the coming thing for lawyers to group themselves along speciality lines, to develop continuing legal education programs for specialists, and to become involved in procedures to certify the expertise thus gained. Where does this leave a society for internationalists?').

8

Participation in the World Trade Organization and foreign direct investment: national or European Union competences

JULIANE KOKOTT

Introduction

As a true international lawyer and multilingual citizen of the world, Detlev Vagts has always shown interest in other legal cultures. He is a close observer and analyst of legal developments in Europe. Through his language abilities, Detlev Vagts has direct access, for example, to German legal thought. I hope that my contribution on German and European approaches to WTO law and foreign investment will attract his interest.

The background to my contribution is set by the Lisbon Treaty. This Treaty was the second attempt to reorganise the European Union (EU) in response to the recent enlargements and the continuing extension of its activities. A first attempt, the Constitutional Treaty, failed after it was rejected in 2005 by referenda in France and The Netherlands. The new Treaty drops most of the symbolism that characterised the Constitutional Treaty but aims to maintain much of its substantial impact – e.g. in the areas of criminal law, fundamental rights and international relations. Following a long and difficult ratification process – including a failed referendum in Ireland, seemingly endless political debate and judicial hurdles before Constitutional Courts – the Lisbon Treaty came into force on 1 December 2009 after Ireland, Germany, Poland and the Czech Republic overcame their respective domestic problems concerning ratification.

As was the case with the earlier Treaty of Maastricht,[1] the German ratification depended on a decision[2] by the German Federal Constitutional

---

[1] Treaty on European Union (TEU), OJ (Official Journal) C 191 of 29 July 1992.

[2] Federal Constitutional Court (Bundesverfassungsgericht, BVerfG), 2 BvR 2134, 2159/92 of 12 October 1993.

Court. That Court was seized with several complaints against the ratification of the Lisbon Treaty by the Federal Republic of Germany. In its judgment of 30 June 2009,[3] the Court allowed ratification but set out additional procedural and substantial conditions for further integration.

These conditions affect my subject in Union law, the Common Commercial Policy (CCP). The relevant provision belongs to the most heavily revised parts of the European Treaties by the Lisbon Treaty. Therefore, the subject is very topical. This concerns especially foreign direct investment (FDI) as well as trade in services and the commercial aspects of intellectual property (Art. 207 (1) TEU). In both fields, the competences of the EU will increase significantly. This implies a shift of powers from the Member States to the EU. However, the German Federal Constitutional Court's interpretation of these provisions could substantially limit this shift.

National responsibility for integration according to the German Federal Constitutional Court

Before dealing with the WTO and FDI, some explanation should be given as to why the German Federal Constitutional Court dealt with the CCP. Member States entrusted the European Court of Justice (ECJ) with interpreting the Founding Treaties. Why then did the German Federal Constitutional Court attempt to limit a shift of powers, agreed upon by the other branches of government?

Legislation accompanying the Ratification Act to the Treaty of Lisbon

According to the Constitutional Court's Lisbon Treaty decision, Germany's accompanying legislation to the ratification, the 'Act Extending and Strengthening the Rights of the Bundestag and the Bundesrat in European Union Matters',[4] infringes Art. 38 read in conjunction with Art. 23 of the German Constitution which concern the fundamental right to take part in elections to the German Federal Parliament and the structure of the EU. Emphasising the 'responsibility for integration' of the German legislature, the Constitutional Court, as in its Maastricht decision of 1993,[5] takes the view that the German

---

[3] BVerfG, 2 BvE 2/08 of 30 June 2009. For further discussion of this case, see chapter 9 by Andreas Paulus in this volume.
[4] Bundestag document 16/8489.   [5] *Supra* n. 2.

legislator – for the sake of democracy – must retain more control over the European integration process:

> The European Parliament can only be a supplementary source of demo-cratic legitimization. 'Measured against requirements in a constitutional state, the European Union lacks, even after the entry into force of the Treaty of Lisbon, a political decision-making body which has come into being by equal election of all citizens of the Union and which is able to uniformly represent the will of the people'.[6] Therefore, further substantial integration steps foreseen by the Lisbon Treaty ('passerelles'[7]) require legislative approval in Germany before the government can agree to the respective steps in the EU's Council of Ministers.

In substance, and the Constitutional Court reserves ultimate control over that, Member States must 'retain sufficient room for the political formation of the economic, cultural and social circumstances of life …, in particular the private space of their own responsibility and of political and social security, which is protected by the fundamental rights, and to political decisions that particularly depend on previous understanding ['Vorverständnisse'] as regards culture, history and language and which unfold in discourses in the space of a political public that is organized by party politics and Parliament'.[8]

For these reasons, the 'Act Extending and Strengthening the Rights of the Bundestag and the Bundesrat in European Union Matters' had to be amended in order to guarantee more democratic participation of the German legislature in the integration process.

The Ratification Act

Whereas the accompanying legislation thus had to be amended before ratification of the Lisbon Treaty, the 'Act Approving the Treaty of Lisbon' (the Ratification Act) itself required no amendments. Thus, Germany was not constitutionally required to renegotiate the Treaty. The Constitutional Court's decision therefore did not prevent Germany from ratifying the

---

[6] BVerfG, 2 BvE 2/08, *supra* note 3, para. 280.

[7] Passerelles are provisions enabling procedural requirements to be reduced, or other adjust-ments made (i.e. reducing the voting requirement from unanimity to qualified majority or reducing the requirements from special legislative procedure to ordinary legislative procedure), without formal Treaty revision. They invariably require unanimity, giving each national government, and in some cases also national parliaments, a veto. On the 'passerelles', cf. also House of Lords, European Union Committee: *The Treaty of Lisbon: An Impact Assessment, vol I: Report* (London: The Stationery Office Limited, 2008), 35 *et seq.*, see www.publications. parliament.uk/pa/ld200708/ldselect/ldeucom/62/62.pdf.

[8] BVerfG, 2 BvE 2/08, *supra* n. 3, Headnote 3.

Treaty as it stands. However, the Ratification Act is only constitutional on the condition that it is interpreted in conformity with the reasoning of the Constitutional Court's judgment. Suggestions have been made to deposit the Constitutional Court's judgment in Rome, along with the Ratification Act, as a reservation to the Lisbon Treaty or to transform that judgment into a reservation under public international law[9] – an approach which no doubt would greatly complicate the integration process.

The Constitutional Court affirms its approach of the limited primacy of Community law over national law, the core of the national constitution being excluded from primacy.[10] It maintains that the primacy depends on the national ratification of the Treaty and therefore may not affect the constitutional identity of the German State.[11] According to the ECJ, however, Community law must enjoy primacy over national law, including national constitutional law, to guarantee the uniform effect of Community law.[12]

The Constitutional Court's approach affects, of course, the relationship between the German Federal Constitutional Court and the ECJ. As the Constitutional Court observes: 'This construction, which is rather theoretical in everyday application of the law because it often does not result in practical differences as regards its legal effects, has, however, consequences for the relation of the Member States' jurisdiction to the European one. Bodies of jurisdiction with a constitutional function may not, within the limits of the competences conferred on them – this is at any rate the position of the Basic Law – be deprived of the responsibility for the boundaries of their constitutional empowerment for integration and for the safeguarding of the inalienable constitutional identity.'[13]

From its concept of national democratic responsibility for the integration process, the Constitutional Court – as guardian of the Constitution – derives its duty to interpret the Lisbon Treaty. On that basis, the Constitutional Court provides its own reading of the Treaty on many subjects, e.g. criminal law (Art. 31 (1) lit. e TEU, Art. 82f. TFEU),[14] family law (Art. 81 TFEU)[15] and the CCP (Art. 207 TFEU).[16]

---

[9] CSU-'Landesgruppe' in the German Bundestag: Leitlinien für die Stärkung der Rechte des Bundestages und des Bundesrates in EU-Angelegenheiten, para. 9.

[10] BVerfG, 2 BvE 2/08, *supra* n. 3, 118, para. 341 *et seq.* With the entry into force of the Lisbon Treaty on 1 December 2009, the term 'Community' has been replaced by the term 'Union'. Here, both terms are being used and are interchangeable since the focus is on the Lisbon judgement of the German Federal Constitutional Court and on past ECJ jurisdiction.

[11] *Ibid.*, 118, para. 343.

[12] ECJ, Case 11/70 *Internationale Handelsgesellschaft* [1970] ECR, 1125, para. 3.

[13] BVerfG, 2 BvE 2/08, *supra* n. 3, 115, para. 336.   [14] *Ibid.*, 28ff, para. 65 *et seq.*

[15] *Ibid.*, 129, para. 369.   [16] *Ibid.*, 129 ff, para. 370 *et seq.*

With regard to the CCP, the Constitutional Court specifically deals with WTO participation of the EU and its Member States (III) and national or EU competence in the area of FDI (IV), which I shall investigate below.

Participation in the World Trade Organization

The Constitutional Court's approach to the participation of the Member States and the EU in the World Trade Organization

The German Federal Constitutional Court is concerned that 'the membership of the Member States of the European Union in the World Trade Organization would no longer exist on a substantial level but only on the institutional and formal level'[17] and about 'the idea, that the Member State's own legal personality status in external relations gradually takes second place to a European Union which acts more and more clearly in analogy to a State . . . To the extent that the development of the European Union in analogy to a State would be continued on the Basis of the Lisbon Treaty, which is open to development in this context, this would be in contradiction to constitutional foundations.'[18] This passage almost creates the impression that Germany would lose its statehood, should it no longer be a member of the WTO.

The Constitutional Court highlights the importance of Member States' legal and diplomatic presence within the WTO, '[e]ven if the Member States will . . . normally be represented by the Commission'.[19] This is the basis for the democratic discourse within the Member States under the German Federal Constitutional Court's model of democratic legitimacy of supranational power: 'When the Federal Government informs the German Bundestag and the Bundesrat of the topics of the rounds of world trade talks and the negotiation directives adopted by the Council (Art. 218 (2) TFEU), thereby permitting them to review adherence to the integration programme and the monitoring of the Federal Government's activities, this is not only the normal exercise of its general task of information; it is constitutionally obliged to do so with a view to the joint responsibility for integration and the differentiation of tasks among the constitutional bodies under the separation of powers.'[20]

But the Constitutional Court understands the Lisbon Treaty as at any rate not requiring the Member States to waive their member status. In

---

[17] *Ibid.*, 131, para. 375.   [18] *Ibid.*, 132, para. 376.   [19] *Ibid.*, 131, para. 375.   [20] *Ibid.*

this regard the Court in particular referred to negotiations on multi-lateral trade relations within the meaning of Art. III.2 of the WTO Agreement. Their possible future content is not determined by the law of the EU, and it could therefore fall within the competence of the Member States, depending on the course of future trade rounds.[21] The Constitutional Court considers that 'the development to date of a membership that is cooperatively mixed and is exercised in parallel might . . . be a model for other international organizations and other associations of States'.[22]

The Common Commercial Policy

At first glance the understanding of the CCP by the Constitutional Court seems to be at odds with the jurisprudence of the ECJ. However, this impression could be misleading as the ECJ itself is moving towards a cautious approach. Nevertheless, the Lisbon Treaty provides for a substantial extension of Union competences in this regard and it remains to be seen whether Member States will retain a substantial role in the future.

Exclusive nature of the Common Commercial Policy

The ECJ has consistently held that the CCP is of an exclusive nature. Member States must not 'lay claim by invoking a concurrent power, so as to ensure that their own interests were separately satisfied in external relations, at the risk of compromising the effective defence of the common interests of the Community'.[23] A crucial characteristic of such exclusive competence is the exclusion of any parallel or concurrent action on the part of the Member States. This aims to exclude unilateral action on the part of the Member States that would lead to distortions of competition.

Scope of the exclusive Common Commercial Policy: services and intellectual property?

Initially, the Commission boldly considered that the Community would enjoy exclusive competence for all matters under the WTO Agreement, including trade in services and trade-related aspects of intellectual property rights (TRIPS). But in its Opinion 1/94,[24] the ECJ rejected the

---

[21] *Ibid.*   [22] *Ibid.*, 132, para. 376.   [23] ECJ, Opinion 1/75 *OECD* [1975] ECR, 1355.
[24] ECJ, Opinion 1/94 *GATS and TRIPS* [1994] ECR, 5267, *ILM*, 34 (1995), 689.

Commission's arguments that trade in services should also be covered by 'commercial policy' or by implied powers or by powers existing in parallel internally and externally. Interpreting the term 'common commercial policy', the ECJ examined which type of trade in services was more like trade in goods and which was not. Under that approach, cross-frontier supplies of services, rendered by a supplier in one country to a consumer in another country, are like trade in goods. But this does not apply to services involving the cross-frontier movement of persons. Only the first, not the second type of services is covered by 'common commercial policy'. In principle, the CCP, as interpreted by the ECJ, comprises only trade in goods and cross-frontier services, but neither other types of services nor trade-related aspects of intellectual property rights.

Under the Treaty of Nice, the Commission again tried to bring trade in services and the trade-related aspects of intellectual property rights within the scope of the CCP and thus within the Community's exclusive competence. But that Treaty did not change the legal situation in this regard. As I set forth in my recent Opinion regarding the accession of Vietnam to the WTO[25]: Exclusive competence for the Community in the fields of trade in services and the commercial aspects of intellectual property would be better suited for ensuring the effective representation of European interests at international level. However, no such competence was acquired by the Community under the rules created by Art. 133 (5) EC. Rather Article 207 (1) of the Lisbon Treaty completes this step by means of placing the *new* fields of commercial policy on the same footing as the conventional fields, therefore expressly assigning the CCP to the exclusive competence of the Union (Art. 3 (1) lit. e TFEU). Until it entered into force, the Community's competence under Art. 133 (5) EC could, at the most, have been converted into exclusive competence in accordance with the so-called *ERTA*[26] *principles*. However, the Community has not yet acquired by that means a comprehensive exclusive competence for trade in services and the commercial aspects of intellectual property.[27]

In the following, I examine the perspectives, under the Lisbon Treaty, with regard to the German Federal Constitutional Court's three concerns:

[25] ECJ, Opinion of Advocate General Kokott in Case C-13/07 *Commission* v. *Council* (WTO – Accession of Vietnam), *European Yearbook of International Economic Law*, 2 (2011); the Commission withdrew its claim on 15 April 2011 due to the entry into force of the Lisbon Treaty.

[26] ECJ, Case 22–70 *Commission* v. *Council* ('European Agreement on Road Transport – ERTA') [1971] ECR, 263.

[27] WTO – Accession of Vietnam, *supra* n. 25, paras. 63–64.

whether the Member States' legal personality might take second place with the EU acting like a State, whether participation in international agreements might be cooperatively mixed, and whether the competence to participate in the WTO might be exercised in parallel.

Member States' legal personality taking second place with the EU acting like a State?

According to the ECJ's cautious interpretation, the exclusive CCP basically comprises trade in goods and cross-frontier services not requiring the movement of persons. Under European Law prior to the Lisbon Treaty, Member States were able to play a considerable role in the WTO, with trade in services and FDI becoming ever more important.

But under the Lisbon Treaty, these important subjects shift to the EU level and Europe's representation within the WTO thus will be more efficient. The Lisbon Treaty extends the CCP's scope explicitly to trade in 'services, and the commercial aspects of intellectual property, foreign direct investment, the achievement of uniformity in measures of liberalization, export policy and measures to protect trade',[28] thus to most areas covered by WTO law. Therefore, some authors have even raised the question whether membership of the EU Member States alongside the EU would still make sense under the Lisbon Treaty or whether there is a Community law duty – flowing from Art. 307 EC analogously read in conjunction with Art. 10 EU (Art. 351 TFEU and Art. 4 (3) TEU) – of the Member States to withdraw from the WTO.[29]

I would not go so far as to agree with this position. Formal membership of EU Member States in the WTO does not appear to be at risk. However, only the future will show whether negotiations on multilateral trade relations will cover sufficiently important other new subjects which do not fall under exclusive EU competence, so that Member States can still in substance fulfil their role within the WTO as assigned by the German Federal Constitutional Court.

---

[28] Art. 207 (1) TFEU.
[29] Cf. e.g. M. Burgenberg, 'Außenbeziehungen und Außenhandelspolitik', *EuR*, Beiheft 1 (2009), 195–216, 205–6; C. Tietje, 'Das Ende der parallelen Mitgliedschaft von EU und Mitgliedstaaten in der WTO' in C. Herrmann, G. Krenzler and R. Streinz (eds.), *Die Außenwirtschaftspolitik der Europäischen Union nach dem Verfassungsvertrag* (Baden-Baden: Nomos, 2006), 161–73; C. Herrmann, 'Die Rolle der erweiterten Union in der WTO. Das Integrationsmodell der Union als geeignetes Leitbild für die Mitwirkung?' in T. Bruha and C. Nowak (eds.), *Die Europäische Union. Innere Verfasstheit und globale Handlungsfähigkeit* (Baden-Baden: Nomos, 2006), 229–36, 232.

Participation in cooperatively mixed international agreements

Outside the scope of application of the exclusive CCP, both the Member States and the EU are, in principle, competent to take external action. This applies to the negotiation phase as well as to the conclusion of international agreements – e.g. in the fields of development aid and environmental protection.

The practice of concluding mixed agreements with the Community as well as its Member States on the one side and third countries on the other side has been subject to critique. This practice does not serve legal certainty, because the question of national or Community competence may be avoided.[30] Also, the procedure to conclude mixed agreements is burdensome, because all EU Member States besides the Commission need to be integrated into the negotiation process, and ratification by all EU Member States is required. Therefore, the Commission's policy is to interpret the CCP broadly and thus to reduce the need to have recourse to 'mixed agreements'.

The ECJ also started from the basis that the CCP may not be interpreted restrictively on the ground that to do so would risk causing disturbances in intra-Community trade by reason of the disparities which would then exist in certain sectors of economic relations with non-member countries.[31] It recognised the legitimate concern of the Commission that the Community's unity of action *vis-à-vis* the rest of the world would be undermined and its negotiating power greatly weakened through separate and individual actions of the Member States. The solution, however, is not judicial extension of the scope of application of the exclusive CCP, but cooperation. The ECJ

> stressed, first, that any problems which may arise in implementation of the WTO Agreement and its annexes as regards the coordination necessary to ensure unity of action where the Community and Member States participate jointly cannot modify the answer to the question of competence, that being a prior issue. As the Council has pointed out, resolution of the issue of the allocation of competence cannot depend on problems which may arise in administration of the agreements. Next, where it is apparent that the subject-matter of an agreement or convention falls in part within the competence of the Community and in part within that of

---

[30] Cf. C. Vedder and S. Lorenzmeier, 'Article 133' in E. Grabitz and M. Hilf (eds.), *EUV/ EGV*, 5 vols. (Munich: Beck, 2008), vol. II, para. 26.

[31] Cf. ECJ, Opinion 1/78 *International Agreement on Natural Rubber* [1979] ECR 2871, para. 45; K. Lenaerts and P. van Nuffel, *Constitutional Law of the European Union*, 2nd edn. (London: Sweet & Maxwell, 2005), 828–43, 829.

the Member State, it is essential to ensure close cooperation between the Member States and the Community institutions, both in the process of negotiation and conclusion and in the fulfilment of commitments entered into.[32]

The ECJ thus recognises the imperative of cooperating, particularly within the WTO. But the scope of application of the duty to cooperate shrinks in reverse proportion to the increase of the exclusive CCP. Against this background, the German Federal Constitutional Court's judgment assumes and suggests a restrictive interpretation of the exclusive CCP.

Membership exercised in parallel?

At first glance the German Federal Constitutional Court seems to point towards parallel competences as a way to ensure a sufficient role of the Member States in the CCP. The issue of parallel external competences regarding commercial policy has recently been discussed in two procedures.[33] However, as we shall see, already under current law parallel competences are excluded as far as the CCP is concerned; parallel competences also seem to be excluded in the areas of trade in services and the commercial aspects of intellectual property. The Lisbon Treaty would not step back behind this *acquis*. Moreover, it is doubtful, whether – as the Constitutional Court held – parallel competences may arise as far as commercial policy is combined with political issues.

Parallel competences under Community law

Regarding trade in services and the commercial aspects of intellectual property, it would be 'permissible for the Member States to be involved alongside the Community on the basis of Article 133 (5) EC only if there were *parallel competences* of the Community and the Member States in relation to trade in services and the commercial aspects of intellectual property'.[34] The Treaty sometimes confers parallel competences to the EC and the Member States, e.g. in Art. 181 EC on development policy whose wording is similar to Art. 133 (5) EC. Under the ECJ's case-law, parallel competence under Art. 181 (2) EC means that the

---

[32] Opinion 1/94 *GATS and TRIPS, supra* n. 24, paras. 107–8.

[33] WTO – Accession of Vietnam, *supra* n. 25, and Opinion 1/08, not yet published in the ECR, on modification to the agreements regarding limitations and withdrawals of specific engagements of new Member States of the EU under the General Agreement on Trade in Services (GATS).

[34] WTO – Accession of Vietnam, *supra* n. 25, para. 67, emphasis in the original Opinion.

Member States are entitled to enter into commitments themselves *vis-à-vis* non-Member States concerning development cooperation, either collectively, individually, or jointly with the Community.[35] Parallel competences also exist in the areas of economic, financial and technical cooperation with third States, in a similar manner as they exist in competition law (Arts. 81 EC and 82 EC). Because Community and national competition law consider restrictive practices from different perspectives, it is consistent with the case-law of the ECJ that they are applicable in parallel. Here again, it is consistent with the meaning and purpose of the relevant rules of the EC Treaty to assume that the Community and the Member States have parallel powers.[36]

Parallel competences for trade in services and the commercial aspects of intellectual property?

Teleological interpretation, *effet utile* Despite the similarity of wording, the same reasoning does not necessarily apply to development cooperation (Art. 181 (2) EC) and to commercial policy. 'Thus, in the field of development cooperation, Community policy only complements that of the Member States in that field (Art. 177 (1) EC). Independent action by the Member States in that field, whether collectively, individually or jointly with the Community, can share out the financial and technical burdens of development cooperation in Europe over several shoulders.'[37] In the end, more development aid or more economic, financial and technical cooperation with third States may result.

In the field of external trade, the situation is different. In negotiations where the interests of the Community and its Member States must be represented, especially against other significant trading partners, the negotiating position of both Member States and the Community is weakened the more players are involved at the international level. In the CCP, agreements where both the Community as well as the Member States are parties, are 'consequently out of place'. A voluntary involvement of the Member States alongside the Commission, representing the Community, is thus not permissible in matters concerning Art. 133 (5) EC. This provision calls for a concurrent or shared competence, meaning that the Member States may no longer exercise their powers

---

[35] ECJ, Case C-316/91 *Parliament* v. *Council* ('European Development Fund – EDF') [1994] ECR I-625, paras. 26 and 34.
[36] WTO – Accession of Vietnam, *supra* n. 25, para. 71.   [37] *Ibid.*, para. 70.

when the Community exercises its own powers in the area of trade in services and the commercial aspects of intellectual property.[38]

Art. 133 (5) sub-para. 4 EC   Nevertheless, the Council has argued that Art. 133 (5) sub-para. 4 EC provides for parallel competences.[39] It lays down that '[t]his paragraph shall not affect the right of the Member States to maintain and conclude agreements with third countries or international organizations in so far as such agreements comply with Community law and other relevant international agreements'. Member States must thus observe Community law when exercising their reserved competences. Parallel competence might appear to result from 'the right of the Member States to maintain and conclude agreements with third countries or international organisations'.

But, Art. 133 (5) sub-para. 4 EC may also be understood 'simply as an expression of the concurrent nature of the new powers in relation to external trade'.[40] This concurrent nature is expressed in particular in the ERTA case-law. Under ERTA, internal Community legislation in a particular field entails an implied corresponding external competence.[41] Such competences are concurrent in so far as they allow independent Member State legislation as long as they have not been exercised by the Community. And '[b]earing in mind the objective of representation of Community interest at international level which should be as effective as possible, the Member States cannot be allowed, without restriction, to maintain or conclude agreements with non-member countries or international organizations in the fields of trade in services and the commercial aspects of intellectual property, but may do so only in so far as the Community itself does not act'.[42]

In other words, the competence for trade in services and the commercial aspects of intellectual property is concurrent and not parallel. The same approach should apply to further aspects of the CCP as introduced by the Lisbon Treaty.

Parallel competences under the 'new'
Common Commercial Policy?

Already under the Treaty regime prior to Lisbon, the EC often combined various political objectives with its external policy in the same

---

[38] *Ibid.*, paras. 72 and 74 *et seq.*   [39] *Ibid.*, para. 50 *et seq.*   [40] *Ibid.*, para. 77.
[41] Cf. *supra* nn. 26 and 27.   [42] WTO – Accession of Vietnam, *supra* n. 25, para. 77.

agreement.[43] The Lisbon Treaty reinforces that trend: pursuant to the Lisbon Treaty the CCP 'shall be guided by the principles, pursue the objectives and be conducted in accordance with the general provisions laid down in Chapter 1 of Title V of the Treaty of the European Union [general provisions on the area of freedom, security and justice]'.[44] This among other things refers to democracy, the rule of law, human rights, the general principles of law, the Charter of the United Nations, sustainable development, integration of developing countries into the world economy, environmental protection and global governance.[45] Such politicisation of the CCP[46] may introduce all kinds of subjects to negotiations on multi-lateral trade relations which – according to the German Federal Constitu-tional Court – might fall within the competence of the Member States in the future, depending on the course of future trade rounds.[47]

It remains to be seen whether the ECJ will share this approach. Arguments against the Constitutional Court's approach would be that the Lisbon Treaty only takes up an already existing development: CCP has, for decades, also pursued political goals. Already in 1995, the ECJ held that a measure 'cannot be treated as falling outside the scope of the common commercial policy on the ground that it has foreign policy and security objectives'.[48] Moreover, under the Lisbon Treaty the exclu-sive CCP is part of the general external action by the Union which shall be guided by political principles (cf. Arts. 205 and 206 TFEU read together with Art. 21 TEU).

To sum up, parallel competences in the area of the CCP are excluded. Whether 'new political' subjects in trade agreements might lead to a parallel competence of the Community and Member States for such negotiations and agreements remains doubtful.

Investment law

The ECJ has not yet had to answer the question whether FDI is covered by the CCP as it stands. Even though it would not be linguistically impossible to include FDI in the CCP, legal doctrine rejects this

---

[43] Cf., e.g., C. Tietje, 'Die Außenwirtschaftsverfassung der EU nach dem Vertrag von Lissabon', *Beiträge zum Transnationalen Wirtschaftsrecht*, 83 (2009).

[44] Art. 205 TFEU.   [45] Cf. Art. 21 (2) TEU.

[46] Tietje, 'Die Außenwirtschaftsverfassung', *supra* n. 43, 19–20.

[47] BVerfG, 2 BvE 2/08, *supra* n. 3, 131, para. 375.

[48] ECJ, Case C-70/94 *Werner* [1995] ECR I-3189, 3223, para. 10; see also ECJ, Case C-83/94 *Leifer* [1995] ECR I-3231.

proposition.[49] An important argument is that the proposal to create an explicit Community competence for FDI in the Treaty of Nice had been rejected. The Commission had proposed to reformulate Art. 133 (1) EC as follows:

> The common commercial policy shall be based on uniform principles, particularly with regard to changes in tariff rates, the conclusion of tariff and trade agreements relating to trade in goods and services, and the commercial aspects of intellectual property, foreign direct investment, the achievement of uniformity in measures of liberalization, export policy and measures to protect trade such as those to be taken in the event of dumping or subsidies.[50]

As this proposal was rejected it must be assumed that FDI, along with trade in services and intellectual property, are not covered by the classical concept of 'common commercial policy'. Only the Lisbon Treaty finally took up this proposal and included FDI in Art. 207 (1) TFEU. In view of the legislative history it should be understood as a constitutive, not merely declaratory provision.

The German Federal Constitutional Court on foreign direct investment

The German Federal Constitutional Court also comments on the extension of the CCP to FDI. It highlights the differences of opinion on the protection of property on the international level: 'For decades, far-reaching ideologically motivated differences have existed concerning the socio-political importance of the fundamental liberty right to property'.[51] The supranationalisation of FDI is of great impact: 'The vast majority of foreign assets, which for the Federal Republic of Germany amounted to 5,004 billion Euros in 2007, falls under the scope of application of 126 investment protection agreements currently in force. At the end of 2007, a total of 2,608 bilateral investment protection agreements existed worldwide.'[52]

Under Art. 207 (1) TFEU, the exclusive CCP explicitly includes FDI.

---

[49] E.g. M. Hahn 'Article 133', in C. Calliess and M. Ruffert (eds.), *EUV/EGV*, 3rd edn. (Munich: Beck, 2007), para. 48.

[50] COM(2000) 34 final, 'Adapting the institutions to make a success of enlargement. Commission Opinion in accordance with Article 48 of the Treaty on European Union on the calling of a Conference of Representatives of the Governments of the Member States to amend the Treaties', 49.

[51] BVerfG, 2 BvE 2/08, *supra* n. 3, 132, para. 377.   [52] *Ibid.*, 132, para. 378.

The German Federal Constitutional Court considers this an extension of the CCP which should be interpreted narrowly *ratione materiae* as well as *ratione temporis*. *Ratione materiae*, according to the Constitutional Court '[m]uch . . . argues in favour of assuming that the term "foreign direct investment" only encompasses investment which serves to obtain a controlling interest in an enterprise'.[53] Consequently, an exclusive competence of the Union would exist only for investment of this type whereas investment agreements that go beyond must be concluded further on as mixed agreements.

Rationae temporis, the Constitutional Court invokes Art. 351 TFEU (Art. 307 EC) according to which 'rights and obligations arising from agreements concluded before 1 January 1958 . . . between one or more Member States on the one hand, and one or more third countries on the other, shall not be affected by the provisions of this Treaty', from which it concludes that '[t]he continued legal existence of the agreements already concluded is not endangered. International agreements of the Member States that were concluded before 1 January 1958 shall in principle not be affected by the Treaty establishing the European Community (Art. 307 (1) EC; Art. 351 (1) TFEU). In many cases this provision is not directly applicable because bilateral investment protection agreements have, as a general rule, been concluded more recently,[54] but the legal concept that a situation in the Member States which qualifies as a legal fact will in principle not be impaired by a later step of integration.'[55]

'Direct investment' under the EC Treaty

The EC Treaty uses the term 'direct investment' only in Art. 57 EC with regard to the free movement of capital. This is the only fundamental freedom that not only applies to movement between the Member States but also extends to third countries. Art. 57 (1) and (2) EC provide for the continued application of existing restrictions with regard to third countries and for the adoption of new measures. In this context they refer to 'direct investment – including in real estate – establishment, the

---

[53] *Ibid.*, 133, para. 379.
[54] The world's first bilateral investment treaty was signed in 1959 between Germany and Pakistan; cf. A. Zampetti and P. Sauve, 'International Investments', in A. Guzmán and A. Sykes (eds.), *Research Handbook in International Economic Law* (Cheltenham: Edward Elgar, 2007), 211–70, 215.
[55] BVerfG, 2 BvE 2/08, *supra* n. 3, 133, para. 380.

provision of financial services or the admission of securities to capital markets'.

Many questions regarding the definition of FDI under Community law are still unanswered: (a) whether Art. 57 (1) EC covers only investment serving to obtain a controlling interest in an enterprise as set forth by the German Federal Constitutional Court; (b) whether 'direct investment' in Art. 57 EC is the same as 'foreign direct investment' in Art. 207 (1) TFEU, whether 'direct' in the sense of FDI under Art. 207 EC is to be construed broadly or restrictively and whether investment protection is covered as well as investment liberalisation; and finally (c) the applicability of Art. 307 EC *ratione temporis*.

'Direct investment' under Art. 57 EC

Legal doctrine and the ECJ take Council Directive 88/361[56] as an indicator for interpreting the concept of direct investment.[57] In its 2006 judgment in *Test Claimants in the FII Group Litigation*[58] the ECJ held:

> As regards, more particularly, the concept of 'direct investment', it must be stated that this is not defined by the Treaty. Nevertheless, that concept has been defined in Community law in the nomenclature of the capital movements set out in Annex I to Council Directive 88/361/EEC of 24 June 1988 for the implementation of Article 67 of the Treaty [article repealed by the Treaty of Amsterdam], which sets out 13 categories of capital movements. It is settled case-law that, inasmuch as Article 56 EC substantially reproduced the content of Article 1 of Directive 88/361, . . ., that nomenclature retains the same indicative value, for the purposes of defining the term 'movement of capital', as it did before their [now Arts. 56–60 EC] entry into force, subject to the qualification, contained in the introduction to the nomenclature, that the list set out therein is not exhaustive. The same indicative value must be given to that nomenclature in interpreting the concept of direct investment. The first section of that nomenclature, entitled 'Direct investments' includes the establishment and extension of branches or new undertakings belonging solely to the person providing the capital and the acquisition in full of existing undertakings, participation in new or existing undertakings with a view to establishing or maintaining lasting economic links, . . . and reinvestment of profits with a view to maintaining lasting economic links. As that list

---

[56] Council Directive 88/361/EEC of 24 June 1988 for the implementation of Article 67 of the Treaty, OJ L 178, 8.7.1988, 5–18.

[57] Cf. ECJ, Case C-446/04 *Test Claimants in the FII Group Litigation* [2006] ECR I-11753, para. 178 *et seq.* with references to earlier cases; see also the Opinion of Advocate General Geelhoed, para. 117 *et seq.*

[58] *Test Claimants in the FII Group Litigation, supra* n. 57, para. 177 *et seq.*

and the relative explanatory notes show, the concept of direct investments concerns investments of any kind undertaken by natural or legal
persons and which serve to establish or maintain lasting and direct links
between the persons providing the capital and the undertakings to which
that capital is made available in order to carry out an economic activity.[59]

The following passage from the ECJ's judgment is interesting when
compared with the German Federal Constitutional Court's approach
according to which 'much ... argues in favour of assuming that the
term "foreign direct investment" only encompasses investment which
serves to obtain a controlling interest in an enterprise'.[60] According to
the ECJ, '[a]s regards shareholdings in new or existing undertakings, as
the explanatory notes confirm, the objective of establishing or maintaining lasting economic links presupposes that the shares held by the shareholder enable him, either pursuant to the provisions of the national laws
relating to companies limited by shares or otherwise, to participate
effectively in the management of that company or its control'.[61]

It remains to be seen whether to 'participate effectively in the management' (ECJ) of a company or its control is the same as 'serves to obtain a
controlling interest in an enterprise' (German Federal Constitutional
Court).

The ECJ did not interpret FDI restrictively in other respects. Thus,
the ECJ held that 'the restrictions on capital movements involving direct
investment or establishment within the meaning of Article 57 (1) EC
extend not only to national measures which, in their application to
capital movements to or from non-member countries, restrict investment or establishment, but also to those measures which restrict payments of dividends deriving from them'.[62]

The underlying Annex I to Directive 88/361 emphasises the element of
time – establishment or maintenance of *lasting* economic links – rather
than that of control. Although both criteria often coincide, they do not
always overlap.

Nevertheless, 'much argues in favour', as the Constitutional Court put
it, that foreign *direct* investment, as opposed to foreign investment,
involves direct management of the investment by its foreign controller,[63]
and hence that short-term portfolio investments are not covered.

---

[59] *Ibid.*, para. 77 *et seq.*   [60] Cf. *supra* n. 53.
[61] *Test Claimants in the FII Group Litigation, supra* n. 57, para. 182.   [62] *Ibid.*, para. 183.
[63] S. Daya Amarasinha and J. Kokott, 'Multilateral Investment Rules Revisited', in
     P. Muchlinski, F. Ortino and C. Schreuer (eds.), *The Oxford Handbook on
     International Investment Law* (Oxford University Press, 2008), 119–54, 120.

'Foreign direct investment' under Art. 207 TFEU

The question remains whether 'direct investment' under Art. 57 EC is identical with 'foreign direct investment' under Art. 207 TFEU.[64] The wording is similar, but the two provisions fulfil different functions: Art. 57 EC is a transitory provision, exceptionally allowing restrictions to the free movement of capital. As a general rule, exceptions are to be construed narrowly.[65] Art. 207 TFEU defines the foreign commercial policy and thus the reach of the exclusive EU competence. The interpretation rule for exceptions therefore does not apply.

Wording   Generally, identical terms in one document should be interpreted as having the same meaning. Therefore, the elements of long-time establishment or maintenance of economic links as well as effective participation in the management or control are equally relevant under Art. 207 TFEU. Those two elements reflect the public international law approach to direct investment.[66] But international law provides no clear-cut criteria for a definition of investment. Under the draft Multilateral Agreement on Investment of 1998, as well as under NAFTA, the definition of investment is very wide, even including portfolio investment; most bilateral investment treaties equally apply broad definitions of investment.[67] However, when the reference specifically is to *direct* investment, portfolio investments are excluded. Foreign investment can indeed be divided into FDI and indirect – or portfolio – investment where the element of direct management of the investment by its foreign controller is absent.[68] In his book on *Transnational Legal Problems*,[69] Detlev Vagts refers to '[t]he decision to seek profits by direct participation in the economic life of another country – through establishment of a foreign branch or wholly-owned subsidiary, or through a company owned jointly with nationals of the foreign country'.

---

[64] Cf. also Tietje, 'Die Außenwirtschaftsverfassung', *supra* n. 43, 16.

[65] On Art. 57 EC, see also ECJ, Opinion of Advocate General Geelhoed in *Test Claimants in the FII Group Litigation*, *supra* n. 57, para. 117.

[66] Cf. J. Ceyssens, 'Towards a Common Foreign Investment Policy? – Foreign Investment in the European Constitution', *Legal Issues of Economic Integration*, 32 (2005), 259–91, 274–5) with references.

[67] Amarasinha and Kokott, 'Multilateral Investment Rules', *supra* n. 63, 138 with references.

[68] *Ibid.*, 120.

[69] D. F. Vagts, H. J. Steiner and H. H. Koh, *Transnational Legal Problems*, 4th edn. (Westbury, NY: Foundation Press, 1994).

Therefore, it appears reasonable to assume that portfolio or indirect investments are not covered by the newly formulated commercial policy under Art. 207 TFEU. But room remains for clarifying the precise criteria for the 'direct' in 'foreign direct investment' – e.g. participation in the management or control, or serving 'to obtain a controlling interest in an enterprise'.

Moreover, even though the Treaty of Lisbon clearly lists FDI as an EU competence, it is not clear whether this includes both investment protection and investment liberalisation. Some maintain that only investment liberalisation is covered.[70] However, I believe that the distinction between these two fields would be difficult to maintain in practice.

'*Effet Utile*' and implied powers as applied to the Common Commercial Policy Against this background it is useful to examine whether one should start from a more generous understanding of the common commercial policy in the sense of '*effet utile*' or implied powers, or whether one should adopt a restrictive understanding of that exclusive Community competence when interpreting FDI.

'*Effet utile*' and implied powers are recognised principles for the construction of Community law. As the German Federal Constitutional Court phrased it: 'Whoever relies on integration must expect the independent opinion formation of the institutions of the Union. What must therefore be tolerated is a tendency towards maintaining the *acquis communautaire* and to effectively interpreting competences along the lines of the US doctrine of implied powers or the principle of *effet utile* under the law of international agreements. This is part of the mandate of integration which is wanted by the Basic Law.'[71]

Accordingly, under the ERTA case-law the ECJ held that the system of internal Community measures cannot be separated from that of external relations. Rather, internal competences may imply external competences. Thus, the Community's authority to enter into international agreements arises not only from an express conferment by the Treaty – as is the case with Art. 113 of the EEC Treaty (after modification now Art. 133 EC) and 114 of the EEC Treaty (in the meantime repealed) for tariff and trade agreements and with Art. 238 of the EEC Treaty (after modification now Art. 310 EC) for association agreements – but may equally flow from other

---

[70] Cf. S. Woolcock, 'The Potential Impact of the Lisbon Treaty on European Union External Trade Policy', *European Policy Analysis*, 8 (2008), 1–6.

[71] BVerfG, 2 BvE 2/08, *supra* n. 3, 77, para. 237.

provisions of the Treaty and from measures adopted, within the framework of those provisions, by the Community institutions.[72]

However, the ECJ did not always interpret the scope of the CCP extensively using the *effet utile* or implied powers doctrines. Rather, in its Opinion 1/94,[73] it rejected the Commission's arguments that trade in services should also be covered by 'commercial policy' or by implied powers or as powers existing in parallel internally and externally.[74]

Therefore it cannot be generally assumed that '*effet utile*' and implied powers can be relied on to extensively interpret external Community competences.

The principles of subsidiarity and proportionality as applied to the Common Commercial Policy

Subsidiarity   The German Federal Constitutional Court reserved its right to review whether legal instruments of the European institutions adhere 'to the principle of subsidiarity under Community and Union law [and] keep within the boundaries of the sovereign powers accorded to them by way of conferred power'.[75] The principle of subsidiarity,[76] however, applies only to areas which do not fall within the exclusive competence of the Union. It is in the first place a principle governing the exercise of concurrent Community competences, but it may also influence the interpretation of the reach of an exclusive competence. '[E]xclusive Community competence is the exception and, as a rule, the Community shares its areas of competence with the Member States because only in that way is it possible to ensure that the principle of subsidiarity, a fundamental stipulation of the Treaties which applies only to non-exclusive competence (second paragraph of Art. 5 EC), has appropriate scope for application ... Against that background it by no means necessarily follows that the exclusive nature of the competence under Article 133 (1) EC also extends to the new competence under Article 133 (5) EC created by the Treaty of Nice.'[77] A similar argument could be made for interpreting 'foreign direct investment' under Art. 207 (1) TFEU restrictively.

Proportionality   Similarly, the principle of proportionality may influence the interpretation of Union competences in a way to protect

---

[72] *ERTA* case, *supra* n. 26, paras. 15–16.   [73] Opinion 1/94 *GATS and TRIPS, supra* n. 24.
[74] Cf. *supra* n. 24.   [75] BVerfG, 2 BvE 2/08, *supra* n. 3, Headnote 4.
[76] Art. 5 (2) EC; also Art. 5 (3) TEU as amended by the Lisbon Treaty.
[77] WTO – Accession of Vietnam, *supra* n. 25, paras. 55–56.

national powers and national sovereignty.[78] 'Under the principle of proportionality, the content and form of Community action shall not exceed what is necessary to achieve the objectives of the Treaties.'[79]

Interim conclusion   The preceding overview shows the ECJ's careful approach to the exclusive Community competences under the CCP. The ECJ has not always interpreted the CCP extensively. Rather, it is sensitive to the concerns of EU Members States regarding their external powers, even in a context where this remarkably complicates international negotiations. The principles of subsidiarity and proportionality further support such an approach.

The Lisbon Treaty seems to leave room for mixed investment agreements, at least with regard to portfolio investments.

Applicability of Art. 307 EC *ratione temporis*: Investment Agreements Concluded Before 1 January 1958 or Before Accession

According to Art. 307 EC '[t]he rights and obligations arising from agreements concluded before 1 January 1958 or, for acceding States, before their accession, between one or more Member States on the one hand, and one or more third countries on the other, shall not be affected by the provisions of this Treaty'.

In the absence of any empirical case in this particular policy-field of bilateral investment treaties, the German Federal Constitutional Court assumes that the concept of Art. 307 EC also covers subsequent agreements when the competence of the Community results from a subsequent step of integration.[80] This is in accordance with legal practice[81] and doctrine. Only some authors require in addition that the development of a Community competence in the subject matter was not

---

[78] Lenaerts and van Nuffel, *Constitutional Law, supra* n. 31, 112 *et seq.*
[79] Art. 5(3) EC; also Art. 5(4) TEU as amended by the Lisbon Treaty.
[80] BVerfG, 2 BvE, 2/08, *supra* n. 3.
[81] COM(2002) 649 final, 'Communication from the Commission on the consequences of the Court judgements of 5 November 2002 for European air transport policy', 7–9, paras. 30, 33, 38, 39; Regulation (EC) No. 847/2004 of the European Parliament and of the Council of 29 April 2004 'on the negotiation and implementation of air service agreements between Member States and third countries', OJ L 195 of 2 July 2004, 3–6, para. 6; cf. also F. Hoffmeister, 'Bilateral Air Transport Agreements between Several EU Member States and the United States ("Open Skies")', *AJIL*, 98 (2004), 567–72, 571.

predictable.[82] In view of the dynamics of integration, the latter condition would not be easy to fulfil.

Obligation to eliminate incompatibility

In any event, the Member States 'shall take all appropriate steps to eliminate the incompatibilities established' (Art. 307 EC). The ECJ has recently emphasised this duty with regard to investment treaties the respective Member States concluded with third States prior to their accession.[83] Such incompatibilities typically arise from substantial provisions – e.g. the basic freedoms – but not from violation of concurrent external competences of the Community as such. As long as the Community does not exercise concurrent competences, Member States in principle remain free to act. However, specific competences may result in more far-reaching obligations. Because the powers to adopt financial sanctions under Art. 57 (2) EC, 59 EC and 60 (1) EC are granted to allow immediate Community action, Member States must abolish potential loopholes to future sanctions even before they are adopted by the Community.[84] Therefore, in these cases the mere existence of a competence was sufficient to require an alignment of Member State agreements. In contrast, there is no obvious reason why a concurrent Community competence to enter into agreements on FDI as such should be affected by existing Member State agreements.

Concluding remarks

Based on its role as guardian of the Constitution and of German sovereignty, the German Federal Constitutional Court has given its own interpretation of the articles of the Lisbon Treaty concerning membership in the WTO and FDI. Until now, the development of this field of the law, the CCP, as well as of other fields of Community law, appear as the result of the interaction between the Treaty-making powers of the governments and Treaty interpretation by the ECJ. Now, the Constitutional Court strives to intervene as a third player.

---

[82] See, e.g., J. Kokott, 'Article 307', in R. Streinz (ed.), *EUV/EGV* (Munich: Beck, 2003), para. 7; K. Schmalenbach, 'Article 307', in Calliess and Ruffert (eds.), *EUV/EGV*, *supra* n. 49, para. 5; P. Manzini, 'The Priority of Pre-Existing Treaties of EC Member States within the Framework of International Law', *EJIL*, 12 (2001), 781–92, 786.

[83] Cases C-205/06 *Commission* v. *Austria* [2009] ECR I-1301 and C-249/06 *Commission* v. *Sweden* [2009] ECR I-1335.

[84] *Ibid.*, paras. 28 and 29.

It is not so much the content of the German Federal Constitutional Court's judgment on the Lisbon Treaty that is remarkable. It is rather the fact that – as well as the extent to which – a national constitutional court deals with the interpretation and application of the Lisbon Treaty, a function which the Member States conferred upon the ECJ in view of ensuring a uniform interpretation throughout the EU.

The German Federal Constitutional Court makes clear that Germany – and within Germany, the Constitutional Court – controls the integration process. In part, the decision could be read as only mandating the German legislature to control the process. The procedural requirements laid down by the Court on the one side require Parliament to decide on the degree of integration, while on the other side the Court lays down substantial limits to integration. Thereby, it takes away from Parliament at least some of the powers pertaining to it as an equally supreme branch of government. The Constitutional Court protects Parliament against itself. It thus makes sure that Parliament does not transfer too much power to the EU, even if integration is politically wanted and even if the directly elected representatives of the people come to the conclusion that some powers can be exercised more efficiently on the supranational level.[85] Still, a positive effect of the Constitutional Court's decision can lie in better information of Parliament by the government and a more lively parliamentary debate in European matters.

The practical consequences of the Lisbon judgment will depend on the standard of scrutiny which the Constitutional Court itself is going to apply. Fortunately for European integration, the judgment hints at a low standard: 'It is a consequence of the continuing sovereignty of the Member States that at any rate if the mandatory order to apply the law is *evidently* lacking, the inapplicability of such a legal instrument to Germany is established by the Federal Constitutional Court'.[86]

What I find most peculiar – beyond the specific case of the Lisbon judgment – is the self-image of the German Federal Constitutional Court. The decision reads like a piece of mandatory advice from a council of wise statesmen, rather than a judgment of a court which typically decides cases and controversies between parties. One might also wonder why the newly introduced unilateral right to leave the Union (Art. 50

---

[85] For judicial self-restraint in view of the separation of powers, cf. Czech Constitutional Court, Lisbon Treaty II, Judgement of 9 November 2009, para. 111 *et seq.*

[86] BVerfG, 2 BvE 2/08, *supra* n. 3, 116, para. 339 (emphasis added).

TEU as amended by the Lisbon Treaty) is not sufficient proof of the Member States' continuing sovereignty.

It remains to be hoped that the judgment supports, or at least does not undermine, the effective representation of German interests at the European level. Particularly with regard to the WTO and FDI, Europe hopefully will become a more efficient partner in multilateral trade negotiations now that the Lisbon Treaty has entered into force.

9

From dualism to pluralism: the relationship between international law, European law and domestic law

ANDREAS L. PAULUS[*]

Introduction

As a young German Visiting Researcher at Havard Law School in 1994–5, Detlev Vagts' class on Transnational Legal Problems opened up a new perspective on international law for me: pragmatic and pluralist rather than doctrinal and separated into public law, private law and criminal law.[1] In addition, the Jubilee impressed me with his keen interest in German law and culture. Thus, while being forced to rethink the traditional German approach to all things legal, Detlev made the young German student feel at home both intellectually and personally. The following contribution to his *Festschrift* attempts to follow Detlev's example.

For one of the fathers of the transnational law approach, it will hardly come as a surprise that both the German and the US legal orders are faced with an increasing fragmentation of the legal landscape, in which domestic law cannot but pay attention to European, international and, at times, foreign law. However, both are also concerned with democratic legitimacy and the preservation of domestic prerogatives of parliaments and courts. In Europe, the matter becomes even more complicated. While European law is not 'domestic' in character, but has been established

[*] Parts of this chapter were presented at a panel of the American Society of International Law (ASIL) 2009 meeting on the domestic enforcement of international tribunal judgments. This chapter was completed in January 2010. I thank Morten Jonas, Neels Lamschus and Matthias Lippold for their valuable research assistance; as well as Helmut Aust and Frank Schorkopf for their thoughtful comments and important critique.
[1] H. J. Steiner and D. F. Vagts (eds.), *Transnational Legal Problems*, 4th edn. (Westbury, NY: Foundation Press, 1994).

by a treaty between States,[2] its law is 'supranational', e.g. directly applicable to individuals in its Member States. Thus, the European legal order faces an additional difficulty when faced with international decisions: it must first decide 'on which side it is', in other words, whether it regards its own legal order, in a monist perspective, as part of international law, or as a separate legal order that faces international law the same way as a domestic legal order.[3]

A European may be forgiven for considering the US debates on the very citation of foreign law sources[4] as slightly retrograde and illusionary, pretending that the US system could ignore international and foreign law sources altogether. But recent decisions of the European Court of Justice (ECJ) and the German Federal Constitutional Court (Bundesverfassungsgericht) demonstrate that US and European courts use similar concepts in response to the implementation of international decisions.

After the ECJ, in its *Kadi* judgment,[5] had required the European Commission to give reasons for the listing of terrorists, Jack Goldsmith and Eric Posner concluded that 'European nations today are like the American States agreeing to form a federal union in the 18th century . . . Their devotion to their Union is real. Their devotion to international law – even the U.N. Charter – is less pronounced . . . Here, as in other settings, Americans and Europeans have more in common than meets

---

[2] For consolidated versions of the TEU and the TFEU in the version of the Lisbon Treaty that entered into force on 1 December 2009, see *Official Journal* (OJ) C 115 (9 May 2008). For consolidated versions of the preceding Nice Treaty and the accession treaties of Bulgaria and Romania, see Treaty on European Union and Treaty Establishing the European Community (consolidated texts), OJ C 321E, 29 December 2006.

[3] *Kadi* v. *Council of the EU*, Judgment (Grand Chamber), Cases C-402/05P, C-415/05P [2008]; *CMLR*, 45 (2009), 213–39 can be considered as having settled this question in favour of a dualist (or, rather, pluralist) perspective, see p. 135. On pluralism in general, see N. Walker, 'The Idea of Constitutional Pluralism', *Modern Law Review*, 65 (2002), 317–59; A. Paulus, 'The Emergence of the International Community and the Divide Between International and Domestic Law', in A. Nollkaemper and J. E. Nijman (eds.), *New Perspectives on the Divide between International Law and National Law* (Oxford University Press, 2007), 228–34 with further references.

[4] See, e.g., A. Scalia and S. Breyer, 'Constitutional Relevance of Foreign Court Decisions', American University, 13 January 2005, www.wcl.american.edu/secle/founders/2005/050113.cfm; A. Scalia, 'Keynote Address. Foreign Legal Authority in the Federal Courts', *ASIL Proceedings*, 98 (2004) 505. For the discussion within the Supreme Court, see also *Roper* v. *Simmons*, 543 US 551 (2005) 551, 575; *Atkins* v. *Virginia*, 536 US 304, 316, n. 21; *ibid.*, 321, 325 (Rehnquist, CJ, dissenting) and 536 US, 337 (Scalia J., dissenting) with further references.

[5] *Kadi*, *supra* n. 3.

the eye.'[6] The opinion article by two of the leading US sceptics on international law[7] raises many questions – whether international law is a 'belief', whether the US/European framework is correct, whether the comparison between the European Union (EU) and the eighteenth-century founding of the United States makes sense,[8] and whether European law and international law are to be treated differently in the domestic realm.

The judgment of the German Federal Constitutional Court on the compatibility of the Lisbon Treaty on European Union[9] with the German Constitution[10] casts doubt on Goldsmith's and Posner's contention that domestic European courts do indeed differ that much in their attitudes towards international and European law. As far as Europe is concerned, we will deal with the implementation of Security Council resolutions by the European legal order, as well as with the impact of European law on domestic law in general. For the first problem, I discuss the *Kadi* judgment of the ECJ; for the latter, I review the Lisbon decision of the German Federal Constitutional Court.[11] This latest judgment will take up the largest part of this chapter.

It transpires that European courts share the concerns of their American brethren regarding the democratic legitimacy of international decisions, and use similar concepts to draw the line between the implementation of international decisions and their control on democratic and individual rights grounds.

Thus, while the 'friendliness' or openness of German courts towards international and European law, as the German Federal Constitutional Court calls it,[12] suggests a more forthcoming European attitude towards international regulation, it appears that Goldsmith and Posner are correct in

---

[6] J. L. Goldsmith and E. Posner, 'Does Europe Believe in International Law?', *The Wall Street Journal*, 25 November 2008, 15.

[7] See J. L. Goldsmith and E. A. Posner, *The Limits of International Law* (Oxford University Press, 2005).

[8] For a fruitful comparison, see R. Schütze, 'On "Federal" Ground: The European Union as an (Inter)national Phenomenon', *CMLR*, 46 (2009), 1069–1105.

[9] Treaty of Lisbon amending the Treaty on European Union and the Treaty establishing the European Community, signed at Lisbon, 13 December 2007, *OJ* C 306, 17 December 2007.

[10] BVerfG, 2 BvE 2/08, 30 June 2009, www.bverfg.de/entscheidungen/es20090630_2bv-e000208en.html (hereafter, Lisbon judgment). See also chapter 8 in this volume.

[11] See *supra* n. 10.

[12] BVerfGE 31, 58, 75–6; *Görgülü*, BVerfGE 111, 307, p. 317; 112, 1, 26. On the concept in general, see A. Paulus, 'Germany', in D. Sloss (ed.), *The Role of Domestic Courts in Treaty Enforcement. A Comparative Study* (Cambridge University Press, 2009), 209–42.

maintaining that the United States and Europe, including Germany, are far more sceptical towards international law and international tribunals than it appears on first sight. However, while Europe and the United States are indeed more similar than it appears, international law plays a larger role in both legal systems than the sceptics are prepared to concede.

The European Court of Justice and the Security Council: legal control in all but name

In *Kadi*, the ECJ struck down the EU regulation regarding the implementation of UN sanctions against alleged terrorists.[13] The Court held that the inclusion of one individual and of a foundation on a terror list violated the rights to defence, in particular the right to be heard, the principle of effective judicial protection, and the right to property under European law.[14]

What has been less mentioned, however, is that the Court did not hold the whole sanctions regime to be impermissible. Rather, the Court upheld the annulled regulations for another three months to give the EU organs time to bring EU practice in compliance with both European and international law.[15] In addition, the ECJ held that 'the restrictive measures imposed by the contested regulation constitute restrictions of the right to property which might in principle be justified'.[16]

As a result, the European Commission informed the claimants on the 'narrative summaries of reasons' given by the Sanctions Committee and renewed the addition of the two claimants to the list, arguing that their listing continued to be 'justified for reasons of [their] association with Al-Qaeda'.[17] Thus, the judgment did not put 'Terrorism Financing Blacklists at Risk', as *The Washington Post* had feared;[18] rather, the Sanctions Committee was

---

[13] Council Regulation (EC) No. 881/2002 (27 May 2002) imposing certain specific restrictive measures directed against certain persons and entities associated with Usama bin Laden, the Al Qaeda network and the Taliban.

[14] *Kadi, supra* n. 3.   [15] *Ibid*., 375–6   [16] *Ibid*., 366, 374.

[17] Commission Regulation (EC) No. 1190/2008, 28 November 2008, OJ L 322/25 (2 December 2008). The information was provided by the Security Council Committee established pursuant to resolution 1267 concerning Al Qaeda and the Taliban and associated individuals and entities ('1267 Committee'), see Jan K. F. Grauls, Security Council, 63rd year, 6015th meeting, November 12, 2008, S/PV.6015, 6. Kadi's challenge of the latter regulation is pending before the European Court of First Instance (CFI), *Kadi v. Commission*, Case No. T-85/09, 2009 OJ (C90/37); see also P. Fromuth, 'The European Court of Justice *Kadi* Decision and the Future of UN Counterterrorism Sanctions', *ASIL Insight* 30 (2009), Issue 20.

[18] C. Whitlock, 'Terrorism Financing Blacklists At Risk', *The Washington Post*, November 2, 2008, A1.

forced to give at least some reasons for its decisions, and the EU simply transmitted them to the individuals concerned.

In a situation that involves the delegation of powers to an international organisation, the European Court of Human Rights, in its *Bosphorus Airways* decision relating to EU sanctions against Milošević's Yugoslavia, had ruled that the delegating member State would be held responsible for the actions of that organisation if the organisation lacked an equivalent system of human rights protection.[19] In case such system was in place, the Court created a rebuttable presumption that it was not deficient in the protection of human rights.

In *Kadi*, however, the ECJ has chosen another path. Whereas earlier judgments could have been understood as following a 'monist' interpretation of European law with regard to international law, the Court now emphasises the 'constitutional' character of the European Treaties that did not allow for the violation of its basic principles, in particular human rights (Art. 6 §1 TEU).[20] Whereas the Court of First Instance (CFI) arguably misinterpreted the extent of human rights protection in the law of the UN Charter,[21] the ECJ refused to acknowledge that, as the only independent court with jurisdiction in the matter, it should have included the relationship between international and European law in its terms of reference.

Thus, the ECJ has been criticised – correctly, in my view – because the multiplicity of legal orders requires not blindness, but dialogue,[22] and for its disregard for the Charter claim of prevalence under Art. 103. But if we look at the result in the specific case, the judgment indeed has opened such a dialogue with the Council. Even before the publication of the judgment, the Security Council, in resolution 1822 (2008), had further

---

[19] *Bosphorus* v. *Ireland*, [2005] ECHR-VI. Cf. *Kadi*, *supra* n. 3, paras. 322–6.

[20] *Kadi*, *supra* n. 3, paras. 283–5, 316.

[21] In this sense also Human Rights Committee, *Sayadi* v. *Belgium*, Communication No. 1472/2006, Views, 22 October 2008, Doc. CCPR/C/94/D/1472/2006, Ind. Op. Iwasawa, 34; N. Rodley, *ibid.*, 36 (arguing that Council action needs to be interpreted as intending to maintain human rights).

[22] For a similar critique, see J. Weiler, 'Editorial', *EJIL*, 19 (2008), 895–6; A. Gattini, 'Comment', *CMLR*, 46 (2009), 213–14, 226–7; G. de Búrca, 'The EU, the European Court of Justice and the International Legal Order after *Kadi*', *HILJ*, 51 (2009); D. Halberstam and E. Stein, 'The United Nations, the European Union, and the King of Sweden. Economic Sanctions and Individual Rights in a Plural World Order', *CMLR*, 46 (2009), 13–72, 71–2. See also the position taken by the European Commission in *Kadi*, *supra* n. 3, paras. 269–70, 319; but see B. Kunoy and A. Dawes, 'Plate Tectonics in Luxembourg. The *ménage à trois* between EC Law, International Law and the European Convention on Human Rights following the UN Sanctions Cases', *CMLR*, 46 (2009), 73–104, 103–4.

amended the sanctions regime by providing for the publication of the reasons for listing and an annual review.[23] Ideally, this would also lead to an identification of the provider of information that could be sued before domestic courts.

Thus, the ECJ, by interpreting European law in accordance with the most recent international decisions, did much more to accommodate an internationalist point of view than Posner and Goldsmith would make us believe.[24]

The German Constitutional Court and the Lisbon Treaty: dualism under the cloak of pluralism

Contrary to the intentions of its drafters, the example of the treatment of international law by the ECJ apparently has not been lost on another court, namely the German Federal Constitutional Court. In its judgment on the compatibility of the Lisbon Treaty on European Union[25] with the German *Grundgesetz* (Basic Law), the *Bundesverfassungsgericht* explicitly cites the ECJ for the proposition that '[t]here is . . . no contradiction to the aim of openness to international law if the legislature, exceptionally, does not comply with the law of international agreements . . . provided this is the only way in which a violation of fundamental principles of the constitution can be averted', adding that this was 'familiar in international legal relations as reference to the ordre public as the boundary of commitment under a treaty'.[26]

This view has important consequences, allowing the Constitutional Court to claim a residual power of oversight over European integration with regard to human rights protection,[27] the respect for the limits of competences transferred to the Union,[28] and for the protection of the

---

[23] Security Council resolution 1822 (2008), paras. 13, 25, 26. For the further introduction of an ombudsperson, see Security Council resolution 1904 (2009), paras. 20 and 21.

[24] See Goldsmith and Posner, 'Does Europe Believe', *supra* n. 6. [25] Cf. *supra* n. 10.

[26] Lisbon judgment, *supra* n. 10, para. 340, citations omitted.

[27] *Ibid.*, para. 191; the Court explicitly confirms its famous '*Solange*' ('as long as')-Rechtsprechung, BVerfGE 37, 271; BVerfGE 73, 339 in this regard, and adds another '*Solange*' regarding the respect for the principle of limited powers, *ibid.*, para. 262: 'As long as, and to the extent to which, the principle of conferral is adhered to in an association of sovereign States with clear elements of executive and governmental cooperation, the legitimation provided by national parliaments and governments, which is complemented and sustained by the directly elected European Parliament is, in principle, sufficient.' For an overview, see Paulus, 'Germany', *supra* n. 12.

[28] *Ibid.*, paras 238–9.

core of 'national identity'.[29] Just like its earlier Maastricht ruling,[30] the German Federal Constitutional Court now places not only the ECJ, but all European and State organs, including the national German Parliament, under its own supervision.[31] The irony has not been lost on observers that the Court – itself only indirectly democratically legitimated – thus claims a right of supervision over the democratically elected Parliament in the very name of democracy.[32]

Early commentary on the judgment, while highly critical, has centred on the Court's treatment of the 'democratic deficit' of the EU and its concomitant 'State law' approach, according to which the transfer of competences to the EU requires the consent of the domestic legislative bodies rather than the executive branch only.[33] In the absence of popular consent as expressed in the failed referenda on the Lisbon Treaty in Ireland and the preceding Constitutional Treaty in France and The Netherlands, however, the Court is correct to point out that the EU derives its legitimacy not directly from the people, but from the Member States that ratified its constituent treaties.[34] However, the Court apparently fails to understand that a return to classical sovereignist solutions would not lead to more democratic decision-making in the EU.

It is remarkable that the *Bundesverfassungsgericht* seems to regard European law in a similar way as international law in general. It thus uses

---

[29] *Ibid.*, para 240. Art. 79 §3 *Grundgesetz* reads: 'Amendments to this Basic Law affecting the division of the Federation into Länder, their participation on principle in the legislative process, or the principles laid down in Articles 1 and 20 shall be inadmissible.' Art. 20, in turn, contains the principles of democracy, of the rule of law (*Rechtsstaat*), and the 'social state' (*Sozialstaat*).

[30] BVerfGE 89, 155 (hereafter, Maastricht judgment).

[31] See C. Tomuschat, 'Die Europäische Union unter der Aufsicht des Bundesverfassungsgerichts', *Europäische Grundrechtezeitschrift*, (1993), 489–96, commenting on the Maastricht judgment. However, as representative of the Federal government in the oral proceedings on the Lisbon Treaty, Tomuschat seemed to have warmed up to such control of the outer limits of European integration; Lisbon judgment, *supra* n. 10, para. 240.

[32] C. Calliess, 'Unter Karlsruher Totalaufsicht', *Frankfurter Allgemeine Zeitung*, 27 August 2009, 8; M. Nettesheim, 'Entmündigung der Politik', *Frankfurter Allgemeine Zeitung*, 27 August 2009, 8; M. Nettesheim, 'Ein Individualrecht auf Staatlichkeit? Die Lissabon-Entscheidung des BVerfG', *NJW*, (2009), 2867; see also D. Halberstam and C. Möllers, 'The German Constitutional Court says "Ja zu Deutschland!"', *German Law Journal*, 10 (2009), 1241–58, 1252–3; C. Schönberger, '*Lisbon* in Karlsruhe. Maastricht's Epigones At Sea', *German Law Journal*, 10 (2009), 1201–18, 1216–18.

[33] Lisbon judgment, *supra* n. 10, paras. 296–7.

[34] *Ibid.*, paras. 231–2. For the contrary position, see, for example, I. Pernice, 'Multilevel Constitutionalism and the Treaty of Amsterdam. European Constitution-Making Revisited?', *CMLR*, 39 (1999), 703–50, 717; but see Schütze, *supra* n. 8, 1079, n. 47.

the same terminology of 'friendliness' – or, in the quasi-official translation of 'Freundlichkeit', 'openness' – as it does with regard to international law.[35] The direct effect between individuals that distinguishes EU law from the bulk of public international law does not impress the Court in this regard, because it exacerbates the democratic deficit rather than attenuating it. The Court thus challenges the European orthodoxy according to which European law constitutes a decisive advance over international law by being directly legitimated at citizen level.[36] The main justification for the autonomy of the Community legal order lies, as with international law, in the benefits all its members derive from membership, which might be endangered if every one of them can decide for itself whether or not to implement collective decisions.

But I do not intend to go into detail here. Rather, I shall concentrate on four points that demonstrate the attitude of the Court towards international law. The first point relates to the effects of European – or international – acts that are regarded as *ultra vires* by domestic institutions – a central part of the judgment that builds on the famous passage of the Maastricht judgment creating the theory of the 'ausbrechenden Rechtsakt',[37] e.g. European legal acts not respecting the limits of EU powers.[38] Secondly, I address the claim that international law contains a 'principle of reversible self-commitment'[39] with regard to international unions in general. Thirdly, I comment on the related point that international law – or, for that matter, the German Constitution – allows for a tacit reservation of the domestic *ordre public* when concluding international treaties. Finally, I look at the extensive attempt by the Court to substantiate a 'domaine réservé' for States that cannot be transferred to international organisations.[40] As a result, I come to the conclusion that the judgment reverts to a view of European and international law that has a lot in common with the judgment of the US Supreme Court in *Medellín*,[41] but seems ill-equipped for the twenty-first century challenge to democratise international relations.

---

[35] *Ibid.*, paras. 225, 240, 340. On the openness to international law, see *supra* n. 12.

[36] See, e.g., J. Weiler and U. R. Haltern, 'The Autonomy of the Community Legal Order – Through the Looking Glass', *HILJ*, 37 (1996), 411–48, 420; against T. Schilling, 'The Autonomy of the Community Legal Order', *HILJ*, 37 (1996), 389.

[37] Maastricht Judgment, *supra* n. 30, 188.

[38] Lisbon Judgment, *supra* n. 10, para. 240 ('obvious transgressions of the boundaries').

[39] *Ibid.*, para. 233.   [40] *Ibid.*, paras. 249, 352 ff.

[41] *Medellín* v. *Texas*, 552 US 491 (2008); see also *Sanchez-Llamas* v. *Oregon*, 548 US 331, 126 S Ct 2669 (2006). For a comparative analysis, see C. Hoppe, 'Implementation of *LaGrand* and *Avena* in Germany and the United States. Exploring a Transatlantic Divide in Search of a Uniform Interpretation of Consular Rights', *EJIL*, 18 (2007), 317–36.

Ultra vires: *a return to an international framework?*

From the primacy of State over European or international models of democracy, the Court concludes that democracy prohibits a European *Kompetenz-Kompetenz* (competence-competence) in the broad sense of the term – i.e. a competence of the Union to extend its competences without Member State consent, and requires a narrow reading of the competences of the EU.[42] It thereby espouses a universalist Statism that regards electoral democracy within the national State as the only model of democracy.[43] My Göttingen colleague Frank Schorkopf emphasises that, with its new *ultra vires* terminology, 'the Lisbon treaty both linguistically and dogmatically follows international law by taking up the classical notion of public power acting without competence'.[44]

The *Certain Expenses* Opinion of the ICJ agrees with the proposition that, in the absence of delegation to an international organisation, Member States retain freedom of action.[45] But it also emphasises that the organisation benefits from a presumption of legality when acting within its purpose.[46] In international law, the consequences of international organisations arguably acting beyond their competences are

---

[42] Lisbon judgment, *supra* n. 10, paras. 233, 236, 240. However, the overbreadth of some ECJ judgments invited such a response.

[43] *Ibid.*, paras. 268–72. See F. Schorkopf, 'The European Union as An Association of Sovereign States. Karlsruhe's Ruling on the Treaty of Lisbon', *German Law Journal*, 10 (2009), 1219–40, 1221.

[44] See Schorkopf, *supra* n. 43, 1231. Interestingly, Schorkopf's citations to Gerhard Leibholz and Rudolf Bernhardt rather point to limitations of the domestic invocation of the *ultra vires* quality of international acts; see G. Leibholz, 'Das Verbot der Willkür und des Ermessensmißbrauches im völkerrechtlichen Verkehr von Staaten', *ZaöRV*, 1 (1929) 77–125, 94; referring to A. V. Dicey and A. B. Keith, *A Digest of the Law of England with Reference to the Conflict of Laws*, 4th edn. (London: Stevens, 1927), 23 (regarding *ultra vires* as an example of the French doctrine of *excès des pouvoirs* and abuse of rights and applying it to States); R. Bernhardt, 'Ultra Vires Activities of International Organizations', in J. Makarczyk (ed.), *Theory of International Law at the Threshold of the 21st Century. Essays in Honour of Krzysztof Skubiszewski* (The Hague: Kluwer, 1996), 599–611, 604 (arguing for primacy of international determinations of *ultra vires* acts).

[45] *Certain Expenses of the United Nations, Advisory Opinion*, ICJ Rep. 1962, 151 (168).

[46] 'But when the Organization takes action which warrants the assertion that it was appropriate for the fulfillment of one of the stated purposes of the United Nations, the presumption is that such action is not *ultra vires* the Organization.' This jurisprudence has been confirmed in the Lockerbie Preliminary Measures Case, *Questions of Interpretation and Application of the 1971 Montreal Convention arising from the Aerial Incident at Lockerbie (Libya v. UK)*, ICJ Rep. 1992, 3 (15), para. 39.

unclear. Just as in European law, traditional approaches emphasise the auto-interpretation of States that may disregard decisions of international organisations they deem unlawful under international law, whereas others give primacy to the view of the organisation, even in the absence of a judicial interpretation by an international court.[47] Others are resigned to the insolvability of the riddle of who is the final arbiter of the lawfulness of acts of international organisations.[48]

In the presence of an international court, however, whose task precisely is to decide questions of competences for all, collective determination, such as the one by the ECJ, is clearly preferable,[49] with the possible exception of egregious cases of abuse. Only obvious violations of the powers of international organisations can thus be disregarded by States with the *ultra vires* argument.[50] The international implied powers doctrine that the Court seems to embrace in the judgment[51] shows that such overstepping of competences cannot lightly be presumed.[52] Whatever one thinks of some ECJ judgments, it is difficult to maintain that they fall under this category.

The best approach to what constitutes a decision or judgment *ultra vires* would probably take up the '*Solange*' criteria as developed in the case-law of the *Bundesverfassungsgericht*.[53] In other words, only if the EU organs systematically disregarded the legal basis of their activity,

---

[47] In this vein, see Bernhardt, *supra* n. 44, 604.

[48] J. A. Frowein, 'The Internal and External Effects of Resolutions by International Organizations', *Heidelberg Journal of International Law*, 49 (1989), 778–90, 783.

[49] That was also the position of L. Gross, 'States as Organs of International Law and the Problem of Autointerpretation', in *Essays on International Law and Organization* (Dobbs Ferry, NY: Transnational Publishers, 1993), vol. I, 367, 394, strangely invoked by T. Schilling, *supra* n. 36, 389, 404, for the opposite conclusion; on the whole matter, see Weiler and Haltern, 'The Autonomy of the Community', *supra* n. 36, 425–8.

[50] In the same vein, more recently, see N. Weiß, *Kompetenzlehre internationaler Organisationen* (Heidelberg: Springer, 2008), 420–3, 436, See also Art. 46 of the 1969 Vienna Convention on the Law of Treaties, (VCLT), 1155 UNTS 331, on the related problem of treaties violating a domestic constitution. See also the identical provision in the Vienna Convention on the Law of Treaties between States and International Organizations or between International Organizations, *opened for signature* 21 March 1986 (not yet in force), UN Doc.A/CONF.129/15 (1986), *ILM*, 25 (1986), 543.

[51] Lisbon judgment, *supra* n. 10, para. 237.

[52] On implied powers, see *Reparation for Injuries Suffered in the Service of the United Nations*, ICJ Rep. 1949, 174 (182); K. Schmalenbach, 'International Organizations or Institutions, General Aspects', in R. Wolfrum (ed.), *Max Planck Encyclopedia of International Law*, 3rd edn. (Oxford University Press, 2009), www.mpepil.com, paras. 47–9.

[53] See *supra* n. 27.

namely the treaties establishing the Union, resulting in a general 'decline below the required standard'[54] of treaty interpretation, could Germany and its courts end their practice of implementing the judgments of the ECJ. I consider such a scenario highly unlikely.

Thus, the *Bundesverfassungsgericht* cannot point to international law for extending Member States' control over arguable *ultra vires* acts of the organisation, even less so because the Member States have entrusted that task to an independent court.[55]

The right to withdrawal in international law

In the very same paragraph in which the Court draws the conclusion from its analysis by excluding the transfer of *Kompetenz-Kompetenz* to the EU, it also provides that:

> withdrawal from the European union of integration (*Integrationsverband*) may, regardless of a commitment for an unlimited period under an agreement, not be prevented by other Member States or the autonomous authority of the Union. This is not a secession from a State union (*Staatsverband*), which is problematical under international law, but merely the withdrawal from an association of sovereign states (*Staatenverbund*) which is founded on the principle of the reversible self-commitment.[56]

In this translation the passage is difficult to understand. It intends to say that while secession from a federal State is problematic under international law, an international federation (*Staatenverbund*, a term coined by the Court for the European Union) must allow for an individual right of withdrawal, and this proposition is supposed to be in accordance with international law.

First, the statement by the Court is *obiter* because one of the central modifications introduced by the Lisbon Treaty is an explicit right to withdrawal (Art. 50, para. 1) coming into effect through the conclusion of a treaty with the Union on its modalities.[57]

---

[54] *Bananenmarktordnung* (Banana Market Regulation), BVerfGE 102, 147, 164, BVerfG, 2 BvL 1/97, 6 July 2000, para. 39, www.bverfg.de/entscheidungen/ls20000607_2bvl000197en.html.

[55] Weiler and Haltern, 'The Autonomy of the Community', *supra* n. 36, 423–4, refuting the misconstruction of auto-interpretation of international law by Schilling, 'The Autonomy of the Community Legal Order', *supra* n. 36, 407.

[56] Lisbon judgment, *supra* n. 10, para. 233, citation omitted.

[57] Art. 50, para. 1, TEU (L): 'Any Member State may decide to withdraw from the Union in accordance with its own constitutional requirements.' For the previous situation, see

Secondly, a right to withdrawal is highly controversial in international law. A State may withdraw from a treaty – institutional or other – if and to the extent one of the parties is in 'material breach' of the treaty, or in case of a fundamental change of circumstances (*clausula rebus sic stantibus*).[58] In other cases, Art. 56, para. 1 of the Vienna Convention on the Law of Treaties provides that a

> treaty which contains no provision regarding its termination and which does not provide for denunciation or withdrawal is not subject to denunciation or withdrawal unless
>
> (a) it is established that the parties intended to admit the possibility of denunciation or withdrawal; or
> (b) a right of denunciation or withdrawal may be implied by the nature of the treaty.

While Art. 53 TEC in the pre-Lisbon version,[59] according to which the treaty is 'concluded for an unlimited period', indicates that the parties originally did not intend to allow for denunciation or withdrawal, the matter depends on whether the 'nature' of a treaty of a regional supranational organisation implies an individual right to withdrawal. Letter (b) was added by the Vienna Conference. The original draft of the Convention by the ILC had not contained this provision.[60] As the ILC commentary indicates, there was no agreement on the matter.[61] Contemporary writers hold divergent views.[62]

K. Schmalenbach, in C. Calliess and M. Ruffert, EUV/EGV 2007, Art. 312 EGV, para. 4 with further references.

[58] See Arts. 60 and 62 VCLT. [59] OJ C 321E (29 December 2006), (consolidated version).

[60] See Art. 53 of the ILC draft articles, *ILC Yearbook 1966*, vol. II, 250, www.un.org/law/ilc. Letter b was added by a majority of one vote in the Drafting Committee of the Vienna Conference on the Law of Treaties with the purpose of providing a remedy in case of treaties that did not contain a clause on their unlimited duration; see Report of the Committee of the Whole, in UN Conference on the Law of Treaties, Official Records, 177, para. 490 (c) as well as the proceedings in 2 UN Conference on the Law of Treaties, 336 (Cuba) and 339 (F. Vallat for the United Kingdom). For an overview of the drafting history, see I. Sinclair, *The Vienna Convention on the Law of Treaties*, 2nd edn. (Manchester University Press, 1984), 186–8, who tends to the view that the unlimited nature of a treaty counsels against the application of Art. 56.

[61] *Ibid.*, 251.

[62] See A. Aust, *Modern Treaty Law and Practice*, 2nd edn. (Cambridge University Press, 2007), 398 favouring such right; but see his main source, K. Widdows, 'The Unilateral Denunciation of Treaties Containing No Denunciation Clause', *BYBIL*, 53 (1982), 83–114, 102, with extensive analysis to practice; see also T. Christakis, in O. Corten and P. Klein (eds.), *Les Conventions de Vienne sur le Droit des Traités* (Brussels: Bruylant, 2006), vol. III, 2008–9 (arguing in favour of an explicit provision in the European treaties).

The practice of international organisations is not very helpful. The UN Charter does not contain any clause regarding withdrawal. The matter was discussed at the San Francisco Conference and resolved in favour of a declaration according to which 'if . . . a Member because of exceptional circumstances feels constrained to withdraw, and leave the burden of maintaining international peace and security on the other Members, it is not the purpose of the Organization to compel that Member to continue its cooperation in the Organization'.[63] One may understand this resolution as a statement on the law. It can also be read as merely allowing for a withdrawal on the basis of the *clausula rebus sic stantibus*.[64] The better reading appears to be that it was designed to maintain constructive ambiguity.

When Indonesia 'withdrew' its membership on 20 January 1965, and asked for re-entry one year later on 19 September 1966, it simply 'resumed' membership without re-admission.[65] Thus, the claim of a right to withdrawal was ignored, and Indonesia re-assessed its own interests in the membership of the organisation. In the time between withdrawal and resumption, however, Indonesia seems not to have been counted as a UN member.

The Court thus presents a highly controversial matter as one of course. If anything, the language of the German Constitution that provides for German cooperation in the establishment of the Union (Art. 23, para. 1, Preamble, sentence 1) argues against a withdrawal as long as the Union remains faithful to its founding treaties.

A general reservation of 'ordre public'?

The Court's views on withdrawal and of 'reversible self-commitment' only constitute a sub-set of a larger argument according to which States are only bound under reservation of their *ordre public*. The doctrine stems from private international law according to which States may decline to apply foreign (not international!) law if and to the extent it

---

[63] UNCIO Documents, vol. VII, 267, Doc. 1043, I/2/70, 17 June 1945. The remainder of the resolution dealt with a special case – namely the adoption of an amendment by majority against the will of a member. For a thorough review of the debates in San Francisco on the matter, see N. Feinberg, 'Unilateral Withdrawal From an International Organization', *BYBIL*, 39 (1963), 189–219, 199–202.

[64] Feinberg, *supra* n. 63, 201; K. Widdows, *supra* n. 62, 100.

[65] K. Ginther, in B. Simma (ed.), *The Charter of the United Nations. A commentary*, 2nd edn. (Oxford University Press, 2002), Art. 4, para. 40.

violates their *ordre public* – e.g. the body of rules containing the core principles of the forum State. As such it is a domestic, not an international legal concept[66] and does not affect the foreign rule as such, but merely its impact in the forum State.[67] In addition, it only applies to private international law conventions when explicitly permitted therein; and courts need to keep in mind the need of uniform interpretation in all State Parties.[68] In addition, the *ordre public* may limit the recognition and enforcement of foreign judgments and arbitral awards in the domestic legal sphere.[69]

The German Federal Constitutional Court invokes this doctrine in the passage in which it cites the ECJ view held in *Kadi*:

> The Basic Law ... does not waive the sovereignty contained in the last instance in the German constitution ... There is therefore no contradiction to the aim of openness to international law if the legislature, exceptionally, docs not comply with international treaty law – accepting, however, corresponding consequences in international relations – provided this is the only way in which a violation of fundamental principles of the constitution can be averted.[70]

This passage correctly argues, from a dualist viewpoint, that the domestic legal order may reject foreign law in exceptional cases, when it is ready to suffer the consequences for violating a rule of international law, namely State responsibility.[71]

While this first passage suggests that the Court was aware that such unilateral derogation is contrary to international law (while, strangely enough, the Court speaks of 'consequences in international relations' rather than using the legal term 'State responsibility'), a second passage of the same paragraph sounds quite different: 'Such a legal construct is not only familiar in international legal relations as reference to the *ordre public* as the boundary of a treaty commitment; it also corresponds, if used constructively, to the idea of contexts of political order which are not structured according to a strict hierarchy.'

But it will remain the Court's secret how it can, by allowing for the violation of international law, be 'constructive'. 'Constructive' it could only be by beginning a dialogue, but not by derogating outright from the binding commitments of a Member State. This was the secret behind the success of

---

[66] See M. Gebauer, 'Ordre Public (Public Policy)', in Wolfrum (ed.), *Max Planck Encyclopedia of International Law, supra* n. 52, paras. 1–11.
[67] *Ibid.*, para. 10.   [68] *Ibid.*, para. 9.   [69] *Ibid.*, para. 14.
[70] Lisbon judgment, *supra* n. 10, para. 340.   [71] See *Görgülü, supra* n. 12, 317–18.

the famous *'Solange'*-jurisprudence of the Court.[72] But the dialogue it now seems to contemplate is the *'dialogue des sourds'*. The consequence of breach is not dialogue, but responsibility and eventual reparation.

In addition, by speaking consistently of 'international relations' rather than 'international law', the Court maintains a profound ambiguity as to the source of the proposed reservation of the *ordre public*. The ambiguity of the Court suggests that a State could violate its international obligations with impunity, even with a sense of righteousness. On the contrary, every violation of an international agreement is unlawful and entails international responsibility, including a duty to provide full reparation of the injury caused to others.[73] Thus, wilful disregard of international obligations contradicts any pretension to an 'openness' or 'friendliness' towards international law.

The objectivation of the domaine réservé: history of a failure

While the *ultra vires*, right to withdrawal and *ordre public* points are of a similar nature – emphasising domestic control over the extent of international integration – the fourth point is different: it does not constitute a direct challenge to international or European law as such, but rather constitutes an attempt to defend an objective, substantive view of the 'minimum State' *vis-à-vis* international and European law. According to the Court:

> [t]he principle of democracy as well as the principle of subsidiarity . . . therefore require factually to restrict the transfer and exercise of sovereign powers to the European Union in a predictable manner particularly in central political areas of the space of personal development and the shaping of living conditions by social policy. In these areas, it is particularly necessary to draw the limit where the coordination of cross-border situations is factually required.[74]

While thus paying lip service to the 'great successes of European integration'[75] and recognising that there is no 'hard core' of State competences not open to transfer,[76] the Court uses the language of democracy to

---

[72] On this point, see A. Paulus, 'Germany', *supra* n. 12; F.C. Mayer, 'The European Constitution and the Courts', in A. von Bogdandy and J. Bast (eds.), *Principles of European Constitutional Law*, 2nd edn. (Oxford: Hart, 2010), 399.

[73] See only Art. 1 and 31 of the ILC Articles on State responsibility, in Responsbility of States for Internationally Wrongful Acts, GA res. 56/83 of 12 December 2001, Annex.

[74] Lisbon judgment, *supra* n. 10, para. 251 references omitted.   [75] *Ibid.*

[76] *Ibid.*, para. 248.

defend national prerogatives. By identifying substantial areas in which democracy requires domestic freedom of decision, the Court thus contradicts international developments with regard to the *domaine reservé*, as contained in Art. 2 §7 of the UN Charter, according to which domestic jurisdiction is determined by the current state of international law rather than by objective criteria. In the *Nationality Decrees* case, the Permanent Court of International Justice (PCIJ) held: 'The question whether a certain matter is or is not solely within the jurisdiction of a State is an essentially relative question: it depends on the development of international law.'[77] In other words: when States are not only free to remain outside international organisations, but also are free to enter into international obligations,[78] it appears impossible to arrive at a 'hard core' of domestic competences.

As Halberstam and Möllers have pointed out, it has proved impossible to determine a precise list of 'State tasks'.[79] Instead, the Court draws up a list of competences currently not delegated to the EU. In other words, the Court's theory of sovereign prerogatives is equivalent to a statement aimed at bringing further losses of sovereignty under its control.

However, at a time when international law covers almost every area of international life, the unlimited freedom of States to assume international obligations towards other States reduces the area of domestic jurisdiction to the point where it ceases to exist. In the words of Georg Nolte, '[t]he development of international law after the Second World War ... has led to the coverage of so many fields by (consensual or customary) rules of international law that the definition ... by the PCIJ does not leave very much room for this concept any longer'.[80] The addition of the words 'essential' to the domestic jurisdiction in Art. 2 §7 of the UN Charter constituted an attempt to reserve certain competences for States.[81] Instead of defining a substantive hard core of State

---

[77] *Nationality Decrees in Tunis and Morocco*, PCIJ, Ser. B, No. 4, 7 February 1923, p. 24.

[78] See famously, *SS Wimbledon*, PCIJ, Ser. A., No. 1, 1923, 24.

[79] Halberstam and Möllers, 'The German Constitutional Court', *supra* n. 32, 1250: 'But is there any theory or argument behind this list? We find none in the opinion. The Court merely refers to its own imagination of past sovereignty.' And further, *ibid.*, 1251: 'The deep irony of this part of the decision lies in the fact that the alleged theory of the sovereign State simply stems from a negative reading of the European Treaties ... What the Court deems to be protected are merely the leftovers of European integration recycled as necessary elements of State sovereignty.'

[80] G. Nolte, in B. Simma (ed.), *The Charter of the United Nations*, *supra* n. 65, Art. 2 (7), para. 29.

[81] *Ibid.*, para. 32.

sovereignty, however, Georg Nolte has proposed to regard Article 2 §7 'as encompassing a principle of proportionality'.[82] In other words, international intervention should only go as far as necessary. It is not by accident that Nolte invokes the principles of subsidiarity and proportionality as contained in Article 5 §§3 and 4 TEU for this proposition. Again, it turns out that an 'internationalist' and a 'European' view on the Lisbon Treaty arrive at the same conclusions.

While aiming at drawing an outer limit to European integration, the Court does not devise these areas as absolute limits, but seems to regard them as considerations for a proportionality analysis in which 'the coordination of cross-border situations is factually required'. There is some contradiction in the way the Court first defines these areas as limits to internationalisation and then nevertheless allows for regulation of 'cross-border situations'. This reintroduces subsidiarity and proportionality in the way that Nolte has proposed. It opens up the possibility for the Court to limit the 'identity protection' review of European decisions.

But the Court thus fails to provide, just like Article 2 §7 of the UN Charter, a clearly defined area of domestic jurisdiction. The protection of the domestic area remains both relativist and indeterminate. This has two consequences: first, it empowers the Court to determine the outcome of the analysis, instead of the domestic Parliament or the ECJ and, secondly, it comes down to a relative rather than absolute protection of the 'hard core'. Legal certainty is, in spite of the substance of the list, basically lost.

Let us now briefly look to the substance of the list of the Constitutional Court:

> Particularly sensitive for the ability of a constitutional state to democratically shape itself are decisions on substantive and formal criminal law (1), on the disposition of the monopoly on the use of force by the police within the state and by the military towards the exterior (2), fundamental fiscal decisions on public revenue and public expenditure, the latter being particularly motivated, *inter alia*, by social policy considerations (3), decisions on the shaping of living conditions in a social state (4) and decisions of particular cultural importance, for example on family law, the school and education system and on dealing with religious communities (5).[83]

---

[82] *Ibid.*, para. 75.   [83] Lisbon judgment, *supra* n. 10, para. 252 references omitted.

As to criminal law, which played a large role in the oral proceedings, this is a reaction to the perceived overbearing of the ECJ in these matters.[84] As to the monopoly of the use of force, this is a criterion which certainly makes sense regarding the domestic use of the military. In view of current military realities, the second component of this element, the military monopoly on the use of force towards the exterior, appears particularly dubious, however. Thereby, the Court seems to intend to immunise the parliamentary prerogative – according to which the German armed forces are a 'parliamentary army' – against centralised European decision-making.[85] The historical and constitutional irony of this step, however, is that the European Defence Community (EDC) devised by some of the very framers of the German *Grundgesetz*[86] is now apparently held to be unconstitutional, whereas the concept of the 'parliamentary army' was an invention by the Court by which it successfully arbitrated a constitutional dispute within government and Parliament enabling Germany to participate in military operations abroad after the end of the Cold War.[87] The assertiveness by which the Court counts external security under sovereign prerogatives appears ironic if one looks at the constitutional requirement to use armed forces only in a system of collective security (Art. 24.2 of the *Grundgesetz*[88]). In fact, Germans are well aware that the German armed forces could not even move their personnel without the support of its allies. National abilities do not match national prerogatives. This is exactly a situation where subsidiarity requires communal decision-making at a higher level. It remains unclear, however, whether, according to the judgment, a truly European army would be permissible that includes German contingents not belonging to the *Bundeswehr*.[89]

---

[84] See, e.g., *Environmental Penalties, Commission v. Council*, Case C-176/03, [2005] ECR I-7879 (7928), paras. 48, 52.

[85] See Lisbon judgment, *supra* n. 10, 254, speaking of a 'similarly determined limit'.

[86] BGBl (German Federal Gazette), II 1954, 343 Among the spiritual fathers of the EDC was Konrad Adenauer, the chairman of the Parliamentary Council drafting the German *Grundgesetz* and first Chancellor of the Federal Republic.

[87] *AWACS/Somalia*, BVerfGE 90, 286, 382.   [88] See *ibid.*, 344 *et seq.*

[89] Lisbon judgment, *supra* n. 10, para. 255; the Court emphasises that '[t]his, however, does not raise an insurmountable obstacle under constitutional law to a technical integration of a European deployment of armed forces … Only the decision on any specific deployment depends on the constitutive approval of the German *Bundestag*.' See also C. D. Classen, 'Legitime Stärkung des Bundestages oder verfassungsrechtliches Prokrustesbett?', *Juristenzeitung*, (2009), 881–7 (espousing a sceptical view as to the permissibility of a European Army under the judgment).

The other three considerations – fiscal, social, cultural – relate both to the financial interests of the largest economy in Europe, as well as to the alleged threat of forced cultural homogenisation. Even though I doubt that the latter will ever happen, it merits mention that the true equalising force of culture in Europe certainly does not emanate from Belgian chocolate or French movies, but from a globalised cultural industry. To protect cultural sovereignty, the Court determines that the Member States need to remain members of the WTO even when they have lost all their competences justifying their presence.[90] Whether cultural protectionism will help nation States to maintain their identity, however, remains to be seen.

The list as a whole has no basis in the text of the Constitution, but in the circumstances of the case, in particular in the list of complaints (from neo-liberal hardliners to reformed communists). Rather than having a strong legal basis, the list is based on a particular social theory that combines traditional (sovereignty) and postmodern (reflexivity) elements.[91] But was the political expediency of some of the rulings of the ECJ not precisely the reason for Karlsruhe's intervention?

In view of the relativism of the criteria for both the substance of the prerogatives and for their application, it appears that the mass of *obiter dicta* will not shape the future of European integration, but rather will constitute a concession to populist, but transient sentiments.

The Lisbon judgment and international law

In conclusion, in the Lisbon judgment, the Court not only treats European law as, at the core, still suffering from the traditional deficiencies of international law – namely, ineffectiveness and democratic deficit – but it seems to have missed important developments in international law itself. It is thus difficult to square the Lisbon judgment with the earlier case-law of the Karlsruhe Court with regard to the domestic effect of international law. On the other hand, ironically, the Court takes up the sceptical elements of the US jurisprudence of the *Medellín* variety at a time when its moment in the United States seems to be waning. While this conclusion would ignore the considerable difference between the density of European integration and the much less intrusive ICJ

---

[90] *Ibid.*, para. 375.   [91] *Ibid.*, para 249.

jurisprudence, a considerable nexus between the two judgments is hard to deny.

Nevertheless, the earlier Karlsruhe case-law also shows that the theoretical dualism of the German Federal Constitutional Court, in practice, often gives way to a pragmatic approach in favour of implementing international as well as European law, as demonstrated by the *Görgülü* and *LaGrand* decisions. As in the human rights cases, the Court is not in a position to serve as a court of last resort towards the ECJ. When it invokes the 'idea of contexts of political order which are not structured according to a strict hierarchy'[92] the Court makes clear that it shares, in principle, a pluralist approach with regard to the relationship of legal orders, but demands the last word for itself as the guardian of democracy and of the core principles of the domestic constitutional order.

This is not worrying in itself. But it is precisely the necessity for tackling common problems such as global warming or transnational terrorism that has spurred the creation of international organisations with collective decision-making processes. National parliaments, as well as national courts, are incapable of fine-tuning these decisions. They can only provide a check on the executive branch *before*, and on the implementation of the results *after*, their international adoption. Only in a limited set of cases, however, will they be able to influence outcomes. They may destroy, not build. This counsels for a cautious use of domestic prerogatives in order to maintain the ever-precarious international process of decision-making indispensable to the solution of international problems. In the age of globalisation, the existence of and the participation in such machinery is in the common interest as well as in the national interest. In the German case, it is even mandated by its Constitution.[93] The future will show how carefully the Court will make use of its self-attributed powers of review of international decisions.

---

[92] *Ibid.*, para. 340. Unfortunately, however, this approach is not fully in line with the claim of primacy in the same paragraph, see H. P. Aust, Case Note, *International Law in Domestic Courts (ILDC)*, 1364 (DE 2009), www.oxfordlawreports.com.

[93] See the preamble: 'Conscious of their responsibility before God and man, Inspired by the determination to promote world peace as an equal partner in a united Europe, the German people, in the exercise of their constituent power, have adopted this Basic Law', as well as Art. 23: 'With a view to establishing a united Europe, the Federal Republic of Germany shall participate in the development of the European Union that is committed to democratic, social and federal principles, to the rule of law, and to the principle of subsidiarity, and that guarantees a level of protection of basic rights essentially comparable to that afforded by this Basic Law.'

At the same time, the democratic legitimacy of international decisions is one of the central challenges in a globalising world.[94] This is the reason why it appears troubling when the Court correctly emphasises, on the one hand, the need not to schematically subject international organisation to models of domestic democracy, but appears to shut the door, on the other hand, to a practical realisation of supranational democracy by the introduction of 'degressive proportionality' in the European Parliament (Art. 14, para. 2 TEU) and by the inclusion of elements of 'participatory democracy' (Art. 11 TEU).[95] At least, the Court recognises that participatory elements can 'ultimately increase the level of legitimisation'.[96] Indeed, they were never intended 'to replace the majority rule which is established by an election'. But it remains to be emphasised that while strictly majoritarian democracy may not be suitable for the international level, seeking consensus among stakeholders should not be discarded lightly as an alternative that may indeed, and not only 'ultimately', increase the legitimacy of international decision-making.

Towards a dialogue of courts in a multi-level and pluralist legal system

By way of conclusion, I wish to emphasise the following points:

(1) The relationship between international and local law – and even less so between international and domestic courts – cannot be described by a simplistic monist or dualist framework. Rather, in the contemporary world, every legal regime must relate, in one way or the other, to other legal systems and their judicial 'products'.[97]

(2) Every legal system will also attempt to maintain its distinct character and its main source of legitimacy, in particular popular sovereignty,

---

[94] For a more comprehensive treatment, see S. Besson, 'Institutionalizing global demoi-cracy', in L. Meyer (ed.), *Justice, Legitimacy and Public International Law* (Cambridge University Press, 2009), 58–91; A. Paulus, 'Subsidiarity, Fragmentation and Democracy. Towards the Demise of General International Law?', in T. Broude and Y. Shany (eds.), *The Shifting Allocation of Authority in International Law. Considering Sovereignty, Supremacy and Subsidiarity* (Oxford: Hart, 2008), 198–206, 193; J. H. H. Weiler, *The Constitution of Europe* (Cambridge, 1999), 264–85 each with further references.

[95] See Lisbon judgment, *supra* n. 10, para. 219, on the one hand, and paras. 279–95, on the other.

[96] *Ibid.*, para. 294.

[97] Similarly H. H. Koh, 'International Law as Part of Our Law', *AJIL*, 98 (2004), 43–56; A.-M. Slaughter, 'A Global Community of Courts', *HILJ*, 44 (2003), 191–219, 192; S. D. O'Connor, 'Keynote Address', *ASIL Proceedings of the 96th Annual Meeting*, 96 (2000), 348.

and protect the basic rights of its citizens. Through judicial control, international cooperation can therefore be balanced with constitutional values.

(3) On the other hand, the implementation of international obligations and of international adjudication constitutes a value in itself that is recognised both by the US and the German Constitutions. Digressions must therefore be exceptional and reserved for extreme cases. Thus, I will not hide my preoccupation with suggestions that domestic courts should preserve an 'option of noncompliance' with international obligations[98] or could rely on a domestic *ordre public* for not implementing international decisions. I am also concerned about the parochial European human rights absolutism of the ECJ that ultimately helps neither human rights nor collective interests. Rather, courts must try to accommodate different legal systems while preserving their distinctness. Dialogue, however, presupposes open engagement with other legal systems.

I know very well that, in the United States as well as in Europe, many people are anxious that giving too much space to international courts would abrogate democracy at home. But in a globalised world, human beings do not live in isolation, and common problems such as climate change or a return to financial sanity require common responses, even at the price of national prerogatives. Accommodation as advocated here means neither abdication nor parochialism. Domestic courts may serve as defenders of national rights, but only to the extent strictly necessary for maintaining the rule of law. While States are sovereign, international rules as well as decisions by international organisations are binding on States that freely undertook to observe them.

Does Europe believe in international law? Certainly. But it also believes in human rights and democracy. Bringing these principles into a principled and practical balance is the province of contemporary jurisprudence. In other words: transnationalism liveth.

---

[98] *Medellín, supra* n. 41.

10

Transnational law comprises constitutional, administrative, criminal and quasi-private law

ANNE PETERS

Introduction: transnational law oversteps traditional categories

In their book *Transnational Legal Problems*, first published in 1968, Detlev Vagts and Henry Steiner espoused Philip Jessup's term 'transnational law' as 'more than congenial' to them.[1] 'Transnational law' was meant by Jessup 'to include all law which regulates actions or events that transcend national frontiers. Both public and private international law are included, as are other rules which do not wholly fit into such standard categories'.[2] In their seminal book, Steiner and Vagts sought to give principal attention to problems that were 'relevant not only to governments but also to the private participants – individual or corporate – in transnational life'.[3] They defied 'rigid compartments', and instead dealt with all kinds of legal issues, including foreign investment and multinational enterprises (MNEs), 'on a spectrum between the extremes of "national" and "international" law, or on one between "private" and "public" law'.[4]

With that approach, Detlev Vagts contributed to overcoming the public–private split in international law. That catchword denotes the distinction between a public and a private realm of life, and goes hand in hand with the distinction between State and society, or between State and market. The blurring of these spheres seems particularly obvious with regard to economic law, and has been reinforced by the phenomenon which became generally known as globalisation in the 1990s. But although the erosion of the public–private split can usefully be captured with the

---

[1] H. J. Steiner and D. F. Vagts, *Transnational Legal Problems*, 2nd edn. (Westbury, NY: The Foundation Press, 1976), xv.

[2] P. C. Jessup, *Transnational Law* (New Haven, CT: Yale University Press, 1956), 2.

[3] Steiner and Vagts, *Transnational Legal Problems*, *supra* n. 1, xvi.   [4] *Ibid.*, xvii.

notion 'transnational', conceptual ambiguities and potential misunderstandings with regard to the key terms remain. After describing traditional international law as private law 'writ large', this chapter addresses these ambiguities. The chapter then argues – and this its thesis – that international (or transnational or global) law has started to go through a process of *structural* differentiation which complements the differentiation along issue-areas. It concludes by discussing the problems and merits of the suggested new structural order of international law.

The old international law as private law 'writ large'

Traditional international law (being mainly interstate law) has long been conceived as 'private law writ large'.[5] Hersch Lauterpacht famously stated that 'formally, international public law belongs to the *genus* private law'.[6] The roots of this conception lie in the infancy of the discipline of *ius naturae et gentium*, where States were viewed as analogous to human beings in the State of nature.[7] *Ius gentium* was the law of

---

[5] T. Holland, *Studies in International Law* (Oxford. Clarendon, 1898), 152. Montesquieu described international law as 'le droit civil de l'univers dans le sens que chaque peuple est un citoyen'. (Charles de Secondat Montesquieu, *De l'esprit des lois* (Geneva: Barrilot & Fils, 1748), livre vingt-sixième. Des lois dans le rapport qu'elles doivent avoir avec l'ordre des choses sur lesquelles elles statuent; chapitre premier – idée de ce livre).

[6] H. Lauterpacht, *Private Law Sources and Analogies in International Law* (London: Longmans, Green & Co, 1927), 81.

[7] See on the analogy between States and individuals as one of the most decisive features of the teachings of Hugo Grotius, seminally, H. Lauterpacht, 'The Grotian Tradition of International Law', first published in *BYBIL*, 23 (1946), 1–53, here as published in E. Lauterpacht (ed.), *International Law. Being the Collected Papers of Hersch Lauterpacht*, vol. 2 (Cambridge University Press, 1970–8), 307–65, e.g. 336. See, for a nuanced treatment, C. Wolff, *Ius Gentium Methodo Scientifica pertractorum*, vol. II, trans. J. H. Drake (Frankfurt, 1764), in J. B. Scott (ed.), *The Classics of International Law* (Oxford: Clarendon, 1934), preface (p. 5 of the translation) and §§2–3 (9); E. De Vattel, *Le droit des gens ou principes de la loi naturelle, appliqués à la conduite et aux affaires des Nations et des Souverains*, vol. I (London, 1758), in J. B. Scott (ed.), *The Classics of International Law, supra, passim* (e.g. préliminaires, para. 18; book II, chap. III (285); J.-J. Rousseau, *Du contrat social* (Paris: Garnier, 1954 (orig. 1762)), livre I, chap. VII (245): 'à l'égard de l'étranger, il [the state] devient un être simple, un individu.' Draft of *Abbé Grégoire* for a declaration of the rights of peoples of 23 April 1793: '2. Les peuples sont respectivement indépendants et souverains, quel que soit le nombre d'individus qui les composent et l'étendue du territorie qu'ils occupent. Cette souveraineté est inaliénable. 3. *Un peuple doit agir à l'égard des autres comme il désire qu'on agisse à son égard; ce qu'un homme doit à un homme, un peuple le doit aux autres*', in W. G. Grewe (ed.), *Fontes Historiae Iuris Gentium. Sources Relating to the History of the Law of Nations*, Bd. 2 (Berlin: de Gruyter, 1988), 660 (emphasis added).

nature, applied to States. The personification of the State through the monarch, and the romantic view of States as living organisms, added underpinnings to this picture of the State as a super-person.

The roots of sovereignty in the institution of property reflect another strand of 'privatism'. In the feudal system preceding the emergence of the State as an institution, the Lord's *dominium* over the land (and by extension over its inhabitants) had been conceived as private property.[8] Only Hugo Grotius and contemporaries re-discovered the ancient Roman law distinction between *dominium* (the power over things and unfree persons) and *imperium* (the more limited and what we would now call 'political' power of magistrates over persons), and began to analyse the State's authority as *imperium* rather than *dominium*.[9] But even in 1867, Carl Victor Fricker found it necessary to discuss at length and to combat the idea of territory as the State's property, because 'doubtlessly the private law view has not yet been overcome in this context'.[10]

Moreover, international law has a horizontal structure which corresponds to the ideal-typical private law-like structure. Because States as the principal international legal subjects are equally sovereign, they must be imagined as sitting on a horizontal plane without any hierarchy among them. This image is aptly captured in the old-fashioned German term '*genossenschaftliches Recht*' for international law.[11]

In private law, the typical form of legal interaction is the 'horizontal' conclusion of contracts as opposed to the 'top-down' enactment of laws. International treaties are in many ways analogous to private law contracts.[12] Along that line, the WTO Appellate Body described the WTO Agreement of 1994 as follows: 'The WTO Agreement is a treaty – the

---

[8] F. Kratochwil, 'Sovereignty as *Dominium*. Is there a Right of Humanitarian Intervention?', in M. Mastanduno and G. M. Lyons (eds.), *Beyond Westphalia? State Sovereignty and International Intervention* (Baltimore, MD and London: Johns Hopkins University Press, 1995), 21–42, esp. 25–33. Cf. also N. Jansen and R. Michaels, 'Private Law and the State', *RabelsZ*, 71 (2007), 345–97, repr. in N. Jansen and R. Michaels (eds.), *Beyond the State. Rethinking Private Law* (Tübingen: Mohr Siebeck, 2008), 15–67, 60.

[9] H. Grotius, *De Jure Belli ac Pacis libri Tres*, chap. III, sec. IV, vol. II, trans. F. W. Kesley *et al.* (Oxford: Clarendon, London: Humphrey Milford, 1925).

[10] C. V. Fricker, *Gebiet und Gebietshoheit, Anhang. Vom Staatsgebiet* (Tübingen: Laupp, 1901 (orig. 1867)), 100–12, quote on 100, trans. by the author.

[11] F. Berber, *Lehrbuch des Völkerrechts, I. Band, Allgemeines Friedensrecht*, 2nd edn. (Munich: Beck, 1975), 16–19.

[12] This analogy was notably exploited in the heyday of German private law scholarship in the second half of the nineteenth century. See C. F. Gerber, *Über öffentliche Rechte* (Tübingen: Laupp & Siebeck, 1852), 40: 'With regard to inter-state treaties, the legal form is private law, despite the political contents. The various contracting States oppose

international equivalent of a contract. It is self-evident that in an exercise of their sovereignty, and in pursuit of their own respective national interests, the Members of the WTO have made a bargain. In exchange for benefits they expect to derive as Members of the WTO, they have agreed to exercise their sovereignty according to the commitment they have made in the WTO Agreement.'[13] Also the 1969 Vienna Convention on the Law of Treaties (VCLT) draws heavily on legal institutions ultimately derived from (Roman) private law, such as full powers, void-ability, or denunciation. Before international law prohibited the use of force, the possibility of pressuring another State into concluding an international treaty under threat or use of military force was the most important difference compared to private contracts, consent to which is vitiated by duress.[14] This crucial difference has been tempered by the VCLT provision that a treaty is void if it has been procured by the threat or use of military force (Art. 52 VCLT), but has not fully disappeared. There is still no prohibition of duress against States in all forms (beyond the threat of military force). The exercise of economic and political pressure in order to force a treaty upon a weaker State is still a common practice in international relations.

The best-known examples are the Bilateral Immunity Agreements (BIAs) concluded by the United States with some 100 mostly indigent countries. These agreements seek to shield US citizens from the jurisdiction of the International Criminal Court (ICC) by providing that US government officials, military and other personnel, and US nationals, would not be transferred to the ICC by the contracting party. Countries were pressured into concluding the agreements by the threat of reduction of US Military Education and Training and Military Financing. Numerous States lost all US aid in the fiscal years 2004 and 2005 after refusing to

each other as right-holding single individuals. In the law of nations, a State is treated in the same way as an individual, as in private law the human being' (trans. by the author).

[13] Cf. WTO Appellate Body, *Japan – Taxes on Alcoholic Beverages* (4 October 1996) WT/DS8/AB/R, WT/DS10/AB/R, WT/DS11/AB/R, 15.

[14] H. Kelsen, *Principles of International Law*, 2nd edn. (New York: Holt, 1962), 464. See for the interwar period under the reign of the League of Nations' limitations on resort to war and the contractual prohibition of war by the 1928 Kellogg–Briand Pact, L. Oppenheim, *International Law*, 5th edn, vol. I (London: Longmans, Green & Co, 1937), 702–3 (§499)). Here Oppenheim relates that prior international law 'disregarded the effect of coercion in the conclusion of a treaty imposed by the victor upon the vanquished States', and that for States not bound by the contractual instruments 'there is room for the continuance of the traditional rule disregarding the vitiating effect of physical coercion exercised against a State'.

sign such an agreement.[15] US aid for States such as Benin and Lesotho was completely cut back, but was granted after these States signed the respective BIA.[16] The exercise of economic pressure such as with regard to the conclusion of the BIAs does not render any treaty resulting from it void.[17]

The international law of State responsibility has also been characterised as private-law like.[18] It serves to protect the rights of one State against infringements by others. So the concern of this body of rules is more the protection of 'subjective' individual rights and not of an 'objective' legality which would encapsulate a general public interest. In that respect, the law of international responsibility shares a dominant feature of private law, and is not like public law.

Publification or privatisation of international law?

Against the background of this traditional image of international law, two antagonistic legal trends can be discerned. On the one hand, international law is being publified, on the other hand, it seems to be moving ever more in the direction of private law.

Publification

Both the emergence of new public-law like features of the international legal order, and new readings of pre-existing structures have contributed to the perception of an ongoing publification of international law. And this publification is mostly welcomed as creating a *normativité renforcée* of that order.

One example for such a reconstruction is the feminist one. The feminist claim is that international law rests on and reproduces the dichotomy between the private and the public sphere because matters 'private' to States are considered to be within domestic jurisdiction, whereas matters of international 'public' concern are seen to be regulated by

---

[15] Overall, the US policy resulted in cut-back of development aid of an estimated $10 billion in 2005.

[16] All information on the BIAs is available at www.iccnow.org/?mod=bia.

[17] The 'Declaration on the Prohibition of Military, Political or Economic Coercion in the Conclusion of Treaties', Annex 1 of the Final Act of the Conference on the Law of Treaties (*ILM*, 8 (1969), 733) does not foresee the nullity of a treaty concluded under non-military coercion.

[18] A. Nollkaemper, 'Constitutionalization and the Unity of the Law of International Responsibility', *Indiana Journal of Global Legal Studies*, 16 (2009), 535–63, 542–3.

international law.[19] This approach actually reverses the traditional private law image of international law by proclaiming this body of law to be 'public' law *par excellence* and by questioning the distinction as such.

Beyond this reconstruction, a first tangible aspect of the publification of international law lies in the emergence and acknowledgement of hierarchy. The relations between international bodies (organisations, treaty bodies, agencies, courts, tribunals) and States are 'vertical' ones. These bodies are empowered to render reports, views, decisions and judgments which are in some instances legally binding, and in any case exert a serious compliance pull. Many of these legal texts are adopted in majoritarian proceedings and to that extent escape the consensual 'private law' paradigm. The novel types of international law-making, especially the practice of the global conferences of the 1990s, have therefore been characterised as 'law-making in the public interest'.[20]

A second and related aspect is the acknowledgement of *ius cogens* norms. Orakhelashvili (among others) asserts that 'one of the effects of the introduction of peremptory norms in the international legal system is that it partly transforms international law – a horizontal and consensual legal order – into a vertical system of law'.[21] Others, on the contrary, argue that *ius cogens* norms 'may not sweep everything away' and that these norms should not necessarily take formal precedence over other international rules, but should (only) function as interpretative guidelines.[22] But both views accept *ius cogens* as an expression of underlying values, or an international *ordre public*.

A third strand of publification lies in the distinction between bilateral treaties (including multilateral treaties of a bilateral type, consisting of a bundle of bilateral obligations) and collective treaties which cannot be divided into bilateral obligations. Assuming such a distinction, only the truly bilateral treaties are analogous to (private law) contracts. In contrast, collective treaties, such as human rights treaties, are concluded in the pursuit of a collective interest which transcends the individual

---

[19] H. Charlesworth, C. Chinkin and S. Wright, 'Feminist Approaches to International Law', *AJIL*, 85 (1991), 613–45, 625.

[20] J. Delbrück (ed.), *New Trends in International Lawmaking – International 'Legislation', The Public Interest* (Berlin: Duncker & Humblot, 1997). See also S. Peter, *The Idea of Public Interest in International Law* (PhD, Basel, 2009).

[21] A. Orakhelashvili, *Peremptory Norms in International Law* (Oxford University Press, 2006), 9. In that sense see also D. Shelton, 'Normative Hierarchy in International Law', *AJIL*, 100 (2006), 291–323.

[22] A. Bianchi, 'Human Rights and the Magic of Jus Cogens', *EJIL*, 19 (2008), 491–508, 503–5.

interests of the parties. They are therefore comparable to constitutions (public law) rather than to contracts (private law).

A fourth strand of 'publification' (or even 'constitutionalisation') concerns the traditional 'private-like' bilateral law of international responsibility as described above. This body of law has been publified most of all by eliminating the requirement of a legal injury as a condition for responsibility. According to the 2001 Articles of the International Law Commission on the Responsibility of States for Internationally Wrongful Acts,[23] international State responsibility can arise regardless of legal injury of any particular State, but out of 'objective' breaches of international law. Moreover, the acknowledgement of the rights of all States to invoke responsibility in case of breaches of norms protecting the collective interest (Art. 42 lit. b) and Art. 48(1) lit. b) ILC Articles), and the imposition of obligations on all States to respond to a serious breach of peremptory norms (Art. 41 ILC Articles) have added a stronger 'public law' dimension to the law of responsibility.[24]

Finally, the work of international organisations and courts has been opened for scrutiny by the public, mostly in response to civil society's pressure for transparency. Publicity is being achieved through the publication of working documents and through the admission of the interested public to certain meetings and court sessions. To a limited extent, the traditionally secret mode of negotiating diplomacy has been substituted by an open mode of deliberative governance. Overall, international law is becoming 'public' law in the dual sense of the word: a law not only in the global public interest, but also open to the public.

Privatisation

The contrary trend is the privatisation of international law. But the term 'privatisation' is in the international sphere as imprecise as in national law. It is used to designate four quite different things.

First, privatisation means the resort to private law instruments by public authorities, such as entering into contracts with citizens, creating corporations in order to deliver services and so on. In this weak variant of privatisation, public authorities remain public in substance, and merely rely on or make use of a private form.

[23] UN Doc. A/63/10.
[24] Nollkaemper, 'International Responsibility', *supra* n. 18, 545–9 (qualifying this evolution even as 'constitutionalization').

Second, 'privatisation' is used as a short-hand for the increase of (political) power of private actors. In that sense, globalisation is a gigantic privatisation, because it shifts power from States to markets. This power shift is most obvious where private actors take over formerly public functions, such as patrolling streets, controlling traffic, or running jails. This variant of privatisation is deep, because here the State and public authorities withdraw from activities that have traditionally been regarded as incumbent on the State. More and more often, privatisation in this sense is at the same time a transnational phenomenon, transgressing the boundaries between domestic and international. The most salient example are the private military and security contractors which support national armies abroad.[25]

On the international level, a specific variant of the rise to power of non-State actors is their recognition as at least partial subjects of international law. This means that these actors become the direct addressees and beneficiaries of international rules, ranging from human rights to investment protection.

Of course the public–private categories are fluid here as well. For instance, international investment law displays public law and private law features. An element of privatisation is present in the conclusion of so-called 'State contracts' between private investors and States.[26] These contracts are to some extent denationalised through their reference to and incorporation of international legal principles, and by the fact that they are enforceable by private actors before international investment tribunals. But investment arbitration is distinct from traditional commercial (private) arbitration, because the core of investment disputes are the State's powers to regulate investment, which the State claims to exercise in the national public interest.[27] The International Convention on the Settlement of Investment Disputes between States and Nationals of other States (ICSID) also differs from commercial arbitration, where two private parties agree freely on arbitrators because, in ICISD, the

---

[25] See on this issue the international code regulating the activities of private military and security companies, the Montreux Document of 17 September 2008, Annex to UN Doc. A/63/467-S/2008/636 (2008). See from the literature P. W. Singer, *Corporate Warriors. The Rise of the Privatized Military Industry* (Ithaca, NY: Cornell University Press, 2003).

[26] Steiner and Vagts, *Transnational Legal Problems, supra* n. 1, 495–513; U. Kischel, *State Contracts* (Stuttgart: Boorberg, 1992).

[27] G. van Harten, *Investment Treaty Arbitration and Public Law* (Oxford University Press, 2007), esp. 95–6.

State's consent is prospective, and because the arbitration can be triggered only by the investor.

Third, privatisation also can mean that private actors increasingly enact law in the form of general rules with effect for third parties.[28] Law-making in that sense is distinct from concluding contracts by which the contracting parties only bind themselves. The creation of such (general) norms is arguably a typically public function which from the traditional perspective is reserved for public authorities, precisely because it has effects on bystanders.

On the international plane, that third type of privatisation means that non-State actors participate in the creation of international law in various forms. Non-governmental organisations (NGOs) are observers and partly active participants in international conferences, organisations, and bodies, and thereby become, at least informally, co-law-makers. Transnational business actors adopt corporate codes of conduct. Representatives of entire industries elaborate technical, financial and book-keeping standards, often in collaboration with civil society representatives and governments.

Fourth, the term 'privatisation' is sometimes associated with the question whether a legal order contains different sub-fields called 'public law' and 'private law'. In those domestic orders which acknowledge the distinction, the rules called 'private law' are State-made, and come in the form of codes such as the French *Code Civil* or the German *Bürgerliches Gesetzbuch*. These private law codes provide the framework for private actors to conclude contracts, and thereby allow them to regulate their own affairs in an autonomous fashion. In contrast, private law generally does not allow those private actors to impose standards on others in the style of a legislator. Private autonomy, which is a fundamental element of the citizens' freedom, legitimises private contracting.

On the international plane, privatisation is mostly of the second and third type. The analytical questions arising here are which legal status private (economic or civil society) actors have and their effects on law-making. The normative question is whether they are legitimately entitled to make and to enforce international law. From the traditional

---

[28] For an interdisciplinary study on this issue, see A. Peters, L. Koechlin, T. Förster and G. Fenner Zinkernagel (eds.), *Non-State Actors as Standard Setters* (Cambridge University Press, 2009); from a private law perspective, see G. Bachmann, *Grundlagen ziviler Regelsetzung* (Tübingen: Mohr Siebeck, 2006).

perspective, private rule-making and enforcement can only be explained and justified as delegation by the State, whereas a legal pluralist approach considers non-State actors as original law-producers.

New structures within international law

It is the thesis of this chapter that international (or transnational or global) law has started to go through a process of *structural* differentiation. Structural as opposed to issue-specific differentiation means the emergence of transnational constitutional, administrative, private and criminal law.

The acknowledgement of these four structural branches provides a useful grid for refining the traditional, issue area-wise description of international law, ranging from the law of the sea and diplomatic relations over human rights law to international environmental and climate law. These issue-areas have been much expanding, have developed at unequal speed and have shaped different legal institutions. These dynamics, taken together with the establishment of specialised courts and tribunals, have even given rise to the fear of a fragmentation of international law[29] – a fear which might be alleviated by the insight that there is some order in the apparent chaos after all.

Constitutional law

Since the beginning of the twentieth century, scholars have suggested that there is something like an international constitution.[30] Seen from a less static and more dynamic perspective, one might say that, within international law, a special category of constitutional law is emerging.[31] However, it is difficult to exactly delineate and define this evolving special category.

---

[29] Raising the spectre of fragmentation, see G. Guillaume, 'The Future of International Judicial Institutions', *ICLQ*, 44 (1995), 848–62; but see for an optimistic assessment R. Higgins, 'A Babel of Judicial Voices', *ICLQ*, 55 (2006), 791–805.

[30] A. Verdross, *Die Verfassung der Völkerrechtsgemeinschaft* (Vienna: Julius Springer, 1926), preface; G. Scelle, *Précis de droit des gens. Principes et systématique, Deuxième Partie: Droit constitutionnel international* (Paris: Recueil Sirey, 1934), esp. 4, 9–11; H. Waldock, 'General Course on Public International Law', *RdC*, 106 (1962–II), 5, 7.

[31] J. Klabbers, A. Peters and G. Ulfstein, *The Constitutionalization of International Law* (Oxford University Press, 2009).

Relying on the classic notion of the State constitution as formulated by Emer de Vattel,[32] I submit that international constitutional law is a sub-set of fundamental international rules and principles which regulate the political activity and relationships in the global polity. Because of their material importance, these norms deserve the label 'constitutional'. They are not codified in one single document, but are dispersed in various treaties, 'soft' law texts and customary law. In particular, the UN Charter is not the World Constitution. The absence of a constitutional document means that international constitutional law cannot be easily identified through formal criteria. The distinction between constitutional law and other international law therefore hinges merely on the rules' substance and importance and is necessarily fuzzy. But this problem is well known from the British and other unwritten State constitutions.

Whether the international norms (rules and principles) of potential constitutional quality are superior to ordinary international norms, whether they are created by States or by other actors as well, whether they are always 'hard' legal norms, whether they embody a specific set of material principles, and whether they are 'constitutional' only to the extent that they are enforceable by some form of judicial review, warrants further reflection and debate.

Administrative law

Recent scholarship has identified a special branch of international (or transnational, or global) administrative law.[33] This branch of law has been defined 'as comprising the mechanisms, principles, practices, and supporting social understandings that promote or otherwise affect the

---

[32] '[L]e règlement fondamental qui détermine la manière dont l'Autorité Publique doit être exercée est ce qui forme la Constitution de l'Etat.' E. de Vattel, *Le droit des gens ou principes de la loi naturelle appliqués à la conduite et aux affaires de Nations et des Souverains* (London, 1758, repr. Washington, DC: Carnegie Institution, 1916), livre I, chap. III, §27 (in vol. 3, Engl. trans. p. 17). However, a global or transnational constitution cannot be gained by simply zoning up a typical State constitution. We must be aware of the problems of translation. This is one reason why the term 'constitutional law' is preferable to 'constitution'.

[33] See C. Tietje, *Internationalisiertes Verwaltungshandeln* (Berlin: Duncker & Humblot, 2001); S. Cassese, 'Administrative Law without the State? The Challenge of Global Regulation', *New York University Journal of International Law and Politics*, 37 (2005), 663–94; B. Kingsbury, N. Krisch and R.B. Stewart, 'The Emergence of Global Administrative Law', *Law and Contemporary Problems*, 69 (2005), 15–61; E. Schmidt-Aßmann, 'Die Herausforderung der Verwaltungsrechtswissenschaft durch die Internationalisierung der Verwaltungsbeziehungen', *Der Staat*, 45 (2006), 315–38.

accountability of global administrative bodies, in particular by ensuring they meet adequate standards of transparency, participation, reasoned decision, and legality, and by providing effective review of the rules and decisions they make'.[34] Transnational administrative law is said to resemble domestic administrative law to the extent that there are organisations vested with authoritative powers and adopting administrative decisions, and that there are judges empowered to settle disputes.[35]

But even the proponents of transnational administrative law do not draw a watertight line between the transnational public and the private realm. Sabino Cassese has particularly emphasised that the 'line between public and private is hardly clear at the global level'.[36] And Benedict Kingsbury and his collaborators count among the 'global administrative bodies' also 'hybrid public–private regulatory bodies, and some private regulatory bodies exercising transnational governance functions of particular public significance'.[37]

Moreover, core principles such as due process, proportionality, legality and transparency have a dual administrative and constitutional nature. Any administration should also generally be informed by constitutional values. It is therefore difficult to sharply distinguish global administrative law from global constitutional law.

Criminal law

International (or transnational) criminal law is concerned with the criminal responsibility of individuals flowing from international custom or treaty law. International conventions and even custom have defined certain crimes for centuries, but have remained more or less virtual and inconsequential until recently. Only with the establishment of international criminal tribunals and the International Criminal Court (ICC), and through more active prosecution by domestic courts, has international criminal law become a specific structural branch of international law. This branch does not exist in clinical isolation but depends on the sources and processes of general international law, and on the

---

[34] Kingsbury, Krisch and Stewart, 'Global Administrative Law', *supra* n. 33, 17. The authors define as 'global administrative action' rule-making, adjudication, and decision-making that is neither treaty-making nor simple dispute settlement.
[35] Cassese, 'Administrative Law without the State?', *supra* n. 33, 668.   [36] *Ibid.*, 669.
[37] Kingsbury, Krisch and Stewart, 'Global Administrative Law', *supra* n. 33, 17.

domestic criminal law of States.[38] In addition, international criminal law simultaneously derives from and continuously draws upon both international humanitarian law (IHL) and human rights law. Moreover, the enforcement of international criminal law depends first of all on domestic courts, acting as agents of the international community (the principle of complementarity). Therefore, most customary rules of transnational criminal law have primarily evolved from municipal case-law relating to international crimes, chiefly war crimes. Here the courts have derived numerous elements, notably the mental components of crimes, from the criminal laws of the nation-States. Antonio Cassese has therefore concluded that international criminal law 'is an essentially hybrid branch of law: it is public international law impregnated with notions, principles, and legal constructs derived from national criminal law, IHL as well as human rights law'.[39]

The emergence of international criminal law is another aspect of the publification of the old interstate law not mentioned so far. Formally, the establishment of criminal courts and tribunals introduces a strong element of hierarchy into international law. In substance, criminal law foresees the prosecution of crimes by a public prosecutor in the public interest, and punishment in order to achieve certain social objectives such as the prevention of crimes and the re-integration of perpetrators into society.

Antonio Cassese even perceives a major tension between traditional international law (what I call here transnational quasi-private law) and international criminal law, resulting from conflicting philosophies.[40] While interstate law is primarily concerned with reconciling the conflicting entities of sovereign entities, criminal law aims to punish individuals transgressing legal standards while at the same time safeguarding the rights of accused or suspect persons from arbitrary prosecution and punishment. In order to fulfil its purpose, interstate law needs quite a lot of flexibility, whereas criminal law, quite to the contrary, requires very detailed, clear and unambiguous rules, given that the fundamental rights of suspects are at stake. Consequently, the inherent requirements underlying transnational criminal law collide with the traditional characteristics of international law in its old form of 'private law writ large'.

---

[38] I. Bantekas and S. Nash, *International Criminal Law*, 3rd edn. (London: Routledge–Cavendish, 2007), 1–2. See on the 'transnational reach of criminal legislation', Steiner and Vagts, *Transnational Legal Problems, supra* n. 1, 854–931.

[39] A. Cassese, *International Criminal Law*, 2nd edn. (Oxford University Press, 2008), 7.

[40] *Ibid.*, 8–9.

The remainder of international quasi-private law

Which areas of international law remain private law-like? These are all fields where international law regulates interstate relations, such as the international rules of boundaries and on territorial status, the international law of treaties, and most of the international law of State responsibility. Along that line, Joseph Weiler has characterised bilateral treaties – for example, the classic friendship and navigation treaties – as '*private* bilateral arrangements'.[41]

However, the private law character even of bilateral treaties is ambiguous. Friendship and navigation treaties, free trade area agreements, or bilateral investment treaties, are 'microscopically ... indeed, bilateral private contracts among States. But telescopically, taken in aggregate they define a multilateral regime.'[42]

Crucially, is the private law analogy in interstate relations not fundamentally flawed if we take into account that, ideal-typically, private law intends to further private autonomy, whereas public law is intended to serve the general welfare? The flaw arises from the fact that States are – contrary to the individualistic metaphor pervading the discipline of international law – not individuals. States are – unlike natural persons – no end in themselves. They do not enjoy private autonomy in order to further their personal interests, but are moral persons established to facilitate and further the well-being of human beings. So States should act as representatives of their people, and are to that extent not 'private' actors.

However, this liberal conception of the State is not (yet) the one underlying international law. Although international organisations such as the United Nations, the OSCE and the OAS currently pursue a clear democratisation policy, non-democratic States are still accepted as international legal subjects, as treaty partners and as bearers of international legal responsibility.[43] The private law analogy therefore still corresponds to the structure of international law as it stands in all sub-fields where States act as unitary actors, meet on an equal footing, and are subjects of attribution, and where their rights and interests as moral persons are at stake.

---

[41] J. Weiler, 'The Geology of International Law – Governance, Democracy and Legitimacy', *ZaöRV*, 64 (2004), 547–62, 553, 554 (emphasis added).

[42] *Ibid.*, 554. See also S. W. Schill, *The Multilateralization of International Investment Law* (Cambridge University Press, 2009).

[43] Cf. J. d'Asprémont, *L'Etat non démocratique en droit international* (Paris: Pedone, 2008).

Critique of the new structural order

The re-ordering of international (or transnational) law into constitutional, administrative, criminal and quasi-private law faces objections. The first one is that the sub-division of the body of international law into constitutional, administrative, private and criminal is false, because international law is neither public nor private but 'simply "international"'.[44] Although there is merit in the warnings against false domestic analogies, this does not compel international lawyers to refrain from differentiations. The ongoing development and expansion of international law has transformed its rudimentary and oft-stated 'primitive' character. This development and refinement requires adequate conceptualisations. There is no need to invent new categories if existing ones help map the field. If the problem of translation is kept in mind, no harm is done.

The second important objection is that the categories suggested here are historically and geographically contingent.[45] Most famously, the Common law has been very reluctant to espouse a public law – private law distinction. The notion of English public law is specially contested, as if there were something un-English about public law.[46] One historical explanation for this reluctance is that the reception (or rather re-invention) of the ancient Roman distinction between *ius publicum* and *ius privatum* had not taken place on the British Isles in the same way as it had on the European continent.[47] Second, Albert Dicey, in his influential constitutional treatise, opposed the idea of an English public law and somewhat overstated the difference between English (Common) law and the French *droit administratif*.[48]

In that tradition, some administrative lawyers have argued against the need for a distinction between public and private law in the English legal

---

[44] A. Pellet, 'Can a State Commit a Crime? Definitely, Yes!', *EJIL*, 10 (1999), 425–34, 433.

[45] Seminally on the contingency of the public law–private law distinction, see M. Bullinger, *Öffentliches Recht und Privatrecht* (Stuttgart: Kohlhammer, 1968).

[46] M. Freedland, 'The Evolving Approach to the Public/Private Distinction in English Law', in J.-B. Auby and M. Freedland (eds.), *La Distinction du droit public et du droit privé. Regards français et britanniques* (Paris: éditions Panthéon-Assas, 2004), 101–20, 103.

[47] See on this re-invention, M. Stolleis, 'Öffentliches Recht und Privatrecht im Prozeß der Entstehung des modernen Staates', in W. Hoffmann-Riehm and E. Schmidt-Aßmann (eds.), *Öffentliches Recht und Privatrecht als wechselseitige Auffangordnung* (Baden-Baden: Nomos, 1996), 41–61, 45–51.

[48] A. V. Dicey, *Introduction to the Study of the Law of the Constitution* (London: Macmillan, 1959; repr. Indianapolis, IN: Liberty Fund, 1982), chapter XII 'Rule of law compared with *droit administratif*', 213–73.

system.[49] In contrast, other English authors maintain and defend the distinction.[50] Given that controversy, it cannot be said that the distinction between private law and public law is unknown in the Common law in order to use this as an argument against the viability of the distinction on the international plane.

The third objection is that especially the distinction between administrative and private law is notoriously problematic because the employed criteria (such as public interest versus private interests, or hierarchy versus horizontality) do not give rise to unequivocal results. For instance, in probably all modern codifications of private law, many public interests are endorsed, ranging from the protection of consumer and tenants to antidiscrimination. And private international law, formally adopted and developed by national law-makers, has the (global) 'public' function of regulatory ordering by effecting a regulatory system of distributed 'peer governance', whose objective is to reduce conflicts.[51] It is therefore unsurprising that some areas of domestic law – such as competition law, public procurement law, or intellectual property law – do not clearly fit into one of the categories, and are therefore treated either as a part of public law or as a part of private law in different jurisdictions.

A related aspect is that the current trends of liberalisation and privatisation mentioned above have further undermined the already fuzzy distinction between public and private law. Governments and bureaucracies increasingly make use of private law instruments and tools, ranging from new public management over benchmarking to auctions. All these considerations counsel against insisting on a clear-cut distinction between public and private law.

A fourth objection is that the erection of a new public–private split in transnational relations is backward-looking, runs counter to the modern trend and risks reduplicating artificial barriers that have already been overcome in domestic law. In that sense, the 'public/private classification'

---

[49] C. Harlow, 'Public and Private Law. Definition without Distinction', *Modern Law Review*, 43 (1980), 241–65. See further for an argument against the distinction between public and private law in English law, O. Dawn, *Common Values and the Public-Private Divide* (London: Butterworths, 1999). The author argues that both fields of law are about the control of power, are concerned to uphold authority and to protect the interests of good administration, and have to balance conflicting considerations (11). See also chapter 11 (248–66): 'There is no public–private divide.'

[50] Freedland, 'The Evolving Approach', *supra* n. 46, 115. Still, Freedland perceives an unduly deep split both at the practical or positive law and at the theoretical or doctrinal level.

[51] A. Mills, *The Confluence of Public and Private International Law* (Cambridge University Press, 2009), esp. 299, 308.

has been condemned as being 'wholly irrelevant to the organization of modern society', and as 'nothing more than an attempt by the judiciary to shield from public criticism some highly executive-minded decisions'.[52]

The final objection is the one to be expected by authors like Detlev Vagts, namely that the line between public and private law is especially fuzzy at the global level, and that this is exactly what the term 'transnational' seeks to signify.[53]

However, as demonstrated on pp. 160–3, the so-called erosion of the public and the private sphere is a complex issue which encompasses very different strands, especially on the global plane. It was right and important to call into question the existence of a bright and clear distinction. Moreover, the lasting analytical contribution of the concept of transnational law has been that it encompasses all kinds of law *not made* by States, and that it shifts the focus from the creators of legal rules to those rules' functioning and real effects. But the ongoing process of sophistication of international law now requires a fresh look. Generally speaking, the public law – private law distinction has not proven epistemically worthless and normatively undesirable, and should not be abandoned lightly. The fundamental reason is that this distinction reflects the difference between *iustitia distributiva* (to be realised through distributive policies) and *iustitia compensativa* (as realised in the private sphere and through the market).[54] It is therefore unsurprising that, in structural terms, differences between both areas of law concerning the regulatory objectives, the structure of interests involved, the steering conceptions and steering modes, the sanctions and the culture of implementation do persist in important jurisdictions.[55] The conclusion is that it might be worth considering keeping both fields of law distinct while legal techniques should be employed to facilitate their adequate interaction

---

[52] Harlow, 'Public and Private Law', *supra* n. 49, 256, 265.

[53] But note that the erosion of the public–private distinction is *not* mentioned as a characteristic feature of transnational economic law by C. Tietje and K. Nowrot, 'Laying Conceptual Ghosts of the Past to Rest. The Rise of Philip Jessup's "Transnational Law" in the Regulatory Governance of the International Economic System', in C. Tietje, A. Brouder and K. Nowrot (eds.), *Philip Jessup's Transnational Law Revisited. On the Occasion of the 50th Anniversary of its Publication* (Halle and Saale, Beiträge zum Transnationalen Wirtschaftsrecht 50, February 2006), 17–43, 28–9.

[54] Jansen and Michaels, 'Private Law and the State', *supra* n. 8, 62.

[55] See, for German law, W. Hoffmann-Riehm, 'Öffentliches Recht und Privatrecht als wechselseitige Auffangordnungen – Systematisierung und Entwicklungsperspektiven', in W. Hoffmann-Riehm and E. Schmidt-Aßmann (eds.), *Öffentliches Recht und Privatrecht als wechselseitige Auffangordnung* (Baden-Baden: Nomos, 1996), 261–337.

and mutual complementation. I submit that this should be the research programme for international (or transnational) law as well.

Conclusion: towards a new structural order

What is the epistemological and practical use of introducing or transplanting the categories of constitutional, administrative and criminal law into the international sphere? First, the acknowledgement of different structural branches of transnational (or international) law helps to identify the appropriate types of legal instruments and institutions for the different branches. For instance, international criminal law requires a public prosecutor, and arguably international climate law, forming part of international administrative law, requires a similar institution. In contrast, the enforcement of a bilateral visa regime can be left to the involved States.

Second, it is in this perspective conceivable that different principles apply in the different structural branches. For example, formality is not important in quasi-private interstate relations. In contrast, international criminal law must observe strict legality and formality, whereas this is somewhat less important in international administrative law (although not entirely negligible, because formality safeguards the accountability of the international administrative bodies). For this reason, it would be important to qualify the freezing of assets of individuals on the basis of UN Security Council antiterrorism resolutions either as a measure of criminal law or as administrative action. Depending on that qualification, a different set of rights accrues to the affected individual, and the presumption of innocence applies, or does not.

The reconstruction proposed here implies that international constitutional law furnishes the overarching principles which should serve as a guideline for the interpretation of all other international rules. But it also provides an argument against the overconstitutionalisation of international law. It leads to the insight that not all fields of international law suffer from similar legitimacy deficits and that not all fields equally need democratisation.

Third, the structural ordering acknowledges that, although the human being is the ultimate subject of all law, including international law,[56] individual interests are not equally affected in all areas of international

---

[56] G. Scelle, *Précis de Droit des Gens, Principes et Systématique*, vol. I, Introduction, le milieu intersocial (Paris: Sirey, 1932), 42: 'Les individus seuls sont sujets de droit en droit international public.' See also H. Kelsen, 'Les Rapports de Système entre le Droit Interne

law and by all types of international and transnational governance. International law also protects and should protect the national interest of States (which act ideally, but not always in reality as representatives of their citizens). Finally, international law protects and should even more strongly protect the (global) public interest which cannot in all situations be simply deduced from the sum of individual well-being, but which necessarily transcends individual preferences to some extent.[57]

This also means that sovereignty plays a different role depending on the structural branch of international law in question. In the private law-like areas, State sovereignty indeed plays a role akin to property.[58] Seen as analogous to private property, sovereignty allows States to exclude others from their territory, and to use and convey their territories (and those territories' inhabitants) at will. Sovereignty-as-property guarantees States a manoeuvring space and shields them against foreign interference. Crucially, sovereignty-as-property also shields the sovereign-owner from moral considerations, because a property right entitles the owner even to do immoral things, as long as she remains within her territorially limited domain. In contrast, in the more administrative law-like areas of transnational law, sovereignty must be conceived of as popular sovereignty, with the State acting as an agent or trustee. And this leads to the idea of sovereignty as engendering a responsibility to protect.

In the law of treaties, the distinction between private law-like treaties and public law-like treaties has important practical effects concerning the responses to breaches of treaties through adjudication or countermeasures.[59] One consequence is that with regard to multilateral treaties which only contain a bundle of parallel bilateral obligations (private law-like treaties), individual parties should be allowed to renegotiate their 'contract' as long as they do not affect the individual rights of other parties to that treaty. A defaulting State should be allowed to pay compensation instead of being forced to comply with the treaty if this engenders welfare

---

et le Droit International Public', *RdC*, 14 (1926/IV), 231–329, 281: 'L'idée qu'il y aurait entre l'État et les individus, et par suite d'État à État, des rapports qui ne seraient pas des rapports entre individus est une simple illusion, qui ne s'explique que par l'inadmissible hypostase de l'État en un surhomme.' J. L. Brierly, 'Règles Générales du Droit de la Paix', *RdC*, 58 (1936/IV), 5–237, 47: 'en dernière analyse, seuls les individus sont susceptibles d'être sujets de ce droit-là [i.e. international law].'

[57] This is the case notably with regard to the preservation of global commons, ranging from world peace over the climate and tropical forests to the humane genome.

[58] See the text accompanying nn. 8 and 9.

[59] For an excellent discussion, see J. Pauwelyn, 'A Typology of Multilateral Treaty Obligations. Are WTO Obligations Bilateral or Collective in Nature?', *EJIL*, 14 (2003), 907–52.

gains for the involved parties (the idea of an 'efficient breach'). In contrast, in the event of a breach of a genuinely collective (public law-like) treaty, a party breaching the contract should not be allowed to buy itself out of compliance through paying compensation, just as a perpetrator and a victim cannot settle on a crime because of the public interest in not having that breach or crime committed in the first place.

Overall, the account of emerging international constitutional, administrative, private and criminal law allows us to better understand the differences between some sub-areas, but also highlights commonalities between others. It helps to order the apparent chaos and thereby it is apt to alleviate the fear that the normative power of international law might be weakened by conflicting rules and contradictory judgments and decisions issued by the multiple international courts and bodies. The insights gained by the identification of different structural branches help us to appraise the current developments as normal and potentially even benign processes of differentiation rather than as malignant dispersion and as a source of conflict and confusion.

Most importantly, the reconstruction – or, rather, re-ordering – of international law suggested here enables legal analysts to resolve the current puzzle presented by the simultaneous existence of seemingly contradictory trends such as the erosion of sovereignty on the one hand *and* the unwavering importance of statehood on the other hand, and of 'privatisation' on the one side, *and* 'publification' on the other. These seemingly contradictory trends show a process of differentiation. The structural order proposed here might have some explanatory power and offers a normative guideline in that regard.

11

Founding myths, international law, and voting rights in the District of Columbia

SIEGFRIED WIESSNER[*]

Introduction

The idea of a self-governing people lies at the heart of the American experience.[1] It is deeply enshrined in the justification to the world for the abrupt breach, bloody indeed, with the British Empire. "Taxation without representation" is more than a bumper sticker or an inscription on a Washington license plate. It is the basis for the claim in the founding document of the United States, the Declaration of Independence,[2] for secession, the centerpiece of the nascent country's case to a "candid world" against King George III's "injuries and usurpations," including the rationale "for imposing Taxes on us without our Consent." As Thomas Jefferson penned, in his perennial prose, "[t]o secure these [unalienable] rights [among them Life, Liberty, and the pursuit of Happiness], Governments are instituted among Man, deriving their just powers from the consent of the governed."

---

[*] This chapter is based on the author's keynote address to the University of the District of Columbia Law Review's March 27, 2009 symposium on "The Struggle to Vote. The Right to Political Self-Determination in the District and Beyond." Detlev Vagts was born in Washington, DC.

[1] B. Bailyn, *The Ideological Origins of the American Revolution* (Cambridge, MA: Belknap Press of Harvard University Press, 1972 (original 1967)); R. Middlekauff, *The Glorious Cause. The American Revolution, 1763–1789* (Oxford University Press, 1985); G. S. Wood, *The Radicalism of the American Revolution* (New York: Alfred A. Knopf, 1992). The ideals of its democratic revolution have become a model for the world. G. S. Wood, *The American Revolution. A History* (New York: Modern Library, 2002); R. R. Palmer, *The Age of the Democratic Revolution, vol. I. The Challenge* (Princeton, NJ: Princeton University Press, 1959).

[2] C. L. Becker, *The Declaration of Independence. A Study on the History of Political Ideas* (New York: Harcourt, Brace & Co., 1922).

This was indeed a revolutionary statement, foreshadowed, in the American context, only by philosophers of natural rights and the Enlightenment movement in England and France and the colonies themselves.[3]

Surprisingly, though, the denial of statehood for the District of Columbia (DC) and the effective exclusion of its residents, citizens of the United States, from participating in the election of the legislative structures and functions of the Federal government has left a gaping hole in the implementation of the benefits promised by this original document – not unlike the equally great promise of an equally unalienable right, i.e., that "all men are created equal."

Domestic law

It is the US Constitution and the creation of a ten-square-mile Federal district that are blamed for the departure from this foundational myth. As to the composition of the US House of Representatives, Art. 1, section 2, clause 1 of the US Constitution mandates, in pertinent part:

> The House of Representatives shall be composed of Members chosen every second Year by the People of the several States . . .

As to the US Senate, Art. I, section 3, clause 1 provides:

> The Senate of the United States shall be composed of two Senators from each State . . .

The prevailing interpretation of these two provisions is that the members of both Federal legislative bodies have to come from the various States of the Union – i.e. be elected by the US citizens resident in the various States with qualifications as determined by the States.[4] This would exclude US

---

[3] Ch.W. Morris, "Natural Rights and Political Legitimacy," *Social Philosophy and Policy*, 22 (2005), 314–29.

[4] See, e.g., *Adams* v. *Clinton*, 90 F.Supp. 2d 35, 45–6 (DDC 2000), with further references, aff'd 531 US 941 (2000); *Banner* v. *United States*, 428 F.3d 303, 309, 312 (DCCir. 2005) (*per curiam*); J. Turley, "Too Clever by Half. The Unconstitutionality of Partial Representation of the District of Columbia in Congress," *George Washington Law Review*, 76 (2008), 305–74, 320–8; M.S. Scarberry, "Historical Considerations and Congressional Representation for the District of Columbia: Constitutionality of the DC House Voting Rights Bill in Light of Section Two of the Fourteenth Amendment and the History of the Creation of the District," *Alabama Law Review*, 60 (2009), 783–894; J.C. Fortier, "The Constitution Is Clear: Only States Can Vote in Congress," *Yale Law Journal Pocket Part*, 116 (2007), 403.

citizens resident in the District of Columbia, other Federal enclaves, and US territories, now mostly overseas, from representation in Congress.

The District of Columbia, in particular, was created as a location outside of the territory of any State to serve as the seat of the Federal government. This was done due to the twofold fears that: (1) the executive forces of the "hosting" State might not protect Congress against possible physical attack, as had happened in 1783 in Philadelphia[5]; and (2) that a State in which the Federal government was placed would have unacceptable advantages, in terms of both commercial prowess and political influence, over the other States.[6]

Congress alone controlled this "Federal district." As foreseen in the so-called District Clause, Art. I, section 8, clause 17, it has the power

> To exercise exclusive Legislation in all Cases whatsoever, over such District (not exceeding ten Miles square) as may, by Cession of particular States, and the acceptance of Congress, become the Seat of the Government of the United States, and to exercise like Authority over all Places purchased by the Consent of the Legislature of the State in which the Same shall be, for the Erection of Forts, Magazines, Arsenals, dock-Yards, and other needful Buildings.

The District of Columbia was established in 1790 by Congressional acceptance of cessions of land along the Potomac River by Virginia and

---

[5] The Continental Congress had met in 1783 in Philadelphia, where they were confronted by angry Revolutionary War veterans demanding their back pay, which was long overdue. When Congress asked Pennsylvania State officials to call out the State militia for their protection, the officials refused. See *Journals of the Continental Congress 1774–1789*, 25 (Washington, DC: Government Printing Office, 1922), 973 (1783). While this confrontation did not erupt into violence, it made Congress "flee, first to Princeton, NJ, then to Annapolis, and ultimately to New York City." J. Turley, "Right Goal, Wrong Means", *The Washington Post*, December 5, 2004, B8. This ignominious flight was still on the minds of the Framers when they met in Philadelphia again, in the summer of 1787, to draft the Constitution, and Madison, among others, called for the creation of a Federal district as the seat of the Federal government, which was "independent of any State and protected by federal authority"; only this solution could prevent "public authority" from being "insulted and its proceedings ... interrupted, with impunity." Turley, "Too Clever by Half," *supra* n. 4, 311 with further references.

[6] Even before the Constitution was proposed, there had been fierce competition over the site of the capital, as it was perceived that it would "confer massive wealth, power, and population upon the winning State." R. Chernow, *Alexander Hamilton* (New York: Penguin, 2004), 325; K. R. Bowling, *The Creation of Washington, DC. The Idea and Location of the American Capital* (Fairfax, VA and Lanham, MD: George Mason University Press, 1991). "No doubt those who fought to have the capital in their region sought not just financial gain but also the honor of hosting the federal capital and the prospect of having special influence on the federal government to further regional interests." Scarberry, "Historical Considerations," *supra* n. 4, 884.

Maryland[7] "to establish the capital city" between Alexandria and Georgetown.[8] When the capital was finally moved from Philadelphia to the Federal enclave of Washington, DC in December 1800 and Congress established its Federal jurisdiction over the District via the Organic Act of 1801,[9] the former residents of Virginia and Maryland living in the District lost their voting rights to the Federal legislature.[10] In 1846, the former territories of Virginia (Alexandria County) were ceded back to Virginia,[11] and citizens living there could now vote again as part of the Virginia electorate.[12] Washington, DC now consists solely of former territory of Maryland; its residents are still deprived of the right to vote for and be represented by a Congressperson of their choice.

The fight for their enfranchisement goes back to the beginning of the Union.[13] Its grounding in the founding myth of the US makes it particularly compelling.[14] Still, the hurdles to changes of the US Constitution are eminently high: a majority of two-thirds of the members of both houses is required, as well as three-fourths of the States.[15]

---

[7]   1788 Md. Acts 46, 13 Va. Statutes at Large, ch. 32, reprinted in DC Code Ann. §§33–34 (2001), including Alexandria County and Washington County, respectively.

[8]   Senator Orrin G. Hatch, "'No Right Is More Precious in a Free Country': Allowing Americans in the District of Columbia to Participate in National Self-Government", *Harvard Journal on Legislation*, 45 (2008), 287–310, 289. Actually, "[f]or the first 70 years, there were separate local governmental structures for Washington, Georgetown, and – until the retrocession of the Virginia portion of the District in 1846 – Alexandria." *Adams* v. *Clinton, supra* n. 4, 47, n. 19.

[9]   2 Stat. 103 (1801).

[10] *Adams* v. *Clinton, supra* n. 4, 47–56. DC residents still had voted in national elections in Virginia and Maryland, respectively, from 1790 to 1800. According to *Adams*, this was part of the territory's transition from being part of a State, whose residents could vote, to the status of the seat of Federal government, whose residents could not. The last act that completed this status change was the Organic Act of 1801. *Ibid.*, 62.

[11] Act of July 9, 1846, ch. 35, 9 Stat. 35.

[12] Fortier, "The Constitution Is Clear," *supra* n. 4, 105.

[13] Turley, "Too Clever by Half," *supra* n. 4, 334 *et seq.* (referencing criticism during the ratification debates such as New York leader Thomas Tredwell's statement that the non-voting status of DC residents "departs from every principle of freedom," *ibid.*, 334; and thereafter, e.g., Republican House Member John Smilie's 1801 objection that "the people of the District would be reduced to the level of subjects, and deprived of their political rights," quoted *ibid.*, 342).

[14] As the US District Court for the District of Columbia stated in *Adams* v. *Clinton*, there is a "contradiction between the democratic ideals upon which this country was founded and the exclusion of District residents from Congressional representation," 90 F.Supp. 2d, 72.

[15] Art. V, US Constitution (another process to amend, even more cumbersome, can be initiated by application of the legislatures of two-thirds of the States calling for a convention for proposing amendments, *ibid.*).

The claim for statehood for DC has not met with success; a constitutional amendment that would have granted DC residents full representation in the Senate and the House[16] passed the US Congress in 1978 by more than two-thirds majorities,[17] but garnered only sixteen States in the required time period ending in 1985.[18] The only constitutional change that passed was the 23rd Amendment allowing for the voting of DC citizens in presidential elections.[19]

Statehood for DC, another strong claim advanced by its residents – unlike, say, in Puerto Rico, a Federal territory whose people have defeated statehood proposals several times – is an option which did not meet with success either. The only action moving the ball forward was the passing of Congressional legislation in 1970 which, based on the District Clause mentioned above, allowed for the representation of DC (and, for that matter, Puerto Rico) by one delegate with floor privileges and office space who could be a member of, and vote in, House committees without restrictions,[20] and who could, since 1993, cast a vote in the committee of the whole – but only if her vote was not decisive – i.e. did not break a tie.[21]

Enter the 2009 Congress where full voting rights were intended to be given to representatives of DC in the District of Columbia House Voting Rights Act of 2009;[22] balanced by another representative from Utah, thereby

[16] District of Columbia Voting Rights Amendment, HRJ Res. 554, 95th Cong. §1 (1977).

[17] 125 Cong. Rec., 5272–73 (1978); 125 Cong. Rec., 27,260 (1978).

[18] E. Boyd, *District of Columbia Voting Representation in Congress. An Analysis of Legislative Proposals* (Congress Research Service, 2007), 6.

[19] Amendment XXIII, US Constitution. It was proposed by Congress on June 17, 1960 and ratified by the States on March 29, 1961. Its pertinent first section reads:

> The District constituting the seat of Government of the United States shall appoint in such manner as the Congress may direct: A number of electors of President and Vice President equal to the whole number of Senators and Representatives in Congress to which the District would be entitled if it were a State, but in no event more than the least populous State; they shall be in addition to those appointed by the States, but they shall be considered, for the purposes of the election of President and Vice President, to be electors appointed by a State; and they shall meet in the District and perform such duties as provided by the twelfth article of amendment.

[20] District of Columbia Delegate Act, Pub. L. No. 91–405, sec. 202, 84 Stat. 845, 848 (1970).

[21] Such voting was allowed for the delegates from DC, American Samoa, Guam, and the US Virgin Islands as well as Puerto Rico's resident commissioner. It is, at least in Turley's eyes, "entirely symbolic." He reports that this "rule was changed in 1994 but then reinstated again in 2007," with reference to Voting by Delegates and Resident Commissioner in Committee of the Whole, HR Res. 78, 110th Cong. (2007). Turley, "Too Clever by Half," *supra* n. 4, 307, n. 8.

[22] S. 160, 111th Cong. (2009).

increasing the number of House members from 425 to 427.[23] "Adorned" by a gun rights amendment inserted in the Senate version by Republican Senator Ensign (Nevada),[24] it still awaits final passage in the House of Representatives. Its constitutionality is at issue. The issue is whether the District Clause allows for such legislation increasing the membership of the House by representatives elected by citizens without links to a State,[25] or whether it empowers Congress only to govern the District rather than change its citizens' participation in the governance of Congress itself.[26] One argument, from Congressional practice, is that Congress allowed for the voting of US citizen military personnel stationed abroad;[27] the counter-argument is that these service members had their prior residence in a State of the United States, so the link to a State is still preserved.[28]

This link of Federal voting rights to residence in the States is particularly strong with respect to the Senate: this second Federal legislative chamber was created, in the Connecticut compromise of the Constitutional Convention, as the representative of the States in the making of federal law, which, under Art. VI, is the supreme law of the land – i.e. it prevails upon conflicting State law – if it remains within the ambit of the substantive legislative powers of the Federal government. Up to 1913, the ratification of the 17th Amendment,[29] the Senators were even chosen by the States' legislatures, not the States' people.[30] Thus, due to the respect owed a

---

[23] S. Rep. No. 110–123, 1–2 (2007), analyzing a similar bill introduced in the 110th Congress, the District of Columbia House Voting Rights Act of 2007, S. 1257, 110th Cong. (2007). For details of the legislative history, see Scarberry, "Historical Considerations," *supra* n. 4, 785, n. 3.

[24] Senator Ensign's amendment, passed by the US Senate by a vote of 62–36, would repeal much of DC's existing gun control legislation and severely restricts the District's authority to enact such legislation in the future. See 155 Cong. Rec., S2, 538 (daily edn. February 26, 2009). Due to opposition to the gun control amendment, the House has not yet taken action on S. 160. Scarberry, "Historical Considerations," *supra* n. 4, 785, n. 3.

[25] In the affirmative, Senator Hatch, *supra* n. 8, 297 *et seq.*

[26] Turley, "Too Clever by Half," *supra* n. 4, 350–2 (e.g. *ibid.*, 351: "Congress cannot ... use its authority over the internal operations of the District to change the District's political status *vis-à-vis* the States").

[27] Hearing on HR 1433 Before the H. Comm. On the Judiciary, 110th Cong. 8, 18 (testimony of Viet D. Dinh, co-authored by Adam H. Charnes), referring to Uniformed and Overseas Citizens Absentee Voting Act, Pub.L. No. 99–410, 100 Stat. 924 (1986).

[28] *Attorney-General of Guam* v. *United States*, 738 F.2d 1017, 1020 (9th Cir. 1984) (agreeing with calling the legislation a "reasonable extension of the bona fide residence concept").

[29] In pertinent part, Amendment XVII, section 1 provides: "The Senate of the United States shall be composed of two Senators from each State, elected by the people thereof ..."

[30] The original language of Art. I, section 3, clause 1 was: "The Senate of the United States shall be composed of two Senators from each State, *chosen by the Legislature thereof*" (emphasis added).

co-equal sovereign, the principle of federalism trumped the principle of democracy in the rationale for this second chamber.

Besides the District Clause, another argument has been advanced: the Equal Protection Clause, in its interpretation as guaranteeing the implied fundamental right to vote, should be extended to allow DC residents the right to vote as well via judicial interpretation[31] – similar to the protection of gender groups[32] when the Equal Rights Amendment foundered, and similar to the invalidation of the poll tax.[33] The problem is that any such judge-made extensions of the franchise did not arguably collide with an express provision of the Constitution that could be interpreted as a *lex specialis* compared to the Equal Protection Clause.

As it stands, US courts have upheld the denials of effective participation of DC residents in the making of national laws that affect them on the formal basis of the supremacy of the express text of the US Constitution over all other laws, even the equal protection clause of the 14th Amendment and its implied fundamental right to vote, key concepts of the very same document.[34] Art. I, section 2 and the District Clause in section 8, clause 17, the courts say, prevent the Congress and the courts from giving DC residents the fundamental democratic rights for which blood was shed in the creation of this country, the global standard bearer for democracy. These restrictions, clarified through the Organic Act of 1801,[35] it is said, cannot be lifted by Congress now.

Unfortunately, as the US Supreme Court implied in its most infamous decision, the *Dred Scott* case[36] igniting the Civil War, the Declaration of Independence is not a super-constitution that would outrank, legally

---

[31] J. B. Raskin, "Is This America? The District of Columbia and the Right to Vote," *Harvard Civil Rights–Civil Liberties Law Review*, 34 (1999), 39–97.

[32] J. B. Raskin, "Is There a Constitutional Right to Vote and Be Represented? The Case of the District of Columbia," *American University Law Review*, 48 (1999), 589–727, 697 (suggesting that the DC Voting Rights Amendment follow the example of the equally rejected Equal Rights Amendment: after the rejection, "the Court comes, through the independent evolution of equal protection jurisprudence, to adopt the very viewpoint of the rejected constitutional amendment"). For the latest, high standard of judge-made gender equal protection law, despite, or because of, the defeat of the ERA, see Justice Ginsburg's "exceedingly persuasive justification" requirement formulated in *United States* v. *Virginia*, 518 US 515 (1996).

[33] *Harper* v. *Virginia State Bd of Elections*, 383 US 663 (1996).

[34] The partial dissent in this case, however, would have held "that both *Article I* and principles of equal protection require this Court to declare that qualified residents of the District have a constitutional right to vote for voting representation in the House of Representatives." *Adams* v. *Clinton*, *supra* n. 4, 74 (J. Oberdorfer, dissenting).

[35] See *supra* n. 9.   [36] *Dred Scott* v. *Sandford*, 60 US 393 (1856).

prevail over, the positive law framework of the highest order, the Constitution of 1781.[37] In fact, according to this opinion, it could not have meant what it said.[38]

So, if progress in domestic legal systems, at least in the judicial branch, has ground to a virtual halt, a harder look might be given to the second legal system we are part of and said to be governed by – i.e. international law.

International law

Can it be the basis for an independent assessment of the legality of the status quo? At least, if we find some leeway for construction in the US Constitution itself, it could be bringing closer to full reality the shining light of the American Revolution: the quest for a government "of the people, by the people, and for the people."[39]

Looking at this body of law, we have to state that it is difficult to locate its relationship to domestic law – many countries envision the two legal systems as independent of each other, as two ships passing in the night.[40]

---

[37] "It is not the province of the court to decide upon the justice or injustice, the policy or impolicy, of these laws. The decision of that question belonged to the political or law-making power; to those who formed the sovereignty and framed the Constitution. The duty of the court is, to interpret the instrument they have framed, with the best lights we can obtain on the subject, and to administer it as we find it, according to its true intent and meaning when it was adopted." *Ibid.*, 405.

[38] "The general words above quoted [i.e. 'all men are created equal'] would seem to embrace the whole human family, and if they were used in a similar instrument at this day would be so understood. But it is too clear for dispute, that the enslaved African race were not intended to be included, and formed no part of the people who framed and adopted this declaration; for if the language, as understood in that day, would embrace them, the conduct of the distinguished men who framed the Declaration of Independence would have been utterly and flagrantly inconsistent with the principles they asserted; and instead of the sympathy of mankind, to which they so confidently appealed, they would have deserved and received universal rebuke and reprobation." *Ibid.*, 410.

[39] On November 1, 1863, President Abraham Lincoln proclaimed, in his famous address on the battlefield of Gettysburg, that "these dead shall not have died in vain – that this nation, under God, shall have a new birth of freedom – and that government of the people, by the people, for the people, shall not perish from the earth."

[40] W. M. Reisman, M. H. Arsanjani, S. Wiessner, and G. Westerman, *International Law in Contemporary Perspective* (Westbury, NY: Foundation Press, 2004), 122–5, as to the various permutations of monist and dualist theories of the relationship between international and domestic law.

Art. VI of the US Constitution provides some linkage, as it includes treaties as supreme law of the land.[41] The US Supreme Court has stated, however, that only self-executing treaties can be used as decision-making standards in domestic court,[42] and the definition of such has been significantly narrowed by the most recent *Medellín* decision.[43] On the other hand, customary international law can still be used as a decision-making standard in US court, as subsidiary Federal Common law,[44] although this idea is under attack as well.[45]

How, if at all, can international law, in particular these two main sources, address the situation at hand?

Before 1945, international legal claims of citizens against their government were virtually unknown. Rights were limited to the management of diplomatic protection of nationals abroad. Citizens were left with the legal remedies their governments offered them in domestic fora; there were virtually no rights or remedies against their own potentially and actually abusive governments outside the country, on the international level.

This situation changed dramatically after the Second World War, primarily driven by the experience of the *Shoah*, the Holocaust in Nazi Germany. A new, values-based international legal order was created, with human rights and self-determination at the center of its concern. The sovereign could no longer deal with its citizens as it pleased.

This process led to the recognition, under international law, of the pre-eminent prescriptive claims of the Declaration of Independence: the

---

[41] Art. VI, section 2, US Constitution: "This Constitution, and the Laws of the United States which shall be made in Pursuance thereof; and all *Treaties made, or which shall be made, under the Authority of the United States,* shall be the supreme Law of the Land; and the Judges in every State shall be bound thereby, any Thing in the Constitution or Laws of any State to the Contrary notwithstanding" (emphasis added).

[42] Chief Justice Marshall, in *Foster* v. *Neilson*, 27 US 253 (1829) introduced this previously unknown distinction; for details of the ensuing jurisprudence, see *Restatement (Third) of the Foreign Relations Law of the United States* §111, Reporter's Note 5 (1987); see also Reisman *et al., International Law in Contemporary Perspective, supra* n. 40, 1310 *et seq.*

[43] 128 S. Ct. 1346 (2008); for critical assessments by several authors, see 'Agora *Medellín*', *AJIL,* 102 (2008), 529–72.

[44] *Restatement (Third), supra* n. 42, §111, Reporter's Note 4; Reisman *et al., International Law in Contemporary Perspective, supra* n. 40, 123; M. N. Shaw, *International Law* (Cambridge: Grotius Publications, 1991), 118; J. J. Paust, *International Law as Law of the United States* (Durham, NC: Carolina Academic Press, 1996), 9.

[45] Cf. C. A. Bradley and J. L. Goldsmith, "Customary International Law as Federal Common Law. A Critique of the Modern Position," *Harvard Law Review,* 110 (1997), 815–76.

principle of self-determination of peoples, and the recognition of inalienable (human) rights of individuals. Let us look at these two concepts and evaluate what impact they might have on the situation in the District of Columbia.

The principle of self-determination

Self-determination, in the prevailing positivist paradigm, is a collective right, held by a community, referred to as a "people," which makes it anathema to some, while individual rights are held by individual human beings. Let us deal first with self-determination, as it was appropriately listed as the first right of humans in the International Covenant on Civil and Political Rights (ICCPR) of 1966: ultimately all of these entitlements against the State have the objective of allowing human beings the full range of self-realization – within a group, the family, the State, or individually.

Self-determination is commonly divided into two aspects: an external one, and an internal one. As far as the *external* aspect is concerned, it is considered a right of colonial peoples, albeit within the confines of *uti possidetis* and the procedures of the United Nations. Beyond colonized peoples, the Canadian Supreme Court, in its famed Reference on the Secession of Québec,[46] suggested that "oppressed peoples" may also hold such a right "where a definable group is denied meaningful access to government to pursue their political, economic, and cultural development."[47] This issue became relevant in the context of the disintegrating former Yugoslavia, where recognition of seceding entities was often made dependent upon compliance with the principle of *uti possidetis*, with the possible exception of Kosovo, the lawfulness of whose declaration of independence was the issue of an Advisory Opinion of the International Court of Justice (ICJ).[48]

In our context, however, the context of DC, such remedy, secession from the United States, is generally not sought. What has been sought,

---

[46] Reference Re Secession of Québec, August 20, 1998, reprinted in *ILM*, 37 (1998), 1340–77, 1373.
[47] *Ibid.*, para. 138. The Supreme Court left open the issue whether this is actually an accepted international legal standard.
[48] "Accordance with International Law of the Unilateral Declaration of Independence by the Provisional Institutions of Self-Government of Kosovo," UN General Assembly Request for Advisory Opinion, October 10, 2008; Advisory Opinion of 22 July 2010, text available from the ICJ website, www.icj-cij.org.

however, by an important segment of the US citizens resident in DC, is statehood – i.e. under the choices available to qualifying peoples in the decolonization context according to UN General Assembly resolutions 1514 and 1541[49] – if it were applicable, "full integration" into the colonizing State, in this case possibly statehood and full voting rights in Federal elections. Still, as the people of DC cannot be considered a colony of the United States, the UN decolonization procedures do not apply.

The other issue is whether the *internal* aspect of self-determination of peoples would be of help – i.e. the granting of some sort of autonomy. Such form of self-government has been recognized for the special category of indigenous peoples in the 2007 UN Declaration on the Rights of Indigenous Peoples[50] – a document which, although not formally legally binding, exacts "maximum compliance" from States[51] and partially reflects or engenders pertinent customary international law.[52] Articles 3 and 4 of that document provide for indigenous peoples' self-government in their local and internal affairs. The reason for this is the necessity of preservation and development of their traditional cultures which are inextricably linked to their age-old forms of internal decision-making. Article 5, in addition, gives indigenous people the choice to "participate fully, if they so choose," in the "political, economic, social, and cultural life of the State." This provision might argue for, at least, a full international legal right to participate in the democratic procedures of the modern State. Alas, the US citizens resident in the country's capital cannot, by any stretch of the definition, be considered "indigenous peoples." Thus, the collective right of self-determination, whether of peoples in general or of indigenous peoples in particular, is of no help to the dwellers of DC.

---

[49] UN General Assembly resolutions 1514(XV) (14 December 1960) and 1541(XV) (15 December 1960).

[50] United Nations Declaration on the Rights of Indigenous Peoples, GA res. 61/295, Annex, UN Doc. A/RES/61/295 (13 September 2007).

[51] Clarification by United Nations Office of Legal Affairs on the Legal Status of General Assembly Declarations, Report of the Commission on Human Rights, UN Doc. E/3616/ Rev. l, para. 105, 18th session, Economic and Social Council, 19 March–14 April 1962, United Nations, New York.

[52] S. J. Anaya and S. Wiessner, "The UN Declaration on the Rights of Indigenous Peoples. Towards Re-Empowerment," *Jurist*, 3 October 2007, http://jurist.law.pitt.edu/forumy/ 2007/10/un-declaration-on-rights-of-indigenous.php. See also S. Wiessner, "Indigenous Sovereignty: A Reassessment in Light of the UN Declaration on the Rights of Indigenous Peoples," *Vanderbilt Journal of Transnational Law*, 41 (2008), 1141–76.

Individual human rights: the right to vote

There remains the realm of individual rights and, in particular, the international legal right of citizens to vote. The right to vote can be considered, in many ways, the most exalted right: the right that does not only require the government to stay out of one's affairs (a negative right, right of *status libertatis*), or that forces the government to provide individuals with something (a positive right, right of *status positivus*); it affirms in the post-Westphalian democratic nation-State, the ideal that the individual *is* the government (right of *status activus*). The right to vote, at least in national elections, is exclusively reserved to citizens,[53] and is their most treasured right. Even if, in most cases, individual citizens are not allowed to make substantive decisions, they most of the time affirm a constitution that sets up a legal system and structures of authority which act for them, subject to periodic re-election and possible recall.

Thus, Art. 21(1) of the first universal human rights instrument, the 1948 Universal Declaration of Human Rights,[54] spells out that "[e]veryone has the right to take part in the government of his country, directly or through freely chosen representatives." Art. 21(3) affirms that "[t]he will of the peoples shall be the basis of the authority of government; this will shall be expressed in periodic and genuine elections which shall be by universal and equal suffrage." This document, seen by many in various respects as reflective of customary international law, is now being enforced through the universal periodic review procedure of the UN Human Rights Council,[55] which envisions that by 2011, and beyond that, every four years, every Member State of the United Nations will have been reviewed for compliance with, *inter alia*, these standards in an interactive process involving State reports, NGOs, treaty-monitoring bodies, etc.

Clearly binding, for every ratifying State, is the 1966 ICCPR, mentioned *supra*, which states in Art. 25(2) that "[e]very citizen shall have the right and the opportunity, without any of the distinctions mentioned in Article 2 . . . and *without unreasonable restrictions*: (a) to take part in the

---

[53] S. Wiessner, *Die Funktion der Staatsangehörigkeit* (Tübingen: Tübingen University Press, 1989), 396–7.

[54] Adopted by UN General Assembly res. 217A (III) (10 December 1948).

[55] Human Rights Council, Annex to res. 5/1 of 18 June 2007 – United Nations Human Rights Council: Institution Building (Universal Periodic Review Mechanism), http://ap.ohchr.org/documents/E/HRC/resolutions/A_HRC_RES_5_1.doc.

conduct of public affairs, directly or through freely chosen representatives; (b) to vote and be elected at genuine periodic elections which shall
be by universal and equal suffrage" (emphasis added).

The UN Human Rights Committee, in its pertinent General Comment
No. 25 (1996), states, in para. 5, that Art. 25(2)(a) "covers all aspects
of public administration, and the formulation and implementation of
policy at international, national, regional, and local levels."[56] Para. 4
allows only for "objective and reasonable restrictions,"[57] while para. 22
recommends that "State reports should describe laws and procedures
which ensure that the right to vote can in fact be freely exercised by *all*
citizens" (emphasis added).[58]

While the United States has ratified the Covenant, it has attached
a declaration according to which the substantive guarantees of the
treaty were to be considered non-self-executing – i.e. not legal standards
that can be used as such in American courts.[59] Still, the UN Human
Rights Committee is charged with monitoring the performance of each
Member State under the Covenant, including the United States' record
of compliance. The Human Rights Committee has indeed addressed
the issue. It noted, in para. 36 of its Concluding Observations on the
Second and Third Report of the United States, issued on 18 December
2006:

> The Committee, having taken note of the responses provided by the delega-
> tion, remains concerned that residents of the District of Columbia do not
> enjoy full representation in Congress, a restriction which does not seem to be
> compatible with article 25 of the Covenant.
>
> The State party should ensure the right of residents of the District of
> Columbia to take part in the conduct of public affairs, directly or through
> freely chosen representatives, in particular with regard to the House of
> Representatives.[60]

---

[56] Human Rights Committee, General Comment 25 (57), adopted by the Committee at its
1510th meeting, UN Doc. CCPR/C/21/Rev.1/Add.7 (1996), para. 5.

[57] *Ibid.*, para. 4 ("Any conditions which apply to the exercise of the rights protected by
article 25 should be based on objective and reasonable criteria," an example being the
setting of a minimum age for voting.)

[58] *Ibid.*, para. 22.

[59] The United States declared, at the time of its ratification of the ICCPR on June 8, 1992,
that "the provisions of articles 1 through 27 of the Covenant are not self-executing."
United Nations Treaty Collection, Status as at 18 September 2009, International
Covenant on Civil and Political Rights.

[60] Human Rights Committee, Concluding Observations on the Second and Third Reports
of the United States of America, UN Doc. CCPR/C/USA/CO/3/Rev.1 (18 December
2006), para. 36.

The 2003 Inter-American Commission on Human Rights Report No. 98/03: Statehood Solidarity Committee v. United States

Another avenue of some potential international legal redress is the Inter-American human rights system. As the United States has not ratified the Inter-American Convention on Human Rights, the only pertinent standards come, strictly speaking, from the American Declaration of Human Rights   in particular, its Art. XX, which reads:

> Every person having legal capacity is entitled to participate in the government of his country, directly or through his representatives, and to take part in popular elections, which shall be by secret ballot, and shall be honest, periodic and free.[61]

In fact, on 1 April 1993, Mr. Timothy Cooper, on behalf of DC's Statehood Solidarity Committee, petitioned the Inter-American Commission on Human Rights to conclude that the United States was responsible for violations of Art. II (right to equality before law)[62] and XX (right to vote and participate in government).[63] More than ten years later, on 29 December 2003, the Commission did in fact conclude "that the State [i.e. the United States] is responsible for violations of the Petitioners' rights under Arts. II and XX of the American Declaration by denying them an effective opportunity to participate in their federal legislature."[64]

On the merits,[65] the Petitioners claimed that, as a consequence of having no effective vote in the US legislature, they have no right to legislative, budgetary, or full judicial autonomy that citizens of States have – in their view a violation of Art. II.[66] They also suggest that the

---

[61] American Declaration of the Rights and Duties of Man, adopted by the Ninth International Conference of American States, Bogotá, Colombia, 1948, www.cidh.org/Basicos/English/Basic2.American%20Declaration.htm.

[62] Ibid., Art. II: "All persons are equal before the law and have the rights and duties established in this Declaration, without distinction as to race, sex, language, creed or any other factor."

[63] Inter-American Commission on Human Rights, Report No. 98/03, Case 11.204, Statehood Solidarity Committee v. United States, December 29, 2003, para. 1.

[64] Ibid., para. 117.

[65] The report deals at length with contested issues such as the exhaustion of domestic remedies. Ultimately, the Commission affirmed its jurisdiction and declared the case admissible. For the purposes of this chapter, only the decision on the merits will be reviewed.

[66] Ibid., para. 41.

District's status now may be motivated by an "animus against a particular racial group" as the population of DC "has now evolved to encompass a majority of African American citizens." The appropriate test for
such differential treatment under Art. II, it is presented, is whether it is
"reasonable," irrespective of motive or intent.[67] Here the distinction is
claimed to be "unjustified and arbitrary," and that there is "no relationship between the means employed and the aim sought to be realized," as
the fears of the Founding Fathers relating to the physical security of the
Federal seat of government are unjustified today, in the light of the
present-day military capabilities of the United States. As the US
Department of Defense, in 1994, employed 1,607,844 men and women
in the Armed Services of the United States, it was "impossible to imagine"
that the people of DC "could conceivably pose a viable threat to the seat
of government."[68]

They also contend that they are "denied representation in their country's
government through freely elected representatives contrary to Article XX of
the Declaration." By having no meaningful representation in the US House
of Representatives and none at all in the US Senate they are "excluded from
participating in national and international policy-making decisions" and
cannot vote through their representatives on key issues such as "tax policies,
economic plans, and health care legislation."[69] Also, the United States stands
alone in the Western hemisphere in not allowing their citizens resident in a
Federal district capital full voting rights in national elections.[70]

The US government contends that the decision of the drafters of the
Constitution to make the capital a "separate enclave rather than a state"
was "not motivated by animus against a group of citizens, nor did it
reflect an effort to disenfranchise its residents." It rather was "a consequence of a federal structure of the United States, of the division of
responsibilities between the States and the federal government, and,
more specifically, of the desire to protect the center of federal authority
from undue influence of the various States,"[71] including the concern that
"residents of the District might enjoy disproportionate influence on
government affairs by virtue of their contiguity to, and residence
among members of the national government."[72] It is geography and
the Federal system of government that motivate the special status of
DC residents rather than individual characteristics such as race which
would bring into play Art. II.

---

[67] *Ibid.*, para. 42.   [68] *Ibid.*, para. 43.   [69] *Ibid.*, para. 44.
[70] *Ibid.*, para. 45.   [71] *Ibid.*, para. 52.   [72] *Ibid.*, para. 53.

As to Art. XX, the US government contends that it does not specify the "modalities of participation in government" – such as decisions on proportionate or majority election systems, parliamentary or presidential structures of government, or federalism. Those "matters relating to governmental structure ought to be determined by the citizens of each nation."[73] This domestic discretion ought to apply to the US decision that "only States shall be directly represented in the House of Representatives and Senate and that the seat of the federal government shall not be a State."[74] This decision also does not mean that DC residents are excluded from the political process in the United States voting, as they are, in presidential elections, electing a mayor and city council, and choosing a non-voting delegate in the US House of Representatives with "floor privileges, office space, committee assignments and committee voting rights," as well as "electing two non-voting senators and one non-voting representative whose roles are to advocate the cause of statehood."[75]

Finally, the US government reiterates, the matter involves "delicate issues of constitutional law and federal structure that call into question the very organization of the United States" and therefore should be left in the realm of political debate and decision-making.[76]

The Commission starts its discussion of the merits with a reaffirmation[77] of its statement in *Aylwin Azocar et al.* v. *Chile*[78] that "there is a conception in the inter-American system of the fundamental importance of representative democracy as a legitimate mechanism for achieving the realization of and respect for human rights; and as a human right itself, whose observance and defense was entrusted to the Commission."[79] Thus, the Commission concludes, the provisions of the American Declaration that guarantee political rights, including Art. XX, "must be interpreted and applied so as to give meaningful effect to [the] exercise of representative democracy in this the hemisphere."[80]

Also, in a key leap, the Commission states that "insights regarding the specific content of Article XX of the Declaration can properly be drawn

---

[73] *Ibid.*, para. 55. [74] *Ibid.* [75] *Ibid.*, para. 56.
[76] *Ibid.*, para. 57. [77] *Ibid.*, para. 86.
[78] Case 11.863, Report No. 137/99, Annual Report of the Inter-American Commission of Human Rights 1999, 536.
[79] *Ibid.* [80] Report No. 98/03, *supra* n. 63, para. 87.

from Article 23 of the American Convention [on Human Rights] and the Commission's previous interpretation of that provision."[81]

In its prior interpretations of Art. 23, the Commission had recognized that "a degree of autonomy must be afforded to States in organizing their political institutions so as to give effect to these rights, as the right to political participation leaves room for a wide variety of forms of government."[82] "This does not mean, however," the Commission continues, "that the conduct of States in giving effect to the right to representative government, whether by way of constitutions or otherwise, is immune from review by the Commission."[83]

Referring to a "similar" statement by the UN Human Rights Committee on the limits to its Art. 25,[84] the Commission reaffirmed that its role is "to ensure that any differential treatment in providing for this right lacks [probably meant: does not lack] any objective and reasonable justification." It also stated its agreement with the case-law of the European Court of Human Rights on its pertinent guarantee, Art. 3 of Protocol I to the European Convention which, in the case of *Mathieu-Mohin and Clerfayt*,[85] a complaint against Belgian legislation placing linguistic restrictions on minority language groups' representation in governmental bodies, allowed for a "wide margin of appreciation" for States in implementing this right while the restrictions must not "curtail the rights in question to such an extent as to impair their very essence

---

[81] *Ibid.* This provision reads in full:

> *Article 23. Right to Participate in Government*
>
> 1. Every citizen shall enjoy the following rights and opportunities:
>   a. to take part in the conduct of public affairs, directly or through freely chosen representatives;
>   b. to vote and to be elected in genuine periodic elections, which shall be by universal and equal suffrage and by secret ballot that guarantees the free expression of the will of the voters; and
>   c. to have access, under general conditions of equality, to the public service of his country.
> 2. The law may regulate the exercise of the rights and opportunities referred to in the preceding paragraph only on the basis of age, nationality, residence, language, education, civil and mental capacity, or sentencing by a competent court in criminal proceedings.

American Convention on Human Rights, 22 November 1969, OAS Treaty Series No. 36, 1144 United Nations Treaty Series 123, entry into force 18 July 1978, Art. 23.

[82] *Ibid.*, para. 88.   [83] *Ibid.*, para. 89.   [84] *Ibid.*, para. 90, n. 85 and para. 93, n. 95.

[85] European Court of Human Rights, Case of *Mathieu-Mohin and Clerfayt* v. *Belgium*, No. 9/1985/95/143 (28 January 1987).

and deprive them of their effectiveness; that they are imposed in pursuit of a legitimate aim and that the means employed are not disproportionate. In particular, such conditions must not thwart "the free expression of the opinion of the people in the choice of the legislature."[86] They must also be assessed "in the light of the political evolution of the country concerned."[87]

Applying these standards to the DC context, the Commission, in light of its finding that the vote of the DC delegate in the US House of Representatives "has no chance of affecting the ultimate result of matters coming before the Committee [of the Whole] and is therefore 'meaningless,'" as the US courts themselves have proclaimed,[88] states that it "cannot accept this arrangement as providing the Petitioners with effective participation in their legislature."[89]

In fact, to the extent that the Petitioners do not have the "right to vote for a representative in their national legislature who has an effective opportunity to influence legislation considered by Congress," they have been denied "an equal right under law" in the sense of Art. II of the Declaration, and their rights under Art. XX have been restricted.[90] As far as the allegations of racially discriminatory intent are concerned, the Commission did not find itself "adequately briefed" so as to allow for a "specific determination."[91]

The restrictions on the Petitioners' rights, however, to participate in their national legislature "have been curtailed in such a manner as to deprive [them] of the very essence and effectiveness of that right, without adequate justification being shown by the State for this curtailment."[92]

First, the Commission examines the Petitioners' claim in the light of the political structure of the United States, taking into account the federal allocation of legislative powers, and the US Congress' "extensive powers to consider and enact legislation in areas such as taxation, national defense, foreign affairs, immigration and criminal law" as well Congress' total "legislative control over the District."[93] Despite the Congress' exercising this "expansive authority over the Petitioners," it

---

[86] *Ibid.*, para. 52.   [87] *Ibid.*

[88] The Commission refers to the US District Court for the District of Columbia's statement to that effect in *Michel* v. *Anderson*, 817 F.Supp. 126 (DDC 1993), aff'd 14 F.3d 623, 304 US App. DC 325 (CADC 1994). The District Court had opined: "In a democratic system, the right to vote is genuine and effective only when, under the governing rules, there is a chance, large or small, that, sooner or later, the vote will affect the ultimate result. The votes of the Delegates in the Committee of the Whole cannot achieve that; by virtue of Rule XXIII they are meaningless." *Ibid.*, 147–8.

[89] Report No. 98/03, *supra* n. 63, para. 97.   [90] *Ibid.*, para. 98.   [91] *Ibid.*

[92] *Ibid.*, para. 101.   [93] *Ibid.*, para. 102.

is "in no way effectively accountable to the Petitioners or other citizens residing in [DC]," thus depriving them "of the very essence of representative government namely that title to government rests with the people governed."[94]

As to the original justifications for this denial – i.e. the concern that the seat of the Federal government "may be disproportionately threatened, or the position of a State correspondingly enriched, by placing Congress within a State,"[95] the Commission points out that it has to interpret the Declaration "in the context of current circumstances and standards." It states that "[n]ot only has the State failed to offer any present-day justification for the denial of effective representation in Congress," but "modern developments" within the United States and in this hemisphere "more broadly indicate that the restrictions imposed by the State . . . are no longer reasonably justified."[96]

The US Government's judicial branch has "specifically concluded" that the historical rationale for the District Clause "would not today require the exclusion of District residents from the Congressional franchise," accepting that "denial of the franchise is not necessary for the effective functioning of the seat of government."[97] The justifications proffered were just seen as anachronistic. Also, the Equal Protection Clause of the US Constitution and its one-person, one-vote principle, according to US courts again, does not justify the aforementioned restrictions; it is only overcome by the limitation's location in the Constitution itself.[98] The American Declaration, however, "prescribes no similar limits or qualifications upon the guarantees of the rights under Articles II and XX"; its standards apply to all municipal law, "including its constitutional provisions."[99]

The Commission also "considers it significant" that no other Federal State in the Western hemisphere today denies the citizens resident in their nation's capital the right to vote in national elections.[100] This goes for the City of Ottawa, which is part of the Province of Ontario,[101] as well as for the residents of the City of Buenos Aires, Argentina;[102] Brasilia,

---

[94] *Ibid.*, para. 103.   [95] *Ibid.*, para. 104.   [96] *Ibid.*, para. 105.

[97] *Ibid.*, para. 106, referring to *Adams* v. *Clinton, supra* n. 4, 66. See also *Adams*, 50 ("It is . . . true . . . that the historical rationale for the District Clause – ensuring that Congress would not have to depend upon another sovereign for its protection – would not by itself require the exclusion of District residents from the congressional franchise").

[98] *Ibid.*, referring to *Adams* v. *Clinton*, 66 *et seq.*   [99] *Ibid.*   [100] *Ibid.* para. 108.

[101] Constitution Act 1867 (Canada), sections 32, 37, 40, First Schedule, Item 38.

[102] Constitution of the Nation of Argentina (1994), Title II, sections 125–9; C. W. Harris, *Congress and the Governance of the Nation's Capital. The Conflict of Federal and Local Interests* (Washington, DC: Georgetown University Press, 1995), 255.

Brazil;[103] Caracas, Venezuela;[104] and Mexico City, Mexico[105] – all of them federal districts or enclaves, but still enjoying full voting rights to their national legislatures.

A caveat ends the report: in order to comply with Arts. II and XX of the Declaration, the US government need not necessarily grant the Petitioners "the same means or degree of participation as residents of States in the United States."[106] These provisions only mandate that the Petitioners be granted "the opportunity to exercise a meaningful influence on those matters considered by their governing legislature, and that any limitations and restrictions on those rights are justified by the State as reasonable, objective and proportionate, taking due account of the context of its political system."[107]

While this is "generally achieved through the election of representatives . . . who may cast a vote on matters before the legislature that has a meaningful possibility of affecting the outcome of those deliberations," "the mechanisms through which the State may afford these opportunities are clearly a matter for the discretion of the State concerned."[108]

Expressis verbis, thus, the Commission does not require that the DC's resident US citizens be given the right to vote for a representative of their choice with full voting powers in the House. As the status quo is, however, declared in violation of the Declaration, there is no other way imaginable to comply with this provision in the political context of the US House of Representatives as the legislative body representative of the people of the United States. National discretion here appears to be reduced to zero: the principle of democracy is the only constitutional guiding light undergirding this body. The US Senate, however, might be a different story, as it was conceived, in the Founders' grand Connecticut Compromise, as a device to provide to the Federal legislative process the input of the States – as second legislative chambers are in various countries to give a special voice to territorial components of federations, be they called States, provinces, *Länder* or regions, or to influential social

---

[103] Constitution of the Federative Republic of Brazil (1999 as amended), ch. V, section 1, Art. 32; Harris, *Congress and the Governance of the Nation's Capital, supra* n. 102, 255.

[104] Constitution of the Bolivarian Republic of Venezuela (1999), Title II, Arts. 16–18; Title IV, Art. 186; Harris, *Congress and the Governance of the Nation's Capital, supra* n. 102, 245.

[105] Political Constitution of the United Mexican States (1917, with reforms to 1998), Title II, Arts. 53, 54, 56; Title V, Arts. 122–9; Harris, *Congress and the Governance of the Nation's Capital, supra* n. 102, 245.

[106] *Ibid.*, para. 110.   [107] *Ibid.*   [108] *Ibid.*

groups or institutions. One idea behind such bicameral schemes is to alleviate the specter of the tyranny of the majority.[109] The original design of the US Senate, in particular, was based at least as much on the bedrock principle of federalism as it was on the concept of democracy. This political context of the community of the United States of America, namely its constitutive idea of dual sovereignty, would thus appear to allow a rationale for the exclusion of citizens not linked, by residence, to a particular State from voting for members of this second chamber. On the other hand, the 17th Amendment mandating direct election of its members by the people of the various States rather than by State legislatures[110] has moved the scales markedly in the direction of the democracy rationale.

Finally, international law might also require the granting of such voting rights if it is found, by evidence of very widespread State practice and *opinio juris*, on a global level, that the right to vote has joined the range of human rights under customary international law and that residency in the capital is no longer considered a reasonable ground for exclusion from the franchise to determine who represents a country's citizens at the level of the national government. Such an inquiry, however, is beyond the confines of this chapter.

Appraisal

The Federal judiciary of the United States, the one branch structurally transcending the pressures of the day, ideally the last refuge for minorities of any kind, is quite uncomfortable with the exclusion of full citizenship rights for DC's residents. In fact, in various key decisions it articulates this split feeling.[111] As summarized in *Adams* v. *Clinton*,[112] "many courts have found a contradiction between the democratic ideals upon which America was founded and the exclusion of District residents from congressional representation. All, however, have concluded that it is the Constitution and judicial precedent that create the contradiction."[113] The court in *United States* v. *Thompson*[114] concluded: "[F]or residents of the District, the right to vote in congressional

---

[109] Cf. G. Tullock, "Problems of Majority Voting," *Journal of Political Economy*, 67 (1959), 571.

[110] See *supra* n. 29.

[111] Reminding one of Goethe's Faust's predicament: "*Zwei Seelen wohnen, ach, in meiner Brust*" (Two souls, alas!, reside within my breast).

[112] *supra* n. 4.   [113] *Ibid.*, 72, with further references.   [114] 452 F.2d 1333 (DC Cir. 1971).

elections is ... totally denied. This regrettable situation is a product of historical and legal forces over which this court has no control."[115] Courts feel bound to uphold the US Constitution as written, bound by "text, history, and precedent."[116] After all, the US Supreme Court had decided, in *Tidewater*,[117] following Chief Justice Marshall's opinion in *Hepburn and Dundas*,[118] that the District was no State, and, in *Heald*,[119] that there is no constitutional prohibition of taxation without representation.[120]

Is there any way out of this judicial cul de sac? Obviously, the issue of the denial of voting rights, while clearly a violation of the principle of democracy, does not rise to the level of *Dred Scott*[121] or the Nuremberg Laws,[122] which would mandate the intercession of natural law. Change can, however, be brought about by artful reinterpretation of the Constitution in light of its guiding principles spurred by political action such as statutory institution of representation, its interpretation in light of international law, or by the cleanest of solutions, an amendment to the Constitution.

Such artful constitutional reinterpretation has been urged by no less a proponent of fidelity to text and original intent than Utah Senator Orrin Hatch.[123] In his *volte face* on this issue,[124] in support of a statute that would enlarge the US House of Representatives by one representative of DC and one from the State of Utah,[125] the Senator started his argument with the statement in the Declaration of Independence that government derives its "just powers from the consent of the governed."[126] He

---

[115] *Ibid.*, 1341.   [116] *Adams v. Clinton, supra* n. 4.
[117] *National Mutual Insurance Company of the District of Columbia v. Tidewater Transfer Co., Inc.*, 337 US 582, 586 (1949) (plurality opinion of Jackson, J.).
[118] *Hepburn and Dundas v. Ellzey*, 6 US (2 Cranch) 445, 453 (1805) (for purposes of diversity jurisdiction, a citizen of DC does not equate a citizen of the different States).
[119] *Heald v. District of Columbia*, 259 US 114 (1922).
[120] *Ibid.*, 124 ("There is no constitutional provision which so limits the power of Congress that taxes can be imposed only upon those who have political representation").
[121] G. L. Neuman, in "Is There a Constitutional Right to Vote and Be Represented? The Case of the District of Columbia," *American University Law Review*, 48 (1999), 589–727, 694 ("I do not think that the level of injustice here rises quite to the level of the injustice of the *Dred Scott* decision, which was an even greater national disgrace").
[122] Cf. D.F. Vagts, "International Law in the Third Reich," *AJIL*, 84 (1990), 661–704.
[123] Cf. his article, *supra* n. 8.
[124] As he candidly observed, "[his] position regarding House representation has changed." *Ibid.*, 305–6.
[125] Such a bill was introduced in 2007 (S. 1257), and reintroduced in 2009, see *supra* n. 22.
[126] *Ibid.*, 298.

considered the principle of popular sovereignty "so fundamental to our Constitution, the existence of the franchise so central, that it ought to govern absent actual evidence that America's founders intended that it be withheld from one group of citizens."[127] "[F]ar from indicating an intent to disenfranchise," he states, "the evidence shows that America's founders intended that District residents retain the franchise and be represented in Congress."[128]

In addition, courts have recognized that "Congress may, under its exclusive and plenary legislative authority over the District, treat the District like a State for certain purposes."[129] Hatch distinguishes *Adams* by noting that the court denied relief only "on the basis that the Constitution does not itself grant such representation."[130] So he concludes that "Congress may do what the Constitution does not by providing for House representation by legislation."[131]

One might also argue, based on Chief Justice Marshall's endorsement of implied Federal powers in *McCulloch* v. *Maryland*,[132] that the meaning of the Constitution itself is evolving, and that might be true for the Chief Justice's own holdings and *rationes decidendi*.

Besides changes in judicial interpretation and legislative action, a second way to give effect to the centrality of the franchise is to honor our commitments under international law. Detlev Vagts has shown the way in this respect, as he has many times admonished administrations to respect, not give short shrift to, the mandates of international law.[133] Regarding the observance of treaty obligations, in particular, he has insisted on the

> need to make clear to the public how much our policies abroad depend on our being able to negotiate treaties and to obtain compliance with them from our foreign counterparts. Some of these agreements require other countries to make drastic changes in their domestic legal systems ... A reputation for playing fast and loose with treaty commitments can only do harm to our capacity to be a leader in the post-Cold War world.[134]

---

[127] *Ibid.*, 298–9.   [128] *Ibid.*, 299.   [129] *Ibid.*, 300.   [130] *Ibid.*, 303.

[131] *Ibid.*, 305.   [132] 17 US 316 (1819).

[133] D. F. Vagts, "Editorial Comment. Taking Treaties Less Seriously," *AJIL*, 92 (1998), 458–62; *idem.*, "The United States and Its Treaties.: Observance and Breach," *AJIL*, 95 (2001), 313–34; *idem.*, "International Relations Looks at Customary International Law," *EJIL*, 15 (2004), 1031–40; *idem.*, "Hegemonic International Law," *AJIL*, 95 (2001), 843–8; and *idem.*, "American International Law: A Sonderweg?," in K. Dicke, S. Hobe, K. U. Meyn, A. Peters, E. Riedel, H. J. Schütz, and C. Tietje (eds.), *Weltinnenrecht. Liber Amicorum Jost Delbrück* (Berlin: Duncker & Humblot, 2005), 835–47.

[134] Vagts, "Taking Treaties Less Seriously," *supra* n. 133, 462.

While this statement was written in the context of economic obligations, the depth of its truth extends to all areas of substance our global and globalizing law – in the framework of interpenetrating transnational law – now manages to reach. It certainly includes the law of human rights, the development of which has been spearheaded by the United States. Ideally, domestic laws should be interpreted in a way that is in harmony with America's international obligations.

The denial of the right to vote, with no rational justification remaining, is, in effect, a denial of an individual's right to self-realization. The addressees of the law should also be its ultimate creators. In the crucible between positive law on one side and international law on the other, we could do worse than follow the guiding light of a world public order of human dignity.[135] As law anywhere should serve human beings, it should be constructed and construed in a way to allow individuals ever-increasing, ideally maximum, access to all things they desire of life[136] including, as citizens of a community, power over their own destiny. As soon as such participation in the political processes affecting them is ensured, for all presently unreasonably excluded, the founding myth of the American Republic will be reconciled with its reality.

[135] S. Wiessner and A. R. Willard, "Policy-Oriented Jurisprudence and Human Rights Abuses in Internal Conflict. Toward a World Public Order of Human Dignity," *AJIL*, 93 (1999), 316–34.
[136] *Ibid.*, 324.

12

The tormented relationship between international law and EU law

JAN WOUTERS

Introduction

This chapter is dedicated in high esteem and friendship to Professor Detlev Vagts. Throughout the conversations I had with him during my stay as a Visiting Researcher at Harvard Law School in 1990–1, I was consistently impressed with his unique understanding of intersecting legal orders. For this reason, I chose to look into one of these interactions – namely, the relationship between European Union ('EU') law and public international law. Given that much has been written on this subject over the last four decades, this chapter highlights some of the more recent developments in this field.

The relationship between EU law and public international law is, more than one would expect, a complex one. Throughout the years, it has gone through various stages in the case-law of the European Court of Justice ('ECJ' or 'Court'). From the early 1960s, the ECJ has distinguished the EEC Treaty[1] ('EEC') from 'ordinary treaties' and shied away from relying on traditional international law, including customary international law, in its attempts to build an autonomous Community legal order. This initial position evolved over time and a certain relaxation was noticeable in the Court's case-law. In the *Racke* case[2] (1998), the ECJ even showed an unprecedented openness to customary international law as a ground for assessing the validity of EU legislation.

---

[1] Treaty establishing the European Economic Community, signed in Rome on 27 March 1957. The term 'Economic' was removed by the Treaty on European Union, signed in Maastricht on 7 February 1992.

[2] Case C-162/96 *Racke* [1998] ECR I-3655.

However, ten years later the Court's *Kadi* judgment[3] (2008) strongly re-emphasised the autonomy of Community law *vis-à-vis* international law, even in the face of binding resolutions of the UN Security Council. Other recent ECJ judgments like *Intertanko*[4] (2008) add to the perception that the Court is again reconsidering the relationship between EU law and international law.

It is worth reviewing these recent cases here in an attempt to assess their impact on the relationship between EU law and international law. First, however, it is useful to recall the broad evolution which the ECJ's case-law has undergone, from an initial reticence to a more open attitude *vis-à-vis* international law.

From initial reticence towards a more open attitude

A chilly start

Unlike many constitutions of EU Member States, the EU's founding treaties do not contain any provision on the relationship between EU law and public international law. With the coming into force of the Lisbon Treaty[5] on 1 December 2009 this remains the case, although it should be noted that the new EU Treaty makes 'the strict observance and the development of international law' one of the EU's external relations objectives.[6] If this constitutes one of the aims of the EU's relationship with the wider world, it is hard to imagine that matters would be otherwise for the EU's observance of international law *within its own legal order*: this seems implied by Art. 21(1) of the Treaty on European Union ('TEU'), as 'respect for the principles of ... international law' is listed among 'the principles which have inspired its [i.e. the Union's] own creation, development and enlargement, and which it seeks to advance in the wider world'.

In the absence of explicit Treaty provisions, it befell to the ECJ to elaborate on the aforementioned relationship. From the early 1960s on, the ECJ has emphasised the *sui generis* nature of the European

---

[3] Joined Cases C-402/05P and C-415/05P *Kadi and Al Barakaat* v. *Council and Commission* [2008] ECR I-6351.

[4] Case C-308/06 *Intertanko* [2008] ECR I-4057.

[5] Lisbon Treaty amending the Treaty on European Union and the Treaty establishing the European Community, signed at Lisbon, 13 December 2007, OJ 2007, C 306/1.

[6] Art. 3(5) TEU. For other references to international law, see Arts. 21(1), 21(2)(b) TEU and Arts. 77(4) and 214 Treaty on the Functioning of the European Union ('TFEU').

construction and distinguished European Community law ('EC law' or 'Community law') from international law. In *Van Gend & Loos* (1963), the ECJ stressed that 'the Community constitutes a new legal order of international law for the benefit of which the States have limited their sovereign rights, albeit within limited fields, and the subjects of which comprise not only Member States but also their nationals'.[7]

In *Costa* v. *ENEL* (1964), the Court ruled more comprehensively:

> By contrast with ordinary international treaties, the EEC Treaty has created its own legal system which, on the entry into force of the Treaty, became an integral part of the legal systems of the Member States and which their courts are bound to apply. By creating a Community of unlimited duration, having its own institutions, its own personality, its own legal capacity and capacity of representation on the international plane and, more particularly, real powers stemming from a limitation of sovereignty or a transfer of powers from the States to the Community, the Member States have limited their sovereign rights, albeit within limited fields, and have thus created a body of law which binds both their nationals and themselves.[8]

As Timmermans has observed, in so holding, 'the Court has tried to ensure and protect the autonomy of European Community law both *vis-à-vis* national law and international law'.[9] The initial position of the ECJ *vis-à-vis* international law can be easily understood. In truth, in those early days that position was entirely defensible, and even of existential importance for the establishment of the Community legal system. By stressing the uniqueness of Community law as a legal order rooted within the legal systems of EU Member States, the Court avoided the pitfalls caused by national constitutional doctrines *vis-à-vis* international law – such as dualism, which in a number of Member States would have resulted in according priority to more recent national laws over EC law.

Sometimes the ECJ's strive for autonomy *vis-à-vis* international law has gone a bit too far, though. One example is *Dyestuffs* (1972), a competition law case in which the Court avoided the problem of the limits which customary international law imposes on the EC's jurisdiction in cartel cases.[10]

---

[7] Case 26/62 *Van Gend & Loos* [1963] ECR 1.

[8] Case 6/64 *Costa* v. *ENEL* [1964] ECR 585. Compare Opinion 1/91 *European Economic Area* [1991] ECR I-6079, para. 21.

[9] C. Timmermans, 'The EU and Public International Law', *European Foreign Affairs Review*, 4 (1999), 181–2.

[10] Case 48/69, *Imperial Chemical Industries Ltd* v. *Commission* [1972] ECR 619.

A gradual warming up to (customary) international law

Delimiting State and Community jurisdiction

Gradually, when Community law had become more firmly established, the ECJ became more receptive to arguments based on international law. Since the mid-1970s, for instance, one notices how the Court uses customary international law to demarcate the boundaries of State or EC jurisdiction and powers. A first illustration of this approach can be found in *Van Duyn* (1974). In the face of a UK measure preventing nationals from other Member States (but not of the United Kingdom itself) from entering and taking up employment on the ground of public policy, the Court took notice of customary international law: 'it is a principle of international law, which the EEC treaty cannot be assumed to disregard in the relations between Member States, that a State is precluded from refusing its own nationals the right of entry or residence'.[11]

Two years later, in *Kramer* (1976),[12] the ECJ implicitly accepted customary international law as a limitation on the Community's powers to adopt measures. In this case the Court examined, *inter alia*, whether the Community had the authority to enter into international commitments for the conservation of the resources of the sea. The ECJ deduced from the relevant Community provisions that the EC does indeed have rule-making authority which '*ratione materiae* also extends – in so far as the Member States have similar authority under public international law – to fishing on the high seas'.[13]

In *Wood Pulp* (1988),[14] the ECJ accepted that customary international law acts as a limit on the powers of the European Commission in competition cases. Wood pulp producers from outside the EC contested a Commission decision holding that these companies had engaged in price concertation in violation of Art. 85 EEC (now Art. 101 TFEU). The applicants submitted that the decision was incompatible with public international law as it exceeded the Community's jurisdiction. Deeming the place of implementation of infringements of Art. 85 to be decisive, the ECJ held, however, that the Commission's decision 'was covered by the territoriality principle as universally recognised in public international law'.[15] In fact,

---

[11] Case 41/74, *Van Duyn* v. *Home Office* [1974] ECR 1337, para. 22.
[12] Joined Cases 3/76, 4/76, 6/76 *Kramer* [1976] ECR 1279.
[13] *Kramer, supra* n. 12, paras. 30–33.
[14] Joined Cases 89, 104, 114, 116, 117, 125 to 129/95 *Ahlström* v. *Commission* [1988] ECR 5193.
[15] *Wood Pulp, supra* n. 14, para. 18. See also Case T-102/96 *Gencor* v. *Commission* [1999] ECR II-753, para. 50.

Wood Pulp was the first case in which the ECJ dealt at length with arguments of customary international law in order to review the legality of EU acts.

In *Poulsen* (1992), a case raising multiple questions concerning the relationship between a Community regulation and the customary international law of the sea, the Court stated explicitly for the first time that 'the European Community must respect international law in the exercise of its powers' and that, therefore, provisions of EC legislation must be interpreted, and their scope limited, in the light of the relevant rules of customary international law at hand.[16] This statement of principle has since become well-established case-law[17] and would, *inter alia*, be recalled by the Court in *Kadi*[18] and *Intertanko*.[19]

International rules of interpretation

Since the early 1980s, the Court has often relied on customary international treaty law in interpreting international agreements to which the EC is a party, or rules of Community law proper. The 1969 Vienna Convention on the Law of Treaties (VCLT, or 'Vienna Convention')[20] especially is frequently invoked before the EU courts and is often applied by them in their interpretation and application of international agreements concluded by the Community and of the EC Treaty ('TEC').[21]

---

[16] Case C-286/90, *Anklagemyndigheden* v. *Peter Michael Poulsen and Diva Navigation Corp.* [1992] ECR I-6019, para. 9. For a more detailed analysis, see J. Wouters and D. Van Eeckhoutte, 'Giving Effect to Customary International Law through European Community Law', in J. M. Prinssen and A. Schrauwen (eds.), *Direct Effect. Rethinking a Classic of EC Legal Doctrine* (Groningen: European Law Publishing, 2002), 181, 189–90.

[17] See also, on the application to treaties to which the EC is a party, Case C-284/95 *Safety Hi-Tech* v. *S & T* [1998] ECR I-4302, para. 22; Case C-341/95 *Bettati* v. *Safety Hi-Tech* [1998] ECR I-4355, para. 20; Case C-61/94 *Commission* v. *Germany* [1996] ECR I-3989, para. 52. See also *Racke*, *supra* n. 2, para. 45; Case C-437/04 *Commission* v. *Belgium* [2007] ECR I-2513, para. 34.

[18] *Kadi*, *supra* n. 3, para. 291.   [19] *Intertanko*, *supra* n. 4, para. 51.

[20] Vienna Convention on the Law of Treaties (VCLT), done at Vienna, 23 May 1969 (UNTS, vol. 1155, p. 331). There is also the Vienna Convention on the Law of Treaties between States and International Organisations or between International Organisations, done at Vienna, 21 March 1986 (UN Doc. A/CONF.129/15), but it has not yet entered into force and the Community has not become a party to it.

[21] See, apart from the *Racke* and *Opel Austria* cases, *supra* n. 2 and *infra* n. 26, respectively, Case C-158/91, *Levy* [1993] ECR I-4287, para. 19; Case C-432/92, *The Queen* v. *Minister of Agriculture, Fisheries and Food, ex parte Anastasiou* [1994] ECR I-3087, paras. 43, 50; Case C-25/94 *Commission* v. *Council* [1996] ECR I-1469, para. 33; Case C-62/98, *Commission* v. *Portugal* [2000] ECR I-5171, para. 44; Case C-84/98, *Commission* v. *Portugal* [2000] ECR I-5215, para. 53; Case T-2/99, *T. Port* v. *Council* [2001] ECR II-2093, para. 81; Case T-231/04 *Greece* v. *Commission* [2007] ECR II-63, paras. 85–6.

The cardinal rule on the law of treaties, expressed in Art. 26 of VCLT, is *pacta sunt servanda*: 'Every treaty is binding upon the parties to it and must be performed by them in good faith'.[22] Since *Kupferberg* (1982), the ECJ has often relied on this rule.[23] There are plenty of other cases in which the ECJ has relied on the customary rules of treaty law as reflected in VCLT. For instance, the Court has repeatedly referred to the rules of treaty interpretation laid down in Art. 31 of VCLT.[24] The Court of First Instance ('the CFI'; since the Lisbon Treaty: 'the General Court') has applied this interpretative rule to the WTO Anti-Dumping and Anti-Subsidy Agreements, adding that '[t]hat rule of interpretation corresponds to the rule applied by the Community judicature when called upon to interpret a provision of Community law'.[25]

The latter observation is an interesting one in the light of the inclination sometimes displayed by the EU courts to 'internalise' rules of international law into EU law by equating them with established principles of Community law. An interesting illustration of this 'transformation' approach can be found in the CFI's *Opel Austria* judgment (1997). Although the CFI accepted that 'the principle of good faith is a rule of customary international law whose existence is recognized by the International Court of Justice . . . and is therefore binding on the Community', it continued its analysis of the case exclusively on the basis of EC law, after having observed that 'the principle of good faith is the corollary in public international law of the principle of protection of legitimate expectations which, according to the case-law, forms part of the Community legal order'.[26]

---

[22] Art. 26, VCLT.

[23] Case 104/81 *Hauptzollamt Mainz* v. *Kupferberg* [1982] ECR I-3641, para. 18; Case C-149/96 *Portugal* v. *Council* [1999] ECR I-8395, para. 35. See also Case C-61/94 *Commission* v. *Germany* [1996] I-3989, para. 30.

[24] See Opinion 1/91 *EEA Agreement I* [1991] ECR I-6079, para. 14; Case C-312/91, *Metalsa* [1993] ECR I-3751, para. 12; Case C-416/96, *El-Yassini* v. *Secretary of State for Home Department* [1999] ECR I-1209, para. 47; Case C-268/99, *Jany* v. *Staatssecretaris van Justitie* [2001] ECR I-8615, para. 35; Case C-344/04 *IATA and ELFAA* [2006] ECR I-403, para. 40; Case C-118/07 *Commission* v. *Finland* [2009] ECR I-000, para. 39. See also *Anastasiou, supra* n. 21, para. 43.

[25] CFI, Case T-45/06 *Reliance Industries* v. *Council and Commission* [2008] ECR II-2399, paras. 100–101.

[26] CFI, Case T-115/94 *Opel Austria* v. *Council* [1997] ECR II-39, paras. 90 and 93, respectively. In para. 91, the CFI refers to Art. 18 of the VCLT as a codification of the principle of good faith. See, for a further analysis, Wouters and Van Eeckhoutte, 'Giving Effect', *supra* n. 16, 208–14. In Case T-231/04 *Greece* v. *Commission*, paras. 85–7 almost

International rules to fill gaps

Since the early 1990s, the ECJ from time to time has also relied on rules of customary international law as 'gap-fillers' when EC law itself displays lacunae in respect of a certain issue.[27] With regard to EC fisheries law, the Court has repeatedly held, starting with *Factortame II* (1992), that in the absence of specific Community rules on the registration of vessels, 'it is for the Member States to determine, in accordance with the general rules of international law, the conditions which must be fulfilled in order for a vessel to be registered in their registers and granted the right to fly their flag'.[28] A similar reference to customary international law has been made with regard to the conditions for granting nationality: in *Micheletti* (1992), the Court held that '[u]nder international law, it is for each Member State ... to lay down the conditions for the acquisition and loss of nationality'.[29]

However, the reference to international law in these cases is not unconditional. In the fisheries cases, the Court pointed out that, 'in exercising that power, the Member States must comply with the rules of Community law',[30] while in *Micheletti* it added that 'due regard' was to be given to Community law.[31] Moreover, there are limits to the reliance on customary international law in order to fill certain lacunae in Community law. The Court will not accept that Member States can invoke competences which they have under customary international law in order to unilaterally modify obligations which are incumbent upon them under Community law.[32]

---

literally repeat paras. 90–93 of *Opel Austria*. Interestingly, in its appeal judgment in this case, the ECJ held, referring to para. 52 of its *Intertanko* judgment, that 'the Court of First Instance was entitled to invoke, as an additional basis for the obligation thus incumbent on the Hellenic Republic under the memoranda, the customary principle of good faith, which forms part of general international law'. Case C-203/07P *Greece* v. *Commission* [2008] ECR I-8161, para. 64.

[27] An early and rather general reference in this respect can be found in Case 244/80 *Foglia* v. *Novello* [1981] ECR 3045, para. 24.

[28] Case C-221/89, *The Queen* v. *Secretary of State for Transport, ex parte Factortame* [1991] ECR I-3905, para. 17; Case C-246/89 *Commission* v. *United Kingdom* [1991] ECR I-4585, para. 15; Case C-62/96 *Commission* v. *Greece* [1997] ECR I-6725, para. 22.

[29] Case C-369/90 *Micheletti* [1992] ECR I-4239, para. 10.

[30] *Factortame II*, supra n. 28, para. 17; *Commission* v. *United Kingdom*, supra n. 28, para. 17; *Commission* v. *Greece*, supra n. 28, para. 22.

[31] *Micheletti*, supra n. 29, para. 10.

[32] See in particular Case C-146/89 *Commission* v. *United Kingdom* [1991] ECR I-3533, paras. 25–9.

Meanwhile: 'Europeanising' international agreements and giving them precedence over secondary EU law

What one may also observe since the 1970s, in particular the *Haegeman* judgment (1974), is the Court's acceptance that the provisions of an international agreement concluded by the Community 'from the coming into force thereof, form an integral part of Community law'.[33] This 'monist' attitude applies both to mixed (i.e. involving the Community *and* (some) Member States) and non-mixed[34] agreements. This case-law finds its underpinning in the old Treaty provision, laid down initially in Art. 228(2) EEC, later Art. 300(7) TEC, according to which international agreements concluded under the procedure laid down in that article 'shall be binding on the institutions of the Community and on Member States' (now Art. 216(2) TFEU).

Moreover, in the hierarchy of sources, the Court attaches a higher status to such international agreements than to rules of secondary EU law. In other words, EU legislation can be challenged on the basis of international treaties, at least those to which the EU (previously the E(E)C) is a party.[35] In addition, 'the primacy of international agreements concluded by the Community over provisions of secondary Community legislation means that such provisions must, so far as is possible, be interpreted in a manner that is consistent with those agreements'.[36]

Several observations can be made in the light of this case-law. First of all, through this body of cases the ECJ has brought about a considerable 'Europeanisation' of large parts of international law for EU Member States.[37] To the extent that they are binding upon the EU institutions, international treaties become part of the EU legal order and are therefore 'Europeanised': their application and interpretation by EU Member

---

[33] Case 181/73 *Haegeman* [1974] ECR 449, para. 5. For more recent confirmations, see, *inter alia*, Case 12/86 *Demirel* [1987] ECR 3719, para. 7; Case C-321/97 *Andersson and Wåkerås-Andersson* [1999] ECR I-3551, para. 26; Case C-431/05 *Merck Genéricos – Produtos Farmacêuticos* [2007] ECR I 7001, para. 31; Case C-301/08 *Bogiatzi* [2009], para. 23.

[34] See Case 12/86 *Demirel, supra* n. 33, para. 9 and Case C-13/00 *Commission v. Ireland* [2002] ECR I-2943, para. 14.

[35] See, *inter alia*, Case C-311/04 *Algemene Scheeps Agentuur Dordrecht* [2009] ECR I-609, para. 25; *Intertanko, supra* n. 4, para. 42.

[36] Case C-61/94 *Commission v. Germany* [1996] ECR I-3989, para. 52. See also *Algemene Scheeps Agentuur Dordrecht, supra* n. 35, para. 25; Case C-286/02 *Bellio F.lli* [2004] ECR I-3465, para. 33.

[37] For a more comprehensive analysis, see J. Wouters, A. Nollkaemper and E. De Wet (eds.), *The Europeanisation of International Law. The Status of International Law in the EU and its Member States* (The Hague: T.M.C. Asser Press, 2008).

States are no longer solely a matter for the constitutional order of the latter, but in the first place for EU law, notably with a view to ensuring its uniform application and interpretation.[38]

The fact that in the hierarchy of norms, international instruments and norms occupy an intermediate position – i.e. in between primary and secondary EU law (defined in the following paragraph) – also implies that such international instruments and norms can be used as part of the ECJ's and/or the General Court's control of the validity of EU norms, either as part of a direct challenge based on Art. 230 TEC (now Art. 263 TFEU), or as part of a validity check through the preliminary procedure of Art. 234 TEC (now Art. 267 TFEU). In the 2001 *Biotechnical Inventions* case (*Netherlands* v. *European Parliament and Council*, Case c-377/98, [2001] ECR I-7079) the Court held, with regard to the Convention on Biological Diversity, that even if it 'contains provisions which do not have direct effect, in the sense that they do not create rights which individuals can rely on directly before the courts, that fact does not preclude review by the courts of compliance with the obligations incumbent on the Community as a party to that agreement'.[39]

Secondly, in spite of the 'monist' features attributed to this case-law, it is clear that there are limits to the Court's openness to international treaties. The first such limit pertains to the relationship between the agreements concerned and the EU's 'primary law' – i.e. the EU's basic treaties, including the protocols and annexes attached thereto,[40] and general principles of law.[41] The ECJ has never accepted that international agreements to which the EC/EU is a party have priority over EU primary law. This is logical to the extent that the Court has always denied the power to invalidate primary EU law.[42] But it shows that the ECJ's 'monist' attitude does not extend beyond the level of the acts of the institutions. A second limit is that the Court is not willing to accept, as part of the Community legal order, international agreements to which all EU Member States are a party but the EU/EC itself is not. For this reason, the ECJ recently confirmed in *Bogiatzi* (2009) that it does not have

---

[38] See explicitly *Kupferberg, supra* n. 23, para. 15.

[39] Case C-377/98 *Netherlands* v *European Parliament and Council* [2001] ECR I-7079, para. 54 (*Biotechnical Inventions*).

[40] See Art. 51 TEU.

[41] The general principles of law form part of the 'law' the observance of which the ECJ must ensure pursuant to Art. 19(1) TEU (previously Art. 220 TEC).

[42] See, *inter alia*, with regard to TEU, Order of the Court of 13 January 1995 in Case C-264/94P *Bonnamy* v. *Council* [1995] ECR I-15, para. 11.

jurisdiction to interpret the Warsaw Convention.[43] The only exception it makes in this respect is if the EC/EU 'has assumed the powers previously exercised by EU Member States in the field to which an international convention applies and, therefore, its provisions have the effect of binding the Community[/Union]'.[44]

This brings us to a third limit: even though already in *International Fruit Company* (1972) the ECJ admitted that the latter is the case for the General Agreement on Tariffs and Trade ('GATT'), it has persistently refused to grant full effectiveness in the EU legal order to the GATT and its successor international agreement – or rather, set of agreements – to which the EU itself is a party (jointly with its Member States) – i.e. the WTO Agreement and the multilateral and plurilateral agreements of the WTO.[45] The reason behind this stance is that, especially for GATT and WTO agreements, the Court has stressed time and again that, although they are binding upon the EC/EU, the provisions contained in these instruments are not 'capable of conferring rights on citizens of the Community which they can invoke before the courts'.[46]

A climax? Reviewing the legality of EU acts based on customary international law in Racke

From the perspective of the evolution sketched above, the ECJ's 1998 judgment in *Racke* may be seen as a climax point in the Court's opening up to public international law, as it offered the first occasion in which it scrutinised the legality of an act of an EU institution effectively on the basis of an argument of customary international law.

---

[43] *Bogiatzi, supra* n. 33, para. 25. In full: Convention for the Unification of Certain Rules Relating to International Carriage by Air, signed at Warsaw on 12 October 1929, as amended by the four additional protocols signed at Montreal on 25 September 1975.

[44] Joined Cases 21/72 to 24/72 *International Fruit Company and Others* [1972] ECR 1219, para. 18; Case C-379/92 *Peralta* [1994] ECR I-3453, para. 16; *Intertanko, supra* n. 4, para. 48 (the latter two cases concerning the International Convention for the Prevention of Pollution from Ships, the so-called Marpol Convention); compare Case C-188/07 *Commune de Mesquer* [2008] ECR I-4501, para. 85.

[45] See, *inter alia*, Case C-149/96 *Portugal* v. *Council, supra* n. 23, [1999] ECR I-8395, para. 47. Only where the Community has intended to implement a particular obligation assumed in the context of the WTO, or where the Community measure refers expressly to the precise provisions of the WTO agreements, is the ECJ willing to review the legality of the Community measure in question in the light of the WTO rules: see, *inter alia*, Case C-93/02P *Biret International* v. *Council* [2003] ECR I-10497, para. 53.

[46] Thus the language of *International Fruit Company and Others, supra* n. 44, paras. 8 and 27 and operative part 1.

The 1980 Co-Operation Agreement concluded between the EEC and its Member States and the Socialist Federal Republic (SFR) of Yugoslavia had introduced a preferential tariff for the import of wine originating in Yugoslavia. The Council suspended the Co-Operation Agreement unilaterally in 1991 by means of a regulation. The suspension was alleged to be justified by a fundamental change in circumstances (*rebus sic stantibus*) – i.e. Yugoslavia's civil war and subsequent disintegration. Racke, a German company, imported wine from Yugoslavia and was thus prejudiced by the suspension of the tariff concessions. It continued to rely on the preferential tariff installed by the Co-Operation Agreement and contested the validity of the regulation suspending it. Germany's Bundesfinanzhof asked the ECJ whether the regulation was valid in the light of the conditions imposed by customary international law for a suspension on the basis of *rebus sic stantibus*.

The point of departure for the ECJ's reasoning in *Racke* is affirmative and straightforward and builds on *Poulsen* (*supra*, p. 202):

> the European Community must respect international law in the exercise of its powers. It is therefore required to comply with the rules of customary international law when adopting a regulation suspending the trade concessions granted by, or by virtue of, an agreement which it has concluded with a non-member country.
>
> It follows that the rules of customary international law concerning the termination and the suspension of treaty relations by reason of a fundamental change of circumstances are binding upon the Community institutions and form part of the Community legal order.[47]

To the extent any doubts persisted on this subject, they are hereby clearly resolved. Customary international law is part of the Community legal order. The Court continues on its élan and also answers the following two questions in the affirmative:

> In those circumstances, an individual relying in legal proceedings on rights which he derives directly from an agreement with a non-member country may not be denied the possibility of challenging the validity of a regulation which, by suspending the trade concessions granted by that agreement, prevents him from relying on it, and of invoking, in order to challenge the validity of the suspending regulation, obligations deriving from rules of customary international law which govern the termination and suspension of treaty relations.[48]

---

[47] *Racke, supra* n. 2, paras. 45–46.   [48] *Ibid.*, para. 51.

Thus, in the case at hand, the Court accepted the invocability of customary international law to review the legality of an EU act and accorded the rule of customary international law primacy over the conflicting rule of secondary EU law. This position of principle expressed by the ECJ is remarkable and quite progressive. Only a few domestic courts and tribunals of EU Member States have reached a similar conclusion. Nevertheless, given the wording of the *Racke* judgment, one must be very careful not to overstretch the scope of the Court's ruling. First of all, the judgment is restricted to the situation in which an individual invokes a rule of customary international law in order to review the legality of an EU act. As a matter of fact, the Court ruled that the case did not concern the question of 'direct effect' of the rule of customary international law, but that it concerned the question of 'direct effectiveness' of the Co-Operation Agreement: 'the plaintiff is incidentally challenging the validity of a Community regulation under those rules in order to rely upon rights which it derives directly from an agreement of the Community with a non-member country. This case does not therefore concern the direct effect of those rules'.[49] *Racke* therefore does not resolve the question of invocability of customary international law in order for an individual to derive a right from it.

Secondly, the invocability of a rule of customary international law to review the legality of an EU legal act is furthermore restricted to the situation in which this EU legal act is in fact an implementation of the invoked role of customary international law. Indeed, the contested regulation explicitly provided that it was issued on the basis of the rule of *rebus sic stantibus*.

Thirdly, the Court seems to restrict its ruling to rules of customary international law of a fundamental nature: '*Racke* is invoking fundamental rules of customary international law against the disputed regulation, which was taken pursuant to those rules and deprives Racke of the rights to preferential treatment granted to it by the Co-Operation Agreement.'[50] Although the Court does not expand on what fundamental rules of customary international law are, the 'basic rules of a contractual nature',[51] such as the principle of *pacta sunt servanda* and the rule of *rebus sic stantibus*, qualify as such.[52]

Finally, the Court did not only restrict the scope of the invocability of rules of customary international law in order to review the legality of a Community act, but it rather surprisingly also watered down the legality

---

[49] *Racke, supra* n. 2, para. 47.   [50] *Ibid.*, para. 48.   [51] *Ibid.*   [52] *Ibid.*, paras. 49–50.

test itself when rules of customary international law are at stake: 'because of the complexity of the rules in question and the imprecision of some of the concepts to which they refer, judicial review must necessarily, and in particular in the context of a preliminary reference for an assessment of validity, be limited to the question whether, by adopting the suspending regulation, the Council made manifest errors of assessment concerning the conditions for applying those rules.'[53]

This last restriction is not only undesirable, it is also legally unacceptable. First of all, it is a misconception and oversimplification to hold that rules of customary international law are vague, uncertain and imprecise. Moreover, the customary rule of *rebus sic stantibus* has been codified in Art. 62 VCLT and in Art. 62 of the 1986 Vienna Convention.[54] Hence, the rule of customary international law, as laid down in the law of treaties, has similar characteristics as a treaty provision. It is hard to explain how in reviewing the legality of an EU act on the basis of a rule of customary international law only a marginal appreciation test should apply, whereas this should not be the case in reviewing the legality on the basis of a treaty provision. Secondly, the marginal appreciation test is incompatible with the rule of *rebus sic stantibus*. The corollary of a court's decision to proceed with a marginal appreciation test is the granting of a discretionary competence or a large margin of appreciation to the government body. However, the rule of *rebus sic stantibus* does not accord such a large margin of appreciation. As an exception to the fundamental principle of *pacta sunt servanda*, that rule ought to be interpreted restrictively; a liberal interpretation could jeopardise the stability of international relations.[55] For that same reason, Art. 62, para. 1, of the 1969 VCLT deliberately employs a negative wording[56] and may only be invoked under strict conditions cumulatively satisfied.[57]

---

[53] *Ibid.*, para. 52.

[54] See International Law Commission (ILC), 'Draft Articles on the Law of Treaties', UN Doc. A/CONF.39/11/Add.2, Official Records, II, 76, para. 2; ILC, 'Report of the ILC to the General Assembly' (1963, II) *Yearbook of the ILC*, 207, para. 2; *Fisheries Jurisdiction Case (UK v. Iceland)*, 1973 ICJ Rep. 3, para. 36; *Fisheries Jurisdiction Case (Federal Republic of Germany v. Iceland)*, [1973], ICJ Rep. 63, para. 36; *Case Concerning the Gabčikovo-Nagymaros Project (Hungary v. Slovakia)*, 1997 ICJ 7, paras. 46 and 104.

[55] See ILC, 'Draft Articles on the Law of Treaties between States and International Organisations or between International Organisations', UN Doc. CONF.129/16/Add.1, Official Records, II, 42.

[56] 'A fundamental change of circumstances ... may not be invoked ... unless:' Art. 62, paras. 1–2, VCLT.

[57] See Art. 62, paras. 1–2, and Art. 65–7, VCLT.

In spite of this criticism *Racke* is an important case, as it showed that the ECJ is willing to refer to customary international rules not only for the interpretation of EU law but also, in principle, for the review of the legality of EU acts. In that sense, it fits the larger trend, analysed up to this point, towards a more general openness *vis-à-vis* international law in the case-law of the ECJ. *Racke* may have shown the Court from its most international side. The recent *Kadi* and *Intertanko* judgments, though, seem to have given a new twist to the State of affairs.

The *Kadi* case: re-emphasising autonomy *vis-à-vis* international law

It has been stated that '*Kadi* is one of the ECJ's most significant judgments to date: it makes strong statements about the autonomy of the EC legal order, the centrality of fundamental rights protection to that legal order and its relationship with international law'.[58] This may well be true, and both the CFI and ECJ judgments have given rise to an avalanche of commentaries. The analysis hereafter concentrates on the part of the judgments concerning the relationship between Community law and international law. It is useful to compare the attitude of the CFI with that of the ECJ in its appeal judgment. They are worlds apart: whereas the CFI adopts a strictly monist view on the question, the ECJ's judgment displays a dualist mindset.

Background and issues at stake

On 15 October 1999, the UN Security Council adopted, on the basis of Chapter VII of the Charter of the United Nations ('UN Charter'), resolution 1267 (1999), in which it strongly condemned 'the continuing use of the Afghan territory for the sheltering and training of terrorists and planning of terrorist acts' and reaffirmed 'its conviction that the suppression of international terrorism is essential for the maintenance of international peace and security'.[59] More importantly, it decided that all States had to 'freeze the funds and other financial resources, including funds derived or generated from property owned or controlled directly or indirectly by the Taliban'.[60] In para. 6, the Security Council set up a 'Sanctions

---

[58] A. Johnston, 'Frozen in Time? The ECJ Finally Rules on the *Kadi* Appeal', *Cambridge Law Journal*, 68 (2009), 1–4, 3.

[59] SC res. 1267, UN Doc. S/RES/1267(15 October 1999), preamble.   [60] *Ibid.*, para. 4(b).

Committee', which is responsible, in particular, for ensuring that States implement the freezing of funds and other financial resources measures. In its resolution 1333 (2000), the Security Council decided that all States had to freeze without delay funds and other financial assets of these individuals and entities and requested 'the Committee to maintain an updated list, based on information provided by States and regional organizations, of the individuals and entities designated as being associated with Usama Bin Laden'.[61]

In order to implement resolution 1333, the EU Council adopted a Common Position on 25 February 2001 and a Community Regulation on 6 March 2001. Both instruments were replaced in 2002 to implement Security Council resolution 1390 (2002), by Common Position 2002/402/CFSP and Regulation (EC) No 881/2002, respectively.[62] Annex 1 to this Regulation contains the list of persons, entities and bodies affected by the freezing of funds. This list is updated regularly, following the updates of the list prepared by the Sanctions Committee. Mr Yassin Adullah Kadi's name was mentioned on the list. He decided to bring an action seeking annulment of the Regulation, alleging breaches of his fundamental rights and more precisely, breaches of the right to be heard, to respect for property, and to effective judicial review.[63] The EU Courts would be confronted with two main issues: first of all, the question of the legal basis on which the Community had adopted the regulation and secondly, and more importantly in the framework of this chapter, the question whether the EU Courts are competent to review a resolution of the UN Security Council – and, if so, against which norms.

The CFI's analysis: a strictly monist view

The CFI first considered the relationship between the international legal order under the United Nations and the domestic or Community legal order

---

[61] SC res. 1333, UN Doc. S/RES/1333 (13 December 2000), para 8(c).

[62] Respectively, Council Common Position 2002/402/CFSP of 27 May 2002 concerning restrictive measures against Usama bin Laden, members of the Al Qaeda organisation and the Taliban and other individuals, groups, undertakings and entities associated with them and repealing Common Positions 96/746, 1999/727, 2001/154 and 2001/771/CFSP (OJ 2002 L 139/4); Council Regulation (EC) No. 881/2002 of 27 May 2002 imposing certain specific restrictive measures directed against certain persons and entities associated with Usama bin Laden, the Al Qaeda network and the Taliban, and repealing Regulation No. 467/2001 (OJ 2002 L 139/9).

[63] The parallel case before the CFI and ECJ was brought by Yusuf and Al Barakaat International Foundation: see Case T-306/01 *Ahmed Ali Yusuf and Al Barakaat International Foundation* v. *Council and Commission* [2005] ECR II-3533.

and the extent to which the Community was bound by resolutions of the Security Council adopted under Chapter VII of the UN Charter.[64] The CFI affirmed that, based on Art. 103 of the UN Charter, the obligations of EU Member States under the UN Charter prevail over their obligations under any other international agreement and over domestic law obligations.[65] This primacy extends to the decisions contained in UN Security Council resolutions.[66] The CFI boldly derived from both UN Charter and EC Treaty provisions that 'Member States may, and indeed must, leave unapplied any provision of Community law, whether a provision of primary law or a general principle of that law, that raises any impediment to the proper performance of their obligations under the Charter of the United Nations'.[67] As to the EC itself, the CFI held that even though it is, as such, not bound by the UN Charter because it is not a party to it, it must be considered as being bound in the same way as EU Member States, by virtue of the EC Treaty.[68] Consequently, 'in so far as under the EC Treaty the Community has assumed powers previously exercised by Member States in the area governed by the Charter of the United Nations, the provisions of that Charter have the effect of binding the Community' and 'the Community may not infringe the obligation imposed on its Member States by the Charter of the United Nations or impede their performance and . . . in the exercise of its powers, it is bound, by the [EC Treaty], to adopt all measures necessary to enable its Member States to fulfil those obligations'.[69] This, in the eyes of the CFI, justified the adoption of the Common Position and the Regulation freezing Kadi's assets. The CFI explicitly rejected 'the applicant's arguments based on the view that the Community legal order is a legal order independent of the United Nations, governed by its own rules of law'[70] – in short, a dualist vision on the relationship between international and EU law.

As de Búrca notes, the CFI accepted 'the subordination of EC law to binding resolutions of the Security Council, which would suggest that the Court of First Instance could hardly then proceed to review the resolution in question for conformity with principles of EC law, even principles concerning protection for fundamental rights'.[71] Indeed, the CFI affirmed that 'the resolutions of the Security Council at issue fall, in principle, outside the

---

[64] Case T-315/01 *Kadi* [2005] ECR II-3649, para. 178.   [65] *Ibid.*, para. 183.
[66] *Ibid.*, para. 184.   [67] *Ibid.*, para. 190.   [68] *Ibid.*, paras. 192–193.
[69] *Ibid.*, paras. 203 and 204, respectively.   [70] *Ibid.*, para. 208.
[71] G. de Búrca, 'The European Court of Justice and the International Legal Order after *Kadi*', Jean Monnet Working Paper, New York University School of Law, No. 01/09, 25.

ambit of the Court's Judicial review and that the Court has no authority to call in question, even indirectly, their lawfulness in the light of Community law'.[72] But then it took a remarkable direction: 'None the less, the Court is empowered to check, indirectly, the lawfulness of the resolutions of the Security Council in question with regard to jus cogens, a body of higher rules of public international law binding on all subjects of international law, including the bodies of the United Nations, and from which no derogation is possible'.[73] The CFI's indirect judicial review:

> in connection with an action for annulment of a Community act adopted, where no discretion whatsoever may be exercised, with a view to putting into effect a resolution of the Security Council may therefore, highly exceptionally, extend to determining whether the superior rules of international law falling within the ambit of jus cogens have been observed, in particular, the mandatory provisions concerning the universal protection of human rights, from which neither the Member States nor the bodies of the United Nations may derogate because they constitute 'intransgressible principles of international customary law'.[74]

As to the alleged violation of Kadi's fundamental rights, the CFI ruled that the deprivation of property was not arbitrary: the freezing of funds had been adopted in the framework of the international campaign against terrorism, there were humanitarian exceptions, it was only a temporary precautionary measure and the State of nationality or residence could always ask the Sanctions Committee for a review.[75]

Concerning the right to be heard and the right to judicial review, the CFI likewise concluded that they had not been violated. In the light of the temporary precautionary nature of the measure, the CFI considered that observance of fundamental rights 'does not require the facts and evidence adduced against him to be communicated to him, once the Security Council or its Sanctions Committee is of the view that there are grounds concerning the international community's security that militate against it'.[76]

As to the right to judicial review, the CFI concluded that, although there was no judicial remedy available to the applicant, such a limitation is not in itself contrary to *jus cogens* and 'the applicant's interest in having a court hear his case on its merits is not enough to outweigh the essential public interest in the maintenance of international peace and security in

---

[72] *Kadi, supra* n. 64, para. 225.   [73] *Ibid.*, para. 226.   [74] *Ibid.*, para. 231.
[75] *Ibid.*, paras. 243–252.   [76] *Ibid.*, para. 274.

the face of a threat clearly identified by the Security Council in accordance with the Charter of the United Nations'.[77]

Although the CFI's attempts at preserving a monist attitude *vis-à-vis* international law deserve credit, one cannot but be appalled by the manner in which it developed its *jus cogens* reasoning[78] and applied a fundamental rights test to the measures in question.[79]

The ECJ judgment: a revival of dualism?

One will rarely have seen, in the EU judicial system, an appeals judgment which so fundamentally and radically overrides the analysis of the lower court. In its long-awaited judgment of 3 September 2008, the ECJ annulled the contested EC Regulation in so far as it concerned Mr Kadi (and the Al Barakaat International Foundation, whose case had been joined to the *Kadi* case). In essence, the ECJ found that there had been an unjustified restriction of Mr Kadi's right to be heard, his right to an effective legal remedy and his right to property. Unlike the CFI, the Court's opening shots addressing the relationship between the international legal order and Community law exclusively reason from within the constitutional set-up of EC law proper. After recalling its well-known *Les Verts* case-law on the 'rule of law' foundation of the Community,[80] the Court went on to assert that 'an international agreement cannot affect the allocation of powers fixed by the Treaties or, consequently, the autonomy of the Community legal system, observance of which is ensured by the Court'.[81] It also re-affirmed that fundamental rights are part of the general principles of law whose observance the Court ensures and that respect for human rights is a condition for the lawfulness of Community acts.[82] Consequently, 'the obligations imposed by an international agreement cannot have the effect of prejudicing the constitutional principles of the EC Treaty, which include the principle that all Community acts must respect fundamental rights, that respect constituting a condition for their lawfulness which it is for the Courts to review'.[83]

---

[77] *Ibid.*, paras. 285–289.

[78] See, e.g., the criticism by C. Tomuschat, *Common Market Law Review*, 43 (2006), 537–51, 545–51.

[79] Cf. C. Eckes, 'Judicial Review of the European Anti-Terrorism Measures – The *Yusuf* and *Kadi* Judgments of the Court of First Instance', *European Law Journal*, 14 (2008), 74–92, 91.

[80] *Kadi, supra* n. 3, para. 281. *Les Verts* v. *Parliament* (Case 294/83), [1986] ECR 1339.

[81] *Ibid.*, para. 282.   [82] *Ibid.*, paras. 283–284.   [83] *Ibid.*, para. 285.

In other words, in the ECJ's view the EU courts must 'ensure the review, in principle the full review',[84] of the legality of a Council regulation adopted in implementation of a UN Security Council resolution based on fundamental rights as general principles of EC law. In doing so, it found that Mr Kadi's fundamental rights had been violated and that the Regulation had to be annulled in so far as it concerned him: (i) the rights of defence, especially the right to be heard and the principle of effective judicial protection, were violated as the Regulation was adopted 'without any guarantee being given as to the communication of the inculpatory evidence against them or as to their being heard in that connection';[85] and (ii) there had been an unjustified restriction of the right to property, as the Regulation had been 'adopted without furnishing any guarantee enabling him to put his case to the competent authorities, in a situation in which the restriction of his property rights must be regarded as significant, having regard to the general application and actual continuation of the freezing measures affecting him'.[86]

Kritische Würdigung

The ECJ's reasoning certainly offers an interesting narrative from the viewpoint of Community law. From the viewpoint of international law, though, certain considerations come across as rather defensive, if not arrogant. Is it proper to treat the UN Charter, the constituent instrument of the post-Second World War international community and long predating the EC/EU, as simply 'an international agreement', referring thereby to case-law on treaties such as the European Economic Area (EEA) Agreement, the 1982 UN Convention on the Law of the Sea ('UNCLOS') and a number of framework agreements on bananas, which were all concluded by the EC long after it had been established?[87] Why did the ECJ not pay the slightest attention to the ramifications of

---

[84] *Ibid.*, para. 326, confirmed by the ECJ in Joined Cases C-399/06 P and C-403/06P *Hassan and Ayadi* v. *Council and Commision* [2009] not yet published, para. 71.
[85] *Kadi, supra* n. 3, para. 352.   [86] *Ibid.*, para. 369.
[87] The first two treaties concern the cases referred to in para. 282 of the ECJ's *Kadi* judgment which deal with them: Opinion 1/91 [1991] ECR I-6079 (*EEA Agreement*) and Case C-459/03 *Commission* v. *Ireland* [2006] ECR I-4635 (*UNCLOS*); the framework agreements on bananas were at stake in Case C-122/95 *Germany* v. *Council* [1998] ECR 973, referred to in para. 289.

provisions such as Art. 103 and 25 of the UN Charter?[88] What kind of signal did the Court send to the rest of the world, now that it 'subordinated the international obligations of EU Member States under the UN Charter (in particular to carry out Chapter VII resolutions) to Community law?'[89] Was it necessary to stress – not fewer than three times – the 'autonomy' of the Community legal order?[90] Why did the Court disregard the question of the Community being bound by the UN Charter in so far as it had assumed powers previously exercised by EU Member States[91] and duck the question of hierarchy?[92] From an EU law point of view, one may add the question: what remains of this 'autonomy of the Community legal order' since the entry into force of the Treaty of Lisbon, which formally abolished the three-pillar system of the old TEU and saw the Community 'replaced and succeeded' by the Union?[93]

These, and many other questions will continue to animate the debate for some years to come. Meanwhile, the question arises whether some middle-ground solution between the monist and dualist extremes would

---

[88] Rather, the ECJ used the vague terms 'observance of the undertakings given in the context of the United Nations' (paras. 292–293; compare Kadi, supra n. 64, para. 222, using similar language but explicitly mentioning the relevant UN Charter provisions). See also the criticism of the ECJ's reasoning regarding the freedom of States to choose the mode of implementation of Security Council measures in para. 298 in the light of the requirements of Art. 25 of the UN Charter: L. van den Herik and N. Schrijver, 'Eroding the Primacy of the UN System of Collective Security. The Judgment of the European Court of Justice in the Cases of Kadi and Al Barakaat', *International Organizations Law Review*, 5 (2008), 329–38, 335.

[89] A. Aust, 'Kadi. Ignoring International Legal Obligations', *International Organizations Law Review*, 6 (2009), 293–8, 298. See also the concern for a 'fragilisation' of international law expressed in M. Beulay, 'Les arrêts Kadi et Al Barakaat International Foundation. Réaffirmation par la Cour de justice de l'autonomie de l'ordre juridique communautaire *vis-à-vis* du droit international', *Revue du Marché commun et de l'Union européenne*, 524 (2009), 32–40, 39.

[90] *Kadi, supra* n. 3, paras. 282, 316, 317. In this respect, see P. Daillier ('Contribution au débat entre monisme et dualisme de l'ordre juridique de l'Union européenne', *Revue du Marché commun et de l'Union européenne*, 529 (2009), 394–96, 396), who pointedly warns that '[a]ffirmer trop directement la primauté ou l'autonomie d'un ordre juridique qui s'inscrit dans un ordre plus vaste peut porter atteinte à la légitimité et à la crédibilité internationale de cet ordre partiel'.

[91] Compare *Kadi, supra* n. 64, para. 203. The correctness of this consideration has been supported by L. M. Hinojosa Martínez, 'Bad Law for Good Reasons. The Contradictions of the *Kadi* Judgment', *International Organizations Law Review*, 5 (2008), 339–57, 341; compare Tomuschat, *supra* n. 78, 542–3.

[92] See in particular the formulation of the ECJ in *Kadi, supra* n. 3, para. 305.

[93] Art. 1, para. 3, TEU. Compare with *Kadi, supra* n. 3, para. 202, where the ECJ refers to the 'coexistence of the Union and the Community as integrated but separate legal orders'.

not have been possible and even preferable. The present author favours the approach advocated by authors such as de Búrca and Halberstam and Stein. They admit that there are lacunae in the UN human rights system and admit the possibility for regional and national courts to indirectly review Security Council measures on this matter, but they disagree with the path chosen by the ECJ. They argue that local and regional courts, such as the ECJ, should review Security Council measures against customary international human rights law and the general principles of law derived from the constitutions and practice of States.[94]

Oddly enough, neither the judgment of the CFI nor that of the ECJ referred to customary international human rights law. If the ECJ had reviewed the UN sanctions regime not solely on the basis of its 'domestic' fundamental rights standards but rather on the basis of customary international human rights law, 'the Court would have led the way beyond European particularism toward a more productive engagement with international law for all'.[95] De Búrca advocates in this same vein what she refers to as a 'soft constitutional approach', adding convincingly that such approach 'would fit better with the aspirations of the EU as an international actor and with its professed identity as a good international citizen, yet would not give up on the concerns of international accountability and rights-protection'.[96] In the light of the provisions of the Lisbon Treaty emphasising the EU's attachment to 'the strict observance and the development of international law' (see *supra*, p. 199), it is hard to disagree with this approach.

Intertanko: is the ECJ also reconsidering previous case-law on the applicability of customary international law and international agreements?

Exactly three months before *Kadi*, on 3 June 2008, the ECJ handed down its judgment in *Intertanko*, which also appears to be at odds with certain aspects of the Court's previous case-law on the relationship between international law and EU Law.

In *Intertanko*, the Court was asked to pronounce itself on the validity of Arts. 4 and 5 of Directive 2005/35/EC of the European Parliament and

---

[94] D. Halberstam and E. Stein, 'The United Nations, the European Union, and the King of Sweden. Economic Sanctions and Individual Rights in a Plural World Order', *Common Market Law Review*, 46 (2009), 13, 68.

[95] Halberstam and Stein, *supra* n. 94, 72.   [96] G. de Búrca, *supra* n. 71, 55.

of the Council of 7 September 2005 on ship-source pollution and on the introduction of penalties for infringements.[97] The ECJ concluded that it could not assess the validity of the Directive either in the light of the 1973 International Convention for the Prevention of Pollution from Ships and its 1978 Protocol ('Marpol 73/78') or in the light of UNCLOS. In the process, the Court elaborated upon, albeit not without contestation, the relationship between EC law and various norms of international law.[98]

Concerning Marpol 73/78, the Court first observed that the EC is not a party to this Convention and that it has not assumed the powers previously exercised by the Member States in the field to which the Convention applies.[99] It also affirmed that the mere fact that all EU Member States are parties to the Convention and that the Directive has the objective of incorporating certain rules set out in that Convention into Community law is insufficient for the Court to assess the validity of the Directive in the light of Marpol 73/78.[100]

More interestingly, after recalling that 'the powers of the Community must be exercised in observance of international law, including provisions of international agreements in so far as they codify customary rules of general international law',[101] the Court affirmed that the relevant regulations of Marpol 73/78 entailed no such codification.

By contrast to Marpol, UNCLOS is clearly binding upon the EC, which is a party to it. In the light of Art. 300(7) TEC and the Court's well-established case-law regarding the place of such agreements within EC law (see *supra*, p. 205), UNCLOS has primacy over EC legislation, including the Directive. But according to the ECJ, 'the nature and the broad logic of UNCLOS'[102] precludes the examination of the validity of Community measures in the light of its provisions. Its relevant provisions do 'not establish rules intended to apply directly and immediately to individuals and to confer upon them rights or freedoms capable of being relied upon against States, irrespective of the attitude of the ship's flag State'.[103]

---

[97] OJ 2005 L 255/11; *corrigenda* OJ 2006 L 33/87 and L 105/65.

[98] For a closer analysis, see J. Wouters and Ph. De Man, Case Note to European Court of Justice, International Association of Independent Tanker Owners (Intertanko) Case C-308/06, *AJIL*, 103 (2009), 555–60.

[99] *Intertanko, supra* n. 4, paras. 47–48. [100] *Ibid.*, paras. 49–50. [101] *Ibid.*, para. 51.

[102] *Intertanko, supra* n. 4, para. 54. This 'nature and broad logic' criterion appeared first, but in a liberal manner, in Case C-344/04 *IATA and ELFAA, supra* n. 24, para. 39. Similar to *Intertanko*, it was applied in a restrictive manner in Joined Cases C-120/06P and C-121/06P *FIAMM* v. *Council and Commission* [2008] ECR I-6513, para. 110.

[103] *Ibid.*, para. 64.

It is rather disappointing that the ECJ in *Intertanko* relied on the 'direct effect' doctrine to decide whether the provisions of UNCLOS are invocable. The Court's earlier case-law had sparked hopes that such invocability would not have to depend upon whether international agreements have direct effect – i.e. whether their provisions appear unconditional and sufficiently precise – but *Intertanko* shows that, in this respect, appearances can be deceiving. The provisions of UNCLOS lacking direct effect are thus not invocable. Remarkably, the Court failed to take into consideration the possible effects of customary international law codified in UNCLOS. This is quite surprising, because it does consider this question for Marpol 73/78. This is even more peculiar in the light of the Court's acknowledgement in *Poulsen* that many provisions of UNCLOS are 'considered to express the current State of customary international maritime law'.[104] Not only can UNCLOS not be invoked as such because it lacks direct effect, but the Court does not even take into consideration the rules of customary international law that UNCLOS reflects. The ECJ thereby seems to quash all hopes one might have had after *Racke*[105] and *Biotechnical Inventions*[106](see *supra*, p. 206) for a more lenient approach toward the invocability of customary international law and provisions of international agreements binding the Community by firmly re-introducing the requirement of direct effect. Not surprisingly, it has been said that the ECJ takes a 'largely instrumentalist and self-serving approach to international legal obligations'.[107]

Concluding remarks

If anything, this chapter will have shown that the relationship between international law and EU law is far from a straightforward one. This is partly related to the *sui generis* nature of the EU compared with other international organisations and more generally with other subjects of international law. Throughout the past five decades, the ECJ has been struggling with this issue. Whereas in the beginning the relationship was a tense one and was characterised by the need to affirm the autonomy of the Community's legal order, the Court's case-law gradually seemed to

---

[104] *Poulsen, supra* n. 16, para. 10.   [105] See *supra* n. 2 and p. 202.
[106] See *supra* n. 39 and accompanying text.
[107] G. de Búrca, 'Comment. The European Courts and the Security Council: Between Dédoublement Fonctionnel and Balancing of Values. Three Rephes to Pasquale De Sena and Maria Chiara Vitucci', *EJIL*, 20 (2009), 853–62, 853.

be relaxing and moving in the direction of greater openness toward international law. *Racke* (1998)[108] is clearly an illustration of this, as it affirmed, at least in theory, the possible invocability of customary international law for the purpose of reviewing the legality of EU legislation.

Kadi (2008)[109] not only appears to have put an end to this positive evolution, it even made a clear turn back. In *Kadi*, the ECJ adopted a strongly dualist vision of the relationship between EC/EU law and international law, emphasising the autonomy, authority and separateness of the EC legal order. *Kadi* is completely focused on the EC legal order. One would hope that the Court was in the end more prone to ensure the respect of fundamental rights in the fight against terror than to reassert the autonomy of the EC legal order *vis-à-vis* international law.

Lastly, the turn which the Court took in *Intertanko* (2008)[110] seems to confirm that the position of the ECJ *vis-à-vis* international law is becoming more strict again. This type of judgment makes it rather difficult for norms of international law to be effectively applied in the EU legal order.

It is to be hoped that, now that the UN Security Council seems to have responded to *Kadi* by thoroughly adapting the sanctions regime by its resolution 1904 (2009) adopted on 17 December 2009 – *inter alia* by introducing an independent and impartial ombudsperson to receive requests for delisting of individuals and entities – the ECJ will again be receptive to a more harmonious relationship and interactive dialogue between international and EU law.

---

[108] See *supra* n. 2.   [109] See *supra* n. 3.   [110] See *supra* n. 4.

13

International law scholarship in times of dictatorship and democracy: exemplified by the life and work of Wilhelm Wengler

ANDREAS ZIMMERMANN[*]

Introduction

Detlev Vagts has carried out much research on international law during the Nazi period,[1] including on Wilhelm Wengler and his fate during that time.[2] In this *Festschrift* in Detlev's honour, a focus on the life and work of Wilhelm Wengler,[3] an international law scholar who stood in close contact with the German resistance movement to National Socialism, is particularly appropriate. The academic context in which Wengler was working demonstrates the options open to German international law scholars after 1933. These ranged from genuine enthusiasm for National Socialism, over academic and personal adaptation to the 'new realities' and resort to internal or external emigration to insurgency. Wengler's life

[*] I am particularly grateful to Marianne Nilsson for providing extremely valuable help in translating the chapter, as well as to Daniel Peat, LLB (LSE) for reviewing the manuscript. Thanks also go to the archives of the following institutions for enabling access to their files on Wilhelm Wengler: Max Planck Gesellschaft, Humboldt Universität and Freie Universität Berlin, Bundesarchiv Berlin, as well as Bundesbehörde für die Unterlagen des Staatssicherheitsdienstes der ehemaligen DDR (Federal Commissioner for the Documents of the State Security Service of the former GDR).
[1] Cf. D. Vagts, 'International Law in the Third Reich', *AJIL*, 84 (1990), 661–704.
[2] *Ibid.*, 673.
[3] Cf. also F. v. Schlabrendorff, 'Wilhelm Wengler – Wesen und Gestalt', in J. Tittel (ed.), *Multitudo legum – ius unum – Festschrift für Wilhelm Wengler zu seinem 65. Geburtstag* (Berlin: Interrecht, 1973), 1–21; W. Rudolf, 'Wilhelm Wengler zum 70. Geburtstag', *Archiv für Öffentliches Recht*, (1977), 610–12; K. Wähler, 'Wilhelm Wengler zum 75. Geburtstag', *NJW* (1982), 1444; *ibid.*, 'Wilhelm Wengler zum 80. Geburtstag', *NJW* (1987), 2135; F. Sturm, 'Wilhelm Wengler octogenario gratulamur', *JR* (1987), 490–4; E. Jayme, 'Nachruf: Wilhelm Wengler', *JZ* (1995), 1058; C. Kohler, 'Wilhelm Wengler (1907–1995)', *IPrax* 1996, 152–5.

also exemplifies how post-war scholarship in Germany and abroad evaluated the attitude of German scholars before 1945.

Studies, doctoral thesis and scholarly activities at the Kaiser Wilhelm Institute of Comparative and International Private Law and the Kaiser Wilhelm Institute of Comparative Public Law and International Law

Wilhelm Wengler was born on 12 June 1907, to working-class parents in Wiesbaden. After attending secondary school, he studied law and political science at the University of Frankfurt/Main from 1927 until 1931.[4] In Frankfurt, he also passed his First State Exam with distinction, and also met Hans Lewald, who later became his doctoral supervisor. In 1931 he obtained his doctorate in law *magna cum laude* with a thesis on the primacy of international law,[5] as well as his doctorate in political science *summa cum laude* with a thesis on double taxation.[6] Immediately thereafter, he began his practical legal training and simultaneously started working as a research fellow at the University of Frankfurt/Main before moving to the Kaiser Wilhelm Institute of Comparative and International Public Law in Berlin. His first day at work was 1 May 1933, just after the Nazi government seized power (*Machtergreifung*).[7]

Even before his Second State Exam in 1935 Wengler, like all Prussian junior lawyers was obliged to attend, from March to May 1935, a *Gemeinschaftslager* (community camp) in Jüterbog/Brandenburg. This

---

[4] For the history of the Faculty of Law of the University of Frankfurt/Main during the Weimar Republic period, cf. N. von Hammerstein, *Die Johann-Wolfgang-Goethe-Universität Frankfurt am Main: von der Stiftungsuniversität zur staatlichen Hochschule, vol 1: 1914–1950* (Neuwied and Frankfurt/Main: Alfred Metzner Verlag, 1989), 140–4.

[5] W. Wengler, 'Studien zur Lehre vom Primat des Völkerrechts', *Zeitschrift für Völkerrecht* (1936), 322–92.

[6] W. Wengler, *Beiträge zum Problem der internationalen Doppelbesteuerung. Die Begriffsbildung im internationalen Steuerrecht, Beiträge zum ausländischen und internationalen Steuerrecht*, vol. 11 (Berlin: de Gruyter, 1935). Copies of the certificates are located in Wengler's personnel file in the archive of the Freie Universität Berlin.

[7] Letter from Kaiser Wilhelm Institute, 28 February 1933, according to which it was foreseen that Wengler would 'assist Prof. Lewald in his research work on international private law at the Institute, especially for summary reports on the development of particular doctrines home and abroad', cf. Wengler's personnel file at the Freie Universität Berlin, XIV.

initiative of the Prussian Minister of Justice, Hanns Kerrl,[8] was designed to expose young lawyers to paramilitary and ideological training.[9] Wengler's *Lagerzeugnis* (camp certificate) shows both his unambiguously negative view of the Nazi regime and his frankness. The certificate mentions that his attitude to camp life was 'negative from the very beginning', and that his attitude to the Nazi regime was 'anything but not suspicious'.[10] In addition, the certificate testified that Wilhelm Wengler rejoiced in having failed the sports badge of the *Sturmabteilung* (SA), as he regarded the strengthening of the SA as a 'death sentence for the German Armed Forces'.[11] In particular, the certificate attested to Wengler's desire 'to cross the border, to get out of Germany, because here one cannot live and work freely'.[12] Unsurprisingly, he was considered unsuitable for the civil service because of this negative evaluation.[13] In reaction to these statements, the government prosecution service launched a preliminary investigation against him, alleging a misdemeanour according to para. 2 of the 'Law on Malicious Attacks on State and Party'. However, with the approval by the Minister of Justice, this suit was dropped on 23 November 1935. Having passed his Second State Exam, Wengler became a full-time assistant at the Kaiser Wilhelm Institute of Comparative and International Private Law from 1935 until 1944. At the same time, he also worked at the Kaiser Wilhelm Institute of Comparative Public Law and International Law.[14]

---

[8] Decree by the Prussian State Ministry, *Preußisches Justizministerialblatt*, I 10136, 29 June 1933, 210. For more details, see V. Schmerbach, *Das 'Gemeinschaftslager Hanns Kerl' für Referendare in Jüterbog, 1933–1939* (Tübingen: Mohr Siebeck, 2008).

[9] See also the analysis of this system of *Gemeinschaftslager* in the judgment of the International Military Tribunal Nuremberg, IMT, Bd. III, 99.

[10] Certificate of 18 May 1935, 1, Bundesarchiv Sign. R 1501, Aktenbd. 16329, 26799; also available in Max Planck Institute of Comparative Public Law and International Law, archives related to the Institute's history 1927–1934, Annex 1935–1944.

[11] *Ibid.*   [12] *Ibid.*, 2.   [13] *Ibid.*

[14] Cf. also Rudolf, *supra* n. 3, 610. However, the Institute of Comparative Law and International Law did not belong to the Kaiser Wilhelm Society until 1938, but was rather co-financed by the Foreign Office and the Kaiser Wilhelm Society. It became part of the Kaiser Wilhelm Society when the Nazi government came to power in order to restrict governmental influence on the Institute. Cf., generally, the role of the Kaiser Wilhelm Institute of Comparative Law and International Law under national socialism, I. Hueck, 'Die deutsche Völkerrechtswissenschaft im Nationalsozialismus. Das Berliner Kaiser-Wilhelm-Institut für ausländisches öffentliches Recht und Völkerrecht, das Hamburger Institut für Auswärtige Politik und das Kieler Institut für Internationales Recht', in D. Kaufmann (ed.), *Geschichte der Kaiser-Wilhelm-Gesellschaft im Nationalsozialismus–Bestandsaufnahme und Perspektiven der Forschung*, Bd. 2 (Göttingen: Wallstein, 2000), 490, 499.

His early academic work[15] was predominantly devoted to colonial law[16] – his main responsibility as a scientific assistant at the Kaiser Wilhelm Institute of Comparative Public Law and International Law from the beginning.[17] This led to his membership in a working group on 'Colonial Law'[18] of the Academy of German Law.[19] There he devoted increasing attention to methodological issues such as the application of *ius soli* in African colonies.[20] In this context, his preface to a briefer monograph from 1937 on the administrative organisation of colonies in tropical Africa encapsulates his scholarly approach, as well as the increasing necessity for political caution. According to that preface, he intended to focus on comparative law and 'to examine the issues exclusively from the legal point of view', while expressly stating that it was inappropriate 'to criticize the colonial law of other countries'.[21] Nevertheless, it is worth noting that Wengler served as a legal advisor in the Colonial Department of the Nazi Party (NSDAP) until 1943.

[15] A survey of Wengler's œuvre until 1972 is found in his *Festschrift, supra* n. 3, vol. II, 885.

[16] Cf. also Wengler's publication list in his *Festschrift, supra* n. 3, No. 5 (1936), Nos. 10–12 (1937), Nos. 16–17 (1939), Nos. 24–25 (1940), No. 26 (1941), Nos. 27–28 (1942) and No. 28 (1942).

[17] According to Bruns, Wengler himself had realised how he could to some extent keep away the persecutors, namely in considering the fact that the Nazi leaders had an increased interest in colonial issues, but not enough experts. Therefore Wengler planned to write 'comparing works on colonial law without leaving the scientific terrain', W. Wengler, 'Erwiderung', in P. Eisenmann and G. Zieger (eds.), *Zur Rechtslage Deutschlands – innerstaatlich und international* (Munich: Hanns-Seidl-Stiftung, 1990), 16–21, 18.

[18] Cf. W. Schubert (ed.), *Akademie für Deutsches Recht, 1933–1945, Protokolle der Ausschüsse, vol. 12: Ausschuss für Rechtsfragen der Bevölkerungspolitik (1934–1940)*, 1–256 and *Ausschuss für Kolonialrecht mit den Entwürfen des Kolonialpolitischen Amts (1937–1941)* (Frankfurt/Main: Lang, 2001), 411–567, 569–609.

[19] Wengler's essay, 'Die Verwaltungsorganisation der Kolonien im tropischen Afrika', was published in 1937 as vol. 2 in the publication series of the Academy for German Law, Department of Colonial Law. For general information on the work and function of the Academy for German Law, cf. H.-R. Pichinot, *Die Akademie für Deutsches Recht – Aufbau und Entwicklung einer öffentlich-rechtlichen Körperschaft des Dritten Reiches* (PhD thesis, Universität Kiel, 1981).

[20] *Koloniale Rundschau*, 1942, 205–28. However, the contribution on 'Generalklauseln bei der Rechtsanwendung in den Kolonien', for which Wengler had been granted 5000 Reichsmark of research funds by the Federal Research Council in April 1943, was never completed.

[21] W. Wengler, *Die Verwaltungsorganisation der Kolonien im tropischen Afrika – Grundlinien des Kolonialverwaltungsrechts Englands, Frankreichs, Italiens und Belgiens* (Munich and Leipzig: Duncker & Humblot, 1937), 5. For a survey of Wengler's contributions for the Colonial Committee of the Academy for German Law, see W. Schubert, *Akademie, supra* n. 18, 411–16.

Although Wengler's outlines for a 'constitutional law in German colonies', from June 1937,[22] and for the organisation of 'European law in future German colonies'[23] were formulated in a rather neutral manner, his explanations in 1938 concerning the issue of nationality within German colonies 'to be potentially recaptured in the future' not only contained proposals regarding the acquisition or loss of the 'nationality' of these territories ('*Schutzangehörigkeit*'), but differentiated according to their race, as well as between Europeans and indigenous individuals.[24] Whereas the first differentiation could scarcely be avoided under the prevailing political conditions, the second differentiation between Europeans and the indigenous population tracked the legal terminology of the German Colonial Law of 1886.

Apart from colonial law, Wengler also dealt with public and private international law.[25] He developed various essential theories on private international law that are still indispensable today.[26] It might be of special interest in the present context that Wengler's article from 1944, on general principles of private international law,[27] was translated into French and published in the *Revue critique de droit international privé*, only a few years after the Second World War.[28] On the one hand, this serves as proof that his legal thinking was not imbued with the spirit of National Socialism, unlike many of his colleagues. On the other hand, it shows clearly how Wengler's attitude during the time of National Socialism was observed and evaluated abroad after 1945.[29]

In 1937, Wengler had already been nominated for a professorship at the University of Munich, but his appointment failed for political reasons. The Minister for Science, Education and Culture, whose attention had apparently been drawn to Wengler, ordered an investigation in light of Wengler's 'most subversive statements', questioning whether he could stay in his position at the Kaiser Wilhelm Institute.[30] However, thanks to the intervention of the

---

[22] *Ibid.*, 427–34.   [23] *Ibid.*, 538–49, 554–9.   [24] *Ibid.*, 497–501.

[25] Cf. in Wengler's *Festschrift*, *supra* n. 3, No. 1 (1934) as well as No. 14 (1938), 20–2, 24–5 (1940) and No. 31 (1944).

[26] Literal excerpt from E. Jayme, Nachruf auf Wilhelm Wengler, Juristenzeitung 1995, 1058, referring to the legal concepts of '*Vorfrage*' (preliminary question) and '*Substitution*'.

[27] *Zeitschrift für öffentliches Recht* (1944), 473–509.

[28] Wengler, 'Les Principes généraux du droit international privé et leurs conflits', *Revue critique de droit international privé* (1952), 595–622, and (1953), 37–60.

[29] For this issue and his admission to the *Institut de Droit International* in 1950, see *infra* p. 239.

[30] Letter to the President of the Kaiser Wilhelm Society dated 13 April 1937, Wengler's personnel file at the Freie Universität Berlin, 4.

then-director of the Kaiser Wilhelm Institute of Comparative Public Law and International Law, Viktor Bruns,[31] a possible discharge was averted. In the same way, he was denied a lectureship in colonial law which was supposed to become effective as from the winter term 1938/39 at the Faculty of Law and Political Science of the University of Göttingen, due to doubts about Wengler's political reliability. The main motivation for the abovementioned proceedings against him was accusations that he had violated the 'Law on Malicious Attacks on State and Party'.[32]

In the end, however, Wengler had to swallow a bitter pill. On 1 July 1936, he became, like many others, a member of the *NS-Rechtswahrerbund*,[33] i.e. the organisation of legal scholars affiliated with the Nazi party, arguably in order to prove, at least at a minimum, his loyalty to the regime. In 1940 he also became a member of the *NS-Volkswohlfahrt*,[34] as well as a member of the *Reichskolonialbund* (German Colonial League),[35] which was linked to his activities in the Colonial Board of the Academy of German Law.

Role in the Supreme Command of the German Armed Forces (1942–4)

From the beginning of the Second World War, the Kaiser Wilhelm Institute of Comparative Public Law and International Law, by mutual

---

[31] For more details on the role of Viktor Bruns see, e.g., Anna-Maria Gräfin von Lösch, *Der nackte Geist – Die Juristische Fakultät der Berliner Universität im Umbruch von 1933*, (Tübingen: Mohr-Siebeck, 1999), 388–90.; cf. also the obituary by H. Triepel, 'Viktor Bruns †', *ZaöRV* (1942/3), 324.

[32] Letter to the author, Archive of the University of Göttingen, 3 August 2007 (on file with the author).

[33] Regarding the *NS-Rechtswahrerbund*'s tasks and structures, see the detailed description by Sunnus, *Der NS Rechtswahrerbund (1928–1945) – zur Geschichte der nationalsozialistischen Juristenorganisation*, (Frankfurt/Main: Lang, 1990). Like all other Nazi organisations, the NS-Rechtswahrerbund was also liquidated by the Control Council Law No. 2 regarding the termination and liquidation of Nazi organisations, dated 10 October 1945.

[34] See, generally, H. Vorländer, *Die NSV. Darstellung und Dokumentation einer nationalsozialistischen Organisation* (Boppard am Rhein: Harald Boldt, 1988).

[35] The German Colonial League (Reichskolonialbund) was liquidated in 1943 and its funds transmitted to the NSDAP. The 'Law for Liberation from National Socialism and Militarism' of 5 March 1946 (Annex to the 'Gesetz zur Befreiung von Nationalsozialismus und Militarismus vom 5. März 1946', Part A, H., Class I, No. 2) stated that the German Colonial League had been neither a party organisation nor a society affiliated to the NSDAP. It seems that Wengler had applied for membership of the *NS-Dozentenbund* in March 1942, but it is not clear if he was ever admitted.

agreement, advised the Supreme Command of the German Armed Forces on the laws of war. Graf Stauffenberg[36] and Professor Schmitz, both employed at the Institute, acted exclusively as legal advisors for the Naval War Command (*Seekriegsleitung*) and as international legal advisors for the Foreign Section/Counterintelligence Service (Section Canaris) (*OKW Amtsgruppe Ausland/Abwehr* (Office Canaris)), respectively. The aim of the agreement was to expand the Department of International Law, which had already existed within the Supreme Command's Foreign Section since the beginning of the war, to an international law team and an advisory office for international law.[37] After Schmitz's death in 1942, Wengler was posted to that department until his arrest by the Gestapo in January 1944.[38] The advisory office's work aimed first and foremost at securing compliance with the minimum standards of international law and humanitarian law by the National Socialist leadership.[39] The office was significantly influenced by Helmuth James Graf von Moltke, who was a member of the Kreisau Circle, part of the German resistance movement.[40] Without being a member of the Institute, he contributed several articles to the *Zeitschrift für ausländisches öffentliches Recht und Völkerrecht (ZaöRV)*,[41] and had a

---

[36] For more details, see A. Meyer, *Berthold Schenk Graf von Stauffenberg (1905-1944) – Völkerrecht im Widerstand* (Berlin: Duncker & Humblot, 2001), as well as especially on his activities at the Kaiser Wilhelm Institute, 47 *et seq.*, 58 *et seq.*, 63 *et seq.* on the one hand, and at OKW, 70 *et seq.*, on the other.

[37] For further details, see G. van Roon, *Helmuth James Graf von Moltke – Völkerrecht im Dienste des Menschen* (Berlin: Siedler, 1986), 21, as well as the order by the Chief of OKW dated 15 September 1939, *ibid.*, 176.

[38] From 1938 until 1942 the following members of the Kaiser Wilhelm Institute had also been active there: Günther Jaenicke (cf. K.-H. Böckstiegel, 'Laudatio auf Günther Jaenicke anlässlich seines 85. Geburtstages am 5. Januar 1999', in V. Götz *et al.* (eds.), *Liber amicorum Günther Jaenicke – zum 85. Geburtstag, 1998*, VII ff., VIII; and, after the arrest of Wengler, Hermann Mosler.

[39] Some concise examples of the international law issues, which at that time could have been of interest for the circle around Moltke, to which Wengler belonged, can be found at F. v. Schlabrendorff, 'Wilhelm Wengler', *supra* n. 3, 3–5. Cf. also as to the role of the OKW, Vagts, 'International Law', *supra* n. 1, 696–8.

[40] On his personality, see, e.g., G. Brakelmann, *Helmuth James von Moltke 1907–1945: Eine Biografie* (Munich: Beck, 2007), esp. 282–97, 299, 323 concerning the cooperation between Moltke and Wengler. See also Vagts, 'International Law', *supra* n. 1, 681–2.

[41] Cf. H. J. Graf von Moltke, 'Zur Rechtsstellung der Dominions im Britischen Reich', *ZaöRV* (1935), 935–42; *idem.*, 'Verfassungsrechtliche Fragen des Empire im Zusammenhang mit dem Thronwechsel, insbesondere in der Süd-Afrikanischen Union', *ZaöRV* (1937), 634–7; *idem.*, 'Verteilung der gesetzgeberischen Zuständigkeit zwischen Dominion und Provinzen in Canada', *ZaöRV* (1937), 638–43; *idem.*, Die Lossagung Großbritanniens, Frankreichs, Australiens, Neuseelands, Südafrikas und

thorough knowledge of the Kaiser Wilhelm Institute of Comparative Public Law and International Law. On various occasions Moltke commented upon his collaboration with Wengler as thoroughly positive.[42] In return, Wengler heaped praise on Moltke's work at the Supreme Command of the German Armed Forces in his first article after the war in 1948.[43]

It cannot be stated with sufficient certainty, however, whether Wengler had been aware of Moltke's resistance activities.[44] In July 1943, for example, Wengler and Moltke jointly went on an official journey to Istanbul, in order to debate the legal status of French warships that had been confiscated in the Sea of Marmara with Turkish assistance. But as a matter of fact, Moltke wanted, on the one hand, to contact Allied bodies there, and on the other hand, to attempt once more, at significant risk, to gain the support of Franz von Papen, the German Ambassador to Turkey and former Chancellor, for the resistance against Hitler.[45]

Denunciation, dismissal and arrest

Shortly before Wengler was to finish his official trip and return from Istanbul to Berlin, Herbert Kier, an employee at the Institute and a convinced national socialist, denounced him.[46] The reason for the

---

Indiens von den Verpflichtungen der Fakultativklausel, Art. 36 des Statuts des Ständigen Internationalen Gerichtshofes', *ZaöRV* (1939/1940), 620–6; *idem.*, 'Entscheidungen nationaler Gerichte in völkerrechtlichen Fragen. Britisches Reich', *ZaöRV* (1939/1940), 881–907, as well as *idem.*, 'Die britische Order in Council vom 17. Nov. 1939 über die Beschlagnahme deutscher Ausfuhrwaren', *ZaöRV* (1940/1941), 110–26.

[42] Cf. the letters to Günther Jaenicke, 15 January 1944 (printed in van Roon, *Helmuth James Graf von Moltke, supra* n. 37, 278–9, 279 as well as of 4 March 1943, *ibid.*, 289–90.

[43] W. Wengler, 'H. J. Graf von Moltke 1906–1945 (Vorkämpfer der Völkerverständigung und Völkerrechtsgelehrte als Opfer des Nationalsozialismus)', *Friedenswarte* (1948), 297–395. See also the appreciation in the preface to Wengler, *Völkerrecht*, vol. I (Berlin: Springer, 1964), x *et seq.* See also G. van Roon, 'Helmuth James Graf von Moltke als Völkerrechtler', *ZaöRV* (1987), 740–54.

[44] This was addressed, albeit probably negatively, in a letter related to the quarrels with the Max Planck Society on a possible indemnification, expressing that there were 'insinuations, that Herr W. [sic!] had probably also been active for a certain group with Canaris or, actually, for foreign services' ('*Andeutungen, dass Herr W. (sic!) wahrscheinlich auch für eine bestimmte Gruppe bei Canaris oder sogar für ausländische Dienststellen gearbeitet habe*'), Wengler's personnel file, Archive of the Max Planck Society.

[45] See, generally, Brakelmann, *Helmuth James von Moltke, supra* note 40, 282–97.

[46] On the personality of Kier, see Hueck, 'Die deutsche Völkerrechtswissenschaft', *supra* n. 14, 511. Kier had been member of the NSDAP in 1931(!). In 1934, he came to Germany from Austria, became a member of the SS in the same year and started to work at the Institute in 1936, where his principal responsibility was *Volksgruppenrecht* (the law of

denunciation was alleged[47] comments by Wengler to a Dutch member of the German Waffen SS. That Dutch Waffen SS member, in a conversation with Kier, had accused Wengler of having told him in 1942 that he could not understand why a Dutch citizen was fighting for the Germans, as this could not favour The Netherlands. In a letter of 21 October 1943, the then-General Secretary of the Kaiser Wilhelm Society, Ernst Telschow,[48] notified this incident to the Minister for Science, Education and National Culture, and expressed major doubts as to the 'political trustworthiness of Wengler', with reference to the already mentioned 'incident' in the 'Gemeinschaftslager' of 1937.[49] Furthermore, Kier, in his function as liaison officer for the NS Dozentenbund at the Kaiser Wilhelm Institute, informed the leader of the Gestapo headquarters in Berlin. Shortly after, upon his return from Istanbul, on 25 October 1943, the temporary management of the Institute interrogated Wengler (Viktor Bruns had died shortly before Wengler's return). As soon as 26 October 1943, the Ministry had informed the Reichssicherheitshauptamt of the matter and mentioned at the same time Wengler's collaboration with a 'certain Graf von Moltke'.

Wengler in turn reported this to the German Army's Supreme Command. To forestall a possible arrest by the Gestapo, the Army's Central Court immediately, and with Wengler's agreement, initiated an inquiry on his 'subversive statements'. Nevertheless, in January 1944, the Gestapo arrested him. During his imprisonment, the Kaiser Wilhelm

---

minority groups). In addition he was *Unterführer* at the Berlin Faculty of the *NS-Dozentenschaft für die Juristen*, cf. Gräfin von Lösch, *Der nackte Geist*, supra n. 31, 256 et seq. After 1945, Kier apparently applied for another post at the Kaiser Wilhelm Society/Max Planck Society, but failed. For more details regarding the activities of the Academy for German Law on the *Volksgruppenrecht*, see W. Schubert, *Akademic*, supra n. 18, 352–88, 438–49.

[47] Wengler himself always contradicted this statement. Moltke literally stated in a letter to Günther Jaenicke of 15 January 1944 that 'a nasty and totally absurd denunciation had been launched against Wengler by his enemies in the private law institute in cooperation between Kier and the Secretary of the Kaiser Wilhelm Society ... Countering this absurdity will be difficult because the person primarily concerned [probably the Dutch SS Officer in question] is serving at the front'; see G. van Roon, *Helmuth James Graf von Moltke*, supra n. 37, 278–9.

[48] As to Telschow's personality and activity as Secretary General of the Kaiser Wilhelm Society, see also the critical assessment in A. Przyrembel, 'Glum und Telschow – die Generalsekretäre der Kaiser-Wilhelm-Gesellschaft. Handlungsfelder und Handlungsoptionen der "Verwaltenden" von Wissen während des Nationalsozialismus', www.mpiwg-berlin.mpg.de/KWG/Ergebnisse/Ergebnisse20.pdf.

[49] For more details, cf. *supra* p. 224.

Society gave notice of Wengler's instant dismissal in February 1944, which had been approved by the Ministry and the directors of both Kaiser Wilhelm Institutes. At the same time, the Kaiser Wilhelm Society informed the German Army that they were no longer interested in Wengler. In March 1944 the Gestapo transferred Wengler to the German Army, where he remained in custody until May 1944, when the proceedings against him were discontinued and he was released.[50] During his imprisonment Wengler challenged his dismissal before the Berlin Labour Tribunal. The Tribunal declared the dismissal, which was without notice, to be void and converted it into a dismissal with due notice. Shortly thereafter, Wengler was called up for military service effective on 27 July 1944, where he experienced the end of the war as a member of an interpreter platoon in Munich,[51] and shortly thereafter returned to Berlin, where the City Council recognised him as a victim of fascism.[52]

Excursus: the 'Wengler case' and the discussion about Viktor Bruns' successor at the Kaiser Wilhelm Institute of Comparative Public Law and International Law

After his first heart attack in 1942, Viktor Bruns pleaded, in a letter addressed to the head of the Kaiser Wilhelm Society, that 'only Professor Bilfinger, Graf Stauffenberg or Professor Scheuner could be considered as his successor'. He stated that '[i]n [his] opinion, Professor Ritterbusch or State Councillor [Carl] Schmitt are out of the question'.[53] The dissidents against Hitler at the Institute, led by Moltke and including Wengler, tried to convince the Kaiser Wilhelm

---

[50] An extensive presentation may be found in M. Schüring, 'Minervas verstoßene Kinder – Vertriebene Wissenschaftler und die Vergangenheitsbewältigung der Max-Planck-Gesellschaft', Geschichte der Kaiser-Wilhelm-Gesellschaft im Nationalsozialismus, 33 (2006), 240–6.

[51] Maybe this military draft also protected Wengler from further persecution in connection with the failed assassination of Hitler (20 July 1944); that, at any rate, was the appraisal of V. Schlabrendorff, 'Wilhelm Wengler', supra n. 3, 8.

[52] Wengler's curriculum vitae of 24 August 1947 is to be found in his personnel file at Humboldt University, 8.

[53] Archive of the Max Planck Society, personnel file Bruns, cited in Hueck, 'Die deutsche Völkerrechtswissenschaft', supra n. 14, 523. On Bilfinger, see R. Smend, 'Carl Bilfinger †', ZaöRV (1959), 1–4, who reports that Bilfinger had put up with the dictatorial Nazi regime; ibid., p. 3.

On the life and work of Ulrich Scheuner, see H. Ehmke, 'Geburtstagsrede', in H. Ehmke et al. (eds.), Festschrift für Ulrich Scheuner zum 70. Geburtstag (Berlin:

Society to appoint Graf Stauffenberg as the temporary successor of Viktor Bruns, at least until the end of the war.[54] Colonel Oxé, von Moltke's supervisor, submitted this request to Telschow, General-Secretary of the Kaiser Wilhelm Society, who rejected the request.[55] Shortly thereafter, Wengler was denounced by Kier, as previously noted. At any rate, Moltke understood the denunciation as follows: '(t)hey are taking aim at Wengler, in order to deny my right to co-appoint the new director.'[56]

Friedrich Saemisch, the former Prussian Finance Minister and former President of the Federal Auditing Office, was asked to prepare an expert report on a possible successor to Bruns. He confirmed Bruns' pre-screening by also favouring Bruns' cousin (!), Bilfinger, 'whose patriotism should be beyond doubt', whereas he entertained doubts on Stauffenberg's suitability, 'as one could not foresee for the time being in which sense the Institute's main focus would shift in the future'.[57] This decision, later confirmed by the Kaiser Wilhelm Society, had the long-term consequence of spoiling the chances of Wengler returning to the

---

Duncker & Humblot, 1973), 11–18 and U. Huber and K. Schlaich (eds.), *In Memoriam Ulrich Scheuner. Reden gehalten am 24. Oktober 1981 bei der Gedächtnisfeier der Rheinischen Friedrich-Wilhelms-Universität Bonn* (Bonn: Bouvier, 1982). As to Stauffenberg, see *supra* n. 36. On Rittersbusch, who since 1935 had been director of the Institute of International Law at Kiel, (which was renamed the 'Institut für Politik und Internationales Recht'), cf. Hueck, *supra* n. 14, 493–5, as well as F.-R. Hausmann, "Deutsche Geisteswissenschaft" im Zweiten Weltkrieg. Die "Aktion Rittersbusch" 1940–45' (1998). On Carl Schmitt, see B. Rüthers, 'Carl Schmitt im Dritten Reich' (Munich: Beck, 1990), as well as Vagts, 'International Law', *supra* n. 1, 683–4.

[54] Hueck, 'Die deutsche Völkerrechtswissenschaft', *supra* n. 14, 523.

[55] In contrast, Telschow claimed after the war that the circle around Moltke had attempted to involve Admiral Gladisch of the High Command of the Navy in the process of selecting a new director; cf. Wengler's personnel file, Archive of the Max Planck Society. On Gladisch's activities in international law during the Second World War, cf. D. Fleck (ed.), 'The Gladisch Committee on the Law of Naval Warfare. A German Effort to Develop International Law During World War II' (Bochum: Brockmeyer, 1990).

[56] Cited in Brakelmann, *Helmuth James von Moltke*, *supra* n. 40, 300. Wengler took it for granted that there was a causal link between his arrest and the forthcoming replacement of the director at the Kaiser Wilhelm Institute of Comparative Public Law and International Law; cf. Wengler's statements in his answer in Eisenmann and Zieger, *Zur Rechtslage Deutschlands*, *supra* n. 16, 19.

[57] Wengler personnel file, Archive of the Max Planck Society. A further fact was that Bilfinger, born in 1879, and thus by 1944 already sixty-five years old, was considered a mere transitional candidate, which left any possible post-war options open.

Institute, albeit the lawsuit against him had been abandoned[58] and the war had come to an end.[59]

Employment at the Friedrich Wilhelm University, Berlin

Before 1945

In January 1941, during his time at both Kaiser Wilhelm Institutes, Wengler was offered a lectureship in comparative colonial law at the Friedrich Wilhelm University of Berlin,[60] a post that he filled until 1943. Thereafter, in early July 1943, the Berlin law faculty requested Wengler's suspension in connection with the lawsuit announced against him.[61] When that lawsuit had been abandoned in the beginning of July 1944,[62] the faculty requested the renewal of the lectureship, with success.[63] Wengler was then called up for military service; and in February 1945 the Ministry for Science, Education and Culture cancelled the lectureship in colonial law.[64]

After 1945

After a short time in American captivity, Wengler had returned to Berlin by the end of July 1945, where he was first employed as a Deputy Director of the Legal Department of the German Traffic Administration in the Soviet Occupation Zone. In November 1945, Wengler contacted the German Education Administration in the Soviet Occupation Zone concerning a lectureship in International Law and Private International Law

---

[58] On this matter see *supra* p. 230 *et seq.*

[59] On Bilfinger's attitude regarding Wengler's possible return to the Institute after 1945 see *infra* p. 237.

[60] Letter of the Minister for Science, Education and Culture dated 10 January 1941, Wengler's personnel file, Archive of the Humboldt University Berlin. In some respect it is astonishing that Carl Schmitt who, on the recommendation of Viktor Bruns in November 1933, had become a scientific member of the Kaiser Wilhelm Institute of Comparative Public Law and International Law, and before having become a full professor at the University of Berlin due to the influence exercised by the Nazi government (for further details see Hueck, 'Die deutsche Völkerrechtswissenschaft', *supra* n. 14, 507), had expressed himself very positively on Wengler in 1941, cf. Letter by Schmitt addressed to the Dean of the Faculty of Foreign Studies at the University of Berlin dated 5 January 1941, Wengler's personnel file, Archive of the Free University Berlin.

[61] For more details see *infra* p. 229 *et seq.*   [62] *Ibid.*

[63] Letter of the Faculty for Foreign Studies of the Friedrich Wilhelm University of Berlin, 5 January 1941, Wengler's personnel file, Archive of the Free University Berlin.

[64] *Ibid.*

at Berlin University, which referred him to Eduard Kohlrausch, then Dean of the Law Faculty. Kohlrausch, who himself had played a problematic role at Berlin University after 1933,[65] answered, at least at first, positively in a letter dated June 1946, explaining that 'in view of his [Wengler's] broad and significant publications, a special *Habilitation* thesis was not mandatory'.[66] Yet, a note in the files of the Education Administration in the Soviet Occupation Zone, of November 1946, shows that Kohlrausch had held up Wengler's application for a Habilitation, and that the then-Dean Peters had approved Wengler's academic qualification, on the one hand, but, on the other hand, had deemed him to be a 'problematic person'. The note continued to State that the Faculty had considered offering the lectureship in international law to Karl von Lewinski, the former German General Consul in the United States of America and Kohlrausch's protégé, without any publications in international law, instead of to Wengler.[67] However, the remark continued that Wengler ought to be treated as a victim of Nazi persecution and thus ought to be privileged.[68]

In November 1946, the new Dean of the Law Faculty, Professor Peters, pointed out that Wengler was as a matter of principle obliged to present a new and unpublished *Habilitation* thesis, a precondition hard to comply with in the light of the prevailing circumstances. At the same time, Wengler was advised to apply for a *Habilitation* at another faculty.[69] Wengler answered by way of an open letter to the *Neue Zeitung*

---

[65] For extensive references, see Gräfin von Lösch, *Der nackte Geist, supra* n. 31, 161–75, in particular 170–5, 385–6. Therefore, Kohlrausch could remain in his position after his sixty-fifth birthday due to a formal approval by the Reichskanzlei. Cf. also his 'scientific' statements: E. Kohlrausch, 'Rasseverrat im Ausland', *Zeitschrift der Akademie für Deutsches Recht*, 15 May 1938, as well as E. Kohlrausch, 'Die Strafbarkeit der Umgehung des Blutschutzgesetzes', *ibid.*, 21 June 1941.

[66] Wengler's personnel file, Archive of the Humboldt Universität Berlin, vol. II, 37.

[67] Before the war, Karl von Lewinski was General Consul in New York and had participated as the Reich's representative in the Reparation Conferences in Washington in 1922, although he ultimately had only worked on comparative law concerning US law (cf. *Das Recht der Vereinigten Staaten von Amerika*, Berlin: Heymanns, 1930). Interestingly enough, however, von Moltke had been working between 1935 and 1939 in von Lewinski's law office in Berlin which specialised in private international law, where he was, not least, occupied with the legal and financial consequences of the Jewish persecution; see Brakelmann, *Helmuth James von Moltke, supra* n. 40, 82, 109.

[68] Wengler's personnel file, Archive of the Humboldt Universität Berlin, vol. II, 28; Wengler had in the meantime also received an offer from Professor Hallstein from Frankfurt/Main.

[69] *Ibid.*, 32.

newspaper in Munich. In his typical frank manner, he pointed out that this policy, in view of the lack of professionals at German universities, was a 'conscious, even if not quite obvious affront against those qualified scholars', who had turned against the Nazi dictatorship after 1933. Furthermore, it could be observed that 'traditional nepotism at German faculties' had not ceased to exist. In some cases qualified scholars, once dismissed for their NS-party membership, were now asked to deliver an expert opinion on the personal and scholarly qualification of other applicants.[70]

At Wengler's suggestion, and side-stepping the faculty, the Education Administration obtained external opinions on Wengler's work, among others from his former academic teacher Hans Lewald, who had been lecturing in Basel since 1935,[71] as well as by Martin Wolff, who had emigrated to London. Both of them expressed themselves very positively on Wengler's aptitude. In May 1947, the Education Administration asked the Berlin Law Faculty to report on the actual State of the *Habilitation* procedure. In July, the Faculty requested an extension of time, because they were awaiting a further expert opinion by Professor Raape from Hamburg 'on Dr Wengler's personality' because there were 'a lot of objections against the personality of Wengler'.[72] However, until the end of September 1947, this expert opinion had still not been requested. Nevertheless, for the winter term 1947–8, Wengler received, for the first time, a one-hour teaching position in private international law and a three-hour position in international law.

On 11 November 1948, the Berlin Law Faculty finally awarded Wengler the *venia legendi* in private and public international law, yet hesitated to appoint him. It was only due to a request by the Education

---

[70] *Ibid.*, 33. This remark can possibly be traced back to Professor Kohlrausch's regret about not having requested an expert opinion from Carl Schmitt (since then arrested); Wengler's personnel file, Archive of the Humboldt University Berlin, vol. II, 30. Moreover, it seems that Kohlrausch had also asked Bilfinger to deliver an expert opinion: he, after all, had endorsed Wengler's dismissal in 1944, *Ibid.*, 30. Peters, Kohlrausch's successor as Dean of the Law Faculty, had recommended asking, among others, Professor Jahrreiss, an expert who had delivered a celebratory speech on 30 January 1940 (the so-called 'Anniversary of National Revival', on 'Chamberlain's peace plan and the British claim to create a new world order'. After 1945, he had defended General Jodl in the Nuremberg Trials. According to Wengler, he was no longer allowed to teach at universities at that time; *ibid.*, 30.

[71] On this matter, cf. also Wengler's obituary for H. Lewald, *Annuaire Institut de Droit International*, 51 II (1965), 369.

[72] Wengler's personnel file, Archive of the Humboldt University Berlin, vol. II, 47.

Adminstration that the faculty appointed Wengler as a *Dozent* (associate professor). Soon thereafter, and once again only upon a renewed initiative of the Education Administration, Wengler was appointed as a professor and obtained the *venia legendi* in private and public international law. Finally, by 1 December 1948, the Faculty had requested permission to appoint him as a full professor,[73] a question that became moot, however, as Wengler terminated his employment as of 26 April 1949.[74] He attributed this decision, among other considerations, to the payment of his salary in *Ostmark*, a result of which being that he could not maintain his family and his mother living in West Germany. In addition, he was not allowed to lecture at the (West) Berlin University of Political Science. In his letter of resignation, however, Wengler claimed the right, 'to defend his academic conviction . . . after his change to the newly founded Freie Universität West Berlin, in the same manner as he did during his employment at Humboldt University'.[75]

Wengler's 1947 syllabus for his public international law course[76] reveals the peculiarity of his international legal thinking. His approach became even more noticeable in his textbook on international law some years later. It was characterised by a high level of abstraction, which certainly did not facilitate student participation. Of particular interest with some reservations, is his idea of international law as a global power, combined with further innovative concepts – for example, on the international legal status of armed forces of international organisations or of internationally administered areas. He also reflected on the issues raised by the Nuremberg Trials and their significance for the further development of international law. Presumably, in the immediate post-war years these questions were not self-evident.

Quarrel with the Kaiser Wilhelm/Max Planck Society concerning indemnification

After the end of the Second World War, bitter quarrels arose between Wengler and the still-existing Kaiser Wilhelm Society, as well as its successor, the newly-founded Max Planck Society. Others sometimes characterised this dispute as a 'proper mud fight'.[77] The proximate cause was Wengler's demand in 1946 of indemnification from the still-existing Kaiser Wilhelm Society for his politically motivated dismissal in

---

[73] *Ibid.,* 84. [74] *Ibid.,* 95. [75] *Ibid.,* 96. [76] *Ibid.,* 52 *et seq.*
[77] Schüring, 'Minervas verstoßene Kinder', *supra* n. 50, 240.

1944. This request was denied by the then President, Max Planck, arguing that in 1944 the Kaiser Wilhelm Society had been unable to act in a different way.[78] But Planck advised Wengler to apply for a position at the Institute of International Law at Dahlem, then under construction and managed by General Consul von Lewinski.[79] Wengler reacted vehemently to this proposal, as his primary aim was his moral rehabilitation.

In turn, Professor Bilfinger, who had become director of the Kaiser Wilhelm Institute of Comparative Public Law and International Law when Viktor Bruns died in 1943, rejected any collaboration with Wengler. In his view, it was totally unacceptable to employ him at the Berlin branch of the Institute.[80] A similar event occurred at the Institute of Comparative and International Private Law, located at Tübingen since its evacuation in 1944. The so-called 'Tübingen Circle' – consisting of Professors Erbe, Zweigert and Rupp and the Institute's director – had categorically objected to Wengler's appointment as a professor at Tübingen. Nonetheless, the first post-war volume of RabelsZ published a notice that 'the former member of the Institute [of Comparative and International Private Law], Professor Dr. Dr. Wilhelm Wengler in Berlin ... ought to be admitted to our circle as a regular member, because during Third Reich he was politically persecuted and temporarily deterred from his academic work at the Institute'.[81]

The quarrels between Wengler and, at least parts of, the Kaiser Wilhelm Society hit its peak when Wengler accused the former (and still!) General Secretary of the Kaiser Wilhelm Society, Ernst Telschow, of having committed crimes against humanity pursuant to Art. 2, para. 1 lit. c Control Council Law No. 10 due to his behaviour during Wengler's dismissal and arrest.[82] In return, Telschow questioned Wengler's reliability by referring to his activity at the Colonial Policy Office of the NSDAP. Furthermore, he spread the rumour that Wengler had threatened to denounce other employees to the Gestapo if they continued to make his private life public,[83] or that he had even initiated

---

[78] Wengler's personnel file, Archive of the Max Planck Society.
[79] On this matter, cf. *supra* n. 67.
[80] Wengler's personnel file, Archive of the Max Planck Society.
[81] Preface by the editor H. Dölle, RabelsZ (1949/50), 3. On the other hand, Wengler's appraisal in *NJW* (1951), 555, of the restarted publication of the ZaöRV was much more critical about Bilfinger, who in 1943 had written an article on the tenth 'anniversary' of the rise of the Nazi government.
[82] More details in Schüring, 'Minervas verstoßene Kinder', *supra* n. 50, 241–6.
[83] *Ibid*, 244 with further references.

the transport of looted books from Paris to Berlin during the war. Finally, the proceedings were closed with the statement that Telschow's actions 'exposed the Kaiser Wilhelm Society to severe risks' and, moreover, had no influence whatsoever on the Ministry's further steps.[84]

In 1964, the Max Planck Society finally refused an indemnity, arguing that no harm had been caused to Wengler because he had become a full professor after the war, whereas his former posts at both institutes had been no more than being a *Referent*. The whole discussion continued until the early 1970s[85] and seems to have been finally settled when Wengler, in 1970, talked to the then-President of the Max Planck Society, Adolf Butenandt, and presented an outline for a new, interdisciplinary-oriented Max Planck Institute of Research on Developing Countries which did not materialise.[86]

Professor at the Freie Universität Berlin

Because of the growing tensions among the Allied Powers in Berlin and the increasing challenge to academic liberty at Humboldt University (until 1949 Friedrich-Wilhelm-Universität), the newly founded Freie Universität Berlin began its teaching under rather primitive conditions at the facilities of the former Kaiser Wilhelm Society in Berlin Dahlem during the Winter term of 1948-9.[87] Wengler moved to the Freie Universität during 1949, where he was appointed by May 1949 to the chair of international law and comparative law – based on a positive expert opinion from, among others, Walter Jellinek. Previously, in the winter term of 1948-9, he had already been recommended for the chair of public law by the Heidelberg Law Faculty.[88] During the summer term

---

[84] *Ibid.* The appeal proceedings initiated by Wengler were also unsuccessful.

[85] This is documented in a letter from Telschow to the head office dated 1972; see Wengler's personnel file, Archive of the Max Planck Society.

[86] When the Federal President, at the suggestion of the Bavarian State Government, intended to bestow the *Bundesverdienstkreuz am Bande* upon Wengler in 1978, the latter refused it with the explanation that this merit had also been bestowed on a man who had initiated his arrest in the Nazi period, his dismissal from the Kaiser Wilhelm Institutes and the prevention of an indemnification by the Max Planck Society (on this matter, see G. Zieger, 'Zum 80. Geburtstag', in Eisenmann and Zieger, *Zur Rechtslage Deutschlands, supra* n. 17, 11) – presumably referring to Telschow, the former General-Secretary of the Kaiser Wilhelm Society/Max Planck Society.

[87] For further references, see J. Tent, *Freie Universität Berlin 1948–1988. Eine deutsche Hochschule im Zeitgeschehen* (Berlin: Copress, 1988), 207–8.

[88] Expert opinion by Walter Jellinek on Wilhelm Wengler, 14 April 1949, Wengler's personnel file, Archive of Freie Universität Berlin.

of 1949 he started his lectures with a two-hour introduction to comparative law and a four-hour course on international law. In 1950, he was elected dean.

After his appointment to the Freie Universität, the esteem that Wengler enjoyed, especially abroad, became quickly apparent, reflecting the fact that he had never been involved with National Socialism. As early as 1950, he was elected as a member of the *Institut de Droit International*, probably also thanks to the influence of his academic teacher, Hans Lewald, then also a member of the *Institut*. Wengler was, after Rudolf von Laun und Walther Schätzel,[89] the third German citizen who became a member of the Institut after the war and, at the age of forty-three, the youngest as well. He was to become president from 1973 to 1975.[90] Moreover, he repeatedly acted as a judge and counsel in proceedings before domestic and international courts.[91]

Wengler's two magisterial textbooks on international private law and public international law are probably his main works, but neither is easy to read and neither received general approval.[92] Nonetheless they contain advanced ideas that remain highly relevant more than forty and

---

[89] On the person and works of Schätzel, cf. especially Hans Wehberg, 'Geleitwort', in F. Brüel *et al.* (eds.), *Internationalrechtliche und Staatsrechtliche Abhandlungen – Festschrift für Walter Schätzel zu seinem 70. Geburtstag* (Düsseldorf: Hermes, 1960), vii–ix.

[90] Cf. *Annuaire Institut de Droit International*, vol. 43 II (1950), 427. Moreover, Wengler presided over the Conference in Wiesbaden in 1975; as to his activities at the *Institut de Droit International*, see also the obituary by Christian Dominicé, *Annuaire Institut de Droit International*, vol. 66 II (1996), 52 *et seq.* Cf. also W. Wengler, 'Zur Einführung', in W. Wengler (ed.), *Justitia et Pace – Festschrift zum 100 jährigen Bestehen des Institut de Droit International* (Berlin: Duncker & Humblot, 1974), 7–10.

[91] He participated, for example, in 1959 as counsel in the proceedings before the ECJ, in 1965 as arbitrator in the French–Algerian Arbitral Tribunal and as the representative of the State of Bavaria in the proceedings regarding the constitutionality of the Basic Treaty of the Relations between the Federal Republic of Germany and the German Democratic Republic.

[92] Such as the perception of the textbook on international law; see V. Schlabrendorff, 'Wilhelm Wengler', *supra* n. 3, 1, who attributed that to the fact that the work in question could only be understood 'by means of the author's personality and his experiences', despite the 'preeminent conciseness and brilliance of the terminology and rational thinking'. Cf., moreover, the review of Wengler's textbook on international private law by P. Lalive, 'Un traité magistral: le "droit international privé" de Wilhelm Wengler', *Journal de Droit International* (1983), 769–78; P.-H. Neuhaus, 'Kollisionsrechtliche Besinnung. Zu Wilhelm Wengler, Internationales Privatrecht', *RabelsZ* (1981), 627–52, as well as J. Kropholler, 'Elastische Anknüpfungsmomente für das Internationale Vertrags- und Deliktsrecht? Zugleich eine Besprechung von Wenglers Internationalem Privatrecht', *RIW* (1981), 359–63, who refers to 'the methodological presentation that is

twenty-five years after publication, respectively.[93] Last but not least, Wengler's personality comes through his statements in the prefaces and dedications. For example, the preface to his public international law textbook refers to people who after 1933 'searched for their own kind of humanity in miserable weakness' transformed by the political currents of their times into 'dull debris with a lawyer's mentality'.[94]

Concluding remarks

The life and personality of Wilhelm Wengler was, for various reasons, atypical of his era, particularly as far as German scholarship on private and public international law is concerned. It begins with his biographical background but includes the fact that Wengler was one of the very few German experts on international law that were deeply familiar with both public and private international law. The Wengler case is probably an exception to the rule. Very early on and sometimes also avowedly, Wengler always remained true to himself, turned against the national socialist dictatorship, and had to realise later on, how some people were more flexible and more adaptive to 'new realities', making compromises and avoiding quarrels, not to mention the convinced national socialists.

Even if one came to believe that Wengler's attitude helped him after 1945, one has to realise that even after the liberation from the Nazi dictatorship, there were many people who were quicker than he (quite frequently also quicker than those who emigrated to escape persecution) in returning to their positions of employment, or even being able to remain in their functions. They – unlike Wengler – had not been afraid to

difficult to access', an 'eccentric treatment of the subject matter' and delicate ramifications, 'under which of course sometimes the essential is suffering'; finally, see F. Rigaux, 'Une importante synthèse allemande en droit international privé. Le traité du professeur Wengler', *Revue critique de droit international privé* (1982), 245–72. Regarding his textbook on international law, cf. B. Conforti, 'Il trattato di diritto internazionale del Wengler', *Rivista Diritto Internazionale* (1965), 252–64, as well as Ch. Rousseau, 'Book Review. Wilhelm Wengler: Völkerrecht', *RGDIP* (1964), 566–7, the key sentences of which are: 'le plus important ouvrage de droit international général publié en Allemagne depuis vingt ans – on pourrait même dire depuis trente ans ... L'analyse est toujours d'une extrême rigueur et la maîtrise avec laquelle l'auteur domine et oriente ses dé veloppements est impressionnante'. In contrast, H.-J. Schlochauer is more critical 'Besprechung: Wilhelm Wengler Völkerrecht', *AVR* (1966/7), 129–34.

[93] Cf. also his two courses at the Hague Academy of International Law, W. Wengler, 'The General Principles of Private International Law', *RdC*, 104 (1961 II), 273–469 and W. Wengler, 'Public International Law – Paradoxes of a Legal Order', *RdC*, 158 (1977 V), 9 *et seq.*

[94] W. Wengler, 'Vorwort, X–XI', in W. Wengler, *Völkerrecht*, vol. 1, *supra* n. 43.

adapt, by some means or other, to the regime. It must have been even more depressing for Wengler and others in a comparable situation to realise that it were quite often the same colleagues, who could (again) act as gatekeepers to academia for 'someone like' Wengler. On the other hand, after 1945, Wengler very quickly gained scholarly approval abroad – his early admission into the *Institut de Droit International* and the great number of foreign authors who contributed to the *Festschrift*[95] published on the occasion of his sixty-fifth anniversary provides the best proof.[96] In this sense this biographical outline represents more than just a life story, but rather contains an important aspect of German academic history.

[95] Cf. *supra* n. 3.
[96] However, only thirteen of the eighty authors of the *Festschrift* were German.

PART II

Transnational economic law

PART II

14

Sovereignty-plus in the era of interdependence: toward an international convention on combating human rights violations by Transnational Corporations

OLIVIER DE SCHUTTER

Introduction

Communications today are faster and less expensive than before. Barriers to the movement of capital, goods and services are fewer. The tastes of consumers have become largely homogenous, shaped by the same advertising practices. As a result, the sphere of activity of most corporations typically reaches beyond national borders. They source their supplies from abroad, and they serve clients overseas. They invest and establish subsidiaries outside their State of origin. Sometimes, they are directly present abroad, by creating an agency in another State. The wedge increases between the jurisdiction of the State, which is primarily territorial, and the activity of the corporation, which is increasingly without borders.

In this context, State sovereignty must redefine itself. The assertion by each State of its exclusive competence to regulate activities on its national territory will result in a situation in which States compete with one another to attract companies, whether as buyers or as investors. As buyers of goods, companies act as gatekeepers to global markets: for developing countries' producers, they guarantee access to the high-value markets of industrialised nations, whose purchasing power is many times more significant than that of consumers in developing countries; or they may have unique processing capabilities, allowing raw commodities to be transformed for sale to the final consumer. As investors, companies bring in much-needed capital. Their presence can be a source of local employment opportunities. It can lead to transfers of technologies and know-how to local entrepreneurs. It can produce a 'multiplier effect' on the local economy, as foreign investors source many inputs locally. Unsurprisingly, States change their domestic regulations in order to become more hospitable to foreign capital – for example, by abstaining from imposing performance requirements, by offering tax incentives, by guaranteeing to the investor a right to repatriate profits, or by entering into investment agreements that ensure 'fair and equitable treatment' to the investor.[1] And they aim to improve the competitiveness of the undertakings established on their territory, thus facilitating their ability to expand their market share.

This results in a prisoner's dilemma situation in which the choices made individually by each State may be less optimal than if States were to cooperate in controlling transnational corporations (TNCs), to ensure that globalisation works for the benefit of the full realisation of human rights and human development. The most obvious implication is that States should join their efforts and agree on common frameworks regulating investment. In the absence of such collective action, certain groups of States could be caught in a 'race to the bottom', with few incentives to impose strong obligations on foreign investors, and with such concessions being made to foreign investors that the very benefits of their presence might be increasingly elusive.[2] Another implication is that the classical rules that restrain the exercise by States of their extraterritorial jurisdiction may have to be reinterpreted in the light of this interdependency. The traditional understanding is that, when a State adopts regulations that seek to influence situations located outside its national territory, it competes with the sovereignty of the territorially competent State, and that such regulations should therefore only be allowed in the most exceptional circumstances, since they may run counter to the principle of sovereign equality of States. However, if the adoption by the State of origin of the investor of extraterritorial regulations in fact facilitates the role of the host State in regulating that

---

[1] The fact that States compete in order to attract foreign direct investment (FDI) is well illustrated by figures indicating that the regulatory changes adopted by countries are overwhelmingly favourable to FDI, rather than imposing restrictions on investors. According to the 2004 *World Investment Report*, for instance (UNCTAD, *World Investment Report 2004. The Shift toward Services*), 8, there were 1,771 regulatory changes favourable to FDI over 1991–2003, and 114 less favourable to FDI over the same period.

[2] B. Simmons, Z. Elkins and A. Guzman, 'Competing for Capital. The Diffusion of Bilateral Investment Treaties, 1960–2000', *International Organization*, 60 (2006), 811–46, reprinted in M. Waibel *et al.*, *The Backlash against Investment Arbitration. Perceptions and Reality* (The Hague: Kluwer Law International, 2010), 369–407.

investor, thus ensuring that the investment will contribute to human development and will benefit local communities, this enhances, rather than restricts, the exercise by the host State of its sovereignty. To the extent that it serves universal values, unilateral action may thus contribute to the achievement of multilaterally set goals, such as the Millennium Development Goals (MDGs): the regulation of TNCs becomes a global public good, to which each State should contribute in accordance with its ability.[3]

By putting forward the need to move towards a duty of the home State of the TNC to regulate their corporations, this chapter seeks to ground existing legal practice on international law principles. National courts increasingly accept jurisdiction over cases that concern activities of corporations abroad, provided that these corporations present sufficiently strong links to the forum. The most spectacular example is the revival since 1980 of the Alien Tort Claims Act in the United States, which has allowed foreign victims of serious human rights abuses committed by corporations having sufficiently close links to the United States to seek damages.[4] The US Federal courts have agreed to read this provision as implying that they have jurisdiction over enterprises either incorporated in the United States or having a continuous business relationship with the United States, where foreigners, victims of violations of international law,[5] wherever such violations have taken place, seek damages for such violations committed by these enterprises or in which they are complicit.[6]

This is not an isolated example. Under Council Regulation (EC) No. 44/2001 of 22 December 2000 on jurisdiction and the recognition and

---

[3] The notion of 'global public good' has revived since the 1990s. See, in particular, W. D. Nordhaus, *Managing the Global Commons* (Cambridge, MA: MIT Press, 1994), and the contributions emanating from the UN Development Programme (UNDP), in particular, I. Kaul, I. Grundberg and M. A. Stern, *Global Public Goods. International Cooperation in the 21st Century* (Oxford University Press, 1999); Office of Development Studies, 'Global Public Goods. Taking the Concept Forward', Discussion Paper, 17 (New York: UNDP, 2001); and I. Kaul, P. Conceição, K. Le Goulven and R. U. Mendoza (eds.), *Providing Global Public Goods. Managing Globalization* (Oxford University Press, 2003).

[4] 28 USC §1350.   [5] On this notion, see *Sosa* v. *Alvarez-Machain*, 542 US 692 [2004].

[6] See, in particular, *John Doe I* v. *Unocal Corp.*, 395 F.3d 932, 945–946 (9th Cir., 2002) (complicity of Unocal with human rights abuses committed by the Burmese military); and *Wiwa* v. *Royal Dutch Petroleum Co.*, 2002 WL 319887, *2 (SDNY, 2002) (complicity of Shell Nigeria and its parent companies Shell UK and Royal Dutch in the human rights abuses committed by the Nigerian police).

enforcement of judgments in civil and commercial matters[7] – which ensures the integration in EC law of the 1968 Brussels Convention on Jurisdiction and the Enforcement of Judgments in Civil and Commercial Matters[8] – the Member States of the EU are obliged to recognise the jurisdiction of their national courts when civil claims are filed against persons (whether natural or legal persons) domiciled on their territory,[9] wherever the damage has occurred, and whatever the nationality or the place of residence of the claimants, including in situations where an alternative forum open to the claimants would appear to present closer links to the dispute or to be more appropriate:[10] this rule may be used in the context of human rights litigation, for violations committed abroad, especially in developing countries where European multinationals (MNCs) operate, as has been explicitly envisaged by the European Parliament.[11]

This chapter examines the questions of international law raised by these developments. It focuses on the question of the jurisdiction of States over the activities of TNCs, emphasising how the duty of the host State to regulate corporations operating on its territory could be more easily discharged if home States of TNCs made a more principled use of extraterritorial regulation. These two sovereignties are not as much competing with each other than they are mutually supportive: the adoption of a new international instrument allocating responsibilities to control TNCs could codify in treaty form what is already, arguably, emerging customary international law. This chapter also argues that, until a consensus emerges about the desirable division of tasks between the host State and the home State in controlling investors, the adoption by the home State of extraterritorial legislation addressed directly to the parent company, but imposing on that company a duty to exercise control on its subsidiaries, may be the best route forward.

---

[7] OJ L 12 of 16 January 2001, 1.   [8] OJ L 299, 31 December 1972, 32.

[9] Art. 2 (1) of Regulation No. 44/2001 imposes an obligation on all the national courts of EU Member States to accept jurisdiction over civil suits filed against a defendant domiciled in the forum State. While an identical rule was already present in the 1968 Brussels Convention, Regulation No. 44/2001 adds, for the sake of legal certainty, that for the purposes of the Regulation, 'a company or other legal person or association of natural or legal persons is domiciled at the place where it has its: (a) statutory seat, or (b) central administration, or (c) principal place of business'.

[10] See the judgment of the ECJ of 1 March 2005 in Case C-281/02, *Owusu* [2005] ECR I-1383.

[11] See European Parliament resolution on the Commission Green Paper on Promoting a European Framework for Corporate Social Responsibility (COM(2001) 366 – C5-0161/ 2002 – 2002/2069(COS)) (30 June 2002), para. 50.

The home State of TNCs could best fulfil its role in protecting human rights threatened by the activities of such corporations, I argue, by providing remedies to victims before its domestic courts, where the victims are unable to obtain redress before the courts of the State where the damage occurred. This chapter examines the conditions under which home States of TNCs may be justified in providing such remedies. Because it argues in favour of the exercise of 'indirect' extraterritorial jurisdiction by the home State, which consists in imposing on the parent company domiciled in the home State a due diligence obligation to control its subsidiaries or business partners, it discusses in greater detail the obstacle resulting from the corporate veil to remedies exercised by victims before the courts of the home State. It then places these questions against the background of international law, explaining why the exercise by States of their duty to protect human rights in transnational situations should be guided by the adoption of a multilateral instrument allocating the respective tasks of the different States concerned. The chapter ends with a brief conclusion.

The jurisdiction of States over the activities of transnational corporations

The problem

Where a TNC[12] develops relationships with a country other than its country of origin, either directly or through the establishment of subsidiaries or by contractual relationships, both the State of incorporation of the leading (parent) company, referred to as the 'home State', and the State where the TNC conducts its activities, or 'host State', may potentially assert jurisdiction over the corporation's activities. 'Positive conflicts of jurisdiction' may occur as a result, where both the 'home State' and the 'host State' seek to control the activities of the TNC, thus running the risk of imposing conflicting requirements on the corporation.[13]

---

[12] Peter Muchlinski has defined the transnational corporation as an entity that 'owns (in whole or in part), controls and manages income generating assets in more than one country', P. Muchlinski, *Multinational Enterprises and the Law* (Oxford: Blackwell, 1995), 12. The notion is used here in a broader sense, as including corporations that have suppliers, sub-contractors, or franchisees in countries other than in their country of origin.

[13] It is this risk in particular which the Declaration on International Investment and Multinational Enterprises adopted within the OECD sought to address, when it was adopted on 21 June 1976.

Conversely, where neither the home State, nor the host (territorial) State, effectively controls the activities of the TNC, this may result in a situation of effective impunity for human rights violations.

Positive conflicts of jurisdiction take different forms, depending on the choices made between various types of extraterritorial jurisdiction. Home States may impose on parent corporations an obligation to comply with certain norms wherever they operate (i.e. even if they operate in other countries), or an obligation to impose compliance with such norms on the different entities it controls (its subsidiaries, or even in certain cases its business partners). This form of extraterritoriality may be referred to as *parent-based extraterritorial regulation*. Home States may also seek to impose certain prescriptions directly on the foreign subsidiaries of companies incorporated under their jurisdiction, either by targeting such foreign subsidiaries directly, or by addressing the regulation they adopt to the TNC as such – i.e. the group composed of the parent company and its subsidiaries or affiliates. This form of extraterritoriality may be referred to as *foreign direct liability*. Similarly, host States may seek to regulate the activities of TNCs operating on their territory, either by imposing certain obligations on the subsidiaries incorporated under their jurisdiction – which does not raise a question of extraterritoriality – or by seeking to impose a liability directly on the parent company 'controlling' such a subsidiary or, when the prescriptions are addressed to the group (the TNC considered in its economic unity), on the TNC as such. In these latter two cases, host States resort to forms of extraterritorial jurisdiction in order to control entities whose activities have an impact on their territory, even though these entities either are not incorporated under their jurisdiction (when the foreign parent company is targeted), or are not corporate bodies at all (when the group is targeted).

International law imposes limits to the exercise of extraterritorial jurisdiction that vary depending on the type of extraterritoriality concerned. The risk of the home State interfering with the sovereignty of the territorial State is greatest as regards the imposition of a form of foreign direct liability since, here, the home State seeks to regulate entities (the subsidiaries of the parent company domiciled under the home State's jurisdiction) incorporated under another State's jurisdiction, for activities performed by those entities in the territory of that State. However, the precise restrictions that are imposed by international law to these various instances of extraterritorial jurisdiction remain contested.

The general question of extraterritorial jurisdiction

There is no general agreement within legal scholarship as to the circumstances in which extraterritorial jurisdiction is admissible.[14] As noted by Rosalyn Higgins in 1984, 'the underlying problem is still unresolved – namely, is it necessary to show a specific basis of jurisdiction, or may one assert jurisdiction without reference to a specific basis, so long as one is acting reasonably?'[15] Some authors take the view that States remain free in principle to exercise extraterritorial jurisdiction, in the absence of an explicit prohibition. This position is based on the *Lotus* case of the International Court of Justice (ICJ).[16] In this approach, the only restriction on the acceptability of extraterritorial jurisdiction being exercised by a State resides in the prohibition to interfere with the internal affairs of another State. However, it seems unlikely that the adoption by a State of an extraterritorial statute imposing human rights obligations on a TNC could be described as falling under this prohibition. In the words of the ICJ, the principle of non-intervention 'forbids all States ... to intervene directly or indirectly in internal or external affairs of other States. A prohibited intervention must accordingly be one bearing on matters in which each State is permitted, by the principle of State sovereignty, to decide freely ... Intervention is wrongful when it uses methods of coercion in regard to such choices, which must remain free ones.'[17] But it has long been acknowledged that internationally recognised human rights – such as those included in the Universal Declaration on Human Rights – impose limits to State sovereignty, and that such matters therefore cannot be said to belong to the exclusive national jurisdiction of the territorial State. Moreover, it is doubtful that one may speak here of 'coercion', in the meaning attached to this term in international law. By seeking to regulate the activities of foreign investors in the host States through the adoption of extraterritorial legislation, other States are not imposing on the territorial State that it comply with these norms itself, or that it imposes compliance with these norms on the local corporations: without prejudice of its obligations under the international law of human

---

[14] See generally Cedric Ryngaert, *Jurisdiction in International Law* (Oxford University Press, 2008).

[15] R. Higgins, 'The Legal Basis of Jurisdiction', in C. J. Olmstead, *Extra-Territorial Application of Laws and Responses Thereto* (Oxford: ILA and ESC, 1984), 14.

[16] The *Case of the SS 'Lotus'* (*France* v. *Turkey*), Judgment No. 9 of 7 September 1927, PCIJ Reports 1928, Series A, No. 10.

[17] ICJ, *Case Concerning Military and Paramilitary Activities in and Against Nicaragua* (*Nicaragua* v. *United States of America*) (merits), Judgment of 27 June 1986, para. 205.

rights, that State remains free to legislate upon activities on its national territory.[18]

More generally, while the restrictions that international law imposes on extraterritorial jurisdiction remain debated, the interpretation of existing rules should take into account the specific nature of State regulations that seek to impose compliance with human rights or that seek to contribute to multilaterally agreed goals such as the MDGs. Although the significance of this *dictum* in the *Barcelona Traction* judgment referring to this specific character of international norms relating to 'the basic rights of the human person'[19] has been widely debated – and its consequences probably exaggerated by some commentators[20] – the *erga omnes* character of at least a handful of internationally recognised human rights may justify allowing the exercise by States of extraterritorial jurisdiction, even in conditions which might otherwise not be permissible, where this seeks to promote such rights. Similarly, the realisation of the MDGs is of interest to all States. Extraterritorial jurisdiction seeking to promote human rights or the achievement of the MDGs is not a case where one State seeks to impose its values on another State, as in other cases of extraterritorial jurisdiction.

Specific bases for extraterritorial jurisdiction

Quite apart from how this controversy will develop in the future – and whether or not States will be authorised to resort to forms of

---

[18] Solutions may have to be found in exceptional situations where obligations imposed by the home State on foreign investors contradict those which would be imposed by other States, including the home States of the investors concerned.

[19] The ICJ declared in the *Barcelona Traction* judgment that 'an essential distinction should be drawn between the obligations of a State towards the international community as a whole, and those arising *vis-à-vis* another State in the field of diplomatic protection. By their very nature the former are the concern of all States. In view of the importance of the rights involved, all States can be held to have a legal interest in their protection. They are obligations erga omnes. Such obligations derive, for example, in contemporary international law, from the outlawing of acts of aggression, and of genocide, as also from the principles and rules concerning the basic rights of the human person, including protection from slavery and racial discrimination. Some of the corresponding rights of protection have entered into the body of general international law; others are conferred by international instruments of a universal or quasi-universal character.' ICJ, *Case Concerning the Barcelona Traction, Light and Power Co. Ltd (Belgium* v. *Spain)* (second phase – merits), 5 February 1970, 1970 ICJ Rep. 3, paras. 33–34.

[20] See Ian Seiderman, *Hierarchy in International Law. The Human Rights Dimension* (Antwerp, Groningen and Oxford: Hart–Intersentia, 2001), chapter IV; Maurizio Ragazzi, *The Concept of International Obligations Erga Omnes* (Oxford University Press, 2000).

extraterritorial jurisdiction in order to extend the protection of human rights to all situations which they may influence – their competence to legislate extraterritorially is generally accepted in at least five situations.[21]

The 'effects' doctrine

A State may seek to influence, by the adoption of legislation which has an extraterritorial reach, activities which have a substantial, direct and foreseeable effect upon or in its national territory.[22] This doctrine, alternatively called the 'effects' doctrine or the 'objective territoriality' principle, must be relied upon only with great care, at least when it is invoked to justify the extraterritorial application of legislation other than competition law where its use has become customary. As noted by Roth, 'as economic effects can be remote and general, an unlimited acceptance of extraterritorial jurisdiction based on economic effects could clearly lead to extensive interference in the internal affairs of other States'.[23] The *Restatement (Third) of the Foreign Relations Law of the United States* prepared under the auspices of the American Law Institute, and to which Detlev Vagts made such an important contribution, stipulates therefore that, while a State 'has jurisdiction to prescribe law with respect to ... conduct outside its territory that has or is intended to have substantial effect within its territory', such jurisdiction is not unlimited, since a State 'may not exercise jurisdiction to prescribe law with respect to a person or activity having connections with another State when the exercise of such jurisdiction is unreasonable'.[24] Despite these notes of caution, and the occasional criticisms to which it has been subjected,[25] this basis

---

[21] See, *inter alia*, paras. 11 and 12 of the Explanatory Report to the the Council of Europe Convention on the Transfer of Proceedings in Criminal Matters, *opened for signature* on 15 May 1972, and which entered into force on 30 March 1978 (CETS No. 73).

[22] See F. A. Mann, 'The Doctrine of International Jurisdiction Revisited after Twenty Years', *RdC*, 1984-III, vol. 186, 30–1; A. F. Lowenfeld, *International Litigation and the Quest for Reasonableness* (Oxford: Clarendon Press, 1996), 20–8. See *Hartford Fire Ins. Co.* v. *California*, 509 US 764 (1993) ('the Sherman Act applies to foreign conduct that was meant to produce and did in fact produce some substantial effect in the United States') and *F. Hoffmann–La Roche Ltd* v. *Empagran SA*, 123 S. Ct 2359 (2004).

[23] P.M. Roth, 'Reasonable Extraterritoriality. Correcting the "Balance of Interests"', *ICLQ*, 41 (1992), 245–86, 285.

[24] Sections 402(1)(c) and 403(1) of the *Restatement (Third) of the Foreign Relations Law of the United States*, 2 vols. (St. Paul, MN: American Law Institute, 1987).

[25] The 'effects' doctrine was explicitly referred to by the United States Congress when it adopted the Helms–Burton Act in 1996 (Cuban Liberty and Democratic Solidarity (Libertad) Act of 1996 (Codified in Title 22, Sections 6021–6091 of the US Code) PL

for the exercise of extraterritorial jurisdiction has never been formally abandoned.[26] Some authors even consider that it has been revived when the European Court of Justice (ECJ) decided to rely on a similar reasoning, in particular in order to justify the application of EC competition law to foreign companies, whose practices might impact the internal market.[27] A result similar to that obtained by the 'effects' doctrine may be achieved where a corporation is subjected to criminal liability, in combination with the criminal law doctrine of ubiquity, according to which an offence is considered to have been committed within the territory of a State either if one of the physical acts constituting an element of the offence was perpetrated there, or if the effects of the offence became manifest there.[28]

104–114). Most remarkably, section 302 of the Act (Liability for trafficking in confiscated property claimed by US nationals), which is located under Title III of the Act (Protection of Property Rights of United States Nationals), stipulates that 'any person that, after the end of the 3-month period beginning on the effective date of this title, traffics in property which was confiscated by the Cuban Government on or after January 1, 1959, shall be liable to any United States national who owns the claim to such property for money damages'. Among the findings on which Congress based its adoption of Title III of the Helms–Burton Act is that: 'International law recognizes that a nation has the ability to provide for rules of law with respect to conduct outside its territory that has or is intended to have substantial effect within its territory' (section 301 (9)). This begs the question what such effect actually consists in, and whether it is substantial enough to justify such an exercise of extraterritorial jurisdiction. For strong critiques of this justification, see A. F. Lowenfeld, 'Congress and Cuba. The Helms–Burton Act', *AJIL*, 90 (1996), 419–34, 430–2 and B. Stern, 'Vers la mondialisation juridique? Les lois Helms–Burton et D'Amato–Kennedy', *RGDIP*, 1996, 979–1003, 992–5.

[26] See, for a comparison between the positions of the United States and those adopted in Europe, B. Stern, 'L'extraterritorialité revisitée, où il est question des affaires Alvarez-Machain, Pâte de bois et de quelques autres', *AFDI*, 38 (1992), 251–2.

[27] Famous examples include Case 22/71, *Béguelin Import/GL Import Export*, [1971] ECR 949, para. 11; Case 48/69, *Imperial Chemical Industries Ltd.* v. *Commission*, [1972] ECR 619, paras. 125–130; Case 36/74, *Walrave and Koch/Association Union Cycliste Internationale and Others*, [1974] ECR 1405, para. 28; and Joined Cases 89, 104, 114, 116, 117, 125, 126, 127, 128, 129 and 185/85, *Wood Pulp Cartel Case*, [1988] ECR 5193. See Lowenfeld, *International Litigation*, *supra* n. 22, 33–41; D. W. Bowett, 'Jurisdiction. Changing Patterns of Authority over Activities and Resources', *BYBIL*, 53 (1982), 1–26, 7. In their joint separate opinion to the judgment of 14 February 2002 delivered by the ICJ in the Case Concerning the *Arrest Warrant of 11 April 2000 (Democratic Republic of the Congo* v. *Belgium)*, [2002] ICJ Rep. 3, Judges Higgins, Kooijmans and Buergenthal seem to share this reading of developments in EU law.

[28] *Extraterritorial Criminal Jurisdiction*, Report prepared by the Select Committee of Experts on Extraterritorial Jurisdiction (PC-R-EJ), set up by the European Committee on Crime Problems (CDPC), Council of Europe, 1990, 24.

The fundamental interests of the State

A State may exercise jurisdiction with respect to persons, property, or acts abroad which constitute a threat to the fundamental national interests of the State. Although there is no consensus about what such fundamental interests may be,[29] it is clear that, while these interests may include the security and creditworthiness of the State, they do not extend to the protection of its wider economic interests,[30] or to its foreign policy objectives. It would therefore not be acceptable for a State to justify exercising extraterritorial jurisdiction over a foreign entity, for the activities of such an entity abroad, simply because certain human rights abuses committed by that entity – for instance, violations of basic labour rights – would place the undertakings conducting their activities on the territory of that State at a competitive disadvantage, or as a means to exercise pressure on the host State in order to bring about a change of that State's policies.[31]

The principle of universality

Under the principle of universality, certain particularly heinous crimes may be prosecuted by any State, acting in the name of the international community, where the crime meets with universal reprobation. It is on this basis that, since times immemorial, piracy could be combated by all States: the pirate was seen as the *hostis humanis generis*, the enemy of the human race, which all States are considered to have a right to prosecute and punish. The international crimes for which treaties impose the principle *aut dedere, aut judicare*, or which are recognised as international crimes requiring that all States contribute to their prevention and repression by investigating and prosecuting such crimes where the author is found on their territory unless the suspected author is extradited, also belong to this list.[32] International crimes justifying the

---

[29] CDPC, *Extraterritorial Criminal Jurisdiction, supra* n. 28, 13.

[30] See ICJ, *Case concerning the Barcelona Traction, Light and Power Co. (Belgium v. Spain)* (second phase – merits), 5 February 1970, [1970] ICJ Rep. 3, para. 87 (rejecting the argument that, in the absence of a treaty between the States concerned, a State could exercise its right to diplomatic protection in order to protect investments by its nationals abroad, such investments being part of a State's national economic resources).

[31] In addition, this may constitute a form of economic sanction prohibited under international law.

[32] See the joint separate opinion by Judges Higgins, Kooijmans and Buergenthal, *Arrest Warrant* case, *supra* n. 27, para. 46 (citing Cherif Bassiouni, *International Criminal Law*, vol. III. *Enforcement*, 2nd edn. (Ardsley, NY: Transnational Publishers, 1999),

exercise of universal jurisdiction are war crimes,[33] crimes against humanity,[34] genocide,[35] torture[36] and forced disappearances.[37] In prosecuting these crimes, States are not seen to act in their own interest; they act as agents of the international community.

228); T. Meron, 'International Criminalization of Internal Atrocities', *AJIL*, 89 (1995), 554–77, 576.

[33] Art. 49 of the Geneva Convention (I) for the Amelioration of the Condition of the Wounded and Sick in Armed Forces in the Field, 12 August 1949; Art. 50 of the Geneva Convention (II) for the Amelioration of the Condition of Wounded, Sick and Shipwrecked Members of Armed Forces at Sea, 12 August 1949; Art. 129 of the Geneva Convention (III) relative to the Treatment of Prisoners of War, 12 August 1949; Art. 146 of the Geneva Convention (IV) relative to the Protection of Civilian Persons in Time of War, 12 August 1949; and Art. 85(1) of the Protocol Additional to the Geneva Conventions of 12 August 1949, and relating to the Protection of Victims of International Armed Conflicts (Protocol I), 8 June 1977.

[34] The *jus cogens* character of the prohibition of crimes against humanity is generally considered to imply an obligation to contribute to their universal repression: see C. Bassiouni, 'Crimes against Humanity. The Need for a Specialized Convention', *CJIL*, 1994, 457–94, 480–1; K. C. Randall, 'Universal Jurisdiction Under International Law', *Texas Law Review*, 66 (1988), 785–832, 829–30; the Principles of international cooperation in the detection, arrest, extradition and punishment of persons guilty of war crimes and crimes against humanity adopted by the UN General Assembly resolution 3074 (XXVIII) of 3 December 1973 (G.A. Res. 3074 (XXVIII), UN GAOR, 28th Sess., Supp. No. 30, at 78, UN Doc. A/9030 (1973)).

[35] See the Advisory Opinion delivered on 28 May 1951 by the ICJ relating to the *Reservations to the Convention on the Prevention and Punishment of the Crime of Genocide 1951*, ICJ Rep. 15, 1951, 23 (noting that 'the principles underlying the Convention [on the Prevention and Punishment of the Crime of Genocide, approved and proposed for signature and ratification or accession by General Assembly resolution 260 A (III) of 9 December 1948, 78 UNTS 1021] are principles which are recognized, by civilized nations as binding on States, even without any conventional obligation', and that 'both . . . the condemnation of genocide and . . . the co-operation required "in order to liberate mankind from such an odious scourge" (Preamble to the Convention)' have a 'universal character' – i.e., are obligations imposed on all States of the international community). On the *erga omnes* character of the obligations imposed by the Convention, implying that 'the obligation each State . . . has to prevent and to punish the crime of genocide is not territorially limited by the Convention', see the Judgment of 11 July 1996 delivered in the *Case Concerning the Application of the Convention on the Prevention and Punishment of the Crime of Genocide (Bosnia-Hezegovina v. Yugoslavia)*, Preliminary objections, ICJ Rep., 1996, 615–16, para. 31.

[36] Art. 5(2) of the Convention against Torture and Other Cruel, Inhuman or Degrading Treatment or Punishment *adopted and opened for signature, ratification and accession* by UN General Assembly resolution 39/46 of 10 December 1984, *entered into force* on 26 June 1987.

[37] Art. 9(2) of the International Convention for the Protection of All Persons from Enforced Disappearance, Human Rights Council, Report to the General Assembly on the First Session of the Human Rights Council, at 32, UN Doc. A/HRC/1/L.10 (2006).

The principle of passive personality

A State may be justified in legislating extraterritorially if the person directly affected (the victim) has its nationality. The invocation of this principle of passive personality has sometimes been considered with suspicion, as it could serve as a means to circumvent the rules of the exercise of diplomatic protection, which constitutes the normal means through which a State may seek to protect its nationals situated under another State's jurisdiction;[38] it has, however, gained general acceptance, at least when the nationality link is genuine, and when combined with the principle of double criminality in order to respect the principle of legality where criminal extraterritorial jurisdiction is concerned.[39]

The principle of active personality

Under the principle of active personality, a State may regulate the conduct of its nationals abroad. However, in the absence of any particular mode of determination of the nationality under international law, there is a risk that the modes of determination of the nationality of the corporation will be manipulated in order to allow a State, relying on the principle of active personality, to extend its jurisdiction to extraterritorial situations – including acts adopted by companies incorporated abroad – which it might otherwise be prohibited under international law to reach.[40] In particular, doubts have sometimes been expressed as to

---

[38] See, for instance, the reaction of the Inter-American Juridical Committee to the US Helms–Burton Act, which the US Congress intended to justify, in part, by the need to protect the property rights of US citizens whose assets had been confiscated in Cuba after 1 January 1959: 'When a national of a foreign State is unable to obtain effective redress in accordance with international law, the State of which it is a national may espouse the claim through an official State-to-State claim . . . The domestic courts of a claimant State are not the appropriate forum for the resolution of State-to-State claims', Organisation of American States, *Inter-American Juridical Committee opinion examining the US Helms–Burton Act*, 27 August 1996, reproduced in *ILM*, 35 (1996), 1331.

[39] See *Extraterritorial Criminal Jurisdiction*, supra n. 28, 12. In their joint separate opinion appended to the judgment delivered by the ICJ in the *Case Concerning* the *Arrest Warrant of 11 April 2000 (Democratic Republic of the Congo v. Belgium)*, judges Higgins, Kooijmans and Buergenthal conclude that passive personality jurisdiction, 'for so long regarded as controversial, is now reflected not only in the legislation of various countries (the United States, Ch. 113A, 1986 Omnibus Diplomatic and Antiterrorism Act; France, Art. 689, Code of Criminal Procedure, 1975), and today meets with relatively little opposition, at least so far as a particular category of offences is concerned' (para. 47).

[40] Y. Hadari, 'The Choice of National Law Applicable to the Multinational Enterprises', 1 *Duke Law Journal* (1974), 1–57, 16 (noting that the determination by the United States of the rules of the nationality of the corporation has occasionally been relied upon in order

whether it should be considered allowable for States to treat as their 'nationals' legal persons incorporated under the laws of another country, but which are managed, controlled, or owned, by natural or legal persons of the State concerned. The *Barcelona Traction* case of the ICJ did seem to exclude, at least in the context of diplomatic protection, basing nationality of the corporate entity on the nationality of its shareholders. In finding that Belgium lacked *jus standi* to exercise diplomatic protection of shareholders in a Canadian company with respect to measures taken against that company in Spain, the Court recalled that, in municipal law, a distinction is made between the rights of the company and those of the shareholders, and that 'the concept and structure of the company are founded on and determined by a firm distinction between the separate entity of the company and that of the shareholders, each with a distinct set of rights'.[41]

However, this ruling does not necessarily prohibit a State from treating a company incorporated in another State but controlled by a parent company incorporated in the State seeking to exercise extraterritorial jurisdiction, as having the nationality of that State for the purposes of exercising such jurisdiction. Already in its *Barcelona Traction* judgment of 5 February 1970, the ICJ noted that the veil of the company may be lifted in order to prevent the misuse of the privileges of legal personality, in both municipal and in international law.[42] Therefore, where the separation of legal personalities is used as a device by the parent company to limit the scope of its legal liability, the lifting of the veil may be justified. In addition, the recent proliferation of bilateral investment treaties (BITs) under which States seek to protect their nationals as investors in foreign countries even in cases where they have set up subsidiaries under the laws of the host country, has shed further doubt on the validity of the classical rule enunciated by the *Barcelona Traction* judgment, according to which a State may not claim a legal interest in the situation of foreign companies, even where its nationals are in control.[43] The 2004 version of the Model US Bilateral Investment Treaty, for

---

       to allow for an extension of US law to corporations whose main connections may be to foreign countries).

[41] ICJ, *Case Concerning the Barcelona Traction, Light and Power Co. (Belgium v. Spain)* (second phase – merits), 5 February 1970, [1970] ICJ Rep. 3, 184.

[42] *Ibid.*, 38–9.

[43] Doubts were raised at an early stage concerning the relevance of the *Barcelona Traction* case beyond the exercise of diplomatic protection: see S. D. Metzger, 'Nationality of Corporate Investment Under Investment Guaranty Schemes – The Relevance of Barcelona Traction', *AJIL*, 65 (1971), 532–43.

instance, defines as an 'investor of a Party' protected under such a treaty 'a Party or State enterprise thereof, or a national or an enterprise of a Party, that attempts to make, is making, or has made an investment in the territory of the other Party', the 'investment' meaning in turn 'every asset that an investor owns or controls, directly or indirectly, that has the characteristics of an investment, including such characteristics as the commitment of capital or other resources, the expectation of gain or profit, or the assumption of risk'. There is no doubt that, under these definitions, investments made by US nationals in a State bound by a BIT concluded with the United States are protected under the treaty, even when (and, indeed, in particular when) their investment consists in a controlling participation in a corporation incorporated in the host country. Similarly, under the draft Multilateral Agreement on Investment (MAI) negotiated within the framework of the OECD between 1995 and 1998, the investments made in each Contracting Party by investors from another Contracting Party comprised 'Every kind of asset owned or controlled, directly or indirectly, by an investor', including, *inter alia* 'an enterprise (being a legal person or any other entity constituted or organised under the applicable law of the Contracting Party, whether or not for profit, and whether private or government owned or controlled, and includes a cor poration, trust, partnership, sole proprietorship, branch, joint venture, association or organisation)' and 'shares, stocks or other forms of equity participation in an enterprise, and rights derived therefrom'.

The practice of determining the nationality of the corporation on the basis of the nationality of its shareholders, particularly of the nationality of a controlling parent company, while not usual, is not unknown. For instance, while the practice of the United States has generally been to determine the nationality of the corporation on the basis of the company's place of incorporation,[44] it is occasionally defined by reference to the nationality of its owners, managers, or other persons deemed to be in control of its affairs. This is the case, in particular, in the tax area;[45] but

---

[44] *Restatement (Third) of the Foreign Relations Law of the United States* (1987), 213, n. 5. On this question, see generally L. A. Mabry, 'Multinational Corporations and US Technology Policy. Rethinking the Concept of Nationality', *Georgetown Law Journal*, 87 (1999), 563–631.

[45] As noted by Mabry (*supra* n. 44), this allows the aggregation of the different corporate entities integrated within the multinational group and treating them as one single enterprise whose benefits will be taxed on a consolidated basis, reflecting the operations of both domestic and foreign subsidiaries. She refers to *Container Corp. of America* v. *Franchise Tax Bd*, 463 US 159 (1983). This decision upheld California's unitary basis test, which consists in taking into account 'the combined world-wide income of all of the

there seems to be no reason why this could not also justify the exercise of foreign direct liability regulation in other domains. It should therefore not come as a surprise if *The Restatement (Third) of the Foreign Relations Law of the United States* of the American Law Institute (ALI) does not exclude the regulation of foreign corporations – i.e. corporations organised under the laws of a foreign State, 'on the basis that they are owned or controlled by nationals of the regulating State'.[46]

The *Restatement* adds, however, that in the exceptional cases where this may be justified in principle, 'the burden of establishing reasonableness [is] heavier . . . than when [the direction] is issued to the parent corporation'.[47] Indeed, parent-based extraterritorial regulation as described above will by definition be easier to justify, since it raises no question of extraterritoriality: certain obligations are imposed on the parent corporation by the State of which it has the 'nationality' (or where it is domiciled). The impacts on situations located outside the national territory are merely indirect: any such impacts would result from the parent company being imposed an obligation to control its subsidiaries, or to monitor the supply chain. Indeed, the most promising avenue is one that imposes such an obligation on the parent company (or, *mutatis mutandis*, on the buyer). The advantages of this solution are also apparent once we examine another major obstacle to ensuring the protection of human rights throughout the corporation's activities, even when such activities span different jurisdictions.

The question of the 'corporate veil'

While disagreements about the existence of a 'genuine link' between the State seeking to legislate extraterritorially and the corporation whose conduct it seeks to influence may, in certain cases, constitute an obstacle to the exercise of extraterritorial jurisdiction, in practice it is the problem of piercing the corporate veil that is the most acute, and it is this hurdle that is the most difficult for the victims to overcome. Within the MNC as a group of companies, the parent (controlling) corporation, on the one hand, and its (controlled) subsidiary, on the other, form two distinct legal

---

corporate components of the enterprise'. However, the two questions are not necessarily linked: the choice to treat on a consolidated basis the benefits of the MNE for taxation purposes does not follow necessarily from the choice to consider as 'American' the subsidiaries controlled by the American parent corporation.

[46] *Restatement (Third) of the Foreign Relations Law of the United States* (1987), §414.

[47] *Ibid.*

entities, each with their own juridical personalities. In addition, according to the doctrine of limited liability, the shareholders in a corporation may not be held liable for the debts of that corporation beyond the level of their investment.[48] These doctrines combined make it difficult for victims of the conduct of the subsidiary to seek reparation by filing a claim against the parent company, before the national jurisdictions of the home State of that company. Three paths may be explored in order to overcome the problem of the separation of legal entities.

Three ways of overcoming the problem of the corporate veil

The first approach: piercing the corporate veil

The classical 'piercing the corporate veil' approach requires a close examination of the factual relationship between the parent and the subsidiary in order to identify whether the nature of that relationship is not more akin to the relationship between a principal (the parent) and an agent (the subsidiary), or whether, for other motives, there are reasons to suspect that the separation of corporate personalities does not correspond to economic reality. Thus, in exceptional circumstances, the US courts will allow claimants to establish that the parent company exercises such a degree of control on the operations of the subsidiary that the latter cannot be said to have any will or existence of its own,[49] and that treating the two entities as separate (and thus allowing the parent to shield itself behind its subsidiary) would sanction fraud or lead to an inequitable result.[50] In such cases, the 'piercing of the corporate veil' will be

---

[48] *Anderson* v. *Abbott*, 321 US 349, 362 (1944) ('Normally the corporation is an insulator from liability on claims of creditors. The fact that incorporation was desired in order to obtain limited liability does not defeat that purpose. Limited liability is the rule, not the exception' (citations omitted)); *Burnet* v. *Clark*, 287 US 410, 415 (1932) ('A corporation and its stockholders are generally to be treated as separate entities').

[49] Taken alone, neither majority or even complete stock control, nor common identity of the parent's and the subsidiary's officers and directors, are sufficient to establish the degree of control required. What is required is 'control ... of policy and business practice in respect to the transaction attacked so that the corporate entity as to this transaction has at the time no separate mind, will or existence of its own' (*Lowenthal* v. *Baltimore & Ohio RR Co.*, 287 NYS 62, 76 (NY App. Div.), aff'd, 6 NE2d 56 (1936), cited by Ph. I. Blumberg, 'Accountability of Multinational Corporations: The Barriers Presented by Concepts of the Corporate Juridical Entity', *Hastings International & Comparative Law Review*, 24 (2001), 297–330, 304).

[50] See *Taylor* v. *Standard Gas Co.*, 306 US 307, 322 (1939) ('the doctrine of corporate entity, recognized generally and for most purposes, will not be regarded when to do so would work fraud or injustice').

admitted, on the basis that the subsidiary has been a mere instrument in the hands of the parent company[51] or that the parent and the subsidiary are 'alter egos'.[52]

Alternatively, it may be shown that the subsidiary was acting in a particular case as the agent of the parent company.[53] This will be allowed, again in exceptional cases, where the parent company controls the subsidiary and where both parties agree that the subsidiary is acting for the agent: in such a case, 'the acts of a subsidiary acting as an agent are, from the legal point of view, the acts of its parent corporation, and it is the parent that is liable'.[54] An example is the reasoning followed in the case of *Bowoto* v. *Chevron Texaco*, where Judge Illston concluded that CNL, the subsidiary of Chevron in Nigeria, which allegedly had acted in concert with the Nigerian military in order to violently suppress protests against Chevron's activities in the region, could be considered as the agent of Chevron, in view in particular of the volume, content and timing of communications between Chevron and CNL, notably on the day of a protest when 'an oil platform was taken over by local people'.[55] These and other indicia showed that Chevron 'exercised more than the usual degree of direction and control which a parent exercises over its subsidiary'.

In order to establish either that the corporate form has been abused – by a parent artificially seeking to shield itself from liability by establishing a subsidiary which has in fact no existence of its own – or that the subsidiary has been acting in fact as the agent of the parent corporation, it will be required to bring forward a number of circumstances which will serve to demonstrate that the separation of legal personalities is a mere legal fiction to which the economic reality does not correspond and

---

[51] *Chicago, M & St PR Co. Assocn* v. *Minneapolis Civic and Commerce Assn*, 247 US 490, 501 (1918) (principles of corporate separateness 'have been plainly and repeatedly held not applicable where stock ownership has been resorted to, not for the purpose of participating in the affairs of a corporation in the normal and usual manner, but for the purpose . . . of controlling a subsidiary company so that it may be used as a mere agency or instrumentality of the owning company').

[52] See, e.g., *United States* v. *Betterfoods*, 524 US 51 (1998).

[53] As Justice (then Judge) Cardozo summarized in *Berkey* v. *Third Avenue R Co.*, 244 NY 84, 95, 155 NE 58, 61 (1927): 'Dominion may be so complete, interference so obtrusive, that by the general rules of agency the parent will be a principal and the subsidiary an agent.'

[54] Blumberg, 'Accountability', *supra* n. 49, 307.

[55] *Bowoto* v. *Chevron Texaco*, No. C 99–2506 SI, 2004 US Dis LEXIS 4603 (ND, Cal 2004). The case is discussed by S. Joseph, *Corporations and Transnational Human Rights Litigation* (Oxford: Hart Publishing, 2004), 132–3.

which should not be admitted, as this might sanction fraud.[56] This approach thus may constitute a source of legal insecurity, since the criteria allowing the 'piercing of the veil' are many, without either the list of admissible criteria or their hierarchisation being authoritatively identified; and it imposes a heavy burden on complainants seeking to invoke the indirect liability of the parent corporation for the acts of its subsidiary. The result is that, in fact, very few such attempts to 'pierce the veil' end up succeeding.[57]

The ECJ has taken a quite similar view in antitrust cases.[58] In the leading case of *Imperial Chemical Industries*,[59] the Court considered that where an undertaking established in a third country, in the exercise of its power to control its subsidiaries established within the Community, orders them to carry out a decision amounting to a practice prohibited under the competition rules of the EC, the conduct of the subsidiaries must be imputed to the parent company. The separation of legal personalities should not shield the parent company from liability for the acts of its subsidiaries, 'in particular where the subsidiary, although having separate legal personality, does not decide independently upon its own conduct on the market, but carries out, in all material respects, the

---

[56] See, e.g., *Labor Board* v. *Deena Artware*, 361 US 398, 402 (1960).

[57] Since the New Deal period, therefore, an alternative line of cases has emerged in the US courts, which has led a number of them to set aside the classical tests for allowing the piercing of the corporate veil in order to ensure that the legislative policy will not be defeated by the choice of corporate forms. See, e.g., *Anderson* v. *Abbott*, 321 US 349, 362–3 (1944) ('It has often been held that the interposition of a corporation will not be allowed to defeat a legislative policy, whether that was the aim or only the result of the arrangement'); *Bangor Punta Operations, Inc.* v. *Bangor & Aroostook R Co.*, 417 US 703, 713 (1974) ('the corporate form may be disregarded in the interests of justice where it is used to defeat an overriding public policy'); *First National City Bank* v. *Banco Para El Comercio Exterior de Cuba*, 462 US 611, 630 (1983) ('the Court has consistently refused to give effect to the corporate form where it is interposed to defeat legislative policies'). However, the abandonment of the classical 'piercing-the-corporate-veil' test has been piecemeal rather than systematic, and this has not contributed to legal certainty.

[58] See generally on the approach followed in European Courts, E. J. Cohn and C. Simitis, '"Lifting the Veil" in the Company Laws of the European Continent', *ICLQ*, 12 (1963), 189–225; Y. Hadari, 'The Structure of the Private Multinational Enterprise', *Michigan Law Review*, 71 (1973), 729–806, 771, n. 260; J. M. Dobson, '"Lifting the Veil" in Four Countries. The Law of Argentina, England, France and the United States', *ICLQ*, 35 (1986), 839–63; K. Hofstetter, 'Parent Responsibility for Subsidiary Corporations. Evaluating European Trends', *ICLQ*, 39 (1990), 576–98; L. Bergkamp and W.-Q. Pak, 'Piercing the Corporate Veil. Shareholder Liability for Corporate Torts', *Maastricht Journal of European and Comparative Law*, 8/2 (2001), 167–88.

[59] Case 48/69, *Imperial Chemical Industries Ltd.* v. *Commission*, [1972] ECR 619.

instructions given to it by the parent company'.[60] The parent company and the subsidiary will be considered to form one single 'economic unit' – allowing for the acts of the subsidiary to be imputed to the parent company – where two cumulative conditions are fulfilled: first, the parent has the power to influence decisively the behaviour of the subsidiary;[61] second, it has in fact used this power on the occasion of the adoption of the contested acts.[62] In such circumstances, 'the formal separation between these companies, resulting from their separate legal personality, cannot outweigh the unity of their conduct on the market for the purposes of applying the rules on competition'.[63]

The second approach: the presumption of control in the integrated enterprise

A second approach is based on the idea that MNCs are groups of formally separate entities, but whose interconnectedness is such that it may be justified to establish a presumption according to which any act committed by one subsidiary of the group should be treated as if it were adopted by the parent. In this perspective, the TNC is seen as 'a conglomeration of units of a single entity, each unit performing a specific function, the function of the parent company being to provide expertise, technology, supervision and finance. Insofar as injuries result from negligence in respect of any of the parent company functions, then the parent should be liable.'[64]

This technique has been used in the United States not only in New Deal legislation and by courts and agencies seeking to ensure that legislation protecting employees would not be circumvented by the abuse of the corporate form, but also in order to define the conditions under which certain legislations protecting employees from discrimination could extend to the operations of subsidiaries of American undertakings operating overseas.[65] The 1990 American with Disabilities Act is

---

[60] *Ibid.*, para. 133.

[61] Thus, the Court remarks that 'at the time the applicant held all or at any rate the majority of the shares in those subsidiaries' (para. 136) and 'was able to exercise decisive influence over the policy of the subsidiaries as regards selling prices in the common market' (para. 137).

[62] *Ibid.*, paras. 137–9.   [63] *Ibid.*, para. 140.

[64] R. Meeran, 'The Unveiling of Transnational Corporations', in M. Addo (ed.), *Human Rights Standards and the Responsibility of Transnational Corporations* (The Hague: Kluwer Law International, 1999), 170.

[65] Blumberg, 'Accountability', *supra* n. 49, 313–15.

an example. The Act prohibits discrimination against persons with disabilities, as committed by any employer, employment agency, labour organisation, or joint labour–management committee. It provides for the extraterritorial scope of the prohibition, by establishing a presumption according to which 'If an employer controls a corporation whose place of incorporation is a foreign country, any practice that constitutes discrimination under this section and is engaged in by such corporation shall be presumed to be engaged in by such employer'.[66] Remaining within the boundaries of extraterritorial jurisdiction as defined by the principle of active personality, this section does not apply with respect to 'the foreign operations of an employer that is a foreign person not controlled by an American employer'.[67] This is equivalent to imposing on all American employers covered by the Act an obligation to monitor the compliance of all the corporations they control in foreign countries with the prohibition of discrimination on grounds of disability. The Act also provides that

> the determination of whether an employer controls a corporation shall be based on –
> (i) the interrelation of operations;
> (ii) the common management;
> (iii) the centralized control of labor relations; and
> (iv) the common ownership or financial control, of the employer and the corporation.[68]

Similar provisions may be found, for instance, in Title VII of the Civil Rights Act of 1964.[69] Although the amendments made to the Civil Rights Act in 1991 seriously restricted the extraterritorial reach of this statute – following those amendments, only employees who are citizens of the United States are covered by the protection afforded under Title VII of the Civil Rights Act[70] – American employers are presumed, under this statute, to engage in any discriminatory practice engaged in by a corporation whose place of incorporation is a foreign country, if they control such foreign corporation. The modalities of determining the

---

[66] Pub. L. 101–336, title I, §102, July 26, 1990, 104 Stat. 331; amended by Pub. L. 102–166, title I, §109(b)(2), November 21, 1991, 105 Stat. 1077; codified as 42 USC §12112 (c)(2)(A) (1994).

[67] 42 USC §12112 (c)(2)(B) (1994).   [68] 42 USC §12112 (c)(2)(C) (1994).

[69] Pub. L. 88–352, title VII, 42 USC §2000e and ff., as amended by the Civil Rights Act of 1991 (Pub. L. 102–166).

[70] 42 USC §2000e, (f), and §2000e-1, (a).

existence of such control are identical to that provided for in the American with Disabilities Act.[71]

In the *Amoco Cadiz Oil Spill* case, it is such an 'enterprise' approach which the District Court of Illinois adopted, even in the absence of any legislative mandate, in order to conclude that the parent corporation should be held liable for environmental damage caused by an oil spill from a tanker off the coast of France: the close degree of control of the parent corporation over its subsidiaries allowed the court to overcome the separation of legal personalities.[72] It has also been proposed in legal doctrine to adopt a similar approach in the Alien Tort Claims Act where, it has been argued, the fact that the subsidiary has allegedly violated the law of nations should be sufficient to allow for piercing the veil, and impose a liability on the parent (controlling) company, unless it is proven by the latter that 'no reasonable effort would have discovered evidence from documents of any applicable government, non-governmental organizational documents and reports, employee information, or anecdotal information in the State that would have moved a reasonable person to inquire further'.[73]

Insofar as it is based on the presumption that the 'controlling' parent company may effectively influence the behaviour of the subsidiary – which justifies attributing to the parent company the acts of the subsidiary – the 'integrated enterprise' approach is in line with the contemporary evolution of multinational firms. The ability of the multinational firm to move large volumes of goods swiftly and cost-effectively, as well as the standardisation of products across the globe, has transformed the classical understanding of the relationship between the parent and the subsidiary. In many cases, the multinational appears as a coordinator of the activities of its subsidiaries, which function as a network of organisations working along functional lines rather than

---

[71] 42 USC §2000e-1, (b) and (c).

[72] See *Amoco Cadiz Oil Spill*, 1984 AMC 2123, 2 Lloyd's Rep. 304 (ND Ill. 1984): 'As an integrated multinational corporation which is engaged through a system of subsidiaries in the exploration, production, refining, transportation and sale of petroleum products throughout the world, Standard [the American parent corporation] is responsible for the tortious acts of its wholly owned subsidiaries and instrumentalities AIC and Transport.'

[73] S. Coye-Huhn, 'No More Hiding behind Forms, Factors and Flying Hats. A Proposal for a per se Piercing of the Corporate Veil for Corporations that Violate the Law of Nations under the Alien Tort Claims Statute', *University of Cincinatti Law Review*, 72 (2003), 743–70, 758. In contrast with this proposal, however, the presumption established under statutes such as the Civil Rights Act or the American With Disabilities Act is nonrebuttable.

according to geographical specialisation: 'In the past, parent companies typically made little effort to coordinate strategically the activities of their foreign subsidiaries. Foreign affiliates were treated as distant appendages – as 'stand-alone fiefdoms' that operated independently and merely paid a dividend to the home office. Today, ... some multi-nationals are integrating their previously nationally focused and auton-omous production and distribution operations in various countries along regional and global lines. Thus foreign subsidiaries that in the past produced and marketed products only in the country in which they were based, are now supplying regional or worldwide markets, including in many cases the parent company's home market.'[74] In this process, the new organisational structures 'give global corporate managers authority over country and regional managers'; incentive systems are devised to 'encourage cooperation among employees working for different affili-ates'; and 'programs and practices designed to instill in diverse groups of employees scattered around the globe a common sense of purpose and common methods of operation':[75] in sum, the head office reasserts its role, as the integration of the group is deepened.

The third approach: the direct liability of the parent corporation for failure to exercise due diligence

Finally, a third avenue consists in abandoning the idea of linking the behaviour of the subsidiaries to that of the parent altogether, and focus-ing instead on the direct liability of the parent company arising from the failure to exercise due diligence in controlling the acts of the subsidiaries it may exercise control upon. The liability of the parent corporation thus relates not only to the action of the parent firm, but also to its omissions. Indeed, in the absence of an obligation to exercise control over the activities of the subsidiary, there would be a risk that an attempt to substitute a direct liability approach to an indirect liability approach will result in creating a disincentive on parent companies to monitor the behaviour of their subsidiaries, because any amount of 'excessive' control might allow us to conclude either that the subsidiary is merely acting as an agent of the parent, or that the implication of the parent in the operations is such that it should be held liable alongside the subsidiary. In that sense, where direct liability attaches to parent com-panies only in cases of actions rather than omissions 'parents will be

---

[74] Mabry, 'Multinational Corporations', *supra* n. 44, 565.   [75] *Ibid.*

discouraged from intervening in their subsidiary's operations, even though they may have superior knowledge and technical expertise. Alternatively, parent companies might maintain "strategic control" but avoid responsibility by delegating operational matters, which are more likely to give rise to tortious consequences.'[76]

The case of *Connelly* v. *RTZ Corporation plc and Others* may serve as an illustration.[77] The claimant in that case was a former employee for Rossing Uranium Ltd. (RUL), a Namibian subsidiary of the defendant corporation (RTZ Corporation plc, incorporated in the United Kingdom). He had been employed by RUL in a uranium mine. It was discovered three years after his return that he was suffering from cancer of the larynx, apparently due to exposure to radioactive material in the mine. According to the description by the House of Lords, the claim was based on the allegation that 'RTZ had devised RUL's policy on health, safety and the environment, or alternatively had advised RUL as to the contents of the policy', and that 'an employee or employees of RTZ, referred to as RTZ supervisors, implemented the policy and supervised health, safety and/or environmental protection at the mine'. The argument was therefore not (as in classical piercing-the-veil analysis) that separation between the parent and the subsidiary should be treated as a mere fiction, a fraudulent means of limiting the liability of the parent corporation, without any correspondence to economic reality: it was that RTZ corporation had itself contributed, by its acts, in causing the damage for which the victim sought compensation. Such an argument would have had no chance to succeed if, instead of being involved in defining the policy of its subsidiary on health and safety or environmental issues, RTZ Corporation had simply ignored any risks associated with the mining of uranium, and had acted merely as a shareholder, monitoring the financial performances of its subsidiary, but without seeking to be informed about, let alone participate in, the definition of its everyday policies in such areas.

In *Connelly*, the direct liability of the parent corporation was asserted on the basis of the *actions* it had taken in defining the policies of its subsidiary. By contrast, the *omissions* of the parent corporation were at stake in *Lubbe and 4 Others* v. *Cape plc*, which the House of Lords was

---

[76] Joseph, *Corporations*, *supra* n. 55, 134. See also J. Cassels, 'Outlaws. Multinational Corporations and Catastrophic Law', *Cumberland Law Review*, 31 (2000), 311–35, 326.

[77] *Connelly* v. *RTZ Corp. plc and Others* [1997] UKHL 30; [1998] AC 854; [1997] 4 All ER 335; [1997] 3 WLR 373.

presented with again only three years later.[78] Over 3,000 plaintiffs claimed damages for personal injuries (and in some cases death) allegedly suffered as the result of exposure to asbestos in South Africa, either upon working in mines owned by the defendant (until 1948) or by a fully owned South African subsidiary of the defendant, or as a result of living in an area contaminated by the mining activities of the defendant or its subsidiaries. As noted by the leading opinion of Lord Bingham of Cornhill, 'the claim is made against the defendant as a parent company which, knowing (so it is said) that exposure to asbestos was gravely injurious to health, *failed to take proper steps to ensure that proper working practices were followed and proper safety precautions observed throughout the group.* In this way, it is alleged, the defendant breached a duty of care which it owed to those working for its subsidiaries or living in the area of their operations (with the result that the plaintiffs thereby suffered personal injury and loss).'[79]

Central to the *Cape plc* case was, therefore, the question 'whether a parent company which is proved to exercise de facto control over the operations of a (foreign) subsidiary and which knows, through its directors, that those operations involve risks to the health of workers employed by the subsidiary and/or persons in the vicinity of its factory or other business premises, owes a duty of care to those workers and/or other persons in relation to the control which it exercises over and the advice which it gives to the subsidiary company'.[80]

The choice between these approaches

To summarise, the obstacles created by the separation of legal personalities within the corporate group may be overcome in three ways : first, we may seek to affirm the derivative liability of the parent corporation for the acts of its subsidiary, where the corporate veil could be lifted because it has been abused ; second, the 'integrated enterprise' approach could be adopted, which is an intermediate approach predicated on the understanding that the multinational enterprise (MNE) is organised as

---

[78] [2000] 4 AU ER 268. On 14 December 1998, the House of Lords had already refused to allow leave to the defendants to file a further appeal against an initial decision by the Court of Appeal. Following this, over 3,000 new plaintiffs emerged, fundamentally transforming the nature of the litigation presented before the UK courts.

[79] Emphasis added.

[80] As indicated by the opinion of Lord Bingham of Cornhill, this is the issue as reformulated during the first Court of Appeal hearing in the case.

an integrated group, allowing for a presumption that the acts committed by the subsidiary will be imputed to the parent; third, the direct liability of the parent corporation could be affirmed for its own actions or omissions, including the omission to exercise due diligence in controlling the subsidiary. Two important consequences follow from this distinction.

First, the first approach, based on the 'derivative liability' of the parent corporation, creates a disincentive on the parent company to exercise a strict control over the activities of the subsidiary, even in situations where it could in fact exercise such control. Indeed, to the extent that the relationships between the parent and the subsidiary remain fully consistent with the norms of corporate behaviour – i.e. do not lead to the suspicion that the parent–subsidiary separation has been misused in order to artificially insulate the parent from liability for the behaviour of the subsidiary – the corporate veil will not be pierced : only where it has been established that the control by the parent company is such that the subsidiary has no existence of its own (has no 'separate mind'), will the separation of legal personalities be overcome. Thus, insofar as this serves to limit its potential legal liability, it will be in the interest of the parent company not to monitor closely the everyday operations of the subsidiary, but on the contrary to abandon broad discretion to the subsidiary as to how to implement the general policies set for the multinational group. By contrast, if – under the 'integrated enterprise' approach – we establish a presumption that the parent is liable for all the acts adopted by the subsidiaries within the multinational group, or if we seek to engage the 'direct liability' of the company for failing to exercise due diligence in controlling the activities of its subsidiary, close monitoring of the subsidiary will be in the interest of the parent: instead of making it vulnerable to attempts to pierce the corporate veil, it may be seen as a way to avoid liability or as an insurance against the risk of being accused of being negligent in exercising oversight over the subsidiary's activities.

The second consequence of this distinction is related to the question of State jurisdiction. The *Imperial Chemical Industries* case of the ECJ presents us with a rather unfamiliar situation where the applicability of the law of the forum was extended to the acts of a parent company, incorporated in a foreign country, because of the acts committed by the subsidiaries of that company on the territory of the forum (more precisely in the *ICI* case, the behaviour of the subsidiaries produced effects on the common market of the European Economic Community,

EEC).[81] In general however, the situation is exactly the reverse: the extraterritorial application of the law of the forum State is sought to be justified by the fact that the subsidiaries, though established in foreign States, in fact are controlled by the parent company, domiciled in the forum State. In this scenario, direct liability of the parent TNC or the adoption of the 'integrated enterprise' approach[82] present over derivative liability the advantage that they can be based on the territoriality principle, combined with the criminal law doctrine of ubiquity where the extraterritorial legislation is of a criminal nature, or at least on the active personality principle. In addition, in litigation before the US Federal courts based on the Alien Tort Claims Act, the adoption of the 'direct liability' or the 'integrated enterprise' approaches would facilitate overcoming the barrier represented by the *forum non conveniens* doctrine, since the connection to the forum will be stronger if the parent company is sued directly for its own actions, rather than for those of its subsidiaries.[83]

By contrast, under the first approach based on the derivative liability of the parent for the acts of its subsidiaries, it may be more difficult to justify imposing on foreign subsidiaries the law of the forum State, even if the objective is to reach, via the direct liability of the subsidiaries, the parent corporation itself.

---

[81] A situation with certain similarities presented itself in the *Doe* v. *Unocal* case, in which the US District Court for the Central District of California considered that it had no personal jurisdiction over Total, the French partner in the Yadana pipeline project in Burma of the Californian company Unocal (*Doe* v. *Unocal*, 27 FSupp 2d 1174 (CD Cal 1998), aff'd 248 F 3d 915 (2001)). Under the ATCA, in order for US Federal courts to be able to exercise 'personal jurisdiction', the defendant must have 'minimum contacts' with the forum, and this in principle requires 'systematic' and 'continuous' contacts with it (see *International Shoe* v. *Washington*, 326 US 310 (1945); cf. *Hanson* v. *Deckel*, 357 US 235 (1958), and their progeny). The US District Court for the Central District of California took the view that it had no 'personal jurisdiction' over Total, since the Californian subsidiaries of Total were not its 'alter egos' in the classical 'piercing-the-veil' approach

[82] Under the 'integrated enterprise' approach, the law of the forum State is extended to foreign corporations on the basis that they are part of one single economic group, coordinated by the parent corporation: indeed, as illustrated by the examples of the Civil Rights Act and the American With Disabilities Act mentioned above, this approach has been adopted precisely in order to justify the extraterritorial reach of the relevant statutes.

[83] Joseph, *Corporations*, *supra* n. 55, 134, citing M. J. Rogge, 'Towards Transnational Corporate Liability in the Global Economy. Challenging the Doctrine of *Forum non Conveniens* in *Re: Union Carbide, Alfaro, Sequihua,* and *Aguinda*', *Texas International Law Journal*, 26 (2001), 299–330, 313–14.

For both these reasons, the most advisable solution to avoid the parent corporation from shielding itself behind the subsidiary where it would have been able to control the subsidiary more effectively would seem to consist in imposing directly on the parent corporation an obligation, defined by statute, to effectively monitor the behaviour of the subsidiaries which it 'controls'. The notion of 'control', for the purposes of the application of such a statutory obligation, should be defined on the basis of the stock ownership,[84] without there being a need to identify, on a case-to-case basis, whether the parent company has in fact been involved in the policies of the subsidiary or whether the latter has a 'mind of its own'. Only where the parent company could demonstrate that it was unable to effectively avoid the contested behaviour of the subsidiary company from occurring, despite having exercised due diligence and despite its best efforts to seek information about such behaviour and to react accordingly, should its liability be excluded. Just as in the 'integrated enterprise' approach above, a presumption should therefore be established that the acts committed by the subsidiaries which it 'controls' may be attributed to the parent company as such, although such a presumption could conceivably be rebutted in certain instances where, despite the safeguards in place, the parent company failed to prevent certain tortious or otherwise illegal acts from being adopted.

Transforming international law

Extraterritorial obligations

While the adoption of legislation imposing on the parent company certain due diligence obligations to control compliance with human rights in the group or down the supply chain may be desirable, it is not a requirement under the existing international law of human rights. In principle, the international responsibility of a State may not be engaged by the conduct of actors not belonging to the State apparatus unless they are in fact acting under the instructions of, or under the direction or control of, that State in carrying out the conduct.[85] Although

---

[84] For instance, sections 747–6 and Schedules 24–6 of the UK Income and Corporation Taxes Act 1988 rely on the notion of the 'controlled foreign company', defined as a foreign company in which the resident company owns a holding of more than 50 per cent.

[85] To paraphrase Art. 4 of the ILC's Articles on State Responsibility, which itself is of course directly inspired by the position adopted by the ICJ in *Case Concerning Military and Paramilitary Activities in and Against Nicaragua (Nicaragua* v. *United States of America)*

the private–public distinction on which this rule of attribution is based is mooted (though not contradicted) by the imposition under international human rights law of positive obligations on States – implying that the State must accept responsibility not only for the acts its organs have adopted, but also for the omissions of these organs, where such omissions result in an insufficient protection of private persons whose rights or freedoms are violated by the acts of other non-State actors – this has been recognised only in situations falling under the 'jurisdiction' of the State – i.e. in situations on which the State exercises effective control. Outside the national territory, it is not presumed that the State exercises such control, and only in exceptional circumstances will it be considered that the power its organs exercise on persons or property located abroad amounts to that State having 'jurisdiction' in a sense which would justify the extension of the positive obligations derived from any international human rights instruments binding upon it.[86] Thus, in the current State of development of international law, a clear obligation for States to control private actors such as corporations, operating outside their national territory, in order to ensure that these actors will not violate the human rights of others, has not yet crystallised.

This classical view may be changing, however, especially as far as economic and social rights are concerned. There is a growing recognition that the fact of the interdependency of States should lead us to impose an extended understanding of State obligations, or an obligation on all States to act jointly in the face of collective action problems faced by the international community of States. Art. 2(1) of the International Covenant on Economic, Social and Cultural Rights (ICESCR) refers to international assistance and cooperation as an instrument to ensure the realisation of economic, social and cultural rights, and Art. 23 specifies the different forms international action for the achievement of the rights recognised in the Covenant may take: such international action 'includes such methods as the conclusion of conventions, the adoption of

---

(merits), [1986] ICJ Rep., 14. The Articles on State Responsibility for internationally wrongful acts were adopted by the ILC on 9 August 2001; the UN General Assembly has taken note of the Articles in Res. 56/83 adopted on 12 December 2001, 'Responsibility of States for Internationally Wrongful Acts'.

[86] On the extraterritorial application of human rights treaties see, among many others, the essays collected in F. Coomans and M. Kamminga (eds.), *Extraterritorial Application of Human Rights Treaties* (Antwerp and Oxford: Intersentia, 2004), M. J. Dennis, 'Application of Human Rights Treaties Extraterritorially in Times of Armed Conflict and Military Occupation', *AJIL*, 99 (2005), 119–41 and T. Meron, 'Extraterritoriality of Human Rights Treaties', *AJIL*, 89 (1995), 78–82.

recommendations, the furnishing of technical assistance and the holding of regional meetings and technical meetings for the purpose of consultation and study organised in conjunction with the Governments concerned'.

The preparatory work shows that, in adopting these provisions relating to international assistance and cooperation, the drafters of the ICESCR did not wish to impose an obligation on any State to provide such assistance or cooperation at any specified level.[87] However, this is not to say that no other obligations may be derived from the reference made in Art. 2(1) of the Covenant to international assistance and co-operation – that, in other terms, 'the relevant commitment [would be] meaningless'.[88] The Committee on Economic, Social and Cultural Rights derives from this provision an obligation to protect the rights that would be threatened by the activities of private actors whose behaviour a State may decisively influence, even outside the national territory.[89] There is also a strong tendency within legal doctrine to insist on the need to impose on States an obligation to seek to influence extraterritorial situations, to the extent that they may exercise influence in fact – or, in other terms, to align the scope of their international responsibility to the degree of their effective power to control.[90] Sornarajah has argued that 'developed States owe a duty of control to the international community and

---

[87] Ph. Alston and G. Quinn, 'The Nature and Scope of States Parties' Obligations under the International Covenant on Economic, Social and Cultural Rights', *Human Rights Quarterly*, 9 (1987), 156–229, 186–92.

[88] *Ibid.*, p. 191. Alston and Quinn add that: 'In the context of a given right it may, according to the circumstances, be possible to identify obligations to cooperate internationally that would appear to be mandatory on the basis of the undertaking contained in Article 2(1) of the Covenant.'

[89] See Committee on Economic, Social and Cultural Rights, General Comment No. 14 (2000), *The right to the highest attainable standard of health (article 12 of the International Covenant on Economic, Social and Cultural Rights)*, UN Doc. E/C.12/ 2000/4 (11 August 2000), para. 39; and Committee on Economic, Social and Cultural Rights, General Comment No. 15 (2002), *The right to water (articles 11 and 12 of the International Covenant on Economic, Social and Cultural Rights)*, UN Doc. E/C.12/2002/ 11 (26 November 2002), para. 31. For comments, see W. Vandenhole, 'Completing the UN Complaint Mechanisms for Human Rights Violations Step by Step', *Netherlands Quarterly of Human Rights*, 21, No. 3 (2003), 423–62, 445–6 and M. Craven, *The International Covenant on Economic, Social and Cultural Rights. A Perspective on Its Development* (Oxford University Press, 1995), 147–50.

[90] See, e.g., S. Skogly, *Beyond National Borders. States' Human Rights Obligations in International Cooperation* (Antwerp and Oxford: Intersentia, 2006), esp. chapter 3 ('Extraterritorial Human Rights Obligations').

do in fact have the means of legal control over the conduct abroad of multinational corporations'.[91] He sees the imposition of such an obligation as the logical counterpart of the extensive protections afforded to foreign investors under both general public international law and conventional international law. While this statement would seem to refer to international law as it should be rather than as it is, this position is not isolated, even if we take it as a statement about the positive State of the law.[92]

From unilateralism to multilateralism

Whether or not, in the current State of international law, there exists an obligation on each State to protect human rights (especially the rights of the ICESCR) threatened by the activities of private actors which the State is in a position to control, at a minimum, the community of States cannot ignore the fact of the interdependencies created by the activities of such transnational actors, and the need to devise an adequate reaction to the problem of externalities thus posed. El Hadji Guissé, a Special Rapporteur of the UN Commission on Human Rights, has expressed with particular clarity that

> The violations committed by the transnational corporations in their mainly transboundary activities do not come within the competence of a single State and, to prevent contradictions and inadequacies in the remedies and sanctions decided upon by States individually or as a group, these violations should form the subject of special attention. The States and the international community should combine their efforts so as to

---

[91] M. Sornarajah, *The International Law on Foreign Investment*, 2nd edn. (Cambridge University Press, 2004), chapter 4.

[92] Magdalena Sepúlveda writes, for instance, that 'according to the Committee, developed States have an obligation to discourage practices which lead to violations of economic, social and cultural rights in third parties [sic: this should probably read as 'in third countries', although the correct expression would be 'in foreign countries'; or perhaps the author meant 'by third parties'], by penalising harmful behaviour and through the adoption of measures to prosecute perpetrators at the domestic level (e.g. in countries where the headquarters of transnational corporations are based)' (Magdalena Sepúlveda, 'Obligations of "International Assistance and Cooperation" in an Optional Protocol to the International Covenant on Economic, Social and Cultural Rights', *Netherlands Quarterly of Human Rights*, 24, No. 24, 271–303, 282). See also *The Right to Food*, Report submitted by the Special Rapporteur on the right to food, Jean Ziegler, in accordance with Commission on Human Rights resolution 2002/25, UN Doc. E/CN.4/ 2003/54, 10 January 2003, para. 29.

contain such activities by the establishment of legal standards capable of achieving that objective. [93]

The preparation of a new International Convention on Combating Human Rights Violations by Transnational Corporations would therefore not move into entirely unchartered territory. The main value of such an instrument would consist in establishing a clear division of responsibilities between the host State and the home State in the regulation of TNCs. The primary responsibility of the host State, on the territory of which the TNC conducts its activities, should be reaffirmed. But the home State of the TNC should be imposed a subsidiary responsibility to exercise control on the TNC over which it may have jurisdiction on the basis of the principle of active nationality. A clarification of the division of tasks would thereby be achieved. This would meet the concern of the business community that the development of extraterritorial jurisdiction on a unilateral basis – exercised by the home State in the absence of any bilateral or multilateral framework – might be a source of legal uncertainty. The International Chamber of Commerce (ICC), in particular, encourages governments to 'consider greater use of intergovernmental organisations . . . as vehicles for discussion and resolving disputes related to the extraterritorial application of national laws. In this regard, the ICC further encourages governments to explore the feasibility of an international convention on the extraterritorial application of national laws providing for means of resolving extraterritoriality disputes, where appropriate, by way of consultation, cooperation, conciliation, or arbitration'.[94] In order to understand the sources of the potential uncertainties linked to an anarchic use of extraterritorial jurisdiction, it is useful to briefly examine this problem, before turning to other issues raised by the adoption of an International Convention on Combating Human Rights Violations by Transnational Corporations.

It is clear that the exercise of extraterritorial jurisdiction may result in positive conflicts of jurisdiction between the host State and the home State concerned, even though it may be well intended, and be

---

[93] *The Realization of Economic, Social and Cultural Rights, Final report on the question of the impunity of perpetrators of human rights violations (economic, social and cultural rights)*, prepared by Mr El Hadji Guissé, Special Rapporteur, pursuant to Sub-Commission resolution 1996/24, UN Doc. E/CN.4/Sub.2/1997/8, 27 June 1997, para. 131.

[94] *Extraterritoriality and Business*, prepared by the Task Force on Extraterritoriality of the International Chamber of Commerce, 13 July 2006 (doc. 103–33/5 final), para. 7 of the recommendations.

defended as an instrument through which the impunity of TNCs for human rights violations may be combated. The problems caused by such positive conflicts of jurisdiction fall into two categories. First, the interests of States may diverge. The territorial State may consider that the extraterritorial jurisdiction exercised by another State, which seeks to extend the reach of its national legislation to situations arising on the territory of the first State, violates its sovereignty or constitutes an intervention in its internal affairs. Moreover, conflicts may arise between different States seeking to exercise extraterritorial jurisdiction over the same situations, to which they intend to attach diverging solutions.[95] Second, the addressee of different domestic laws – in particular, the TNC having to comply simultaneously with different prescriptions – may encounter certain difficulties in the face of extraterritorial legislations. Where the criteria for the extraterritorial application of any State legislation are not defined with the required precision – for example, as regards the determination of the nationality of the corporation or as regards the conditions under which a foreign corporation is considered to be 'controlled' by a corporation considered to possess the 'nationality' of the forum State – a problem may arise as regards the principle of legality, especially where criminal extraterritorial jurisdiction is

---

[95] In the extraterritorial application of their antitrust legislation, for instance, the policy choices of the EU, of Canada, of Japan and of the United States may differ, and there is a risk, where the respective antitrust legislations of these States all are applicable to the same anticompetitive arrangements concluded by undertakings, that these choices be undermined – as when a settlement negotiated under the relevant competition rules of the EC would be threatened by the availability of a remedy before US courts, for competitors of the undertakings concerned, on the basis of the US Sherman Act. This question was at the heart of *F. Hoffmann–La Roche Ltd.* v. *Empagran S.A.*, 123 SCt 2359 (2004). In this case, the Supreme Court unanimously held that where anticompetitive behaviour, such as a price-fixing agreement, 'significantly and adversely affects both customers outside the United States and customers within the United States, but the adverse foreign effect is independent of any adverse domestic effect', plaintiffs who allege that they have been injured by the 'foreign effect' cannot invoke the jurisdiction of US antitrust laws or courts. In the case presented to the Court, producers of vitamin products from various countries had joined in a price-fixing conspiracy by fixing their prices worldwide over a period of several years. The Court was moved to interpret restrictively the extraterritorial reach of the Sherman Act under the Foreign Trade Antitrust Improvements Act of 1982 (FTAIA), by noting that it should 'assume that legislators take account of the legitimate sovereign interests of other nations when they write American laws. [This statutory construction] thereby helps the potentially conflicting laws of different nations work together in harmony – a harmony particularly needed in today's highly interdependent commercial world. No one denies that America's antitrust laws, when applied to foreign conduct, can interfere with a foreign nation's ability independently to regulate its own commercial affairs.'

concerned. Moreover, the simultaneous application of more than one State legislation to a same situation may lead to situations where the TNC will face conflicting requirements.

The risks of positive conflicts of jurisdiction arising from the extension of extraterritorial legislation may be attenuated either by an attitude of the forum State aimed at limiting the risks involved, or by measures adopted in a bilateral or multilateral framework. The Annex appended in 1991 to the OECD Declaration on International Investment and Multinational Enterprises[96] contains a series of general considerations and practical approaches aimed at avoiding or minimising the imposition of conflicting requirements on MNEs by governments. Under the 'general considerations', the OECD governments recommend that the forum State seeking to exercise extraterritorial jurisdiction do so within the confines of the principle of reasonableness:

> In contemplating new legislation, action under existing legislation or other exercise of jurisdiction which may conflict with the legal requirements or established policies of another Member country and lead to conflicting requirements being imposed on multinational enterprises, the Member countries concerned should:
> (a) Have regard to relevant principles of international law;
> (b) Endeavour to avoid or minimise such conflicts and the problems to which they give rise by following an approach of moderation and restraint, respecting and accommodating the interests of other Member countries[97];
> (c) Take fully into account the sovereignty and legitimate economic, law enforcement and other interests of other Member countries.

In line with the general philosophy thus advocated within the OECD, the State seeking to exercise extraterritorial jurisdiction may envisage a number of measures in order to minimise positive conflicts of jurisdiction with other States. It may avoid legislating unless there is a clear basis, recognised under international law, for doing so (effects doctrine, active or passive personality principle, principle of protection, or principle of

---

[96] The Declaration was adopted by the Governments of the OECD Member Countries in 1976. It has been adhered to by the thirty OECD Member Countries, but has also been subscribed to, in addition, by Argentina (22 April 1997), Chile (3 October 1997), Brazil (14 November 1997), Estonia (20 September 2001), Lithuania (20 September 2001), Slovenia (22 January 2002), Israel (18 September 2002), Latvia (9 January 2004) and Romania (20 April 2005).

[97] In a footnote, the 'general considerations' explain that this is in accordance with 'the principle of comity, as it is understood in some Member countries, which includes following an approach of this nature in exercising one's jurisdiction'.

universality), and provided the principle of reasonableness is complied with. To the extent the State authorities have a certain discretion whether or not to exercise extraterritorial jurisdiction in specific instances under extraterritorial legislation allowing for this possibility, they may use this discretion in order to accommodate the interests of other States: this could guide, for instance, the prosecuting authorities under the principle of expediency; or it could guide the courts in deciding whether or not to accept jurisdiction, under a doctrine such as the *forum non conveniens* rule relied upon by common law jurisdictions, or equivalent doctrines of subsidiarity. Finally, where the exercise of criminal extraterritorial jurisdiction is concerned, the forum State may consider extending respect for the *non bis in idem* rule to situations where a criminal defendant has already been prosecuted for the same acts, when the said acts are offences under the laws of another State having exercised jurisdiction. It may also only apply a criminal statute to extraterritorial situations under the condition of double criminality; or, at a minimum, it may decide that a particular conduct will not constitute unlawful behaviour when such behaviour is prescribed by the territorial State, thus avoiding the need to impose conflicting obligations on the addressee.

Most of the measures which a State may adopt in order to avoid positive conflicts of jurisdiction out of respect for the sovereignty of other States, in accordance with the principle of comity between nations, will simultaneously benefit the addressee of the extraterritorial legislation concerned, by relieving it from certain obligations which might otherwise have been imposed. In general, the attitude of restraint in the adoption of extraterritorial legislation, in particular where the legislature avoids regulating extraterritorial situations unless there exists a clear connecting factor to the forum State and unless the criterion of reasonableness is complied with, thus will risk respecting other States' interests at the expense of combating certain forms of unacceptable behaviour. This apparent dilemma, however, is not unavoidable. On the contrary, a number of doctrines aimed at ensuring self-restraint in the exercise of extraterritorial jurisdiction, while justified by the principle of comity towards foreign nations, will not fundamentally modify the legal situation of the addressee of such extraterritorial legislations, insofar as such doctrines will affect not the very *possibility* of extraterritorial jurisdiction being exercised, but only the *exercise*, in any individual case, of extraterritorial jurisdiction. Thus, the rule of reason in the exercise of criminal extraterritorial jurisdiction is essentially used in order to guide the decision whether or not to prosecute, in accordance with the principle of expediency or of opportunity. Similarly, the doctrine of *forum non conveniens*, as applied by the United States and other Common law jurisdictions,[98] shows a certain degree of deference to foreign jurisdictions, without depriving the applicable extraterritorial legislation of its deterrent effect, and allowing extraterritorial jurisdiction to be exercised where, in its absence, certain forms of behaviour would remain unpunished or the victims left without remedies.

It is true that reliance on such doctrines presents certain disadvantages: they imply that a balancing of the interests involved shall be performed within the forum State, by the prosecuting authorities, or by the courts, which may impair the objectivity of the exercise; and the case-to-case approach they imply makes the outcome essentially unpredictable. However, it is also the flexibility of these doctrines which constitutes their strength: they allow an escape from the dilemma of not taking into account the interests of the other States in exercising extraterritorial jurisdiction, on the one hand, and leaving certain violations unpunished or certain victims without remedies, on the other hand, since the exercise of extraterritorial jurisdiction will be considered justified to the extent that the balancing of the interests clearly weighs in favour of such exercise, rather than deferring to the choices of the territorial State in the face of human rights violations committed by TNCs or in which such corporations are complicit.

Similarly, the exercise of criminal extraterritorial jurisdiction, when combined with the requirement of double criminality, is fully compatible with other States' interests, and in particular with the interests of the territorial State concerned. Indeed, it may be seen as a gesture by which the forum State puts its institutions at the disposal of the effective enforcement of the territorial State's laws; and to the extent that those laws are not in fact enforced by the territorial State concerned, because of the inability or the unwillingness of the national authorities to do so, the enforcement of their requirements through the machinery of another State asserting jurisdiction may be beneficial to transparency, obliging each State to behave consistently with its own laws.

---

[98] Although not by the UK or Ireland courts when their jurisdiction is based, in civil cases (in particular where a suit is filed alleging tortious behaviour by the defendant company domiciled in the United Kingdom or in Ireland), on the 'Brussels I' Regulation, Council Regulation (EC) No. 44/2001 of 22 December 2000 on jurisdiction in civil and commercial matters referred to above.

This complementarity between the accommodation of the interests of the territorial State and the fight against impunity may also be ensured by other techniques mentioned above. In particular, a State adopting extraterritorial legislation may exempt from the obligation to comply with such legislation addressees whose conduct, while in violation of that legislation, might be obligatory under conflicting requirements imposed under the territorial legislation applicable. For instance, while it extends its prohibitions to all corporations controlled in foreign countries by the employers covered under the Act, the 1990 American with Disabilities Act[99] provides that 'It shall not be unlawful under this section for a covered entity to take any action that constitutes discrimination under this section with respect to an employee in a workplace in a foreign country if compliance with this section would cause such covered entity to violate the law of the foreign country in which such workplace is located'. Similarly, under the 1964 Civil Rights Act as amended in 1991, although foreign corporations controlled by an American employer and established abroad are prohibited from engaging into certain unlawful employment practices as defined by sections 703 and 704 of the Act, as regards at least American employees, such entities may 'take any action otherwise prohibited . . ., with respect to an employee in a workplace in a foreign country if compliance with [the prohibition of unlawful employment practices as defined under the Act] would cause such [entity] to violate the law of the foreign country in which such workplace is located'.[100]

The measures cited above are unilateral measures adopted by a State seeking to exercise extraterritorial jurisdiction, the aim of which is to limit the risks of positive conflicts of jurisdiction and infringements on the sovereignty of the territorial State which this potentially implies. The adoption of an International Convention on Combating Human Rights Violations by Transnational Corporations would go beyond such unilateral measures. It would seek to minimise positive conflicts of jurisdiction by clarifying the conditions under which, where the host State authorities remain passive, the home State should compensate for such passivity by exercising extraterritorial jurisdiction over corporations of its nationality.[101] This instrument could provide, for instance, that the

---

[99] 42 USC §12112 (c)(1)(1994).   [100] 42 USC §2000e-1, (b) (1991).

[101] By defining such conditions, such an instrument would also protect the interests of the host State against unreasonable attempts by the home State concerned to exercise extraterritorial jurisdiction over activities conducted on its national territory. This would constitute an incentive for States joining the instrument since, if they are not

home State is obliged to take such measures as may be necessary, in accordance with its legal principles, to establish the liability of legal persons for certain serious violations of human rights, unless the host State has acted in order to protect these rights under its jurisdiction and effective remedies are available in that State to victims. In addition, in order to minimise the risks of positive conflicts of jurisdiction, it could provide for consultations between both States where the home State intends to exercise extraterritorial jurisdiction.[102] The very fact that the home State of a TNC would be requesting to hold such consultations could constitute a powerful incentive on the host State to adopt the necessary measures ensuring that the human rights violations be remedied and, if necessary and in compliance with the legal principles of its national legal system, sanctioned. Moreover, as noted by the *Extraterritorial Criminal Jurisdiction* study prepared by the Council of Europe in 1990, 'consultations may reveal whether the proposed legislation will miss its mark and thereby have unintended harmful effects which cannot be repaired without considerable loss of face'.[103] Finally, the instrument could also include provisions allowing a State on whose territory certain violations have taken place in which a TNC is implicated, to request the home State of the parent company to file proceedings against this company, international cooperation thus being put at the service of the effective implementation of the host country's legislation.[104]

---

parties, the general regime of public international law would apply to the relations between both States, implying that the home State may exercise extraterritorial jurisdiction over TNCs controlled by companies incorporated under their jurisdiction in a wide variety of situations, without being obliged to respect a condition of subsidiarity.

[102] This would be in line with the Annex to the OECD Declaration on International Investment and Multinational Enterprises containing a series of general considerations and practical approaches aimed at avoiding or minimising the imposition of conflicting requirements on MNEs by governments.

[103] *Extraterritorial Criminal Jurisdiction, supra* n. 28, 33. This study concludes on this point that 'Unusual as such prior consultations are under certain circumstances, they nevertheless appear to be an important instrument in keeping conflicts between States within acceptable proportions' (*idem.*).

[104] Inspiration could be sought from the Council of Europe Convention on the Transfer of Proceedings in Criminal Matters, *opened for signature* on 15 May 1972, and which entered into force on 30 March 1978 (CETS No. 73). The principle of this convention is that when a person is suspected of having committed an offence under the law of a Contracting State, that State may request another Contracting State to take proceedings against that person, *inter alia*, if the suspected person is ordinarily resident in the requested State; if the suspected person is a national of the requested State or if that State is his State of origin; if proceedings for the same or other offences are being taken

Conclusion

There is general agreement that States have an obligation to protect human rights which could be threatened by the activities of corporations. But the territorially competent State, where the violation takes place, may be unwilling or unable to effectively regulate the conduct of the corporation concerned, particularly when the latter is in the hands of foreign investors and may be protected by investment agreements, or when imposing too far-reaching obligations on the corporation would create the impression that the host State is not a hospitable destination for foreign investment.

One solution to overcome this difficulty is to strengthen the obligation imposed on the home State of the TNC under international law, to discharge its obligation to protect human rights by regulating that corporation, preferably by imposing on the parent company an obligation to control its subsidiaries operating overseas. But because of the risks of positive conflicts of jurisdiction and because of the potential sensitivity of the host State towards such exercise of extraterritorial jurisdiction, another and more promising approach would be to work towards a Convention on Combating Human Rights Violations by Transnational Corporations. Such a convention could impose on the home States of TNCs an obligation to adopt parent-based extraterritorial regulation, allowing the home State to exercise extraterritorial jurisdiction where this appears necessary to avoid impunity, or where victims would have no effective remedy before the national courts of the host State. Thus, the States parties to this convention would impose on the parent companies of multinational groups which have their nationality that they respect internationally recognised human rights, over and above the locally applicable legislation, in all their activities, and that they monitor the behavi-our of their subsidiaries, affiliates and business partners, by includ-ing provisions imposing a similar obligation to respect internationally recognised human rights in the agreements they conclude with these partners.

against the suspected person in the requested State; if it considers that transfer of the proceedings is warranted in the interests of arriving at the truth and in particular that the most important items of evidence are located in the requested State; or if it considers that it could not itself enforce a sentence if one were passed, even by having recourse to extradition, and that the requested State could do so. The requested State may refuse the request for the transfer of proceedings only in limited circumstances (see Arts. 6, 8(1) and 11).

The advantages of such a multilateral approach would be considerable. In the law of the sea, States which agreed to register vessels accepted certain obligations to control them, because it was realised that a purely territorial understanding of jurisdiction would not be effective. Similarly, in the high seas of economic globalisation, certain powerful actors seem to escape any effective regulation of their activities as long as we remain wedded to the classical concept of jurisdiction. In an interdependent world, only sovereignty that is shared can be exercised effectively.

15

The noisy secrecy: Swiss banking law in international dispute

JEAN NICOLAS DRUEY

Introduction

I did not choose the subject of this chapter just for its current relevance, but in an attempt to reflect a lesson which I learned from Detlev Vagts. I remember, among other lessons, a specific one in the context of the dispute regarding accounts of Holocaust victims held with Swiss banks.[1] He argued on pertinent issues of international law for the banks and showed how a jurist can be truly independent from all the semi-truths typically associated with that kind of case. Detlev Vagts can draw from his roots a rarely found ability to 'think international'. But there is more to it: he personifies the power of pure juridical argument over politics.

At the time of writing of this chapter addressing the subject of Swiss banks, the case pursued by the US Internal Revenue Service (IRS) against Union Bank of Switzerland (UBS), which presently is Switzerland's biggest bank, is in the process of settlement. But there is also pressure from the EU and the OECD, and litigation may continue in the United States. I will not describe all the ramifications of the UBS litigation, which of course are manifold. Instead, I will attempt to offer a bird's-eye view. I am confident that my observations will retain some of their relevance after the specific cases have been settled in one way or another.

Of course, the issues at stake, while being of eminent importance for Switzerland, are of rather remote concern in the United States, and only slightly more so in Switzerland's neighbouring countries. This evidently has to do with the difference in relative size of the matters, although a comparison with the epic battle between David and Goliath would be to overstate the matter. Modern Davids are usually not winners, because

---

[1] D. F. Vagts, 'Switzerland, International Law and World War II', *AJIL*, 91 (1997), 466–75.

they are Davids for the very reason of thinking too national and not having established reliable allies. The tremendous asymmetry in national impact is enhanced by a secondary effect, in that it heats up the *internal* political atmosphere and reawakens old antagonisms, which in turn complicates the negotiators' job.

I personally am fortunate to be a mere external observer. But I must confess that, when I heard US Senator Carl Levin state on Swiss radio that 'the Swiss hold out bank secrecy as a national value, in the same way the US prize freedom and democracy',[2] I felt hurt as a Swiss national. I do not think that by granting banking secrecy a country gives up its claim to be a free and democratic State. The opposite might be true, as I will try to show.

Senator Levin's statement also raises the issue of how to conduct this kind of dispute. Of course, the statement was addressed to a US Senate Subcommittee and not to the international community. However, it still reflects that kind of self-attribution of morality which tends to increase international barriers instead of removing them. But I am also convinced that Switzerland has in turn not done enough in this international dispute. As I also wish to show, things cannot continue in Switzerland as they used to. This is not just a matter of changing the law, but of better reflection on the arguments. My personal hope as a Swiss citizen is that the shock wave may not be too strong, but strong enough to bring about that change.

Secrecy, privacy, privilege, confidentiality

It should be understood, last but not least by my own compatriots, that there is no such thing as a bank secret. Any banker, including a Swiss banker, will naturally try to keep silent on certain matters; but he does so like any businessman in the world of any business branch would, just as they will in certain circumstances do the opposite when they think it desirable to inform people about certain facts. What is so special about banking secrecy that could justify particular legal provisions?

As Swiss bankers rightly insist, it is actually the *client's* secrecy that the banks are obliged to safeguard. In this sense, they speak of 'Bank-*Kunden*-Geheimnis'. But new questions arise. At the practical level, one

---

[2] Opening Statement of Senator Carl Levin, US Senate Permanent Subcommittee on Investigations, Hearing on Tax Haven Banks and US Tax Compliance: Obtaining the Names of US Clients with Swiss Accounts, 4 March 2009, www.levin.senate.gov/newsroom/release.cfm?id=309057.

question concerns the impression of a certain opportunism in applying the client's right. One example is the interbank credit rating system. Of course, feeding client information into these systems without asking the client for permission is often justifiable because of the client's presumable interest, but secrecy should mean that the client's actual wishes, rather than her presumable interests, govern.

On the level of *basics*, the question remains: what is so special about banks? Why not protect clients of other industries in the same way? Is the service of the store at the corner of the street selling me my daily bread in any sense less valuable than the services provided by bankers? To be sure, there is an important difference. Bread is for everyone; that I eat some of it regularly is nothing of interest. Money, on the other hand, is spread much more individually. News in that respect offers more information.

But questions remain nevertheless: is having money something private and therefore protected, and eating bread a fact belonging to the public domain? One could well reverse the statement: food is more private, more personal, compared with the extremely neutral medium of money. The play on the arguments can be continued endlessly.

Indeed, if one interviews some Swiss bankers or reads the experts' books, one will most certainly be told that the client's *privacy* is what it is all about. But they do not discuss the subject further, they do not ask what privacy exactly means, despite – or maybe because of – the intense struggle with other jurisdictions which has lasted for so many years already. The discussion has petrified, so to speak. The reaction to questions like those I raise above may even be 'No jokes on serious matters, please!' The Swiss, similar to the Americans in my view, are pragmatic people; their actions, particularly in the economic field, are not driven by the stars of a philosophical heaven, but by the immediate interests as they appear in clear daylight. But nowadays, in criminal, tax and other matters, a *conflict of values* has arisen.

Values are the most important rhetorical weapons, nationally and internationally, and for that the value concepts must be precise. That is their chance to survive against opposing values. I might put it in this way: not dollars but ideas, not daylight of regular business but the leading stars in the dark sky, and the actors should not be Herodes' killers but the three magical . . .

Privacy, however, is an ambiguous value. Almost everyone, in every situation, can pretend to it. Thus, it is a weak weapon. To state that privacy is the motive behind banking clients' protection is neither right nor wrong, since the question still is what lies behind all of this: why should we bother about privacy, and in what situations?

If one looks at the history of the banks' duty to keep their customers' data secret, one obtains the following hints: although practised already as long as banks exist, explicit wording was introduced into Swiss legislation by the Banking Act (*Bankengesetz*) of 1934,[3] in particular Art. 47. In a world in which money no longer should be kept under a private mattress, banks were considered as *confidents nécessaires* – i.e. as entities rendering services on which the public is depending and requiring individual information from the client. A line was drawn relative to the other, mostly classical professions placed under a similar regime: physicians, priests and ministers, lawyers and accountants. Specific motives were extended to banks, including, to give one example, the protection of the Jewish monies then flowing from Germany.

This special position of certain professions in the English vocabulary is usually denoted by the word *privilege*, thereby stressing its function in civil and criminal *procedure*. In the European Continental systems, however, the primary source is *substantive* criminal law. Thus, the feature distinguishing these professions is the penal *sanction* that is placed on transmitting information received through the client and/or the mandate. Art. 321 of the Swiss Criminal Code is the general source of professional secrecy, providing a list of the professions involved. The procedural privilege, which used to be a matter left to the Swiss Cantons, is sometimes tied to this provision (cf. on professional secrecy, p. 297).

The banker does not appear on this list. Banking secrecy has its systematic source in a special law, not in the provision on professional secrecy contained in the Swiss Criminal Code. The Banking Act was promulgated several years before the Criminal Code came into effect. These circumstances notwithstanding, Art. 47 of the Swiss Banking Act is so clearly moulded in the same fashion that the common origin is beyond doubt. Some differences do, however, exist. While they call for an explanation (see also p. 292), they do not alter the general idea.

Viewed in this light, the motive behind Art. 47 Banking Act is reasonably clear.[4] It is the insertion of the banker's activity into the list of

---

[3] *Bundesgesetz vom 8. November 1934 über die Banken und Sparkassen*, Systematic Collection of the Federal Laws (SR) 952.0.

[4] The wording is somewhat ambiguous in this respect. The Article fails to name the client as the holder/addressee of the right and, similar to Art. 321 of the Swiss Criminal Code regarding the professions covered there, it does not explicitly provide that the client can relieve the bank of its duty. Nevertheless, the provision is so construed. See G. Stratenwerth, 'Note 25 to Art. 47', in R. Watter, N. P. Vogt, Th. Bauer and Ch. Winzeler (eds.), *Basler Kommentar (BSK) zum Bankengesetz (BaG)* (Basel, Geneva and Munich: Helbing & Lichtenhahn, 2005), 690;

confidents nécessaires being criminally sanctioned for the breach of the banker's duty of confidentiality. It is not the banks' or bankers' secrecy, but bank*ing* secrecy: it is generated by the bank's *activity*.[5] In my view, this position taken by the Swiss legislator in 1934 cannot be called unreasonable or even arbitrary at the outset. Professional secrecy is called for when the services rendered are necessary and are of a complex nature, with the consequence that the client is obligated to confide a relatively large amount of information, since it is only the expert receiving the information who can assess its relevance. We can leave it to the individual taste if one prefers to speak in this context of the client's 'privacy'. Even then, the logic must be that privacy is at stake *because* confidentiality is granted, and not that it is granted because there is a case of privacy.

The State's authority to interfere with confidentiality

For many reasons, legitimacy may be claimed for an interest to find out what deposits a person holds at her bank and/or *where* the means originated from, or *who* has been paid from them, or *when* the debit and credit entries occurred.

Such interests may be those of *private* persons. Typical examples are those of creditors who need to assess whether to grant a credit or how good the credits are which they already granted. Another is the spouse or the heirs for whom the money available and debts outstanding may be of vital importance. In Switzerland, as elsewhere, there is a distinction between the time a holder is alive and the position of her heirs. During

---

M. Aubert, P.-A. Béguin, P. Bernasconi, J. Graziano-von Burg, R. Schwob and R. Treuillard (eds.), *Le secret bancaire suisse*, 3rd edn. (Berne: Stämpfli, 1995), 106 *et seq.* Moreover, §3 explicitly employs the term '*Berufsgeheimnis*' (professional secrecy), in parallel to Art. 321. Commentators also tend to support professional secrecy, although the lack of clarity illustrates that little attention is paid to this kind of 'philosophical' issue. E.g. B. Kleiner, R. Schwob and C. Winzeler (eds.), *Kommentar zum Bundesgesetz über die Banken und Sparkassen* (Zurich: Schulthess, 2006), Art. 47, n. 1, use the title '*Bankkundengeheimnis als Berufsgeheimnis*', but go on to say that the basis lies in Art. 13 of the Swiss Constitution, which protects individual privacy (n. 4) and the *Persönlichkeitsrecht* (right to personality, which in Switzerland is understood as the source of the right to privacy; Art. 28 Civil Code). Stratenwerth, 'Note', *supra*, Art. 47, n. 1 and P. Nobel, *Swiss Finance Law and International Standards* (Berne, The Hague and Boston: Stämpfli, Kluwer Law International, 2002), 890 *et seq.*, §15, n. 83, point to a double root in contract law (Art. 398 Code of Obligations) and in the right to personality.

[5] Rightly, Nobel, *Swiss Finance Law and International Standards*, *supra* n. 4, heading preceding n. 77.

a person's lifetime, she may have multiple obligations to inform others on matters regarding her assets or debts, but her bank is no source of inquiry for those interested. The client's duty is not by itself a duty of all third parties who, like the banks, can contribute to its execution.[6] The situation becomes different, and varies among States, if requests by heirs, executors, etc. are presented to the bank after the holder's death.

The State also respects a person's control. To execute what it considers to be its claims, certain procedures involving the person must be followed; to cover a tax debt the fiscal authority may not just choose the property best suitable to the State and proceed to confiscate it. The same must be true when the State wants information. It must adhere to certain procedures. It is not that the State is barred from obtaining any specific information; the State always and everywhere can arrogate to itself the power of access. But the way chosen cannot be any one way leading to the goal. This means, among others, that the State's procuring of information must be *proportionate* – i.e. it must be the least intrusive way possible, taking into consideration the individual's protected values which are at stake.

Evidently, confidentiality concerns particular individuals. But it nevertheless concerns the State. The State cannot freely intervene in human interaction without losing its proper *raison d'être* of protecting the State's subjects, anywhere in the world.

In this sense it is, in my view, beyond doubt that individuals have a *right* to engage themselves in communication and thereby create obligations towards their partners, even though legal science and law so far have not tied this right to constitutional human rights in a coherent and uniform manner.[7] And communication necessarily means the possibility

---

[6] Cf., with regard to a spouse's right to information, Art. 170 §2 Civil Code, providing that in an intramarital information procedure the court itself may require a third party such as a bank to provide complementary information. There is no direct claim on the part of the plaintiff against the bank. The court thus is intercalated in order to harmonise best the interests involved. See V. Bräm and F. Hasenböhler, 'Art. 170 Civil Code', in P. Gauch and J. Schmid (eds.), *Kommentar zum schweizerischen Zivilgesetzbuch* (Zurich: Schulthess, 1997), Art. 170 Civil Code, n. 15, 452 *et seq.*; cf. C. Hegnauer and P. Breitschmid, *Grundriss des Eherechts*, 4th edn. (Berne: Stämpfli, 2000), n. 19.12, 199 *et seq.*; but see, for a more generous view, H. Hausheer, R. Reusser and Th. Geiser, *Berner Kommentar*, 2nd edn. (Berne: Stämpfli, 1999), Art. 170 Civil Code, n. 29, 438.

[7] Cf. J. N. Druey, 'Kommunikationsfreiheit – ein Programm', in B. Ehrenzeller, Ph. Mastronardi, R. Schaffhauser, R. J. Schweizer and K. A. Vallender (eds.), *Der Verfassungsstaat vor neuen Herausforderungen. Festschrift für Yvo Hangartner* (St Gallen: Dike Verlag, 1998), 523–36. The constitutional protection is clearer in Germany than in Switzerland; cf. with

of confidentiality. It is personal by its essence; it is always *addressed* to persons, usually to specific ones, but rarely to the public.[8] This fundamental proposition is evidenced when confidentiality is made the object of a *contract* – as is usually the case in the banking industry. Every legal system protects contracts, and attributing some value to them must have repercussions for the State's own conduct.

Thus, forcing a party to disregard confidentiality is *never* irrelevant. If the State disregards or disturbs confidentiality such action must be justified as an *exception*. This means the following:

– The exceptions, as they deny the expectations of those involved, must be based on a set of *general* rules, not just be a case-by-case pondering.
– The exceptions must be part of a *coherent system* in order to justify them.
– The exceptions must be proportionate to the goal pursued by the State.
– For any exceptions to be justifiable, they must be *particular* – i.e. they must be tied to specific informational needs.

Never is the State as such the purpose justifying an exception, nor are any of its agencies.

All of this has nothing to do with any special and one-sided rule of whatever kind concerning banking clients. Confidentiality in general is a constitutional value requiring self-restraint on the part of the State. In addition, then, the account of values must give room to the quality of the profession as *confident nécessaire*.

Art. 47 of the Swiss Banking Act

The basic first paragraph of Article 47 states in pertinent part:

> Who reveals a secret, which has been entrusted to him in his function as an ... employee of a bank ... or which he came to know in such function ..., shall be punished by imprisonment of up to 6 months or a fine of up to CHF 50,000.

The Article goes on to state in §2 that negligence is also punishable, subject to a somewhat milder sanction. Art. 47, §3, provides that the

---

regard to the banking secret (which has no criminal relevance), J. Petersen, *Das Bankgeheimnis zwischen Individualschutz und Institutionenschutz* (Tübingen: Mohr, 2005), 26–8, following the tradition set by Canaris and Hopt; see also P. Wech, *Das Bankgeheimnis* (Berlin: Duncker & Humblot, 2009), 78–88, 147–55.

[8] Cf. J. N. Druey, *Information als Gegenstand des Rechts* (Zurich: Schulthess, 1995), 156–8 *et passim*.

Article also applies to acts committed after termination of the banking mandate.

These paragraphs are followed by a crucial final provision, §4. It reads as follows:

> The Federal and Cantonal provisions about the duty to testify and to disclose information against State agencies remain reserved.

What then is it about this Article that has caused such upheaval? *'Tant de bruit pour une omelette?'* Art. 47, §4, seems to carve out what appears in §1 to be the very essence of the Article and which has produced all the noise, namely, the information given to the *judicial and financial authorities.* How can a Swiss bank be held liable for breach of confidentiality by accepting a governmental request for information in the national interest, if the various branches of government can sweep Art. 47 away by rules proper to their respective purposes?

It is interesting to examine what the Swiss Confederation and the Cantons have done with their power in this respect. The procedures in the courts hitherto were vested in the Cantonal jurisdictions, where one rarely finds an explicit mention of the banks in the rules pertaining to professional privileges. However, those rules often simply refer to the respective provisions in criminal law. Whether these references include Art. 47, and whether they *can* include it, is uncertain.[9] As a whole, the impression is that there is not much eagerness among Cantonal legislators to give the banks procedural privileges. This is confirmed by the harmonised civil and criminal procedures for the whole country implemented in 2007–8.[10]

For one thing, banking does not enjoy the same tradition-born prestige as do the 'classical' professional privileges. Furthermore, banking appears as another kind of activity than those 'classical' ones. The

---

[9] The predominant view is that in civil procedure banking secrecy is included in general legal references like 'professional secrecy', but only if it is preponderant compared with the truth-finding interest in the case (see also *infra* n. 10), whereas in criminal procedure banking is entirely excluded as a privilege. See Aubert *et al.* (eds.), *Le secret bancaire Suisse, supra* n. 4, 135–9 and 147–9; G. Piquerez, *Traité de procédure pénale suisse*, 2nd edn. (Zurich: Schulthess, 2006), n. 778.

[10] *Schweizerische Strafprozessordnung*, 5 October 2007, Art. 173 §2, and similarly *Schweizerische Zivilprozessordnung*, 19 December 2008, Art. 166 §§1–2: an absolute privilege is granted only to the traditional professions, whereas bankers (and other legally protected professions – e.g. auditors) are subject to a weighing of interests. The burden of showing a predominant secrecy interest is placed on the bank.

physician and attorney especially represent the medieval discipline of the liberal arts, whereas a bank is not constituted by the capacities of any particular physical person, but is an organisation.[11] To introduce the banks into the civil procedure laws would, therefore, have triggered quite some debate and pressure on the part of other organisations.

But all of this is not incompatible with the concept of *confident nécessaire* contained in Art. 47 of the Swiss Banking Act. Indeed, the differences in content between that provision and the general criminal provision regarding professional secrecy in Art. 321 of the Swiss Criminal Code are not essential and they are directed to reinforcing the banking client's position.[12] Thus, our intermediary conclusion is that the function of banking secrecy as a privilege in court is well conceivable from its nature as a professional secrecy, albeit that political debate on the subject was avoided and the issue remained somewhat in the background. The procedural privilege is not where the stress of Art. 47 lies, which in comparison to the United States might be due to the lack of a procedure regarding discovery.

The position of the tax authorities

Leaving aside procedural privileges, let us return to our main theme and examine the other loophole left by Art. 47, §4 – namely, the power of agencies within the *government* to request information from the banks. In so doing, I will narrow my focus on one of the main segments, namely, the *tax authorities*. That must mean, primarily, the *Swiss* authorities. The space granted to them in the national context determines the possibilities of *international cooperation*, which hardly can go beyond the power allowed against nationals.[13] This deserves a heading of its own not only because it is presently the source of most debate, but because it puts

---

[11] One Swiss Court has held that the absence of a reference to banks in Art. 321 of the Criminal Code shows that 'the legislator chose those professions which, contrary to the bankers, wear in our society an aura of wisdom, replacing the priests and magicians of primitive times' (Bezirksgericht Affoltern, judgment of 14 March 1989, *SJZ*, 45 (1989), 252) (trans. by the author).

[12] The Banking Act is more far-reaching, not only in that it also includes mere negligence but it drops the requirement contained in Art. 321 that prosecution is to be requested by the client. Thus, enforcement is initiated *ex officio* by the State attorney. The idea behind this provision is that clients abroad might learn about the disclosure only after the time limit for the request of prosecution had expired.

[13] This restriction is, however, no longer accepted by the OECD. Cf. also *infra* n. 15.

the spotlight back on Art. 47. Our findings will be that tax law does not exhaust the discretion granted, but rather professional secrecy and procurement of tax-relevant information live together in a kind of symbiosis based on mutual respect.

The basic observation is the following: tax law does not break the client–bank confidentiality tie.[14] But of course the treasury department does not simply trust the taxpayers' tax returns, and hence it applies a withholding tax at the source of income from securities that will be accounted for in the final assessment of the tax duty based on the return. Besides this regular feature, which is applicable to the tax duties of *physical* persons,[15] there is the exceptional frontal attack on banking confidentiality in specific contexts of *prosecution*, criminal or administrative, in the event that there are sufficient grounds for suspicion of the respective behaviour.

At the *international* level, a considerable network of double taxation and mutual assistance treaties governs this matter, providing specific degrees of informational cooperation of the Swiss authorities and to some extent involving the banks directly.[16] For the investor subject to a tax jurisdiction other than Switzerland, the withholding tax is lost unless she can avail herself of a double taxation treaty.

Considering this primarily national system, the question thus arises again: '*Tant de bruit pour une omelette*?' How can confidentiality be praised as a value when the State forces people to disclosure by subjecting them to a heavy burden if they do *not* disclose? Is it not sanctifying a mere formality when the State restrains itself from addressing the bank directly? The 35 per cent rate of withholding tax for many Swiss is higher than their tax duty on the respective assets; secrecy then becomes a costly luxury instead of a human right. And for those subject to a higher tax

---

[14] *Bundesgesetz über die direkte Bundessteuer DBG, Systematische Sammlung des Bundesrechts*, SR 642.21, Art. 127 §2.

[15] Companies are subject to a stricter regime. Cf. P. Locher, *Einführung in das internationale Steuerrecht der Schweiz*, 3rd edn. (Berne: Stämpfli, 2005), 531.

[16] The Swiss Federal Court has subjected banking secrecy to a weighing of interests featuring an international scope and has declared that there may be a preponderant interest of the Confederation to cooperate with other countries (concerning bribery prosecution in Italy; *Amtliche Sammlung der Bundesgerichtsentscheide 1997* (123), II 160). I consider this case to be very important. It brings an international scope directly into the weighing procedure instead of determining how far national restrictions of confidentiality can be extended to international cooperation of States. The statement, often heard these days, that banking secrecy 'remains intact' is thereby abolished at the international level. At the constitutional level, it raises the question whether a court has the power to decide matters of international policy.

charge, the motive of tax evasion in making use of banking confidentiality is clear enough and thereby abusive.

Herein lies the source of a basic misunderstanding leading friends as well as foes of banking confidentiality to reach exaggerated conclusions. Any right to cut off any flow of information, be it labelled secrecy, privacy, confidentiality, or whatever, is a right to *dispose*, a 'privilege' in the sense used by Hohfeld;[17] the holder of the right has his hand on the switch, so to speak. This particular right belongs to the category of rights such as ownership or the right to enter into contracts or of voting in an assembly, and it is opposed to the rights to *enjoy*, which are characterised by a specific interest, like receiving piano lessons or a neighbour's forbearance from raising swine.[18]

A person accused of a crime might consider that the better tactic is to answer the prosecution's questions. If she remains silent nevertheless and does not follow the direction desired by the State attorney, that is her choice. Her right is not to suffer any disadvantage from her silence, *but to determine her interests by her proper autonomy*. Thus, the withholding tax is not by itself an intrusion into the protected sphere. However, it would be questionable if the rate would be set at a level *excluding* the silence *as a conceivable option*. The rate of 35 per cent also seems to be guided by the intention of a certain neutrality considering the great variety of situations as part of an overall assessment.[19]

In similar vein, it is wrong to criticise confidentiality because it helps taxpayers to evade taxes or furthers other kinds of misuse. *Abusus non tollit usum*: so long as there are cases where secrecy does not cover unlawful practices, it retains its legitimacy despite the remaining possibility of abuse. If tax avoidance rather than evasion is the motive, if tactical advantages of hiding clues to an adversary are at stake, if a son losing all his money in the casino should not be aware of the actual fortune of his father, or if simply a stingy man wants to look poor – such aims are sometimes lawful, and sometimes not, but it cannot be the sense of confidentiality that those interests are evaluated on a case-by-case

---

[17] W. Newcomb Hohfeld, *Fundamental Legal Conceptions as Applied in Juridic Reasoning* (Aldershot: Ashgate, 2001), *passim*.

[18] The distinction has already been alluded to with respect to the limits of case-by-case weighing of interests, *supra* n. 2. Cf. Druey, *Information als Gegenstand des Rechts, supra* n. 8, 206–9.

[19] See M. Beusch, 'Art. 13, n. 2', in M. Zweifel, P. Athanas and M. Bauer-Balmelli (eds.), *Kommentar zum schweizerischen Steuerrecht*, 2 vols. (Basel: Helbing & Lichtenhahn, 2005), vol. II/2, 416 *et seq.* (considering economic interests only).

basis. Confidentiality has its ground in the mere contact with certain persons, not in the particularities of the information received. The justification also is given – I would say, all the more so – when the intentions of the client are unclear to herself at that moment.

The limit of this argument is reached where abuse is dominant or even usual. Given the popularity of Swiss banking secrecy as a means of tax evasion, the Swiss banks have the burden of proof in this respect, politically or even legally.

Conclusion: an omelette is of value everywhere

Our elementary view on the matter is sufficient to draw a conclusion that in turn is elementary. The banking confidentiality as a self-restraint on the part of the State has its basis not in the famous Art. 47 of the Swiss Banking Act, but in the law and practice of the various branches of government. This confirms formally what we had observed when looking at the values involved: confidentiality is an element inherent in all human interaction and a value as such. Art. 47 enters the scene through its determination of the banker as a *confident nécessaire*. It works as a further consideration limiting the State's breaking through confidentiality.

This does not in any way mean that the State must protect confidentiality in an absolute manner, but rather that it is under a duty to safeguard confidentiality whenever it is reasonably possible. The more frontal the attack, the stronger must be the power of this argument. Whether or not investigations are limited to prosecuting tax fraud or also include all or certain types of tax evasion is, under the auspices of banking confidentiality, an important but by no means essential difference. The answer is crucially different if automatic access is to be granted to the fiscal authorities. Such a grant flies in the face of the idea of confidentiality, reaching far beyond banks, banking law provisions and money. In a constitutional State, no citizen has to accept having a microphone attached to her conveying to the listeners whatever she says. And every citizen may choose her partner, and also select a bank of her choice.

The pressure that has been applied to Swiss bank confidentiality has, oddly enough, stirred movements in both directions. On the one hand, progressive politicians argue for the complete *abolition* of the concept. One conservative party proposes, on the other hand, to *reinforce* it by inserting the concept of bank confidentiality into the Swiss Federal Constitution. My answer here is simple: both are right. But both of them need not battle for their positions, because essentially things already are as they wish them to be. If Switzerland were to get rid of Art. 47 of the Banking Act, the situation would not change the State's rights and the level of its international cooperation. In this sense, Art. 47 has no content of its own. But it expresses a constitutional principle. The very core of banking confidentiality, as applied to the State (or to any State), being proportionality and rule-guidance when breaking up confidential relations, finds its origin in the Constitution.

Both movements risk overshooting their goal. This would be the case if the abolition is combined with new State powers directed toward totalitarian information links between the banks and the State. And this would also be the case if a constitutional amendment in an isolated way deals with banks only, and does not address the issue of confidentiality in a broader way.

At the *international* level, the discussion about *values* should be considerably widened and intensified. This is a task primarily incumbent upon Switzerland. But the result, in my view, must be that the basis of freedom and democracy, claimed for the United States by Senator Levin and in fact common to many States, also sets common ground to the value of communication and thereby of confidentiality. Differences in where the stress is placed certainly remain; still, the comparison cannot but bring about convergence.[20]

In this process, the concept of 'bank secrecy' must shed its reputation as a purely Swiss concept and a tax haven specialty, but must not be repelled as such. To the contrary, it should be discovered in every nation based on a free and democratic constitution. Therefore, it should not be an object of competition between States or a source of exploiting national differences. Politically, this is to say that there is no point in fighting over banking secrecy, *no matter whether it is a fight for or against it* – subject to two conditions: first, that both sides recognise what their constitution is saying, and secondly, that they be transparent *vis-à-vis* each other. The right, anyway, is merely formal – it represents a protection of the individual autonomy and, at the international level, of the sovereignty of States, and a warranty of procedures only, not of secrecy. In this sense, the right is as thin as an omelette. But many people in many countries like omelettes.

---

[20] See in this sense the very elaborate comparison of French, Luxemburg and Swiss law by Jérôme Lasserre Capdeville, *Le secret bancaire. Étude de droit comparé* (Aix-Marseille: Presses Universitaires d'Aix-Marseille, 2006), vol. 2, nn. 1062–74, 782–800.

16

Not-for-profit organisations, conflicts of laws and the right of establishment under the EC Treaty

WERNER F. EBKE

Prologue

This *Festschrift* pays tribute to an extraordinary man, a distinguished law professor, a prolific scholar and a thoughtful teacher whose life and work have inspired many students, academics, judges, lawyers, accountants and managers throughout the world. His lucidity of thought and expression, vast knowledge, maturity of judgement, steadiness of temperament, fair-mindedness and exceptional linguistic skills have always impressed me. It was, therefore, a great honour and privilege for me, in 1991, to receive, jointly with Detlev F. Vagts, the Max Planck Research Award for 'internationally outstanding research accomplishments'. We used the generous funds that were attached to the Award to organise an international conference in Constance, Germany, on 'Democracy, Market Economy, and the Law'.[1] The conference took place at a time when the fall of communism and the subsequent dissolution of the Soviet Union had started to change the world's perspectives and the transition to democracy required answers to numerous unprecedented legal, economic and political problems. A few years later, Detlev and I organised a second international conference at Lake Constance. The conference dealt with 'Financial Accounting and Auditing in Global Capital Markets'. At this conference, lawyers and economists from Europe and the United States convened to discuss some of the most pressing issues resulting from the widening gap between European and US Generally Accepted

---

[1] The papers that were presented at the conference are published in W. F. Ebke and D. F. Vagts (eds.), *Democracy, Market Economy, and the Law* (Heidelberg: Verlag Recht & Wirtschaft, 1995).

Accounting Principles (GAAP) and the need for internationally acceptable financial reporting standards that lead to transparency, reliability and efficient capital markets.[2]

Detlev F. Vagts is probably the single most distinguished example of the seminal role that legal writers have played, and continue to play, in the intellectual upheaval of what is now commonly referred to as 'transnational law'. He mastered the enormous complexity of transnational legal problems and grasped the essentials of the growing body of transnational law with a speed, thoroughness, and love for details that must amaze every lawyer familiar with the subject matter. His classic casebook *Transnational Legal Problems*, the first edition of which appeared in 1968,[3] reflects his sensibility for the historical dimensions of transnational law, his broad-based comparative approach, his power of reasoning and his unique blend of analytical abilities and practical experience. The book also emphasises the need to overcome traditional modes of thinking and conceptual distinctions such as the distinction between private und public international law and to understand the interaction between private and public law, both domestically and internationally.[4]

Vagts has been equally influential in the area of corporation law. His *Basic Corporation Law*, first published in 1973, was adopted by many law schools throughout the United States and laid the ground for the law students' comprehension of the fundamental principles of corporate law.[5] In the preface to the 3rd edition, Vagts, who had started teaching Corporations in 1959, pointed out that much had changed since the 1st edition and accentuated the significance of concepts of economics to understand corporate organisational structure and the securities markets.[6] Comparative corporation law and conflicts of corporate laws are also of great interest to him.[7]

---

[2] The papers that were presented at the conference are published in *Wirtschaftsprüferkammer-Mitteilungen*, 36 (Special Issue, June 1997), 1–182.

[3] D. F. Vagts, *Transnational Legal Problems* (Westbury, NY: Foundation Press, 1968). The most recent edition is D. F. Vagts and Henry Steiner, *Transnational Legal Problems*, 4th edn. (Westbury, NY: Foundation Press, 1994).

[4] See also D. F. Vagts, *Transnational Business Problems* (Westbury, NY: Foundation Press, 1986), xix. The most recent edition is D. F. Vagts, W. S. Dodge and H. H. Koh, *Transnational Business Problems*, 4th edn. (Westbury, NY: Foundation Press, 2008).

[5] D. F. Vagts, *Basic Corporation Law* (Westbury, NY: Foundation Press, 1973).

[6] D. F. Vagts, *Basic Corporation Law*, 3rd edn. (Westbury, NY: Foundation Press, 1989), xix.

[7] D. F. Vagts, 'Comparative Company Law – The New Wave', in R. J. Schweizer, H. Burkert and U. Gasser (eds.), *Festschrift für Jean Nicolas Druey zum 65. Geburtstag* (Zürich: Schulthess 2002), 595–605.

His article 'The Multinational Enterprise. A New Challenge for Transnational Law' is generally acknowledged to be one of the most thoughtful and seminal pieces on comparative and international company law.[8] The article was published at a time when the academic community had just started to identify the multinational enterprise (MNE) as a discrete phenomenon and as a major source and force in the international economy.[9]

The multinational spread of US and, later, European enterprises gave rise to novel issues of financial accounting and financial disclosure. The inclusion of foreign subsidiaries in consolidated financial statements and the translation of fluctuating or hyperinflationary currencies posed new challenges for both the accounting profession and legislatures around the globe.[10] Vagts was, once again, among the first legal scholars who grappled with the issues. Rather than focusing upon narrow, albeit important issues, he took a broader conceptual view. His monumental contribution to the *International Encyclopedia of Comparative Law*, entitled *Law and Accounting in Business Associations, and Private Organizations*, marks the beginning of a new branch of comparative law:[11] comparative accounting,[12] which today forms an integral part of transnational law.

The development and practice of transnational law have been accelerated and transformed by globalisation. The increasing cross-border mobility of goods, services, capital, persons and companies requires new modes of thinking and novel regulatory concepts and approaches that go beyond traditional notions and distinctions such as public versus

---

[8] D. F. Vagts, 'The Multinational Enterprise. A New Challenge for Transnational Law', *Harvard Law Review*, 81 (1970), 739–92.

[9] See, e.g., C. P. Kindleberger (ed.), *The International Corporation* (Cambridge, MA: MIT Press, 1971); R. Vernon, *Sovereignty at Bay. The Multinational Spread of US Enterprises* (New York: Basic Books, 1971); B. Grossfeld, *Praxis des Internationalen Privat- und Wirtschaftsrechts – Rechtsprobleme multinationaler Unternehmen* (Reinbek: Rowohlt, 1975).

[10] D. F. Vagts, 'Currency Translation Accounting', *Wirtschaftsprüferkammer-Mitteilungen*, 36 (Special Issue, June 1997), 61–7; see also J. A. Largay and J. L. Livingstone, *Accounting for Changing Prices* (New York: Wiley, 1976); G. Whittington, *Inflation Accounting* (University College Cardiff Press, 1981); S. Siegel, 'Accounting and Inflation. An Analysis and a Proposal', *UCLA Law Review*, 29 (1981–2), 271–95.

[11] D. F. Vagts, 'Law and Accounting in Business Associations and Private Organizations', *International Encyclopedia of Comparative Law*, XIII, ch. 12A (Leiden: Brill, 1972).

[12] *See* B. Grossfeld, 'Comparative Accounting', *Texas International Law Journal*, 28 (1993), 235–68.

private law, national versus international law and governmental versus private ordering.[13] Financial accounting (i.e. the 'language' of enterprises and the central means to portray an enterprise's status and performance in qualitative and quantitative terms) is a ready example in support of this proposition. A global economy calls for internationally accepted financial reporting standards (at least for listed companies)[14] and requires an expansion of the legal horizons beyond the classical view of state-centred standard-setting.[15]

The European conflict-of-corporate-laws revolution is yet another example of the rapid changes of transnational law and the increasing impact of supranational law on norm-making.[16] It is, therefore, against the backdrop of Vagts' fundamental contributions to the development of transnational law, of his vivid employment of the comparative law methodology and of his deep interest in Europe and the law of the European Community (EC) that this chapter on the impact of EC law on the conflicts of the laws of not-for-profit organisations – in particular, not-for-profit foundations – is presented as a modest tribute.

Cross-border activities

Not-for-profit foundations play an increasingly important role in many countries, especially in the European Union (EU).[17] As a general rule, the

---

[13] For details, see W. F. Ebke, 'Global Economy – Global Law?', in J. B. Attanasio and J. J. Norton (eds.), *Multilateralism v. Unilateralism – Policy Choices in a Global Society* (London: The British Institute of International and Comparative Law, 2004), 83–97.

[14] Whether or not there is also a need for international financial reporting standards for non-listed companies is another issue. For details, see, e.g., W. F. Ebke, C. Luttermann and S. Siegel (eds.), *Internationale Rechnungslegungsstandards für börsenunabhängige Unternehmen* (Baden-Baden: Nomos, 2007).

[15] For a more detailed exposition of this view, see W. F. Ebke, 'Accounting, Auditing and Global Capital Markets', in T. Baums, K. J. Hopt and N. Horn (eds.), *Corporations, Capital Markets and Business in the Law – Liber Amicorum Richard M. Buxbaum* (The Hague: Kluwer International Law, 2000), 113–36.

[16] For details, see W. F. Ebke, 'The European Conflict-of-Corporate-Laws Revolution. *Überseering, Inspire Art* and Beyond', *International Lawyer*, 38 (2004), 813–53. For the effects of this revolution on US American enterprises, see W. F. Ebke, 'Conflicts of Corporate Laws and the Treaty of Friendship, Commerce and Navigation between the United States of America and the Federal Republic of Germany', in H.-E. Rasmussen-Bonne, R. Freer, W. Lüke and W. Weitnauer (eds.), *Balancing of Interests – Liber Amicorum Peter Hay zum 70. Geburtstag* (Frankfurt/Main:Verlag Recht & Wirtschaft 2005), 119–39.

[17] See, e.g., K. J. Hopt, W. R. Walz and T. von Hippel, *The European Foundation. A New Legal Approach* (Cambridge University Press 2006); K. J. Hopt and D. Reuter (eds.), *Stiftungsrecht in Europa* (Cologne: Heymanns, 2001); A. Schlüter, V. Then and

activities of such foundations are primarily local or regional in nature and scope. However, a growing number of foundations are engaged in activities abroad as well.[18] In fact, the very objective of many foundations is international, sometimes even exclusively. Cross-border activities of foundations give rise to numerous legal, economic and other issues. Tax issues have been particularly pressing and have attracted a great deal of interest and attention by lawyers, economists, social scientists and politicians.[19] In recent years, legal barriers other than tax barriers have also gained attention. This is particularly true with respect to barriers that make it more difficult, or sometimes even impossible, for foundations to engage in cross-border activities. In the EU, there is a lively debate regarding the question of whether and to what extent, if any, such barriers are compatible with the freedom-of-establishment provisions of the EC Treaty.[20]

Recognition of foreign foundations

As a general rule, all Member States recognise a foundation that has been validly formed in accordance with the laws of one Member State as a foundation. If the State of formation grants a foundation the status of a legal person (*juristische Person*), the status will be recognised by all other Member States. As a legal entity, a foundation may, as a general rule, enter into contracts, hold property, engage in legal activities, and it may sue and be sued. In principle, all Member States allow a domestic foundation to engage in activities abroad. Hence, it is for the foundation to determine whether and to what extent it wishes to engage in activities outside of its home State and, if so, how it wishes to structure and organise its cross-border activities.

P. Walkenhorst (eds.), *Foundations in Europe* (Gütersloh: Bertelsmann Foundation Publishers, 2001), 133–44.

[18] In Germany, for example, 59.5 per cent of activities of German foundations in 2006 were local, 29 per cent national and 11.5 per cent international. See R. Sprengel and T. Ebermann, *Statistiken zum deutschen Stiftungswesen* (Stuttgart: Lucius & Lucius, 2007), 69.

[19] R. Hüttemann, *Gemeinnützigkeits- und Spendenrecht* (Cologne: Dr Otto Schmidt, 2008); B Schäfers, *Die steuerliche Behandlung gemeinnütziger Stiftungen in grenzüberschreitenden Fällen* (Baden-Baden: Nomos, 2005), 367–8.

[20] The author co-authored a Feasibility Study for the European Foundation Statute which addresses, among other issues, the impact of Arts. 43 and 48 EC Treaty (now Arts. 49 and 54 TFEU) on foundations. See K. J. Hopt, T. von Hippel, H. Anheier, V. Then, W. F. Ebke, E. Reimer and T. Vahlpahl, *Feasibility Study on a European Foundation Statute – Final Report* (2009), 105–11, 123–39, http://ec.europa.eu/internal_market/company/docs/eufoundation/feasibilitystudy_en.pdf.

Theoretically, foundations have several options to structure and organise their cross-border activities. A foundation can:

- Operate in a State other than its State of formation (i.e. home state) as a 'foreign' (out-of-state) foundation
- Operate in a State other than its home State through representatives, agents, or branches
- Operate in a State other than its home State through independent subsidiaries (e.g. a local foundation)[21]
- Transfer its centre of administration (*centre d'administration, siège réel*, or *effektiver Verwaltungssitz*) from its home State to another State
- Transfer its registered seat (*siège social* or *Satzungssitz*) from its home State to another State.

National measures

If a foundation engages in activities in a country other than its country of origin, it very often faces national measures and legal prerequisites that go beyond the requirements imposed by its home country. Thus, for instance, in the EU it is not uncommon for Member States to impose national recognition procedures or registration requirements on out-of-State foundations. Moreover, if a foundation decides to transfer, or has effectively transferred, its *siège réel* or *effektiven Verwaltungssitz* to another Member State, Member States applying the 'real seat doctrine' (*Sitztheorie*) will require the foundation to dissolve itself and to reconstitute itself in accordance with the laws of the host Member State – provided, of course, the dissolution is permitted in the first place or approved by the competent government authorities of the foundation's home country. As the dissolution and liquidation of a foundation effectively terminates the will of the original benefactor (founder/settlor),[22] the board's decision to dissolve and liquidate the foundation will, as a general rule, require government approval. Formation of a new foundation in another Member State, in turn, will be subject to a set of entirely new and different laws that may be based on a totally different perception

---

[21] It should be noted, however, that under the law of many Member States not-for-profit foundations, because of their legal nature, may not, as a general rule, hold an interest in another foundation or company. For the pertinent German law, see A. Stengel, *Stiftung und Personengesellschaft* (Baden-Baden: Nomos 1993).

[22] For the role and the significance of the settlor's will, see D. Jakob, *Schutz der Stiftung* (Tübingen: Mohr Siebeck, 2006), 129 *et seq.*

or conception of not-for-profit organisations and foundations. The same is true with regard to the formation of a subsidiary organisation in another Member State if a foundation decides not to dissolve itself in its home State and reconstitute itself in another Member State but rather form a subsidiary organisation in the other Member State in which it wants to engage in activities. Similar problems arise also in cases in which a foundation, duly formed in one Member State, decides to transfer its registered seat to another Member State.

Conflict-of-laws principles

Most Member States apply, with or without variations, general principles of conflict of corporate laws to determine the legal status and the nationality of a foundation (*lex societatis*). While they are codified in some EU Member States, the conflict-of-corporate-laws principles are based on case-law in most Member States. Member States have traditionally differed as to what law governs the internal affairs and the legal status of a corporate entity or foundation. As a general rule, two fundamentally different approaches can be found in the EU: the 'real seat doctrine' and the 'State of incorporation doctrine' (which is sometimes also referred to as the 'internal affairs doctrine').[23]

Real seat doctrine

The real seat doctrine has a long tradition in several Member States (e.g. Austria, Belgium, France, Germany, Poland, Romania, Slovakia and Spain). The real seat doctrine recognises that only one State should have the authority to regulate a foundation's internal affairs, while the most plausible State to supply that law is the State in which the foundation has its real seat (*siège réel* or *effektiver Verwaltungssitz*). The term 'real seat' is commonly understood as referring to the place where the fundamental decisions by the foundation's management are being implemented effectively into day-to-day activities. Thus, in effect, the term 'real seat' refers to the principal place of business (*centre d'exploitation*) of an entity.

The real seat doctrine is based upon the assumption that the State in which an entity has its real seat is typically the State that is most strongly affected by the activities of the entity and, therefore, should have the power to govern the internal affairs of that entity. The real seat doctrine

---

[23] For the following, see Ebke *et al.*, *Feasibility Study*, *supra* n. 20, 105 *et seq.*

stresses the importance of uniform treatment by requiring that all foundations having their real seat in a particular State be formed under that State's law. Thereby, the real seat doctrine creates a level playing field and prevents foundations from evading that State's legal controls through formation in a jurisdiction that has less stringent laws. As a result, under the real seat doctrine all foundations concerned are subject to the same rules and principles of the law of foundations and related laws.

Most Member States that apply the real seat doctrine typically require a foundation not only to have its registered seat (*siège social* or *Satzungssitz*) in the State of formation but also its principal place of business or real seat (*siège réel* or *effektiver Verwaltungssitz*). Under the real seat doctrine, the transfer of the principal place of activities (*centre d'exploitation*) or real seat across State borders from the State of formation (Member State A) to another Member State (Member State B) results, as a general rule, in the loss of the foundation's legal status granted by the State of formation ('emigration' or 'exit' case). In such a case, the foundation would be required to reconstitute itself in Member State B in accordance with that Member State's laws. Similarly, from the perspective of Member State A, a foundation that has been formed in accordance with the law of Member State B and has moved its real seat from Member State B to Member State A ('immigration' or 'entry' case) is considered to have lost its legal status as a foundation in Member State A, provided both Member State A and Member State B apply the real seat doctrine.[24]

State-of-incorporation doctrine

Obviously, the approach of the real seat doctrine is fundamentally different from the conflict-of-corporate-laws principles traditionally employed by courts in Bulgaria, Cyprus, Denmark, Estonia, Ireland, The Netherlands, Sweden, The United Kingdom and, of course, by courts in the United States. Thus, for example, under the laws of Denmark, The Netherlands, and the United Kingdom the founders of a corporate entity are free to choose the State of incorporation. According to the choice-of-corporate-law principles of these countries, the existence of a foundation, as well as its dissolution, are governed by the law of the State of incorporation ('state-of-incorporation doctrine' or

---

[24] If the two countries involved apply different conflict-of-laws principles (e.g. the real seat principle and the state-of-incorporation doctrine), courts are likely to apply the principle of *renvoi*.

Gründungstheorie). The importance of the law of the State of incorporation is greatly enhanced by the fact that the law of the State of incorporation also applies, with rare exceptions, to the internal affairs of the entity.
Obviously, the state-of-incorporation doctrine emphasises, as a general
rule, the founders' freedom to choose the proper law. Thus, the *lex
societatis*, or in the language of English law the *lex domicilii*, is the result
of the founders' own volition. Moreover, the State of incorporation
allows foundations to transfer their real seat across State borders without
any effect on their legal status as a corporate entity under the law of the
State of incorporation, provided the registered office (*Satzungssitz*)
remains in the State of incorporation.

Policy considerations

Clearly, Member States that apply the real seat doctrine aim at effectua-
ting material legal, economic and social values of the country having the
most significant relationship with a particular company. States that
recognise a political, or even a constitutional, need to protect certain
(local) interests will favour the real seat doctrine. In contrast, States that
support the idea of party autonomy (*Parteiautonomie*) in corporate
and foundation law matters will, at least in principle, be in favour
of the State-of-incorporation rule or similar choice-of-corporate-law
principles. If viewed from this perspective, conflict-of-laws rules are, to
some extent, a reflection of the general attitude of a legal culture towards
the socio-economic role of corporations and foundations and the function of complementary substantive and procedural rules of the pertinent
laws for purposes of protecting and furthering the multifarious, and
sometimes hard to reconcile, interests of all those affected by a legal
entity.

It is important to keep in mind, however, that conflict-of-laws rules,
like other legal institutions common to all legal systems, are shaped not
only by efficiency considerations but also by history and politics. Initial
conditions, determined by the accident of history or the design of
politics, influence the path that a conflict-of-laws rule will take. In the
EU, path dependency, or institutional persistence, is, however, not the
only force that influences the direction and objectives of a Member
State's conflict-of-laws rules. Rather, the conflict-of-laws principles of a
Member State, like complementary legal institutions that aim at enhancing the pre-existing conflict-of-laws rules, need to be in compliance with
the supreme law of the EU, especially with the freedom of establishment
guaranteed by Arts. 43 and 48 EC Treaty (now Arts. 49 and 54 TFEU).

The jurisprudence of the European Court of Justice

The European Court of Justice (ECJ) has interpreted Arts. 43 and 48 EC Treaty in a series of seminal decisions involving corporations. The Court's seminal rulings on the right of establishment of corporate entities include its decisions in *Centros*,[25] *Überseering*,[26] *Inspire Art*[27] and *Cartesio*.[28] The Court has never had the opportunity, however, to apply these Treaty provisions to conflict-of-laws issues involving foundations. Therefore, it is necessary to analyse the impact of the pertinent case-law on not-for-profit foundations.[29]

Inbound cases ('immigration' cases)

In order to fully comprehend the significance of Arts. 43 and 48 EC Treaty, it is essential to distinguish between 'inbound' ('immigration') and 'outbound' ('emigration') cases.

Centros The first inbound case was *Centros Ltd* v. *Erhvervs- og Selskabsstyrelsen*.[30] In this case, the Court took exception to a Danish authority's refusal to register a branch of a company validly incorporated in the United Kingdom. According to the Court, the refusal to register the branch constituted a restriction of the English company's right of establishment pursuant to Arts. 43 and 48 EC Treaty which could neither be justified under Art. 46 EC Treaty (i.e. the *ordre public* exception) nor under the four-factor test set forth in *Gebhard* v. *Consiglio dell' Ordine degli Avvocati e Procuratori di Milano*[31] and expressly reconfirmed in *Centros*. While it is debatable whether the English company in *Centros* had actually transferred its seat from England to Denmark – that is, whether the case involved the 'primary' or 'secondary' right of establishment – there can be no doubt that Centros Ltd. had, and continued to have, its registered office in the United Kingdom while its principal place of business or real seat had been in Denmark. In light of

---

[25] Case C 212/97, *Centros Ltd* v. *Erhvervs- og Selskabsstyrelsen*, [1999] ECR I-1459.
[26] Case C-208/00, *Überseering BV* v. *NCC Nordic Construction Baumanagement GmbH*, [2002] ECR I-9919.
[27] Case C-167/01, *Kamer van Koophandel en Fabrieken voor Amsterdam* v. *Inspire Art Ltd*, [2003] ECR I-10155.
[28] Case C-210/06, *Cartesio Oktató és Szolgáltató Bt*, [2009] (16 December 2008).
[29] For the following, see Ebke *et al.*, *Feasibility Study supra* n. 20, 123 *et seq.*
[30] *Centros, supra* n. 25.
[31] Case C-55/94, *Gebhard* v. *Consiglio dell' Ordine degli Avvocati e Procuratori di Milano*, [1993] ECR I-4165.

the Court's holdings in *Centros*, a corporation that is validly incorporated in a Member State enjoys, in principle, the freedom of establishment guaranteed by Arts. 43 and 48 EC Treaty even if it never intended to
do any business in its State of incorporation but was formed in one
Member State only for the purpose of establishing itself in another
Member State where its main, or indeed entire, business is to be conducted. Thus, the freedom of establishment is triggered by the valid
incorporation in any of the twenty-seven EU Member States; provided,
the registered office of the corporation is, and continues to be, in its State
of incorporation. In light of *Centros*, the reasons for which a company
chooses to be incorporated in a particular Member State are, as a general
rule, irrelevant with regard to application of the rules on freedom of
establishment.

Überseering Similarly, in *Überseering BV* v. *NCC Nordic Construction
Baumanagement GmbH*,[32] the ECJ held that Überseering BV, which was
validly incorporated in The Netherlands and had its registered office there,
was entitled under Arts. 43 and 48 EC Treaty to exercise its freedom of
establishment in Germany as a company incorporated under the law of The
Netherlands. According to the Court, the lower German courts' refusal,
under the German version of the real seat doctrine (i.e. the *Sitztheorie*), to
recognise the legal status of Überseering BV as a Dutch corporate entity on
the ground that the corporation had effectively transferred its principal
place of business or real seat (*effektiver Verwaltungssitz*) to Germany,
constituted a restriction on the company's freedom of establishment
which, in principle, is incompatible with Arts. 43 and 48 EC Treaty.
Under Arts. 43 and 48 EC Treaty, a Member State is required to recognise
the legal personality of a corporation validly incorporated in another
Member State as provided for by the *lex societatis*. Most importantly, the
Member State in which the sister State corporation has its real seat (establishment) may not disregard the legal personality of that corporation as
provided for by its *lex societatis* and substitute it by resorting to local forms
of business associations. Also, the Member State may not deny a corporation validly incorporated in another Member State the right to sue or to
be sued.

Inspire Art *Überseering* laid the ground for a much broader application of the freedom of establishment guaranteed by Arts. 43 and 48 EC

---

[32] *Überseering, supra* n. 26, [2002] ECR I-9919.

Treaty, as is evidenced by the Court's decision in *Kamer van Koophandel en Fabrieken voor Amsterdam* v. *Inspire Art Ltd*.[33] The dispute in *Inspire Art* arose because Inspire Art Ltd was not registered in The Netherlands as a 'formally foreign' corporation as required by the Dutch Law of 17 December 1997 on Pseudo-foreign Corporations. Inspire Art Ltd was formed in the legal form of a private company limited by shares under the law of England and Wales, had its registered office at Folkestone (United Kingdom) and a branch in Amsterdam where it carried on business under the business name Inspire Art Ltd in the sphere of dealing in *objets d'art*. Taking the view that Inspire Art Ltd should be registered as a pseudo-foreign corporation, the Chamber of Commerce of Amsterdam applied to the *Kantongerecht* (District Court) of Amsterdam for an order that there should be added to the registration of Inspire Art Ltd in the commercial register the statement that it is a formally foreign corporation.

In accordance with its holding in *Centros*, the ECJ noted that it is 'immaterial', with respect to the application of the European rules on freedom of establishment, that Inspire Art Ltd was formed in the United Kingdom only for the purpose of establishing itself in The Netherlands where its main, or indeed entire, business is being conducted. The Court also pointed out that the fact that Inspire Art Ltd was formed in the United Kingdom for the sole purpose of enjoying the benefits of more favourable legislation with regard in particular to minimum capital and the paying-up of shares, did not mean that the establishment by Inspire Art Ltd of a branch in The Netherlands was not covered by freedom of establishment as provided for by Arts. 43 and 48 EC Treaty, even if the company conducts its activities entirely or mainly in The Netherlands. 'While in this case Inspire Art was formed under the company law of a Member State . . . for the purpose in particular of evading the application of Netherlands company law, which was considered to be more severe, the fact remains', the Court opined, 'that the provisions of the Treaty on freedom of establishment are intended specifically to enable companies formed in accordance with the law of a Member State and having their registered office, central administration or principal place of business within the Community to pursue activities in other Member States through an agency, branch or subsidiary'.

The Court refused to accept the argument that Inspire Art's freedom of establishment was not in any way infringed by The Netherlands' Law

[33] *Inspire Art Ltd*, *supra* n. 27, [2003] ECR I-10155.

on Pseudo-Foreign Corporations. The government of The Netherlands had argued that, under that Law, foreign companies are fully recognised in The Netherlands and are not refused registration in the business register, the Law having the effect of simply laying down a number of additional obligations that were characterised as 'administrative'. However, according to the ECJ, the effect of the Law is, in fact, that the Dutch company law rules on minimum capital and directors' liability are applied mandatorily to foreign companies such as Inspire Art Ltd when they carry on their business activities exclusively, or almost exclusively, in The Netherlands. Therefore, the Court concluded that the Law's provisions relating to minimum capital (both at the time of formation and during the life of the company) and to directors' liability constituted restrictions on freedom of establishment as guaranteed by Arts. 43 and 48 EC Treaty. The reasons for which the company was formed in the other Member State, and the fact that it carried on its activities exclusively or almost exclusively in the Member State of establishment, do not deprive, the Court ruled, the company of the right to invoke the freedom of establishment guaranteed by the Treaty, 'save where abuse is established on a case-by-case basis'. Having concluded that the Law's provisions relating to minimum capital and directors' liability constituted a restriction of the freedom of establishment of Inspire Art Ltd, the ECJ addressed the question of whether there was any justification for such restriction. While it did not engage in a neat factor-by-factor analysis, the ECJ made it clear in *Inspire Art* that the restriction of the company's freedom of establishment provided for by Arts. 43 and 48 EC Treaty could not survive scrutiny under the four-prong test of *Gebhard* and *Centros*.

The immediate lesson from *Inspire Art* is that, within the EU, both capital requirements and directors' liability are governed by the law of the corporation's State of incorporation. In light of *Überseering* and *Inspire Art*, it is also fair to conclude that all other internal affairs of a corporation that is incorporated in one Member State but carries on business in another Member State are also governed by the law of the State of incorporation, its *lex societatis*. Thus, within the EU, the real seat doctrine has been effectively put to rest by the ECJ in regard to corporations formed in any of the twenty-seven Member States. Yet, even after *Inspire Art*, the question remains whether and to what extent a Member State can take measures to prevent certain of its nationals from attempting, under cover of the rights created by the EC Treaty, improperly to circumvent their national legislation or to prevent individuals from improperly or fraudulently taking advantage of provisions of Community law. As the Court noted in *Überseering*, '[i]t is not inconceivable that overriding requirements relating to the general interest, such as protection of the interests of creditors, minority shareholders, employees and even the taxation authorities, may, in certain circumstances and subject to certain conditions, justify restrictions on freedom of establishment'.

Outbound cases ('emigration' cases)

It is important to emphasise that *Centros*, *Überseering* and *Inspire Art* concern 'inbound', 'immigration', or 'entry' cases. The question of whether a corporation that is validly incorporated in one of the Member States may invoke freedom of establishment under Arts. 43 and 48 EC Treaty to transfer its principal place of business or real seat from its State of incorporation to another Member State ('outbound', 'emigration', or 'exit' case) has been equally controversial. In *The Queen v. HM Treasury and Commissioners of Inland Revenue, ex parte Daily Mail and General Trust plc*,[34] the Court addressed the issue for the first time.

Daily Mail   In *Daily Mail*, the Court held that a company could not rely upon the right to freedom of establishment in order to transfer its central management and control to another Member State (The Netherlands) for the purpose of selling a significant part of its non-permanent assets and using the proceeds of that sale to buy its own shares without having to pay the tax normally due on such transactions in the Member State of origin (the United Kingdom). The Court rejected the company's view that the tax authorities had infringed the right of establishment. The Court concluded that 'in the present State of Community law' Arts. 43 and 48 (*ex* 52 and 58) EC Treaty, properly construed, confer no right on a company incorporated under the legislation of a Member State and having its registered office there to transfer its central management and control to another Member State. In para. 23 of its decision in *Daily Mail*, the Court observed that 'the Treaty regards the differences in national legislation concerning the required connecting factor and the question whether – and if so how – the registered office or real head office of a company incorporated under national law may be transferred from one Member State to another as problems which are not resolved by the rules

---

[34] Case C-81/87, *The Queen v. HM Treasury and Commissioners of Inland Revenue, ex parte Daily Mail and General Trust plc*, [1988] ECR 5483.

concerning the right of establishment but must be dealt with by future legislation or conventions'.[35]

Distinguishing *Überseering* Distinguishing *Überseering* from *Daily Mail*, the ECJ held in *Überseering* that, despite the general terms in which para. 23 of *Daily Mail* is cast, the Court did not intend to recognise a Member State as having the power, *vis-à-vis* companies validly incorporated in other Member States and found by it to have transferred their seat to its territory, to subject those companies' effective exercise in its territory of the freedom of establishment to compliance with its domestic company law.[36] The *Überseering* Court saw no grounds for concluding from *Daily Mail* that, where a company formed in accordance with the law of one Member State and with legal personality in that State exercises its freedom of establishment in another Member State, the question of recognition of its legal capacity and its capacity to be a party to legal proceedings in the Member State of establishment falls outside the scope of the Treaty provisions on freedom of establishment, even when the company is found, under the law of the Member State of establishment, to have moved its actual centre of administration to that State.[37]

In *Überseering*, the ECJ made it also clear that the exercise of the freedom of establishment is not dependent upon the adoption of a convention on the mutual recognition of companies within the meaning of Art. 293 EC Treaty. According to the Court, Art. 293 EC Treaty gives Member States the 'opportunity' to enter into negotiations with a view, *inter alia*, to facilitating the resolution of problems arising from the discrepancies between the various laws relating to the mutual recognition of companies and the retention of legal personality in the event of the transfer of their seat from one Member State to another. Pointing to the 'so far as is necessary' clause in Art. 293 EC Treaty and the Opinion of the Advocate General in *Überseering*, the Court concluded that Art. 293 EC Treaty does not constitute 'a reserve of legislative competence vested in the Member States'. It follows that the fact that no convention on the mutual recognition of companies has yet been adopted on the basis of Art. 293 EC Treaty[38] cannot be used by the Member States to

---

[35] *Ibid.*, para. 23.   [36] *Überseering, supra* n. 26, para. 72.

[37] *Überseering, supra* n. 26, para. 73.

[38] The Convention on the Mutual Recognition of Companies and Bodies Corporate of 29 February 1968 did not enter into force for lack of ratification by The Netherlands. It is highly unlikely that the Convention will be 'revitalised' despite proposals for a more positive reappraisal of such a Convention.

justify limiting the full effect of freedom of establishment guaranteed by Arts. 43 and 48 EC Treaty.

Further developments The Court's holdings in *Sevic Systems AG* v. *Amtsgericht Neuwied*[39] can also be cited in support of the legal proposition that Arts. 43 and 48 EC Treaty prohibit restrictions on 'entering' or 'leaving' national territory. Furthermore, in light of the Court's holdings in *Hughes de Lasteyrie du Saillant* v. *Ministère de l'Économie, des Finances et de l'Industrie*[40] and *Cadbury Schweppes*[41] it appeared inconceivable that the Court would construe a corporation's freedom of establishment guaranteed by Arts. 43 and 48 EC Treaty in the event of cross-border transfer of the real seat, principal place of business, or centre of administration to another Member State ('outbound', 'emigration', or 'exit' case) more restrictively than in an 'inbound', 'immigration', or 'entry' case such as *Überseering* or *Inspire Art*. In light of the Court's jurisprudence, it could be argued persuasively that the negation by a Member State of the right of a cross-border transfer of the real seat, principal place of business, or actual centre of administration ('emigration') and the requirement to re-incorporate in the other Member State (i.e. the State of establishment) would be tantamount to outright negation of the freedom of establishment that Arts. 43 and 48 EC Treaty are intended to ensure.

Cartesio This proposition is supported by the opinion of the Avocate General Poiares Maduro of 22 May 2008 in the matter of *Cartesio*.[42] In *Cartesio*, a limited partnership (*betéti társaság*) constituted in accordance with the law of Hungary and registered in the Hungarian city of Baja, submitted an application to the Commercial Court to amend its registration in the local commercial register so as to record an address in Italy as its new operational headquarters (*központi ügyintézés helye*). The Court, however, rejected Cartesio's application on the grounds that Hungarian law did not offer companies the possibility of transferring their operational headquarters to another Member State while retaining their legal status as a company governed by Hungarian law. Therefore, in order to change its

---

[39] Case C-411/03, *Sevic Systems AG* v. *Amtsgericht Neuwied*, [2005] ECR I-4321.
[40] Case C-9/02, *Hughes de Lasteyrie du Saillant* v. *Ministère de l'Économie, des Finances et de l'Industrie*, [2004] ECR I-2409.
[41] Case C-196/04, *Cadbury Schweppes plc & Cadbury Schweppes Overseas Ltd* v. *Commissioners of Inland Revenue*, [2006] ECR I-7995.
[42] Case C-210/06, *Cartesio*, *supra* n. 28.

operational headquarters, Cartesio would first have to be dissolved in Hungary and then reconstituted under Italian law. In the subsequent proceedings pursuant to Art. 234 EC Treaty the Hungarian court submitted, *inter alia*, the question of whether regulation of the transfer of a company's seat is within the scope of Community law or, in the absence of the harmonisation of laws, national law is exclusively applicable.

Advocate General Poiares Maduro stated in his opinion of 22 May 2008 in *Cartesio* that it is impossible to argue on the basis of the current State of Community law that Member States enjoy an absolute freedom to determine the 'life and death' of companies constituted under their domestic law, irrespective of the consequences for the freedom of establishment. Otherwise, Member States would have *carte blanche* to impose a 'death sentence' on a company constituted under its laws just because it had decided to exercise the freedom of establishment.

However, in its judgement of 16 December 2008, the ECJ held that 'as Community law now stands, Articles 43 EC and 48 EC are to be interpreted as not precluding legislation of a Member State under which a company incorporated under the law of that Member State may not transfer its seat to another Member State whilst retaining its status as a company governed by the law of the Member State of incorporation'. The Court reiterated its observation in *Daily Mail* that 'companies are creatures of national law and exist only by virtue of the national legislation which determines its incorporation and functioning' and emphasised that

> in accordance with Article 48 EC, in the absence of a uniform Community law definition of the companies which may enjoy the right of establishment on the basis of a single connecting factor determining the national law applicable to a company, the question whether Article 43 EC applies to a company which seeks to rely on the fundamental freedom enshrined in that article – like the question whether a natural person is a national of a Member State, hence entitled to enjoy that freedom – is a preliminary matter which, as Community law now stands, can only be resolved by the applicable national law.

Consequently, the Court concluded that 'the question whether the company is faced with a restriction on the freedom of establishment, within the meaning of Article 43 EC, can arise only if it has been established, in the light of the conditions laid down in Article 48 EC, that the company actually has a right to that freedom'. The surprising holding of the ECJ in *Cartesio* will disappoint those who had hoped for a liberal, internal market-friendly solution for the recognition of out-of-State corporations in 'outbound' cases. Member States are, of course, free to allow domestic corporations to transfer their real seat (*siège réel* or *effektiver Verwaltungssitz*) to another Member State without losing their legal status as a domestic corporation, and some Member States (e.g. Germany) do that already, as long as the registered seat (*siège social* or *Satzungssitz*) remains in the home State.

Cross-border transfer of registered seat

The cross-border transfer of the registered seat (*siège social* or *Satzungssitz*) is, of course, a different and more complicated issue. For such a transfer, a corporation needs to acquire legal personality in the other Member State and lose it in the home Member State in order to avoid any complications arising from its being registered in two countries. In light of the holdings of the ECJ in *Centros, Überseering, Inspire Art, Sevic, Hughes de Lasteyrie du Saillant, Cadbury Schweppes* and *Cartesio* it is unclear whether the retention of legal personality in the event of cross-border transfer of the *registered* seat is possible within the EU or whether secondary Community legislation, such as a coordination Directive under Art. 44(2)(g) EC Treaty (now Art. 50(2)(9) TFEU), needs to be adopted for these cases. Such legislation would have to provide appropriate safeguards in the Member States to allow companies to exercise their freedom of establishment by transferring their registered office, thereby acquiring legal personality under the law of the other Member State in order to be governed by that law and without having to be wound up in the home Member State. The objective of such a Directive should be to facilitate the cross-border transfer, by way of freedom of establishment, of the registered office of a corporation already formed under the law of a Member State. The EU Commission outlined its views as to the proposal of a 14th Company Law Directive on the Cross-border Transfer of the Registered Office of Limited Companies in a public consultation. Upon re-evaluating the issue, the Commission concluded, however, in December 2007, that no legislative action was needed at EU level. Consequently, work on the 14th Directive was discontinued.

Application to foundations

It is still a largely unsettled question whether and to what extent, if any, the right of establishment guaranteed by Arts. 43 and 48 EC Treaty (now Arts. 49 and 54 TFEU) is applicable to not-for-profit foundations.[43]

---

[43] For recent discussions see, e.g., Ebke *et al.*, *Feasibility Study, supra* n. 20, 106–11, 123–39; S. Leible, 'Die Stiftung im Internationalen Privatrecht', in I. Saenger, W. Bayer, E. Koch

General observations

As a general rule, the principles developed by the ECJ in its jurisprudence are not applicable only to companies but also to foundations. As a result, restrictions by Member State legislation on 'entering' (as opposed to 'leaving') the national territory would be prohibited, regardless of whether those restrictions are substantive or procedural in nature or part of the conflicts-of-laws regime, which would allow a foundation to engage in cross-border activities, including the transfer of its (real) seat from one Member State to another while retaining its legal status as a foundation under the law of the State of formation. It appears to be equally clear from the Court's case-law regarding the right of establishment that the effective exercise of the freedom of establishment requires at least some degree of mutual recognition and coordination of the various systems of rules.

It should also be emphasised that, according to the Court's case-law, Member States may take measures to prevent 'wholly artificial arrangements, which do not reflect economic reality' and which are aimed at circumventing national legislation. In particular, the right of establishment does not preclude Member States from being wary of 'scam' foundations. This follows from the principle of abuse of Community law the applicability of which in the context of Arts. 43 and 48 EC Treaty (now Arts. 49 and 54 TFEU) was expressly mentioned in *Centros* and *Inspire Art*, even though the Court continues to use the notion of abuse with considerable restraint. In addition, restrictions by Member State legislation on the freedom of establishment of a foundation may be justified on grounds of general public interest, such as the prevention of abuse or fraudulent conduct, or the protection of the interests of individuals affected by the activities of a foundation, or the tax authorities.

In search of an answer

As stated above, the ECJ has never had the opportunity to rule on the issue of whether and to what extent Arts. 43 and 48 EC Treaty (now Arts. 49 and 54 TFEU) apply to the recognition of foreign foundations or to the cross-border mobility of foundations within the EU. The Court has, however, interpreted Arts. 43 and 48 EC Treaty in the contexts, for example, of

and T. Körber (eds.), *Festschrift für Olaf Werner* (Baden-Baden: Nomos 2009), 256–74; A. Spickhoff, 'Zum Internationalen Privatrecht der Stiftungen', in I. Saenger, W. Bayer, E. Koch and T. Körber (eds.), *Festschrift für Olaf Werner* (Baden-Baden: Nomos 2009), 241–55.

taxation[44] and Community competition law.[45] Consequently, answers need to be developed in light of the pertinent European law as well as relevant case-law, taking into account the opinions of legal commentators.

Literal interpretation   In view of the language of Art. 54(2) TFEU, an argument could be made that only foundations carrying on a commercial ('for-profit') activity are subject to the right of establishment. Thus, charitable foundations and other not-for-profit foundations engaged in cultural, scientific, or social activities would not be entitled to invoke the right of establishment under Arts. 49 and 54 TFEU , as those activities are not commercial in nature. Such an interpretation of Arts. 49 and 54 TFEU would seem to be rather narrow, however, and inconsistent with other case-law.

Functional approach   Alternatively, rather than construing Art. 54(2) TFEU based only upon its language, one could apply a functional approach taking into account the EC Treaty's provisions – for example, on competition or EU legislation (e.g. Council Directive 77/187/EEC) and the case-law interpreting these provisions. Thus, for example, the Court held in *Motosykletistiki Omospondia Ellados NPID (MOTOE)* v. *Elliniko Dimosio*[46] that the fact that the Automobile and Touring Club of Greece (ELPA) does not seek to make a profit does not prevent the courts from treating it as an undertaking for purposes of Community competition law. Similarly, it should be noted that in *Ministero dell' Economia e delle Finanze* v. *Cassa di Risparmio di Firenze and Others* the Court stated that the fact that the offer of goods or services is made without a profit motive does not preclude a court from characterising an actor as being an undertaking that carries out those operations in the market, since that offer exists in competition with that of other actors who do seek to make a profit. '[W]here a banking foundation, acting itself in the fields of public interest and social assistance uses the authorisation given it by the national legislature to effect the financial, commercial, real estate and asset operations necessary or opportune in order

---

[44] Cf. Case C-386/04, *Centro di Musicologia Walter Stauffer* v. *Finanzamt München für Körperschaften*, [2006] ECR I-8203.

[45] Case C-222/04, *Ministero dell'Economia e delle Finanze* v. *Cassa di Risparmio di Firenze and Others*, [2006] ECR I-289.

[46] Case C-49/07, *Motosykletistiki Omospondia Ellados NPID (MOTOE)* v. *Elliniko Dimosio*, [2008] ECR I-4863.

to achieve the aims prescribed for it', the Court opined, 'it is capable of offering goods or services on the market in competition with other operators, for example in fields like scientific research, education, art or health'.[47] On that hypothesis, which is subject to the national court's assessment,[48] the Court concluded that the banking foundation must be regarded as an undertaking, in that it engages in an economic activity, notwithstanding the fact that the offer of goods or services is made without a profit motive, since that offer will be in competition with that of profit-making operators.

Application   As applied to Arts. 49 and 54 TFEU, this case-law would seem to suggest that, notwithstanding the fact that their offer of goods or services is made without profit motive, not-for-profit foundations may be entitled to the right of establishment if and to the extent that they engage in an economic activity in a market by offering goods or services that are in competition with offerings of commercial offerors seeking a profit. In that regard it must be pointed out that, according to the case-law,[49] the mere holding of shares, even controlling shareholdings, is insufficient to characterise as 'economic' an activity of the entity holding those shares, when it gives rise only to the exercise of the rights attached to the status of shareholder or member, as well as, if appropriate, the receipt of dividends, which are merely the fruits of the ownership of an asset. On the other hand, an entity which, owning controlling shareholdings in a company, actually exercises that control by involving itself directly or indirectly in the management thereof must be regarded as taking part in the economic activity carried on by the controlled undertaking. Similarly, the Court held in *Centro di Musicologia Walter Stauffer* v. *Finanzamt München für Körperschaften* that in order for the provisions relating to freedom of establishment to apply, it is generally necessary that the property of a foundation located in another Member State is 'actively' managed by the foundation.[50] Thus, if, for example, a foundation having charitable status under the law of Italy is the owner of real property located in Germany and the services ancillary to the letting of that property are provided by a property management agent in Germany, the provisions governing freedom of

---

[47] Case C-222/04, *Ministero dell' Economia e delle Finanze* v. *Cassa di Risparmio di Firenze*, [2006] ECR I-289, para. 122; see also Case 382/92, *Commission* v. *United Kingdom*, [1994] ECR I-2435.

[48] *Ibid.*, para. 123.   [49] *Ibid.*, paras. 111–112.

[50] *Centro di Musicologia Walter Stauffer*, *supra* n. 44, para. 19.

establishment are not applicable as the foundation has not secured a permanent presence in the host Member State.

The actual scope of the concept of economic activity is illustrated in *Didier Mayeur* v. *Associations Promotion d'Information Messine (APIM)*.[51] In this case, the Court held that a private non-profit-making association which had legal personality separate from that of the city may be characterised, for purposes of Council Directive 77/187/EEC of 14 February 1977 on the Approximation of the Laws of the Member States relating to the Safeguarding of Employees' Rights in the Event of Transfers of Undertakings, Businesses or Parts of Businesses,[52] as engaging in economic activity if it carries out publicity and information activities on behalf of the city in connection with the services that the latter offers to the public. Thus, the transfer of activities formerly carried out by an organisation or entity established under public law to a not-for-profit organisation formed under private law does not prevent the activity from being characterised as economic activity.

Summary   In light of the foregoing case-law it is reasonable to conclude that a foundation the activities of which are financed neither through its own business operations nor by means of an 'active' management of its property is not engaged in economic activities. Consequently, such a foundation would not be able to claim the benefits of the right of establishment pursuant to Arts. 49 and 54 TFEU. If, however, a not-for-profit foundation is 'actively' managing its assets or engaging in the trading of goods or services that are in competition with activities of commercial offerors seeking a profit, the foundation is entitled to the right of establishment pursuant to Arts. 49 and 54 TFEU.

As to the expenditures of a not-for-profit foundation, one needs to distinguish between grant-making and operating foundations. An operating foundation carries out self-directed not-for-profit projects. If, in the course of such a project, goods or services are being exchanged for value (i.e. consideration), small or large, the foundation is to be qualified as engaging in economic activities. As a result, such an operating foundation would be subject to Arts. 49 and 54 TFEU. The activities of

---

[51] Case C-175/99, *Didier Mayeur* v. *Associations Promotion d'Information Messine (APIM)*, [2000] ECR I-7755; cf. Joined Cases C-173/96, *Francisca Sánchez Hidalgo and Others* v. *Asociación de Servicios Aser and Sociedad Cooperativa Minerva* and C-247/94, *Horst Ziemann* v. *Ziemann Sicherheit GmbH and Horst Bohn Sicherheitsdienst*, [1998] ECR I-8237.

[52] OJ 1977 L 61, 26.

a grant-making foundation, by contrast, are often limited to the distribution of money or similar financial means to individuals, institutions, or projects. A grant-making foundation typically does not offer goods or services in exchange for money and is not competing against for-profit organisations. Hence, a pure grant-making foundation normally does not fall within the ambit of Arts. 49 and 54 TFEU.

In sum, a foundation can only invoke freedom of establishment pursuant to Arts. 49 and 54 TFEU if it operates a business or if it is 'actively' managing its assets or property or if, in the course of its not-for-profit activities, it offers goods or services in exchange for money or similar financial means. If it does not meet any of the aforementioned prerequisites, the foundation will not fall within the ambit of Arts. 49 and 54 TFEU.

Cross-border activities: setting up agencies and branches

If, however, a foundation is entitled to invoke freedom of establishment under Arts. 49 and 54 TFEU, the question arises to what extent, if any, Arts. 49 and 54 TFEU can be utilised to overcome existing private law barriers.[53]

Setting up subsidiaries   Freedom of establishment includes the right to set up and manage subsidiaries under the conditions laid down for its own nationals by the law of the Member State where such establishment is effected. Thus, the formation of a legally independent subsidiary of a foundation requires an act by the foundation or its founders in accordance with the law of the Member State in which the establishment is to be effected; provided, of course, the Member State in which the foundation has been formed allows foundations to set up a subsidiary abroad. The formation of the subsidiary is then governed solely by the law of the State of establishment which is likely to differ, more or less, from the law of the Member State in which the foundation has been formed.

Setting up agencies or branches   Freedom of establishment also includes the right to set up agencies or branches. Obviously, agencies and branches are not legally independent entities. Rather, agencies and branches of a foundation are governed by the law of the State in which the foundation was formed. It follows that not-for-profit foundations that can invoke freedom of establishment are entitled to set up agencies

---

[53] For details, see Ebke *et al.*, *Feasibility Study*, *supra* n. 20, 135 *et seq.*

or branches in another Member State. To the extent that the activities of an agency or branch are within the scope of the foundation's purpose or purposes, the branch or agency does not need to be reconstituted under the non-profit-organisations laws of the host Member State. Thus, the establishment of an agency or branch in another Member State is within the powers of the management of the foundation. If the home State of the foundation imposes restrictions on the right of a foundation to establish an agency or branch in another Member State, such restriction would hinder or make 'less attractive' the foundation's freedom of establishment under Arts. 49 and 54 TFEU and, therefore, would constitute a violation of Arts. 49 and 54 TFEU unless it can be justified under the 'four-factor test' that was first applied by the ECJ in *Gebhard*[54] in the context of Art. 43 EC Treaty and extended by the Court in *Centros*[55] to restrictions on companies' freedom of establishment guaranteed by Arts. 43 and 48 EC Treaty (now Arts. 49 and 54 TFEU) and reconfirmed in *Inspire Art*.[56] Hence, a categorical denial by a Member State of the right to set up agencies or branches in another Member State would deprive foundations within the ambit of Arts. 49 and 54 TFEU of their freedom of establishment. Similarly, attempts by the Member State in which the establishment is effected to impose its more restrictive law (e.g. concerning the purpose of a foundation) on the agency or branch of a foreign (EU) foundation would constitute a violation of Arts. 49 and 54 TFEU unless such violation could be justified in accordance with the jurisprudence of the ECJ.

In light of the case-law mentioned above, a Member State law that requires the branch of a foreign (EU) foundation, that was validly formed in accordance with the law of the foundation's home State, fully to comply with the foundation laws of the branch's host State would seem to be inconsistent with the mandates of Arts. 49 and 54 TFEU unless it could be justified under the 'four-factor test' established in *Gebhard*. Similarly, a law that imposes unnecessarily rigorous requirements on the establishment of an agency of a foreign (EU) foundation would also restrict the foundation's freedom of establishment and could be upheld only if it were justified in light of the *Gebhard* test.

In view of the four-factor test set out in *Gebhard* and expressly reconfirmed in *Centros*, Member States may, however, impose upon out-of-State foundations certain notification or registration requirements (see, e.g., the registration requirements under Czech law) as long

---

[54] *Gebhard, supra* n. 31.   [55] *Centros, supra* n. 25, para. 34.
[56] *Inspire Art Ltd, supra* n. 27, para. 133.

as they are reasonable under the circumstances and not prohibitive. Thus, for example, a Member State may not charge foreign foundations prohibitively high fees or impose excessive waiting periods in connection with the registration.[57] A Member State may, however, require useful information – for example, about the nature of the activities of the foreign foundation, the capitalisation, the management and the persons behind the organisation as well as the tax status in the country of formation.[58] The requirement of some Member States that a foreign foundation follow certain recognition procedures or establish a representative office within the Member State in which it intends to carry on its activities, however, constitutes a highly questionable restriction that can hardly be justified in light of the four-factor test.

Transfer of real seat   Arts. 49 and 54 TFEU apply also to the transfer of the centre of administration or real seat (*siège réel* or *effektiver Verwaltungssitz*). According to the jurisprudence of the ECJ, freedom of establishment includes the right of a company to transfer its centre of administration or real seat (*siège reel* or *effektiver Verwaltungssitz*) to another Member State. The same principles apply to foundations that fall within the ambit of Arts. 49 and 54 TFEU. Measures and instruments of government supervision may be governed by both private or public law. In any event, legal and other measures affecting foreign foundations must be measured against freedom of establishment as Arts. 49 and 54 TFEU mandate that a foundation's freedom of establishment must not be restricted regardless of whether the restriction is part of private and public law. Justifications, if any, need to meet the high standards developed by the ECJ in *Gebhard, Centros, Überseering* and *Inspire Art* ('four-factor test'). As has been explained above, the principles established

---

[57] Cf. Cases C-163/94, C-165/94 and C-250/94, *Lucas Emilio Sanz de Lera and Others*, [1995] ECR I-4821, para. 38 (holding that in cases involving the free movement of capital '[a] prior declaration, giving useful information as to the nature of the planned operation and the identity of the declarant, would enable the Member States to verify the actual use to which means of payment exported to non-member countries was put, without impeding liberalized capital movements, and thereby to ensure observance of any restrictions on capital movements authorized by Article 73c of the Treaty').

[58] Cf. *Centro di Musicologica Walter Stauffer, supra* n. 44, para. 49 (holding that '[t]here is nothing to prevent the tax authorities concerned from requiring a charitable foundation claiming exemption from tax to provide relevant supporting evidence to enable those authorities to carry out the necessary checks. Further, national legislation which absolutely prevents the taxpayer from submitting such evidence cannot be justified in the name of effectiveness of fiscal supervision').

by the ECJ regarding freedom of establishment in the 'immigration' or 'entry' cases are not equally applicable to the 'emigration' or 'exit' cases (*Cartesio*).

Cross-border mergers between, and acquisitions of, foundations

The ECJ has never had an opportunity to rule on cross-border mergers between, and acquisitions or restructurings of, foundations. There is no pertinent secondary EU legislation either. Directive 2005/56/EC applies only to corporations but not to foundations.[59] At the national level, there is hardly any discussion of the relevant issues. In the United Kingdom and The Netherlands, the law does allow foundations to merge. German law permits a foundation to spin off economic activities. The foundation laws of several German provinces (*Länder*) provide that foundations may merge, provided such a merger is expressly permitted in the foundation's articles of formation. Such a merger requires, however, approval by the competent government authorities. In light of the ECJ's decision in *Sevic Systems AG* v. *Amtsgericht Neuwied*,[60] it is fair to conclude that if a Member State allows domestic entities to merge or engage in similar restructuring transactions it must also allow these transactions across State borders. This would seem to apply equally to outbound (*Hinausverschmelzung*) and inbound transactions (*Hineinverschmelzung*).[61]

Conclusions

The preceding analysis illustrates the increasing significance of the right of establishment pursuant to Arts. 49 and 54 TFEU and its potential impact upon not-for-profit foundations. While the ECJ has not yet ruled on any of the issues discussed in this chapter, case-law suggests that the provisions regarding freedom of establishment apply to a not-for-profit foundation if it engages in 'economic activity' – i.e. if it offers goods or services in a market in competition with offers made by persons who operate in that market for profit. In contrast, if the foundation does not carry on an 'economic activity', it cannot invoke the right of

---

[59] Directive 2005/56/EC on cross-border mergers of limited liability companies, OJ L 310/1, 25 November 2005.

[60] *Sevic Systems, supra* n. 39, para. 21.

[61] Opinion of Attorney General Tizzano of 18 March 2004 in *Sevic Systems, supra* n. 39, para. 45.

establishment. Given the theoretically broad scope of the concept of 'economic activity' it is fair to conclude that at least some not-for-profit foundations in the EU are subject to the right of establishment.

Where to draw the line between economic and non-economic activities is, however, not entirely clear. While the Court's jurisprudence does provide some guidance, it does not offer clear, foreseeable and reliable solutions for all possible cases. Thus, for example, it is subject to debate under what, if any, circumstance the management of a foundation's assets can be characterised as 'active' within the meaning of *Stauffer*.[62] Similarly, it is unclear whether the economic activity in question needs to be material and, if so, whether it needs to be quantitatively or qualitatively material or both. The absence of a clear distinction is particularly problematic because the applicability of Arts. 49 and 54 TFEU depends upon the characterisation of the activity of a foundation as an 'economic' one. Only if the activity of a not-for-profit foundation can be characterised as an economic activity may the foundation invoke the right of establishment which allows it, *inter alia*, to engage in cross-border activities. Under the provisions regarding the right of establishment, the not-for-profit foundation even enjoys the freedom to transfer its principal place of business or real seat (*siège réel* or *effektiver Verwaltungssitz*) from its home Member State to another Member State. Specifically, the right of establishment allows a foundation, at a minimum, to immigrate whereas its right to emigrate depends on whether its home State allows such emigration. In contrast, in the current State of European law, the transfer of the registered seat (*siège social* or *Satzungssitz*) will be possible only if legal mechanisms are in place that ensure that the interests of all those affected by such a transfer are taken into account.

It is also clear from the ECJ's case-law that if a foundation enjoys the right of establishment, a Member State may not, as a general rule, restrict this right or make its exercise less attractive, unless the restriction can be justified according to Art. 52 TFEU or pursuant to the 'four-factor' test set out in *Gebhard*[63] and reconfirmed by the ECJ in *Centros*. In light of the case-law, the real seat doctrine would not seem to be a justifiable restriction of a foundation's right of establishment in regard to immigration cases. However, Member States may impose registration requirements on foreign corporations; provided, these requirements are not

---

[62] *Centro di Musicologica Walter Stauffer*, supra n. 44.
[63] *Gebhard*, supra n. 31; *Centros*, supra n. 25.

contrary to the *Gebhard* test. Thus, for example, under Arts. 49 and 54 TFEU the registration authority of a Member State may not charge prohibitively high registration fees or impose unreasonably long waiting periods in connection with the registration. Special recognition requirements for foreign not-for-profit foundations are subject to the same limitations as registration requirements. The requirement imposed by some Member States that a foreign foundation establish a representative office in the State in which it wishes to operate would seem to be an unjustifiable restriction of the foundation's right of establishment.

While for a foundation that is engaged in 'active' economic activities, a cross-border transfer of its principal place of business, real seat, or *siège réel* is possible under Arts. 49 and 54 TFEU, albeit only 'inbound', numerous material problems continue to exist. These result primarily from the supervision and control mechanisms that Member State authorities may exercise over domestic (and sometimes also over foreign foundations). Such control may be necessary, for example, to effectuate the will of the settlor or to ensure compliance with applicable laws, including the law of taxation. The interaction between State supervision and freedom of establishment is still in a state of flux.

17

The meaning of 'investment' in the ICSID Convention

BARTON LEGUM AND CALINE MOUAWAD

The term 'investment' is a gateway that limits access to the dispute resolution mechanism established by the 1965 Convention on the Settlement of Investment Disputes Between States and Nationals of Other States (the 'ICSID Convention').[1] If the term has a narrow and precise meaning, then a number of disputes that the parties have agreed to submit to ICSID may have no forum for resolution. If the term has a broad and flexible meaning, then the ICSID system will be poised to accept most, if not all, of the cases that the parties have consented to submit to ICSID arbitration.

A concrete example serves to illustrate the issue. A company organised under the law of an ICSID Contracting State holds a demand account with a bank in another Contracting State. A bilateral investment treaty is in force between the two countries that provides only for ICSID arbitration of disputes between investors and a State. The host country seizes the funds credited to the company's bank account without any offer of compensation.

Under the definition used in many investment treaties, the funds credited to the bank account could qualify as an 'investment' covered

---

[1] E.g. E. Gaillard, '"Biwater", Classic Investment Bases. Input, Risk, Duration', *New York Law Journal*, 240, 31 December 2008; S. Manciaux, 'La compétence matérielle. Actualité de la notion d'investissement international', paper submitted to the Colloquium on La Procédure arbitrale relative aux investissements internationaux. Aspects récents (Institut des Hautes Études Internationales Université Panthéon-Assas (Paris II), 3 April 2008; D. Krishan, 'A Notion of ICSID Investment', in T. J. Grierson Weiler (ed.), *Investment Treaty Arbitration and International Law* (New York: Juris Publishing, 2008), 61–84; C. McLachlan, L. Shore and M. Weiniger, *International Investment Arbitration – Substantive Principles* (Oxford University Press, 2007), 164; M. Waibel, 'Opening Pandora's Box. Sovereign Bonds in International Arbitration', *AJIL*, 101 (2007), 711–59, 722–32.

by the treaty. The credit is an asset of the company in the territory of the host country, a right conferred by the account agreement with the bank and a claim to money. If the credit indeed qualifies as an 'investment' under the investment treaty, the host country has agreed to submit a dispute concerning its seizure of the credit to ICSID arbitration.

The question then arises as to whether the dispute is one falling within the jurisdiction established by the ICSID Convention: whether the term 'investment' has a content under that Convention that is independent from the definition under the investment treaty and, if so, whether such content is narrower than the treaty definition. As outlined in greater detail below, some arbitral decisions have interpreted the term 'investment' in the ICSID Convention as having an autonomous meaning that requires an expectation of gain, a certain duration and a contribution to the development of the host country. The bank credit in the example could well fail this test. A demand deposit account pays no interest; the funds are committed for no defined period of time and can be withdrawn at any moment; and the contribution of such funds to the development of the host country is difficult to quantify.

If this narrower interpretation is applied, a dispute that two Contracting States to the ICSID Convention have agreed is suitable for ICSID arbitration will be denied access to the ICSID forum. With respect to the class of disputes falling within the investment treaty's broad definition of 'investment' but outside the narrower interpretation of the term in the ICSID Convention, the investor–State arbitration provision in the investment treaty will become a pathological clause, one that envisages submitting a dispute to arbitration but fails to do so.

On the other hand, if the term 'investment' in the ICSID Convention is dependent on the definition contained in the investment treaty, the clause is not pathological and ICSID can hear the dispute that the parties have agreed to submit to it.

This chapter examines the meaning of 'investment' in the ICSID Convention and, in particular, considers the significance of that question for investment treaties that call for ICSID arbitration as the sole means of investor–State dispute resolution. In reviewing these issues, this chapter attempts a rigorous application of the Vienna Convention on the Law of Treaties of 1969 (the 'Vienna Convention', or VCLT). By so doing, it hopes to contribute meaningfully to the debate over 'investment' in the ICSID Convention, since to date many arbitral decisions and awards addressing the topic have not applied the VCLT in as thorough a fashion as might otherwise be desired.

We first review the doctrinal debate to which recent jurisprudence has given rise, on the meaning of the term 'investment' in the ICSID Convention. This chapter then undertakes an analysis of that term using the principles set out in Arts. 31 and 32 VCLT. It begins by summarising those principles. It considers the ordinary meaning of the term 'investment', together with the object and purpose of the ICSID Convention. It examines the context of that term, notably in the preamble to the ICSID Convention and the Report of the Executive Directors of the World Bank that transmitted the ICSID Convention to Member States for their consideration. It studies whether investment treaties can be considered either a 'subsequent practice of States' regarding the interpretation of the ICSID Convention, or a 'relevant rule of international law applicable to the relations between' such States. It addresses the preparatory works for the ICSID Convention. And, finally, it considers whether investment treaties calling exclusively for ICSID arbitration may be seen as 'successive treaties relating to the same subject matter' as the ICSID Convention.

Doctrinal debate on ICSID 'investment'

Recent arbitral awards[2] have sparked a renewed and intensified debate among practitioners and scholars of investment treaty arbitration over the definition of the term 'investment' contained in the ICSID Convention.

Although Art. 25(1) of the ICSID Convention grants ICSID jurisdiction over 'any legal dispute arising directly out of an *investment*, between a Contracting State . . . and a national of another contracting State, which the parties to the dispute consent in writing to submit to the Centre', the ICSID Convention does not define the term 'investment'. This absence of a definition did not result from an oversight by the Contracting States,

---

[2] *Patrick Mitchell* v. *The Democratic Republic of Congo*, ICSID Case No. ARB/99/7, Decision on the Application for Annulment of the Award, 1 November 2006 ('*Patrick Mitchell*'); *Malaysian Historical Salvors* v. *Malaysia*, ICSID Case No. ARB/05/10, Award on Jurisdiction, 17 May 2007, 2009; *Biwater Gauff Ltd* v. *Tanzania*, ICSID Case No. ARB/05/22, Award, 24 July 2008 ('*Biwater*'); *Phoenix Action* v. *Czech Republic*, ICSID Case No. ARB/06/5, Award, 15 April 2009, para. 114 ('*Phoenix*'); *Malaysian Historical Salvors* v. *Malaysia*, ICSID Case No. ARB/05/10, Decision on the Application for Annulment, 16 April 2009, para. 62 ('*MHS Annulment*') *Inmaris Perestroika Sailing Maritime Services GmbH and Others* v. *Ukraine*, ICSID Case No. ARB 108/8, Decision on Jurisdiction, 8 March 2010, paras. 129–30 ('*Inmaris*').

but rather from the latter's inability to agree, despite numerous attempts, on a definition.[3] Given 'the essential requirements of consent by the parties, and the mechanism through which Contracting States can make known in advance, if they so desire, the classes of disputes which they would or would not consider submitting to the Centre (Art. 25(4))',[4] the Contracting States opted to dispense with a definition of 'investment'.

Yet this deliberate silence on the part of the drafters has engendered a heated debate as to the proper meaning of the term 'investment' in the ICSID Convention. Faced with respondent States increasingly challenging the jurisdiction of ICSID tribunals on the basis that the investor-claimant failed to make an 'investment' under the ICSID Convention, tribunals have been required to interpret and give meaning to this term so as to determine their jurisdiction to hear a dispute. Professor Walid Ben Hamida helpfully observes that two distinct theories have emerged from the practice of ICSID tribunals: the objective approach, and the subjective one.[5]

---

[3] Manciaux, 'La compétence matérielle', *supra* n. 1, para. 5 ('L'étude des travaux préparatoires de la Convention de Washington démontre en effet que nombre d'États souhaitaient que l'on définisse précisément la notion d'investissement et que ce n'est que faute d'accord entre les États à ce sujet qu'il fut décidé de ne pas en retenir', emphasis added); W. Ben Hamida, 'Two Nebulous ICSID Features. The Notion of Investment and the Scope of Annulment Control', *Journal of International Arbitration*, 24 (2007) 287–306, 288–9 (citing possible explanations for the absence of a definition, including that 'there was a lack of consensus over the definition of the notion of investment among the representatives of the states'); Waibel, 'Opening Pandora's Box', *supra* n. 1, 719 ('During negotiations, various attempts at defining that term failed; this lack of consensus was the primary reason for the Convention's silence on the definition of "investment"'); G. R. Delaume, 'Convention on the Settlement of Investment Disputes Between States and Nationals of Other States', *International Lawyer*, 1 (1966), 64–80, 69–70 (stating that the lack of a definition was the best solution since any definition would have been too broad to serve a useful purpose while a precise formulation would have been inconvenient in that it might have arbitrarily limited the scope of the Convention); R. Dolzer and C. Schreuer, *Principles of International Investment Law* (Oxford University Press, 2008), 61 (stating that the *travaux préparatoires* of the Convention reveal that several attempts to define an 'investment' were made but failed).

[4] Report of the Executive Directors on the Convention on the Settlement of Investment Disputes between States and Nationals of Other States (18 March 1965), para. 27. See also A. Broches, 'The Convention on the Settlement of Investment Disputes. Some Observations on Jurisdiction', *Columbia Journal of Transnational Law*, 5 (1966), 263–80, 268.

[5] For a different approach, see E. Gaillard, 'Identify or Define? Reflections on the Evolution of the Concept of Investment in ICSID Practice', in C. Binder *et al.* (eds.), *International Investment Law for the 21st Century – Essays in Honour of Christoph Schreuer* (Oxford University Press, 2009), 403–16 (analysing the deductive method of defining an investment and the intuitive method of identifying characteristics of an investment); *Romak SA v. Uzbekistan*, PCA Case No. AA280, Award on Jurisdiction, 20 November 2009, para.

The objective theory posits that there is an objective and autonomous definition of investment for purposes of establishing ICSID jurisdiction.[6] The term investment has an 'independent meaning' and sets the 'outer limits' of Art. 25(1) such that any transaction falling outside the scope of these limits would not be deemed an ICSID investment (and thus would not fall within ICSID jurisdiction), irrespective of any agreement between the parties.[7] This line of cases espouses different variations of the so-called *Salini* test, which identifies five elements of an ICSID investment,[8] namely (a) a contribution of money or other assets of economic value, (b) the regular generation of profits and return, (c) a certain duration, (d) an element of risk and (e) a contribution to the host State's development.[9]

In contrast, the subjective theory considers that the term 'investment' in Art. 25(1) of the ICSID Convention does not have an autonomous meaning but rather is 'subjectively defined by the parties when framing

---

197 ('*Romak*') ('Certain arbitral tribunals have taken a "conceptualist" approach and have considered that there exists a definition of investment that entails certain elements which must be present in order to assert jurisdiction *ratione materiae*. Other tribunals have resorted to a more "pragmatic" approach which avoids any generalization, and considers the presence of certain elements typical of investments – even if they are not always present in every investment – to suffice for the purpose of establishing jurisdiction').

[6] Ben Hamida, 'Two Nebulous ICSID Features', *supra* n. 3, 290; Waibel, 'Opening Pandora's Box', *supra* n. 1, 722–32.

[7] Krishan, 'A Notion of ICSID Investment', *supra* n. 1, 3–4; see also N. Rubins, 'The Notion of Investment in International Investment Arbitration', in N. Horn and S. Kröll (eds.), *Arbitrating Foreign Investment Disputes. Procedural and Substantive Legal Aspects* (The Hague and Boston: Kluwer Law International, 2004), 283–324, 289 (stating that the drafters of the Convention consciously established the objective limitations of ICSID jurisdiction as distinct from the issue of consent, in part to prevent investors from using overweening bargaining power to compel small Host States to submit all disputes to ICSID jurisdiction).

[8] Although these five elements are typically referenced as the *Salini* test, it was the *Fedax* Tribunal that first examined the definition of an 'investment' for purposes of ICSID jurisdiction and discerned these five elements. *Fedax NV v. The Republic of Venezuela*, ICSID Case No. ARB/96/3, Decision of the Tribunal on Objections to Jurisdiction, 11 July 1997, para. 43, *ILM*, 37 (1998), 1378 ('*Fedax*').

[9] *Salini Costruttori SpA and Italstrade SpA v. Kingdom of Morocco*, ICSID Case No. ARB/00/4, Decision on Jurisdiction, 23 July 2001, para. 52, *ILM*, 42 (2003), 609 ('*Salini*'); *Joy Mining Machinery Ltd v. Egypt*, ICSID Case No. ARB/03/11, Award on Jurisdiction, 6 August 2004, paras. 49–50; *Saipem SpA v. Bangladesh*, ICSID Case No. ARB/05/07, Decision on Jurisdiction and Recommendation on Provisional Measures, 21 March 2007, para. 99; *Patrick Mitchell, supra* n. 2, para. 31. One Tribunal adapted and modified these five elements into six elements, namely (1) a contribution in money or other assets; (2) a certain duration; (3) an element of risk; (4) an operation made in order to develop an economic activity in the host State; (5) assets invested in accordance with the laws of the host State; and (6) assets invested *bona fide*. *Phoenix, supra* n. 2, para. 114.

their consent to ICSID arbitration'.[10] Notably, many investment treaties concluded in recent years contain a broad asset-based definition of investment ('any kind of asset', 'every kind of asset', or 'all assets'), thereby 'suggesting that the term embraces everything of economic value, virtually without limitation'.[11] Under the subjective theory, if States expressly agree in their investment treaty to characterise a transaction as an investment, then such agreement would govern for purposes of ICSID jurisdiction.[12] Accordingly, whether a claimant has made an 'investment' for purposes of Art. 25(1) of the ICSID Convention would be dependent on and determined by the terms of the instrument consenting to ICSID jurisdiction (here, the bilateral investment treaty).[13] The 'dependent' content of the ICSID term 'investment' is the key under this theory, and it is perhaps more accurate to describe the dialectic here as one between an 'autonomous' meaning of investment and a 'dependent' one, rather than between an 'objective' and 'subjective' reading of that term.[14]

---

[10] Ben Hamida, 'Two Nebulous ICSID Features', *supra* n. 3, 289.

[11] UNCTAD, *International Investment Agreements: Key Issues*, vol I, (Geneva: UNCTAD, 2004), 119. ('UNCTAD Paper'), www.unctad.org/en/docs/iteiit200410_en.pdf. For a narrow interpretation of an asset-based definition of 'investment' in an investment treaty, see *Romak SA* v. *Uzbekistan*, *supra* n. 5. The *Romak* award arrived at that result by considering the ordinary meaning of the term 'investment' in the investment treaty, even though that term had been specifically defined by the treaty parties. See paras. 174, 176–177, 180. By contrast, the UNCTAD Paper and other authorities consider that, where the term 'investment' has been defined by the parties, the relevant ordinary meaning is that of the terms used in the definition (e.g. 'every kind of asset'), and not that of the term defined by the parties (i.e. 'investment'). See also VCLT Art. 31(4).

[12] Krishan, 'A Notion of ICSID Investment', *supra* n. 1, 3. As noted by this commentator, although the parties' consent may expand or limit ICSID jurisdiction, it does not shed light on the meaning of the term 'investment' contained in Art. 25(1) of the ICSID Convention, nor on whether such meaning should be autonomous. He argues that the task of identifying an 'objective definition' of 'investment' falls to the parties of the treaty (i.e. States), not to individual tribunals sitting in cases of particular investor-State disputes (p. 5).

[13] See, e.g., *Lanco International* v. *Argentina*, ICSID Case No. ARB/97/6, Preliminary Decision: Jurisdiction of the Arbitral Tribunal, 8 December 1998, para. 48, *ILM*, 40 (2001), 457, ICSID Case No. ARB/00/9 (2008); *Mihaly International* v. *Sri Lanka*, ICSID Case No. ARB/00/2, Award, 15 March 2002, para. 55 ('*Mihaly*'); *Generation Ukraine* v. *Ukraine*, ICSID Case No. ARB/00/9, Award, 16 September 2003, para. 8.2; *MCI Power Group* v. *Ecuador*, ICSID Case No. ARB/03/6, Award, 31 July 2007, paras. 159–160 ('*MCI Power*'); *Inmaris*, *supra* n. 2, para. 130.

[14] The authors are grateful to Anthea Roberts for suggesting this distinction between 'autonomous' and 'dependent' interpretations.

In contrast to the subjective theory, application of the objective theory may leave an important gap in the remedy intended to be offered by an investment treaty. If the term 'investment' has an autonomous meaning under Art. 25 of the ICSID Convention that is distinct from and narrower than any such meaning ascribed by States in their investment treaties, this may create a situation where an asset would constitute an investment under an investment treaty but not under Art. 25 of the ICSID Convention. In cases where an investment treaty provides *only* for ICSID arbitration as a forum for resolving investor–State disputes, and to the extent that the objective meaning of 'investment' is narrower than the definition in an investment treaty, a potential investor-claimant may have claims against a Contracting State for breaches of an investment treaty but lack any forum in which to seek and obtain a remedy for such breaches.[15]

While an empirical study of all investment treaties containing a broad definition of 'investment' and providing exclusively for ICSID arbitration is beyond the scope of this chapter, anecdotal evidence shows that such treaties are far from rare. It is notable that a model investment treaty adopted for at least some years by each of the following States falls into this category: Burundi, France, Germany, Malaysia and the United Kingdom;[16] examples of such treaties in force include also at least some treaties for Belgium and Luxembourg, The Netherlands, France and Switzerland.[17]

---

[15] It is precisely this concern, *inter alia*, that recently prompted an *Ad Hoc Committee* to annul an ICSID award. *MHS Annulment, supra* n. 2, para. 62 ('It cannot be accepted that the Governments of Malaysia and the United Kingdom concluded a treaty providing for arbitration of disputes arising under it in respect of investments so comprehensively described, with the intention that the only arbitral recourse provided between a Contracting State and a national of another Contracting State, that of ICSID, could be rendered nugatory by a restrictive definition of a deliberately undefined term of the ICSID Convention, namely, "investment," as it is found in the provision of Article 25(1).').

[16] See prototype treaties collected in the UNCTAD International Investment Agreements Compendium, www.unctadxi.org/templates/DocSearch____780.aspx.

[17] See, e.g., Art. 11 of the Agreement between the Belgo-Luxembourg Economic Union and the Government of the Republic of Albania for the Mutual Encouragement and Protection of Investments, 1 February 1999; Art. 7 of the Agreement between the Government of the French Republic and the Government of the Republic of Armenia for the Mutual Encouragement and Protection of Investments, 4 November 1995; Art. 8 of the Agreement between the Government of the French Republic and the Government of the People's Republic of Bangladesh for the Mutual Encouragement and Protection of Investments, 10 September 1985; Art. 9 of the Agreement on Encouragement and

The conjunction of the broad definition of 'investment' in such treaties, their provision for exclusive ICSID Convention jurisdiction and jurisprudence espousing a narrow view of 'investment' in that Convention raises the question of whether application of the VCLT compels this lacuna in protection for the investor-claimant. Rather, could it be said that the treaty interpretation principles enunciated therein, when applied to the ICSID Convention, dictate an autonomous meaning of the term 'investment' that is broader than that delineated by the *Salini* test such that the aforementioned problem dissipates? Alternatively, could it be said that the meaning of 'investment' is dependent on the terms of operative consent to ICSID jurisdiction? Before exploring each of these questions, however, we must first address whether the VCLT applies at all to the ICSID Convention.

Applicability of the VCLT to the ICSID Convention

Art. 4 of the VCLT reflects the rule against the retroactivity of treaties and generally provides for the application of its rules only to treaties concluded after its entry into force. Because the ICSID Convention was concluded in 1965 – four years before the VCLT was adopted – the question of whether the VCLT supplies the appropriate reference point for interpreting the ICSID Convention naturally arises.

The non-retroactivity principle embodied in Art. 4, however, is '[w]ithout prejudice to the application of any rules set forth in the present Convention to which treaties between one or more States ... would be subject under international law independently of the Convention'. If the rules of interpretation of the VCLT reflect or codify customary international law, then the ICSID Convention would be subject to those rules 'independently' of the VCLT.[18]

This prohibition against retroactivity thus depends on the extent to which the relevant provisions of the VCLT are declaratory of customary law rather than representing a progressive development of the law. The International Court of Justice (ICJ) has held that the VCLT's provisions on interpretation of treaties reflect customary international

---

Reciprocal Protection of Investments between the Kingdom of The Netherlands and the People's Republic of Bangladesh, 1 November 1994; Art. 9(6) of the Accord entre la Confédération suisse et la République de Bolivie concernant la promotion et la protection réciproques des investissements, 6 November 1987.

[18] P. V. McDade, 'The Effect of Article 4 of the Vienna Convention on the Law of Treaties 1969', *ICLQ*, 35 (1986), 499–511, 500.

law.[19] The Court's view accords with those of respected commentators from the time the Vienna Convention was adopted[20] and of the United Nations International Law Commission (ILC), which prepared and proposed the text of the Draft Articles on the Law of Treaties in Chapter II of the 1966 Report of the International Law Commission ('Draft ILC Articles'), the preparatory text for the VCLT, which the Conference adopted in significant part. The ILC confirmed that it sought to 'isolate and codify the comparatively few general principles which appear to constitute general rules for the interpretation of treaties'.[21]

Accordingly, the provisions contained in Part III of the VCLT discussed in the pages that follow, namely Arts. 30–33, constitute customary international law that was codified in the VCLT and are therefore applicable to treaties concluded prior thereto, including the ICSID Convention.[22]

---

[19] *Sovereignty over Pulau Ligitan and Pulau Sipadan (Indonesia–Malaysia)*, Judgment, 17 December 2002, ICJ Rep. 2002, 625, 645, para. 37 (noting that, 'in accordance with customary international law, reflected in Articles 31 and 32 of that Convention: a treaty must be interpreted in good faith in accordance with the ordinary meaning to be given to its terms in their context and in the light of its object and purpose. Interpretation must be based above all on the text of the treaty. As a supplementary measure recourse may be had to means of interpretation such as the preparatory work of the treaty and the circumstances of its conclusion') (internal quotation omitted); ('with respect to Article 31, paragraph 3, the Court has had occasion to State that this provision also reflects customary international law').

[20] I. Sinclair, 'Vienna Conference on the Law of Treaties', *ICLQ*, 19 (1970), 47–69, 65–6 (the treaty interpretation principles set out in Arts. 31–33 VCLT, which were adopted by unanimous vote, 'faithfully reflect the preponderant opinion among jurists and practitioners on the relative value to be attached to the various elements of treaty interpretation').

[21] 'Reports of the Commission to the General Assembly', *YB Int'l L. Comm.*, 2 (1966), 187–274, 218–19 ('ILC Commentaries'). Although these ILC records 'are not technically the records of the Vienna diplomatic conference', they were referred by the United Nations General Assembly to the Conference as 'the basic proposal for consideration by the conference'. H. W. Briggs, 'The *Travaux Préparatoires* of the Vienna Convention on the Law of Treaties', *AJIL*, 65 (1971), 705–12, 711–12. Moreover, given that many of the articles of the VCLT 'are identical with those drafted by the Commission, and in most others the changes are relatively minor' – which is the case for Arts. 30–33 VCLT – 'the records of the Commission may, in particular cases, be an indispensable aid in elucidating the terms appearing in the Vienna Convention' (712).

[22] The *Ad Hoc* Committee in *MHS Annulment* reached the same conclusion when it expressly examined this question, finding that it was on 'firm ground in resorting to the customary rules on interpretation of treaties as codified in the Vienna Convention'. *MHS Annulment, supra* n. 2, para. 56. In contrast, although two other ICSID tribunals referenced the VCLT interpretation principles as being relevant to defining the term 'investment' in Art. 25(1) of the ICSID Convention, neither underwent the foregoing

The fact that the International Bank for Reconstruction and Development (IBRD, or World Bank) signed the ICSID Convention and assumed certain obligations thereunder gives rise to another applicability question. If the Bank were to be considered a 'party' to the ICSID Convention (a question addressed further below), the VCLT might not apply since its applicability is generally limited to treaties between States only.[23] However, the VCLT nonetheless applies to 'any treaty which is the constituent instrument of an international organisation and to any treaty adopted within an international organisation without prejudice to any relevant rules of the organisation'.[24] Since the ICSID Convention is both the constituent instrument for ICSID, an international organisation, and was adopted within the World Bank, the VCLT clearly applies to it under this article.

Interpreting the term 'investment' in Art. 25(1) ICSID Convention

The Vienna interpretation principles

The elements of interpretation in Art. 31 VCLT – namely, the ordinary meaning of the terms, the context and the object and purpose of the treaty – 'all relate to the agreement between the parties *at the time when or after it received authentic expression in the text*'.[25] The various elements are set forth in a logical progression, not a hierarchical order, and are intended to be applied as part of a 'single combined operation', consistent with the spirit of the unity of the process of interpretation.[26]

Putting aside the element of 'good faith' interpretation, which is assumed here, the 'ordinary meaning' is not only the 'normal' or 'usual' meaning of the terms,[27] but also encompasses a temporal element. The 'ordinary meaning' generally implies the meaning associated with those terms at the time of the conclusion of the treaty because other approaches

---

analysis on the retroactivity – and thus applicability – of the VCLT in the first place. See *Fedax, supra* n. 8, para. 20; *Patrick Mitchell, supra* n. 2, para. 25.

[23] Art. 1 VCLT ('The present Convention applies to treaties between States'); Art. 3 VCLT (noting '[t]he fact that the present Convention does not apply to international agreements concluded between States and other subjects of international law').

[24] Art. 5 VCLT.

[25] ILC Commentaries, *supra* n. 21, 220 (emphasis in original).   [26] *Ibid.*, 219–20.

[27] M. K. Yasseen, 'L'interprétation des traités d'après la Convention de Vienne sur le droit des traités', *RdC*, 151 (1976), 26 (1978).

could result in a meaning not intended by the drafters.[28] Alternatively, a context specific to a treaty – for example, one that establishes an international organisation or that uses legal terms of art – can indicate an intent for a more dynamic approach to treaty interpretation: one that supports the notion that such a term or such a treaty should evolve over time to keep pace with developing norms of international law or the needs of the Member States of the organisation.[29]

The 'ordinary meaning' of treaty terms also must be discerned in light of the treaty's 'object and purpose', which are usually set out in the preamble. In the event the treaty is silent in this regard, the entire text and its context will shed light on the treaty's object and purpose.[30]

With respect to the 'context' of the terms of a treaty, Art. 31(2) sets out the various elements that form part of such context – namely, the text with its preamble and annexes, any related agreement made by all parties in connection with the conclusion of the treaty, and any instrument made by one or more parties in connection with the conclusion of the treaty and accepted by the other parties to it. Thus, each treaty provision must be read in such context so as to discern its meaning.[31] To the extent that the preamble might give rise to a meaning incompatible with the provisions of the treaty, however, such meaning may not be

---

[28] *Ibid.*, 26–7.

[29] *Ibid.*, 66–7 ('[Certaines catégories de traités] peuvent *de par leur nature* se prêter à une interprétation évolutive, notamment les traités normatifs qui énoncent des règles de droit et surtout les traités de codification et de développement progressif de droit international . . . Quant aux termes qui visent des concepts juridiques, c'est encore le traité qui en fait l'usage qui détermine si ces termes désignent un concept figé, immuable ou un concept évolutif'); B. Fassbender, *UN Security Council Reform and the Right of Veto. A Constitutional Perspective* (The Hague: Kluwer Law International, 1998), 131–2 ('A constitution, we argued, typically emancipates itself from the forces that brought it about. To use judge Alvarez' wonderful metaphor, constitutions "can be compared to ships which leave the yards in which they have been built, and sail away independently, no longer attached to the dockyard" [*Reservations to the Genocide Convention*, Adv. Op., 1951 ICJ Reports 15, 53 (Alvarez, J., dissenting)]. Hence, an interpretation based on the original will of the parties ("static-subjective interpretation") is inappropriate. It would unduly . . . impede the solution of contemporary problems. Instead, an interpretation of a [UN] Charter provision must aim at establishing, at the time of interpretation, its objective meaning in the light of the concrete circumstances of the case in question, thus taking account of the dynamic character and inherent incompleteness of any constitution'); *Dispute Regarding Navigational and Related Matters (Costa Rica v. Nicaragua)*, Judgment, 13 July 2009, para. 63 (quoted and discussed *infra* n. 93 and accompanying text).

[30] Yasseen, 'L'interprétation des traités', *supra* n. 27, 57.

[31] *Ibid.*, 34. See generally *ibid.*, 34–6.

maintained.[32] The remaining contextual elements in the form of an agreement or instrument made by the parties must be related to the treaty and must be made at the time of its conclusion so as to be taken into account in the interpretation of the treaty.[33]

Together with the context, Art. 31(3) VCLT also looks to any subsequent agreement between the parties regarding the interpretation or application of the treaty, any subsequent practice in the application thereof, and any relevant rules of international law applicable between the parties. The subsequent practice of States in applying a treaty is particularly enlightening 'for it constitutes objective evidence of the understanding of the parties as to the meaning of the treaty'[34] and represents a means of 'authentic interpretation' of a treaty, independent of the clarity (or lack thereof) of its terms.[35] However, although such practice should be 'agreed, shared and consistent',[36] it will only be binding on those States that have engaged in such practice.[37] A State that has not engaged in, nor objected to, the practice nonetheless may be deemed to have acquiesced or silently approved such practice. In all events, the applicable rules of international law at the time of a treaty's

---

[32] *Ibid.*, 35. See *ADF Group, Inc.* v. *United States of America*, ICSID Case No. ARB(AF)/00/01, Award, 9 January 2003, para. 147 ('We understand the rules of interpretation found in customary international law to enjoin us to focus first on the actual language of the provision being construed ... The provision under examination must of course be scrutinized in context; but that context is constituted chiefly by the other relevant provisions of NAFTA. We do not suggest that the general objectives of NAFTA are not useful or relevant. Far from it. Those general objectives may be conceived of as partaking of the nature of lex generalis while a particular detailed provision set in a particular context in the rest of a Chapter or Part of NAFTA functions as lex specialis. The former may frequently cast light on a specific interpretive issue; but it is not to be regarded as overriding and superseding the latter'); cf. *Oil Platforms (Islamic Republic of Iran* v. *United States of America)*, 1996 ICJ Rep. 803, 814, 12 December 1996 (rejecting argument that the United States had breached an article of the treaty providing that 'there shall be firm and enduring peace and sincere friendship' between the parties, holding that the aforementioned article 'must be regarded as fixing an objective, in light of which the other Treaty provisions are to be interpreted and applied', but could not be the basis on which a breach of the treaty might be found).

[33] Yasseen, 'L'interprétation des traités', *supra* n. 27, 37–8. See also I. Sinclair, *The Vienna Convention on the Law of Treaties*, 2nd edn. (Manchester University Press, 1984), 129 (stating that the agreement or instrument should be related to the treaty, concerned with the substance of the treaty and with clarifying certain concepts in the treaty or limiting its field or application, and must be equally drawn up on the occasion of the conclusion of the treaty).

[34] ILC Commentaries, *supra* n. 21, 221.

[35] Yasseen, 'L'interprétation des traités', *supra* n. 27, 49.   [36] *Ibid.*, 48.   [37] *Ibid.*, 52.

interpretation – which may arise from another treaty, customary international law, or general legal principles – will apply.[38]

Once the application of the interpretation principles set out in Art. 31 VCLT yields a meaning, reference may nonetheless be made to the 'preparatory work of the treaty and the circumstances of its conclusion' either to confirm such meaning or, if such meaning is 'ambiguous', 'obscure', or leads to a result that is 'manifestly absurd or unreasonable', to determine the meaning.[39] Although the probative value of preparatory works has been called into question,[40] it was nonetheless included in the treaty interpretation principles because it was recognised that, in practice, international tribunals and States have recourse to subsidiary means of interpretation, such as preparatory works, not only when the interpretation principles fail to yield a clear meaning but also to confirm such meaning, both of which are reflected in Art. 32 VCLT.[41]

Finally, Art. 33 VCLT applies to the interpretation of treaties authenticated in two or more languages. Although the plurality of texts 'may be a serious additional source of ambiguity or obscurity in the terms of the treaty', it may also facilitate the interpretation of treaties by providing a clear and convincing meaning in one language that is lacking in another language.[42] That being said, the existence of a treaty in multiple languages does not change the fact that only a single treaty exists with a single set of terms subject to the aforementioned

---

[38] *Ibid.*, 63.   [39] Art. 32 VCLT.

[40] See, e.g., ILC Commentaries, *supra* n. 21, 220 ('it is beyond question that the records of treaty negotiations are in many cases incomplete or misleading, so that considerable discretion has to be exercised in determining their value as an element of interpretation'); Yasseen, 'L'interprétation des traités', *supra* n. 27, 85–6 ('il est à remarquer que l'obscurité du texte trouve souvent son origine dans les travaux préparatoires. D'ailleurs cette obscurité peut n'être que le résultat d'une situation qui n'a pas été clarifiée ou n'a pu être clarifiée lors des négociations ... Et puis les comptes rendus des séances d'une conférence ne reflètent pas toujours fidèlement ce qui s'est passé ... Tout cela démontre combien il est illusoire souvent de compter sur les travaux préparatoires pour apporter au texte la clarté qui lui fait défaut. La plus grande prudence s'impose donc dans le recours aux travaux préparatoires').

[41] ILC Commentaries, *supra* n. 21, 223. See also *MHS Annulment*, *supra* n. 2, para. 57 ('In any event, courts and tribunals interpreting treaties regularly review the *travaux préparatoires* whenever they are brought to their attention; it is mythological to pretend that they do so only when they first conclude that the term requiring interpretation is ambiguous or obscure').

[42] ILC Commentaries, *supra* n. 21, 225.

interpretation principles.[43] In practice, the equality of the texts means that every reasonable effort should be made to find a 'common meaning for the texts before preferring one to another' and 'to ascertain the intention of the parties by recourse to the normal means of interpretation'.[44]

Applying the Vienna interpretation principles to the ICSID Convention

The application of these interpretation principles should thus lead to a meaning of the undefined term 'investment' in Art. 25(1) of the ICSID Convention.

Ordinary meaning: object and purpose

Turning to the ordinary meaning of the term 'investment' at the time that the ICSID Convention was concluded, a dictionary roughly contemporaneous with the ICSID Convention defined 'investment' in most pertinent part as follows:

> 1 a: an expenditure of money for income or profit or to purchase something of intrinsic value : capital outlay . . . 2: the commitment of funds with a view to minimizing risk and safeguarding capital while earning a return – contrasted with *speculation* 3: the commitment of something other than money to a long-term interest or project.[45]

Similarly, contemporaneous dictionary definitions of the French term '*investissement*' and the Spanish term '*inversión*' in the authentic text of Art. 25(1) of the ICSID Convention in those languages are '[p]lacer des fonds./Investir des capitaux dans une entreprise' and 'hablando [de caudales] emplearlos en aplicaciones productivas'.[46] It also appears that, by the mid-twentieth century, an increasingly common form of foreign investment was in the form of equity stock in companies, particularly in the primary sector (e.g. concession agreements for natural

---

[43] *Ibid.* [44] *Ibid.*

[45] *Webster's Third New International Dictionary* (Springfield, MA: Webster–Merriam, 1971), vol. II, 1190 (emphasis in original).

[46] *Petit Larousse Illustré* (Paris: Librarie Larousse, 1968), 555 ('INVESTIR: Placer des fonds./Investir des capitaux dans une entreprise . . . INVESTISSEMENT: Nouveau moyen de production./Placement des fonds'); *Diccionario General Ilustrado de la Lengua Española* (Barcelona: SPES, 1953) ('inversión: acción y efecto de invertir . . . invertir: hablando [de caudales] emplearlos en aplicaciones productivas').

resource extraction), with the protection thereof becoming 'an increasing concern of foreign investment law'.[47]

Thus, based on dictionaries contemporary with the ICSID Convention, the ordinary meaning of 'investment' is both broad and consistent with (1) a notion of investment that 'has changed over time as the nature of international economic relations has changed' and today generally is accepted to encompass such intangible assets as intellectual property,[48] and (2) the findings of several ICSID tribunals that the absence of a definition of the term 'investment' in the ICSID Convention was intended to preserve a certain amount of flexibility as to its content and to leave it to the consent of the parties to determine the parameters thereof.[49]

The ordinary meaning of the term 'investment' must also be viewed in light of the object and purpose of the Convention. The Preamble indicates that the primary object and purpose of the Convention is to respond to 'the need for international cooperation for economic development, and the role of private international investment therein' by providing 'facilities for international conciliation or arbitration to which Contracting States and nationals of other Contracting States may submit such disputes if they so desire'. Such object and purpose give the term 'investment' a dimension of international economic development and of promotion of effective dispute resolution facilities that does not necessarily emerge from dictionary definitions.[50] What

---

[47] UNCTAD, *International Investment Agreements, supra* n. 11, 116.

[48] *Ibid.* 115. See also G. R. Delaume, 'ICSID Clauses. Some Drafting Problems', *News from ICSID*, 1 (1984), 19 ('This lack of definition, which was deliberate, has enabled the Convention to accommodate both traditional types of investment in the form of capital contributions and new types of investment, including service contracts and transfers of technology').

[49] See, e.g., *Fedax, supra* n. 8, paras. 21–22; *Mihaly, supra* n. 13, para. 33 ('the definition was left to be worked out in the subsequent practice of States, thereby preserving its integrity and flexibility and allowing for future progressive development of international law on the topic of investment'); *MCI Power, supra* n. 13, paras. 159–160; *Biwater, supra* n. 2, para. 316.

[50] According to Christoph Schreuer, the 'only possible indication of an objective meaning that can be gleaned from the Convention is contained in the Preamble's first sentence . . . This declared purpose of the Convention is confirmed by the Report of the Executive Directors which points out that the Convention was "prompted by the desire to strengthen the partnership between countries in the cause of economic development."' C. H. Schreuer, *The ICSID Convention. A Commentary* (Oxford University Press, 2005), 124–5. See *also* E. Schlemmer, 'Investment, Investor, Nationality and Shareholders', in P. Muchlinski, F. Ortino, and C. H. Schreuer (eds.), *The Oxford Handbook of*

constitutes economic development and effective dispute resolution in this context is likely to evolve over time and, with it, the types of investments implicated. The ICSID Convention's object and purpose thus tends to support a meaning of 'investment' that evolves over time.

The context

The context of the term 'investment' also strongly suggests a more 'dependent' meaning of the provision. The relevant context for these purposes includes the Preamble to the Convention and, as compelling arguments suggest, the Report of the Executive Directors of the World Bank.

First, the Preamble of the ICSID Convention injects a certain fluidity and flexibility into the term 'investment'. As a preliminary matter, other than in the full name of ICSID and in Art. 25(1), the term 'investment' only appears in a handful of provisions of the ICSID Convention: the first two clauses of the Preamble and Art. 1(2) establishing the purpose of the Centre, none of which provides a definition of the term. Yet, as noted above, the Preamble acknowledges the role of private international investment in international cooperation for economic development and the need for a forum for resolving investment disputes that arise from time to time. This aspect of the context suggests that the meaning of the term 'investment' should be flexible and capable of evolving with changing times and development and dispute resolution needs.

Second, the Report of the Executive Directors of the World Bank, which accompanied the ICSID Convention, strongly suggests that the meaning of 'investment' should be informed in significant part by the terms of the consent of the disputing parties to submit the dispute to ICSID arbitration. In describing Art. 25(1) of the ICSID Convention, the Report first emphasises that '[c]onsent of the parties is the cornerstone of the jurisdiction of the Centre'.[51] On the content of the term 'investment' in Art. 25(1), the Report States as follows:

> No attempt was made to define the term 'investment' given the essential requirement of consent by the parties, and the mechanism through which Contracting States can make known in advance, if they so desire, the

International Investment Law (Oxford University Press, 2008), 49–88, 64–5 (stating that the only limiting factor should be the first preamble sentence of ICSID which speaks of 'the need for *international* co-operation for *economic development* and the role of *private international investment* therein', emphasis in the original).

[51] Report of the Executive Directors, para. 23.

classes of disputes which they would or would not consider submitting to the Centre (Art. 25(4)).[52]

The Report thus suggests a conscious decision *not* to provide the term 'investment' with independent content, but to leave this element to determination by the will of the disputing parties in formulating their individual consent to submit the dispute to ICSID arbitration. An emphasis on the will of the parties also follows from the reference to the mechanism of Art. 25(4) of the ICSID Convention, through which States may indicate their intention not to submit certain classes of disputes to ICSID jurisdiction. The Report thus provides substantial evidence supporting the dependent, rather than the autonomous, definition of the term 'investment'.

The question then arises as to the status of the Report in the hierarchy of sources for treaty interpretation set out in Arts. 31 and 32 of the VCLT. We are persuaded that the Report forms part of the context under Art. 31 (2) VCLT for the reasons that follow.

As a preliminary matter, we respectfully disagree with the suggestion that the Report forms part of the *travaux préparatoires* of the ICSID Convention.[53] Because the Report was not prepared until *after* the text of the ICSID Convention was finalised, it cannot fairly be viewed as a *preparatory* work to the Convention. There was nothing left to prepare at that point. Indeed, the Report itself effectively confirms this point by describing the preparatory work that led to the adoption of the text of the Convention.[54]

In our view, the Report more naturally falls under Art. 31(2) VCLT, which provides as follows:

> The context for the purpose of the interpretation of a treaty shall comprise, in addition to the text, including its preamble and annexes:
> (a) any agreement relating to the treaty which was made between all the parties in connection with the conclusion of the treaty;

---

[52] *Ibid.*, para. 27. Our view is that the phrase 'no attempt was made to define the term "investment"' refers to the absence of a definition of the term in the ICSID Convention, not to the lack of effort by the drafters to reach (unsuccessfully) a shared definition.

[53] C. F. Amerasinghe, *Jurisdiction of International Tribunals* (The Hague: Kluwer Law International, 2002), 301 ('The Report of the Executive Directors on the [ICSID] Convention may be regarded as part of the *travaux préparatoires* to which parties to the Convention subscribe when they sign and ratify the Convention').

[54] See The Report of the Executive Directors, *supra* n. 53, para. 3.

(b) any instrument which was made by one or more parties in connection with the conclusion of the treaty and accepted by the other parties as an instrument related to the treaty.

The Report clearly was made in connection with the conclusion of the treaty and is an instrument or an agreement related to the treaty. The more difficult question is whether it can be considered to have been made 'between all the parties' or 'by one or more parties' in this connection. While the answer is not free from doubt, in our opinion the better view is that it is.

There are essentially two theories on which such a conclusion could be based. The first is that the IBRD (the Bank) may be considered a party to the ICSID Convention, and the Report was made by the Bank and accepted by the other parties as related to the ICSID Convention. Although it is not difficult to view a document unanimously adopted by the Bank's Executive Directors as one 'made by' the Bank, the more difficult question is whether the Bank can be viewed as a 'party'.

As stated in the ultimate clause of the ICSID Convention, the Bank signed the Convention and 'indicated by its signature . . . its agreement to fulfil the functions with which it is charged under this Convention'. In addition to acting as a depository for the Convention, those functions included making available the facilities from which ICSID was to operate and making available its President to serve as the Chairman of ICSID's Administrative Council and to perform certain important tasks such as appointing arbitrators, among others.[55] As an entity that signed the Convention and obligated itself in specific respects, the Bank could be argued to be a party to the Convention.

On the other hand, while having some intuitive appeal, this contention fits with the definitional structure of neither the ICSID Convention nor the VCLT. The ICSID Convention conceives of the 'Contracting States' as its parties; clearly the Bank does not fit this category. The VCLT also defines the term 'party' in terms of States, which is hardly surprising given its scope as a convention addressing treaties between States.[56]

The second theory is that the Executive Directors, in adopting the Report, did so as representatives of the Member States of the Bank and the Report therefore either reflects an 'agreement relating to the treaty which was made between all the parties in connection with the

---

[55] Arts. 3, 5, 38, ICSID Convention.   [56] Art. 2(1)(g) VCLT.

conclusion of the treaty' or constitutes an 'instrument' along the same lines. There is, in our view, substantial support for this proposition.

In the Bank, Member States are represented by Governors, each of whom is appointed by his or her respective Member State.[57] The Board of Governors may delegate to the Executive Directors the authority to perform a number of acts, with limited exceptions not applicable here.[58] As noted in the Report, by Resolution dated 10 September 1964, the Board of Governors requested the Executive Directors 'to formulate a convention establishing facilities and procedures which would be available on a voluntary basis for the settlement of investment disputes between contracting States and Nationals of other contracting States through conciliation and arbitration'.[59] The Board also directed that '[t]he Executive Directors shall submit the text of such a convention to member governments with such recommendations as they shall deem appropriate'.[60] The Board, and the member governments represented on the Board, thus delegated to the Executive Directors of the Bank the authority to adopt the text of the ICSID Convention, and to submit that text to member governments 'with such recommendations as they shall deem appropriate'.

The process resolved by the Governors may be seen as analogous to that of a multilateral conference convened for the purpose of adopting the text of a convention for subsequent approval by States. The Executive Directors were delegated the authority to adopt the text of the ICSID Convention, within the internal framework of the Bank's procedures.[61] The Executive Directors' role resembles that of representatives of States accredited to an international conference for the purpose of adopting a proposed multilateral convention, within the framework of procedures established by the conference. The Report thus may be seen as analogous, if not equivalent, to 'the Final Act of a conference incorporating the text' of the treaty adopted at that conference, and thereby establishing that text as 'authentic and definitive' within the meaning of Art. 10 VCLT.[62] As noted above, the resolution of the Board of Governors authorised the Executive Directors not only to adopt the text of the Convention but also to forward it, with their recommendations, to Member States for consideration. The Governors therefore may be seen

---

[57] See Articles of Association of the Bank, Article V, sec. 2(a).

[58] See *ibid.* Article V, sec. 2(b).

[59] See The Report of the Executive Directors, *supra* n. 53, para. 1 (quoting Resolution No. 214 of 10 September 1964).

[60] *Ibid.*   [61] Art. 7(2) and Art. 9(1) VCLT.   [62] Art. 10 VCLT.

to have authorised the Directors to issue the Report. The Report may therefore be seen as reflecting an 'agreement relating to the treaty which was made between all parties' within the meaning of Art. 31(2)(a) VCLT, or, at a minimum, an 'instrument which was made by one or more parties ... and accepted by the other parties as an instrument related to the treaty' within the meaning of Art. 31(2)(b).[63]

This conclusion is reinforced by the similar status given to similar instruments in international law. For example, Draft Protocols to the European Convention of Human Rights are accompanied by an Explanatory Report of the Ministers' Deputies who approve the text of the draft and submit it for adoption to the Committee of Ministers. These explanatory reports are considered by both commentators and the European Court of Human Rights (ECHR) as part of the context of the treaty, and not as a secondary source for interpretation.[64]

We conclude that the Report of the Executive Directors should be considered part of the context of Art. 25(1) of the ICSID Convention, and on the same plane as the text of the Convention, including its preamble. That Report, in turn, strongly supports a dependent interpretation of the term 'investment' in Art. 25(1), in accordance with the subjective approach taken by some of the jurisprudence on that term.

Subsequent practice

As 'objective evidence' of the Contracting States' understanding of the meaning of the term 'investment', the subsequent practice of States that can be deemed 'agreed, shared and consistent' may properly be 'taken into account' in interpreting a treaty's text, under Art. 31(3)(b) VCLT.[65] Recent scholarship has highlighted the importance of subsequent practice in

---

[63] As the Chairman of the Drafting Committee that adopted Arts. 31–33 VCLT noted, there is no requirement that an 'agreement' within the meaning of Art. 31(2) be labelled as such or take any particular form; he mentions a United Nations General Assembly resolution adopting a treaty text as an example of such an agreement. See Yasseen, 'L'interprétation des traités', *supra* n. 27, 38–9.

[64] See Sinclair, *The Vienna Convention*, *supra* n. 33, 129; *Kozacıoğlu v. Turkey* ECHR, Application No. [GC], No. 2334/03, para. 32, Judgement of 19 February 2009 (including the explanatory report as an integral part in describing the relevant law applicable to the case: 'the Council of Europe Framework Convention on the Value of Cultural Heritage for Society, adopted on 27 October 2005, and its Explanatory Report').

[65] ILC Commentaries, *supra* n. 21, 221; Yasseen, 'L'interprétation des traités', *supra* n. 27, 48. It should be noted that the application of Art. 31(3) VCLT presupposes that another treaty is compatible with the ICSID Convention; to the extent that this may not be the case, Art. 30 VCLT would then become relevant to the interpretation analysis.

international investment law.[66] While we have considered other sources of subsequent State practice in the application of the ICSID Convention as potentially relevant,[67] our view is that State practice agreeing to investment treaties providing exclusively for ICSID arbitration is the most relevant of such sources to the question under consideration.

The instruments in which States have consented to submit 'investment' disputes to ICSID jurisdiction (i.e. investment treaties) contain specific definitions of the term 'investment'. Looking across investment treaties for any particular State or, if applicable, at a model bilateral investment treaty prepared by a State,[68] a consistent definition of this term will often emerge as a reflection of a State's deliberate policy in this regard. If, in turn, a number of States were found consistently to use a similar definition of 'investment', such a definition could be said to constitute State practice for – and to be binding on – these given States.[69]

This form of State practice could be particularly enlightening and persuasive in cases where investment treaties provide only for ICSID

---

[66] A. Roberts, 'Rethinking the Interpretation of Investment Treaties. The Dual Role of States', *AJIL*, 104 (2010).

[67] State practice might express itself through Art. 25(4) of the ICSID Convention, pursuant to which a State may notify the Centre of certain classes of disputes that it wishes to exclude from ICSID jurisdiction. However, the manner and extent to which a State may avail itself of this mechanism offers limited insight into the content of the term 'investment' under the ICSID Convention. Indeed, although this provision clearly affords a State control over the types of disputes that it may choose to subject to ICSID jurisdiction, it remains a matter of State consent rather than one of autonomous meaning of the term 'investment'. Cf. Broches, 'The Convention', *supra* n. 4, 266, 268 ('the requirement that the dispute must have arisen out of an "investment" may be merged into the requirement of consent to jurisdiction. Presumably, the parties' agreement that a dispute is an "investment dispute" will be given great weight in any determination of the Centre's jurisdiction, although it would not be controlling'). At most, by availing itself of this provision, a State can signal the types of disputes – and, potentially investments (depending on the specific wording of the exclusion) – that it deems to fall within the scope of ICSID consent, thereby necessitating an express exclusion. To date, only seven States have availed themselves of this provision. The classes of disputes identified by these States, however, are such that no consistent State practice can be said to have emerged in this regard. See, e.g., Guatemala's exclusion of disputes arising from a compensation claim against the State for damages due to armed conflicts or civil disturbances, or Jamaica's exclusion of disputes arising directly out of an investment relating to minerals or other natural resources, see Contracting States and Measures Taken by Them for the Purpose of the Convention, ICSID, April 2008.

[68] See US Model BIT 2004 and Norwegian Model BIT 2007, both of which import a *Salini*-type test to investor–State arbitration irrespective of the forum by requiring that the asset 'have the characteristics of an investment, such as the commitment of capital or other resources, the expectation of gain or profit, or the assumption of risk'.

[69] See Krishan, 'A Notion of ICSID Investment', *supra* n. 1, 8.

jurisdiction (as opposed to various arbitration fora in addition to ICSID). Established principles of treaty interpretation suggest that, in conferring various protections to their nationals under international law and providing for ICSID arbitration of disputes concerning those protections, States intended for the ICSID arbitration provision of such treaties to be *effective* with respect to the full range of disputes covered by the consent to ICSID jurisdiction expressed therein.[70] In other words, there is little basis for considering that such States intended for there to be a gap between the definition of 'investment' under the investment treaty and the content of that same term in the ICSID Convention, given that the Convention was chosen as the sole means for resolving investment disputes under the treaty. Such treaties can therefore fairly be viewed as reflecting a subsequent practice in the application of the ICSID Convention that evidences an agreement at least by the States Parties to such treaties that ICSID Convention jurisdiction extends to a broad range of 'investment disputes'.

As previously noted, while a comprehensive review of all investment treaties in effect is far beyond the scope of this chapter, preliminary consideration of model investment treaties elaborated by a range of States suggests that there are a substantial number of treaties in force that provide only for ICSID resolution of disputes concerning 'investments' as defined by such treaties. Notably, model treaties published by Burundi, France, Germany, Malaysia and the United Kingdom, among others, either provide only for ICSID arbitration, or provide for it as the exclusive means of resolution of investor–State disputes under the treaty in the event that the Convention has entered into force for both State Parties to the investment treaty in question.[71] Each of these models provides for a broad definition of investment, most covering 'any kind of asset'.[72] To return to the example provided at the beginning of this chapter, each of these model treaties arguably would cover a demand

---

[70] See *Territorial Dispute (Libya v. Chad)*, 1994 ICJ Rep. 6, para. 51 (collecting authorities supporting 'one of the fundamental principles of interpretation of treaties, consistently upheld by international jurisprudence, namely that of effectiveness'); *Accord Anglo-Iranian Oil Co. (UK v. Iran)*, 1952 ICJ Rep. 93, 105 (the principle 'that a legal text should be interpreted in such a way that a reason and a meaning can be attributed to every word in the text ... should in general be applied when interpreting the text of a treaty'); *Corfu Channel (UK v. Albania)*, 1949 ICJ Rep. 4, 24 ('It would indeed be incompatible with the generally accepted rules of interpretation to admit that a provision of this sort occurring in a special agreement should be devoid of purport or effect').

[71] See *supra* n. 16 and accompanying text.

[72] France: Art. 1 (1) *UNCTAD International Investment Agreements Compendium*, vol. III, 159; Germany: Art. 1 (1), *ibid.*, vol. III, 167–8, Art. 1 (1), *ibid.*, vol. VII, 297; Malaysia:

deposit account and contemplate ICSID arbitration as the means for resolving disputes concerning such an asset.

In short, the practice of States in entering into investment treaties with broad definitions of 'investment' and calling exclusively for ICSID arbitration of disputes concerning investments so defined can fairly be viewed as a 'subsequent practice in the application of the treaty which establishes the agreement of the parties regarding its interpretation',[73] at least with respect to the States entering into such investment treaties.

The question then remains of whether the prevalence of such investment treaties – those providing both a broad definition of 'investment' and exclusively for ICSID arbitration of disputes concerning such 'investments' – is sufficiently 'agreed, shared and consistent' to reflect a subsequent practice of *all* Contracting States to the ICSID Convention. Responding to such a question with empirical evidence (i.e. a cross-referencing of ICSID Contracting States and parties to investment treaties with such characteristics) is beyond the scope of the present chapter. However, our initial assessment is that it is indeed possible that most if not all ICSID Contracting States are also parties to investment treaties containing a broad definition of 'investment' and providing exclusively for ICSID arbitration. If this assessment is proven correct, a general 'subsequent practice' may have emerged among ICSID Contracting States that 'shall be taken into account' under Art. 31(3) VCLT.

Relevant rules of international law

Art. 31(3)(c) also requires a treaty interpreter to 'take into account ... any relevant rules of international law applicable in the relations between the parties'. According to at least one respected commentary on the VCLT, this provision applies both to conventional obligations (such as investment treaties) as well as to obligations established under customary international law.[74] The drafting history of this provision of the VCLT leaves little doubt that it was intended to include both rules of international law existing at the time of the

---

Art. 1 (1), *ibid.*, vol. V, 309; Burundi: Art. 1 (4), *ibid.*, vol. IX, 288; United Kingdom: Art. 1 (1), *ibid.*, vol. III, 185.

[73] Art. 31(3)(b) VCLT.

[74] Sinclair, *The Vienna Convention, supra* n. 33, 139 ('But what does this reference to "relevant rules of international law" mean? Every treaty provision must be read not only in its own context, but in the wider context of general international law, *whether conventional or customary*') (emphasis added).

conclusion of the treaty and those developed or agreed between the parties thereafter.[75]

Thus, on its face this provision of the VCLT would accept the relevance of subsequent treaty practice concerning the content of 'investment' in the ICSID Convention, such as the definitions of that term in investment treaties providing only for ICSID arbitration. However, Art. 31(3)(c) is limited to rules applicable in the relations between the parties to a treaty – presumably, its ambit is limited to rules applicable in the relations between *all* parties. For the ICSID Convention, it would appear to require that each of the 140 Contracting States be a party to at least one ICSID-only investment treaty with a broad definition for investment for this rule to come into play.[76] As noted above, it may be the case that each such Contracting State is a party to such a treaty, but such an empirical study is beyond the scope of the present chapter.

Preparatory works

Finally, as mentioned above, the *travaux préparatoires* of the ICSID Convention show that several attempts were made to define the term 'investment'. The First Draft introduced a definition of investment as 'any contribution of money or other assets of economic value for an indefinite period or, if the period be defined, for not less than five years'.[77] This

---

[75] Commentary of draft Art. 27 §3c), *Yearbook of the ILC* (1966), vol. II, 222 ('On re-examining the provision, the Commission considered that the formula used in the 1964 text ["in the light of the general rules of international law *in force at the time of its conclusion*"] was unsatisfactory, since it covered only partially the question of the so-called intertemporal law in its application to the interpretation of treaties and might, in consequence, lead to misunderstanding. It also considered that, in any event, the relevance of rules of international law for the interpretation of treaties in any given case was *dependent on the intentions of the parties*, and that to attempt to formulate a rule covering comprehensively the temporal element would present difficulties. It further considered that correct application of the temporal element would normally be indicated by *interpretation of the term in good faith*') (emphasis added).

[76] An argument could be advanced that the broad definition of 'investment' is sufficiently common that it has entered into customary international law. But *Glamis Gold* v. *United States of America* explains why it is difficult for bilateral treaty obligations to crystallise into a rule of customary international law, *Glamis Gold.* v. *United States of America*, NAFTA Award, 8 June 2009, paras. 598–618. It is even more difficult to imagine that a *definition* in a bilateral treaty which, on its own, ordinarily sets out no obligation whatsoever, could be viewed as reflecting a general and consistent practice of States followed with a sense of obligation.

[77] Schreuer, *The ICSID Convention*, *supra* n. 50, 122. Other attempts included the following proposed definitions: 'the acquisition of (i) property rights or contractual rights (including rights under a concession) for the establishment or in the conduct of an industrial, commercial, agricultural, financial or service enterprise; (ii) participations or shares in

proposed definition attracted criticism, *inter alia*, as being 'unsatisfactory' by lacking in precision and for introducing a specific time element.[78] Some counterproposals 'emphasised aspects of money and profit, property rights or the host State's interest in development',[79] even seeking to introduce a quantitative limit so as to exclude investments falling below a certain level.[80] Yet, ultimately, no definition was adopted. As noted above, the Report of the Executive Directors eventually acknowledged that in the final text 'no attempt was made to define the term "investment"'.[81] The drafters of the ICSID Convention thus explicitly contemplated various definitions of the term 'investment', but deliberately chose to be silent in this regard.

In any event, in light of the various possible definitions of 'investment' proposed by the drafters, it cannot be said that the *travaux préparatoires* confirm – much less clarify – the meaning of this term.[82]

Investment treaties as successive treaties of the ICSID Convention

For the sake of completeness, we also consider here one other theory to which the definition of 'investment' contained in investment treaties calling for ICSID arbitration could be relevant – namely, that these investment treaties could be considered 'successive treaties relating to the same subject matter' within the meaning of Art. 30 VCLT.[83]

As a preliminary matter, we have little difficulty in concluding that a later investment treaty calling for ICSID arbitration can be considered a successive treaty 'relating to the same subject matter' as the ICSID Convention for purposes of Art. 30 – namely the promotion of foreign direct investments (FDI) and effective dispute resolution mechanisms. We believe such is the case for several reasons. First, a variation of the first clause of the Preamble of the ICSID Convention[84] consistently appears in the preamble of investment treaties, thereby not only echoing

---

any such enterprise; or (iii) financial obligations of a public or private entity other than obligations rising out of short term banking or credit facilities' (121–5).

[78] *Ibid.*, 122.   [79] *Ibid.* (internal references omitted).   [80] *Ibid.*, 123.

[81] The Report of the Executive Directors, *supra* n. 53, para. 27.

[82] Yasseen, 'L'interprétation des traités', *supra* n. 27, 85–6 ('il est à remarquer que l'-obscurité du texte trouve souvent son origine dans les travaux préparatoires. D'ailleurs cette obscurité peut n'être que le résultat d'une situation qui n'a pas été clarifiée ou n'a pu être clarifiée lors des négociations').

[83] Art. 30 VCLT.

[84] 'Considering the need for international cooperation for economic development, and the role of private international investment therein'.

but also implementing and furthering the same strategic goals that motivated the drafters of the ICSID Convention.[85] Second, the terminology and types of provisions contained in investment treaties (e.g. investment, nationality of investors, consent) again echo the ICSID Convention, thereby evidencing a continuation – indeed, a succession – as between the two. Third, both investment treaties and the ICSID Convention contain provisions for a dispute resolution mechanism in investor–State disputes. Fourth, when an investment treaty calls for ICSID arbitration, it is hard to dispute that such treaty and the ICSID Convention relate to the same subject matter, namely arbitration of foreign investment disputes.

Art. 30 VCLT sets out the principles for the application of successive treaties relating to the 'same subject matter'. Specifically, when the parties to a later treaty do not include all of the parties to the earlier one, and both treaties are still in force, then as between the States that are parties to both treaties, 'the earlier treaty applies only to the extent that its provisions are compatible with those of the later treaty'. This rule is 'no more than an application of the general principle that a later expression of intention is to be presumed to prevail over an earlier one'.[86]

In most every respect, later investment treaties are entirely compatible with the ICSID Convention. Thus, the question of the application of the ICSID Convention does not arise: the provisions of the earlier and the later treaty being compatible, both continue to apply and their simultaneous application poses no particular difficulty.

In the scenario under consideration, however, a difficulty could indeed arise: the term 'investment' in Art. 25 of the ICSID Convention could have a narrow autonomous meaning, while the investment treaty could envisage ICSID arbitration for a wider range of investment disputes, such as a dispute concerning our example of the demand deposit account. What result would Art. 30 VCLT compel under such circumstances, where an incompatibility within the meaning of that article could indeed be at issue?

---

[85] See, e.g., Agreement on Encouragement and Reciprocal Protection of Investments between the Government of the Kingdom of The Netherlands and the Government of Romania, 19 April 19 1994; Agreement on the Reciprocal Encouragement and Protection of Investments between the Government of the Republic of Lebanon and the Government of the Republic of Mauritania, 15 June 2004; Agreement between Australia and the Republic of Poland on the Reciprocal Promotion and Protection of Investments, 7 May 1991.

[86] ILC Commentaries, *supra* n. 21, 217.

Interestingly, and assuming for these purposes a narrow, autonomous definition of 'investment' in the ICSID Convention, the answer under Art. 30 VCLT appears to be different for the two State Parties to the investment treaty and the other Contracting States to the ICSID Convention. Under Art. 30(4): 'When the parties to the later treaty do not include all the parties to the earlier one: (a) as between States Parties to both treaties the same rule applies as in paragraph 3', i.e. the later-in-time rule. Thus, as between the two Contracting States party to the investment treaty, the broader definition contained in that treaty would appear to apply. With respect to the demand deposit case, the version of the ICSID Convention as modified between those two States in the investment treaty would appear to provide ICSID jurisdiction and obligate those two States to respect and enforce the award as an ICSID Convention award.

With respect to other ICSID Contracting States, however, only the 'original' ICSID Convention with the assumed narrow, autonomous meaning of 'investment' would appear to apply. Under Art. 30(4)(b) VCLT, 'as between a State party to both treaties and a State party to only one of the treaties, the treaty to which both States are parties governs their mutual rights and obligations'. Thus, imagining a scenario where an ICSID tribunal held that Art. 25(1) reflected a narrow, autonomous meaning of the term 'investment' but nonetheless retained jurisdiction under the ICSID Convention as modified by the subsequent investment treaty, other ICSID Contracting States might not be obligated to enforce the tribunal's award as an ICSID award. However, as noted above, the two State Parties to the investment treaty would be so obligated (and of course the award might remain enforceable under the New York Convention or other treaty on the recognition and enforcement of arbitral awards).

This somewhat surprising result, however, could arise only if there is an incompatibility between the definition of 'investment' in an investment treaty and the content of that undefined term in the ICSID Convention. Nonetheless, it raises a policy dimension relevant under Art. 41(1)(b) VCLT that highlights the uniqueness of the ICSID Convention.[87] If some States agree between themselves that certain assets should constitute 'investments' for purposes of ICSID jurisdiction and consent thereto – with all of the limitations on sovereignty that it may imply (e.g. 'application of international law (Art. 42), recourse against

---

[87] Art. 41(1) and Art. 30(5) VCLT.

awards limited to an ad hoc committee')[88] – why should they be barred from so doing? What harm to other ICSID Contracting States could result from investment treaty State Parties defining 'investment' how they wish?

Some commentators argue that, if the term 'investment' is ascribed a definition that is dependent on the will of State Parties to investment treaties and that is so broad so as to encompass any kind of economic operation, 'even those without any connection to "authentic" investment', ICSID would become 'just another arbitration institution competing with a range of others' and this would render meaningless these important limitations on sovereignty accepted by the Contracting States when signing the Convention.[89] Yet a State that might adopt such a broad definition would do so fully knowing that it was renouncing various State sovereign prerogatives.[90] Others consider that if ICSID jurisdiction were to become solely a matter of consent between States as expressed in investment treaties, this would render 'superfluous the requirement of "investment" under the convention'.[91] Yet this argument presupposes its own conclusion, i.e. that the term 'investment' in the ICSID Convention has an autonomous meaning that is at odds with any meaning that may be ascribed by the States.

From our perspective, and as noted above, the interest that Contracting States to the ICSID Convention hold in a definition of 'investment' voluntarily adopted in an investment treaty by other Contracting States is evident, if at all, in the area of enforcement. Contracting States have agreed to recognise an ICSID award as enforceable and not to subject it to any court review. That agreement, which encompasses both a commitment of national resources (to enforce the

---

[88] F. Yala, 'The Notion of "Investment" in ICSID Case Law. A Drifting Jurisdictional Requirement? Some "Un-Conventional" Thoughts on Salini, SGS and Mihaly', *Journal of International Arbitration*, 22 (2005), 105–25, 125.

[89] *Ibid.*, 117 ('there are serious problems with admitting an operation within the ambit of ICSID jurisdiction simply because it falls under a category of investments protected by a BIT containing an ICSID clause').

[90] But see Manciaux, 'La compétence matérielle', *supra* n. 1, para. 9 ('Définir la notion d'investissement est donc nécessaire, et pas seulement pour des raisons académiques; abstraction faite de l'avenir du Cirdi, c'est une question de sécurité juridique pour les investisseurs étrangers et les Etats récepteurs d'investissements, . . . il semble en outre difficile de concevoir que la portée *ratione materiae* de ce traité multilatéral . . . dépende d'instruments bilatéraux comme des TBI qui ne sont à son égard que de simples textes d'application. Ce serait faire primer le texte secondaire sur le texte principal').

[91] Gaillard, '"Biwater"', *supra* n. 1.

award) and an unusual abandonment of any national control of the content of the award, arguably is limited to awards expected to fall within the ICSID Convention's grant of jurisdiction. An award reflecting a bilateral agreement on 'investment' far afield from the autonomous meaning of that term could arguably betray the expectations on which that commitment of resources and abandonment of sovereignty were based. On a more mundane level, to the extent that an expansive definition of 'investment' in investment treaties might lead to an unexpected growth in the number of cases brought before ICSID, various case management issues would likely arise for the Secretariat, as well as costs for the Contracting States as a whole, since they bear ICSID costs that are not directly covered or reimbursed by the parties, such as a portion of the costs related to ICSID counsel serving as Secretary of the Tribunal and various other costs for administrative facilities and services.[92]

However, in our view, we are not entirely convinced that these policy concerns are sufficiently pressing to impact significantly the analysis. To return again to the demand bank account scenario, we do not find it shocking to consider that the taking of a credit in such an account could give rise to ICSID jurisdiction. We also see no evidence to date of a risk to ICSID's effectiveness and success as a dispute resolution forum and mechanism resulting from such definitions of 'investment'.

Conclusion

The ICJ recently had occasion to make the following, important observation on treaty interpretation:

> there are situations in which the parties' intent upon conclusion of the treaty was, or may be presumed to have been, to give the terms used – or some of them – a meaning or content capable of evolving, not one fixed once and for all, so as to make allowance for, among other things, developments in international law. In such instances it is indeed in order to respect the parties' common intention at the time the treaty was concluded, not to depart from it, that account should be taken of the meaning acquired by the terms in question upon each occasion on which the treaty is to be applied.[93]

[92] Art. 17, ICSID Convention.
[93] *Dispute Regarding Navigational and Related Matters (Costa Rica v. Nicaragua)*, Judgment, 13 July 2009, para. 63.

Our review above of the ICSID Convention term 'investment' through the prism of the VCLT identified a number of factors arguing for a similarly flexible and evolving approach to 'investment' in Art. 25(1):

(a) The approach of considering the content of 'investment' based primarily on the terms of the operative consent to ICSID jurisdiction in each case is the approach strongly suggested by the Report of the Executive Directors. It is our view that such Report qualifies as part of the 'context' of the provisions of the ICSID Convention under Art. 31(2) VCLT. The Report's statement is highly persuasive evidence in favour of the dependent approach to 'investment' in Art. 25(1).

(b) Other elements of the context of the term 'investment', notably the Preamble's reference to foreign private investment's role 'in international cooperation for economic development', tends to support the notion that what constitutes an 'investment' could evolve over time.

(c) Elements of an 'agreed, shared and consistent' State practice favouring a broad definition of 'investment' have emerged in the definitions of the term 'investment' in investment treaties providing only for ICSID arbitration. Similarly, those same treaties could be seen as 'relevant rules of international law applicable in the relations between the parties' within the meaning of Art. 31(3)(c) VCLT. Whether this State practice is sufficiently general and consistent to reflect a common view among ICSID Contracting States is a question for empirical study that is beyond the scope of the present chapter.

By contrast, our analysis has not found substantial support in a VCLT analysis for an autonomous definition of the term 'investment' as exemplified by the five-part *Salini* test. This is not a criticism of the autonomous approach *per se* – we consider *Salini* and its progeny to represent a logical use of inductive reasoning to arrive at a definition of 'investment'. The difficulty, however, from the viewpoint of a VCLT analysis, is that there is little to suggest that the Contracting States intended for the term 'investment' to have an autonomous definition, much less for the *Salini* test to reflect *the* definition. As noted further above, the ordinary meaning of 'investment' at the time the ICSID Convention was concluded does not accord with the autonomous approach exemplified by the *Salini* test. The context – notably in the form of the Report of the Executive Directors – is contrary to the autonomous approach: that Report states that the decision not to include a specific definition of 'investment' was intentional and that this element was considered adequately addressed by the terms of the consent required in each individual case. The subsequent practice of ICSID Contracting States that we have considered also does not support the autonomous approach. While the *travaux préparatoires* to the ICSID Convention provide conclusive support neither for the autonomous nor the dependent approach, they do suggest that the negotiating parties considered a number of different definitions and were unable to reach agreement on any of them. *Salini*'s definition is a fine definition for what it is, but application of the VCLT does not lead to the conclusion that the term 'investment' has an autonomous definition or that such definition has a specific content.

Jan Paulsson, in a recent award in a case in which he sat as sole arbitrator, framed the issue as follows:

> Indeed in the context of BITs the notion of an autonomous investment requirement would be of a different nature than the 'legal dispute' and 'Contracting States' requirement [also stated in ICSID Art. 25(1)]. It would deny Contracting States the right to refer legal disputes to ICSID if they have defined investments too broadly. One may wonder about the purpose of such a denial. If the words of the Convention nevertheless said so that would of course be decisive. But there is no such express limitation. The drafters of the Convention decided not to define 'investments'. Does this mean that the matter is left to the determination of States?
>
> For ICSID arbitral tribunals to reject an express definition desired by two States-party to a treaty seems a step not to be taken without the certainty that the Convention compels it.[94]

For the reasons stated above, we consider that a VCLT analysis of 'investment' in the ICSID Convention does not provide such certainty.

---

[94] *Pantechniki SA Contractors & Engineers* v. *Albania*, ICSID Case No. ARB/07/21, Award, 30 April 2009, paras. 41–42 (para. numbers omitted) See also *Inmaris, supra* n. 2, para. 130.

18

Toward a proper perspective of the private company's distinctiveness

GEORGE C. NNONA

Introduction

Leafing through a dog-eared copy of his book[1] at the library of the Institute of Advanced Legal Studies, Lagos, Nigeria, I got acquainted with Professor Detlev Vagts long before I met him. I got acquainted with him not in transnational law, the field in which he has made the greatest impact, but rather in the field of corporate law, where he also has left his mark. Such is the range of his scholarly reach. It is, therefore, fitting that I celebrate his contributions to the scholarly enterprise with an examination of aspects of company law in a comparative context.

A 'private company' is usually identified by reference to certain distinctive features, which typically include express restrictions on key aspects such as the size of its membership, the transferability of its shares and invitations to the public to subscribe its securities. These sorts of restrictions may currently be found in section 755 of the Companies Act 2006[2] in England and Article 26(5) of the Model Articles for Private Companies,[3] as well as in section 22 of the Companies and Allied Matters Act (hereafter, 'CAMA'),[4] the basic legislation governing companies in Nigeria. The restriction on invitations or offers to the public to subscribe its securities is thought to be the basic distinguishing feature of the

---

[1] D. F. Vagts, *Basic Corporation Law*, 2nd edn. (Westbury, NY: Foundation Press, 1979), cited in G. C. Nnona, 'The Requirements of Company Incorporation in Nigerian Law. An Analysis of Underlying Philosophies', *RADIC*, 7 (1995), 568–609, 576.

[2] C. 46.

[3] In Schedule 1 of the Companies (Model Articles) Regulations 2008, made pursuant to section 19 of the Companies Act 2006, available at www.berr.gov.uk/files/file45533.doc. These Regulations came into force on 1 October 2009. See Art. 1 of the Regulations, SI 2008/3229.

[4] Cap. C20, Laws of the Federation, 2004.

private company in English and Nigerian law.[5] A 'public company', on the other hand, has none of these restrictions. In tandem with the restrictions on private companies come some privileges, especially by way of reduced disclosure and procedural requirements.

Given the abiding nature of the public–private company distinction in Anglo-Nigerian law, it would not be far-fetched to call it an article of faith among company law scholars and policy-makers. It is central to the way most lawyers conceptualise the field: a somewhat bifurcated regulatory regime under which a company is held to varying standards in key respects, depending on whether it is classified as private or public. For instance, a private company is held, in appropriate circumstances, to different standards in terms of types of meeting required,[6] auditing and financial reporting requirements[7] and even the methods by which

[5] See P. L. Davies, *Gower and Davies' Principles of Modern Company Law*, 7th edn (London: Sweet & Maxwell, 2003), 12, defining private companies as those which are not permitted to offer their securities to the public. See also H. R. Hahlo and J. R. Farrah, *Hahlo's Cases and Materials on Company Law*, 3rd edn. (London: Sweet & Maxwell, 1987), 44, noting that the essential difference between a private company and a public company is that a public company can, but a private company may not, offer its securities for sale to the public.

[6] A private company is not required to hold a statutory meeting under section 211(1) of the CAMA. Indeed, in England the private company's obligations to hold annual general meetings has been dispensed with. The requirement of Annual General Meetings in section 336 of the Companies Act 2006 is made with reference to public companies only.

[7] In England, section 388(4) of the Companies Act 2006 mandates private companies to retain accounting records for only three years, as against six years for public companies. Also, under section 430 only quoted companies are obliged to make their annual accounts and reports available on a web site. Generally, under Part 15 of the Companies Act 2006, even more dispensations are granted to private companies which qualify as small companies. See, e.g., section 398, which dispenses with the obligation for a small company that is a parent company to prepare group accounts. In Nigeria, section 377(2) of the CAMA permits small companies to completely avoid the requirement that copies of a company's financial statement be annexed to its annual returns. Additionally, section 350 of the CAMA exempts a small company from the requirement of delivering full financial statements, if a modified financial statement conforming to Part I of Schedule 7 to the Act is delivered. (Note that although section 350 refers to Schedule 6, the Schedule containing the details of the modified financial statement is actually Schedule 7. The reference to Schedule 6 is apparently a drafting error.) Note also that section 351 stipulates that only a private company can qualify as a small company. Section 334(3) of the CAMA exempts a private company from some elements of a full financial statement – namely, the statement of accounting policies, the statement of source and application of funds, the annual statement of value added and the five-year financial summary. A private company is also exempt from the requirement of preparing and filing, with the Corporate Affairs Commission, a statutory report pursuant to section 211(6) of the CAMA, as a corollary to its non-amenability to the requirement of a statutory meeting required of public companies by section 211(1).

decisions of the general meeting can be taken.[8] This reality is broadly reflected in section 23 of the CAMA.[9] Section 23 provides that any private company which defaults in meeting the conditions stipulated in section 22 shall 'cease to be entitled to the privileges and exemptions conferred on private companies ... as if it were not a private company'. Section 24 of the CAMA, just like section 4(1) of the English Companies Act 2006, states explicitly that a company which is not a private company shall be a public company, the net result being that a company which ceases to be entitled to the privileges and exemptions of a private company assumes *ipso facto* the full obligations of a public company. The proposed European Private Company (SPE)[10] takes these exemptions further by giving each private company the leeway to set the form which its meeting would take, including electronic, video conferencing, or other forms.[11]

The fundamental nature of the public–private company distinction to the conceptualisation of companies in Anglo-Nigerian law is further borne out by the fact that the Nigerian Law Reform Commission, whose recommendations led to the promulgation of the CAMA in 1990, considered the possibility of adjusting the distinction through the creation of further categories of companies but rejected the idea, in line with the general view in the memoranda it received on the matter.[12]

---

[8] In private companies, written resolutions may be circulated and passed by members without an actual physical meeting being held. See section 288(1) of the Companies Act 2006 in England, which defines written resolutions in terms of the private company only. See also the procedure in section 234(b) of the CAMA for written resolutions of private companies. On this, see G. C. Nnona *et al.*, 'Resolutions in Lieu of General Meetings. Possible Landmines Under Nigeria's Companies Act', *The Nigerian Juridical Review*, 7 (1998–9), 1–32, esp. 2–3, 10–11, 32.

[9] Indeed, in the broader context of common law jurisdictions generally, Henry Manne's comments that there are indeed two corporate legal orders – that applicable to public listed corporations and that applicable to small private companies – reflects a unifying reality. H. G. Manne, 'Our Two Corporation Systems. Law and Economics', *Virginia Law Review*, 53 (1967), 259–84, 259.

[10] Societas Privata Europaea, or Société Privée Européenne. This is a new form of business organisation being introduced at the EU level as a community-wide regulation. On this see Document COM(2008) 396/3 2008/Xxxx (CNS), Proposal for a Council Regulation on the Statute for a European Private Company (Presented by the European Commission) [SEC(2008) 2098][SEC(2008) 2099]. See also the accompanying press release IP/08/1003 of 25 July 2008.

[11] See Arts. 26(2) and 27(3) of the proposed Regulation of the Statute of SPE, as amplified by the Citizens Summary prepared by the European Commission in support of the proposal.

[12] See The Nigerian Law Reform Commission, *Working Papers on the Reform of Nigerian Company Law*, vol. I (1988), Part II: para. 29, entitled 'Incorporation of Companies and Incidental Matters'.

But is the distinction between private and public companies optimal in the manner in which it has been implemented in the various Anglo-Nigerian company legislation? In essence, does Anglo-Nigerian company law reflect a nuanced appreciation of the true nature of the private company and the important policy purposes which it serves, or ought to serve? This chapter answers these questions in the negative. Using the United Kingdom's Companies Act 2006 and the Nigerian CAMA as primary points of reference, together with the regimes of private company legislation in the United States and under the proposed SPE Statute, the chapter argues that the attributes of the private company which receive primacy in the current conceptualisation and understanding of the private company in Anglo-Nigerian jurisprudence (such as the small size of the private company, the prohibition against the public issue of securities and its freedom from certain disclosure obligations) do not constitute the defining essence of the private company under a proper understanding of its nature. Rather they point to and help secure a more fundamental and defining element of the private company – namely, the intimacy which undergirds the private company as the transposition of a personal relationship into a business setting. This intimate and personal character of the private company rationalises and justifies all the attributes usually given primacy in the definition of such a company. The chapter goes on to work out some of the implications of such an understanding of the private company.

Background and baseline problem

English company law has for long distinguished between private companies and public companies.[13] This distinction is, however, relatively recent. In the days when incorporation occurred only by way of royal charters, letters patent and other specific exercises of direct governmental prerogative, all incorporated companies were essentially public companies, to the extent that they had none of the restrictions now imposed on private companies and were thus able to sell securities to the public and raise capital without the current restrictions. The first Act of Parliament permitting routine incorporation of companies in England, the Joint Stock Companies Registration, Incorporation and

---

[13] P. L. Davies, *Gower and Davies' Principles of Modern Company Law*, *supra* n. 5, 12–14, explaining the abiding character and importance of this distinction in British company law.

Regulation Act of 1844,[14] made no distinction between private and public companies. Its focus was rather on the control of large partnerships having freely transferable shares and fluctuating memberships, the indiscriminate formation of which contributed to the stock market abuses which precipitated the Bubble Act of 1720.[15]

The distinction between private and public companies first appeared in England in the Companies Act of 1907,[16] which created special exemptions from disclosure for private companies as encouragement for the use of the company by small businesses.[17] The 1907 Act was consolidated in the better-known Companies (Consolidation) Act of 1908,[18] which provided the basic structure for the first company legislation in Nigeria – the Companies Ordinance of 1912.[19] The distinction between the private company and the public company in English law, as reflected in the 1908 Act, has been carried forward in Nigerian companies legislation ever since, Nigerian company law being in significant measure a progeny of English law.

Just like its English antecedents,[20] section 19 of the CAMA prohibits, with a few exceptions, the formation of unincorporated companies of more than twenty persons. This is in essence a prohibition of large unregulated partnerships, given the market abuses to which such large partnerships have historically been prone. This prohibition implicitly endorses the relatively benign nature of unincorporated commercial associations of twenty persons or fewer, while simultaneously responding to the dangers in larger unincorporated commercial associations by compelling their incorporation. The logic of this prohibition points to a putative regulatory regime embodying a broad distinction between unincorporated associations of twenty persons or fewer and incorporated bodies of largely more than twenty persons.[21] Such a regime, having brought business associations of more than twenty persons within the heightened oversight of the companies statute, would treat all such

---

[14] 7 & 8 Vict., c.110.   [15] 6 Geo. 1, c.18.   [16] 7 Edw. 7, c.50.

[17] On this, see J. Freedman, 'Small Businesses and the Corporate Form. Burden or Privilege?', *Modern Law Review*, 57 (1994), 555–84, 569.

[18] 8 Edw. 7, c.69.

[19] See The Nigerian Law Reform Commission, *Working Papers on the Reform of Nigerian Company Law*, *supra* n. 12, Part I: Para. 1, entitled 'Introduction'.

[20] See section 716(1) of the UK Companies Act 1985, which has now been repealed by Schedule 16 of the Companies Act 2006 and Art. 2 of the prior Regulatory Reform (Removal of 20 Member Limit in Partnerships, etc.) Order 2002 (SI 2002/3203).

[21] Largely more than twenty persons because the law would still permit two or more persons to form a company, as is currently allowed by section 18 of the CAMA.

companies alike. The private–public company distinction detracts from this putative regime by further sub-classifying companies under the CAMA into two, so that notionally we have three classes – namely, unincorporated associations of twenty persons or fewer, private companies of twenty-one–fifty persons[22] and public companies with more than fifty persons. While technically private and public companies do not need to have memberships conforming in number to these gradations, it is within these gradations that the distinction is intrinsically and practically most important. Private companies of twenty persons or fewer exist, but here the private company is not critical because the association could as well be an unincorporated association – i.e. a partnership.[23] Similarly, public companies of fifty persons or fewer can exist, but what would be the purpose of undertaking the expense and trouble of becoming a public company with such a small membership, since the company could as well exist as a private company or as a partnership of twenty persons or less?

The gradation under the UK Companies Act 2006 differs somewhat from that under the Nigerian CAMA. The former appears to have jettisoned the approach of having a specific bright-line upper limit on the number of members which a private company may have. Of course, there remains an implied limit derived from the prohibition of public offerings by private companies in section 755 of the Companies Act 2006. This prohibition is largely a ban on the sale of the securities of a private company to persons who lack a pre-existing connection with the company. With such limitation the likelihood of a large membership for private companies becomes significantly reduced. Indeed, the definition of private offering in section 756(4)(a) of the Companies Act 2006 seems to reinforce the view that the private company is for members who have an intimate knowledge of one another. This is because one of the indicia of a non-public (i.e. private) offering is the offer of securities to someone with whom the issuing company has a pre-existing connection. Such pre-existing connection is stated expressly in section 756(5) to mean, *inter alia*, connections arising from marriage to an existing member or employee of the company, or from other familial relationships.

---

[22] Section 22(3) of the CAMA restricts the membership of a private company to a maximum of fifty persons.

[23] While it may seem that limited liability is a reason for avoiding partnerships, the existence of limited partnerships in England and Nigeria takes the edge off that difference.

The putative regime first mentioned above is the original regime reflected in the early English Companies Acts, where there was no distinction between private and public companies, but only a requirement that associations of more than twenty-five members not be formed without incorporation. In England, prior to the Joint Stock Companies Act of 1856,[24] the Joint Stock Companies Registration, Incorporation and Regulation Act of 1844[25] and the Limited Liability Act of 1855[26] specified only the maximum number of persons – i.e. twenty-five persons – permitted to carry on business as an association – i.e. as a partnership – without incorporation. The introduction of the private company exposed an intermediate regulatory zone between the unincorporated partnership and the public company – a zone the precise delineation of which has since proved problematic. This is quite apart from the basic problem of ascertaining the very conceptual nature of the zone. In this regard, the private company zone is like a piece of territory the existence of which can be known in the abstract by deduction, but the exact dimensions and nature of which are not amenable to easy ascertainment, thus implicating quantitative difficulties (i.e. difficulties of boundary delineation) and qualitative difficulties (i.e. difficulties of ascertaining the nature of the territory).

The existence of the private company zone has been obvious ever since it became clear that the paradigm of the public company, in connection with which most of the basic rules of English company law were developed, did not fit many of the companies that emerged in the wake of public statutes permitting routine incorporation of companies by registration. Many of these companies were effectively partnerships incorporated in order to secure limited liability, perpetual succession and the other benefits attendant upon incorporation. They did not fit the classical mould of companies – associations of numerous persons joined together for the purpose of aggregating capital in pursuit of a joint undertaking, under the directorship of a few to whom the leadership of the association was vested in trust. They were anything but associations formed for raising capital, being often owner-originated, owner-financed and owner-managed. The need to treat this class of companies differently from the classic company – i.e. the need to recognise the existence of the private company zone and delineate it – was thus easily acknowledged quite early. Determining the exact scope of the companies to which the different treatment should be extended was not, however, as easy, and

---

[24] 19 & 20 Vict. c.47.   [25] 7 & 8 Vict. c.110, *supra* n. 14.   [26] 18 & 19 Vict. c.133.

this has been at the core of the difficulties with the private–public company distinction in company law. There has in this regard remained the possibility that too narrow a definition of the private company will make it underinclusive, therefore eliminating from its coverage many of the very entities which the class was meant to recognise and grant differential treatment. On the other hand, too broad a definition would be overinclusive and would likely capture many companies not coming within the group contemplated by the class as originally conceived.[27] This problem of determining the scope of the private company – i.e. its range – dovetails into, and perhaps originates from, the problem of determining the very nature of the private company itself: is it simply a smaller version of the public company or is it something completely different; something *sui generis*? The answer given to this question is crucial to the delimitation of the private company's zone.

The true nature of the private company

Towards conceptual clarity in articulating the nature of the private company

The Nigerian Law Reform Commission, in making provisions for the private company under the CAMA, considered the nature and essence of the private company. Reflecting the definitions referenced earlier,[28] the Commission stated that '[a] private company is designed for small, especially family business although it is also commonly used for subsidiary and holding companies. A public company on the other hand is designed to involve the public through the offer of its shares and debentures for subscription.'[29] Going further, the Commission stated that:

---

[27] On this definitional problem and how it structures debate on the private company and alternative forms of business organisations, see generally Freedman, 'Small Businesses and the Corporate Form', *supra* n. 17, esp. 558–9. Regarding the problem of delimiting private companies so as to exclude *de facto* public companies from using or abusing the privileges associated with private companies, Freedman writes, *ibid.* 569, that the introduction of the private company was followed by the 'abuse of the privileges of the private company by public companies running their businesses through private companies thereby maintaining secrecy in relation to aspects of their dealings'. The Nigerian Law Reform Commission also showed an awareness of the difficulties here. See The Nigerian Law Reform Commission, *Working Papers on the Reform of Nigerian Company Law*, *supra* n. 12, Part II: para. 26.

[28] See *supra* n. 5.

[29] See The Nigerian Law Reform Commission, *Working Papers on the Reform of Nigerian Company Law*, *supra* n. 12, Part II: para. 23.

> [t]he aim and purpose of a private company in the Nigerian context should be to provide a means of running small or family businesses on a status higher than that of a business name, for example, by providing the advantages of incorporation such as perpetual succession, the right to sue and the liability to be sued, and the right to own and deal with property as a beneficial owner, and to provide for limited liability.[30]

The Commission's conceptualisation of the private company is clearly in sync with generally accepted notions concerning the nature of the private company. Yet it betrays a long-lasting misunderstanding of the true essence of the private company.[31] This misunderstanding does not arise from the incorrectness of the attributes ascribed to the private company, such as the prohibition of securities offerings to the public and reduced reporting requirements. Rather it arises from the centralisation of these attributes as the core of the private company. In effect, these attributes, which are at best like spokes radiating outwards from the hub (core) of a wheel, are conflated with the hub itself, thus mischaracterising the nature of the private company. A closer look reveals, however, that the multiplicity of entities and situations in which the private company is used – the multiplicity captured in Judith Freedman's observation that there exists 'a continuum from the one person firm, through the husband and wife company, the family company, the private company which brings in outside finance',[32] rather than just one clear-cut type of private company – is captured by focusing on one thing – namely, the intimacy between the members in a private company. It is this intimacy more than anything else which constitutes the core or essence of the private company: its distinguishing quality and the marker by which the province of the private company can truly be defined or delineated. This intimacy is apparent, for instance, in the average small or family business – the sort of business often identified with the private company.

An examination of the purposes or policy underpinnings of the usual definitional attributes ascribed to the private company – i.e. restriction on the transfer of shares, limits on the number of shareholders or members, non-offer of its securities to the public, etc. – sheds light on the centrality of intimacy as an organising framework for the private company. When we focus on these attributes, we ordinarily observe that they serve as investor or creditor protection devices which shield the public from being harmed by an association such as the private company which

---

[30] *Ibid.*, para. 26.   [31] As exemplified by the references, *supra* n. 5.
[32] Freeman, 'Small Businesses and the Corporate Form', *supra* n. 17.

is subjected to attenuated regulation by way of reduced disclosure requirements and otherwise. Thus, the prohibition of offers or sale of private company securities to the public can be rationalised as a prohibition aimed at shielding the investing public from the unscreened securities of companies which attract reduced regulation. Similarly, the restriction on transfers of existing securities as well as the restriction stipulating a maximum size in the membership of the private company can be rationalised as devices for protecting the investing public from the hazards of the private company as a less rigorously regulated type of business association. Yet viewing these attributes simply as investor or creditor protection devices eludes the more fundamental question of why the private company came into being in the first place – its *raison d'être*. The private company certainly did not come into being in order to present investor and creditor with protection problems, the solutions to which would be ends in themselves – ends attained through the derivation of, and focus on, the usual private company attributes under consideration. Rather, the utility of these attributes in addressing the heightened investor protection problems raised by the private company makes sense only as a second-order justification or reason for the attributes – i.e. as a reason secondary to a primary antecedent reason for the existence of the attributes. This primary antecedent reason is the intimacy between the members of a private company: the intimacy reflected in the idea of a private company as a business association founded on a personal relationship. It is this intimacy which is secured by the attributes under consideration, being attributes which essentially prevent or inhibit the admission of outsiders into the private company in disruptive numbers. Thus, restrictions such as those against the sale of private company shares to the public and the free transferability of shares already sold, while appearing to be primarily for the protection of the public, serve the real purpose of shielding the existing membership of the private company from the disintegrating erosion of an enlarged, fluctuating membership of barely acquainted individuals. The attributes under consideration serve the purposes of securing and reinforcing the intimacy existing between members of a private company – the intimacy which is central to the nature of the company. In a sense, these attributes may then be seen as being primarily for the protection of the private company from the public, rather than the other way round.

When we consider the various attributes traditionally ascribed to the private company as a means of defining it, we observe that they all make sense as tools for securing the intimate relationship between the members of a private company, rather than as simply tools for investor protection. Securing this intimate relationship is thus the fundamental reason which animates the attributes. This fundamental reason rationalises all the attributes usually ascribed to the private company and organises them around itself, just as the hub of a wheel organises the spokes around itself in the service of a central purpose. Thus the prohibition of sales of securities to the public can simply be explained as a protocol for maintaining the intimate, personal character of the association, since sale and dissemination of the company's securities to a wide fluctuating body of investors inevitably leads to impersonality and anonymity of the sort which impairs or jeopardises the close knit character of the association. Similarly, restrictions on the size of the company's membership and restrictions on the transfer of its securities to third parties serve to secure the intimacy of the underlying relationship by preventing an unwieldy size and ensuring a business context conducive to the management of the benefits and burdens attendant upon the conduct of business by persons bound together by ties running deeper than merely formal business connections. When private companies are thought of as preponderantly small or family businesses, such thinking ties into the reality of the private company as a company whose size and other features are geared towards securing the personal character of the relationship among its members. Indeed, the privileges conferred on private companies – privileges such as minimised reporting and procedural requirements – may also be rationalised as serving the very same purpose as the prohibitions or restrictions placed on the private company. The privileges of reduced reporting requirements and procedural informalities help in particular to secure and enhance the privacy (and hence intimacy) of the association's affairs as well as the flexibility which should attend such a relationship. By shielding the affairs of the private company from the prying eyes of the public,[33] such privileges help to secure the intimacy existing between the members of the company in the same manner as the restrictions already discussed. That such privileges are viewed as ends in themselves – i.e. as the primary purpose or end of having a private company – evinces a disarticulation of their full worth and purpose.

---

[33] In terms of privacy, section 485 of the UK Companies Act 2006 is notable in permitting the directors of a private company to dispense with the obligation of appointing external auditors. See also section 444(2), which complements this by allowing small companies to dispense with the auditor's report on the directors' report.

The implications of recognising the
private company's true nature

The foregoing analysis regarding the true nature of the private company naturally leads on to an exploration of the implications of the new appreciation of the private company's true nature. In this regard it can be said, at the very least, that the definitional problem which has historically beset the private company and led to so much difficulty in delineating its limits or zone, should become attenuated as a result of this new appreciation. Judith Freedman's frustrations with the difficulties of capturing the full range of situations encompassed by the private company given the continuum of possibilities available[34] should no longer be warranted. Wherever we find a company set up in such a manner as to secure and enhance an underlying intimacy or closeness between its members, we should concede the existence of a private company, and wherever such intimacy is lacking, be the company ever so small, there also should we deny the existence of a private company. Along this line of analysis, definitions based, for instance, on size of a company's business (turnover, revenue, etc.) become largely irrelevant. While the number of members in a company would remain relevant in determining whether it is a private company, no hard and fast number need be stipulated as has been done under section 22(3) of the CAMA, the context and peculiarities of each company providing the key indicia for determining whether that company is one that can lay claim to the intimacy which is so essential.[35] This is the basic contour of the definitional project to which private company regulation should commit itself for the future. The dominant definitional approach involving the centralisation of private company attributes – such as restrictions on sale or transfer of company securities, or the small size of such companies – should be abandoned, since it engenders the very definitional problems which beset private company regulation. If, for instance, we see the private company as a small company, then we are left with the problem of delimiting the boundaries of the small company – the point where 'small' ends and 'big' commences. In general, because of the multiplicity of these attributes,

---

[34] Freeman, 'Small Businesses and the Corporate Form', *supra* n. 17.

[35] A reverse safe-harbour rule would, however, not be out of place: for instance, a rule stating that while remaining at or below any particular maximum number of members is not sufficient to guarantee a company's designation as a private company, a specified threshold in number, once reached, would raise a rebuttable presumption that a company is not a private company.

centralising them as the essence of the private company multiplies the definitional problems which beset the private company concept, since not only do we have to streamline the relationship of the attributes *inter se*, we also have to define or delimit each attribute individually.

Refining the approach in the Companies Acts

Setting the private company on a proper course in pursuit of its true purpose

The Nigerian Law Reform Commission, in preparing the CAMA, focused on the same second-order attributes often emphasised by the courts[36] in crafting a definition of the private company. Specifically, the Commission recommended as follows:

> After considering this problem and the solutions proffered in some other jurisdictions we are satisfied that the present division into private and public should be maintained. Indeed, that was the general view in the memoranda received. Instead of creating specific categories of private companies, special privileges of non-disclosure of affairs should be granted to every private company which is not a holding company and has no alien member, and the directors hold at least 51% of the issued share capital. Such a company is more likely to meet the definition of a small business which according to one of the memoranda is 'one that is self-initiated, self-financed and self-managed'. Furthermore, a private company should not have a corporation as a director or have a member which is a corporate body or a State ... As to the maximum number of members, we do not subscribe to the view that there should be no upper limit, for unless there is, the private nature of the company will be easily destroyed and a private company will readily become a de facto though not a de jure public company ... While we are of the view that a maximum number should be fixed, we see no justification for the number 'fifty'. If a partnership cannot have more than twenty members, and a private company is designed to be used for a small or family business, it does not seem consistent or logical to allow the membership of a private company to rise to fifty. If anything, it should be less than twenty.[37]

Following from the Commission's recommendation, the draft Companies Decree did not make a two-way distinction between private companies and public companies, but rather a three-way distinction between public

---

[36] See, e.g., *Galler* v. *Galler*, 32 Ill.2d 16 (1965) (S. Ct of Illinois), 27–8.

[37] See The Nigerian Law Reform Commission, *Working Papers on the Reform of Nigerian Company Law*, *supra* n. 12, Part II: paras. 29–31.

companies, private companies generally and small companies; small companies being a derivative of the private company.[38] To small companies it extended enhanced public disclosure exemptions. This three-way distinction in the CAMA is also manifest in the Companies Act 2006 in England, which makes a similar distinction between the public company, the private company and the small company.[39] While there are differences between both statutes in the way in which they define the private company and the small company, these differences are not significant save in one respect – namely, the CAMA's retention of an upper limit of fifty members for the private company, a limit lacking in the Companies Act 2006. Instead of an upper limit in members, the Companies Act 2006 uses an upper limit in employees, albeit in relation only to small companies and medium-sized companies as defined under the Act.[40] It would appear, though, that this focus on number of employees instead of number of members, shorn of the apparent veneer of egalitarianism, is little more than the adoption of another index of size. In essence, the number of employees is a new rendition of the same old theme in private company regulation, by which quantitative features such as size is emphasised as a parameter for defining its essence. As already argued in this chapter, such features are secondary and subsidiary to the real determining feature of the private company – its character as the transposition of a personal relationship into a business setting and the intimacy which is in consequence imported into its affairs. To set the private company on a proper course in pursuit of its true purpose, this characteristic must receive primacy of place in private company regulation. When this is done, we shall see, for instance, that a good case can be made for the substantial elimination of financial reporting and disclosure obligations for all private companies, and not just small companies or other private companies which satisfy special requirements; such elimination being quite conducive to the confidential and interpersonal nature of a private company and necessary for the full realisation of its potential as such.

Other arguments can be advanced for the elimination of such financial reporting and disclosure. Notable is the fact that the market can take

---

[38] See section 351(1) and 376(2) of the CAMA on the features of the small company.
[39] See sections 4, 381 and 382 of the Companies Act 2006.
[40] Section 383(4) prescribes a limit of fifty employees for companies qualifying as small companies. Section 465(3) similarly uses an upper limit on the number of employees as one of the indicia for delimiting companies qualifying as being of medium size, the limit being 250 employees. A medium-sized company must be a private company since section 467(1)(a) expressly excludes public companies from qualifying as medium-sized companies.

care, on an ad hoc basis, of such disclosure as becomes necessary. The putative beneficiaries of the disclosure requirements placed on private companies are primarily contract creditors. The protection pertains primarily to contract creditors because private companies do not raise capital through the public sale of shares, so that investor protection through disclosure serves primarily the interest of creditors of all sorts who, unlike shareholders, may not otherwise have statutorily provided access to key information on company performance. Yet, such creditors often do not need such disclosure, because surrogate sources of reliable information concerning the affairs of such companies are available. Most important here is the fact that the private company's business partners usually have a long-standing knowledge of the company, particularly with regard to the shareholders' probity, integrity and overall business circumstances. Beyond this, however, is the reality that ultimately, in myriad transactions, it is impractical and inefficient for one to conduct due diligence by examining information on the company one is transacting with, even when such information is publicly available. This would often be because the value of the transaction or other aspects thereof does not warrant the expense of such due diligence. The regulator should, therefore, ordinarily be content in the knowledge that on those occasions presenting a genuinely meaningful need for such disclosures, concerned creditors can request and obtain the disclosures by specifically contracting for it with the private company and its shareholders. Usually, this would be in relatively high-value, sensitive, or otherwise specialised transactions of the type which would warrant the expense of a due diligence.[41]

Correcting company law's biases in the regulation of the private company

While company regulation was originally preoccupied with arresting abuses of the corporate form, especially abuses arising from freely transferable shares in large unincorporated associations,[42] it has subsequently come to assume a facilitative role as well,[43] with company law now also

---

[41] On this see *infra*, text related to nn. 44 and 45.

[42] Those abuses gave rise to the Bubble Act of 1720 and other early company statutes in England.

[43] Among facilitative company law statutes, the Delaware General Corporation Law remains the Northern Star.

being aimed at the overt encouragement of entrepreneurial activity. In the treatment of the private company by the Nigerian law-maker, for instance, we see the manifestation of a continuing struggle between these two competing aims. On the one hand is the objective of protecting the public investor from the hazards of unregistered securities or other investments of the private company. On the other hand is the aim of ensuring that the private company is not unduly encumbered by restrictions which ultimately impede entrepreneurial activity. These aims clash in determining the permissible level of dispensation from disclosure obligations for the private company and how tightly the private company concept should be defined. Too much dispensation from disclosure obligations could endanger the public by providing too little information concerning the affairs of the company to outsiders who may have dealings with it. Likewise, too broad a definition of the private company could extend the disclosure dispensations granted it to an unduly large number of complex entities, thereby leaving the public investor unprotected in their dealings with such companies. The position taken in this chapter – namely, that private companies ought to be defined as all those where there is a pre-existing personal relationship between the members and that the disclosure dispensation and other advantages of the private company be granted to all such companies – amounts to an assertion that *in this context*, the public interest in facilitating entrepreneurial activity by persons whose business affairs are undergirded by a personal relationship predominates over the public interest in investor protection. It also amounts to an assertion that the case for protection of the public investor through disclosure obligations – as distinct from supervision by the regulatory authorities or other forms of case-by-case intervention by such authorities – is overstated in this context.

Much of the investor protection risks for private companies lie in the area of protecting the trade creditor, rather than the public investor in securities of the private company. (Indeed, no private company could offer securities to the public and still claim that the affairs of the company are undergirded by a meaningful degree of intimacy between the members. In essence, a private company which offers securities to the public ceases *ipso facto* to be a private company.) As already argued, however,[44] the risks to such trade creditors are risks for which those creditors could seek additional contractual protection, where the transaction involved is

---

[44] *Supra* text in paragraph related to n. 41.

sufficiently substantial or otherwise special and the risks are therefore significant. Alternatively, they are risks which even in the best of circumstances are too minimal to be efficiently investigated and provided for *ex ante* by the rational creditor, simply because the cost of such investigative efforts – even where information for the necessary due diligence is publicly available – are disproportionate to the risks sought to be mitigated.[45] In this regard it is noteworthy that a regulatory scheme reflecting the foregoing realities is already functional in the United States for close corporations, even though it is not necessarily anchored on a conceptual appreciation of the close corporation as being *sui generis* on account of the intimate character of the association. There is generally no obligation for close corporations in most of the United States to make regular disclosures to the authorities as an investor protection measure, merely on account of the size of their business undertakings.[46] If a corporation has not offered securities to the public it has little public disclosure obligations, and trade or other special creditors must rely on special contractual arrangements with the close corporation or other sources if they need additional information about the corporation's affairs. Practically speaking, the average trade creditor often needs no such information from the company, however, relying instead on other surrogate indicia of corporate performance for an assessment of its well-being.[47] The disclosure requirements for private companies under the Companies Act 2006 and the CAMA should, therefore, be adjusted to reflect this reality.

In considering the scheme of protection for investors in relation to private companies, it is fruitful to think of two constituencies – i.e. the external constituency and the internal one. The former encompasses all those who are not members of the company but who may be led to transact with it, especially potential creditors and potential purchasers of its securities. The latter includes persons already within the company as members – i.e. existing shareholders. Even though the private company

---

[45] An example would be an occasional supplier of minor confectionery to a start-up private company for the entertainment of the occasional guest.

[46] This is, however, not to gainsay that there could be significant creditor protection problems for such companies since, even with a very small membership, a close corporation with a substantially sized business undertaking can imply heightened creditor protection problems on account of the vast number of people who transact business with it and who may be led to extend credit in one form or another to it. But disclosure is not an efficient or effective response to this creditor protection problem.

[47] *Supra*, text in paragraph related to n. 41.

was introduced into English law to ease the burdens on the small entrepreneur operating through an incorporated company, it does not seem that this can be viewed as official enthusiasm for, or endorsement of, heightened use of the private company by such businesses.[48] The law did not, therefore, go very far in crafting nuanced and well-adapted rules for the private company, but instead hewed close to the pre-existing rules which were designed by default for public companies. Consistent with company law's pre-existing bias towards the protection of the external constituency against potential abuses arising from use of the corporate form, stringent rules aimed at protecting the external investor were put in place for the private company, while the protection of the internal constituency from perils peculiar to the private company was neglected, no special rules being made to meet them. Rules articulated for the public company thus came to be applied to the private company. This reality is reflected in the current regulatory scheme of the Companies Act 2006 in England as well as the CAMA, under which the bulk of the provisions apply equally to public and private companies, especially in the area of internal governance and disclosures – the areas in respect of which the day-to-day affairs of the private company differ most markedly from the public company, because of the personal character of the relationship between the members, and where such companies ought, therefore, to receive very differentiated regulatory treatment.

Recognising that the private company is *sui generis*, by virtue of the intimate character of the relationships which undergird it, as argued in this chapter, would conceptually facilitate the adoption of rules properly aimed at enhancing the appeal of the private company to individual entrepreneurs by correcting the bias inherent in the current scheme of company law regulation. There are several aspects to such correction. One aspect would be modification of specific company law rules in order

---

[48] There are indications that Lord Chancellor Loreburn's Committee, whose 1906 report gave rise to the private company in England, did not envisage the great popularity of such a company as a vehicle for small business. Indeed, the legislature were ambiguous about the use of the incorporated company for small business from the inception of limited liability. Egalitarian impulses indicated that the limited liability company ought to be made available for small entrepreneurs as well, even as the expectation was expressed that small entrepreneurs should not be able to use the limited liability company on account of the expense involved in using such entities for small business. The introduction by the House of Lords of a provision requiring a minimum of twenty-five members into the Limited Liability Bill of 1855 was indeed a means of ensuring that only groups which were not too pipsqueak would be able to use the corporate form for business. See, generally, Freedman, 'Small Businesses and the Corporate Form', *supra* n. 17, 568.

to tailor them to the private company. There could also be a broader statutory recognition of the overarching role of equity in regulating the internal governance of the private company, beyond the basic power to wind up a company on just and equitable grounds. Along these lines, consider the well-established rule of company law in section 379(1) of the CAMA and Art. 30(2) of the Model Articles for Private Companies in England[49] that a company can only declare dividends on the recommendation of directors. This rule works well enough in the context of the large public company where most shareholders would have little knowledge of the affairs of the company *vis-à-vis* the directors and, therefore, would have less of a basis for overriding directorial recommendations as to the propriety or otherwise of dividends. In the average private company, on the other hand, shareholders are more likely to have a fair knowledge of the affairs of the company, so that relying on the recommendation of directors for dividend declaration becomes less necessary, and granting the power exclusively to directors *ab initio* becomes less meaningful.

A better rule might be to allow either directors or the general meeting to declare dividends. This could make a big difference in private companies in which all shareholders do not serve as directors. Indeed, giving such prerogatives to directors can prove troublesome in the private company context, as for example where the directors and officers, because they already receive significant benefits from the company by way of salaries and allowances, decide to deny other (non-director and non-officer) company members the financial benefits accruing from membership in the company by refusing to recommend dividends. The private company member affected by this act of bad faith has little prospects for relief, in the light of the current provisions on the recommendation of dividends by directors. Yet this member is in a position quite different from, and indeed worse than, a similarly positioned public company shareholder who not only can sell her shares in the open market with little restriction, but also typically has a smaller proportion of her wealth and income-generating resources locked into a single company than the average private company member. Failure to recommend dividends therefore has a greater impact on the private company shareholder and can be an instrument of oppression.

Another aspect to correcting the biases against the private company inherent in the current regulatory scheme would be the collection of

---

[49] *Supra* n. 3.

those CAMA and Companies Act 2006 provisions peculiar to private companies within one segment or part of the Act, to facilitate easy access and comprehension. Such consolidation is necessary because ascertaining the rules peculiar to the private company in the form in which they are currently scattered throughout the Acts is a tedious and perhaps error-prone act. This is more so in England, given the labyrinthine nature of the Companies Act 2006 with its far-flung provisions. It is instructive that this is the approach adopted by the EU in the Statute of the SPE,[50] which is a consolidated statute designed exclusively for the regulation of private companies community-wide.

For the CAMA, perhaps one way to ease the problem would be to move more of the provisions in the CAMA pertaining to the public company to a special securities statute, the Investment and Securities Act (ISA),[51] in so far as these provisions properly pertain to the public issue of securities by the public company. Granted, it is not always easy to draw a line between provisions which are aimed at investor protection in relation to the public issue of securities and those which function as internal governance mechanisms for companies generally. However, most disclosure obligations seem to be either intrinsically linked to the public sale of securities or to be more meaningful in connection with companies which have gone through that process, for whom the need to keep widely dispersed shareholders informed is heightened. It would, therefore, not be disruptive to move provisions which help in meeting this need from the general companies legislation to a special securities statute. Indeed, the case for such a move would be more apparent if private companies are granted substantial dispensation from disclosure following from a refocused definition as canvassed in this chapter. There would in that event be little purpose in retaining provisions pertaining to disclosure by companies with publicly traded securities in a companies statute which deals with basic governance for both public and private companies, given the existence of special statutes regulating the public sale of securities – the defining attribute of the public company in connection with which disclosure is needed.

The SPE in critical perspective

The recitals in the preamble to the proposed Regulation on the Statute of the SPE[52] place considerable emphasis on party autonomy. Thus, in

---

[50] *Supra* n. 10.   [51] Cap. I 24, Laws of the Federation of Nigeria 2004.   [52] *Supra* n. 10.

para. 3 of the preamble the drafters affirm that 'as many matters as possible should be left to the contractual freedom of shareholders'. Towards this and other ends, para. 6 of the same preamble emphasises the need to provide for a 'list of matters to be set out in an Annex, in respect of which the shareholders of the SPE are obliged to lay down rules in the articles of association'. An examination of the articles of association in Annex I to the Statute shows that it differs markedly from the articles of association in the traditional tables or schedules to the various companies Acts. Unlike the traditional Articles, the Articles in the SPE Statute do not contain default rules which bind a private company unless adjusted by the incorporators. Rather, pursuant to Arts. 4(1) and 8(1) of the Statute, Annex I lists items which incorporators of the SPE must provide for in the Articles in order to obtain incorporation. It effectively forces the incorporators to actively choose the character of the private company. Also, unlike the traditional Articles, the Articles in the SPE Statute encompass several items which are traditionally governed by substantive provisions of the Companies Acts – items such as the permissibility of the company's acquisition of its own shares and the related question of capital reduction, as well as whether the company is to have an auditor or not.

In essence, the SPE regime is a blank slate of sorts on which incorporators must inscribe the details they have chosen to govern the internal relationship of the members. They may thus design the company's internal affairs in such a manner that the company becomes a private company properly so called, with the close-knit intimate character of the association fully secured. Alternatively, they may design the structure in such a way that the association is no more than a smaller version of the general conception of the limited liability company. This versatility may well be one of the greatest achievements of the SPE regime.

Indeed, in this regard the SPE regime potentially approximates that for close corporations in the United States, since a corporation's status as a close corporation is mostly determined by the manner in which its incorporators and managers tweak its internal affairs post-incorporation. The approach in the English Companies Acts and their progenies differs from the foregoing, because the Acts have not provided the same flexibility and opportunity to conform the private company to the needs of a business relationship founded on intimacy. The provisions of these Acts have been more rigid and peremptory, which is paradoxical in the light of the inbuilt expectation that the Acts will be all things to all people. These Acts, with their rigid structure, have been deployed to meet the needs of the close-knit business as well as the requirements of more sophisticated actors who use the private company for complex corporate transactions. The Acts end up falling short at least of satisfying the element of intimacy, which is conceptually antecedent under a proper view of the nature of the private company.

From the foregoing discussion it is clear that, while not conforming itself to the dictates of the private company as a formal manifestation of a personal relationship, the EU regime for private companies under the SPE Statute has left some room for incorporators to arrive at a business structure geared towards that end. The design of Annex I to the Statute, as well as substantive provisions such as that in Art. 3(1)(d),[53] account in large part for this success.

Conclusion

The various company legislations have treated the privileges granted the private company as ends in themselves – i.e. as the *raison d'être* for the private company. The logic of this legislative treatment would require a person who is asked to explain the existence of the private company to state no more than that the company exists to secure the benefits of reduced disclosure and other attenuated corporate obligations, and that the restrictions imposed by company law on the private company constitute the price paid for these benefits. By treating the attributes of the private company in this way, these legislations decouple the attributes from the true purpose underlying them – namely, the need to secure the intimacy which attends the private company as the transposition of a personal relationship into a business context. When these privileges are thus decoupled from the *raison d'être* of the private company, it becomes easy to parcel out the privileges or attributes piecemeal, without regard to their interconnectedness as portions of a mechanism meant to serve, in a unified manner, a central purpose. The attributes of the private company effectively end up balkanised and even mutually contradictory,[54] unable

---

[53] Prohibiting the public sale of private company statutes.

[54] The Companies Act 2006 does not provide for a maximum number of members, a factor supporting the position that the private company is conceptually independent of the number of persons involved and is properly a function of the personal character of their relationship *inter se*. On the other hand, it applies the same rules to the private and public company in the area of dividend declaration and also curiously permits (in section 567) the exclusion of shareholder pre-emption rights by private companies. Similarly, the Statute of the SPE is generally successful in recognising that a separate legislation is required for the private company, a factor which acknowledges the private company as *sui generis*. On the other hand, the Statute in Art. 4(1) consigns the regulation of the

to fulfil the ideal which truly informs their existence. The net result is that in none of the legislation under examination, including the Statute of the SPE, can we discern any central, consistently manifest, conceptual underpinning of the attributes of the private company embodied therein. The private company appears, then, to have been pressed into service in pursuit of disparate objectives determined largely by a combination of contingency and expediency. Looking, for instance, at the English Companies Act 2006, we see a private company regime which is amenable to use in just about any circumstance that does not involve a public offering of securities. The same can be said of the private company formed under the Statute of the SPE as well as the private company under the CAMA. None of them shows fidelity to the essence of the private company. They end up making the private company just another incarnation of the broad conception of the limited liability entity, which is not what the private company truly is, or ought to be.

The personal, intimate character of the relationship implied by the private company is its fundamental distinguishing feature. This feature is conceptually antecedent to all the other features and attributes by which the private company has come to be defined through the years. Fidelity to its conceptual primacy would yield not just intellectual or theoretical harmony, but also pragmatic dividends by way of a properly focused regulatory scheme for private companies which targets its essence with precision, and in so doing deftly draws together other basic aspects of the private company, rationalising and harmonising them efficiently. While the analysis offered herein has proceeded primarily on the basis of English and Nigerian company law, with reference to EU and US law, English and Nigerian company law embody the same conceptual or theoretical difficulties which generally afflict the conceptualisation and treatment of the private company in regulatory regimes derived under, or in the shadows of, the common law tradition.[55] This gives the analysis in this chapter an overarching relevance to company law and its improvement across multiple common law jurisdictions.

private company's disclosures to the company law rules of the various countries of the EU, thus treating it in this essential respect as if it were not distinct from the other forms of business association obtaining in those countries. Under the CAMA in Nigeria, a maximum number of members is stipulated for the private company, indicating that the drafters misconceived size to be of the essence of the private company. Yet the drafters correctly maintained the basic ban against public offerings by private companies.

[55] See, e.g., the regulatory regime for private companies under Ghana's companies code of 1963 and related legislation.

19

Administrative law and international law: the encounter of an odd couple

HERNÁN PÉREZ LOOSE

Introduction

It is hard to find a branch of law that has not been affected by globalisation. As one might expect, the legal areas most influenced by this phenomenon have been those whose core principles and concepts involve economic relations. Important issues of commercial law, intellectual property and competition law, to mention just a few, have been largely reshaped by the forces of this economic transformation.

But there have been other fields of the law that have proven to be more resistant to the winds of globalisation. In general, they are fields of law involving political relations between the State and its nationals. One such field is administrative law. A branch of the law long regarded as the bastion of the nation-State, administrative law, is perhaps the quintessential legal field that is purely domestic in character. Its rise as an autonomous area of the law, with its distinctive principles, rules, traditions and discourse, was closely linked with the construction of the modern State.[1] Few branches of law can claim to be more immune to affairs occurring beyond the national borders than administrative law.

---

[1] For the rise of the 'administrative State' from a US perspective, see L. M. Friedman, *A History of American Law* (New York: Simon & Schuster, 1973), 384–408; S. Skowronek, *Building a New American State. The Expansion of National Administrative Capacities, 1877–1920* (Cambridge University Press, 1982); Robert Rabin, 'Federal Regulation in Historical Perspective', in P. H. Schunck (ed.), *The Foundations of Administrative Law* (Oxford University Press, 1994), 33–8. The European experience is generally associated with the direction adopted by France's public institutions after the French Revolution, see E. García de Enterría, *Revolución Francesa y Administración Contemporánea*, 4th edn. (Madrid: Civitas 2005); J. Alli-Arangueren, *Los paradigmas de la legalidad y la justicia en el Derecho Administrativo francés* (Navarra: Universidad Pública de Navarra, 2008), 61–267.

Nonetheless, recent developments in international law seem to suggest that this may no longer be the case. Under the impressive network of bilateral investment treaties (BITs)[2] and the International Convention for the Settlement of Disputes between States and Nationals of other States (ICSID),[3] and the growing jurisprudence produced by international tribunals – a remarkable feature of today's international scene[4] – administrative law, as developed and applied by the States that are parties to these international instruments, is becoming more and more relevant to international law. After all, administrative law shares a concern with international instruments: the treatment given to individuals by the State and in particular by its administrative agencies.

Although an international tribunal will examine the conduct of the State toward the investor through the lenses of international law, and the finding of a State's liability is a matter to be decided in accordance with international legal standards,[5] domestic law is not wholly irrelevant to investment disputes. In fact, in most cases the applicable substantive law turns out to be a combination of both international and domestic law, although in the event of a conflict international law will prevail.[6] The need to take into consideration domestic law explains why both respondents and claimants in international investment disputes often call in experts in administrative law to convince arbitrators that the State actions under review were adopted in conformity with the rules and

---

[2] By the end of 2006 2,573 BITs had been signed, see L. Sachs and K. Sauvant, 'BITs, DTTs, and Flows. An Overview', in K. Sauvant and L. Sachs, (eds.), *The Effect of Treaties on Foreign Direct Investment. Bilateral Investment Treaties, Double Taxation Treaties, and Investment Flows* (Oxford University Press, 2009), xxxiv.

[3] The International Convention for the Settlement of Disputes between States and Nationals of other States (ICSID Convention) was *opened for signature* in 1965. There are currently 156 signatory States to the Convention. Of these, 144 States have also deposited their instruments of ratification, acceptance or approval of the Convention and have become Contracting States. See also chapter 17 in this volume.

[4] For analysis of the political impact of the BIT phenomenon in the world scenario, see Z. Elkins, A. T. Guzman and B. Simmons, 'Competing for Capital. The Diffusion of Bilateral Investment Treaties, 1960–2000', *International Organization*, 60 (2006), 811–46; R. Desbordes and V. Vicard, 'Foreign Direct Investment and Bilateral Investment Treaties. An International Political Perspective', *Journal of Comparative Economics*, 37 (2009), 372–86.

[5] A. Newcombe and A. Paradel, *Law and Practice of Investment Treaties* (The Hague: Kluwer, 2009), 99.

[6] R. Dolzer and C. Schreuer, *Principles of International Investment Law* (Oxford University Press, 2008), 271; *LG&E* v. *Argentina*, ICSID Case No. ARB/02/1, Decision on Liability, 3 October 2006, 94, *ILM*, 46 (2007), para. 94; *CDSE* v. *Costa Rica*, Award, 17 February, 2005, 5 ICSID Rep., 153, paras. 64–65; *Duke Energy* v. *Perú*, Decision on Jurisdiction, 1 February 2006, para. 162.

principles of domestic administrative law or, on the contrary, that they constitute a violation of them. It is through this narrow and unusual portal that administrative law and international law have started to meet each other.

This chapter attempts to bring attention to this crossroads which, although marginal and fragmented at present, is becoming an unrecognised step toward a larger pattern of transnational law. It was precisely to the understanding of this process that Professor Detlev Vagts devoted much of his generous academic life.

I start by reviewing some common features of the cases registered at the ICSID Centre. Then I will comment on certain developments that have taken place in administrative law, particularly in the Civil law tradition, which may be relevant to international investment law. Finally, I will review some of these issues through the prism of certain decisions by international arbitration tribunals. The chapter ends with some conclusions.

Investment disputes

As of the writing of this chapter, some 180 investment disputes have been resolved under the ICSID Convention, while an additional 121 cases are still pending. Although there are to be sure a number of investment disputes outside the ICSID system, ICSID data will be sufficient for the purposes of the present chapter. Considering the total number of cases – resolved and pending – managed under the auspices of the Centre, it is possible to group most of them into seven categories, according to the type of dispute involved, as follows:

- Concessions for the distribution of potable water services
- Construction of highways
- Operation of gas pipelines
- Exploration and exploitation of oil
- Contracts for the purchase of power
- Telecommunication services
- Contracts for the construction of airports.

The ICSID cases have not been limited to those involving disputes arising out of contracts between the host State and the foreign investor. There are also an increasing number of disputes arising out the State's exercise of its regulatory power. These disputes include those involving the regulation of industries as diverse as banking, cement, textile, automobile, beer, gambling, leasing and the production of oil from flowers. There are even cases of denial of justice.

One of the features common to these disputes is that they derived from legal relations (contractual or otherwise) which from a domestic point of view are relations that typically concern administrative law.[7] To scholars or practitioners in this field of the law, especially in countries with a Civil law tradition, these controversies are very familiar ones. In the case of contractual disputes, they are premised on the existence of a contract whereby one of the parties is the host State or a public instrumentality, and the other is a private party, usually a legal entity. Under the national law of many States, including those that appear in the ICSID registry, these contracts fall into the category of 'administrative contracts', since their objects are closely linked to the provision of public services.[8]

The other line of ICSID cases involves disputes about the regulatory power of the host State. These disputes do not concern the breach of any administrative contract. Instead they revolve around public decisions (statutes, regulations, etc.) which affect the investor's business in the host country. Although in some instances such actions are adopted with the aim of affecting existing administrative contracts with the

---

[7] In the tradition of Civil law countries, administrative law encompasses a wide range of issues. They include the rules applicable to the internal organisation of governmental bodies, their conduct toward private individuals, the rights of those affected by that conduct, the status of civil servants, the regime applicable to public domain, administrative contracts, State liability for torts and the judicial review of administrative decisions. See A. Von Mehren, *The Civil Law System* (Englewood Cliffs, NJ: Prentice Hall, 1957), 250–336.

[8] The concept of 'administrative contract', as an autonomous category of contract, has not been free from controversy. While discrepancies still occur – including voices which question even the existence of such a contractual category – there is a relative consensus that such contracts can be differentiated from contracts governed by private law, when (a) the State, or one of its instrumentalities is the contracting party; (b) the purpose of the agreement is directly linked with the provision of a public service; and, (c) the contract contains some clauses which grant the contracting entity of prerogatives, the so-called 'exorbitant clauses', since they are not found in the general law of contract. These clauses may include the right to modify the scope of the contract for public reasons, to terminate the contract anticipatorily, to impose fines on the contractor, to render binding interpretations of the agreement while in progress and to extend the contract term. While these decisions are self-executing, the contractor retains the right to challenge them subsequently, before a court or Arbitration Tribunal. For a general discussion, see M. A. Bercaitz, *Teoría General de los Contratos Administrativos* (Buenos Aires: Depalma, 1980), 145–217. For a cautionary view of the risks and pitfalls of an expansive notion of administrative contracts, see H. Mairal, 'De la peligrosidad o inutilidad del concepto de contrato administrativo', in *El Derecho*, 179, 18 September 1998, 655–700.

foreign investors, in most cases such actions are simply carried out for the purpose of advancing one or more public goal.

From the perspective of domestic law, the disputes arising out of the regulatory power of the State are also a recognisable feature of administrative law. The issue that is commonly associated with these conflicts is the proper exercise of such regulatory power and the remedies available to the injured individuals. On numerous occasions these disputes have involved not only questions of administrative law but also issues of constitutionality.

Some new developments in administrative law

Two of the areas where these trends have been most visible have been in the administrative contracts area and in the area of the State's regulatory power. We will examine first the developments in the sphere of administrative contracts.

The law of administrative contracts

Contract relations with States are not easy ones, especially in nations where, for historical reasons, governments play an overwhelming role in their political and social structure. The power displayed by these States, both in terms of financial resources and political capabilities, makes them a very peculiar contracting partner. In the field of administrative contracts the principal concern that has been emphasised during recent decades has been to strengthen the private contractor's position *vis-à-vis* the contracting State. These efforts have contributed significantly to overturning the image sometimes associated with the concept of administrative contract as a type of agreement wherein a private contractor is deprived of any legal protection from its contracting counterpart.

The economic financial equation doctrine

Today, the view is widely accepted that private parties to administrative contracts are agents who come to assist the State in the fulfilment of its responsibilities. While this particular feature, not found in private contracts, places upon the contractor a certain burden in term of its performance, it also underscores the collaborative attitude that is expected to govern these contracts. Under this approach the contracting State or public entity must not remain indifferent to the fate of its contractors. Their relationship needs to be understood in terms of partnership and alliance, not of confrontation. This approach has by no means under-mined the power of the State over the performance of these contracts, but rather has only set certain limits to that power.

The concept of the administrative contract, as developed especially in the Civil law tradition, is understood as a legal mechanism created by the State to meet the demands of public services more efficiently. At the same time, it is assumed that no entity other than the State is better equipped to organise public service delivery. This special position of the State, moreover, explains its power to modify these contracts while they are still being performed, the so called *ius variandi*.[9]

However, this power to modify administrative contracts unilaterally is not absolute. Just as with any other power in a democratic State, the *ius variandi* has significant constraints.[10] In the absence of such limitations the very notion of a contract will be destroyed. The fact that this type of agreements is characterised as 'administrative' does not deprive it of its contractual nature.[11] The most important of these limitations, albeit not the only one, is the requirement to maintain intact the eco-nomic arrangement agreed to by the parties in order to compensate the work, investment and risk assumed by the private contractor. This economic arrangement has become known in administrative law as the 'economic–financial equation'.[12] It is short-hand for a legal doctrine, developed by courts and legal scholars, to shield private contractors from

[9]   E. García de Enterría and T.-R. Fernández, *Curso de Derecho Administrativo*, 12th edn., 2 vols. (Madrid: Thompson–Civitas, 2004), vol. I, 698. These modifications may include the adoption of new technologies for the provision of public services, the construction of additional facilities to those originally agreed upon, or changes in the original designs of public infrastructures to meet new demands.

[10]   A. de Laubadère, F. Moderne and P. Devolvé, *Traité de contrats administratifs*, 2 vols. (Paris: Librairie Générale de Droit et Jurisprudence: 1984), vol. II, 403–8.

[11]   H. Escola, *Tratado Integral de los Contratos Administrativos*, 2 vols. (Buenos Aires: Depalma:, 1977), vol. I, 396–8.

[12]   In addition to maintaining the economy of the contract as originally agreed upon, the modifications to the contract cannot be of such nature that they would amount to a different contract. Moreover, it is expected that the decision of the contracting authority must be adopted in *bona fide* – that is, absent of hidden motives like, for example, the renegotiation of the contract. In many systems, the idea that the *ius variandi* is an implicit power of the public administration is not fully accepted because it may represent a breach of the 'legality principle'. See A. de Laubadère *et al.*, *Traité de contrats, supra* n. 10. Therefore, to the foregoing requisites is usually added the need for a specific statutory legislation authorising the modification of administrative contracts or the inclusion of that power among the clauses of the respective contract. The European Commission has raised some concern with regard to the possibility of modifying public contracts once they are signed. In a 2007 letter addressed to the Spanish government, the

the power of public entities to modify unilaterally their contracts with private persons. In exchange for the prerogatives that public entities enjoy in terms of modifying administrative contracts, the contractor has the right to have the economic equation of its contract preserved.

The first antecedent of this doctrine is found in the 1910 ruling of the French Conseil d' État (Council of State) in the case *Compagnie nouvelle du gaz de Déville-lès-Rouen* v. *Déville-lès-Rouen*.[13] The Conseil held that the contracting entity had not breached a concession agreement for urban transportation, as the claimant had argued, when it ordered the concessionaire to expand the network of railways to cover new urban developments. Although neither the expansion of the network nor the power to order such expansion was contemplated in the original contract, the Conseil found that the contracting authority had acted legitimately. Its power to modify the concession did not arise from the agreement, but from its capacity as a public entity. As administrative contracts are intended to provide public services, they are subject to modifications by the contracting agencies since the need for such services may evolve over time. A concession contract with a private enterprise does not deprive the service provided by that enterprise of its public nature.

The Conseil, however, accepted the position held by the representative of the French government during the proceeding, the jurist Léon Blum. He had argued that the modifications introduced to the transportation concession, as legitimate as they were, could not be introduced at the expense of the contractor's economic rights. For Blum a 'financial equation' between the obligations assumed by the contractor and the price he will receive was implicit in any concession contract, an equation that must remain unaffected during the life of the agreement. The Conseil declared, therefore, that the contractor was entitled to economic compensation.[14]

Commission expressed its concern for the way the government had conceived this power in the draft of new legislation on public contracts. Because the explanations by the Spanish authorities did not satisfy the Commission, and the legislation was eventually approved, the Commission issued a report on 27 November 2008, finding that the new legislation was incompatible with European Law. See J. Vásquez, 'La modificación de los contratos administrativos. reflexiones en torno a la STJCE de 29 de abril de 2004 y la Ley de Contratos del Sector Público', *Revista Española de Derecho Administrativo*, 143 (2007), 531–62. The author examines the *ius variandi* under Spanish law in light of the finding of the Commission and the *CAS Suchi di Frutta* ruling of the ECJ, (*CAS Suchi di Frutta SpA* v. *Commission of the European Communities*, Case C-497/06P) [2009].

[13] *Compagnie nouvelle du gaz de Déville-lès-Rouen* v. *Déville-lès-Rouen*, Sirey 1902, III, 563.

[14] See M. Long, P. Weil, G. Braibant, P. Delvolvé and B. Genevois, *Los Grandes Fallos de la Jurisprudencia Administrativa Francesa*, trans. L. Torres, H. Mora and M. L. Crépy

Although the doctrine of the economic and financial equation was first formulated within the particular context of public service concessions, the principle behind it was later extended to other administrative contracts.[15] The doctrine has helped to strike a balance between the rights of the contractor to the economic rewards that he has bargained for, and the power of the State to oversee the provision of public services in the way that is best suited to society at large.

The *pacta sunt servanda* principle in administrative contracts

The economic and financial equation doctrine has helped to underscore two aspects present in any administrative contract and the different regimes that apply to them. One is the economic formula of the contract. The other comprises its object and the set of duties assumed by the contractor. It is in this latter area where the principle of *pacta sunt servanda* may recede somewhat.[16] It is in this area that the State can exercise, under exceptional circumstances, and within certain limits, the so-called *ius variandi*.[17]

The same cannot be said with regard to the 'economic zone' of the administrative contract. Here the principle *pacta sunt servanda* rules unequivocally.[18] Once the price of the contract, or the formula to calculate it, is fixed by the parties, it must remain unaffected during the life of the agreement.[19] It is here where the principle of equality between the parties governs the relation between the contracting State and its private

(Bogotá: Librería del Profesional, 2000), 87–90. The Conscil d'État's ruling in this case has been regarded as a complement to a previous ruling where the Conseil had established the 'mutability' doctrine of administrative contracts, Conseil d'État, 10 January 1902, *Compagnie nonvelle du gaz de Déville-lès-Rouen* v. *Déville-lès-Rouen*, Sirey 1902, III, 563. The 1910 decision was further developed in subsequent cases. See Long, *et al.*, *Los Grandes Fallos*, *supra*, 89–90.

[15] M. Waline, *Droit administratif* (Paris: Sirey, 1963), 617–18. Escola, *Tratado Integral*, *supra* n. 11, 452–4. For a study of the 'cumulative impact' and the economic equation of administrative contracts, see M. Safar, *Impacto cumulativo y equilibrio economic en el contrato estatal* (Bogotá: Externado, 2006).

[16] Rercaitz, *Teoría General*, *supra* n. 8, 348–51.

[17] M. Diez, *Derecho Administrativo*, 6 vols. (Buenos Aires: Ultra, 1979), vol. III, 166.

[18] For an analysis of the French case-law on these two aspects present in administrative contracts, see G. Vedel, *Droit administratif*, 2 vols. (Paris: Presses Universitaires de France, 1992), vol. II, 771–2. See also Bercaitz, *Teoría General*, *supra* n. 8, 348–51.

[19] If any adjustment to the price formula is permitted (inflation, etc.), it is for the protection of the contractor's rights. As put by Parra, 'the unilateral modification of the contract shall never consist in a reduction of the financial advantages of the contractor'. W. Parra, *Los Contratos Estatales* (Bogotá: Ibáñez, 1994), 31. Citing some case-law, Dromi says that the 'mutability of administrative contracts does not apply to its price'. R. Dromi, *Derecho Administrativo*, 2 vols. (Buenos Aires: Ciudad Argentina, 1992), vol. I, 406.

counterpart. As it was put very graphically by Barra, it is as if the life of the contract has been frozen, or a photo has been taken of it, at that crucial moment.[20]

Application of the doctrine

Not only has the financial equation formula been accepted in administrative law as a shield to protect the contractor from the power of the contracting State to modify administrative contracts, for public purposes. The doctrine has also been adopted to protect the contractor's price from circumstances other than the unilateral decision of the contracting authority. That is the case of general laws or regulations adopted by the State (*factum principis*) or unforeseen circumstances that may make the performance of the contract so burdensome to the contractor that it may put at risk the provision of a public service or the completion of a public work (*théorie de l'imprévision*).[21]

The rationale for protecting the contractor's price from virtually any risk lies in the peculiar nature of administrative contracts. Since these contracts, unlike private contracts, are linked to the provision of public services, the intended and immediate beneficiary of the contractor's work, investments and skills is society at large, or at least some segments of it. It would be a breach of the constitutional principle of equality of social burdens if the State increased the contractor's duties – from which some part of the community would gain – at the same price as that for which he had agreed he would perform a less onerous work.[22] If the community as a whole is benefiting from public services that are being

---

[20] R. Barra, 'La actualización por desvalorización monetaria del precio contractual', in Asociación Argentina de Derecho Administrativo (eds.), *Contratos Administrativos*, 2 vols. (Buenos Aires: Astrea, 1982), vol. I, 150.

[21] J. Rivero and J. Waline, *Droit administratif* (Paris: Dalloz, 1991), 405–6; E. Granillo, *Distribución de los Riesgos en la contratación administrativa* (Buenos Aires: Astrea, 1990), 103–5; J. Benavidez, *El Contrato Estatal, entre el Derecho Público y el Derecho Privado* (Bogotá: Externado, 2004), 131–9; O. Ottheguy, 'La ecuación económico-financiera y el hecho del príncipe', *Revista de Derecho Público*, 1 (2007), 261–75.

[22] Arts. 4 and 16 of the Argentine Constitution, for example, establish that the contributions that the State may request from the inhabitants of the nation must be equitable and proportional. If by an act, legitimate or not, of a State organ a special sacrifice is imposed upon a particular member of society, the equality among all the inhabitants must be restored, by granting them a compensation which ultimately will be spread among the rest of society. See R. Dromi, *Derecho Administrativo*, 2 vols. (Buenos Aires: Cuidad Argentina, 1992), vol. II, 255. This principle has been applied to shield the economic equation of administrative contracts from disruptions caused by the exercise of the *ius variandi* by the contracting agency as well by the occurrence of a *factum principis* or

provided by one of its members, that community as whole must bear the cost of such work.[23]

The other basis for securing the economic equation of administrative contracts is found in the constitutional protection of property rights. From a constitutional perspective, the concept of property includes rights which are derived from contracts. As assets forming part of a person's patrimony, contracts rights deserve full constitutional protection.[24] Administrative contract rights need not be an exception. Moreover, private parties to administrative contracts need more protection since in these contracts the State plays the dual role of both contracting partner and political authority. Therefore, any change in the financial equation of administrative contracts to the contractor's detriment amounts to an infringement of the contractor's property rights if the State does not re-establish the economic equation to the point where it was originally bargained for and agreed.[25]

Arbitration in administrative contracts

Another development that has been taking place in the field of administrative contracts is the growing recognition of mechanisms such as mediation and arbitration to solve disputes arising out of these agreements. This is certainly a remarkable departure from the view, held very firmly until recently, that rejected these mechanisms, and in particular arbitration, in the field of administrative contracts. While in continental Europe the trends have been less even – Italy, for example, being more open to it than France – in Latin America the movement has gained more ground.[26]

---

unforeseeable and extraordinary event that made performance of the contract extremely burdensome to the contractor (*théorie de l'imprévision*). See M. Marienhoff, *Tratado de Derecho Administrativo*, 2nd edn., 5 vols. (Buenos Aires: Abeledo-Perrot, 1978), vol III-A., 498–514.

[23] G. Jèze, *Principios Generales de Derecho Administrativo*, 7 vols. trans. Julio Almagro (Buenos Aires. Depalma, 1950), vol. IV, 234.

[24] A. Jana Linetzky and J. C. Marín González, *Recursos de Protección y Contratos* (Santiago: Editorial Jurídica de Chile, 1996), 42; G. Bidart, *Tratado Elemental de Derecho Constitucional Argentino*, 2 vols. (Buenos Aires: Ediar, 2003), vol. II-A, 67–8.

[25] M. Marienhoff, *Tratado de Derecho*, supra n. 22, 472–3; M. Bercaitz, *Teoría General*, supra n. 8, 409.

[26] The reluctance to allow arbitration has been rooted in the notion that public officials are not allowed to waive the enforcement of the State's duties. A critical analysis of this position is found in M. Del Signore, *La compromettibilitá in arbitrato nel Diritto Ammnistrativo* (Milan: Giuffrè, 2007).

The increasing acceptance of arbitration as a mechanism to solve administrative contract disputes has significantly enhanced the position of private contractors *vis-à-vis* the State. Given the preponderant role that the State enjoys in many nations, and the entrenched position of administrative tribunals within the political structure of the State, arbitration is a positive step to correct that unbalanced relationship. Arbitration is also being explored as an alternative mechanism in taxation.[27]

Administrative relations outside the contractual sphere

The other field of administrative law where there have been important developments which, in our view, are relevant to investment disputes, is the area of regulatory power. During recent decades, the administrative law of many Western European countries has significantly changed; changes that in many respects amount to profound transformations,[28] and which have had considerable influence upon other regions.[29] As the wave of democratisation gained strength during the 1980s, many nations began to dismantle the authoritarian features that had characterised their public administration structures.

Control over discretionary decisions

One important step was the abandonment of the traditional doctrine which prevented judicial review of administrative decisions adopted in the exercise of 'discretional powers'.[30] This shift was part of larger movement toward the elimination of most enclaves of State immunity.[31]

The doctrine of excluding discretional decisions from judicial control were gradually weakened, and in many cases rejected altogether. The

---

[27] For a review of the arbitration in administrative contracts in the national laws of Latin America, see A. Zapata de Arbeláez, S. Barona and C. Esplugues (eds.), *El Regimen Jurídico de Arbitraje Interno e Internacional en América Latina* (Bogotá: Externado: forthcoming, on file with the author).

[28] For an in-depth examination of these trends, see M. Ruffert (ed.), *The Transformation of Administrative Law in Europe* (Munich: Sellier European Law Publishers, 2007).

[29] The changes in Latin America are reviewed in S. González-Varas (ed.), *Derecho Administrativo Iberoamericano* (Madrid: Instituto Nacional de Administración Pública, 2005). See also V. Hernández-Mendible (ed.), *Derecho Administrativo Iberoamericano*, 3 vols. (Caracas: Paredes, 2007).

[30] J. Sesín, *Administración Pública, actividad reglada, Discrecional y Técnica. Nuevos mecanismos de control judicial* (Buenos Aires: LexisNexis Depalma, 2004).

[31] For an historical account of this process, see E. García de Enterría, *La lucha contra las inmunidades del poder en el Derecho Administrativo* (Madrid: Civitas, 1983).

principle that all public officials must act in accordance with prior legislative authorisation ('principle of legality') included both 'regulated' and
'discretionary' powers. The distinction between these two categories of
powers has been held to be an artificial one. In any discretionary decision
there are elements of legality that are susceptible to judicial scrutiny.[32]
More importantly, a discretionary power free from judicial control may
easily lead to an arbitrary decision.

Reasoning

Another step in the same direction has been the renewed emphasis on the
reasoning of administrative decisions. Until recently in many countries
the lack of written justification of an administrative act was not a ground
for its nullity. At most it was seen as a failure to comply with good
administrative practices. Today, however, written justification itself is
being considered as an essential element of an administrative act. The
aim of this trend is clear: to reduce the margin of arbitrariness by
administrative agencies.[33]

Proportionality

One mechanism that has been introduced to curb the danger of arbitrary
government decisions is the principle of proportionality. Administrative
agencies in adopting actions that may harm private parties who are
subject to their regulatory power are now asked to balance the objectives
of the legislation, on the one hand, and the administrative goals embodied in the decision to be made, on the other, so that the least harmful
outcome is achieved. This balancing process implies that the actions
adopted by agencies will not prejudice the interests of private parties
disproportionately in relation to the expected public benefits.[34]

---

[32] For an analysis of the evolution of this doctrine in France, see G. Bermann, 'The Scope of
Judicial Review in French Administrative Law', *Columbia Journal of Transnational Law*,
16 (1977), 194–274. For later developments, see J. Morand-Deviller, *Cours de droit
administratif* (Paris: Montchrestien, 2003), 272–8. See also G. Vedel, *ibid.*, 203. The
influence of this evolution on Latin America is found in S. González-Varas, *Derecho
Administrativo Iberoamericano, supra* n. 29.

[33] One study on this subject is G.S. Tawil and L. Monti, *La Motivación del Acto
Administrativo* (Buenos Aires: Depalma, 1998). See also Laubadère *et al.*, *Traité de
contrats supra* n. 10, vol. II, 607–8.

[34] For a general review of the growing importance of the principle of proportionality in
contemporary administrative law, see N. Emiliou, *The Principle of Proportionality
in European Law. A Comparative Study* (New York: Aspen, 2002); D. Sarmiento, *El
principio de proporcionalidad en el Derecho Administrativo. Un análisis jurídico desde el*

One of the events that spread proportionality in the field of administrative law, in many countries, was the fact that agencies began to enjoy an unprecedented power to impose administrative sanctions. This trend led many legislatures to subject this inflation of administrative sanctions to the traditional principles of criminal law, including the principle of proportionality.[35]

The principle, however, has transcended the field of administrative sanctions to become a focal point in many other areas. Proportionality is now considered as a principle that must be taken into consideration by administrative agencies in diverse settings.

The principles of good faith and juridical certainty

In many countries, the principle of good faith has now been introduced into administrative law. While the principle has had a long tradition in civil and commercial contracts, it was hardly considered relevant to administrative relations. As a result of this new trend, doctrines such as promissory estoppel, *Nemo auditur propriam turpitudimem allegans* (no one alleging his own turpitude is to be heard), the interdiction of abuse of rights as well as the duty to protect legitimate expectations – all progenies of the good faith principle – have entered into the legal discourse of administrative law.

Another significant development has been the introduction of the principle of 'juridical certainty' in the process of administrative adjudication.[36] The principle had been the subject of theoretical discussion for many years, particularly with respect to problems of statutory retroactivity and the principle's constitutional implications. However, its scope has now been broadened so that it has become one of the key standards of conduct of public entities in their dealings with private persons and enterprises.[37]

Derecho español (Bogotá: Externado, 2007); S. Villamena, *Contributo in tema di proporzionalitá* (Milan: Giuffre, 2008). For a study of proportionality in the Mexican legal system, including its judicial application, see R. Sánchez, *El principio de proporcionalidad* (México City: UNAM, 2007). For an American perspective, see E. T. Sullivan and R. Frase, *Proportionality Principles in American Law. Controlling Excessive Government Actions* (Oxford University Press, 2008).

[35] A. Nieto, *Derecho Administrativo Sancionador* (Madrid: Civitas, 2005).

[36] For an analysis of how good faith became a recognised principle in public law discourse, see F. Merusi, *Buona Fede e Affidamento nel Diritto Pubblico. Dagli anni 'Trenta' all' 'Alternanza'* (Milan, Giuffrè, 2001). A challenge to the traditional idea that good faith has historically not been a relevant principle in public law is found in F. Manganaro, *Principio di buona fede e attivita delle admministrazione pubbliche* (Catanzaro: Edizione Scientifiche Italiane, 1995).

[37] S. Schonberg, *Legitimate Expectations in Administrative Law* (Oxford University Press, 2001); M. Viana, *El principio de Confianza Legítima en el Derecho Administrativo colombiano* (Bogotá: Externado, 2007); J. González Pérez, *El principio general de buena*

As applied by courts and commented upon by scholars, the core of the principle of 'juridical certainty' is to guarantee a framework of normative stability, certainty and transparency so that individuals can estimate with a reasonable degree of confidence the future consequences of their actions. The effects of this principle have been far-reaching since they pose a severe limit to unexpected modifications of polices and regulations that contradict previous positions of administrative agencies in similar situations. The principle has generated a spate of scholarly debates on its scope in the field of administrative law, which in turn have been galvanised by court rulings in some countries.[38]

General evaluation

There have also been analogous transformations in other administrative law areas such as State liability for damages caused to private individuals,[39] and the judiciary's powers to execute their decisions.[40] The common denominator of these trends has also been the search for a more responsive, transparent and predictable public administration.

An original feature of the transformations occurring in the field of administrative law is their constitutional imprimaturs. Administrative law has been the traditional province of legislatures, and the framework

fe en el Derecho Administrativo (Madrid: Civitas, 2009); H. Mairal, La doctrina de los actos propios y la administración pública (Buenos Aires: Depalma, 1988); E. Arana, La alegación de la propia torpeza y su aplicación al Derecho Administrativo (Granada: Comares, 2003).

[38] An analysis of the application of this principle in Europe is found in J. Raitio, The Principle of Legal Certainty in EC Law (The Hague: Kluwer, 2003). For a Latin American perspective, see M. Madariaga, Seguridad Jurídica y Administración Pública para el Siglo XXI (Santiago: Editorial Jurídica de Chile, 1993); G. Kaufman, Seguridad Jurídica y Progreso Económico (PhD thesis, Universidad de Buenos Aires, 1993); F. Arcos, La Seguridad Jurídica. Una teoría formal (Madrid: Dickinson, 2000).

[39] In this field, the major shift has been the rise of the objective (strict liability) standard and the increasing number of actions, some of them completely legitimate, for which the State may now be held liable. D. Fairgrieve, State Liability in Tort. A Comparative Law Study (Oxford University Press, 2003); P. Craig, 'The Domestic Liability of Public Authorities in Damages. Lessons from the European Community?', in J. Beatson and T. Tridimas (eds.), New Directions in European Public Law (Oxford: Hart Publishing, 1998), 75–90; L. Parejo, Lecciones de Derecho Administrativo (Valencia: Tirant Lo Blanch, 2008), 697–718.

[40] Some countries have introduced reforms to grant administrative tribunals more powers to control the conduct of public administration. One example is the power to issue preliminary measures and injunctions against administrative agencies. The reforms adopted by France in the mid-1980s were an important step in that direction. For the experience of several Latin American nations, see V. Hernández-Mendible, Derecho Administrativo, supra n. 29, vol. II, 1079–1412.

designed by the legislatures was seen as self-sufficient. This enduring paradigm, rooted to large extent in the historical role played by the principle of legality in the French tradition,[41] has slowly been replaced by a new vision that regard public administration as too important – and perhaps too powerful – to be left solely in the hand of legislatures.[42] It is not uncommon today to find constitutional reforms which have included provisions and even chapters dealing with traditional issues of administrative law.[43]

However, new developments in the field of administrative law have not always crystallised into new patterns of conduct on the part of administrative agencies or legislatures. In nations with weak judicial institutions these innovations may have dubious relevance for their nationals. But this simply means that the struggle to modernise traditional institutions of administrative law have moved to a different camp, not that the struggle has been lost.

Are these legal trends relevant to international law, in particular with regard to investment disputes? To what extent? I am not sure if these questions can be answered in a comprehensive and satisfactory fashion. What seems clear, at least to the author of this chapter, is that some of the concerns that run through the new trends that have shaken the traditional foundations of administrative law are not so far removed from

---

[41] J. Alli-Arangueren, *Los paradigmas, supra* n. 1, 341–73.

[42] The constitutionalization of administrative law is addressed in the introduction of M. Ruffert, *The Transformation of Administrative Law, supra* n. 28. Some of the principles that I have briefly reviewed before (proportionality, motivation, juridical certainty, etc.) are principles that have gained constitutional status in many legal systems. This step has not only helped to strengthen to individuals' rights and scrutiny upon administrative agencies' doings. It has also helped to limit the discretion of legislatures in matters affecting administrative law. Proportionality, for example, has been recognised in Mexico's constitutional jurisprudence, see Sánchez, *El principio, supra* n. 34.

[43] For an evaluation of the first two decades of the constitutionalisation of Spain's public administration under its 1978 Constitution, see E. Alvarez (ed.), *Administraciones Públicas y Constitución. Reflexiones sobre el XX aniversario de la Constitución Española de 1978* (Madrid: Ministerio de Administraciones Públicas, 1998). An interesting study of the same process in the case of Chile is found in R. Pantoja, *El Derecho Administrativo. Clasicismo y modernidad* (Santiago de Chile: Editorial Jurídica de Chile, 1994). The case of the 1991 Colombia Constitution is studied in G. González, *Fundamentos constitucionales de nuestro Derecho Administrativo en la Constitución de 1991* (Bogotá: Doctrina y Ley, 1994). For the case of the 1999 Venezuela Constitution, see A. Brewer-Carías, 'Marco Constitucional del Derecho Administrativo', in González-Varas (ed.), *Derecho Administrativo Iberoamericano, supra* n. 29, vol. I, 183–220. For the case of the 2008 Ecuador Constitution, see J. Zavala, 'La Constitución de 2008 y la Administración Pública en Ecuador', in *La Constitución Ciudadana* (Madrid: Taurus, 2009). The interaction between constitution and public administration in Italy is analysed in *La Pubblica Amministrazione nella Costituzione* (Milan: Giuffrè, 1993).

some of the issues that are being disputed in the field of international investment law. This is the subject of the next section.

International investment disputes and administrative law

At the centre of international investment disputes is the conduct of the host State toward the foreign investor, individuals, or corporations. Unlike the scrutiny that administrative law exerted over the behaviour of the State, the standard against which the State is examined by international arbitration tribunals is the standard of international law. Although both standards differ in their origin and scope, how much they differ in substance is an issue that has received diffuse attention. My purpose in this section is not to analyse in depth the degree to which both standards differ from one another, but rather to identify some of the issues that cut across both standards. This rather limited scope is perhaps a necessary first step for further research.[44]

The economic equation of administrative contracts

In some cases the host State has attempted to take refuge in the concept of an administrative contract to justify the introduction of unilateral modifications to agreements that it had signed with investors, and even the repudiation of the contract itself. A common argument of the host States has been that those modifications have been adopted to improve the provision of public services; and that therefore they should not be scrutinised by an Arbitration Tribunal without severely impairing the State's sovereign regulatory authority. However, as discussed above, the doctrine of *ius variandi* as applied to administrative contracts has certain limits within the tradition of administrative law.

The use of the 'administrative contract' argument was seen, for example, in *Southern Pacific Properties (Middle East) Ltd (SPP) v. Arab Republic of Egypt*.[45] There, the investor had entered into a joint venture agreement with an instrumentality of the Egyptian government for the

---

[44] An important inquiry along these lines is R. Dolzer, 'The Impact of International Investment Treaties in Domestic Administrative Law', *New York University Journal of International Law and Politics*, 37 (2005), 953–72. See also B. Kingsbury and S. Schill, 'Investor–State Arbitration as Governance. Fair and Equitable Treatment, Proportionality and the Emerging Global Administrative Law', www.iilj.org/publications/2009.

[45] *Southern Pacific Properties (Middle East) Ltd (SPP) v. Arab Republic of Egypt*, ICSID Case No. ARB/84/3, Award, 20 May 1992, *ILM*, 32 (1993), 937–87.

development and construction of two tourist sites, the Pyramid Oasis Project and the Ras Wl Hekman Project. At one point during the performance of the agreement, the Egyptian government, invoking reasons of public benefit, ordered the cancellation of the Pyramid Oasis Project at the site previously chosen, and requested that the investor proceed with the other project. It was the plaintiff's position that the cancellation of the Pyramid Oasis Project led – in addition to other government measures – to the financial collapse of the entire investment which, in turn, amounted to an expropriation.

The government's response was that its decision to cancel the Pyramid Oasis project amounted only to a modification of the agreement since the investor was advised to move the cancelled project to another site. The government claimed that since the agreement signed by the investor was an administrative contract the government had the authority to modify it.[46]

The Tribunal summarised the positions of the parties as follows: 'The Respondent argues that the Claimants were required to accept the Sixth of October City as a modification of the contract because the contract under Egyptian law belonged to the special category of contracts known as "administrative contracts". The Respondent adds that it was in the exercise of the powers concerning "the mutability of administrative contracts in response to the requirements of public service" that it decided to allocate to ETDC (Claimants) the usufruct rights over an area of six thousand feddans of land in an around the Sixth of October City, in compensation for the usufruct granted to ETDC on the Pyramids Plateau. The Respondent contends that it was the Claimant's refusal to accept this modification on the contract that made them 'responsible for the total failure of the project.'[47] The Claimant's response to this was that the alternative site was not a viable alternative since the proposed site was unsuitable for tourist purposes.[48]

While the Tribunal seems to have agreed with the Respondent's assertion that the agreement with the investors was, under Egyptian law, an 'administrative contract', it did not accept the government's conclusion that such a type of contract allowed governments to modify the contract's terms without certain conditions being met. The Tribunal cited with approval the opinion of the *Aminoil* Tribunal when confronted with the same argument:

> In the *Aminoil* v. *Kuwait* case, the tribunal referred to the doctrine of administrative contract 'as it was originally developed in French law and

[46] *Ibid.*, 169.   [47] *Ibid.*, 174.   [48] *Ibid.*, 175.

subsequently in other legal systems such as those of Egypt and Kuwait' (Lloyds Ar. Rep. 1988, at 195). The French doctrine of 'la mutabilité des contrats administratifs' authorizes the public administration to introduce unilateral modifications to administrative contracts or concessions or even to put an end to them provided that certain conditions are fulfilled. The first such condition is that the modification be made in the public interest and concerned with what is called in France a 'service public', the second condition is that modification be accompanied by adequate compensation designed to preserve what is described as 'l'equilibre financier du contract'.[49]

Then the Tribunal added: 'The conditions upon which the State may modify or terminate an administrative contract were described by the tribunal in the *Aminoil* case as follows: "The public authority can require a variation in the extent of the other party's liabilities (services, payments) under the contract. This must not however go as far as to distort (unbalance) the contract; and the State can never modify the financial clauses of the contract – nor, in particular, disturb the general equilibrium of rights and obligations of the parties that constitute what is sometime known as the contract's "financial equation"'.[50]

The Tribunal found that the change of the project's site from the one previously agreed upon to the one that was later proposed by the Egyptian authorities would have involved much more than a mere variation of the original contract. In the Tribunal's view such modification 'would have changed the Parties' bargain and the underlying financial assumptions'.[51] The Tribunal held, therefore, that the Egyptian government had to compensate the investors for the cancellation of the project.

Administrative contracts *and* factum principis

In *Sempra Energy International* v. *Argentine Republic*[52] the issue of the stability of administrative contracts was viewed through a different prism. In this case, what came under the scrutiny of the Tribunal was not an express modification of a single contract but the impact of general

---

[49] *Ibid.*, para. 176.   [50] *Ibid.*, para. 177.   [51] *Ibid.*, para. 178.
[52] *Sempra Energy International* v. *Argentine Republic*, ICSID Case No. ARB/02/16, Award, 28 September 2007. Although Argentina has routinely claimed that its conduct should be evaluated under its domestic administrative law – a request that has been mostly ignored – this is one of the few cases where an ICSID Tribunal undertook such an evaluation.

decisions adopted by the State on the financial equation of administrative contracts and the right of the contractor to be compensated.

The dispute arose out of the measures promulgated by the Argentine government during 2000–2 in the wake of its financial turmoil. The Claimant had a security interest in two companies (Camuzzi Gas Pampena and Camuzzi Gas del Sur) that had obtained government licences to operate as distributors in the newly liberalised gas market.[53] According to the investor the measures adopted by the Argentine government, which included the prohibition of adjusting tariffs according to the US Producer Price Index (PPI), the elimination of the calculation of the tariff in US dollars, the unilateral modification of the Licence by the government, and the failure to reimburse some subsidies owed, not only represented a full reversal of the regulatory framework that had induced its venture in Argentina,[54] but also destroyed the value of its contract rights, for which it was entitled to a full compensation.

One of the arguments advanced by Respondent was that because the dispute evolved around the government decisions about licences which were related to public services, a proper legal analysis required that the issues be considered from the perspective of the law applicable to administrative contracts, including its principles and jurisprudence, and not only to the law of private contract.[55]

The Tribunal did not reject the Claimant's proposed analysis, and consequently went on to examine the situation under the lens of administrative law. It started by recalling that the Argentina Supreme Court had developed a broad definition of the right to private property, which comprises 'every right that has a value recognized as such under the law, whether it originates in private law relations or is born from administrative decisions (subjective rights of public or private nature)'.[56] While the Tribunal acknowledged that under certain circumstances these rights must yield to the public interest, it also underlined the fact that under Argentine law the State is obligated to compensate the affected person.[57]

On the issue of whether the State is immune from liability for the effects that its regulations may cause in the economic equation of administrative contracts – a point which was strongly argued by the Respondent – the Tribunal said the following:

> The opinion of learned authors equally imposes very specific conditions on the operation of the doctrine of the 'fait du prince' which is applicable

---

[53] *Ibid.*, paras. 82–92.   [54] *Ibid.*, para. 93.   [55] *Ibid.*, para. 262.   [56] *Ibid.*, para. 263.
[57] *Ibid.*, para. 264.

> to administrative acts that would alter the contractual relationship to the detriment of the other party. Among such conditions is the requirement that the administrative act be of a general nature and attributable to the public authority, that it would alter the economic balance of the contract, and that it was unforeseeable at the time of the contract's execution. All these lead to the right to compensation for the affected party.[58]

The Tribunal shared the Claimant's expert view that the government measures under examination were issued while the government itself was at the same time a party to the contract executed with the licence holders, and that such measures were unforeseen when the licences were granted. It added that '[T]here is also a direct causal relationship between the act and the damage suffered by the other party, all of it fundamentally altering the economic equation of the contract and thereby leading to the inescapable conclusion that compensation must be paid'.[59]

More importantly, the Tribunal concurred with the long-standing doctrine in the field of administrative law that forbids the State from placing upon certain persons (whether natural or legal) the burden of a public policy designed to benefit the rest of society without compensation. The Tribunal accepted that, in such situations, the principle of equality of public burdens applies and therefore the Claimant had to be compensated for its loss. The Tribunal concluded its analysis by noting that its findings with respect to the liability of the Respondent would not vary substantially whether its conduct were examined under the rules and principles of administrative law or under those of the bilateral investment treaty and international law.[60]

A similar approach is found in *CMS Gas Transmission Company v. Argentina*,[61] another dispute between a foreign investor in the gas industry and the Argentina government. As in the *Sempra* case, here the Tribunal tested the conduct of the host State from the administrative law angle. In doing so the Tribunal applied well-known doctrines of French administrative law to conclude that the host government was liable.

Proportionality in investment disputes

Proportionality, as we have been, is an issue which is receiving growing attention in recent international investment disputes. The issue has become relevant because the lack of proportionality of actions adopted

---

[58] *Ibid.*, para. 265.   [59] *Ibid.*, para. 266.   [60] *Ibid.*, para. 268.

[61] *CMS Gas Transmission Company* v. *Argentina* ('CMS'), ICSID Case No. ARB/01/08, Award, 12 May 2003.

by the State against a foreign investor is a good indication that the 'fair and equitable' standard has been broken.

In the well-known case of *Tecnicas Medioambientales Tecmed SA* v. *The United States of Mexico*[62] the issue of proportionality was at the centre of the ruling. The dispute arose out of the decision of a Federal agency of the Mexican Government (the National Institute of Ecology, or 'INE') not to renew the Claimant's licence to operate an industrial site for the deposit and processing of dangerous wastes. The Claimant had acquired the property rights for this site, including buildings, a lot of land and certain facilities, from a decentralised agency of the City of Hermosillo, State of Sonora, after a public bid.[63]

Prior to the bid, the processing plant had been operated first by a local public corporation under a licence issued by the Federal authorities and then by the Claimant. But when the time for the renewal of the licence came the INE decided to deny it and ordered the closing of the facility.[64] The Mexican government justified its decision on the ground that Claimant had committed certain breaches of its obligations under the licence.[65]

During the arbitration the investor contended that Mexico's decision not to renew the plant and its order to close the site was disproportionate and therefore arbitrary because it lacked a reasonable relation to the *motives* invoked in the resolution. The Tribunal agreed with the Claimant. 'There must be a reasonable relationship of proportionality between the charge or weight imposed on the foreign investor and the aim sought to be realized.'[66] The Tribunal found that the resolution of the Mexican authorities was mainly a response to political pressures and that it was disproportionate because the investor had not 'seriously or imminently affect[ed] public health, ecological balance or the environment', and 'the infringements committed were either remediable or remediated or subject to minor penalties'.[67]

Unlike the *Sempra* Tribunal, in *Tecmed* the Tribunal found Mexico liable without examining its conduct under its domestic law – in particular, under the rules and principles of its internal administrative law. However, the line of argument of the Tribunal on the proportionality principle is virtually the same as that found in the general field of administrative law, including Mexico's.

---

[62] *Tecnicas Medioambientales Tecmed SA* v. *the United States of Mexico* ('*Tecmed*'), ICSID Case No. ARB(AF)/00/2, Award, 29 May 2003.
[63] *Ibid.*, para. 38.   [64] *Ibid.*, para. 39.   [65] *Ibid.*, para. 50.   [66] *Ibid.*, para. 122.
[67] *Ibid.*, para. 130.

In its reasoning, the *Tecmed* Tribunal appealed to the 1986 ruling of the European Court of Human Rights (ECHR) in the *James* case, a case dealing with the proportionality principle in the context of government measures that affected a person's property rights.[68] The Tribunal remarked that the reasoning of the ECHR in that case was also applicable to actions adopted by the State in the exercise of its powers 'as administrator, and not only when it acts as legislator'.[69] It is, in fact, in the sphere of the State as administrator where the principle of proportionality is being applied by administrative tribunals, with considerable support from the academic authorities. This is a process in which the European Court of Justice (ECJ) has played a key role in the European space and beyond.

The frustration of legitimate expectation

One of the most salient issues in today's international investment disputes revolves around use of the principle of 'legitimate expectations'. This principle is being used to shield investors from the harmful effects of unexpected reversals of State policies and attitudes toward foreign investors. With few exceptions, the host State's policies toward foreign investment play an important role in the decision-making process of investors intending to venture abroad. These attitudes may include a variety of 'messages' on which the foreign investor may rely. Because this communicative framework is commonly built to encourage foreign enterprises to invest their capital in the host country – or at least make it predictable that such messages will be incorporated into the bases of the investor's plans – the resulting expectations cannot be subsequently betrayed by the host State without compensation.

Although the precise shape of the principle is still being carved out, legitimate expectations have already gained wide acceptance. One reason that may explain its role as protagonist is the fact that, just like the proportionality doctrine, the legitimate expectation principle has become a useful guide when applying the otherwise broad fair and equitable standard.[70] Moreover, the close link between the protection

---

[68] *Ibid.*, para. 122. *James and Others* v. *The United Kingdom*, ECHR Application No. 8793/79; *In the Case of James and Others*, 8 EHRR 123 (1986).

[69] *Ibid.*, para. 122.

[70] UNCTAD Series on Issues on Issues on International Investment Treaties, *Fair and Equitable Treatment* (1999), 22. In *Waste Management*, the Tribunal acknowledged that 'the standard is to some extent a flexible one which must be adapted to the circumstances

of legitimate expectations with the principle of good faith, a principle that has a long history in international law, has contributed to solidifying its reputation as a useful tool among international tribunals.

The *Tecmed* ruling is also a reference point in the 'legitimate expectation' debate. While previous tribunals, such as those in the *Metalclad* and *CMS* cases, had suggested that failures of the host State to act according to previous assurances given to the investor would be a breach of the fair and equitable treatment standard, the Tribunal in *Tecmed* took the step of using the investor's legitimate expectation as the key test to assess the breach of the standard. For the Tribunal, that standard is breached when the treatment given to the foreign investor by the host State 'affect(s) the basic expectations that were taken into account by the foreign investors to make the investment'.[71]

The Tribunal underscored lack of consistency and transparency as relevant elements in defining the breach of the legitimate expectation principle, thereby triggering a fair and equitable claim. 'The foreign investors expect the host State to act in a consistent manner, free from ambiguity and totally transparently in its relations with the foreign investor, so that it may know beforehand any and all rules and regulations that will govern its investments . . . to be able to plan its investment and comply with such regulations'.[72]

Since then, a progression of tribunals has considered, explicitly or implicitly, the *Tecmed* holding as a framework within which the legitimate expectation principle is applied to the disputes they have at hand. These cases have added important elements to the *Tecmed* approach, which in turn has infused some degree of predictability to the fair and equitable standard. To the need for consistency and transparency enunciated by *Tecmed*, later tribunals have added, for example, the need to examine closely the conduct of the investor in the production of the assurance;[73] the degree of formality of the assurance given to the

of each case', *Waste Management* v. *The United Mexican States*, ICSID Case No. ARB (AF)/00/3, 11 *ICSID Reports* 361, 2004; *ICM*, 43, 967 (2004); *AJIL*, 98, 838–40, 2004.

[71] *Tecmed*, supra n. 62, para.154; *Metalclad Corp.* v. *United Mexican States*, ICSID Case No. ARB(AF)/97/1 (2000); *CMS, supra* n. 61.

[72] *Ibid.*

[73] See, e.g., *International Thunderbird Gaming* v. *The United Mexican States* ('Thunderbird') (UNCITRAL) (NAFTA), Award, 26 January 2006. (The investor's conduct in disclosing the nature of its investment was held relevant to examine his 'legitimate expectation' argument.) Another case where the conduct of the investor was found relevant, and eventually had an impact in assessing the amount of damages he received, was *MTD Equity Sdn Bhd and MTD Chile SA* v. *Republic of Chile* ('MTD Equity'), ICSID Case No. ARB/01/7, Award, 25 May 2004.

investor, including the presence or not of a contract with the State;[74] the whole economic and political climate of the host country;[75] and the source of disappointment of the expectations.[76] It is expected that the principle will be refined further in the near future along such lines.

Most, if not all, issues raised by the *Tecmed* Tribunal and by successive tribunals are well known in administrative law. The very expression 'legitimate expectations' was coined to protect the rights of citizens that have relied on positions adopted by administrative agencies from future policy changes. The ongoing debate as to the scope, limits and conditions of this principle is virtually the same as that which has been taking place among scholars of administrative law.[77]

The administrative roots of the legitimate expectation principle have not been overlooked by the international legal investment community. For example, the dissenting arbitrator in the *Thunderbird* case – one of the most important rulings on the fair and equitable standard – the late Thomas Wälde, while concurring with the majority's approach to the 'legitimate expectation principle', made some important remarks in a separate opinion.[78] He noted that whereas the principle had been applied by international tribunals in international commercial cases and in disputes among sovereign States, in the field of international investment law it played a different role. There, the principle served to protect the investor from the unfamiliar cultural environment of the host State and 'hidden forms of collusion between administrators and local

---

[74] For the CMS Tribunal, for example, the fact that the investor and the State had signed a formal agreement was critical to the creation of legitimate expectations on the part of the investor. Similarly the MTD Equity Tribunal found that a State contract is a good 'indication [to the investor] that, from the Government point of view, the Project is not against Government policy'. *MTD Equity, supra* n. 73, para. 189.

[75] In *Parkerings-Compagniet AS* v. *Republic of Lithuania*, ICSID Case No. ARB/05/08, Award, 11 September 2007, the Tribunal found that the investor should have taken into account the economic and political turmoil Lithuania was experiencing as the nation moved from a communist regime to a capitalist system.

[76] There is certain consensus that a breach of the investor's legitimate expectation will amount to a breach of the fair and equitable standard if that breach springs from actions adopted by the State's higher levels of political or administrative centres. A commercial breach will not be sufficient. In the *CMS* case, for example, the Tribunal gave considerable weight to the fact that the reversal of the tariff regime was a decision of the State's higher levels of government.

[77] Schonberg, *Legitimate Expectations, supra* n. 37.

[78] *Thunderbird, supra* n. 73 (Separate Opinion of Professor Thomas Wälde) ('Thunderbird Separate Opinion').

businessmen', as well as to provide balance for the investor's lack of a trading partner against whom he might retaliate.[79]

Wälde contends that if there is a field of law where we should look for guidance when applying the legitimate expectations principle in international investment disputes, it is administrative law. He goes on to argue that the entire development of the international law of investment disputes will profit considerably from consideration of administrative law developments:

> The common principles of the principal administrative law systems are ... an important point of reference for the interpretation of investment treaties to the extent [that] investment jurisprudence is not yet firmly established.[80]

Some final remarks

Transnational law is a process that may follow different paths. One of them is the type of legal encounter that we have briefly reviewed here. Both the international law of investment and administrative law have the conduct of the national State as their major concern. Critics of the emerging international legal regime for foreign investment argue that international arbitral tribunals pay little or no attention to the domestic law of host States. As a result of this neglect, in their view, foreign investors have been granted privileges that are not enjoyed by nationals of the host country. Moreover, the regime is perceived as weakening the host States' capability of governance by imposing serious limits on its ability to establish and modify public policies in accordance with its preferences.

These claims are unsubstantiated. On the one hand, the scarce attention that these tribunals pay to domestic law is explained by their international origin and the fact that, despite the deference they may have to domestic law, international law is the law that ultimately prevails. On the other hand, the argument that local investors are discriminated against in favour of their foreign counterparts ignores the different positions of both categories of investors within the host nation, a difference that Wälde forcefully underlines in his dissent. It also overlooks the fact that the standards of treatment of the foreign investor that are emerging from the international law investment jurisprudence (proportionality, legal certainty, etc.), are not as different from the standards that contemporary administrative law has been trying to enforce in the last

---

[79] *Ibid.*, para. 34.   [80] *Ibid.*, para. 28.

quarter of century in the domestic sphere. A task that has not always been easy.

The lack of strong judicial institutions capable of enforcing such principles in many countries, despite their formal acceptance in constitutions and legislative statutes, is another matter. The developments witnessed in administrative law since the 1990s have sought to strengthen the position of private individuals *vis-à-vis* the State across various fields. They have also aimed to put an end to the arbitrary behaviour of public officials and administrators. A major concern of this trend has been to remove the vestiges of the authoritarian model of the State that inspired the contours of classic administrative law for many decades. The successive waves of democratisation that have over taken many countries have been a powerful force behind these transformations.

Viewed from this perspective, international investment law – like international human rights law from a different angle – is a welcome development. It is becoming an additional source of scrutiny of State actions, a task assumed by administrative law long ago within the domestic context. It is a complex process where both administrative law and international law – despite their theoretical distance – may benefit and reinforce each other. It is novel, and at the same time, a classic case of transnational law.

20

Making transnational law work through regime-building: the case of international investment law

JESWALD W. SALACUSE*

Introduction

Transnational law, in Philip Jessup's words, 'includes all law which regulates actions or events that transcend national frontiers'.[1] For Jessup, Detlev Vagts and others who established its foundations as a field of study, transnational law is not just about rules; it is especially about behaviour – not only the behaviour of States but also of corporate entities, private persons, and other non-State actors who engage in transactions transcending national boundaries. As scholars, their fundamental concern has not been just the nature of legal doctrine but the way transnational law works in practice. They have had a vision of international law that is dynamic, transactional, multidisciplinary and especially problem-focused. As Henry Steiner and Detlev Vagts write in the Preface to the 3rd edition of *Transnational Legal Problems*, their purpose is 'to develop a conceptual framework for understanding problems involving more than one legal and political system' and to study 'problems that are relevant not only to governments in their dealings with each other, but also to private participants, individual or corporate, in their relations to governments'.[2]

One of the ways in which transnational law becomes a reality in the sense of actually affecting the behaviour of both States and private parties is through the creation of international regimes. A regime, according to

* Jeswald Salacuse is privileged and grateful to have been a student of Detlev Vagts at Harvard.
[1] P. Jessup, *Transnational Law* (New Haven, CT: Yale University Press, 1956), 2.
[2] H. J. Steiner and D. F. Vagts, 'Preface', in H. J. Steiner and D. F. Vagts, *Transnational Legal Problems*, 3rd edn. (Westbury, NY: Foundation Press, 1986), xix.

one accepted definition consists of 'principles, norms, rules and decision-making procedures around which actors' expectations converge in a given area of international relations'.[3] For over two decades, international relations scholars have worked to develop a theory of regimes to explain the phenomenon of cooperation in an otherwise anarchic world. Although regime theory as a body of scholarly endeavour has been the almost exclusive province of political scientists, rather than international lawyers, some of its insights and frameworks may be useful in explaining how and why transnational law works in the way it does. Accordingly, this chapter will examine international investment law, a vitally important part of transnational law, through the lens of regime theory in an effort to understand how that law is made to work.

A background to international investment law

Since the end of the Second World War, the nations of the world have been engaged in building a global regime for investment through the negotiation of investment treaties. Investment treaties, often referred to as 'international investment agreements' (IIAs), are essentially instruments of international law by which States (1) make commitments to other States with respect to the treatment they will accord to investors and investments from those other States and (2) agree on some mechanism for the enforcement of those commitments. A fundamental purpose of investment treaties, as indicated by their titles, is to protect and promote investment.[4]

States undertook this effort to build an international regime for investment because they considered that the existing international law at the end of the Second World War did not offer the foreign investments of their nationals an adequate level of protection. At that time, foreign investors and their home governments seeking the protection of international investment law encountered an ephemeral structure consisting

---

[3] S. D. Krasner, 'Structural Causes and Regime Consequences. Regimes as Intervening Variables', *International Organization*, 36 (1982), 185–205.

[4] E.g. Treaty Concerning the Reciprocal Encouragement and Protection of Investment (United States–Armenia), 23 September 1992, s Treaty Doc. No. 1993103–11; Treaty Concerning the Promotion and Reciprocal Protection of Investments (Germany–Poland), 10 November 1989, *ILM*, 29 (1990), 333; Agreement for the Promotion and Protection of Investments (Indonesia–United Kingdom), 27 April 1976, Treaty Series No. 62. US BITs tend to refer to the 'encouragement of investment', rather than the 'promotion of investment'. Based on an analysis of BIT provisions, it appears that the two terms, 'encouragement' and 'promotion', have the same meaning.

of scattered treaty provisions, a few questionable customs and some contested general principles of law. Foreign investors considered the existing international legal structure to be seriously deficient in several respects. First, the applicable international law failed to take into account contemporary investment practices and needs and to address important issues of concern to foreign investors.[5] For example, customary international law had virtually nothing to say about the right of foreign investors to make monetary transfers from a host country or to bring foreign managers and technicians into a host country to operate their investments. Second, the principles that did exist were often vague and subject to varying interpretations. For example, although there was strong evidence that customary international law required the payment of compensation upon nationalisation of an investor's property, no specific principles had crystallised as to how that compensation was to be calculated.

Third, the existing international legal framework was a subject of strong disagreement between industrialised countries and capital-importing developing nations. For example, while capital-exporting States claimed that international law imposed an obligation on host countries to accord foreign investors a minimum standard of protection and required that States expropriating the property of foreign investors pay compensation, many non-Western countries denied the existence of such international rules. The Soviet Union's massive nationalisations without compensation of foreign investments at the time of the Russian Revolution and Latin America's Calvo doctrine represented long-standing challenges to Western views on the content of international investment law. With the advent of decolonisation after the Second World War, many developing countries, asserting that they had played no part in the development of Western conceptions of international law and believing that existing international rules served only to maintain their poverty, also challenged Western views of international

---

[5] In 1970, the ICJ in the *Barcelona Traction* case found it 'surprising' that the evolution of international investment law had not gone further and that no generally accepted rules had yet crystallised in light of the growth of foreign investments and the expansion of international activities by corporations in the previous half-century. *Case Concerning the Barcelona Traction, Light and Power Co., Ltd (Belgium v. Spain)*, 1970 ICJ Rep. 3, 46–7. As recently as 2004, one scholar of international investment law stated: 'There are few customs in this sense in the field of foreign investment', M. Sornarajah, *The International Law on Foreign Investment*, 2nd edn. (Cambridge University Press, 2004), 89.

investment law. They demanded that the international legal order take account of their particular needs and circumstances.[6] Their position on foreign investment was incorporated into Art. 2 of the 1974 United Nations Charter of Economic Rights and Duties of States,[7] which was adopted by the United Nations General Assembly over the opposition or abstention of developed countries.

Finally, existing international law offered foreign investors no effective enforcement mechanism to pursue claims against host countries that seized investments or refused to respect contractual obligations. As a result, investors had no assurance that investment contracts and arrangements made with host country governments would not be subject to unilateral change at some later time. An affiliate of the World Bank, the International Centre for Settlement of Investment Disputes under the International Convention for the Settlement of Disputes between States and Nationals of other States (ICSID) was formally established in 1966 to resolve disputes between host countries and foreign private investors,[8] but it required the specific consent of the parties to an ICSID Tribunal to exercise jurisdiction over an investor–State dispute. As a result, the Centre did not hear its first case until 1972. Injured foreign investors who were unable to negotiate a satisfactory settlement, secure an arbitration agreement with a host government, or find satisfaction in the local courts had few options other than to seek diplomatic protection from their home country governments. By its very nature, the process of diplomatic protection was more political than legal and, in any event, yielded results that were always uncertain and invariably slow.

---

[6] Inspired by the success of the oil-producing countries in raising petroleum prices in 1973–4, developing countries had hoped that by building a numerically strong coalition among themselves, they would be able to bring about desired change in various international fora. As a result of the debt crisis in the early 1980s, the internal economic restructuring demanded by international financial institutions (IFIs), such as the International Monetary Fund (IMF) and the World Bank, and the abandonment of command economy models by developing countries, the movement for a 'New International Economic Order' (NIEO) lost steam and was virtually dead by 1990. T. Wälde, 'Requiem for the "New International Economic Order"', in G. Hafner et al. (eds.), Festschrift für Ignaz Seidl-Hohenveldern (Cologne: C. Heymann, 1998), 771–804. See generally, J. Hart, The New International Economic Order (London: Macmillan, 1983); J. N. Bhagwati (ed.), The New International Economic Order. The North–South Debate (Cambridge, MA: MIT Press, 1977).

[7] UNGA Res. 3281 (XXIX), 12 December 1974; UN Doc. A/RES/3281 (XXIX) (1974); ILM, 14 (1975), 251.

[8] International Convention on the Settlement of Investment Disputes between States and the Nationals of other States, 18 March 1965; 17 UST 1270; 575 UNTS 159.

In sum, then, as global economic expansion began to accelerate in the years following the Second World War, the existing international law on foreign investment was for most foreign investors incomplete, vague, contested and without an effective enforcement mechanism. Because of these defects, investors and their home governments needed to find another means to protect foreign investments from the injurious actions of host country governments. To protect the interests of their companies and investors, capital-exporting countries sought to build an international regime for investment that, to the extent possible, would be: (1) complete, (2) clear and specific, (3) uncontestable and (4) enforceable. The means to achieve that end would lie in negotiating investment treaties.

The nature of investment treaties

The movement to negotiate investment treaties, driven by capital-exporting countries, began in the 1950s, has steadily gained momentum since that time and has taken place at both the bilateral and multilateral level among States.[9] Three basic types of investment agreements have evolved during that period: (1) bilateral investment treaties, commonly known as 'BITs', (2) bilateral economic agreements with investment provisions and (3) other investment-related agreements involving more than two States.

Bilateral investment treaties

BITs, as their name indicates, govern investment relations exclusively between two signatory States. As of the beginning of 2008, the total number of BITs in existence was 2,608, and 179 countries were parties to at least one of them.[10] The degree to which individual countries have participated in concluding BITs has varied. For example, 41 per cent of all BITs concluded as of 2008 were between a developing and a developed country, while only 9 per cent were between developed countries.[11] And while Germany, the first country to negotiate a BIT, had concluded

---

[9] For background on the investment treaty movement, see J. W. Salacuse and N. P. Sullivan, 'Do BITs Really Work? An Evaluation of Bilateral Investment Treaties and Their Grand Bargain', *HILJ*, 46 (2005) 68–75.
[10] UNCTAD, *World Investment Report 2008* (New York: United Nations, 2008) 14.
[11] *Ibid.*, 16.

nearly 140 individual BITs as of 2008,[12] certain other States had ratified very few.

Bilateral economic treaties with investment provisions

In addition to BITs, which concern investment only, various other bilateral economic agreements also contain investment provisions. Among the most important of these are modern free trade agreements, such as those pursued by the United States,[13] and economic partnership and cooperation treaties, like those advanced by Japan,[14] which contain chapters on investment that replicate many, if not most, of the provisions in BITs. As of 2008, 254 such agreements were in existence. In addition, one must also consider earlier bilateral commercial and trade agreements, such as the Treaties of Friendship Commerce and Navigation negotiated by the United States with numerous countries, which often include provisions that affect foreign investments and can become the basis for international litigation to protect investor interests.[15] Many of these early treaties contain provisions, such as promises of 'full protection and security' that BITs would subsequently incorporate and develop.

Multilateral investment treaties

Investment treaties as a group include more than strictly bilateral agreements. Numerous treaties with more than two State parties set down important enforceable international rules concerning foreign investment. These include the North American Free Trade Agreement (NAFTA),[16] a treaty among the United States, Canada and Mexico, in which Chapter Eleven is itself an investment treaty, and the Energy

---

[12] *Ibid.*, 15.

[13] E.g. United States–Colombia Trade Promotion Agreement, 22 November 2006.

[14] M. Yasushi, 'Economic Partnership Agreements and Japanese Strategy', *Gaiko Forum*, 6, No. 3 (Fall 2006), 53.

[15] E.g. *Case Concerning Elletronica Sicula SpA (ELSI) (United States of America v. Italy)*, 20 July 1989, ICJ Rep., 15 (applying the 1948 Treaty of Friendship, Commerce and Navigation Between Italy and the United States); *Case Concerning Oil Platforms (Islamic Republic of Iran v. United States of America)*, 6 November 2003, 1996 ICJ Rep., 803 (applying 1955 Treaty of Amity, Economic Relations, and Consular Rights between the United States and Iran).

[16] North American Free Trade Agreement (NAFTA, United States–Canada–Mexico), 17 December 1992, *ILM*, 32 (1993), 289.

Charter Treaty,[17] a multilateral convention among fifty-one countries setting down rules for trade and investment in the energy sector. Also included in the group of multilateral treaties are various regional international arrangements such as the Unified Agreement for the Investment of Arab Capital in the Arab States,[18] the ASEAN Agreement for the Promotion and Protection of Investments,[19] and Latin America's Mercosur.[20] The provisions of these agreements are remarkably similar to the BITs and were clearly influenced and informed by the BIT experience.

As a result of the surge in treaty-making undertaken by States since the end of the Second World War, the total number of treaties with meaningful provisions relating to foreign investment as of the beginning of 2009 probably exceeded 3,000. That number is certain to grow as States continue to negotiate significant numbers of investment treaties each year.[21]

Although each of the 3,000 investment treaties is legally separate and distinct and therefore binds only the States that have concluded them, investment treaties as a group bear a remarkable similarity to one another with respect to structure, purpose and principles. It is for this reason that one may view them, despite individual differences in their text, as constituting a single international regime for investment. For example, nearly all international investment agreements cover the following nine topics: (1) definitions and scope of application; (2) investment promotion and the conditions for the entry of foreign investment and investors; (3) general standards of treatment of foreign investors and investments; (4) monetary transfers; (5) expropriation and dispossession; (6) operational and other conditions; (7) losses from armed conflict or internal disorder; (8) treaty exceptions, modifications and terminations; and (9) dispute settlement. In addition, the language used in expressing these principles is often identical, so that it is not uncommon, for example, to find that both counsel and arbitrators will refer to arbitral

---

[17] European Energy Charter Treaty, *ILM*, 34 (1995), 360.

[18] 'Unified Agreement for the Investment of Arab Capital in the Arab States', in *Economic Documents* (Tunis: League of Arab States), No. 3, www.unctad.org/sections/dite/iia/docs/Compendium//en/36%20volume%202.pdf.

[19] ASEAN Agreement for the Promotion and Protection of Investments of 1987, *ILM*, 27 (1988), 612.

[20] Protocol of Colonia for the Promotion and Reciprocal Protection of Investments in Mercosur, 17 January 1994, MERCOSUR/CMC/DEC No. 11/93.

[21] For example, UNCTAD determined that in 2007 alone forty-four new BITs were signed and at least seventy non-BIT international investment agreements among 108 countries were under negotiation, UNCTAD, *World Investment Report, supra* n. 10, 15–16.

decisions in cases interpreting one type of investment treaty – for example, the investment chapter of NAFTA – to interpret a similar provisions in a totally separate and unrelated treaty, for example a BIT between Chile and Malaysia.[22]

An important support mechanism for this emerging international investment regime has been ICSID, which was formally established to resolve disputes between host countries and foreign private investors. Although ICSID, as we have seen, did not hear its first case until 1972, it has become an important institution for international investment dispute resolution. It is through the dispute resolution process that substantive treaty commitments toward investments and investors from other treaty countries are given meaning and made a reality.

The significance of investment treaties

The six decades since the end of the Second World War have thus witnessed a widespread *treatification*[23] of international investment law. Today, unlike the situation that prevailed before the Second World War, foreign investors in many parts of the world are protected primarily by international treaties, rather than by customary international law alone. For all practical purposes, treaties have become the fundamental source of international law in the area of foreign investment.[24] Indeed, in 2003, an Arbitral Tribunal that included a former president of the International Court of Justice (ICJ) suggested that the 2,000 BITs then in existence had shaped the customary international law with respect to the rights of investors.[25]

---

[22] See, e.g., *MTD Equity Sdn Bhd & MTD Chile S A* v. *Republic of Chile*, ICSID Case No. ARB/01/7.

[23] The word 'treatification', while not recognised by any standard English dictionaries, has been used on rare occasions. See, for example, the executive summary on missile proliferation on the web site of the Canadian Department of Foreign External Affairs. Foreign Affairs and International Trade Canada, www.dfait-maeci.gc.ca/arms/MTCR/page2-en.asp. The origin of this derivation of the word 'treatify' may perhaps be found in the 1908 Nobel lecture of the Peace Prize Laureate Frederik Bajer, who urged that a treaty be established to govern the canals between the North and Baltic seas, stating 'there is a need to "treatify", if I may coin this expression, the waterways – the French call them "canaux interocéaniques" – which connect the two seas'. See J. W. Salacuse, 'The Treatification of International Investment Law', *Law and Business Review of the Americas*, 13 (2007), 155–66.

[24] P. Juillard, 'L'evolution des sources du droit des investissements', *RdC*, 250 (1994), 74–216.

[25] *Mondev International Ltd* v. *United States of America*, ICSID Case No. ARB(AF)/99/2, NAFTA, Award, 11 October 2002, *ILM*, 42, 85, para. 125.

This shift from customary international law to treaty law in the domain of international investment has been anything but theoretical. For one thing, it has imposed a discipline on host country treatment of foreign investors. In those cases in which host governments have failed to abide by their commitments to investors, governments have found themselves involved in international arbitration proceedings (some 288 at the end of 2007[26]), and in many cases arbitral tribunals have held them liable to pay substantial damage awards to injured investors.[27] The decisions in investor–State arbitrations are becoming an increasingly important source of international jurisprudence on the respective rights of foreign investors and the States in which they invest.

In sum, international investment treaties are playing and will continue to play a growing role in international business and economic relations. An intensified knowledge of international investment treaties is therefore vital for government officials who negotiate, interpret and apply them, as well as for those who manage relations with actual and prospective foreign investors in their territories. Many officials and their government have learned at significant cost that international investment treaties are not just 'expressions of good will' but are binding instruments of international law that impose enforceable legal obligations on host country governments.

Similarly, international business executives, bankers and their lawyers must take account of relevant investment treaty provisions in planning, executing and managing foreign investment projects. International investment treaties have become, and will remain, vital elements in evaluating political risk in any country in which such professionals hope to operate. And when, as a result of changes in circumstance or policy, conflict arises between investors and host countries, international investment treaties usually play a significant role in their resolution. The treaty enforcement provision whereby individual investors are given the right to initiate arbitration against host countries has led to the development of an increasingly important area of legal practice. Law firms and practising lawyers need to understand, interpret and apply international

---

[26] UNCTAD, *World Investment Report*, *supra* n. 10, 16.

[27] One notable example is the case of *CME Czech Republic B V* v. *The Czech Republic*, an UNCITRAL arbitration under The Netherlands–Czech Republic BIT, which resulted in an award and payment of $355 million to an injured investor in 2003, one of the largest awards ever made in an arbitration proceeding up to that time, 14 March 2003, Final Award; P. Green, 'Czech Republic Pays $355 Million to Media Concern', *New York Times*, New York, May 16, 2003, W1.

investment treaties in order to effectively advise clients and represent them before arbitral tribunals – and, in some cases, national courts. Thus, international investment agreements have a growing significance for the conduct of international business, finance and legal practice.

But beyond the application of specific treaties to individual investors, one may well ask: What is the significance as a whole of all of this treaty-making over the last six decades? Just what does it all add up to? On the one hand, certain scholars have said that each of these 3,000 treaties are *lex specialis* that do nothing more than define specific rules for regulating investments between individual pairs of countries that are parties to the treaties.[28] According to this view, the whole is merely the sum of its parts. On the other hand, in view of the strong similarity among treaties and the common concepts, language, structure and processes they employ, other scholars have argued that given the large number of countries involved in the movement to negotiate international investment agreement these treaties constitute customary international law.[29] This debate is not new. Indeed, virtually since the beginning of the BIT movement, scholars have debated the extent to which BITs constitute or form customary international law with respect to foreign investment. One argument is that BITs 'establish and accept and thus enlarge the force of traditional conceptions' of the law of State responsibility for foreign investment.[30] Others have countered that, despite their prevalence, BITs have effect only between the parties to them because they are not sufficiently uniform to establish custom accepted by the international community.[31]

A regime for international investment

Without resolving the debate as to whether or not investment treaties constitute customary international law, one may conceptualise the mass of investment treaties made over the last sixty years in yet another way. Borrowing from international relations theory, one can think of the

---

[28] E.g. Sornarajah, *The International Law on Foreign Investment, supra* n. 5, 267.

[29] A. Lowenfeld, 'Investment Agreements and International Law', *Columbia Journal of Transnational Law*, 42 (2003), 12; S. M. Schwebel, 'The Influence of Bilateral Investment Treaties on Customary International Law', *Proceedings of the 98th Annual Meeting of the American Society of International Law* (2004), 27–30.

[30] F. A. Mann, *British Treaties for the Promotion and Protection of Investments*, BYBIL, 52 (1981), 241–9, 249.

[31] B. Kishoiyian, 'The Utility of Bilateral Investment Treaties in the Formulation of Customary International Law', *Northwest Journal of International Law & Business*, 14 (1994), 327–9, 329; Sornarajah, *The International Law on Foreign Investment, supra* n. 5, 267.

existing body of investment treaties as constituting a *regime*. As indicated at the outset of this chapter, a leading scholar of international relations has defined an international regime as 'principles, norms, rules and decision-making procedures around which actors' expectations converge in a given area of international relations'.[32] International regimes, according to two other scholars, 'constrain and regularize the behavior of participants, affect which issues among protagonists are on and off the agenda, determine which activities are legitimized or condemned, and influence where, when, and how conflicts are resolved'.[33]

Regimes, then, are instances of international cooperation in an otherwise anarchic world of independent sovereign States. States form international regimes in order to deal with problems in a manner that advances their interests. Their aim in building a global investment regime has been to facilitate the flow of capital and related technology among States so as to promote economic development and prosperity by solving the problem of foreign investment insecurity caused by the risk of adverse actions by governments in host countries. The basic building block for this emerging international investment regime has been the investment treaty.

The application of regime theory to examine the mass of investment treaties has the advantage of capturing the dynamics of the relationships established by these treaties among States and their nationals and of highlighting the systemic nature of what States have created through the investment treaty-making process. Examining the accumulated treaties through the lens of treaty analysis alone, on the other hand, yields a static picture that does not fully reflect the dynamism and fluidity of the resulting system that such treaties have created.

The application of regime theory to investment treaties

Regime elements

Following the 'consensus definition' quoted above, a regime consists of four elements: (1) principles; (2) norms; (3) rules; and (4) decision-making processes.[34] Each of these elements is examined below in connection with the regime created by investment treaties.

---

[32] Krasner, 'Structural Causes', *supra* n. 3, 2.

[33] D. J. Puchala and R. F. Hopkins, 'International Regimes. Lessons from Inductive Analysis', *International Organization*, 36 (1982), 245–76.

[34] A. Hasenclever *et al.*, *Theories of International Regimes* (Cambridge University Press, 1997), 9.

Regime principles

The first element of a regime is principles. By 'principles', regime theorists mean something different from what lawyers and legal scholars usually understand by that term. Within the context of international regimes, principles may be defined as 'beliefs of fact, causation, and rectitude'.[35] Regimes are based on a belief by their participants that cooperation in a particular area will lead to some desired outcome. Thus, for example, one may say that a regime for the prevention of nuclear proliferation is based on the principle that the proliferation of nuclear arms increases the likelihood of nuclear war and that a regime to control proliferation will achieve the desired outcome of reducing that likelihood.[36] What, then, are the principles upon which the international investment regime is based? An examination of investment treaty texts indicates a set of more or less common principles that the participating States have believed in negotiating them.

A first principle is the belief that increased investment between and among contracting States will increase their prosperity, economic development and business activity, and will lead to heightened economic cooperation among them.[37] Thus, the treaties' ultimate goal, as envisioned by their contracting States, is not just to increase the flow of capital and to protect individual investors.

A second principle is that favourable conditions in host States will, all other things being equal, lead to increased investment. The reference to 'favourable conditions' does not merely mean the natural state of things; it refers in particular to conditions that can be affected by host government actions and it recognises that such actions can either encourage or discourage investment. Thus, the title of virtually all investment treaties states that the agreement is to 'promote' or 'encourage' investment, and the targets of that promotion are investors of the other contracting party.

---

[35] Krasner, 'Structural Causes', *supra* n. 3.

[36] H. Muller, 'The Internationalization of Principles, Norms, and Rules by Governments. The Case of Security Regimes', in V. Rittberger (ed.), *Regime Theory and International Relations* (Oxford: Clarendon Press, 1993), 361–8. See also Hasenclever, *Theories of International Regimes, supra* n. 34.

[37] For example, the preamble to 1995 BIT between Mongolia and Singapore States: 'RECOGNIZING that the encouragement and reciprocal protection of such investments will be conducive to stimulating business initiative and increasing prosperity in both States', Agreement Between the Government of Mongolia and the Government of the Republic of Singapore on the Promotion and Protection of Investments, 24 July 1995.

A third principle of the investment regime is that the law and administrative decisions of host States can influence investment by giving increased predictability to the rules under which investors make their investments and conduct their activities. Underlying this principle, one may cite the work of the noted German sociologist, Max Weber, who sought to understand why capitalism arose in Europe. He concluded that one of the reasons was the nature of European law, which allowed what he called the 'calculability' of transactions. Weber emphasises the role that law plays in raising the probability that actions will take place. Calculability, according to Weber, encourages investment transactions. For Weber three conditions were necessary for law to be calculable: (1) the legal text must lend itself to prediction; (2) the administration and application of the legal text must not be arbitrary; and (3) contracts must be enforced.[38] Similarly, the goal of investment treaties has been to increase the calculability of foreign investment transactions

A fourth principle underlying the treaty regime is that the means to promote investment is to protect it. The promise of investment protection results in investment promotion. Thus the titles of nearly all investment treaties state that their purpose is not only to promote investment, but to protect it. The connection between promotion and protection lies in investor concepts of risk and predictability.

The general premise of investment treaties is that investment promotion is to be achieved by the host country's creation of a stable legal environment that favours foreign investment. The basic working assumption upon which investment treaties rest is that clear and enforceable rules that protect foreign investors reduce investment risk, and a reduction in risk, all other things being equal, promotes investment. Investment treaties, on the other hand, do not generally bind a home country to encourage its nationals and companies to invest in the territory of a treaty partner.

The risk for any foreign investor is that once the investment is made the host State may change the rules. A sudden, unexpected change in the rules is a principal form of political risk, perhaps its very essence. In order to encourage investment within their territories, host States make various kinds of commitments to investors in many different ways, including the provisions of foreign investment codes, investment agreements, development contracts, public service concessions and tax stabilisation

[38] R. Swedberg, 'Max Weber's Contribution to the Economic Sociology of Law', *Annual Revue of Law and Social Sciences*, 2 (2006), 61–81.

agreements, to mention only a few. Such instruments contain important commitments upon which investors rely in deciding to invest their capital in projects in the host country. The continuing respect by the State of such commitments is usually crucial for the profitability of the investment, and sometimes for its very survival. Since these arrangements are governed by the law of the host country and subject to the actions of its institutions, their continued stability faces the risk that the host government will unilaterally modify or terminate them at some later time, a phenomenon that has in fact taken place on numerous occasions. Such obligations made by host States to foreign investors are, in the oft-quoted words of the late Professor Raymond Vernon of the Harvard Business School, 'obsolescing bargains' between the investor and the host country.[39] The cause of their obsolescence has much to do with the decline in bargaining power of the investor during the life of the investment, and with changes in circumstance within the host country. At the time that an investor is proposing an investment to a country, the investor has a certain amount of bargaining power with the host government to secure favourable treatment and conditions for its investment; however, once the investor makes the investment and thereby places its capital under the sovereignty of the host State, its bargaining power diminishes and the commitments received risk becoming obsolete in the eyes of the host government.

The fifth principle of the investment regime is that international rules with effective enforcement mechanisms will deal with the problem of the obsolescing bargain by restraining the actions of the host government towards foreign investment in its territory. Rules and enforcement mechanisms are seen as a basic means to protect investment.

Regime norms

Norms are the second element of a regime. Norms in regime theory are defined as 'standards of behavior defined in terms of rights and obligations'.[40] Accordingly, investment treaties specify standards of 'treatment' (a term of art in all investment treaties) that host States are obligated to accord to investors and investments from their treaty partners.

---

[39] R.Vernon, *Sovereignty at Bay. The Multinational Spread of US Enterprises* (New York: Basic Books, 1971), 46.

[40] Krasner, 'Structural Causes', *supra* n. 3.

In order to protect foreign investors against the political risk resulting from placing their assets under host country jurisdiction, investment treaties include obligations with respect to the 'treatment' that host countries must give to investors and their investments. Although the treaties do not usually define the meaning of 'treatment', that word in its ordinary dictionary sense includes the 'actions and behaviour that one person takes toward another person'. By entering into an investment treaty, a State makes promises about the actions and behaviours – that is, the treatment – it will give to investments and investors of its treaty partners in the future.[41] The treaty provisions on investor and investment treatment are intended to restrain host country government behaviour and to impose a discipline on governmental actions. They seek to achieve this goal by defining a *standard* to which host countries' governments must conform in their treatment of investors and investments. State actions that fail to meet the defined standard constitute treaty violations that engage the offending State's international responsibility and render it potentially liable to pay compensation for the injury it has caused.

The standards of treatment – that is, the norms of the regime – bear a remarkable similarity in language and concept among investment treaties. Thus, nearly all investment treaties require host States to respect the norms of 'fair and equitable treatment', 'full protection and security', 'most-favoured-national (MFN) treatment', 'national treatment' and 'non-discriminatory treatment' with respect to protected investors and their investments. At the same time, it should be emphasised that treatment standards in treaties are almost always expressed in general and even vague terms so as to render difficult the task of applying them to concrete, complex fact situations of the type that usually arise in investment disputes. Indeed, the stated norms of the regime are breathtaking in their generality, vagueness and lack of specificity. The application of these vague norms in investment treaties has been the work of investor–State arbitration tribunals, the primary decision-making bodies of the international investment regime.

One norm in particular appears consistently in investment treaties and has become 'an almost ubiquitous presence in investment litigation':[42]

---

[41] In *Suez*, the Tribunal defined 'treatment' as follows: 'The word "treatment" is not defined in the treaty text. However, the ordinary meaning of that term within the context of investment includes the rights and privileges granted and the obligations and burdens imposed by a Contracting State on investments made by investors covered by the treaty.' *Suez, Sociedad General de Aguas de Barcelona SA and Vivendi Universal SA* v. *The Argentine Republic*, ICSID Case No. ARB/03/19, Decision on Jurisdiction, 3 August 2006, para. 55.

[42] R. Dolzer, 'Fair and Equitable Treatment. A Key Standard in Investment Treaties', *The International Lawyer*, 39 (2005), 87.

fair and equitable treatment. Indeed, it is so prevalent that one may say the term 'fair and equitable treatment' seems to be viewed by contracting States as the basic standard of treatment to be accorded to investors. Indeed, to borrow the terminology of Hans Kelsen,[43] it is no exaggeration to say that the obligation of a host State to accord fair an equitable treatment to foreign investors is the *Grundnorm* or basic norm of the international investment regime. The basic purposes of investment treaties, as stated in their titles, are to promote and protect investments. Certainly, neither of those purposes could be achieved if treaties promised foreign investors treatment that was less than fair and less equitable.

Regime rules

Rules are the third element of a regime. For purposes of regime theory, rules are defined as 'specific prescriptions or proscriptions for actions'.[44] Although the difference between a 'norm' and a 'rule' is not always clear, one finds rules, in the form of prescriptions for action, in two places in the investment regime. First, the treaty texts contain many specific prescriptions for action. Thus, in addition to norms, the treaties express rules about such matters as expropriation, monetary transfers and compensation of injured investors because of war, revolution and civil strife. The second set of rules lies in the decisions of arbitral tribunals which apply the regime norms to specific fact situations. For example, fair and equitable treatment, according to many investment tribunals, means that the host government must respect 'the legitimate expectations' which it has created in the investor.[45] Indeed, one cannot fully know or understand the rules of the investment regime without studying the decisions of the arbitral tribunals that have applied often vague treaty terms to concrete fact situations.

Regime decision-making

The fourth and final regime element is decision-making procedures, which are defined as 'prevailing practices for making and implementing collective choice'.[46] The international regime for investment has no

---

[43] H. Kelsen, *Pure Theory of Law* (Berkeley, CA: University of California Press, 1978).

[44] Krasner, 'Structural Causes', *supra* n. 3.

[45] See R. Dolzer and C. Schreuer, *Principles of International Investment Law* (Oxford University, 2008), 119–49.

[46] Krasner, 'Structural Causes', *supra* n. 3.

422   J E S W A L D   W.   S A L A C U S E

centralised governing council with the power to administer and apply its rules, or the authority to make and implement collective choice. In that respect, it is unlike other international regimes such as the European Union (EU), the World Trade Organization (WTO), or the United Nations. Decision-making processes and authority are decentralised and diffused throughout the investment regime by individual treaties. Investment treaties provide for decision-making in basically four ways: (1) by consultation between the State parties to the treaty; (2) by arbitration between State parties in cases where they are unable to resolve conflicts through consultation and negotiation; (3) by consultations and negotiations between the investor and the State; and (4) by investor–State arbitration.

This last decision-making procedure has become the most important of the four. It is a unique feature of the regime, for two reasons. First, there are few instances in the international system where international law gives private persons and companies the right to compel a sovereign State to appear before a Tribunal and defend its sovereign actions, ostensibly taken to protect the public interest. The WTO, for example, has dispute resolution processes, but States, and States alone, are participants in those processes. Thus, the global investment regime has granted a private right of action to investors and has thereby also privatised the decision process to a large extent since arbitrators are private persons compensated by the disputants, not officials of governments or international organisations. Second, it is within investor–State arbitrations that most important decisions about the regime are decided. The first two of the abovementioned decision-making processes, while they exist in treaty law, are rarely employed by States. One exception is the North American Free Trade Agreement (NAFTA), which has created a Free Trade Commission (FTC) with the power to make binding interpretations of NAFTA provisions that NAFTA tribunals must follow in rendering their decisions.[47]

The decisions of arbitral tribunals in the nearly 300 investor–State disputes that have arisen under investment treaties have not only resolved a vast array of investor–State conflicts but they have also shaped the rules and norms of the regime. International law contains no doctrine of binding precedent, making the decisions of an international judicial or arbitral body in one case binding upon international judicial or arbitral

---

[47] Articles 2001–2002 NAFTA. The Commission has exercised this power on occasion. See NAFTA Free Trade Commission, *Notes of Interpretation of Certain* Chapter 11 *Provisions*, 31 July 2001.

bodies deciding similar, future cases.[48] Art. 59 of the Statute of the ICJ specifically states that '[t]he decision of the Court has no binding force except between the parties and in respect of that particular case'. Similarly, Art. 1136(1) of NAFTA, in virtually identical language, makes it clear that decisions of investment arbitral tribunals under Chapter 11 do not constitute binding precedent for the future. The treaty states '[a]n award made by a Tribunal shall have no binding force except between the disputing parties and in respect of the particular case'. Neither the ICSID Convention nor individual investment treaties contain a similarly specific prohibition, but neither do they expressly recognise that investment arbitration awards constitute precedent.[49] On the other hand, Art. 38 (d) of the Statute of the ICJ, in defining the sources of international law, recognises 'judicial decisions and the teachings of the most highly qualified publicists of the various nations as subsidiary means for the determination of rules of law'.[50] Thus, in applying international law international, courts and tribunals may refer to previous judicial decisions and arbitral decisions to determine the applicable rules of international law.

In international investment arbitration, counsel for the parties regularly cite prior cases in support of their positions, and tribunals, while reaffirming that they are not bound by previous arbitral decisions and awards, nonetheless constantly refer to earlier awards and decisions in interpreting investment treaty provisions and deciding investment disputes. Various factors have supported this trend. First, the vague and general language of many investment treaties, and the fact that treaties employ common legal concepts and phrases, naturally leads lawyers and tribunals to refer to decisions in other cases to determine how such provisions should be interpreted. Second, a recognised goal of international investment law is to establish a predictable, stable legal framework for investments, a factor which causes tribunals to pay attention to previous decisions on similar issues. Third, tribunals, like courts, are motivated by the underlying moral consideration that 'like cases should

---

[48] G. Kaufmann-Kohler, 'Arbitral Precedent. Dream, Necessity or Excuse?', *Arbitration International*, 23 (2007), 357.

[49] Art. 53(1) ICSID Convention States: 'The award shall be binding on the parties.' Schreuer suggests that this provision may be interpreted as 'excluding the applicability of the principle of binding precedent to successive ICSID cases'. He also notes that there is nothing in the preparatory work of the Convention suggesting that the doctrine of precedent should be applied to ICSID arbitration. C. Schreuer, 'A Doctrine of Precedent?', in P. Muchlinksi *et al.* (eds.), *The Oxford Handbook of International Investment Law* (Oxford University Press, 2008), 1190.

[50] Art. 38(1)(d) ICJ Statute.

be decided alike', unless a strong reason exists to distinguish the current case from previous ones.

The growth in investor–State arbitration in recent years has led to a significant expansion in the jurisprudence of investment treaties. The commonality of language and provisions among investment treaties makes an understanding of judicial and arbitration decisions important to their interpretation and application. Thus, this essentially private method of decision-making has played a crucial role in the development and maintenance of the regime set in place by investment treaties.

Why have States chosen to privatise this important method for implementing collective choice concerning the investment regime? No doubt capital-exporting countries believed that granting investors a private right of action for violation of regime rules would be an effective way of assuring that such rules were respected. But investor–State arbitration as a decision-making procedure has another advantage for home countries: it is a way for capital-exporting governments to reduce the governmental transaction costs arising out of the investments made by their nationals. Under the previous systems, government had to deal with their nationals seeking diplomatic protection and other forms of interventions with host country governments. That method potentially entailed significant diplomatic, political and economic costs since it might impact on and complicate important multi-faceted international relationships between a host State and an investor's home State. Investor–State arbitration relieves home countries of those costs. In effect, it allows them to say to their nationals and companies aggrieved by host government acts: 'You have your own remedy in the treaty. Use it if you wish. Go away and don't bother us.'

A different kind of regime

While the approximately 3,000 investment treaties together would seem to meet the definition of an international regime, one must acknowledge that this emerging regime has significant differences from other international regimes. Two of the most important are, first, that the regime has largely been constructed bilaterally, rather than multilaterally and, second, that it gives broad scope to private decision-making.

Bilateral construction

First, the investment regime has been constructed largely through bilateral negotiations, rather than multilateral ones. Most other international regimes – like the WTO, the International Criminal Court (ICC), the international human rights regime and the nuclear non-proliferation regime – have been the product of multilateral, indeed global, negotiations. Thus, for example, at the same time that the nations of the world have been building a global regime for investment, they have also been hard at work developing an international trade regime, primarily through the General Agreement on Tariffs and Trade (GATT)[51] and, since 1995, the WTO.[52] But whereas the trade regime has been developed on a *multilateral* basis through a succession of multilateral negotiating rounds leading to multilateral conventions, the investment regime has been built largely on a *bilateral* basis as numerous pairs of countries have negotiated similar rules and enforcement mechanisms that apply to their nationals and their investments in the territory of the other country. On the other hand, efforts to negotiate a global treaty on investment, such as the OECD initiative to conclude a Multilateral Investment Agreement (MIA), have failed.[53]

An interesting question is *why* the nations of the world have been willing to conclude bilateral investment treaties in growing numbers over the last fifty years but have generally resisted global agreements on investment. There is both a technical and a political explanation for this. The technical explanation is that a bilateral treaty must accommodate the interests of only two parties and is therefore far less complicated to negotiate than a multilateral, global treaty, which must accommodate the interests of many countries.[54] The political explanation is that, given the asymmetric nature of bilateral negotiations between a strong, developed country and a usually much weaker developing country, the bilateral setting allows the developed country to use its power more effectively than does a multilateral setting, where that power may be much diluted. For example, in multilateral settings, developing countries have the

---

[51] General Agreement on Tariffs and Trade, *opened for signature* on 30 October 1947, 55 UNTS 308.

[52] Agreement Establishing the World Trade Organization, Marrakesh, 15 April 1994.

[53] OECD, Multilateral Agreement on Investment: *The Original Mandate*. See also G. Kelley, 'Multilateral Investment Treaties. A Balanced Approach to Multinational Corporations', *Columbia Journal of Transnational Law*, 39 (2001), 483.

[54] For a discussion of the differences between bilateral and multilateral negotiations, see F. O. Hampson, *Multilateral Negotiations. Lessons from Arms Control, Trade, and the Environment* (Baltimore, MD: Johns Hopkins University Press, 1995), 1–51, 345–60; I. W. Zartman (ed.), *International Multilateral Negotiation. Approaches to the Management of Complexity* (San Francisco, CA: Jossey-Bass, 1994), 1–10, 213–22.

opportunity to form blocking coalitions with like-minded States to enhance their power in the negotiations, something that is impossible in bilateral negotiations. Moreover, the prospects of investment capital from specific developed countries, along with other political and economic benefits arising from a definite bilateral relationship, may make a developing country more willing to enter into a BIT with a specific developed country than it would a multilateral agreement where those benefits may seem more tenuous and theoretical. Moreover, whereas developed countries would be willing to enter into bilateral treaties with developing countries for investment liberalisation, knowing full well that little if any enterprises from the developing country would ever invest in the developed State, they have been unwilling to enter into treaties that would grant such liberalisation to investors from other developed States, who could become strong competitors to the host countries' own enterprises.[55]

Viewed from a different perspective, one may also say that the 2,600 bilateral investment treaties, although bilateral in form, have not really been negotiated on a strictly bilateral basis. One may view them as the product of 'serial multilateralism', instead of the traditional 'conference multilateralism' which has produced most of the world's international regimes. That is to say, capital-exporting States, which have driven the treaty-making process, have done so on the basis of prepared models or prototypes which they then proceeded to negotiate with many individual countries, showing little willingness to deviate significantly from the model they had prepared. Thus, from the outset, those capital-exporting States contemplated engaging in a multilateral process of negotiating with other States one at a time.

The similarity in models used by capital-exporting States has, of course, led to a similarity in treaties actually concluded. What explains the similarity of the models that States have used to negotiate BITs? Do they represent a grand conspiracy among capital-exporting States? Certainly there has been communication among capital-exporting States over the years as they have developed and refined their models. But an even more important factor has helped to shape the investment treaty regime: the epistemic community of international lawyers and scholars. Epistemic communities are defined as 'networks of professionals with recognised expertise and competence in a particular domain

---

[55] Such a problem arose during the negotiation of the failed OECD MIA, conducted between 1995 and 1998. See Kelley, 'Multilateral Investment Treaties', *supra* n. 53.

and an authoritative claim to policy relevant knowledge within that domain or issue area'.[56] Epistemic communities are vital to regime creation and maintenance because, according to Haas, they 'are crucial channels through which new ideas circulate from societies to government as well as from country to country'.[57] Since the movement to negotiate investment treaties began, the epistemic community of international lawyers, scholars, jurists and arbitrators has through their advising, writing, advocacy and judicial and arbitral decisions shaped the regime. They are now the principal actors for maintaining and operating it.

Privatised decision-making

A second important difference from other international regimes is the strong roles that non-State actors play in formulating, elaborating and applying the rules of the regime. In effect, the investment regime 'privatises' decision-making, whereas in other regimes, such as the WTO, decision-making remains firmly in the hands of Member States.

In most other regimes, States and their representatives are entrusted with the crucial function of elaborating and defining the rules of the regime. Thus, for example, State representatives may meet periodically to negotiate new rules, and institutions under the control of States are usually entrusted with the task of applying those rules to specific cases. A similar model of decision-making does not prevail in the international investment regime. Instead the regime, through investment treaties, has delegated decision-making to private persons – arbitrators, who are not representatives of States, and are not, unlike diplomats, able to pursue State policy. Indeed, arbitral rules of conduct require them to decide and act 'independently', which means that they may not be influenced by States, governments, the parties, or anybody else for that matter. Other private parties – lawyers and law firms representing investors and States – also play an important role in the decision-making process. Through their advocacy, they strongly influence both the process of decision-making and its end result. Thus, to a significant extent, regime elaboration and operation are largely in the hands of private parties who are not accountable to the States that have created the regime.

---

[56] P. Haas, 'Introduction: Epistemic Communities and International Policy', in P. Haas, 'Introduction: Epistemic Communities and International Policy Coordination', *International Organization*, 46 (1992), 1–35, 3.
[57] *Ibid.*, 27.

In theory, of course, arbitrators only decide disputes. They have no authority to make rules, and their decisions do not formally constitute legal precedent. But in practice, the approximately 300 decisions that have emanated from tribunals are consistently cited by lawyers and other tribunals and have a powerful influence on the making of future regime decisions.

Regime challenges

Regime theorists recognise that regimes are not permanent. The fact that at a given moment in time the parties' expectations may have 'converged' around a given set of principles, norms, rules and decisions in the investment area of international relations to form a regime does not mean that those expectations have converged permanently. Thus, despite the fact that the international investment regime is founded on 3,000 treaties solemnly concluded by some 180 different States, one cannot assume that it will endure.

For regime theorists, the endurance of a regime depends on two factors: regime effectiveness and regime robustness.[58] 'Regime effectiveness' requires the continued willingness and ability of its members to abide by its rules and to pursue its objectives and purposes. 'Regime robustness' refers to the ability of the regime to withstand external threats and challenges. The effectiveness and robustness of the international investment regime is by no means assured. It faces four salient challenges: two internal to the regime, and two external.

(1) The investment regime has been founded on the assumption that it will increase international investment, which in turn will lead to increased prosperity and economic development. Much research has questioned whether investment treaties have in fact increased investment flows to poor countries.[59] If the regime is ultimately judged not to have achieved its fundamental objective of promoting investment, then the justification for its continued existence becomes problematic.

(2) While public opinion generally seems to accept the norms and rules of the regime, its decision-making processes have been seriously

---

[58] Hasenclever, *Theories of International Regimes, supra* n. 34, 2.

[59] M. Hallward-Driemeier, 'Do Bilateral Investment Treaties Attract FDI? Only a Bit . . . and They Could Bite', World Bank, Working Paper No. 3121, June 2003; Salacuse and Sullivan, 'Do BITs Really Work?', *supra* n. 9, 66.

called into question. Host governments and elements of civil society have challenged the decision-making process on many grounds: that it is not transparent, that it does not account for the disparity in economic situation of regime members, that arbitrators are not truly independent, that they have an investor bias and that their decisions infringe on the legitimate exercise of sovereignty by host States.[60] For these alleged reasons, Bolivia in 2007[61] and Ecuador in 2010[62] formally withdrew from ICSID, an important pillar of the regime.

(3) The 'Washington Consensus' – the shared belief or, in the language of regime theory, 'the converged expectations' of many countries from the late 1980s until the end of the 1990s, that increased investment, open economies, privatisation and economic deregulation would result in increased global prosperity and economic development – was a powerful force for the spread of investment treaties and the development of the regime that they created.[63] Many parts of the world have lost faith in the ability of the 'Washington Consensus' to bring prosperity, and they therefore are looking for alternative ways of economic development.[64] The shattering of the 'Washington Consensus' may constitute the loss of an important support for a global investment regime based on treaties.

---

[60] J. A. Van Duzer, 'Enhancing the Procedural Legitimacy of Investor–State Arbitration Through Transparency and Amicus Curiae Participation', *McGill Law Review*, 52 (2007); S. D. Franck, 'The Legitimacy Crisis in Investment Treaty Arbitration. Privatizing International Law Through Inconsistent Decisions', *Fordham International Law Review*, 73 (2005), 1521; M. Sornarajah, 'A Coming Crisis. Expansionary Trends in Investment Treaty Arbitration', in K. Sauvant (ed.), *Appeals Mechanisms in International Investment Disputes* (New York: Oxford University Press, 2008), 39.

[61] ICSID News Release, 16 May 2007.

[62] ICSID News Release, 9 July 9 2009, announcing Ecuador's denunciation of the ICSID treaty with effect from 7 January 2010.

[63] The term 'Washington Consensus' is said to have been coined by economist John Williamson in 1989. It consisted of ten broad reforms: (1) fiscal discipline; (2) reordering public spending priorities away from politically powerful groups, such as the military, and toward basic services and infrastructure; (3) tax reform; (4) financial liberalisation; (5) competitive, stable exchange rates; (6) trade liberalisation; (7) reduction in barriers to foreign investment; (8) privatisation of State enterprises; (9) deregulation; and (10) property rights reform. S. Flanders, 'A New Washington Consensus', *The Financial Times*, 14 March 1997, 2. See also J. W. Salacuse, 'From Developing Countries to Emerging Markets. A New Role for Law in the Third World', *International Lawyer*, 33 (1999), 875.

[64] M. Hudson and J. Sommers, 'The End of the Washington Consensus', *CounterPunch*, December 12–14, 2008.

(4) Serious regional and global economic crises, like the one that struck Argentina in 2001 and the entire world in 2008, pose important external threats to the international investment regime. Countries under great stress, faced with potential social and political upheaval as a result of rapidly declining standards of living, often seek radical solutions and are impatient with international investment rules that may restrict their scope for action. For example, during times of economic crisis, they may be unwilling to grant national treatment to foreign investors, to avoid changing regulations in the name of 'fair and equitable treatment' and to refrain from seizing vital national resources held by foreigners just because they have made treaty promises not to expropriate.

These threats are real and they have the potential power to cause a divergence of State expectations and thus undermine the regime that has been painstakingly constructed over the last sixty years. The international investment regime will require wise management and flexible leadership in the future if it is to withstand the challenges.

21

Creditor protection in international law

MICHAEL WAIBEL

Introduction

When I arrived at Harvard Law School in the Fall of 2007, Professor Vagts had already retired from the faculty. Yet he was still very much present on campus. As a central pillar of the international law pantheon at Harvard, he continued supervising and giving advice to any student eager to learn about international law. Even though I never had the privilege of being taught by him, I am immensely grateful to him for all the guidance I received during my LLM year and for taking an active interest in my development as an international lawyer.

His door in Langdell was always open. Soon after my arrival, I became a regular visitor to Langdell 337. He would put aside the newest article he was working on. Invariably, a fascinating conversation would follow, which often took unexpected turns. What made the conversations with Detlev so delightful was that he provided not just many academic insights but drew on his lifelong wisdom as a scholar and dedicated internationalist. He was most generous with his time. I would also meet him regularly at the German lunch tables that he organised. For decades, he has served as the cultural bridge for Europeans who came to study at Harvard Law School, especially those from German-speaking countries.

Ever so often, I would wander to my pigeon hole in the Hark and find a letter from Professor Vagts. These letters contained press clippings, drawing my attention to developments within my own particular research area, the law of sovereign debt – which he often discovered earlier than I. When an article of mine appeared in the *American Journal of International Law*, Detlev was the first to send me a congratulatory note. He also served as the external examiner of my thesis, a task which he undertook with tremendous speed and efficiency.

One of his most recent scholarly contributions concerns the implications of the global financial crisis internationally.[1] He also wrote about the debt servicing difficulties of States, comparing the financial situation of the German Reich and Iraq after Saddam Hussein, and the measures taken by the international community to put both States in a position to start anew after the forcible removal of brutal dictatorships.[2] And then there is, of course, his magisterial essay on the occasion of ASIL's Centenary, charting the evolution of international economic law over the course of the twentieth century.[3] International financial law occupies an important place in this intellectual history of the discipline. In line with these interests of Detlev, my chapter examines the protection of creditor claims in international law.

Assume that a government puts a major financial institution during a systemic banking crisis into administration, or takes the financial institution into public ownership. Time is of the essence. In the crisis, the government decides to give priority to the bank's depositors – one type of creditor – and subordinates all other creditors, despite a rule of equal treatment of creditors before the crisis provided for by statute. Is a general unsecured creditor of the bank able to bring an international claim against the government in this situation?

In October 2008, Iceland's entire banking system collapsed. A financial institution that purchased medium-term notes issued by Landsbanki and Kaupthing, two large Icelandic banks, brought a claim against Iceland before the EFTA Surveillance Authority for discriminating against its creditors, allegedly in violation of Arts. 4 and 30 European Economic Area (EEA) Agreement.[4] In the crisis, the Icelandic authorities gave priority to depositors over other unsecured creditors by emergency legislation.[5]

In its preliminary assessment, the EFTA Surveillance Authority concluded that the Icelandic emergency measures did not run afoul of the non-discrimination provisions of the EEA Agreement. In view of their

---

[1] D. F. Vagts, 'The Financial Meltdown and its International Implications', *AJIL*, 103 (2009), 684–91.

[2] D. F. Vagts, 'Sovereign Bankruptcy, In re Germany (1963), In re Iraq (2004)', *AJIL*, 98 (2004), 302–6.

[3] D. F. Vagts, 'International Economic Law and the American Journal of International Law', *AJIL*, 100 (2006), 769–82.

[4] Agreement on the European Economic Area, *ILM*, 27 (1988), 281.

[5] Art. 6, Act No. 125/2008 (Iceland), Authority for Treasury Disbursements due to Unusual Financial Market Circumstances, amending Art. 103 of the Icelandic Act 161/2002 on Financial Undertakings.

essential role for the stability of the financial system, depositors and other unsecured creditors were not in a comparable situation. The response of the Icelandic authorities, who according to the Authority enjoyed a wide margin of discretion in economic policy matters, was deemed to be proportionate to the economic calamity Iceland faced. Therefore, the difference in treatment did not constitute discrimination.[6]

This Icelandic scenario is far from unique, and raises important questions about the scope of protection for creditor claims in international law. This chapter reviews some of the decisions of international courts and tribunals on creditor claims, and indicates general tendencies on the protection of such claims. The first section looks at the protection of creditor claims domestically, especially in constitutional law. The second section reviews the historical evolution of creditor protection in international law, while the third section examines the protection of creditor claims before national claims settlement institutions. The fourth and final section looks at creditor protection in international law, especially under modern investment treaties.

The conclusion reached is that creditor protection in international law, even today, is more limited than commonly assumed.[7] There is a rich literature on shareholder protection in international law;[8] by contrast, academic writing on creditor protection in international law is comparatively limited.[9]

The term 'creditor' covers a wide range of claims, including leases, mortgages, liens and pledges – security interests – and also debt securities such as bonds, loans, promissory notes and debentures, and more generally, all claims to money against a borrower. The focus of this chapter is on creditors who have money claims. The distinction between secured and unsecured creditors is important in this context.

---

[6] EFTA Surveillance Authority, Case No. 66935, Event No. 539094, Preliminary Assessment, 10 December 2009 (on file with the author).

[7] D. J. Bederman, 'Creditors' Claims in International Law', *International Lawyer*, 34 (2000) 235–53, 237 (concluding that both secured and unsecured creditors are substantially protected in international claims practice).

[8] E.g. F. A. Mann, 'The Protection of Shareholder Interests in Light of the Barcelona Traction Case', *AJIL*, 67 (1973), 259–74; R. B. Lillich, 'Two Perspectives on the Barcelona Traction Case', *AJIL*, 65 (1971), 522–32.

[9] E. Borchard, 'Contractual Claims in International Law', *Columbia Law Review*, 13 (1913), 457–99 (creditors generally lack standing); Bederman, 'Creditors' Claims', *supra* n. 7; W. M. Hauschild, 'Creditor Protection in the European Community', *ICLQ*, 31 (1982), 17–35; for a political economy perspective on creditors in international affairs, see J. Frieden, 'Capital Politics. Creditors and the International Economy', *Journal of Public Policy*, 8 (1988), 265–86.

Protection for creditors under international law depends on whether their claims may be considered a bundle of internationally protected rights ('international property'). International law has its own autonomous definition of property, though with considerable input from domestic law.[10] It is thus instructive to review the treatment of creditor claims in domestic law, before turning to the status of creditor claims in international law.

Creditor claims in domestic law

The term 'property' has several meanings in *foro domestico*. Domestic law knows at least three notions of property: a private, criminal and constitutional law definition.[11] A second dimension of variation is across countries, with the private law definition of property differing significantly by jurisdiction.[12]

Traditionally, continental European legal systems limited the notion of property to corporeal things, adopting a *numerus clausus* of property rights. The separation between the law of things and the law of obligations, which has its origin in Roman law, remains the dominant analytical framework.[13] Common law jurisdictions typically take a broader

---

[10] R. Dolzer, *Eigentum, Enteignung und Entschädigung im geltenden Völkerrecht* (Berlin and New York: Springer, 1985), 171 (concluding on the basis of custom, treaty and general principles that the autonomous definition of property adopted by public international law encompasses all rights of private parties that have a financial value); *Ivcher Bronstein* v. *Peru*, Inter-American Court of Human Rights, 6 February 2001, Series C. No. 74 (defining property as 'those material objects that may be appropriated, and also any right that may form part of a person's patrimony; this concept includes all moveable and immoveable property; corporal and incorporeal elements, and any other intangible object of any value'); *Awas Tingni Community* v. *Nicaragua*, (Inter-American Court of Human Rights, 31 August 2001, Series C. No. 79, para. 144) ('Property can be defined as those material things which can be possessed, as well as any right which may be part of a person's patrimony; that concept includes all movables and immovables, corporal and incorporal elements and any other intangible object capable of having value').

[11] U. Kriebaum, *Eigentumsschutz im Völkerrecht. Eine vergleichende Untersuchung zum international Investitionsrecht sowie zum Menschenrechtsschutz* (Berlin: Duncker & Humblot, 2008), 43.

[12] A. R. Coban, *Protection of Property Rights within the European Convention on Human Rights* (Aldershot: Ashgate, 2004), 10.

[13] Cf. Art. 544 of the French Code Civil: 'La propriété est le droit de jouir et de disposer *des choses* de la manière la plus absolue pourvu qu'on fasse pas un usage prohibé par les lois et les règlements' (emphasis added). S. Pavageau, *Le droit de propriété dans les jurisprudences des juridictions suprêmes françaises, européennes et internationales* (Paris:

view of property,[14] but there, too, the notion of property has its limits. Financial claims, in particular pensions and other welfare benefits, are commonly carved out.[15]

The constitutional notion of property underlying constitutional property clauses also varies across countries. Art. 14's scope of protection in the German *Grundgesetz* (Basic Law) is wide. The concept of constitutional property in Germany expanded over the course of the twentieth century to cover not only real property but a wide array of private claims.[16] Property covered includes both rights to physical property and contractual commitments; rights with their origin in private and in public law.[17] Protected assets also include intellectual property rights, stocks and social security benefits.[18] Excluded from constitutional protection are gratuitous welfare benefits.[19]

Debts are increasingly regarded as property protected by constitutional property clauses.[20] Van Der Walt observes that 'debts and claims

Librairie Générale de Droit et de Jurisprudence, 2006), 131–204; J.-R. Sieckmann, *Modelle des Eigentumsschutzes. Eine Untersuchung zur Eigentumsgarantie des Art. 14 GG* (Baden-Baden: Nomos, 1998), 108 *et seq.*; and F. Rey Martínez, *La propiedad privada en la Constitución española* (Madrid: Centro de Estudios Constitucionales, 1994), 253–81, cover the concept of property in three continental jurisdictions. See, generally, J. E. Penner, *The Idea of Property in Law* (Oxford University Press, 1997) and L. S. Underkuffler, *The Idea of Property. Its Meaning and Power* (Oxford University Press, 2003).

[14] *Belfast* v. *OD Cars*, [1960] AC 490, 517 ('very wide import, including intangible and tangible property'). See generally, T. Allen, *The Right to Property in Commonwealth Constitutions* (Cambridge University Press, 2000), chapter 5 ('The Meaning of Property').

[15] *US* v. *Teller* 107 US 64 (1882) (pension no vested legal right). C. A. Reich, 'The New Property', *Yale Law Journal*, 73 (1964), 733–87, argues in favour of accrued protection for governmental benefits against arbitrary deprivation by public officials; see *Goldberg* v. *Kelly*, 397 US 254 (1970) (following Reich).

[16] RGZ 109, 310 (319); M. Wolff, *Reichsverfassung und Eigentum* (Tübingen: J.C.B. Mohr, 1923), 5, 23.

[17] BGHZ 6, 270 (278).

[18] A. J. Van Der Walt, 'The Constitutional Property Clause', in Van Der Walt, *Constitutional Property Law* (Claremont: Juta, 2005), 84 ('all valuable rights which a person can use for her own benefit in the social context'); H. Mostert, *The Constitutional Protection and Regulation of Property and its Influence on the Reform of Private Law and Landownership in South Africa and Germany. A Comparative Analysis* (Berlin, Heidelberg and New York: Springer, 2002), 230. See also BVerfGE 42, 263 (*Contergan*).

[19] BVerfGE 69, 272 (1985) (only benefits that exist due to contributions by recipient protected).

[20] Cf. *Queensbury Industrial Society Ltd* v. *William Pickles and Others* (1865) LR 1 Exch 1, 4–5 ('any ordinary person would certainly think it strange, if he were told that a debt due to him was not part of his property'); *Jones* v. *Skinner* (1835) LJ Ch 87, 90 (property is 'the most comprehensive of all terms . . . every possible interest the party can have').

that sound in money have been recognized as constitutional property in most jurisdictions'.[21] The constitutional notion of property is of particular interest for the protection of creditor claims internationally.

Several decisions affirm the proprietary quality of debts.[22] In the *Hewlett* case, the Zimbabwean High Court addressed the threshold question of whether public debt was protected property only briefly, and affirmed this by reference to the ordinary meaning of the term and adopting a wide conception of tangible and intangible property that included debt.[23] Relying on a close textual reading of the property guarantee, the Court found that there was no violation on account of a repudiation of State debt. Art. 15 of the Zimbabwean Constitution says, in pertinent part, that 'no property ... shall be compulsorily acquired'. Ultimately, the court declined to find, however, that Zimbabwe acquired any property interest in destroying a debt by statute.[24]

In *Shah* v. *Attorney-General* (*No. 2*), the Ugandan High Court analysed a similar case through a different prism.[25] The case concerned a private contractor's judgment debt against the State rendered unenforceable by statute. Again, the debt easily met the threshold test of being a protected property interest. In contrast to *Hewlett*, the court in *Shah* found there was a clear benefit to the Uganda State due the destruction of its payment obligation. With this in mind, the Court affirmed an acquisition of property. But note that this case concerned a judgment debt, rather than a general, unsecured creditor claim.

The Australian High Court adopted a similar approach to *Shah*. The *Georgiadis* case concerned the cancellation of a Common law negligence claim by statute. The High Court established the principle that it is sufficient for a deprivation if the State receives a 'direct benefit

---

[21] Van Der Walt, *Constitutional Property Law, supra* n. 18, 96.

[22] *Rao Jiwaji Rao Scindia* v. *Union of India*, AIR 1971 SC 530 (India); *Georgiadis* v. *Australian and Overseas Telecommunications Corp.* (1994) 179 CLR 297 (Australia); *A&B Company* v. *Federal Republic of Germany* 14 DR 146 (1978); *Peverill* v. *Health Insurance Commission* 104 ALR 449 (FC) (1991) (Australia); *Shah* v. *Attorney-General* (*No. 2*), [1970] EA 523 (UHC) (State debt) (Uganda).

[23] *Hewlett* v. *Minister of Finance and Another* 1982 (1) SA 490 (ZSC) (Zimbabwe), 497 ('the ordinary meaning of property clearly includes a debt payable to a person'). Cf. also *Attorney-General* v. *Lawrence*, [1985] LRC (Const.) 921 (CA) (St Christopher and Nevis) and *Shah, supra* n. 22.

[24] *Hewlett, supra* n. 23; T. Allen, 'Limitations on Constitutional Property Rights', in P. Jackson (ed.), *Property Law. Current Issues and Debates* (Aldershot: Gower, 1999), 187–207, 192–3, explains that this is one common way of limiting the scope of compensable interference in creditor claims.

[25] *Shah, supra* n. 22.

or financial gain'.[26] Since the Australian government enhanced its resources, the challenged measure amounted to a deprivation. Judge Brennan explained that there is not only deprivation of property, but also acquisition if the freeing of the State from liability is the 'correlative' of the creditor's claim.[27]

In *Peverill* v. *Health Insurance Commission*, a doctor's right to payment for medical services rendered to the State was cancelled by statute with retroactive effect. This State action, the Australian Federal Court found, clearly amounted to an acquisition of property in terms of section 51(xxxi), the property guarantee of the Australian Constitution. By abrogating its own payment obligation, a financial benefit undoubtedly accrued to the State.

But the High Court of Australia overturned the lower court's decision.[28] The court reasoned that the plaintiff had no vested right, since it was created by legislation and subject to withdrawal and even outright cancellation at any time. Whether constitutional protection is available hence depends on the vested character of the claim to money.[29] Ephemeral claims create no legitimate expectations of future stability in the contractual relation. They are subject to legislative modification at any time.

In summary, most of the case-law takes a sceptical view of the expropriability of creditor claims in domestic law. Either these claims do not fall under constitutional property clauses in the first place or, absent a clear repudiation by the government, the non-payment of a sum due does not amount to an expropriation. Let us now turn to how the protection of creditor claims evolved in international law.

A short history of creditor protection in international law

Before the First World War, creditors, or their governments, generally failed to obtain compensation before arbitral tribunals and mixed

---

[26] *Georgiadis, supra* n. 22, 305. This is consistent with the influential article by J. Sax, 'Takings and the Police Power', *Yale Law Journal*, 74 (1964), 36, where Sax posits that the purpose of constitutional property guarantees is to prevent government from arbitrarily realising profit opportunities. *Mutual Pools and Staff Pty Ltd* v. *The Commonwealth of Australia*, (1994) 179 CLR 155 follows this approach (upholding a direct tax refund of an improperly collected tax to homeowners against challenge by intermediary).

[27] *Ibid.*, 311. [28] *Peverill* v. *Health Insurance Commission* 179 CLR 226 (1994).

[29] Van Der Walt, *Constitutional Property Law, supra* n. 18, 223.

claims commissions.[30] Except in limited circumstances, these claims commissions tended to decline 'pure' creditor claims. Some tribunals declined compensation to creditors, seemingly because no clear link of causation ran from a governmental expropriation of some commercial undertaking to the indirect injury suffered by the creditor of that undertaking.[31] This reluctance to accept creditor claims extended to national courts and claims commissions.[32]

It is important to bear in mind that in the late nineteenth and the first part of the twentieth centuries, it was common to equate the private property interests of nationals with those of their home State. A loss of private wealth to a national was deemed to constitute a loss of 'national wealth' – a transfer from the creditor's home country to another State or its nationals. As a principle, this equivalence is already doubtful. But even apart from this basic point, it may be questioned whether this equivalence of State and individual economic loss represents an accurate view today, with the increasing individualisation of international law, and greatly increased mobility of individuals across borders.[33]

A first shift occurred in the interwar period, though consistency in the practice on creditor claims continued to be lacking.[34] Secured debt claims – such as mortgages – started to receive international protection in claims practice.[35] Mortgages are rights *in rem*, and closely related to immovable property.[36] In isolated cases, unsecured claims were deemed

---

[30] J. H. Ralston, *The Law and Procedure of International Tribunals* (Stanford University Press, 1926), 158.

[31] *Mora & Arango Case* (*US* v. *Spain*), Award, 22 February 1883, J. Moore (ed.), *History and Digest of the International Arbitrations to which the United States has been a Party* (Washington, DC: Government Printing Office, 1898), vol. 3, 233; *Alsop* Claim (*US* v. *Peru*), *ibid.*, 1627–28.

[32] *Blagge* v. *Balch*, 162 US 439 (1896) (French Spoliation Acts, 3 March 1891, 26 Stat. 862, 897, 908 (1891) excludes creditors and assignees); *Labadie* v. *United States*, 32 Ct Cl. 368 (1896) (1891 Indian Depredation Act excludes creditors and assignees).

[33] Z. Douglas, *The International Law of Investment Claims* (Cambridge University Press, 2009), para. 337, 162 ('the national contracting State of the claimant has only a marginal interest in the investor/State arbitration proceedings').

[34] Bederman, 'Creditors' Claims', *supra* n. 7, 238.

[35] Bederman, 'Creditors' Claims', *supra* n. 7, 237; A. H. Feller, *The Mexican Claims Commissions 1923–1934. A Study in the Law and Procedure of International Tribunals* (New York: Macmillan, 1935), 116–17.

[36] On the importance of distinguishing rights *in rem* and *in personam*, see Douglas, *The International Law of Investment Claims*, *supra* n. 33, 202–9 ('If the distinction between contract and property is blurred in respect of the threshold question of whether a qualifying investment has been made by the claimant, the consequential error will be

to benefit from protection under international law, too.[37] Most of the time, however, unsecured creditors (or, more precisely, their State of nationality in the days of diplomatic protection) lacked an international law remedy.

Creditor claims raise particular issues of causation and attribution under the secondary rules on State responsibility. In the international law on creditor claims, the question of the immediacy of the damage looms large. Adjudicators realised that a general rule to the effect that any ripple effect of some injury to tangible property or the person on the creditor's repayment or her contractual rights would be problematic. Therefore, the tendency was to look at the connection of the creditor's loss with the direct injuries to person or property. If this link was too remote, the creditor had no claim in international law against the government.

In the *Ziat, Ben Kiran* arbitration, Max Huber categorically rejected that international law protection extended to the person 'who is only a creditor of another upon whom the damage has directly fallen in immediate form'.[38] Only a person 'who has been immediately hit by the damage' could claim relief. Another good example of how the directness criterion operates is the *Dickson Car Wheel Company* case. The Mexican–American General Claims Commission examined the non-payment of a debt arising out of a sale of goods to a Mexican enterprise nationalised soon thereafter. The Commission held that the claimant lacked standing to sue because only a Mexican company suffered the injury, rather than the American creditor.[39]

But the Commission went further, holding that a 'State does not incur international responsibility from the fact that an individual or company of the nationality of another State suffers a pecuniary injury as the corollary or result of an injury which the defendant State has inflicted upon an individual or company irrespective of nationality when the relations between the former and the latter are of a contractual nature'.[40]

the tribunal's application of the substantive obligations of investment protection to a contractual dispute').

[37] *Compagnie Générale des Eaux de Caracas (Belgium v. Venezuela)*, 9 *RIAA* 329, 330–31, 346 (1903) (Venezuela liable for debts of expropriated entity).

[38] *Ziat, Ben Kiran*, Claim 53, 2 *RIAA* 729, 730 (1925), quoted from Bederman, 'Creditors' Claims' *supra* n. 7, 239.

[39] *Dickson Car Wheel Company (USA) v. United Mexican States*, 4 *RIAA* (2002), 669; in *Oil Field of Texas, Inc.* v. *Islamic Republic of Iran*, 1 *Iran–US CTR* (1986), 347, 375, n. 14, the Iran–US Claims Tribunal attributes the denial of the claim in the *Dickson* case at least partly to the fact that the remaining assets and income of Dickson's contractual counter-party 'could be used to satisfy creditor claims').

[40] *Ibid.*, 681.

Commissioner Nielsen dissented on the grounds that the creditor had in fact suffered direct damage due to Mexican government acts.[41] Other awards in that period adopted the same restrictive directness criterion.[42]

In *Hofmann and Steinhardt*, a case concerning bonds issued by a private railway before the American–Turkish Claims Commission, the Commission required 'convincing evidence showing interference by the Turkish government with property rights, resulting, in effect, in confiscation'.[43] The Commission also set out general requirements for successful creditor claims under international law:

> (1) that the claimant has cognizable property interests in another entity, which can include contractual rights or debt obligations; (2) that the government 'exercised control' over the entity 'and interfered with its operation and took action resulting in the destruction of the claimant's property rights in a manner violative of international law'; and (3) 'the claimant has suffered damages that can be estimated with reasonable accuracy'.[44]

Under these conditions, the Commission concluded, the presumption that 'damages sustained were the proximate result of the application of such measures' was warranted.[45] These conditions, taken together, amount to a general rule that creditor claims are compensable provided government action had confiscated an entity along with its contractual and debt obligations.[46] The causation of the injury is therefore the critical element. But the cases provide little further guidance on how causation with respect to creditor claims ought to be assessed.

Creditor claims before domestic claims settlement institutions

Domestic settlement institutions were somewhat more welcoming to creditor claims than mixed claims commissions and other arbitral tribunals.[47]

---

[41] Feller, *The Mexican Claims Commission*, *supra* n. 35, 124, (if 'the Mexican government had taken over the [railway] lines because it wanted to prevent the fulfillment of this or other contracts, it would be easier to say that the damage was "direct" and hold Mexico responsible').

[42] *Société civile des porteurs d'obligations du Crédit foncier mexicain*, Mexican–US Claims Commission, Award No. 79 (unpublished), Feller, *The Mexican Claims Commission*, *supra* n. 35, 122–3; *Debenture Holders of the San Marcos & Pinos Co.* (*UK* v. *Mexico*), 5 *RIAA* 191 (1931) (claim based on debentures secured by mortgage failed).

[43] *Hofmann and Steinhardt*, *infra* n. 47, 291.   [44] *Ibid.*, 293.   [45] *Ibid.*

[46] Bederman, 'Creditors' Claims', *supra* n. 7, 241.

[47] *Laredo Elec. & Ry Co.*, Decision 2-D, in *American Mexican Claims Commission. Report to the Secretary of State*, 247 (1948) (debt of a Mexican company whose assets

After the Second World War, the US Foreign Claims Settlement Commission (FCSC) adjudicated a series of lump-sum agreements.[48] The FCSC is a permanent national commission which adjudicates private claims under a variety of settlement agreements with other countries. The FCSC's applicable law includes international law.[49]

Crucially, Congress limited the FCSC's authority with respect to several lump-sum agreements by expressly excluding creditor claims.[50] By their very nature, lump-sum agreements provide limited compensation, often to a broad pool of claimants.[51] The policy reason behind this limitation is quite obvious. The pool of money available for distribution is limited. Congress provided for compensation payouts to affected American citizens with that financial limitation in mind.[52] These limitations are important, because they provide evidence of State practice on general creditor claims.

---

seized by the government compensable); H. Milne McIntosh, Decision 17-C, *ibid.*, 364–7 (bondholders); *General Finance Co.*, Decision No. 125-E, *ibid.*, 546–8 (mortgage bonds); *Ina M. Hofmann and Dulce H. Steinhardt* v. *The Republic of Turkey American–Turkish Claims Commission*, in F. K. Nielsen (ed.), *American–Turkish Claims Settlement. Opinions and Reports* (Washington, DC: US Government Printing Office, 1937), 286–9 (bonds issued by private railway).

[48] Established by the United States International Claims Settlement Act of 1949. See, generally, R. Lillich and B. Weston, *International Claims. Their Settlement by Lump Sum Agreements* (Charlottesville, VA: University Press of Virginia, 1975).

[49] Section 303, Title III, International Claims Settlement Act of 1949 ('[the] Commission shall determine in accordance with applicable substantive law, including international law, the validity and amount of claims').

[50] Bederman, 'Creditors' Claims', *supra* n. 7, 241.

[51] H. Van Houtte, B. Delmartino and I. Yi, *Post-War Restoration of Property Rights under International Law* (Cambridge University Press, 2008), vol. I, 306 (lump-sum agreements, though not required, often provide for lower compensation than the aggregate of individual damages).

[52] Bederman, 'Creditors' Claims', *supra* n. 7, 241–2 ('Congress chose to conserve the funds distributed in lump-sum settlements and statutorily disqualify many sorts of unsecured creditors' claims'); *Charles D. Siegel* v. *Soviet Union*, Decision, FCSC No. SOV-230, *ILR*, 26 (1959), 275 (Commissioner Clay dissenting on the grounds that since the US government ordinarily did not exercise diplomatic protection on sovereign bonds, a bond denominated in roubles fell outside the jurisdiction of the Commission, emphasising that there were limited monies available for compensation and the aggregate of claims presented greatly exceeded the lump sum); HR Rep. 2227, 85th Cong., 2nd Session (1958), S. Re. 1794 (1958) ('by limiting actions ... to the claims of persons who have been deprived of property without just compensation ... [there may be] no relief to persons whose claims are not based upon an actual interest [in property] ... [since the latter] action would deplete, perhaps seriously, the amounts which could be recovered by Americans whose property was nationalized by Czechoslovakia').

Only mortgage claims and other, similarly secured claims fall generally within the FCSC's remit.[53] In *Ella Wyman*, a debt annulled explicitly by the Czech government was found to be compensable.[54] In *Re Claim of European Mortgage*, the FCSC construed its authority with respect to creditor claims narrowly. It did emphasise, however, that this was the result of the peculiar treaty language. Specifically, it did not imply that 'a creditor claimant could under no circumstances show himself entitled to recover, particularly under a statute with different background, history and language'.[55]

In the *Skins Trading Corp.* case, the Commission denied compensation on unsecured debts in the absence of an annulment or repudiation. It affirmed that 'the nationalization of a debtor company does not constitute a taking of the property of a creditor of the nationalized company, where there has been no annulment or repudiation of the debt'.[56]

The Commission emphasised the general principle that '[w]artime events, postwar economic conditions, foreign currency control restrictions, and chaotic conditions in general very likely played a greater role in weakening the claimant's ability to collect the debt than did the nationalization of the debtor. Final straws are not to be equated with proximate causes.'[57] The Commission relied in part on the legislative history of the settlement, and found that the United States and Czechoslovakia intended to conclude a lump-sum compensation settlement, without taking into account general creditor claims.[58]

---

[53] E.g. *Joseph Singer*, FCSC Czech Claim No. 3,993, 15th *Semi Annual FCSC Report*, December 1961, 20–1; *Benno Pilpel*, FCSC Claim No. CZ-2442, Decision No. CZ-57 (1959); *Virginia Howard*, Docket FCSC Y-1282, Decision Y-1259, 15 September 1954, Foreign Claims Settlement Commission of the United States. Decisions and Annotations (1968), 112–14 (rejected unsecured creditor claim); *Emma Brunner*, FCSC Claim No. Docket Y-1281, Decision Y-1130 (12 August 1954), 116; *Skins Trading Corp.*, FCSC Claim No. CZ-3978, Decision No. CZ-734 (23 May 1960), FCSC Decisions and Annotations, 402–44 ('There was no showing … that the debt which forms the res was ever annulled by the Government of Czechoslovakia so as to constitute a taking of the claimant's property; and a mere failure … to pay a debt will not give rise to a compensable claim under section 404 of the Act').

[54] *Ella Wyman*, FCSC Claim Nos. CZ-4347–4348, Decision No. CZ-3529 (1960).

[55] *FCSC D&A*, 337.

[56] *Skins Trading Corp.* claim, *supra* n. 53 (23 May 1960), Claim No. CZ-3978, Decision No. CZ-734, (1962) ILR, 42, 155–7, 403.

[57] *Ibid.*, 403. [58] *Ibid.*, 404.

In addition, claims based on unsecured debts such as dividends or loans often failed.[59] In *Skins Trading Corp.*, mere non-payment of contractual retirement benefits did not amount to a taking in the absence of annulment or cancellation.[60] Express repudiation, however, triggers the debtor country's international liability.[61] For instance, in the *Bohadlo* case, the Commission affirmed a taking, after Czechoslovakia had blocked payment on domestic currency bonds (koruna) in 1945 and annulled these debt obligations by decree.[62]

In general, mere non-payment of a debt does not amount to a taking. The *Feierabend* v. *Czechoslovakia* Commission found that non-payment of contractual retirement benefits is no taking. A specific action abolishing or annulling creditor rights is required.[63] However, a judgment creditor has a vested right which, if annulled by an arbitral tribunal on behalf of the debtor government, amounts to a taking.[64]

In *Howard* v. *Yugoslavia*, the Commission ruled that an unsecured loan to a Yugoslavian corporation was outside the scope of the 1948 Yugoslav Claims Agreement. At the same time, it affirmed that the enterprise itself was taken.[65] In contradistinction to the enterprise, the loan could not be taken. The Commission relied on the

---

[59] *Ann A. Unger* v. *Czechoslovakia*, Claim Nos. CZ-3137, CZ-3138 and CZ-3142, Decision No. CZ-3538, (1962) 17 *FCSC Semiannual Reports* 262; *Marietta J. Poras* v. *Czechoslovakia*, Claim No. CZ-3020, Decision No. CZ-3528, (1962) 17 *FCSC Semiannual Reports* 256; *Charles Simonek* v. *Czechoslovakia*, 7 September 1960, FCSC Claim No. CZ-3147, Decision No. CZ-2299, (1961) 14 *FCSC Semiannual Reports* 174. *Erwin P. Hexner* v. *Czechoslovakia*, Claim Nos. CZ-2408, CZ-3255 and CZ-3290, Decision No. CZ-2470, (1962) 17 *FCSC Semiannual Reports* 266; *Joseph Smolik* v. *Czechoslovakia*, FCSC Claim No. CZ-4032, Decision No. CZ-3417 (1954).

[60] *Feierabend* v. *Czechoslovakia*, 7 September 1960, Claim No. CZ-2529, Decision No. CZ-1423, (1962) 17 *FCSC Semiannual Reports* 207; *ILR*, 42, 157–61.

[61] *Toni Felix* v. *Czechoslovakia*, FCSC Claim No. CZ-2097, Decision No. CZ-2322, (1962) 17 *FCSC Semiannual Reports* 231.

[62] *Emil Bohadlo*, FCSC Claim No. CZ-1734, Decision No. CZ-379, (1962) 17 *FCSC Semiannual Reports* 196.

[63] *Feierabend* v. *Czechoslovakia*, Cf. also *Skins Trading Corp.* Claim, *supra* n. 53 (creditor claims not compensable) and *Universal Oil Product Company* v. *Romania*, FCSC RUM-39,531 (nationalisation of debtor company, in the absence of annulation or repudiation of the debt, does not amount to a taking).

[64] *John Stipkala* v. *Czechoslovakia*, FCSC Claim No. CZ-1616, Decision No. CZ-135, (1962) 17 *FCSC Semiannual Reports* 191.

[65] *Virginia Howard* v. *Yugoslavia*, 15 September 1954, FCSC Claim No. Y-1282, Decision No. Y-1269, *FCSC D&A* 112–15; *William S. Smyth* v. *Yugoslavia*, FCSC Claim No. Y-1473, Decision No. Y-1354, *FCSC D&A* 116 (debt against private party for goods sold); *Universal Pictures Co., Inc.* v. *Yugoslavia*, Claim USFCSC No. Y-1509, Decision No. Y-361, *FCSC D&A* 117 (debt for rental fee on motion picture).

language of the agreement and the legislative history of the statute. The debt remained valid and had not been taken by Yugoslavia.

For the British equivalent to the FCSC, the Foreign Compensation Commission (FCC), the availability of relief for creditors also depends in large part on the specific statutory instrument for lump-sum settlement.[66] For instance, under the UK–Poland Agreement of 1954, the Commission shall not entertain claims 'in respect of a debt arising out of a bond or in respect of a loss sustained as a result of Polish measures affecting any security constituted under a bond, if the bond formed part of a public issue'.[67] In other cases, such as the UK–Czech Agreement of 1949, No. 62, a subsequent statutory instrument mandated that the Commission register 'a claim in respect of a debt ... outstanding to a British national from the Czechoslovak Government or municipal authority in Czechoslovakia or from a person, corporation, firm, or association (other than a British national) resident in Czechoslovakia'.[68]

As a general rule, State practice points to a hierarchy of creditor claims in international law, depending on the sums available for satisfaction of creditor claims. Some categories of claimants, such as those having personal injury or those whose rights *in rem* have been expropriated, appear more worthy of protection than others. By contrast, those with pure money claims, such as a general unsecured creditor or a bondholder, rank lower in the hierarchy of priorities. The financial institution in the Icelandic example, an unsecured creditor of an Iceland bank, would fall into the latter category.

Creditor claims under international law

Creditor claims may be possessions under Art. 1 of Protocol No. 1 of the European Convention on Human Rights (ECHR). The ECHR adopted a very wide definition of property, considerably wider than the typical notion of property in private law.[69] Art. I of Protocol No. 1 provides that:

---

[66] Established by the Foreign Compensation Act 1950, c. 12, providing for the establishment of a Commission dealing with compensation received from foreign governments; cf. also the UK–Bulgarian Agreement of 1955, No. 79, which discharged all liability of the Bulgarian government and its nationals arising from debts, claims and obligations.

[67] SI, 1957, No. 101.   [68] SI, 1960, No. 849.

[69] Kriebaum, *Eigentumsschutz im Völkerrecht*, supra n. 11, 44, 47. *Handyside* v. *United Kingdom*, 7 December 1976, Series A. N. 24, §62 (the terms 'possessions', 'property' in the authentic English version of the First Additional Protocol, and the French terms 'biens' and 'propriété' are identical).

Every natural or legal person is entitled to the peaceful enjoyment of his possessions. No one shall be deprived of his possessions except in the public interest and subject to the conditions provided for by law and the general principles of international law. The preceding provisions shall not, however, in any way impair the right of a State to enforce such laws as it deems necessary to control the use of property in accordance with the general interest or to secure the payment of taxes or other contributions and penalties.

According to the ECHR's constant jurisprudence, there are two broad categories of 'possessions' – first, existing property rights and, second, existing claims to money or performance with a financial value, provided that the holder may legitimately expect their fulfilment.[70] The Court has also qualified court judgments with no possibility of further appeal as 'possessions'.[71] Kriebaum and Reinisch note that the European Court of Human Rights has refrained from offering any definition of the term 'property'.[72]

It is important to note that the wide definition of possessions under Art. 1 of Protocol No. 1 ECHR is not necessarily co-extensive with the protection of property under general international law, outside the regional European context.

As far as general public international law is concerned, the question whether a contractual claim to payment is protected property in international law is in flux. In many ways, the term 'investment' is synonymous with the notion of property in international law.[73] Only limited authority lends support to the view that creditor claims are protected property as a matter of international law in general. Of particular interest in this respect is the definition of investment in international investment law, and whether contractual rights are susceptible of being expropriated. The answer is more nuanced than is generally acknowledged in the

---

[70] Kriebaum, European Court of Human Rights, Application, *supra* n. 11, 124 (with a detailed analysis of the case-law).

[71] *Brumarescu* v. *Romania*, No. 28342/95, ECHR 1999-VII; *ON* v. *Bulgaria*, European Court of Human Rights, Application No. 35221/97, 6 April 2000 (judgment on a claim for restitution); *Sciortino* v. *Italy*, No. 30127/96, 18 October 2001 (non-enforcement of a national court decision to award the claimant a higher State pension); *Burdov* v. *Russia*, 7 May 2002, ECHR 2002-III, §§39, 40 (tort claim against State which became binding).

[72] U. Kriebaum and A. Reinisch, 'Property, Right to International Protection', in R. Wolfrum (ed.), *Max Planck Encyclopaedia of Public International Law*, www. mpepil.com, 10.

[73] On the notion of investment, see B. Legum and C. Mouawad, 'The meaning of "investment" in the ICSID Convention', chapter 17 in this volume.

literature, despite the broad asset-backed definition of modern investment treaties.

Douglas emphasises the proprietary character of the assets that qualify as covered investments.[74] Schill, by contrast, posits that the notion of investment comprises 'all essential rights and interests necessary for engaging in economic activities in a host State ... it covers not only classical property rights, but also includes protection for investor–State contracts'.[75]

There is no obstacle in principle to creditor claims governed by some municipal law to be submitted to an international court or arbitral tribunal for adjudication.[76] But the central question is often whether general creditor claims are covered by the scope of State consent for adjudication. In many instances, tribunals have declined to answer that question in the affirmative.

There is also the requirement of a territorial link with the host country.[77] Douglas maintains that a territorial connection to the host State is needed, as an emanation of the central economic characteristics of investments.[78] He suggests that the territorial requirement is satisfied if the host country's rules of private international law at the time the investment was made located intangible property rights in the host State. Creditor claims will often lack this territorial nexus, and are therefore unlikely to qualify as an investment.

But some authority also points in the other direction. In *Fedax NV* v. *Republic of Venezuela*,[79] Venezuela disputed the Tribunal's jurisdiction

---

[74] Douglas, *supra* n. 33, Rule 22, 161, and also paras. 343, 353, 359.

[75] S. Schill, *The Multilateralization of International Investment Law* (Cambridge University Press, 2009), 72.

[76] J. G. De Beus, *The Jurisprudence of the General Claims Commission United States and Mexico Under the Convention of September 8, 1923* (The Hague: Martinus Nijhoff, 1938) (the Drago–Porter Convention of 1907, the objective of which is to prevent the use of force to recover debt before arbitration is exhausted, as illustration that contract claims may be the proper subjects for international claims).

[77] *Ceskoslovenska Obchodni Banka AS [CSOB]* v. *Slovak Republic*, Objections to Jurisdiction, ICSID Case No. ARB/97/4, 24 May 24 1994 (characterising CSOB 'as an investor and the entire process as an investment *in* the Slovak Republic within the meaning of the Convention', emphasis added); *Consorzio Groupement LESI–DIPENTA* v. *People's Democratic Republic Algeria*, ICSID Case No. ARB/03/8, Award, para. 72, 10 January 2005, pt. II.2., para. 13 (iv) (a) '[Q]ue le contractant ait effectué un apport dans le pays concerné' ([that] the contracting party has made contributions in the host country) (ICSID's unofficial translation).

[78] Douglas, *The International Law of Investment Claims*, *supra* n. 33, Rule 22, 171.

[79] *Fedax NV* v. *The Republic of Venezuela*, ICSID Case No. ARB/96/3, Decision on Objections to Jurisdiction, 11 July 1997.

on the ground that Fedax had not made an investment 'in the territory' of the contracting parties as prescribed by the BIT. In dismissing Venezuela's argument on a required territorial nexus, the Tribunal explained that it was 'a standard feature of many international financial transactions that the funds involved are not physically transferred to the territory of the beneficiary, but put at its disposal elsewhere'. It was enough that Venezuela, as the beneficiary of the credit, eventually used the money for its governmental purposes in its territory.

In the *SGS* v. *Philippines* case, the Tribunal held that pre-shipment inspection services conducted in a port outside the host country did not preclude qualification as an investment, since the contract's main purpose was the delivery of inspection certificates in the Philippines. Therefore, some business activity related to the investment in the host State is necessary. The *SGS* v. *Pakistan* Tribunal held that 'certain expenditures in . . . Pakistan' and the 'injection of funds into the territory' satisfied the BIT's territorial link.[80] In an *obiter dictum*, the *SGS* v. *Philippines* Tribunal appeared to object to the 'very broad definition of territoriality' in the *Fedax NV* v. *The Republic of Venezuela* Jurisdiction award.[81]

Contractual rights generally

In principle, contractual rights are capable of being expropriated.[82] Some investment arbitration awards affirm the expropriability of contractual rights in principle.[83] However, an analysis of this line of cases suggests

---

[80] *SGS* v. *Philippines*, ICSID Case No. ARB/02/6, Decision on Objections to Jurisdiction, 29 January 2004, *ICSID Reports*, 8, 519, paras. 57, 99–112.

[81] *SGS* v. *Pakistan*, ICSID Case No. ARB/01/13, Decision on Objections to Jurisdiction, 6 August 2003, *ICSID Reports*, 8, 406, paras. 75–77, 136.

[82] G. Sacerdoti, 'Bilateral Treaties and Multilateral Instruments on Investment Protection', *RdC*, 269 (1997), 251, 381 ('All rights and interests having an economic content come into play, including immaterial and contractual rights'); R. Higgins, 'The Taking of Property by the State. Recent Developments in International Law', *RdC*, 176 (1982), 259–348, 263, 271 ('the notion of "property" is not restricted to chattels. *Sometimes* rights that might seem more naturally to fall under the category of contract rights are treated as property') (emphasis added).

[83] *Southern Pacific Properties (Middle East) Ltd. (SPP)* v. *Arab Republic of Egypt*, Award 20 May 1992, *ICSID Reports*, 3, 189, para. 164 ('Nor can the tribunal accept the argument that the term "expropriation" applies only to jus in rem . . . . there is considerable authority for the proposition that contract rights are entitled to the protection of international law and that the taking of such rights involves an obligation to make compensation therefor'); *Wena Hotels Ltd* v. *Arab Republic of Egypt*, ICSID Case

that, as a general rule, only some, rather than all contractual rights *may* be expropriated. There is considerable uncertainty concerning the scope of appropriable contractual rights, and the application of the rules on expropriation to contractual rights.

In the *Norwegian Shipowners' Claim*, an Arbitral Tribunal operating under Permanent Court of Arbitration rules held in a case concerning contracts between individuals and US docks for the construction of ships that contracts may be the subject of expropriation.[84] The Tribunal noted that the US intention was to 'take' and they did in fact take the contracts under which the fifteen hulls in question were constructed. It explained that these 'contracts were the property, or created it, and what the United States calls "physical property" is only one of the elements or aspects of the "property"'.[85]

On the other hand, some decisions of the Iran–US Claims Tribunal treat contractual rights as subject to expropriation only if they are closely related to physical property. In *Starrett Housing Corp.*, the Tribunal noted with approval that the claimants 'rely on precedents in international law in which cases measures of expropriation or taking, primarily aimed at physical property, have been deemed to comprise also rights of a contractual nature closely related to the *physical property*'.[86] The *Phelps Dodge International Corp.* Tribunal declined to find expropriation of the

---

No. ARB/98/4, Award, 8 December 2000, *ICSID Reports*, 6, 89, para. 98 ('an expropriation is not limited to tangible property rights'); *Consortium RFCC v. Kingdom of Morocco*, Award, 22 December 2003, para. 60 ('des droits issues d'un contrat peuvent être l' objet de mesure d'expropriation, à partir du moment ou ledit contrat a été qualifie d'investissement par le Traite lui-même'); *Impregilo v. Pakistan*, Decision on Jurisdiction, 22 April 2005, *ICSID Reports*, 12, 245, para. 274 ('the Tribunal recognises that the taking of contractual rights could, potentially, constitute an expropriation or a measure having an equivalent effect'); *Bayindir Insaat Turizm Ticaret Ve Sanayi AS v. Islamic Republic of Pakistan*, ICSID Case No. ARB/03/29, Decision on Jurisdiction, 14 November 2005, *ICSID Reports*, para. 255 ('it is not disputed that expropriation is not limited to in rem rights and may extend to contractual rights'); *Mondev International Ltd v. United States of America*, NAFTA Award, 11 October 2002, *ICSID Reports*, 6, 192, para. 98 ('it is clear that the protection afforded by the prohibition against expropriation or equivalent treatment in Article 1110 can extend to intangible property interests, as it can under customary international law'); *Methanex Corp. v. USA*, NAFTA Final Award, 3 August 2005 ('the restrictive notion of property as a material "thing" is obsolete and has ceded its place to a contemporary conception which includes managerial control over components of a process that is wealth producing'), Part IV, Chapter D, para. 17.

[84] *Norwegian Shipowners' Claim (Norway v. United States)*, Arbitral Tribunal, Award of 13 October 1992, 1 *RIAA*, 307ff.

[85] *Ibid.*, 334.

[86] *Starrett Housing Corp. v. Islamic Republic of Iran*, 4 *Iran–US CTR*, (1983), 122, 156 (emphasis added).

claimant's contractual rights, because the link with shares was insufficiently direct.[87] That said, authority in the Iran–US Claims Tribunal jurisprudence also exists for the proposition that no link to physical property is needed.[88]

Financial instruments

Commentators lend some support to ICSID jurisdiction over financial instruments.[89] BIT practice on the inclusion of financial instruments varies. Some BITs cover corporate debt.[90]

In *Fedax NV v. The Republic of Venezuela*, the Tribunal regarded promissory notes issued by Venezuela and assigned by another company to Fedax as an 'investment'. The Tribunal reasoned: 'Since promissory notes are evidence of a loan and a rather typical financial and credit instrument, there is nothing to prevent their purchase from qualifying as an investment under the [ICSID] Convention in the circumstances of a particular case such as this.'[91] The Tribunal explained that promissory notes are not like 'volatile capital'; they satisfy the basic features of an investment – that is, 'a certain duration, a certain regularity for profit and return, assumption of risk, a substantial commitment, and a significance for the host State's development'.

In *Ceskoslovenska Obchodni Banka AS [CSOB] v. Slovak Republic*, the second important ICSID case on financial instruments, a consolidation agreement between the Czechoslovak bank CSOB and the Czech and Slovak Ministries of Finance provided for the assignment of certain non-receivables to a specially constituted Slovak collection company that

---

[87] *Phelps Dodge International Corp.* v. *Islamic Republic of Iran*, 10 *Iran–US CTR*, 157, 170 (1986 I).

[88] *Mobil Oil Iran, Inc. et al.* v. *Islamic Republic of Iran*, No. 311–74/76/81/150–3, 14 July 1987, 16 *Iran–US CTR* 3, 25; *Philips Petroleum Co. Iran* v. *Islamic Republic of Iran*, 21 *Iran–US CTR* 79, 1989, 21 *Iran–US CTR* 79, 106; *Amoco International Finance Corp* v. *Iran*, 15 *Iran–US CTR* 222, 1987, para. 108.

[89] G. R. Delaume, 'ICSID and the Transnational Financial Community', *ICSID Review*, 1 (1986), 237, 242; C. Schreuer, 'Commentary on the ICSID Convention. Article 25', *ICSID Review*, 11 (1996), 318, 372; Sacerdoti, 'Bilateral Treaties', *supra* n. 82, 307.

[90] Treaty Between the United States of America and Bahrain Concerning the Encouragement and Reciprocal Protection of Investment, with Annex, Art. 1(d)(2), 29 September 1999, S Treaty Doc. No. 106–25 (2000) ('bonds, debentures, and other forms of debt interests, in a company'); the NAFTA includes debt securities and loans of enterprises, NAFTA, 17 December 1992, 11.39, *ILM*, 32 (1993), 289.

[91] *Fedax NV* v. *The Republic of Venezuela*, ICSID Case No. ARB/96/3, Objections to Jurisdiction, 11 July 1997, *ICSID Reports*, 5, 186 (2002), *ILM*, 37, 1378 (1998), para. 29.

was to be financed by a loan.[92] Slovakia undertook to make good the collection company's losses, enabling repayment of the loan to CSOB. The loan was held to constitute an 'investment' even though the claim was based on an obligation that, standing alone, did not qualify as an investment.

However, to infer from *Fedax* and *CSOB* the general rule that ICSID tribunals have jurisdiction over financial instruments would be erroneous.[93] The two cases depend on special considerations. A number of pending ICSID cases may be expected to provide further guidance on the qualification of debt as investment in due course.[94]

Assignment

A final question is whether international law draws a distinction between the initial creditor and the assignee. In this context, 'assignment' denotes the transfer to a purchaser (assignee) of the rights of the seller (assignor) against an obligor (debtor) with respect to the extension of credit. To the extent of the assignment, a direct creditor–debtor relationship that existed previously between assignor and debtor is created between assignee and debtor.

Contractual rights, such as the right to repayment on moneys advanced, are a form of intangible property, known to the old Common law as 'choses in action'. The old rule was that choses in action could not be assigned. The debtor's obligation to repay was thought to run only personally to the creditor. Assignments were seen to encourage litigation.[95] Modern law reversed this position. The general rule on the assignment of contract rights is now very liberal, reflecting a general distaste for restraints on alienability.[96] In the absence of express and

---

[92] *Ceskoslovenska Obchodni Banka AS [CSOB]* v. *Slovak Republic*, Objections to Jurisdiction, ICSID Case No. ARB/ 97/4, 24 May 1999, *ICSID Review*, 14, 251 (1999).

[93] For a critical perspective on *Fedax*, see M. Waibel, 'Opening Pandora's Box. Sovereign Bonds in International Arbitration', *AJIL* 101 (2007), 711–59, 720–2.

[94] *Beccara* v. *Argentine Republic*, ICSID Case No. ARB/07/5, registered 7 February 2007 (Italian bondholders who refused to go along with Argentina's 2005 restructuring); *Giovanni Alemanni Giordani and Others* v. *Argentine Republic*, ICSID Case. No. ARB/ 07/08, registered 27 March 2007; *Alpi and Others*, ICSID Case No. ARB/08/9, 28 July 2008; *Deutsche Bank AG* v. *Democratic Socialist Republic of Sri Lanka*, ICSID Case No. ARB/09/2, registered 25 March 2009 (derivative used to hedge against oil price fluctuations).

[95] G. Treitel, *The Law of Contract*, 6th edn. (London: Sweet & Maxwell, 1983), 493.

[96] L. Buchheit, 'Legal Aspects of Assignments of Interests in Commercial Bank Loans', in J. Lederman (ed.), *The Commercial Loan Resale Market* (New York: Probus Professional, 1991), 446, 448.

unambiguous restrictions on assignment, the position under English law, as well as New York law, is that contractual claims are freely assignable. As a general rule, the borrower need not be notified of the assignment. The assignability of contractual rights may be restricted by operation of statute or compelling public policy grounds.[97]

There is only limited authority for distinguishing the initial creditor from the assignee. The draftspersons of the ICSID Convention did not conceive of modern financial instruments, which are routinely traded. Even though the ICSID Convention leaves open the question of duration, it is widely recognised that ICSID lacks jurisdiction over short-term financial flows.[98] *Fedax* arguably takes an overly restrictive view of such 'volatile capital', while leaving that term undefined.[99]

With respect to the qualification of endorsed negotiable instruments as investment, Douglas maintains that the key question is 'the nexus between the funds transferred for consideration for the negotiable instrument and the employment of those funds for commercial purposes of the host State. At the one end of the spectrum, it seems clear that trading on the short-term money market in negotiable certificates of deposit or treasury and commercial bills cannot constitute an investment because this nexus is too weak.' The same applies to the long-term capital market in Eurodollar bonds. Douglas rightly concludes that assignments to another creditor will rarely amount to an investment.[100]

Art. 25 of the ICSID Convention is sometimes taken to indicate that the assignee may bring an arbitration claim after acquiring an investment made by another, because the assignment constitutes a new investment. According to this view, if the initial transaction qualified as an investment, then the assignee would automatically step into the shoes of the assignor, even though the assignment does not fulfil the requirements of an investment. *Fedax* appears to lean in the direction that a separate qualification of the assignment as 'investments' is unnecessary. However, the better view is that the assignment must qualify as an investment in its own right to give rise to an investment claim.

---

[97] E.g. the US Restatement (Second) of Contracts, 17(b) provides for the invalidity of assignments 'where the assignment is forbidden by statute or is otherwise inoperative on grounds of public policy'.

[98] The Convention's first draft, albeit inconclusive, might offer a starting point, 'for not less than five years'. Delaume, *supra* n. 89, 242.

[99] *Fedax, supra* n. 91, paras. 42–43.

[100] Douglas, *The International Law of Investment Claims, supra* n. 33, Rule 23, 180–81.

Conclusion

Van Der Walt identified an important trend in the constitutional case-law on debt, the collateral effects doctrine. Accordingly, the cancellation of debt is not compensable if it is 'the incidental side-effect of reasonable, appropriate, and proportionate measures taken to serve a purpose other than to acquire property'.[101] Likewise, in international law, the general rule is that creditor claims that are affected incidentally by governmental measures, such as a nationalisation or insolvency proceedings, do not give rise to an international claim. A nationalisation of a bank, for instance, has only an incidental effect on the bank's creditors, and does not generally trigger State responsibility of the government concerned.

Bederman distinguished two scenarios. Under the customary international law of claims, creditors are said to possess a fault claim on non-sovereign debt in case of 'outright repudiation, discriminatory treatment, or a denial of justice making collection of the debt impossible'.[102] The second, no-fault category concerns the protection of unsecured creditors of an 'entity expropriated or otherwise controlled by a host government'.[103] With respect to the first category of creditor claims, that view is well founded in international law. The central question for the second type of claims is the degree of directness by which separate entities are affected by government action, and in this respect international law remains very much in flux.

It cannot be said, however, that international law admits all creditor claims. State practice does not lend support to the view that general creditor claims are protected in international law as a general matter. The case-law on creditor claims oscillates in its treatment of the type of claim that may be presented before an arbitral tribunal or mixed commission, and of the character of the governmental act that forms the putative basis for governmental liability for private debt. But only exceptionally do creditors possess an international law claim against the State. General creditor claims are compensable only in cases of express repudiation, annulment, or cancellation of specific debt obligations by government decree or regulation of such intensity amounting to a taking.

---

[101] Van Der Walt, 'The Constitutional Property Clause', *supra* n. 18, 226.
[102] Bederman, 'Creditors' Claims', *supra* n. 7, 237.   [103] *Ibid.*

22

Stability, integration and political modalities: some American reflections on the European project after the financial crisis

DAVID A. WESTBROOK*

To those of us concerned with transnational law, and especially the role of German law on the global stage, it does not need saying that Professor Detlev Vagts is highly deserving of that Germanic and traditional scholarly honour, a *Festchrift*. (In this context, 'does not need saying' of course means 'should be said repeatedly'.) We all owe Detlev Vagts, and as a Germanic traditionalist, I would be delighted to contribute to this volume on general principle, even if I did not know the man. But I also have personal reasons for wanting to honour Professor Vagts: he taught the basic course in corporations to generations of students at Harvard Law School. In addition, Vagts was one of the advisors to the Ford Fellows Program, which was designed to foster international law teachers. After being one such student and one such fellow, in due course I became a teacher of international and corporation law, so I owe Vagts a double debt of professional gratitude. And, as with so many other young (or once young) scholars, Vagts has been cordially supportive of my efforts to find my way in the academy, for which I am most grateful.

Such things said, however, there is another reason I am happy to have the chance to contribute to this *Festschrift*. A certain delicacy is called for here, especially since writing for Vagts carries me halfway back to Harvard, where such things are taken so seriously. But enough beating

* Some of the thinking in this chapter was first expressed in the context of 'policy round-tables' hosted by the European Commission's Bureau of European Policy Advisers (BEPA). My thanks to Vitor Gaspar, and to the BEPA, for inviting me to participate in these transnational intellectual exchanges, which I am sure Vagts would have enjoyed. Thanks also to Pierre d'Argent, Jean-Marc Gollier, Rosa Lastra and Dirk Schoenmaker for very helpful comments. The infelicities and outright mistakes are my own.

around the bush: I was not the strongest student in that corporations course. Actually, I was some distance away from the strongest student. In fact, I could not see her. I have excuses, of course, but the bottom line is that this chapter is a chance not only to honour a dedicated scholar and devoted teacher, but also for academic redemption.

I do not seriously propose that the financial policy community adopt the flippant Christian stance with which I am playing here. But this chapter is written as we (appear to) have hit the bottom of the worst financial crisis since the Great Depression. Even if the bottom has been reached, the damage done around the world has been great, and it will take many years to recover. Here in the United States, it is quite possible that some things – a measure of trust in certain key institutions, a sense of workingman's possibility, what might be called republican spirit, perhaps even a degree of national creditworthiness – have passed from the scene. In Europe, the financial crisis revealed not only substantial weaknesses in the internal market, but also, and more troublingly, cracks in the European project itself. Policies and institutions that seemed essentially 'European' in scope and orientation during good times were revealed to be, when conditions got tough, fundamentally national after all. Bluntly, after the crisis it appears that the process of integration begun after the Second World War may not have progressed as far as many believed not so long ago.

It is not my purpose, especially not in the pages of a *Festschrift*, to cast blame. But the fact remains that financial policy on both sides of the Atlantic (and elsewhere) failed in a host of ways; the 'entire edifice' collapsed, as former Chairman of the US Federal Reserve, Alan Greenspan, put it to the US Congress. The failure of a raft of financial policies – to say nothing of the complete absence of collective consideration of a host of topics which proved expensively relevant in the years 2007–09 – ought to give pause to those of us who profess to teach finance. Perhaps we have no need for redemption, but with one in four American children on food stamps and more than the suspicion that the Great Recession was caused by overweening faith in finance itself, I am not so sure. The matter is worth careful thought. Surely, however, the tendency of financial elites to congratulate themselves on navigating 'the tsunami' – on surviving the massive failure of their own policies – is misplaced and, in light of the damage done, more than a little unseemly.

I should immediately point out that Vagts came of intellectual age when the currents which engendered the latest crisis were mere rivulets. In class, he had none of the narrow-minded certainty which marked the heyday of law and economics. His view of the business world and the lawyer's role in it was always more nuanced. Even in the basic course on corporations, Vagts tried to instil an understanding that things were often done differently, elsewhere (an attitude taught by comparative law), and had been done differently, even here, at other times (an attitude taught by history). More deeply still, Vagts was quite aware of human fallibility, and its sometimes awful potential – he freely admitted to being marked by the Second World War. So had we as a nation kept some of these lessons in mind, would our economy be in better shape than it is today? Perhaps, but there are reasons we speak of manias – and even Newton got caught up in the South Seas Bubble.

But it also may be hoped that we learn from crises. We should ask: What aspects of the old understanding of financial markets now seem compromised, perhaps simply wrong? What are the immediate intellectual consequences of this crisis for the political economy, and especially the political economy of Europe? Does this crisis provide us with opportunities as well as problems and, if so, what might those opportunities be?

A caveat: the reader who hopes that this chapter will provide definitive solutions to the practical problems raised by the crisis will be disappointed. Such a reader is asking the wrong question. There are real limitations on the extent to which an intellectual, operating in the abstract, should offer specific advice to responsible decision-makers. The world has plenty of armchair generals, Monday-morning quarterbacks and garrulous academics. Instead of second guesses, we should attempt to take advantage of critical distance to provide a cooler analysis and a longer view than is available to those in the trenches, perhaps accompanied by a few tentative and general suggestions by way of demonstrating a desire to be constructive. As a good friend often puts it, 'I am not in charge', and I offer my sympathies to those who are.

As I write, toward the end of 2009, it is generally acknowledged that the recent economic crisis exposed serious weaknesses in the structure of European financial markets. To sketch the story in abstract terms: in 2008 and 2009, a number of bank crises required government intervention.[1] Although the European Central Bank (ECB) made liquidity available to the central banks of Member States, kept interest rates low and

---

[1] The European financial landscape is, as ever, dominated by banks. The financial crisis that presented across a variety of institutions in the United States was experienced in Europe as essentially a crisis in the banking sector.

has been credited with avoiding panic in the financial markets, no European institution had the legal authority or the resources required to serve as lender of last resort to 'private' institutions. In the same vein, no European institution had the capacity, legal or otherwise, to resolve insolvent financial institutions, or to insure depositors, maintain trading positions, or otherwise intervene to stabilise financial markets. In Europe during the financial crisis, therefore, most government interventions were in fact, and of practical and legal necessity, interventions by Member States – i.e. national governments. In so intervening, generally spending taxpayer money, national governments tended to act on a national, as opposed to a European, basis.

A number of lessons can be learned from this story. Perhaps the first is that monetary integration, European Monetary Union (EMU), may not provide financial stability, even if currency stability is achieved. Using the traditional tools of central banking, the ECB maintained the stability of the Euro as a currency before and throughout the financial crisis. The crisis happened nonetheless. After the fact, it is obvious enough that radically overleveraged institutions may impose systemic risks, even if their balance sheets are reckoned in a then-sound currency. More theoretically, money supply cannot be divorced from the extension of credit, leverage; market confidence cannot be divorced from the volume, character and velocity of trading. Banks and other financial institutions, however, not just central banks, extend credit and trade. Financial stability, therefore, requires not only sound money, a well-managed Euro, but prudent institutions to manage such money. To put matters gently, many European banks were imprudent.

A complication: in (overly positivist legal) theory, much banking regulation is harmoniously conceived at the European level, and implemented at the Member State level. So we may speak of European banking regulation. Supervision and resolution, however, are matters of Member State competence. But positivists tend to forget that law on the books is not what matters to sound policy; law cannot be understood apart from its social context, including its implementation. (This is especially true in the case of financial regulation. For example, US securities law is hardly to be understood by reading the statutes.) At this level of analysis, the once-easy claim that European banking regulation is fairly harmonised begs more than a raised eyebrow: actual Member State implementation of regulation, deeply intertwined with supervision, meant that political constraints (regulation in the broad sense used in US policy discourse) on European banks in the years leading up to the crisis varied considerably from country to country. In short, integrated European banking law leading into the crisis was partially achieved at best, and further fragmented by essentially national responses to the crisis.

At the same time, European banks often operate across borders, indeed have been encouraged to operate across borders in furtherance of European financial market integration. More specifically, transnational financial operations have been intentionally facilitated by the single currency.[2] Access to the European market has meant that the banks of relatively small countries might have considerable operations in much larger economies. Failure of a big bank based in a small country is unlikely to be successfully resolved by the government of that country. Putting this all together, it might be said that transnational systemic risk was facilitated, if not caused, by the emergence of a more integrated European financial market, coupled with the failure of fundamentally national oversight regimes.[3] The desire for financial stability, especially when coupled with monetary integration, would thus seem to imply not only regulatory reform, but financial law that was more integrated in fact, not merely in bureaucratic wish.

However, as noted above, supervision and resolution of financial institutions in Europe are largely matters of Member State competence. Member States guard their jurisdiction over such issues especially jealously because the fisc of, and the asset values within, each Member State are affected. As a result, and as demonstrated in the events of 2008, responses to institutional crisis tend to be national and therefore both partial and fragmented. Conversely, truly integrating European financial policy would require at least substantial burden-sharing for the supervision and especially resolution of financial institutions. A contrast is often drawn with the United States, where the Federal Reserve and the Treasury, operating on the Federal level, not only supervise, but also have the resources to intervene directly. No analogue exists on the European level, and it is difficult imagining European institutions acquiring such competences or resources within the foreseeable future. So, to generalise, the 2008 crisis demonstrates what has been suspected for some time: true

---

[2] This point should not be overdone. Contagion often occurs across currencies, and did in this crisis. Rephrased, a single currency may encourage cross-border operations, but is hardly a *sine qua non* for cross-border problems.

[3] It should immediately be noted that this problem is not unique to Europe; one might say much the same thing on a global level with regard to Lehman Brothers – i.e. national regulatory failure allowed a transnational systemic risk to be realised.

European monetary union is stymied, or at least profoundly constrained, by the lack of European fiscal integration.[4]

In the same vein, although existing national regulation of financial institutions is derived from European directives, and such regulation has been shown to be in need of reform (both weaker and less well integrated than one might have hoped, when times were good), substantial new European directives do not seem likely. Recent political developments – such as the French and Dutch 'no' to the proposed European Constitution; the exceedingly difficult passage of the Lisbon Treaty; and the German Constitutional Court's suggestion that no further derogation to the EU could be allowed under German law – strongly suggest that financial institutions will be governed more on the national, rather than the European, level for the foreseeable future. And, as has also been suggested, since the Union does not have the power to tax and does not look to acquire the power to tax anytime soon, only Member States (indeed, only large Member States) possess the ready cash required to intervene in a banking crisis. Such interventions, however, tend to fragment, rather than integrate, the European financial system. The true integration of European financial law, therefore, seems to be both more necessary, and much farther away, than many people thought even recently.

In a draft paper that has attracted considerable attention in policy circles, Dirk Schoenmaker elegantly if very schematically states this problematic as the 'trilemma' of financial stability: 'a stable financial system, an integrated [European] financial system, and national financial autonomy are incompatible. Any two of the three objectives can be combined but not all three; one has to give.'[5] In the crux of the paper, Schoenmaker argues that in an integrated financial market, defined as a market in which important institutions have substantial cross-border operations, a national regulator may rationally but inefficiently decide not to save some systemically important financial institutions, because the national government does not gain from rescuing banking operations conducted in foreign countries. Exhibit A for this claim would be the failure of Fortis.

---

[4] See, generally, R. Lastra, *Legal Foundations of International Monetary Stability* (Oxford University Press, 2006), chapter 10.

[5] D. Schoenmaker, 'The Trilemma of Financial Stability', draft available at ssrn.com/abstract=1340395. The trilemma image is well established in monetary policy, and Schoenmaker and others have used the image to make versions of this argument for some time. See Lastra, *Legal Foundations*, *supra* n. 4, and the sources cited therein.

Schoenmaker assumes (perhaps slighting the long Dutch tradition of fiscal independence?) that financial stability is self-evidently the cardinal virtue: the trilemma is thus resolved into a conflict between an integrated European financial market, on the one hand, and national control over financial institutions (and their resolution) on the other. From a European (as opposed to a national) political perspective, and from a relatively orthodox liberal economic perspective, both the course of history and the national order favour expansive and integrated financial markets, and so we learn that supervision is 'still' done at the national level. By now, we are on familiar ground. The trilemma is not difficult as an intellectual matter: the desire for financial stability requires integration of regulation, oversight and even resolution on the European level, founded on a degree of fiscal integration, and national financial autonomy has to give way. As a political matter, however, European progress is frustrated, here as elsewhere, by the parochial interests of national governments. The European financial markets, then, seem doomed to some messy combination of halting integration/national fragmentation, coupled with structurally inadequate supervision (and lagging regulation), resulting in financial instability and associated disadvantages in the real economy.

Are matters really as gloomy as the trilemma so logically implies? If not, what is wrong with the broadly shared assessment of the situation of European financial markets and their regulation that the trilemma so elegantly articulates? In short, how should European policy-makers confront the trilemma?

Two implicit aspects of the problematic seem analytically significant to me. First, the trilemma has a complex relationship with liberal economic thought. On the one hand, the choices highlighted by the trilemma were long obscured, in Europe and elsewhere, by a liberal economic orthodoxy that did a fair job of accounting for relatively stable markets. On the other hand, the trilemma is logically dependent on the same liberal economic orthodoxy, which raises issues if one no longer believes.[6]

Second, both the trilemma and what I take to be the dominant understanding of the European project are informed by a particular political imagination that associates scale with centralisation, centralisation with rationalisation and rationalisation with progress. As an intellectual

---

[6] See, generally, D. A. Westbrook, *Out of Crisis. Rethinking Our Financial Markets* (Boulder, CO: Paradigm Publishers, 2009).

matter, I do not think this is correct – to quip, it is to mistake the history of France for the history of globalisation, and also for the deep structure of the European project.[7] But whether or not the imagination of politics dominant in Europe made sense at one time, or even makes sense in the abstract, this imagination does a poor job addressing the problems of economic integration across jurisdictions, either globally or in Europe, and either now or for the foreseeable future. Neither nation-states nor Member States are going to surrender jurisdiction to a government whose scale matches that of the economy.

Consequently, we must find ways to think politically about financial market regulation under conditions of decentralisation. Fortunately, European traditions of law and politics apart from the administrative centralisation associated with the rise of the modern nation-State, and another of Vagts' areas, American commercial law, have things to teach about creating integrated and reasonably well-governed markets across jurisdictions.

In times of relative economic stability, it is easy enough to understand markets as ordinarily efficient and largely self-correcting. In such times, regulation and supervision of banks and most other key financial institutions remain necessary (only a particularly ideological American might think otherwise), but attract relatively little attention (bank failure has not been so interesting for generations). And thus for many years in Europe, banks were encouraged to develop their risk management models; monetary union proceeded without regulatory integration, and that seemed not only politically necessary but untroubling; and Member State governments were left to regulate and supervise the institutions established within their jurisdictions. Moreover, variances among Member State regulation were seen as an impediment to the integration and expansion of financial markets – that is, to cost money and be inefficient, just as variances among regulatory regimes for other goods and services were traditionally thought to be at odds with the achievement of a true single market. So the project was to work national regulatory barriers down, gradually shifting competence to European institutions and, through the Second Banking Directive and otherwise, to encourage financial institutions established in one Member State to do business in others. During these years, the European financial order was relatively stable – a bit sluggish, perhaps, but stable.

---

[7] See, generally, D. A. Westbrook, *City of Gold. An Apology for Global Capitalism in a Time of Discontent* (New York and London: Routledge, 2003).

Under such circumstances, the trilemma's conflicts, among European and national jurisdictions and financial stability, are hardly apparent. It is only when financial markets are unstable, systemically important institutions are failing and massive and decisive government intervention is required, quickly, that the trilemma's questions – 'which governments can effectively do what, for whom'? – arise. Suddenly national regulatory, supervisory and fiscal authorities are seen as not merely anachronisms, but absolutely essential to avoid panic. A general sense of broadly available efficiencies, fostering highly leveraged operations with tight margins arbitraged across great distances, all very well oiled, that for years made 'European' solutions seem so sensible, can be and was quickly replaced by sudden recognition of widespread mispricing, radical uncertainty, especially about counterparty risk, acute problems of illiquidity even among fundamentally solvent institutions, the insolvency of major institutions, negotiations held over weekends, the need for effective power and the indispensability of national institutions. This is so even if national action presents prisoner's dilemma problems – that is, when a coordinated response would have, in theory, been more efficient.

Although the trilemma is most evident when pricing fails, and the intellectual edifice of liberal economics is rumoured to be collapsing, the trilemma itself is very much a product of liberal political economy. In the traditional push toward 'rigour', the trilemma assumes governments that are able to assess the relative costs of different courses of action, and that act in rational and self-interested fashion upon their assessments. Suffice it to say that such rationality does not describe the action of any of the governments going into the 2008 crisis; it is precisely the risk management edifice that failed. Thus, while it is true that many Member State governments acted in the national, rather than the European, interest, it is a stretch to say that such action was particularly rational, or that any of the governments could have had more than the haziest sense of what the ramifications of various courses of action might have been.

The trilemma reflects its roots in liberal economics in another way: government action is thought of as essentially distinct from marketplace action – i.e. politics are distinct from markets, and the purpose of politics is to facilitate markets. The traditional bifurcation between markets and politics is especially implausible in times of financial crisis, when 'private' institutions are supported by direct injections of tax dollars. More generally, the financial markets are hardly independent of political processes, and so the assumption that financial stability is a cardinal virtue for constitutional thought is unwarranted. The analytic question for

political economy is: How do those aspects of social life that we understand as 'political' interpenetrate those aspects of life that we understand
as 'economic'? The normative question for political economy is: 'What
sort of markets do we, as a society, wish to construct'? Such questions
cannot be asked from within liberal orthodoxy, which distinguishes too
strongly between government and market, public and private interest. In
short, much contemporary analysis of the situation of the European
financial structure is subtly dependent on the beleaguered orthodoxies
of liberal economics; it hardly needs saying that the same intellectual
dependency hampers policy thought in the United States.

As sketchy as the foregoing has been, my next point is more spec-
ulative still. It seems that a second implicit, and vital, aspect of much
contemporary European thinking about financial regulation is a particular imagination of politics that silently structures, indeed dominates,
policy thought. Political action is conceived in terms of jurisdiction to
regulate, and is essentially exclusive. Thus, by way of example, the
trilemma assumes that if we wish to have good markets (financial
stability), a choice must be made regarding jurisdiction over those
markets – i.e. a choice between European and Member State regulators
(here again, using 'regulators' in the broadest sense). Moreover, the
choice for national rather than European law that appears to be politically necessary at the moment is understood to be somewhat retrograde;
progress is understood to be the centralisation of vital politics (monetary,
eventually diplomatic and perhaps military) within dedicated European
institutions. From this perspective, which perhaps should be associated
with former European Commission chief Jacques Delors, political progress in Europe essentially maps that of the modern administrative State:
a linear evolution towards ever-more rational, centralised and bureaucratic forms of social life.

It need not be, indeed was not always, thus. For many years, the
European project was publicly and privately said to be 'sui generis'.
The European project was understood, except perhaps by some of the
English, to be more than trade and different from the nation, to be some
sort of new politics. The terms and form of that politics, however, were
admittedly emergent, as yet unclear, hence sui generis. This lack of
definition was fruitful: 'Europe' provided just enough of a horizon to
organise significant political thought and action for decades. At least to
this friendly outside observer, at some point during the 1990s – after
the Single European Act (SEA), perhaps with Maastricht, certainly
by EMU – the European imaginary shifted. Although the phrase

'United States of Europe' remained a bit vulgar, used pejoratively by Eurosceptics, many people in fact started conceiving of Europe as a very diverse, continental, republican, commercial polity – i.e. much like the United States. And such polities, as the United States has demonstrated, need constitutions.[8] From within this perspective, the 'political' require-ment that financial regulation (in practice if not theory) and intervention and resolution (in theory and practice) be conducted on the Member State level is seen as a setback for the European project.

Conversely, from within this same perspective, progress is understood to be the transferral of politics from areas of smaller geographical scope to areas of larger geographical scope; from 'lower' to 'higher' 'levels' of government; and from the Member States to the European institutions. So the trilemma strongly implies that moving the supervision and reg-ulation of financial institutions to the European level will generate financial stability.

A word of intellectual caution is in order here. While constitutional arguments always maintain that better politics will flow from the estab-lishment of a better structure, real life tends to be messier. Assuming perhaps heroically that large Member States do not capture regulatory processes, making the law of financial institutions an essentially European affair *may* remove the structural tendency toward fragmenta-tion demonstrated during this crisis. Merely federalising financial law, however, hardly guarantees its effectiveness. Although the situation in the United States is complicated, it is generally thought that the Federal Reserve did not acquit itself very well in the years leading into the crisis, and numerous mistakes have been made in the management of the crisis itself. And as has long been noted both in Europe and especially in the United States, centralisation of power raises its own dangers.

More generally, the failure to realise a European financial law is only a setback if the European financial order should be highly centralised. But it would be unfortunate if the destiny of Europe was to be a highly centralised State, not least because that destiny will be frustrated for the foreseeable future – that is, European politics will be understood as a failure. Even assuming that it would be a good idea to integrate financial regulation, supervision, resolution and presumably a degree of taxation

---

[8] It can be said that the centralising tendency was always balanced by the countervailing idea of subsidiarity. True enough, but as the name suggests, 'subsidiarity' is a derivative concept, an argument against the presumption of centralisation. Conversely, subsidiarity is hardly a strong argument for politics; it is not constitutive.

on the European level, such integration is not going to happen soon. And, it should be said, the identical argument could be made on a global level: the existence of an integrated global economy requires global regulatory structures – i.e., not just the current flaccid collection of institutions and precatory laws, but a real global government. I am not holding my breath.

But suppose the issue is not merely one of noble (European) ideals frustrated by harsh (national) political realities? Perhaps rationalising centralisation is not, *even in principle*, the only horizon for politics, including the politics of financial regulation? Surely there is much to be said for nations and other polities, even in an age of economic and other integrations? And should the possibility that Europe represents a new form of political life, something that does not appear very often on the world stage, be given up quite so easily?

Visiting the United States, Tocqueville at first wondered at a large country that seemed, to an astounding degree, to function without government. Upon further observation and reflection, Tocqueville realised that he had overlooked the prevalence of local administrations, and had mistaken the absence of centralised administration for a lack of governance. Clearly society in the United States governed itself, indeed constituted a union, implying a substantial degree of centralisation of some sort, even if not the hub and scope organisation of statutory authority radiating out from the capital with which he was familiar. So Tocqueville famously distinguished between 'administrative centralisation' and 'governmental centralisation'.[9] What Tocqueville meant by 'administrative centralisation' is clear enough, exemplified by the France of his day and ours. What he meant by 'governmental centralisation' is more difficult to say: sometimes the phrase is associated with the (national) legislature (that does not have administrative powers under the US Constitution); sometimes with democracy writ large, and sometimes with the sources of strength and unity within a society. Clearly, however, Tocqueville was on to something important: the United States, for all its millions of people and vast spaces and enormous tangle of jurisdictions, is a very unified polity and, critically for present purposes, an integrated financial market. This unification is not a result of jurisdictional unity, for the simple reason that, even after the Civil War and the New Deal, there is no jurisdictional unity. The principles of unity must be

---

[9] My thanks to Nicolas Veron for raising Toqueville's distinction *vis-à-vis* my argument.

found at a deeper, societal or cultural, level. And yet such unity is normative, regulatory, *governmental*.

My thought is that governmental centralisation could be a key way to reconceptualise financial policy – indeed, politics more generally – in Europe, thereby helping to free political discourse from the coils of the jurisdictional fight articulated by the trilemma. And if we look at European history more broadly, we see a great deal of political life without administrative centralisation, that is, across a wealth of jurisdictions. Germany and Italy were political contexts for centuries before they had anything resembling centralised administrations. Since the Middle Ages, the *lex mercatoria* has made commerce possible among traders from many different countries. And for generations the Roman law was 'the' law virtually everywhere in Europe, quite independent of whether or not, or how, it was the positive law in this or that place. In short, history teaches that political economy does not require the degree of unity of authority that is so often presumed.

It might be said, however, that this is an essentially medieval view, that the story of modernity is the subordination of the nobles to the king, of local authority to central administration, of ideal laws and customary trading patterns to positive laws and regulated markets. I disagree. Moving from history to comparison, the United States demonstrates a tightly integrated, highly modern, market – indeed, the paradigmatic diversified economy – and a great number of jurisdictions, and conversely, a notable shortfall in formal administrative centralisation and attendant positive law. The degree of decentralisation in the United States is, on reflection, quite astonishing. Consider the following:

- Property, contract and tort (delict, which stands in lieu of a fair degree of regulation) are all overwhelmingly State law.
- Corporations are State law; there is no national company law.
- Banks may be chartered on either the State or the Federal level. Both individual States and the Federal government regulate banks and similar institutions.
- Insurance companies are regulated almost exclusively by the States.
- Securities law is mostly Federal law, but States retain the authority to regulate securities.
- Criminal law, including matters such as fraud, is both Federal and State.

The point here is not that the United States has it 'right'. Regulations in the United States, like anyplace else, are variously successful, and this chapter is not long enough for thoughtful suggestions about particular aspects of US financial regulation that might be worth European attention, by way of either adoption or avoidance. Moreover, it should not be denied that the multiplicity of jurisdictions in the United States can create waste and confusion. It is quite possible that insurance, for example, should be regulated on the Federal, and not the State, level. Those things said, the point here is that the United States demonstrates that a highly integrated financial market *can* be created among multiple jurisdictions. This fact provides a modicum of hope, because it means that, in a global context of multiple nation-states, or in a European context of multiple Member States, as in a Federal context, politics need not be understood to be coterminous with jurisdiction – i.e. political discourse is not delimited by the authority of the modern administrative nation-state. Therefore, the impossibility of achieving a politics coterminous with jurisdiction does not necessarily imply that political efforts are doomed. More specifically, the fact that Member States are not going to cede supervisory, much less resolution, powers over their financial institutions to European institutions does not mean that European financial policy is at an end. More hopefully still, the realisation that politics may transcend jurisdiction may help renew the spirit of European political invention.

Just suppose that European politics comes to understand itself along the lines suggested here, in terms of governmental centralisation, of a European culture of government. What would such an understanding of European politics mean for policy? What specific programmes should European institutions adopt if they intend to improve financial regulation, even while jurisdiction remains national?

In the absence of authority to proceed positively on the European level, perforce modest starts on European financial reform have been made through international colleges of financial institution supervisors, and through enthusiasm for 'living wills' and other industry initiatives. One might hope that such efforts contribute to a more European, and wiser, collective understanding of financial regulation. At the same time, it should be rather dourly noted that such measures were not legally binding, and were not strong enough to ensure cooperation during the 2008 crisis, raising the question of whether the improved versions currently under discussion will fare any better in a future crisis. More broadly, it should be remembered that meetings among upper-level bureaucrats, trained internationally, in disciplines formed internationally, are hardly new. European elites have generally had international experience and, within limitations, a 'European' perspective. And during the 2008 crisis, such elites acted in national as opposed to European fashion.

So how might a deeper European governmental centralisation be pursued, while respecting the prerogatives of Member State authorities? Two obvious places to start would be education and law, and, fortuitously for the purpose of honouring Vagts, the combination of education and law: legal education. As Tocqueville recognised, and as remains true, Americans exhibit a surprising degree of uniformity in all sorts of regards, despite the land's vast spaces, and the various cultural backgrounds and beliefs of her people. In particular, Americans share beliefs and assumptions about the institutions of commercial society: property, contract and the like. (Americans often and erroneously think that their beliefs about such institutions are natural.) So, Tocqueville also recognised, one of the most important vectors for governmental centralisation in the United States is law. This has become more true since Tocqueville's day, with the development of the modern law school. While the law taught in law schools is largely (not exclusively) State law, it is not the law of any given State – any basic casebook contains laws from multiple jurisdictions at different times, with no direct or authoritative bearing upon one another. Rather than the positive law of any given jurisdiction, what is taught is legal culture in a general American sense. As a result, people trained at Harvard Law School, in the hardly economically dominant State of Massachusetts, can and do practice American (not US) law all over the United States, and indeed around the world.

This is not to say that positive law is unimportant. But, in a precedential system, with fifty States, a Federal government and countless regulators, practitioners are expected to look up the positive law of the relevant jurisdiction, so that they are absolutely current, and can cite the immediately responsible authority. Legal thought, and policy discourse more generally, tends to happen on the cultural plane, rather than that of positive law.

The national legal culture and State jurisdiction are often understood in complementary, mutually reinforcing, fashion. Notably, the licensing of lawyers (and other professionals) is usually a State function. Typically, State bar associations administer an exam. A candidate for the bar is only allowed to sit for the exam, however, if she has graduated from an accredited law school. And law schools are accredited by the American Bar Association (ABA) – i.e. on a national basis. Moreover, in most States, the first day of the exam is the so-called Multistate exam – i.e.

an exam written by the ABA and based on the national understanding of fundamental areas of law, rather than on the particular rules of a given State.

Surely it would be possible to imagine European financial politics along structurally similar lines – as an essentially cultural discourse that informed the thinking of more localised authorities and, as importantly, market participants. The impasse ostensibly revealed by the 2008 financial crisis is an artifact of certain unnecessary assumptions about politics rather than an intractable flaw in the European constitution. But while the political structure of Europe does not preclude serious rethinking of European financial markets, one must not expect too much from mere constitutional reconceptualisations. A lively continental discourse on financial policy, held in an integrated market stretching across any number of jurisdictions, has not always kept the United States from folly, notably in the 2008 crisis. Financial policy, like politics more generally, can be expected to remain difficult.

PART III

Transnational lawyering and dispute resolution

23

Diffusion of law: the International Court of Justice as a court of transnational justice

PIETER H. F. BEKKER

Introduction

This chapter highlights aspects of the process of diffusion of law as derived from the law and practice of the International Court of Justice (ICJ), the principal judicial organ of the United Nations seated at The Hague in The Netherlands. The ICJ is the world's only court having general jurisdiction over disputes between sovereign States. Diffusion of law is inherent in the concept of transnational law, which likewise is informed by interaction between legal systems and legal traditions. As understood here, legal diffusion essentially is a transnational phenomenon. This chapter seeks to increase our understanding of this phenomenon by focusing on the ICJ. Our focus on the ICJ in illustrating how legal diffusion occurs on the international plane comports with the goal to give 'increased attention to public international law and institutions' advocated by the casebook on *Transnational Legal Problems* for which Detlev Vagts has served as primary author/editor.[1] According to that seminal work, the domain of transnational law is formed by international law and institutions together with aspects of national legal systems concerning 'matters foreign'. As such, these constituent elements form 'the legal framework bearing on relationships among nations or among their citizens and business entities'.[2] Nations, citizens and businesses

---

[1] H. J. Steiner and D. F. Vagts, *Transnational Legal Problems*, 4th edn. (Westbury, NY: Foundation Press, 1994), iii. This author, who worked as a legal officer in the Registry of the International Court of Justice between 1992 and 1994, had the honour to serve as Vagts' research assistant for updating that book on his graduation from Harvard Law School in 1991. Of the sixty-five cases listed under 'Decisions of International Tribunals' in the Table of Contents of the book, some thirty-five originate from the ICJ or its predecessor, the Permanent Court of International Justice (PCIJ).

[2] *Ibid.*

are all affected by the ICJ's work and they play various roles in it, as described below.

As a public international lawyer, and for present purposes, I define 'legal diffusion' as the informal process by which the public and private actors involved in international dispute resolution interact with each other, influenced by their national legal traditions and training, with a view to defining the status and content of particular norms of international law which decide a given interstate dispute. How this process plays out in practice may influence the transportation or reception of law on both the international and domestic legal planes. If the administration of international justice is carried out in a just and transparent way through the observance of basic notions of due process and through convincing argument and reasoning, as perceived by the participating actors, those norms may be spread across different jurisdictions and cultures.[3] They may even influence municipal law-making – what William Twining has called 'cross-level diffusion'.[4] It is especially in the field of international dispute resolution through international courts and tribunals, and particularly the ICJ, that one can observe the process of diffusion of law in all its intriguing facets. Thus, while most studies of diffusion of law focus on municipal law, this chapter shall focus on the international law process which the ICJ administers. The adjudicatory process at the ICJ is a particularly instructive mechanism for studying the process of diffusion of law because of the unique nature of the institution, bringing together fifteen or more individuals 'of different races, cultures and philosophies',[5] and the fact that the ICJ sits at the apex of international courts and tribunals. In the ICJ, diffusion of law often is a by-product of the Court's role in contentious cases, which is 'to decide in accordance with international law such disputes as are submitted to it' by sovereign States.[6] The diffusion of law which takes place at this institution forms a catalyst to the development of general international law, and sometimes even domestic law.

---

[3] As Rosenne has explained, 'a State is not only interested in the operative clause of the judgment: and even when the decision goes against it, the wording of the reasons does not lose its general importance for it'. S. Rosenne, *The Law and Practice of the International Court, 1920–1996*, 3rd edn., 4 vols. (The Hague, Boston and London: Martinus Nijhoff, 1997), vol. III, 1126.

[4] W. Twining, 'Diffusion of Law. A Global Perspective', unpublished paper, University College London, 15, www.ucl.ac.uk/laws/academics/profiles/twining/diffusion.pdf.

[5] M. Lachs, 'Some Reflections on the Nationality of Judges of the International Court of Justice', *Pace Yearbook of International Law*, 49 (1992), 49–68, 68.

[6] ICJ Statute Art. 38(1)(d).

After describing the actors involved in this process, as well as some of the normative questions posing themselves in this context, we shall highlight certain mechanisms of diffusion as they may be observed in the ICJ, including judges ad hoc, the Court's deliberative process, and through a case study featuring a transnational corporation (TNC). We shall briefly address the question whether there is a disjunction between theory and practice in this particular field, before presenting our conclusions.

Agents of diffusion

For purposes of studying legal diffusion in the ICJ, the relevant actors, or 'agents of diffusion', are all lawyers (judges and counsel) and officials directly involved in the international dispute resolution process. They belong to the traditional 'participants in transnational life'.[7] Interestingly, the principal actors are no longer only *government* lawyers or officials. A growing cast of characters is involved. Governments increasingly retain outside counsel for high-stakes, highly specialised ICJ cases. In some cases, private lawyers who do not have the nationality of the State which appointed them have led the State's delegation at the ICJ. As Lucy Reed has observed:

> These private lawyers (ideally) bring with them a wealth of practical and legal skills that they will use in any case they try. Government lawyers observe and digest these skills, later applying them in the public interest . . .
> As they become more familiar with international law, domestic lawyers and judges become more comfortable applying it in a variety of cases.[8]

This development benefits especially governments from the developing world, as well as the process of diffusion.

Governments also increasingly appoint national judges or lawyers as judges ad hoc (discussed in more detail below) in ICJ cases, adding to the process of cross-fertilisation which influences legal diffusion. In this way, cross-fertilisation becomes an important factor in the development of international law.

---

[7] Steiner and Vagts, *Transnational Legal Problems, supra* n. 1, iv.

[8] L. Reed, 'Great Expectations. Where Does the Proliferation of International Dispute Resolution Tribunals Leave International Law?', *Proceedings of the American Society of International Law*, 96 (2002), 219–31, 230.

Counsel representing the parties to a particular case can inform and educate their opponents and the ICJ judges and their legal staff of the particulars of an applicable system of law in which they are qualified or are recognised jurisconsults. Judges can inform the participating parties and their counsel, the legal community and the public at large, of the status and content of norms of contemporary international law.

One also may observe an increasing albeit indirect role for civil society and non-governmental organisations (NGOs), especially human rights organisations. While these groups cannot participate as *amici curiae* in ICJ proceedings, ICJ judges and other participating lawyers (including ICJ Registry staff and law clerks assigned to individual judges) increasingly turn to the information found on these organisations' web sites, in professional journals or newsletters published by them, and sometimes even in documents prepared by them in the course of the Court's exercise of its advisory jurisdiction.[9]

This colourful mix of actors makes this field of law, and the ICJ as an institution, particularly apt for interdisciplinary study involving international law specialists, international relations theorists and scholars in social science. Regrettably, few if any works have undertaken this task.

Relevant normative questions

In order to understand the normative questions arising in this context, it must be kept in mind that public international law, which is the law applicable before the ICJ,[10] in some respects is 'an under-developed system as compared with private law'.[11] The relevant body of law is one with limited means of enforcement. Public international law is a genuine blend, or a fusion, of different legal regimes or systems of law. This hybrid legal system derives its content from, amongst others, Civil

---

[9] According to ICJ Practice Direction XII(3), which relates to advisory proceedings, while documents submitted by NGOs are not to be considered as part of the case file, '[w]ritten statements and/or documents submitted by international non-governmental organizations will be placed in a designated location in the Peace Palace', the building in which the ICJ is located. Thus, States and intergovernmental organisations participating in a given advisory proceeding, as well as the ICJ Judges and the ICJ Registry staff, will have access to such documents. See Practice Directions, www.icj-cij.org/documents/index.php?p1=4&p2=4&p3=0.

[10] See ICJ Statute Art. 38(1).

[11] Separate Opinion of Judge Fitzmaurice, in *Case Concerning The Barcelona Traction, Light and Power Co. Ltd (Belgium* v. *Spain)*, Second Phase, Judgment, 1970 ICJ Rep. 3, 76, para. 23.

law (or 'the law of Western Europe and of Latin America, the direct heirs of the Romano-Mediterranean *jus gentium*');[12] Common law; Islamic law; Buddhist law; Muslim law; Hindu law; and the law of Asian and African countries. The fact that international law, or at least the study thereof, is perhaps not as well-developed compared with other bodies of law makes it a legal field for which the process of diffusion is especially critical and useful.

Public international law is a specialised area of the law and, consequently, its sources are not as easily accessible to the lawyers and officials involved as is the case in other areas of law. The sources of authority for international law are diverse, complex and not clearly defined. While this might be seen as a factor hampering diffusion, practice shows that the various actors participate actively in the law-finding process, aided by new sources of communication technology and the ability to 'mould' the developing law.

Particular normative questions which arise from the phenomenon of legal diffusion as it applies before the ICJ are:

- In defining the law within the ICJ's jurisdiction, how is the line drawn between *lex lata* and *de lege ferenda*? In other words, what is contemporary international law and where does the progressive development of the law commence?
- How does one deal with the limitation constituted by Art. 38, para. 1(d) ICJ Statute, according to which judicial decisions and the literature are only subsidiary means for establishing international law? This means that judicial decisions and scholarly writings cannot be relied upon as primary sources in defining the applicable law, which is often not clearly defined.
- How does the absence of *stare decisis*, or binding precedent, affect the process of diffusion? At what point does a rule developed by international courts and tribunals attain the status of a binding norm of international law and how does an authoritative statement by the ICJ influence this process?
- When is it appropriate to treat precedents, of foreign courts or international tribunals, as persuasive authority?
- What weight should be given to the opinions of individual judges appended to an ICJ ruling, especially in cases decided by the casting vote of the ICJ President?

---

[12] See Separate Opinion of Judge Ammoun, in *North Sea Continental Shelf Cases (FRG/ Denmark; FRG/Netherlands)*, 1969 ICJ Rep. 3, 139, para. 38.

We shall attempt to address some of these questions in the sections which follow.

Diffusion mechanisms in the ICJ

Introduction

Diffusion of law is inherent in the work of the ICJ. According to Art. 9 of the Court's Statute, which forms an integral part of the United Nations Charter, its composition as a 'World Court' must give an equitable representation of 'the principal legal systems of the world'.[13] The regular bench consists of fifteen judges, no two of whom may be nationals of the same State. There exists a direct relationship between, on the one hand, the requirement laid down in Art. 9, and, on the other hand, the performance of their judicial tasks by the judges comprising the ICJ bench, especially as it concerns the law to be applied by the Court. As a former ICJ Vice-President has pointed out, Art. 9 results in the ICJ being 'under a particular obligation to search in all these traditions and legal systems for principles and approaches that enrich the law it adminis-ters'.[14] This, in turn, influences and stimulates cross-level diffusion.

In the words of a leading ICJ commentator, '[t]he emphasis of Article 9 upon the principal legal systems of the world indicates that the Court is intended as a world court applying universal international law'.[15] In the case of the ICJ, the combination of the particular composition of the Court and its working methods, especially the collegial nature of its decision-making (described below), makes it a fertile ground for the process of diffusion of law and, therefore, for the development of trans-national law. The background of the judges and the Court's working methods are conducive to the interaction which leads to diffusion of law.

An ICJ judge once suggested that the opinions of the judges of the ICJ derive increased authority from the fact that those judges were elected, according to Art. 9 of the ICJ Statute, so as to assure 'in the body as a whole the representation of the main forms of civilization and of the

---

[13] The full text of Art. 9 reads as follows: 'At every election, the electors shall bear in mind not only that the persons to be elected should individually possess the qualifications required, but also that in the body as a whole the representation of the main forms of civilization and of the principal legal systems of the world should be assured.' See Rosenne, *The Law and Practice, supra* n. 3, vol. I, 369–70; Lachs, 'Some Reflections', *supra* n. 5, 49–68.

[14] Separate Opinion of Judge Weeramantry, in *Maritime Delimitation in the Area Between Greenland and Jan Mayen (Denmark v. Norway)*, 1993 ICJ Rep. 38, 273, para. 234.

[15] Rosenne, *The Law and Practice, supra* n. 3, vol. I, 370.

principal legal systems of the world'.[16] The judge appears to have had sympathy for the argument that the opinion of a large number of dissenting judges places that opinion under the head of 'the teaching of publicists', which are regarded in Art. 38, paragraph 1(d) ICJ Statute as 'subsidiary means for the determination of rules of law'. In our opinion, this view, which can be said to affect diffusion, is problematic, especially in the light of Art. 59 ICJ Statute, according to which '[t]he decision of the Court has no binding force except between the parties and in respect of that particular case'. This provision confirms that the principle of *stare decisis* – the binding nature of precedent – as it exists in Common law jurisdictions has no place in the ICJ, or in international law in general. As Judge Jessup has pointed out, however, in practice '[t]he influence of the Court's judgments is great, even though Art. 59 of the Statute declares that the *decision* "has no binding force except between the parties and in respect of that particular case"'.[17] As aptly summarised by Jessup, 'the influence of the Court's decisions is wider than their binding force'.[18] It also is the case that '[a]lthough the force of *res judicata* does not extend to the reasoning of a judgment, it is the practice of the Court, as of arbitral tribunals, to stand by the reasoning set forth in previous decisions'.[19]

Judges ad hoc

The process of diffusion of law within the ICJ is assisted by another aspect, namely, the role of the judge ad hoc, a unique position that is peculiar to the ICJ[20] and which is comparable to a party-appointed arbitrator in international commercial and investor–State arbitration.[21] According to Art. 31, paras. 2 and 3 ICJ Statute, if the regular bench does not include a judge of the nationality of a State party to ICJ proceedings,

[16] Separate Opinion of Judge Ammoun, in *Barcelona Traction* case, *supra* n. 11, 317, para. 23.

[17] Separate Opinion of Judge Jessup, in *Barcelona Traction* case, *supra* n. 11, 220, para. 106 (emphasis in the original).

[18] *Ibid.*, 163, para. 9.

[19] Separate Opinion of Judge Gros, in *Barcelona Traction* case, *supra* n. 11, 268, para. 1.

[20] Note, however, that Art. 17 of the Statute of the International Tribunal for the Law of the Sea (ITLOS), which had its first session in October 1996, includes a provision that is almost identical to Art. 31, paras. 2–3, of the ICJ Statute.

[21] Rosenne, *The Law and Practice*, *supra* n. 3, vol. III, 1123. While a judge ad hoc is appointed directly by a State Party to an ICJ proceeding, Art. 20 of the ICJ Statute directs that he 'must make a solemn declaration in open court that he will exercise his powers impartially and conscientiously'. For a critical view of the judge ad hoc concept, see H. Lauterpacht, *The Function of Law in the International Community* (Oxford: Clarendon Press, 1933), 215, 233–6.

that State may choose a person to sit as judge. If the bench does not include a judge of the nationality of either party, both parties may appoint a judge ad hoc. Thus, the ICJ bench in a given case between two States may comprise as many as seventeen judges. As one judge ad hoc has explained, 'the institution of the ad hoc judge was created for the purpose of giving a party, not otherwise having upon the Court a judge of its nationality, an opportunity to join in the work of this tribunal'.[22] According to the ICJ Statute, the work, or function, of the ICJ in contentious cases is 'to decide in accordance with international law such disputes as are submitted to it'.[23] While judges ad hoc are never elected as members of the three-member drafting committee charged with preparing the text of the Court's judgment (as described below), they fulfil a useful function in supplying local legal knowledge to the rest of the bench during the meetings of the Court and, as a result, they can be helpful in assisting the Court in defining the international law relevant in a particular case with a view to attaining the peaceful settlement of the legal dispute submitted to the Court.[24] This is especially relevant when the Court is called upon to define an area of international law that is not well developed and for which domestic law may be instructive, as is demonstrated by the *Barcelona Traction* case discussed below. Also, in situations where a parliamentary Act of one of the States Parties is at issue, judges ad hoc, at least those having the nationality of the State Party whose Act is at issue, can play a useful role in educating the rest of the bench about that Act and its national legal context and basis.[25]

---

[22] Separate Opinion of Judge ad hoc Lauterpacht, in *Application of the Convention on the Prevention and Punishment of the Crime of Genocide (Bosnia-Herzegovina v. Serbia and Montenegro)*, Further Provisional Measures, Order of 13 September 1993, 1993 ICJ Rep. 325, 409, para. 5. See also Dissenting Opinion of Judge ad hoc Sir Geoffrey Palmer, in *Request for an Examination of the Situation in Accordance with Paragraph 63 of the Court's Judgment of 20 December 1974 in the Nuclear Tests (New Zealand v. France) Case*, Order of 22 September 1995, 1995 ICJ Rep. 288, 421, para. 118.

[23] ICJ Statute Art. 38(1).

[24] See Rosenne, *The Law and Practice, supra* n. 3, vol. III, 1126 (citing a 1944 report by the Informal Inter-Allied Committee charged with advising the 1945 San Francisco Conference at which the ICJ Statute was adopted).

[25] See, e.g., *Fisheries Jurisdiction (Spain v. Canada)*, 1998 ICJ Rep. 432 (involving a Canadian legislative measure of which Spain complained). In *Fisheries Jurisdiction*, each party nominated a judge ad hoc of its own nationality. The dissenting opinion of the judge ad hoc chosen by Spain, which was denied jurisdiction in the case, is eight pages longer than the Court's decision. The judge ad hoc selected by Canada did not append an individual opinion, presumably because he was satisfied with the text of the judgment.

Judges ad hoc, just like the regular Members of the Court and their legal staff, are influenced by their legal training and their former legal activities in their countries of origin. As one ICJ judge has remarked: 'It is inevitable that every one of us in this Court should retain some trace of his legal education and his former legal activities in his country of origin.'[26] This results in an intricate process of interaction of legal systems and legal traditions.

Besides being of value in convincing a respondent State to participate in proceedings commenced by another State,[27] the participation of a judge ad hoc also can influence the losing State's willingness to abide by the Court's decision, including eventually by changing its laws or policies to conform to international law as authoritatively interpreted by the ICJ.[28] The yardstick for success of a reception of law through curial settlement is the extent of voluntary compliance of a losing State Party, which may or may not be measured by subsequent municipal legislative action corresponding to the international ruling. Argument, especially judicial reasoning, is key, as is the procedure before the ICJ. If the judicial process and reasoning are transparent and convincing, an ICJ ruling itself becomes an important agent of diffusion of law, even though '[t]he decision of the Court has no binding force except between the parties and in respect of that particular case'.[29] In this context, the Court's practice of

---

[26] Dissenting Opinion of Judge Carneiro, in *Anglo-Iranian Oil Co. (UK v. Iran)*, Preliminary Objections, Judgment, 1952 ICJ Rep. 93, 161, para. 14. See also Separate Opinion of Judge Padilla Nervo, in *Barcelona Traction* case, *supra* n. 11, 245 ('The lessons of history and past experience are, after all, the source of the law and of judicial precedents and must have place and weight in the conscience of the judge'). However, as Judge Lachs has pointed out, 'Judges of the same nationality and of the same legal or cultural dimension frequently arrive at opposing views'. Lachs, 'Some Reflections', *supra* n. 5, 63.

[27] See C. Peck and R. S. Lee (eds.), *Increasing the Effectiveness of the International Court of Justice* (The Hague, Boston and London: Martinus Nijhoff/UNITAR, 1997), 391 ('[I]t is a matter of essentially psychological reassurance to States and conduces to their willingness to arbitrate or adjudicate at all, if they can appoint an arbitrator or appoint an ad hoc judge') (comment by S. M. Schwebel). But see *ibid.*, 376 (comment by E. Lauterpacht).

[28] See S. M. Schwebel, 'National Judges and Judges *ad hoc* of the International Court of Justice', *ICLQ*, 48 (1999), 889–900, 892.

[29] ICJ Statute Art. 59. See also Separate Opinion of Judge Tanaka, in *Barcelona Traction, Light and Power Co. Ltd (Belgium v. Spain)*, Preliminary Objections, Judgment, 1964 ICJ Rep. 4, 65 (pointing out that '[t]he more important function of the Court as the principal judicial organ of the United Nations is to be found not only in the settlement of concrete disputes, but also in its reasoning, through which it may contribute to the development of international law').

appending individual opinions of judges, including judges ad hoc, to its decisions plays a particularly important role.[30]

In recent years, the ICJ has promulgated various 'Practice Directions'. These are designed to help increase the Court's efficiency and productivity. Through these Practice Directions, the ICJ is seeking to enhance compliance by States Parties participating in the judicial process which the Court administers. In the absence of further guidance in the Court's constituent documents, which are not likely to be revised anytime soon in light of their cumbersome provisions on revision, it would be desirable for the Court to adopt a new Practice Direction highlighting the specific role and function of judges ad hoc in the process of the diffusion of law. In conjunction with Art. 31, para. 6 ICJ Statute, which expresses the duty of impartiality by which the judge ad hoc is bound, such a Practice Direction would guide litigating States in their selection of judges ad hoc. It is submitted that a candidate's ability to assist in the diffusion of law by supplying local legal knowledge absent in the regular bench, rather than her ability to advocate the position of the party appointing her, is the primary characteristic of an effective judge ad hoc. The fact that there have been few instances in which a judge ad hoc voted entirely against the position of the State Party which appointed her underscores the need for an expression of the proper role of the judge ad hoc in an official document of the Court.[31]

Clearly, the presence and participation of judges ad hoc is not called for in every ICJ case involving two States which do not have a national on the bench. Rather than flatly discouraging the appointment of judges ad hoc in ICJ cases, greater emphasis should be placed on their proper function. Therefore, the statement made by ICJ President Higgins before the UN General Assembly in October 2008 according to which 'the ICJ believes that where two States appear before it, neither of whom having a national on the Bench, they might want to give very careful consideration to' waiving their right to appoint a judge ad hoc in their case is unfortunate.[32] Notwithstanding the financial hardship which judge ad hoc

---

[30] See Separate Opinion of Judge Ammoun, in *Barcelona Traction* case, *supra* n. 11, 316–17 ('in order to assess the value of a judicial decision, it is necessary to be able to ascertain the extent to which it expresses the opinion of the Court, and what objections judges no less qualified than those who supported it were able to bring against it').

[31] See Schwebel, 'National Judges', *supra* n. 28, 895–6; Rosenne, *The Law and Practice*, *supra* n. 3, vol. III, 1128–9. See also Peck and Lee, *Increasing the Effectiveness*, *supra* n. 27, 387–9 (comments by E. Brown Weiss and E. Lauterpacht).

[32] Rosalyn Higgins, ICJ President, Speech to the UN General Assembly, 30 October 2008, 5–6, www.icj-cij.org/presscom/files/5/14835.pdf. See also ICJ Press Release 2008/38 (30 October 2008).

appointments apparently cause the ICJ,[33] the concept overall has proven a useful one, especially from the perspective of promoting legal diffusion as discussed in this chapter.

The Court's deliberative process

A closer look at how the process of diffusion of law takes place within the ICJ will assist in identifying the Court's role in the diffusion universe.

In order to understand the process of legal diffusion as it pertains to the ICJ, it is particularly instructive to examine the Court's unique deliberative process, involving up to seventeen judges in a case between two States.[34] This examination will demonstrate that the pathway of diffusion at the ICJ is both complex and indirect.

Following the more formal, party-driven process of diffusion which typically unfolds during the written and oral phases of an ICJ case,[35] especially a proceeding which turns on the assessment of a municipal measure or the interpretation of a norm of international law which is not well defined, individual judges of the Court, including judges ad hoc,[36] have several opportunities to influence the process of diffusion during the various stages of the deliberative phase of a case.[37] First, the ICJ President submits to all the judges participating in the case an outline of

---

[33] According to ICJ President Higgins, the twenty judges ad hoc appointed in connection with the ICJ's 2008 docket represented 2 per cent of the Court's annual budget in 2008. *Ibid.*, 5.

[34] See R. Jennings, 'The Internal Judicial Practice of the International Court of Justice', *BYBIL*, 59 (1988), 31–47; P. H. F. Bekker, *World Court Decisions at the Turn of the Millennium (1997–2001)* (The Hague, London and New York: Martinus Nijhoff, 2002), 31–2.

[35] While the written pleadings exchanged between the parties to an ICJ case typically remain confidential until the opening of the hearings, the oral proceedings are open to the public. See ICJ Statute Art. 46 and ICJ Rules of Court Art. 53.

[36] As Rosenne has pointed out, '[o]nce the oral proceedings are closed the parties have no further opportunity of bringing their points of view to bear on the Court, and it rests with the national judges or the judges *ad hoc* not so much to plead their countries' cases as to project their countries' interests in the whole process through which the decision is produced and the reasons formulated'. Rosenne, *The Law and Practice, supra* n. 3, vol. III, 1127. See also Schwebel, 'National Judges', *supra* n. 28, 893 ('[judges ad hoc] are charged with ensuring, in so far as they can, that the factual and legal arguments of [the appointing] State are fully understood and considered by the Court').

[37] Deliberations take place behind closed doors and are attended only by the ICJ judges sitting in the case, any judges ad hoc appointed in the case and selected ICJ staff. See ICJ Statute Art. 54(3) ('The deliberations of the Court shall take place in private and remain secret').

the issues dividing the parties. The President's outline is discussed and commented on by the participating judges during the initial deliberative meeting at which individual judges State their preliminary views. Judges then have several weeks to prepare their individual 'Written Notes' in which they offer their tentative views regarding the issues presented in the President's outline. This stage of the deliberations is especially conducive to diffusion, as it allows individual judges, and especially judges ad hoc, to inform their colleagues of their legal tradition, to the extent relevant to the case, and to engage in an exchange of legal ideas on what constitutes the relevant law. Deliberative meetings are then resumed and judges express their views orally and in inverse order of seniority. This means that judges ad hoc express their views before the regular Members of the Court, potentially influencing their view in this way. After this session, the Court proceeds to elect a Drafting Committee comprising three judges. The President will act as chair *ex officio* of the Drafting Committee, unless he or she shares the minority view. The Drafting Committee prepares a preliminary draft judgment on which individual judges may make written suggestions. The Drafting Committee subsequently issues a fresh draft which it submits for first reading. That draft is discussed among the judges at several private meetings of the Court. At this stage, declarations and separate or dissenting opinions, including by judges ad hoc, are made available by individual judges. Such opinions may influence the final vote. Each paragraph of the draft judgment is then read aloud in the two official languages of the Court (English and French), is discussed and is either left unchanged, amended, or referred back to the Drafting Committee. Finally, an amended draft judgment is distributed to the judges, which is then given a page-by-page second reading and may be commented on by the judges. At the end of the second reading, a final vote is taken, with judges voting in inverse order of seniority.

A careful, inclusive deliberative process, as reflected in the reasoning of an ICJ ruling announced in public and in any individual opinions appended to it, can greatly influence a losing State's post-decision behaviour, and indeed the views and conduct of anybody taking note of the Court's ruling.[38] Thus, diffusion often is a function of the reasoning contained in an ICJ ruling. If the reasoning is convincing, as perceived by the participating actors, the ruling becomes a potent agent of diffusion of international law.

---

[38] See *supra* n. 3.

Because international law as developed by international courts and tribunals is a relatively young body of law, legal diffusion in the ICJ is often a two-way process. The Court's authoritative pronouncements on international law do not exclusively act as forces of diffusion influencing municipal law or policy changes. The reverse situation also is encountered, with municipal rules being transposed and received at the international law plane and dictating the outcome of an ICJ case.

Case study: Barcelona Traction

A prominent example of the latter situation, and an especially appropriate subject for discussion given Vagts' pre-eminent scholarship in transnational corporations law,[39] is the *Barcelona Traction* case.[40] In that case, Belgium initiated proceedings against Spain before the ICJ in connection with the adjudicated bankruptcy in Spain of the Barcelona Traction, Light and Power Co. Ltd, a company formed in Canada. Belgium claimed that the company's share capital belonged largely to Belgian nationals and maintained that the acts of judicial and administrative organs of the Spanish State, whereby the company had been declared bankrupt, were in violation of international law. Thus, Belgium based its claim of compensation on injury done to the Belgian shareholders' interests resulting from injury to rights of the company in which they held shares.

In its landmark judgment of 5 February 1970, the ICJ found that Belgium lacked standing to exercise diplomatic protection for shareholders in a Canadian company in respect of measures taken against that company in Spain. In this context, the Court had to address the question whether 'a right of Belgium [had] been violated on account of its nationals' having suffered infringement of their rights as shareholders in a company not of Belgian nationality'.[41] The ICJ observed as follows:

> In this field international law is called upon to recognize institutions of municipal law that have an important and extensive role in the international field. This does not necessarily imply drawing any analogy between its own institutions and those of municipal law, nor does it amount to making rules of international law dependent upon categories of municipal law. All it means is that international law has had to recognize the

---

[39] See, e.g., D. F. Vagts, *Basic Corporation Law*, 3rd edn. (Westbury, NY: Foundation Press, 1989), and the long list of corporation law articles and notes authored by Vagts listed at the end of this volume (p. 655).

[40] *Barcelona Traction* case, *supra* n. 11.   [41] *Ibid.*, 32, para. 35.

corporate entity as an institution created by States in a domain essentially within their domestic jurisdiction. This in turn requires that, whenever legal issues arise concerning the rights of States with regard to the treatment of companies and shareholders, as to which rights international law has not established its own rules, it has to refer to the relevant rules of municipal law.[42]

Following an examination of rules of municipal law common to those legal systems which recognise the institution of companies limited by shares, the ICJ reached the conclusion that, under municipal law, the rights of the company's shareholders are not affected by measures taken against the company in which they hold shares. It follows, the Court held, that the State of which the shareholders in a company are nationals also has no right which might be injured on the international plane by measures taken by another State against the company.

Through what appears to be a transnational analysis of the rights of the corporate entity and its shareholders under municipal private law, the Court concluded that the rules generally accepted by municipal legal systems – especially the general rule that in the case of a corporate person a State may espouse that company's cause internationally only if the company was incorporated in the claiming State and has its registered seat in that State – dictated dismissal of Belgium's claim against Spain for lack of standing. Thus, the Court's decision was based on 'the application of transposition on to the plane of international law of the rules of municipal law concerning the status of a company and its shareholders'.[43]

The Court's examination of the municipal legal order regarding corporate identity influenced its definition of the content of a norm of international law – in this case, the absence of diplomatic protection for shareholders whose company was affected by a foreign State's measures.[44] This raises another normative question: is such a reference, or *renvoi*, to rules of municipal law appropriate for a question of customary international law involving particular States?[45] Interestingly, it has been stated that the judge ad hoc chosen by Belgium, a Dutch national:

---

[42] *Ibid.*, 33, para. 38.
[43] Dissenting Opinion of Judge ad hoc Riphagen, in *Barcelona Traction* case, *supra* n. 11, 343.
[44] The ICJ recognised that 'on the international plane also there may in principle be special circumstances which justify the lifting of the veil in the interests of shareholders'. *Ibid.*, 39, para. 58.
[45] See Separate Opinion of Judge Gros, in *Barcelona Traction* case, *supra* n. 11, 272–9; Dissenting Opinion of Judge ad hoc Riphagen, in *Barcelona Traction* case, *supra* n. 11, 338, para. 7. As pointed out by Judge Morelli, 'in the eyes of an international tribunal,

voted against the otherwise unanimous decision of the Court that Belgium lacked *jus standi*, because it had not established that the acts of Spain had violated an obligation owed under international law by Spain to Belgium. In his dissenting opinion, Judge ad hoc Riphagen argued that the Court should have applied customary international law rather than almost exclusively Spanish municipal law when determining whether rights of the Belgian State had been violated.[46]

It must be pointed out, however, that the Court emphasised that '[i]t is to rules generally accepted by municipal legal systems which recognize the limited company whose capital is represented by shares, and not to the municipal law of a particular State, that international law refers'.[47] The Court added that '[i]n referring to such rules, the Court cannot modify, still less deform them'.[48]

Disjunction between theory and practice?

In the light of the academic nature of, and the predominantly academic participation in, the judicial process which the ICJ administers, there appears to be less disjunction between theory and practice here than might be observed in other fields of the law. Still, much academic work in our view suffers from a lack of practicable solutions offered and is, consequently, discarded by officials and practitioners appearing before international courts and tribunals as well as the judges themselves.

---

questions of municipal law also are questions of fact'. Separate Opinion of Judge Morelli, in *Barcelona Traction* case, *supra* n. 11, 230. Presumably, it lies within the fact-finding powers of the ICJ to define the pertinent municipal law in determining the applicable international law in a given case. See, generally, K. Highet, 'Evidence and Proof of Facts', in L. F. Damrosch (ed.), *The International Court of Justice at a Crossroads* (Dobbs Ferry, NY: Transnational Publishers, 1987), 355; T. M. Franck, 'Fact-Finding before the International Court of Justice', in R. B. Lillich (ed.), *Fact-Finding Before International Tribunals* (Ardsley-on-Hudson, NY: Transnational Publishers, 1992), 21; R. Teitelbaum, 'Recent Fact-Finding Developments at the International Court of Justice', *Law & Practice of International Courts & Tribunals*, 6 (2007), 119–58.

[46] Schwebel, 'National Judges', *supra* n. 28, 898. For a different view, see Separate Opinion of Judge Morelli, in *Barcelona Traction* case, *supra* n. 11, 233–4. Spain had chosen Mr Enrique C. Armand-Ugon, a former President of the Supreme Court of Uruguay, to sit as judge ad hoc in the case brought by Belgium. While he did not append an individual declaration or opinion to the Court's judgment, having voted with the majority, it may be assumed that, as a jurist from Uruguay, Mr Armand-Ugon was familiar with the pertinent municipal law of Spain, or at least he may be considered to have possessed greater knowledge and understanding of Spanish law than the Dutch judge ad hoc appointed by Belgium.

[47] *Barcelona Traction* case, *supra* n. 11, 37, para. 50.   [48] *Ibid.*

Unlike other areas of diffusion, ICJ judges have clear guidance on when it is appropriate to treat foreign precedents and other sources as persuasive authority. According to Art. 38, para. (1)(d) ICJ Statute, judicial decisions and the literature are only subsidiary sources of international law. However, it is clear from the individual opinions of ICJ judges which are attached to a particular ruling that they are heavily influenced by the decisions of other courts and tribunals (including the ICJ), as well as by the writings of leading jurists. International judges and arbitrators are obviously familiar with the internet and take advantage of the wide variety of sources to which this instrument gives them access. This includes web sites of NGOs, institutions of higher learning and other international courts and tribunals. Reference may also be made to the many specialised professional journals which have emerged in the past decade or so. While these sources do not form direct bases for decision-making at the ICJ (one will look in vain for them in the main text of an ICJ ruling), it is safe to say that the judges and their staff are influenced by those sources, which likely affects the way a judge makes up his or her mind in a given case.

Conclusion

Based upon the above analysis of the judicial process which the ICJ administers, the following concluding observations regarding international adjudication as a mechanism of diffusion may be offered.

First, the sources of authority of international law, or of 'importation', are more diverse when compared to other legal fields or disciplines, as a result of which one may observe more cross-level diffusion of law on the international plane than on the domestic plane. Judicial decisions and influential legal writings are potent forms of 'informal' diffusion of international law, arguably more so than in other fields.

Secondly, the authority of the ICJ as the world's only court of general jurisdiction and its unique composition and collegial working methods explain why one may observe more spontaneous diffusion on the international plane. States often accept international norms, and adapt to them domestically through implementation devices, as a gesture of cooperation and compliance, and municipal law is invoked in aid of the definition of international legal norms by States and international judges alike.

Finally, the transportation or reception of legal norms through international tribunals such as the ICJ occurs more gradually and indirectly as part of an informal process. Rather than replacing prior international law, diffusion of law in this context works mostly to define, or to fill gaps in, the existing international law.[49]

The above discussion of the unique features of the diffusion process taking place within the ICJ hopefully will serve to identify the ICJ as an international court of *transnational* justice contributing to the development of 'world law, ... or transnational law according to Jessup, a term which has become standard in international law'.[50] As such, the ICJ is a most suitable subject for diffusion studies. International law scholars, international relations theorists and social scientists should join in studying the ICJ as a prominent phenomenon for helping us better understand the various mechanisms of diffusion of law, especially on the international plane.

---

[49] See Separate Opinion of Judge Ammoun, in *Barcelona Traction* case, *supra* n. 11, 332 (referring to the ICJ's recourse to 'a subsidiary source of international law taken, as a general principle of law, from paragraph 1 *(c)* of [Article 38 of the ICJ Statute], appeal to which is made in order to remedy the insufficiencies of international law and fill in its *logical* lacunae' (emphasis in the original)).

[50] *Ibid.*, 303.

24

Regulating counsel conduct before international arbitral tribunals

CHARLES N. BROWER AND STEPHAN W. SCHILL[*]

The need for regulating counsel conduct in international arbitration

Detlev Vagts had a visionary perspective on the impact of globalisation on the legal profession. He has repeatedly pointed to the problems stemming from the absence of ethical regulation of the transnational practice of law, including dispute settlement before international courts and tribunals.[1] He was already doing so at a time when the proliferation of international dispute settlement bodies was a barely discernible emerging phenomenon,[2] and well before the dramatic increase in

---

[*] Charles N. Brower served as party-appointed arbitrator in the ICSID arbitration in *HEP v. Slovenia, infra* n. 19, discussed in this chapter.

[1] D. F. Vagts, 'The International Legal Profession. A Need for More Governance?', *AJIL*, 90 (1996), 250–62; D. F. Vagts, 'Professional Responsibility in Transborder Practice. Conflict and Resolution', *Georgetown Journal of Legal Ethics*, 13 (2000), 677–98; D. F. Vagts, 'The Impact of Globalization on the Legal Profession', *EJLR*, 2 (2000), 403–14; D. F. Vagts, 'Transnational Litigation and Professional Ethics', in B. Legum (ed.), *International Litigation Strategies and Practice* (Chicago, IL: ABA Publishing, 2005), 25–31.

[2] On the proliferation of international dispute settlement bodies and their impact on the international legal system see, generally, L. Reed, 'Great Expectations. Where Does the Proliferation of International Dispute Resolution Tribunals Leave International Law?', *Proceedings of the American Society of International Law*, 96 (2002), 219–37; R. P. Alford, 'The Proliferation of International Courts and Tribunals. International Adjudication in Ascendance', *Proceedings of the American Society of International Law*, 94 (2000), 160–5; B. Kingsbury, 'Is the Proliferation of International Courts and Tribunals a Systemic Problem?', *New York University Journal of International Law & Politics*, 31 (1999), 679–96; J. Charney, 'The Impact on the International Legal System of the Growth of International Courts and Tribunals', *New York University Journal of International Law & Politics*, 31 (1999), 697–708; C. Romano, 'The Proliferation of International Judicial Bodies. The Piece of the Puzzle', *New York University Journal of International Law & Politics*, 31 (1999), 709–52; see further also the other contributions to a symposium held at New York University School of Law in October 1998 on the proliferation of

treaty-based arbitrations between States and foreign investors under the International Convention on the Settlement of Investment Disputes between States and Nationals of other States ('ICSID Convention') and other arbitral rules that has marked the past decade.[3] In 1996, he predicted that '[a]s the activities of international law agencies, both public and private, involve more countries and more cultures, disputes about standards of behavior can be expected to multiply'[4] and, as a response, recommended that '[a] set of rules to guide the behavior of lawyers before international panels would be useful'.[5]

Equally Detlev Vagts foresaw how difficult it would be to establish formal rules in an institutional context, in which numerous States with various interests and different approaches to the regulation of lawyers interact. He therefore, attributed great potential to private bodies developing guidelines which could then be adopted by dispute settlement institutions. 'The task' for such bodies, he stated, 'would be challenging, given the variety of practices that prevail in national legal systems, but the need of international lawyers for intelligible and, as far as possible, uniform guidance is becoming clearer. The rules should take into account the importance of an international procedure aimed at achieving widespread respect for its integrity, openness and efficiency.'[6]

Today, we still have not advanced much in terms of formal and binding regulations governing the conduct of counsel in transnational dispute settlement,[7] in sharp contrast to the increasingly tight regulation

international courts and tribunals, in *New York University Journal of International Law & Politics*, 31 (1999), 679–933.

[3] See UNCTAD, 'Latest Developments in Investor–State Dispute Settlement', *IIA Issues Note*, No. 1 (2010), 2–3, www.unctad.org/en/docs/webdiaeia2010_en.pdf (recording an aggregate of 357 investment treaty disputes by the end of 2009).

[4] Vagts, 'The International Legal Profession', *supra* n. 1, 250.   [5] *Ibid.*, 260.   [6] *Ibid.*, 261.

[7] While certain guidelines by private bodies, such as the IBA Guidelines on Conflict of Interests in International Arbitration, have been developed, rules regarding issues of professional ethics in arbitral proceedings, such as conflicts of interests or counsels' duties toward the parties, opposing counsel and the arbitrators, largely remain subject to domestic frameworks and supervision by national bar associations, often in themselves insufficient. See, e.g., R. E. Lutz, 'Ethics and International Practice. A Guide to the Professional Responsibilities of Practitioners', *Fordham International Law Journal*, 16 (1992–3), 53–78; E. Godfrey (ed.), *Law without Frontiers. A Comparative Survey of the Rules of Professional Ethics Applicable to the Cross-border Practice of Law* (London: Kluwer Law International, 1995); Vagts, 'Professional Responsibility', *supra* n. 1, 677; C. A. Rogers, 'Fit and Function in Legal Ethics. Developing a Code of Conduct for International Arbitration', *Michigan Journal of International Law*, 23 (2002), 341–424; M. C. Daly, 'Resolving Ethical Conflicts in Multijurisdictional Practice – Is Model Rule 8.5 The Answer, An Answer, or No Answer At All?', *South Texas Law Review*, 36 (2005), 715–98; C. A. Rogers, 'Lawyers Without Borders',

of international arbitrators, above all through guidelines and formal codes governing their duty to disclose information that may affect, or be perceived as affecting, their impartiality and independence.[8] Thus, none of the major international dispute settlement bodies, including the International Court of Justice (ICJ) and the International Centre for Settlement of Investment Disputes (ICSID), has adopted comprehensive binding, or even non-binding, codes of conduct for counsel.[9] In the ICJ, a comprehensive code of professional conduct for counsel is perhaps not necessary in view of the small pool of counsel appearing before the Court. Yet, the need for regulation of the conduct of counsel becomes increasingly pressing, in particular in treaty-based investment arbitrations, the number of which is increasing tremendously, and with it the number and diversity of counsel appearing before such tribunals, each of whom necessarily has been shaped by his or her national rules of

University of Pennsylvania International Law Review, 30 (2009), 1035–86. See also the symposium issue in *South Texas Law Review*, 36 (1995), 657–1105. See further A. Boon and J. Flood, 'Globalization of Professional Ethics? The Significance of Lawyers' International Codes of Conduct', *Legal Ethics*, 2 (1999), 29.

[8] On the regulation of international arbitrators, see C. Giovannucci Orlandi, 'Ethics for International Arbitrators', *University of Kansas City Law Review*, 67 (1998), 93–109; C. A. Rogers, 'Regulating International Arbitrators. A Functional Approach to Developing Standards of Conduct', *Stanford Journal of International Law*, 41 (2005), 53–121; L. Malintoppi, 'Independence, Impartiality, and Duty of Disclosure of Arbitrators', in P. Muchlinski, F. Ortino and C. Schreuer, *The Oxford Handbook of International Investment Law* (Oxford University Press, 2008), 789. Similarly, in the context of domestic arbitration institutions, the regulation of arbitrator conduct is vast. See, e.g., B. Sheppard, 'A New Era of Arbitrator Ethics for the United States. The 2004 Revision to the AAA/ABA Code of Ethics for Arbitrators in Commercial Disputes', *Arbitration International*, 21 (2005), 91. See, generally, on ethics issues regarding arbitrators, C. Menkel-Meadow, 'Ethics Issues on Arbitration and Related Dispute Resolution Processes. What's Happening and What's Not', *University of Miami Law Review*, 56 (2002), 949–1007.

[9] The only exception, in this context, are the international criminal courts that dispose of comprehensive codes of conduct for counsel, see *infra* n. 37. Other international dispute settlement institutions at most selectively address issues of professional conduct and professional ethics. The ICJ, for example, has issued Practice Directions, and updates them regularly, which contain some rules on professional conduct of counsel, in particular on incompatibilities with the role of counsel. See Practice Directions, www.icj-cij. org/documents/index.php?p1=4&p2=4&p3=0. Thus, Practice Direction VIII states that 'it is not in the interest of the sound administration of justice that a person who until recently was a Member of the Court, judge *ad hoc*, Registrar, Deputy-Registrar or higher official of the Court (principal legal secretary, first secretary or secretary), appear as agent, counsel or advocate in a case before the Court. Accordingly, parties should refrain from designating as agent, counsel or advocate in a case before the Court a person who in the three years preceding the date of the designation was a Member of the Court, judge *ad hoc*, Registrar, Deputy-Registrar or higher official of the Court.'

professional conduct and thus professionally socialised in a domestic litigation context. The cacophony of national ethical rules, subjecting counsel to the rules of their home jurisdiction, and perhaps also to the rules in place at the arbitration's *situs*, potentially results in the application of different standards to opposing counsel or even to counsel on the same team.[10] Furthermore, national rules often do not address the specific issues raised by transnational arbitration and are difficult to enforce as domestic authorities are restricted in their actions to the jurisdiction in which they operate.[11]

Indeed, the issues in relation to professional conduct in treaty-based arbitrations that can give rise to concerns are numerous. They include the extent to which *ex parte* communications between counsel and arbitrators are permissible, if at all; whether witness preparation, as is customary, for example, in the United States but forbidden in many Civil law countries, is proper; whether counsel are under a duty to disclose client misconduct, for example regarding corruption; whether counsel have a duty to disclose to the other party and the Tribunal possible conflicts of interest; and whether counsel have a duty of candour toward the Tribunal – for example, to make a full and objective presentation of legal authority.[12]

The need for uniform rules concerning counsel conduct before international tribunals stems not only from a need to ensure that counsel and parties operate on a level playing field.[13] At issue may ultimately be the legitimacy of the international arbitral system as a whole,[14]

---

[10] See Rogers, 'Fit and Function', *supra* n. 7, 357–79; Vagts, 'Professional Responsibility', *supra* n. 1, 689–98.

[11] See Rogers, 'Fit and Function', *supra* n. 7, 342.

[12] See C.A. Rogers, 'Context and Institutional Structure in Attorney Regulation. Constructing an Enforcement Regime for International Arbitration', *Stanford Journal of International Law*, 39 (2003), 1–58, 2. On the duty of candour, cf. A. Watts, 'Enhancing the Effectiveness of Procedures of International Dispute Settlement', *Max Planck United Nations Year Book*, 5 (2001), 21, 27–8 (reporting from personal experience an example of counsel before the ICJ quoting selectively and incompletely in his pleadings from an international convention while omitting to mention an exception in that Convention that would have been unfavourable to the party he was representing).

[13] Vagts, 'The International Legal Profession', *supra* n. 1, 255; J. Paulsson, 'Standards of Conduct for Counsel in International Arbitration', *American Review of International Arbitration*, 3 (1992), 214.

[14] By 'legitimacy' we mean (following T. Franck, *The Power of Legitimacy Among Nations*, Oxford University Press, 1990, 24) acceptance of 'a rule or rule-making institution which itself exerts a pull toward compliance on those addressed normatively because those addressed believe that the rule or institution has come into being and operates in accordance with generally accepted principles of right process'.

in particular inasmuch as, in the case of investment treaty arbitrations, it operates not only retrospectively as a review mechanism for the legality of State conduct under international law,[15] but also prospectively as a mechanism of global governance.[16] In such cases, the differences in policy choices underlying national rules of professional ethics can compromise the legitimacy of the arbitral process if the parties to an arbitration distrust those divergent rules to which opposing counsel are subject and therefore perceive the outcome of an arbitral proceeding as tainted by what appears, from one party's perspective, to be impermissible ethical conduct.[17] Thus the fairness and legitimacy of the administration of international justice may itself be subject to dispute.[18]

A recent example in investment arbitration: *HEP* v. *Slovenia*

Such a situation arose in the ICSID arbitration *Hrvatska Elektropriv-reda d.d. [HEP]* v. *The Republic of Slovenia*, when the Respondent disclosed only shortly before the hearing on the merits that it had retained an English barrister who was a member of the barristers' chambers in which the Tribunal's President was a door tenant.[19] Immediately following such disclosure, the Claimant, pointing to the

---

[15] See G. Van Harten, *Investment Treaty Arbitration and Public Law* (Oxford University Press, 2007), 58–68; T. Wälde, 'The Specific Nature of Investment Arbitration', in P. Kahn and T. Wälde (eds.), *Les aspects nouveaux du droit des investissements internationaux/New Aspects of International Investment Law* (The Hague: Martinus Nijhoff, 2006), 43, 112; G. Van Harten and M. Loughlin, 'Investment Treaty Arbitration as a Species of Global Administrative Law', *EJIL*, 17 (2006), 121, 145–50.

[16] See B. Kingsbury and S. Schill, 'Investor–State Arbitration as Governance. Fair and Equitable Treatment, Proportionality and the Emerging Global Administrative Law', IILJ Working Paper 2009/6 (Global Administrative Law Series), www.iilj.org/publications/2009-6 Kingsbury-Schill. asp. The function of investment treaty tribunals as a governance mechanism operates primarily through the usage and generation of arbitral 'precedent'. The term 'precedent', however, is not used in this context in a technical sense as part of a system of *stare decisis* but in terms of exercising persuasive authority. See, generally, S. Schill, *The Multilateralization of International Investment Law* (Cambridge University Press, 2009), 321–57.

[17] Cf. Rogers, 'Lawyers Without Borders', *supra* n. 7, 1076–82.

[18] Cf. Watts, 'Enhancing the Effectiveness', *supra* n. 12, 28 ('more about knowing what are the proper standards of conduct to be observed in international proceedings, so that the relationship between counsel and the Court – which is fundamental to the sound administration of justice – can be fostered').

[19] *Hrvatska Elektroprivreda d.d. [HEP]* v. *The Republic of Slovenia*, ICSID Case No. ARB/05/24, Tribunal's Ruling regarding the participation of David Mildon QC in further stages of the proceedings of 6 May 2008. For commentary on that decision see also D.J. Branson, 'An ICSID Tribunal Applies Supranational Legal Norms to Banish Counsel from the Proceedings', *Arbitration International*, 25 (2009), 615. After the

International Bar Association (IBA) Guidelines on Conflicts of Interest in International Arbitration,[20] sought information concerning the relationship between Respondent's counsel and the Tribunal's President, inquiring, *inter alia*, as to the role the counsel in question was expected to play in the hearing.[21] After the Respondent declined to disclose that information, arguing that it was not required to do so,[22] the Claimant emphasised that its concerns about the independence and impartiality of the Tribunal's President were such that 'had [it] known at the outset that the lawyer proposed to be President of the Tribunal and one of Slovenia's lawyers were members of the same Chambers, the Claimant would not have consented to that lawyer's appointment as President'.[23] It therefore insisted on being informed as to when the counsel in question had been engaged.

For the Respondent, by contrast, the fact of the counsel in question and the Tribunal's President being associated in the same English barristers' chambers could not cause justified concern as to the President's independence and impartiality, as such practice is common and permissible under English standards of professional ethics. As a result, the Respondent declined to respond fully to the questions the Claimant had posed, arguing that it had no obligation to disclose such information.[24] The Claimant, however, insisted:

---

manuscript of the present chapter was finished, another ICSID tribunal had to deal with a request to ban counsel from further participating in the proceedings because of counsel's earlier employment by a law firm of which one of the arbitrators was a partner. The request, however, was declined because, based on the facts of the case, the integrity of the arbitral process was not at stake. See *The Rompetrol Group N.V.* v. *Romania*, ICSID Case No. ARB/06/3, Decision of the Tribunal on the Participation of a Counsel of 14 January 2010.

[20] General Standard 3 of the IBA Guidelines requires disclosure of arbitrators about 'facts or circumstances that may, in the eyes of the parties, give rise to doubts as to the arbitrator's impartiality or independence'; General Standard 2(b) requires an arbitrator to refuse an appointment or refuse to continue to act as arbitrator 'if facts or circumstances exist, or have arisen since the appointment, that, from a reasonable third person's point of view having knowledge of the relevant facts, give rise to justifiable doubts as to the arbitrator's impartiality or independence'; General Standard 7 requires arbitrators and parties to provide information 'about any direct or indirect relationship between it . . . and the arbitrator'. Under No. 3.3.2 of the Guidelines' 'Orange List' of situations that may give rise to justifiable doubts as to an arbitrator's impartiality and independence is the fact that an 'arbitrator and . . . counsel for one of the parties are members of the same barristers' chambers'. Para. 4.5 of the Background Information, available in *Business Law International*, 5 (2004), 433–58, issued by the Working Group on the Guidelines, further clarifies that this disclosure requirement also applies to English barristers' chambers.

[21] *HEP* v. *Slovenia*, *supra* n. 19, para. 4.

[22] *Ibid.*, para. 6 (the Respondent, however, as well as the Tribunal's President, provided information on the relationship between counsel in issue and the Tribunal's President, confirming that beyond their common chambers membership they had never had any relationship, professional or personal).

[23] *Ibid.*, para. 7.   [24] *Ibid.*, para. 8.

We understand that the Respondent and its London-based legal team believe that a reasonable third person should have no justifiable concerns about the facts that the President of the Tribunal and a lawyer for the Respondent are both members of Essex Court Chambers or that the announcement of Mr. Mildon's participation was made by the Respondents and its legal team on the eve of the hearing. But the community of participants in ICSID arbitrations is much broader than the English bar, and what may not, apparently, be cause for concern in London may well be viewed very differently by a reasonable third person from Africa, Argentina, or Zagreb, Croatia. The Claimant [an entity wholly owned by Croatia] *is* concerned that the President, and a member of the Respondent's legal team, are from the same Chambers. Viewed from the Claimant's cultural perspective, such concerns are justified, and, indeed, they are unavoidable.[25]

As a consequence, the Claimant ultimately requested the Tribunal to exclude the particular counsel in issue from the further proceedings and the Tribunal proceeded to bar him.[26]

In the current situation, in which the legitimacy of investment treaty arbitration increasingly is questioned,[27] private bodies and arbitral institutions may not be able to move toward formally regulating counsel conduct in time to meet the growing need for it. The question Detlev Vagts posed, namely 'who will lay down the rules governing conduct of lawyers operating across borders and how will they be enforced',[28] at least for the moment,

---

[25] *Ibid.*, para. 10 (emphasis in the original).   [26] *Ibid.*, paras. 10, 12.

[27] See M. Sornarajah, 'A Coming Crisis. Expansionary Trends in Investment Treaty Arbitration', in K. Sauvant (ed.), *Appeals Mechanism in International Investment Disputes* (Oxford University Press, 2008), 39–45; A. Afilalo, 'Meaning, Ambiguity and Legitimacy. Judicial (Re-)Construction of NAFTA Chapter 11', *Northwestern Journal of International Law & Business*, 25 (2005), 279–314, 282; S. D. Franck, 'The Legitimacy Crisis in Investment Treaty Arbitration. Privatizing Public International Law through Inconsistent Decisions', *Fordham Law Review*, 73 (2005), 1521–1625, 1523; A. Afilalo, 'Towards a Common Law of International Investment. How NAFTA Chapter 11 Panels Should Solve Their Legitimacy Crisis', *Georgetown International Environmental Law Review*, 17 (2004), 51; C.H. Brower, II, 'Structure, Legitimacy, and NAFTA's Investment Chapter', *Vanderbilt Journal of Transnational Law*, 36 (2003), 37–94; C. N. Brower, C. H. Brower, II and J. Sharpe, 'The Coming Crisis in the Global Adjudication System', *Arbitration International*, 19 (2003), 415; C. N. Brower, 'A Crisis of Legitimacy', *National Law Journal*, 7 October 2002. On 30 April 2008, Venezuela communicated to The Netherlands its intention to terminate the Dutch–Venezuelan BIT as of 1 November 2008; see L. Peterson (ed.), *Investment Arbitration Reporter* (16 May 2008), www.iareporter.com/Archive/IAR-05-16-08.pdf. Bolivia withdrew from the ICSID Convention as of 3 November 2007. See 'Bolivia Denounces ICSID Convention', *ILM*, 46 (2007), 973. On 12 June 2009, Ecuador's Congress voted to withdraw from the ICSID Convention. Discussion of withdrawal from the ICSID Convention has also been reported with respect to Nicaragua, Venezuela and Cuba. See M. Schnabl and J. Bédard, 'The Wrong Kind of "Interesting"', *National Law Journal*, 30 July 2007.

[28] Vagts, 'The Impact of Globalization', *supra* n. 1, 411.

and with all of its limitations and imperfections, must be answered as follows: it is arbitral tribunals themselves that are called upon to develop and enforce uniform and internationally accepted rules of professional conduct of counsel in order to ensure acceptance of the legitimacy of the treaty-based international arbitral process. Accordingly, in the following we shall discuss, first, the power of international courts and tribunals to enforce and develop those rules and, second, the means available to arbitral tribunals to sanction counsel misconduct. In closing, we shall discuss the bases on which arbitral tribunals can draw to develop substantive standards of counsel conduct and the considerations they should keep in mind.

Powers of international arbitral tribunals to develop and enforce rules of counsel conduct

The competence of international courts and tribunals to develop and to enforce standards of professional conduct of counsel appearing before them is often questioned.[29] In the case of *HEP* v. *Slovenia*, for example, the Respondent answered the Claimant's request to exclude counsel from the further proceedings by asserting that it was 'not aware of any inherent jurisdiction or authority in . . . a public international law proceeding . . . LCIA . . . ICC . . . WTO, ICJ, ITLOS . . . which would enable the Tribunal to grant . . . the relief [the Claimant] is seeking'.[30]

Indeed, the consensual foundation of arbitration arguably militates against conferring authority on arbitrators to develop and to enforce rules of professional conduct of counsel. Such authority usually is viewed as inherently governmental and restricted to State institutions, such as national bar associations or State courts in whose jurisdiction counsel is qualified to practice.[31] Thus, the United States District Court for the Southern District of New York decided that 'disqualification of an attorney for an alleged conflict of interest, is a substantive matter for the courts and not arbitrators', observing that '[a]ttorney discipline has historically been a matter for judges and not arbitrators because it

---

[29] See Rogers, 'Context and Institutional Structure', *supra* n. 12, 1.

[30] *HEP* v. *Slovenia*, *supra* n. 19, para. 14.

[31] See Rogers, 'Context and Institutional Structure', *supra* n. 12, 41–57; Paulsson, 'Standards of Conduct', *supra* n. 13, 215 ('[a]rbitrators are named to resolve disputes between parties, not to police the conduct of their representatives, and therefore do not rule on complaints of violations of codes of conduct').

requires an application of substantive state law regarding the legal profession'.[32]

Yet, treaty-based arbitral tribunals are not solely consent-based dispute settlement mechanisms that are limited to the explicit conferral of authority by party consent. They also constitute treaty-authorised bodies with a judicial function on the transnational level that decide and settle disputes based on the rule of law and render final and binding decisions and awards. Such arbitrators' function goes beyond that of a private contractor offering services. Instead, arbitrators in treaty-based arbitrations hold a public office in view of the host State's consent by sovereign act[33] which, like the procedure for appointment of arbitrators, is contained in an international treaty, not in a private law instrument.

Treaty-based arbitration is thus more comparable to a form of international administrative review than it is to purely commercial arbitration, in which the parties themselves have full sovereignty over the proceeding[34] and in which tribunals cannot as readily presume powers to develop and enforce regulations in relation to counsel conduct beyond or independent of the competent national bodies. Unlike in commercial arbitral tribunals, treaty-based tribunals are not constituted by commercial instruments, serving to settle a dispute between two contracting partners, but exercise, in determining the legality of host State conduct under international law, similarly to permanent international courts, a genuinely judicial function in international dispute settlement.[35]

---

[32] *Munich Re America, Inc.* v. *Ace Property & Casualty Co.*, 500 F.Supp. 2d 272, 275 (SDNY 2007) (the Claimant argued that the arbitrators could decide on the question of whether counsel acting for the Claimant should be disqualified based on an alleged conflict of interest arising out of its previous representation of the Respondent). Similarly, *Simply Fit of North America* v. *Poyner et al.*, 579 F.Supp. 2d 371, 383 (EDNY 2008).

[33] See G. Van Harten, 'The Public–Private Distinction in the International Arbitration of Individual Claims against the State', *ICLQ*, 56 (2007), 371, 378–80.

[34] See literature cited, *supra* n. 15.

[35] See J. Paulsson, 'International Arbitration Is Not Arbitration', *Stockholm International Arbitration Review*, 2 (2008), 1; S. D. Franck, 'International Arbitrators: Civil Servants? Sub Rosa Advocates? Men of Affairs?. The Role of International Arbitrators', *ILSA Journal of International & Comparative Law*, 12 (2006), 499–521, 503–4. On the development of arbitration under public international law towards a judicial mechanism of solving disputes and as a frontrunner of the establishment of permanent international courts, see C. H. Brower, II, 'The Functions and Limits of Arbitration and Judicial Settlement under Private and Public International Law', *Duke Journal of Comparative & International Law*, 18 (2008), 259–309, 265–91.

Against this background, it is appropriate for treaty-based arbitral tribunals to resort to inherent or implied powers for the development and enforcement of rules governing the conduct of counsel before them, parallel to the powers of other international courts and tribunals.[36] The recognition of such powers is evidenced by the ethical rules the various international criminal courts and tribunals have adopted, in the form of binding codes of conduct, for defence counsel and prosecutors.[37] These codes are largely based on broad authorisations conferred on the respective court or tribunal to adopt 'Rules of Procedure and Evidence', without explicitly mentioning the regulation of conduct of counsel appearing before them.[38] Comparable to domestic rules, they regulate various issues of professional responsibility and ethics, including rules on advertising by counsel, on counsel–client relationships, on conflicts of interest, on fees and on conduct *vis-à-vis* the court or tribunal. In addition, these codes authorise the imposition of sanctions for counsel misconduct, such as fines, the temporary suspension of the right to appear before the court or tribunal, or even a permanent ban on practising before the institution.

Similarly, Art. 35(1) of the Rules of Procedure of the European Court of Justice (ECJ), which are established by the Court with approval

---

[36] See, generally, C. Brown, 'The Inherent Powers of International Courts and Tribunals', *BYBIL*, 76 (2005), 195; F. Weiss, 'Inherent Powers of National and International Courts. The Practice of the Iran–US Claims Tribunal', in C. Binder, U. Kriebaum, A. Reinisch and S. Wittich (eds.), *International Investment Law for the 21st Century – Essays in Honour of Christoph Schreuer* (Oxford University Press, 2009), 185.

[37] International Criminal Court (ICC), Code of Professional Conduct for Counsel; International Criminal Tribunal for the Former Yugoslavia (ICTY), Code of Professional Conduct for Defence Counsel Appearing before the International Tribunal; International Criminal Tribunal for Rwanda (ICTR), Code of Professional Conduct for Defence Counsel; Special Court for Sierra Leone (SCSL), Code of Professional Conduct for Counsel with the Right of Audience before the Special Court for Sierra Leone.

[38] See, e.g., Art. 14 of the ICTR Statute in connection with Rules 44 and 46 of the Rules of Evidence and Procedure, forming the basis of the Code of Professional Conduct, *supra* n. 37. The codes of conduct of the ICTY and the SCSL have similarly worded bases in the respective statutes authorising the Tribunal, resp. Court, to adopt and modify its Rules of Procedure and Evidence. The ICC Statute, by contrast, confers the power to adopt Rules of Procedure and Evidence on the Assembly of States Parties; see Art. 51(1) of the Rome Statute of the ICC. Accordingly, the ICC's Code of Professional Conduct, *supra* n. 37, was adopted by that organ, not the Court itself.

of the Council[39] lays down the competence of the Court to develop and enforce rules concerning counsel conduct before it. It provides:

> If the Court considers that the conduct of ... [a] lawyer towards the Court ... is incompatible with the dignity of the Court or with the requirements of the proper administration of justice, or that such ... lawyer is using his rights for purposes other than those for which they were granted, it shall inform the person concerned. If the Court informs the competent authorities to whom the person concerned is answerable, a copy of the letter sent to those authorities shall be forwarded to the person concerned.
>
> On the same grounds, the Court may at any time, having heard the person concerned and the Advocate General, exclude the person concerned from the proceedings by order. That order shall have immediate effect.[40]

Likewise, the ICJ has issued, based on the broad authorisation in its Statute to 'frame rules for carrying out its functions', including 'rules of procedure',[41] some directions for the conduct of counsel in its Practice Directions.[42] In addition, it has assumed the power to reprimand parties and counsel in view of their litigation behaviour. Without imposing any formal sanctions, the Court, for example, rebuked counsel for Albania in the *Corfu Channel* case for unduly delaying the proceedings.[43] Such power concerns the organisation and internal administration of the Court and consequently, 'permits the conclusion that what a State may, or may not, do *vis-à-vis* the International Court in a pending case, and the powers of the Court in relation to that State, neither of which concerns the rights of the parties, is a matter of procedure'.[44]

---

[39] Art. 253(6) TFEU.

[40] http://curia.europa.eu/jcms/upload/docs/application/pdf/2008–09/txt5_2008–09–25_17–33–27_904.pdf.

[41] Art. 30(1) ICJ Statute, 1 *United Nations Treaty Series* 993.

[42] See *supra* n. 9. See also H. Thirlway, 'Article 30', in A. Zimmerman, C. Tomuschat and K. Oellers-Frahm (eds.), *The Statute of the International Court of Justice – A Commentary* (Oxford University Press, 2006), 481, 484–5, para. 11 (stating that Art. 30 of the Court's Statute constitutes the basis for the Practice Directions).

[43] S. Rosenne, *The Law and Practice of the International Court*, 2nd edn., (The Hague: Martinus Nijhoff, 1985), 542 (referencing *Corfu Channel*, Pleadings, vol. III, 187–8). See also *Application of the Convention on the Prevention and Punishment of the Crime of Genocide (Bosnia-Herzegovina v. Serbia and Montenegro)*, Provisional Measures, 1993 ICJ Rep. 325, 336–7, para. 21 (Order of 13 September 1993) ('the submission by the Applicant of a series of documents, up to the eve of, and even during, the oral proceedings ... is difficult to reconcile with an orderly progress of the procedure before the Court, and with respect for the principle of equality of the Parties').

[44] Rosenne, *The Law and Practice*, *supra* n. 43, 542.

Furthermore, the power to regulate and sanction counsel conduct exists not only with respect to international courts and tribunals, but also on the domestic level. Thus, the Common law under the concept of contempt of court, and Civil law systems as well, empower courts to conduct and regulate proceedings before them. Occasionally, domestic courts even analogise the role of arbitrators to the role of judges in order to delineate an arbitrator's powers in conducting arbitral proceedings.[45] Consequently, the inherent power of international courts and tribunals to act to preserve the integrity of proceedings, and to ensure the effectiveness of their judicial function, is a general principle of law in the sense of Art. 38(1)(c) ICJ Statute,[46] independent of whether or not such powers are conferred explicitly upon a court or tribunal.[47]

The widespread acceptance of the authority of courts and tribunals to regulate the proceedings before them and to conduct them in an efficient manner further suggests that provisions in the constitutive documents of international courts and tribunals that can reasonably be understood as conferring such powers should be interpreted and applied accordingly. For instance, Art. 44 of the ICSID Convention, giving tribunals the power to decide 'any question of procedure ... which is not covered by [the ICSID Convention] or the Arbitration Rules or any rules agreed by the Parties', should be understood as including the authority to regulate the proceedings before them and to impose sanctions for counsel misconduct, just as such authority is accepted in other international courts and tribunals.[48]

In consequence, it is on this basis that the ICSID Tribunal in *HEP* v. *Slovenia* recognised its 'obligation as guardian of the legitimacy of the arbitral process ... to make every effort to ensure that the Award

---

[45] See, e.g., *Malik* v. *Ruttenberg*, 942 A.2d 136, 139–141 (Sup. Court New Jersey, App. Div. 2008) (analogising arbitrators to judges as regards the extent of their 'quasi-judicial' acts for purposes of determining the scope of civil immunity granted to arbitrators for such acts).

[46] See *supra* n. 41.

[47] Cf. *AM & S Europe* v. *Commission*, Case 155/79, [1982] ECR 1575 (rule of client confidentiality and the privilege to refuse testimony as to client communication is included as a general principle of Community law common to all major legal systems in the Community legal order). On general principles of law in general, see B. Cheng, *General Principles of Law as Applied by the International Court and Tribunals* (Cambridge University Press, 1953).

[48] See also Rule 19 of the Rules of Procedure for Arbitration Proceedings: 'The Tribunal shall make the orders required for the conduct of the proceeding'. On inherent powers of ICSID tribunals, see also C. Schreuer, L. Malintoppi, A. Reinisch and A. Sinclair, *The ICSID Convention – A Commentary*, 2nd edn. (Cambridge University Press, 2009), 688.

is soundly based and not affected by procedural imperfection'[49] and consequently assumed the power to exclude counsel for the Respondent from the further proceedings. It stated:

> The Tribunal disagrees with the contention of Respondent that it has no inherent powers in this regard. It considers that as a judicial formation governed by public international law, the Tribunal has an inherent power to take measures to preserve the integrity of its proceedings. In part, that inherent power finds a textual foothold in Article 44 of the [ICSID] Convention, which authorizes the Tribunal to decide 'any question of procedure' not expressly dealt with in the Convention, the ICSID Arbitration Rules or 'any rules agreed by the Parties'. More broadly, there is an 'inherent power of an international court to deal with any issues necessary for the conduct of matters falling within its jurisdiction'; that power 'exists independently of any statutory reference'.[50]

In sum, the decision in *HEP* v. *Slovenia* puts into practice what Detlev Vagts stated over a decade ago: 'An argument could be made that an international tribunal has inherent power to discipline lawyers who practice before it, that it is sanctioned by general principles of law recognized by civilized nations.'[51] It shows that treaty-based arbitral tribunals have the power to develop and to enforce rules concerning counsel conduct in order to ensure the functioning, the fairness and the legitimacy of the arbitral proceedings before them.

The means available to international tribunals to enforce standards of conduct

Having established that international courts and tribunals have the inherent power to regulate counsel conduct for purposes of ensuring the integrity of the proceedings before them, the means by which arbitral tribunals can do so must be addressed. While the standing international criminal courts and tribunals have adopted ethical codes with sanctions ranging from admonition by a disciplinary panel, to public reprimands

---

[49] *HEP* v. *Slovenia*, *supra* n. 19, para. 15.

[50] *Ibid.*, para. 33 (quoting *Prosecutor* v. *Beqa Beqaj*, Case No. IT-03–66-T-R77, Judgment on Contempt Allegations (27 May 2005), paras. 9 and 10, and *Prosecutor* v. *Duško Tadić*, Case No. IT-94-I-A-R77, Judgment on Allegations of Contempt against Prior Counsel (31 January 2000), para. 13).

[51] Vagts, 'The International Legal Profession', *supra* n. 1, 253 (citing C. W. Wolfram, 'Lawyer Turf and Lawyer Regulation – The Role of the Inherent Powers-Doctrine', *University of Arkansas at Little Rock Law Journal*, 12 (1989), 1–23).

and the imposition of a fine, to the suspension or even a permanent ban on practising before the respective court or tribunal,[52] one-off arbitral tribunals necessarily are more limited in the types of sanctions they can impose. This is particularly so because they constitute dispute settlement bodies established on a case-by-case basis. For this reason, sanctions amounting to a disbarment of counsel from all treaty-based arbitrations or all ICSID arbitrations would be beyond the powers of an individual arbitral tribunal.

Yet, the arsenal of sanctions available to arbitral tribunals is sufficiently well stocked to develop rules of professional conduct and enforce them effectively. While any sanction necessarily depends on the misconduct in question and must be proportionate to it, sanctions can range from reprimanding counsel in the award and imposing costs on the party whose counsel breached standards of professional conduct, to taking into account certain misconduct in weighing evidence presented by a party and even excluding counsel from further proceedings.[53]

Reprimanding counsel in a decision by the arbitral tribunal is a measure that aims at bringing counsel's reputation into play and thereby achieving the latter's adherence to rules of professional conduct. Thus, the Tribunal in *Pope & Talbot* v. *Canada* termed one counsel's behaviour, which was in breach of a confidentiality order of the Tribunal, as 'highly reprehensible'[54] and 'either an intentional violation of the Tribunal's Procedural Order No. 1 or a reckless disregard of that Order'.[55] The Tribunal considered this behaviour as sufficiently grave for its Order to be made public.[56] Such sanctions will be effective in direct proportion to the personal sense of duty of counsel, accompanied by commensurate sensitivity to the disapproval of one's peers.

Arguably more effective is the employment of cost-shifting strategies to sanction counsel misconduct. It involves the imposition of costs

---

[52] See, e.g., Art. 47(c) of the ICTY's Code of Professional Conduct, *supra* n. 37.

[53] See also Vagts, 'The International Legal Profession', *supra* n. 1, 255 (observing that '[i]t appears that, while arbitrators have no authority to suspend or disbar attorneys, they could disqualify attorneys from appearing before them and could impose sanctions for attorney misbehavior when it came to assessing the costs of the arbitration').

[54] *Pope & Talbot* v. *Canada*, UNCITRAL/NAFTA, Decision on Confidentiality of 27 September 2000, para. 6.

[55] *Ibid.*, para. 8. See also the ICJ's use of reprimands of counsel and party conduct, *supra* n. 43, in the Order of 13 September 1993.

[56] *Pope & Talbot* v. *Canada*, *supra* n. 54, para. 13 (although the Tribunal did not order that the decision be made public it stated that it 'moreover assumes that [the lawyer] will make the present Decision public, as he has all of the Tribunal's previous Awards, Decisions and Orders').

against the party whose counsel breaches standards of professional conduct, even though that party would, under normal circumstances, not be responsible for such costs.[57]

In fact, arbitral tribunals in various cases have already availed themselves of this possibility in order to sanction misconduct, not just by a party, but also its counsel. Thus, in *Generation Ukraine, Inc.* v. *Ukraine*, an ICSID Tribunal shifted the total costs of the proceeding to the investor and further ordered the latter to contribute US$ 100,000 towards the Respondent's legal expenses for reasons related to the way the case was presented. It stated:

> [T]he Claimant's written presentation of its case has also been convoluted, repetitive, and legally incoherent. It has obliged the Respondent and the Tribunal to examine a myriad of factual issues which have ultimately been revealed as irrelevant to any conceivable legal theory of jurisdiction, liability or recovery. Its characterisation of evidence has been unacceptably slanted, and has required the Respondent and the Tribunal to verify every allegation with suspicion ... The Claimant's position has also been notably inconsistent ... Moreover, the Claimant's presentation of its damages claim has reposed on the flimsiest foundation ... The Claimant's presentation has lacked the intellectual rigour and discipline one would expect of a party seeking to establish a cause of action before an international tribunal ... Even at the stage of final oral submissions in March 2003, counsel for the Claimant relied on two ICSID awards without mentioning that they had been partially annulled. The Tribunal assumes in counsel's favour that he was unaware of the annulments; that is bad enough, and does no credit to the Claimant.[58]

Likewise, in *Pope & Talbot* v. *Canada*, the investor was ordered to pay US $ 10,000 to the Respondent government because the investor's counsel had breached the obligation under a prior order of the Tribunal not to publish certain material relating to the dispute.[59] This cost-shifting

---

[57] See, generally, on the distribution of costs in investment arbitration, S. Schill, 'Arbitration Risk and Effective Compliance – Cost-Shifting in Investment Treaty Arbitration', *Journal of World Investment & Trade Law*, 7 (2006), 653.

[58] *Generation Ukraine, Inc.* v. *Ukraine*, ICSID Case No. ARB/00/9, Award of 16 September 2003, paras. 24.2–24.7. Similarly, in *Link Trading Joint Stock Company* v. *Department for Customs Control of the Republic of Moldova*, UNCITRAL, Final Award of 18 April 2002, paras. 93 *et seq.*, the cost decision requiring the Claimant to bear the costs of the proceedings and US$ 22,000 for the Respondent's legal expenses appears to have been motivated in part by the Claimant's arbitration behaviour. Thus, the Tribunal observed that additional costs resulted from filing an 'unsolicited further submission of Claimant ... which required a further responsive pleading from Respondent' (*Ibid.*, para. 96).

[59] *Pope & Talbot* v. *Canada*, UNCITRAL/NAFTA, Decision on Confidentiality of 27 September 2000.

approach was essentially intended to constitute a fine for counsel, as the Tribunal 'expresse[d] the wish that [the Claimant's counsel] will recognize that it is his conduct which resulted in this direction being made against the Investor and, consequently, that he will voluntarily personally assume those costs'.[60] Cost-shifting for bad faith arbitration or procedural misconduct is therefore a way not only to discourage inefficient litigation behaviour, but also to regulate the conduct of counsel and sanction breaches of professional ethics. In this sense, cost-shifting serves the 'integrity of the judicial process'.[61]

Where counsel misconduct concerns the presentation of evidence to the Tribunal, arbitrators could react by taking into account the misconduct in evaluating evidence presented, or even by excluding such evidence altogether. If, for example, the parties to an arbitration have agreed that witness preparation by counsel is impermissible, the arbitrators would be entitled to take into account the fact that a witness actually was prepared in evaluating the credibility of that witness or, depending on the gravity of the misconduct, could even exclude the witness statement altogether.[62]

In the *ELSI* case before a Chamber of the ICJ, for example, a typewritten transcript of handwritten minutes of a company board meetings was presented by the United States which, however, omitted certain passages without noting that there were such omissions. Italy, in consequence, suggested that this 'doctored document' should be taken as an admission against interest'.[63] The Chamber's response

---

[60] *Ibid.*, para. 12.

[61] F. K. Zemans, 'Fee Shifting and the Implementation of Public Policy', *Law and Contemporary Problems*, 47 (1984), 187–210, 190 *et seq.* (with examples from US jurisprudence). See also *ReliaStar Life Ins. Co. of NY* v. *EMC National Life Co.*, 564 F.3d 81 (2d Cir. 2009); *Todd Shipyards Corp.* v. *Cunard Line Ltd*, 943 F.2d 1056 (9th Cir. 1991).

[62] Cf. Art. 9(5) IBA Rules on the Taking of Evidence in International Commercial Arbitration, adopted by a resolution of the IBA Council on 1 June 1999 ('[i]f a Party fails without satisfactory explanation to make available any other relevant evidence, including testimony, sought by one Party to which the Party to whom the request was addressed has not objected in due time or fails to make available any evidence, including testimony, ordered by the Arbitral Tribunal to be produced, the Arbitral Tribunal may infer that such evidence would be adverse to the interests of that Party').

[63] See K. Highet, 'Evidence, the Chamber and the ELSI Case', in R. Lillich (ed.), *Fact-Finding before International Tribunals* (Ardsley-on-Hudson, NY: Transnational Publishers, 1992), 33, 65–7. Similarly, in the same case an issue arose regarding the allegedly intentional mistranslation of documents from Italian into English; see Highet, *ibid.*, 67–8.

was simply to rely only on the original, complete handwritten minutes, duly pointing out the passage that had been omitted in the transcript.[64] While the conduct at issue was not directly considered counsel misconduct, but merely as originating from the party he represented, the case at least suggests that one possible sanction for counsel misconduct in relation to the presentation of evidence can be to take such misconduct into account when evaluating the evidence, or even to strike certain evidence from the record.

Finally, exclusion of counsel from further proceedings is a sanction available to arbitrators. In view of the principle that every party has a right to be represented by counsel of its choice, however, such a sanction requires that the counsel's continued presence interfere with the sound and fair administration of justice. This would be the case if counsel displays behaviour that is seriously disruptive of the proceedings, such as preventing opposing counsel from making arguments, or verbally or physically attacking participants in the arbitration. It may also, however, be an appropriate sanction in case the presence of counsel puts the legitimacy of the arbitration into issue, as in *HEP* v. *Slovenia*.[65]

It must be noted, however, that the rationale for that decision was not solely the fact that counsel for one party was a barrister in the same chambers in which the Tribunal's President was a door tenant. Beyond that, the Respondent contributed to the perception of unfairness by not immediately disclosing, contrary to the IBA Guidelines on Conflicts of Interest in International Arbitration,[66] the fact that it had engaged counsel who was in the said relationship with the Tribunal's President and, in addition, had refused to divulge certain information sought by the Claimant about such engagement.[67] Accordingly, the Tribunal considered that the parties were under a continuous obligation to ensure the legitimacy of the arbitral proceedings and could not, by engaging counsel who was in a relationship with any of the arbitrators which, in turn, could give rise to concerns about the arbitrator's impartiality and independence, compromise the arbitral proceedings, in particular considering

---

[64] See *Elettronica Sicula SpA (ELSI) (United States of America v. Italy)*, Judgment of 20 July 1989, 1989 ICJ Rep. 15, para. 26.

[65] *HEP* v. *Slovenia, supra* n. 19.

[66] On the disclosure requirements under the IBA Guidelines, see *supra* n. 20.

[67] See *HEP* v. *Slovenia*, para. 26. The Respondent, in fact, stated that it had considered disclosing the engagement of the counsel in question at the time of his engagement, but concluded that the relationship with the Tribunal's President did not raise any question of conflicts and was irrelevant. See *ibid.*, para. 11.

that the Claimant had indicated that it would not have agreed to the appointment of the President under such circumstances.[68] Such behaviour, the Tribunal reasoned, was contrary to the principle of the immutability of a properly constituted Tribunal.[69] The Claimant's perception of possible bias, coupled with the Respondent's refusal to answer certain of the Claimant's questions, was what endangered the legitimacy of the entire arbitration and thus the sound administration of justice in an international legal proceeding.

At the same time, the Tribunal also made sure that the standard on which it based its decision was not one that would necessarily affect the regulation of ethical behaviour of counsel in any future arbitration. The Tribunal pointedly recorded that its decision was based on the circumstances of the case:

> The Tribunal does not believe there is a hard-and-fast rule to the effect that barristers from the same Chambers are always precluded from being involved as, respectively, counsel and arbitrator in the same case. Equally, however, there is no absolute rule to opposite effect. The justifiability of an apprehension of partiality depends on all relevant circumstances. Here, those circumstances include, first, the fact that the London Chambers system is wholly foreign to the Claimant; second, the Respondent's conscious decision *not* to inform the Claimant or the Tribunal of Mr. Mildon's involvement in the case, following his engagement in February of this year; third, the tardiness of the Respondent's announcement of Mr. Mildon's involvement and, finally, the Respondent's subsequent insistent refusal to disclose the scope of Mr. Mildon's involvement, a matter of days before the commencement of the hearing on the merits. The last three matters were errors of judgment on the Respondent's part and have created an atmosphere of apprehension and mistrust which it is important to dispel.[70]

In sum, arbitral tribunals dispose of sufficient means for sanctioning counsel misconduct and violations of ethical standards in order to ensure the legitimacy of the arbitral proceedings and the sound administration

---

[68] See *ibid.*, para. 26 ('although the Respondent in this case was free to select its legal team as it saw fit prior to the constitution of the Tribunal, it was not entitled subsequently amend [*sic*] the composition of its legal team in such a fashion as to imperil the Tribunal's status or legitimacy').

[69] *Ibid.*, paras. 25–30.

[70] *Ibid.*, para. 31. In view of the circumstances of the case, the Tribunal also distinguished its decision from an earlier decision of a French Court which did not consider an association between counsel and arbitrators, similar to that in the *HEP* case, as affecting the legitimacy of the proceedings; see *ibid.*, para. 35.

of justice. Accepting the existence of such authority already goes far towards filling the apparent void of ethical regulation and enforcement mechanisms in international arbitrations. At the same time, exercising such competence must be done cautiously and considering the effect the tribunal's action may have on the further proceedings.[71] This will require above all that orders sanctioning counsel misconduct are fully and appropriately reasoned, that the sanctioned counsel is given an opportunity to be heard,[72] and that the sanction imposed is proportionate to the conduct it addresses.

Bases of and limitations to the development of ethical rules by arbitral tribunals

Having set out the power of treaty-based arbitral tribunals to develop and enforce rules for counsel conduct and the means to enforce them, the question remains as to the substantive content of such rules. They, of course, cannot be discussed in detail in the present chapter, but some points appear essential in framing how arbitral tribunals should develop them given that arbitral tribunals increasingly may be prompted by the parties to decide on a range of different issues of professional conduct, such as *ex parte* communications between parties and arbitrators or the permissibility of witness preparation.

First, the development of substantive standards of counsel conduct must rely on a functional approach, as argued convincingly by Catherine Rogers.[73] Thus rules of professional conduct should not rely on abstract ethical or moral considerations, but instead should be tied to the functions counsel exercise in treaty-based arbitrations and to the expectations to which they give rise. These expectations may stem not only from the party retaining counsel and from the opposing party and its counsel.

---

[71] Cf. also Vagts, 'The International Legal Profession', *supra* n. 1, 253 ('[e]xercising that power might, however, be diversionary and counterproductive').

[72] An opportunity to be heard, however, will not be necessary if counsel himself is not the subject of a sanction. Thus, in *HEP* v. *Slovenia*, the counsel excluded from participating further in the proceedings was not banned because of personal misconduct, but because his engagement by the Respondents' solicitors, coupled with those solicitors' failure to disclose this information, was the reason for the ban. Accordingly, an opportunity to hear counsel who was subsequently barred was not necessary; see *HEP* v. *Slovenia*, *supra* n. 19, para. 11.

[73] See Rogers, 'Fit and Function', *supra* n. 7, 341; Rogers, 'Context and Institutional Structure', *supra* n. 12, 1; cf. also Rogers, 'Regulating International Arbitrators', *supra* n. 8, 53.

Particularly in treaty-based arbitration, there also may be legitimate expectations in this regard of unrelated third parties, including other States, other investors and what is generally termed 'civil society' as these groups can be affected, albeit indirectly, by the decision-making of arbitral tribunals.[74] Defining the role of counsel in treaty-based arbitrations must thus be the first analytical step. Accordingly, answers must be provided not only as they relate to the party that engaged counsel, and to the opposing party and its counsel, but also as they affect the broader system of international justice.[75]

Second, with this focus on functionality in mind, it appears that a viable avenue for developing standards for counsel conduct lies in examining whether general principles exist in this context. This is the approach the ECJ has adopted in determining whether client confidentiality and the privilege to refuse testimony regarding client communications is a general principle of Community law common to all major legal systems in the Community legal order.[76] Similarly, a comparative approach could form a basis on which to develop rules of counsel conduct during arbitral proceedings. One needs to keep in mind, however, that the function of counsel in different domestic legal orders may be quite different and that their ethical rules are tailored to specific understandings and structures of the dispute settlement process and the respective roles allocated to advocates and decision-makers.[77] Similarly, standards of professional conduct may differ depending on the arbitral rules applied.[78]

Third, arbitral tribunals should aim to develop rules of professional conduct with the cooperation of the parties to the proceedings. This can be done appropriately during the tribunal's first session, in which the Terms of Reference or Terms of Appointment, as well as questions of procedure, are discussed.[79] Thus, addressing questions of professional

---

[74] See *supra* n. 16.

[75] Cf. Vagts, 'Professional Responsibility', *supra* n. 1, 685–7; see further Rogers, 'Regulating International Arbitrators', *supra* n. 8, 97–105.

[76] See *AM & S Europe* v. *Commission*, Case 155/79, [1982] ECR 1575. Likewise, Vagts, 'The International Legal Profession', *supra* n. 1, 253.

[77] See Rogers, 'Regulating International Arbitrators', *supra* n. 8, 97–105.

[78] *Ibid.*, 107, 110–12.

[79] This further helps to improve the effectiveness of arbitration and reduce future conflicts about questions of procedure. See also A. Meier, 'Pre-hearing Conferences as a Means of Improving the Effectiveness of Arbitration', *German Arbitration Journal/Zeitschrift für Schiedsverfahren*, 7 (2009), 152, 156 ('Pre-hearing conferences contribute to the effectiveness of an arbitration. They require little time and effort while their benefits can be significant. Pre-hearing conferences can considerably promote effective communication,

conduct could be made into a default point to be discussed and agreed upon by the parties. Notwithstanding, default rules will continue to be necessary in case no agreement can be reached. Moreover, some rules of professional conduct may not even be overcome by party agreement as they affect expectations of third parties regarding the legitimacy of treaty-based arbitration.

Fourth, any rules arbitral tribunals develop and any sanction they impose for violations of such rules should be sensitive to the cultural diversity that may exist with respect to the domestic rules of professional ethics applicable to different counsel in an arbitration. Likewise, in tailoring sanctions for counsel misconduct, tribunals must take into account a party's right to be represented by counsel in the proceedings and whether the conduct at issue was a deliberate violation of procedural and ethical rules or whether such violation was merely negligent. Accordingly, in *HEP* v. *Slovenia* the Tribunal decided to make procedural adjustments, after excluding counsel for one of the parties from participating in further proceedings, by deferring until a later date the hearing of specific issues the excluded counsel had been engaged to handle.[80] Such deferral, by contrast, would not seem necessary in case of deliberate violations aimed at interrupting the effective course of arbitral proceedings.

Finally, arbitral tribunals must be aware of the limitations that necessarily restrict their ability autonomously to develop detailed rules of professional conduct. After all, they only constitute dispute settlement bodies that are established on a case-by-case basis with a mandate limited to deciding a specific dispute. Similarly, their decision only has binding effect on the parties to the dispute without binding precedential value for future arbitrations.[81] Tribunals therefore should be careful in developing standards of professional conduct so as to do no more than ensure trust in the legitimacy and fairness of the particular arbitral proceeding. Overtaxing a tribunal's inherent power to regulate the proceedings before it may have the contrary effect. The art for international tribunals will be to achieve the appropriate balance between tribunal regulation and party autonomy.

---

de-escalate the conflicts, facilitate agreements on procedural issues, and, thus, ultimately save costs and time.').

[80] See *HEP* v. *Slovenia, supra* n. 19, para. 34 (stating that the Tribunal 'appreciate[s] that the Respondent was under a misapprehension in this regard and will, by making appropriate procedural adjustments, ensure that the Respondent's ability to present its case will not be adversely affected by this ruling').

[81] See Schill, *The Multilateralization, supra* n. 16, 288–92.

The most appropriate institutions to develop precise, binding and uniform rules of counsel conduct in international arbitrations, however, are arbitral institutions themselves.[82] They are best positioned to structure codes regulating the professional conduct of counsel and prescribe what conduct is permissible or impermissible in international arbitration. The ICSID Administrative Council, for example, could thus rely on the powers granted to it in Art. 6(1)(c) of the ICSID Convention to 'adopt the rules of procedure for conciliation and arbitration proceedings' in order to develop rules of professional conduct. This even could involve sanctions such as excluding counsel from all ICSID proceedings for grave violations of professional conduct and the establishment of an ethics and disciplinary committee. Likewise, other arbitral institutions, for example the International Chamber of Commerce, the London Court of International Arbitration or the Permanent Court of Arbitration, as well as bodies such as the United Nations Commission on International Trade Law, could develop rules governing the conduct of counsel.

Until such initiatives materialise, however, arbitral tribunals not only have the competence, but also the obligation to step in where necessary to ensure the fairness of the administration of international justice and foster the legitimacy that parties and non-parties alike expect from, and must be accorded by, the transnational arbitral process. Perhaps the activities of arbitral tribunals in this regard will prompt arbitral institutions to become more active in developing institutional rules of professional conduct.

---

[82] See Rogers, 'Context and Institutional Structure', *supra* n. 12, 26–9.

25

International arbitrators as equity judges

JAN H. DALHUISEN

Introduction

Law, private law in particular, has a capacity – perhaps a natural inclination – to become rigid or even stultify. It may be asked why this is the case. In regulation, the law is what a State orders or decrees it to be and as such it is what it is. But if we step back from the idea that all law, including private law, issues from a sovereign and accepts instead other sources of law besides legislation (or treaty law) and implementing case-law, like fundamental principles (now often human rights-related but earlier often referred to as natural law having a strong moral or even religious connotation),[1] custom or industry practices,[2] general principles (which may be found among the more advanced legal systems or in reason or common sense) and party autonomy, this broader perspective would suggest that there is ample room for private law to reform itself.

One may recognise here the sources of law that for public international law are recognised in Art. 38(1) of the Statute of the International Court of Justice (ICJ). Like public international law, private law may move forward independently in a similar manner, at least at the international level. This is the modern idea of its transnationalisation and, in international commerce and finance, of the modern *lex mercatoria*,[3] which is then perceived as depending on these various sources of law and maintaining a hierarchy of rules emanating from them. It may even accept in this context ever-evolving pressing moral, social and economic values as

---

[1] See J. H. Dalhuisen, 'Legal Orders and Their Manifestation. The Operation of the International Commercial and Financial Legal Order and Its Lex Mercatoria', *Berkeley Journal of International Law*, 24 (2006), 129–91.

[2] See further J. H. Dalhuisen, 'Custom and its Revival in Transnational Private Law', *Duke Journal of Comparative & International Law*, 18 (2008), 339–70.

[3] See J. H. Dalhuisen, *Transnational and Comparative Commercial, Financial and Trade Law*, 4th edn. (Oxford: Hart Publishing, 2010).

legally normative. In business and finance, this includes in particular considerations of efficiency and the results of cost-benefit analysis, which considerations themselves are then also likely to transcend domestic notions and concepts. It is a development that is in full swing and highly significant, but that for the most part still eludes academic analysis.

The first question here is why law, *private* law in particular, nevertheless appears to respond to change with difficulty, now especially clear in the face of globalisation. This is indeed an issue often associated with the effects of legal positivism in private law, the dominance therefore of black-letter law, usually considered the product of some national legislator. This would suggest a static notion of law depending entirely on a State to move it forward. This is usually combined with the notion of law as technique, therefore as a system of rules to be mechanically applied as a matter of logic in deductive or analogical reasoning. Past experiences and insights then dominate and regulate present and future behaviour. In such a world, the freedom that comes from recognising other sources of law remains contested.

Legal formalism of this nature remains particularly strong in Civil law countries because of the nineteenth-century codification ethos in which domestic legislation monopolises the field even of private law. It is supported by systemic thinking which intellectualises the process of law formation and application. It assumes that an intellectual internally coherent national system represents reality and bears in it the answers to all legal questions. In this universe, private law cannot independently develop and starts to lag. Common law countries do not face the same historical constraints, but those of the English variety, at least in academia, are now often not far behind. Thus, private law is then perceived as a domestic system of pre-existing rules that is to be logically applied and, in this view, substantially derives its legitimacy from that state of affairs.

The international *lex mercatoria* here is not law, merely because it is not national. It follows that in modern times we not only see the narrowing forces of legislation and formal system thinking,[4] but also the limiting forces of *nationalism* which together may conspire especially to deprive commercial and financial law – that is, the law in professional dealings – from its flexibility and of a dynamic forward-moving force.

---

[4] See in England for the notion that practice is not law and, therefore, that international practice also is not international law, R. Goode, 'Rule, Practice, and Pragmatism in International Commercial Law', *ICLQ*, 54 (2005), 539–62, 549.

In Civil law countries, this restrictive effect is mitigated only by a strong dose of liberal interpretation of statutory texts, and in Common law countries of the English variety by narrow interpretation of statutes and by judicial pragmatism. However, in either legal system, the interpretative canons are still mostly of a domestic nature and therefore are still likely to be confining, which again is particularly noticeable and relevant in international commerce and finance.

Certainty is here often introduced as a prop for legal formalism and positivism of this nature. Too often it means, however, certainty of a low quality, dictated merely by past experiences at the national level. In any event, given the admitted need for liberal interpretation, certainty was never a realistic proposition, including in codification countries. The emphasis instead should be on transactional finality and otherwise on predictability, which is itself a dynamic concept. Quite apart from the nationalistic undertone, this approach raises the more fundamental question whether we live with an account of human behaviour that can scientifically be clarified and is in essence based on repetition. That is the neo-classical view in economics, often believed to have failed us, but we struggle with the same problem in the law. Or must we accept that the future is different and cannot be systematically captured, in short the Popper vision? It is clear that in a neo-classical atmosphere, private law can hardly develop independently and fulfil its role in a fast-moving environment, now for professional dealings also strongly globalised.

At least on the European continent, it had all been quite different before the nineteenth century. That was the time of the *ius commune*, the time therefore of the reception of Roman law, which was never promulgated but itself considered a higher form of custom, supplemented by natural law notions (in terms of directly applicable fundamental and general principle) and local laws. But even thereafter, the idea of an autonomous non-statist transnational law was never completely abandoned, nor fully forgotten, at least in commerce. Upon a proper analysis, we have always seen autonomous non-statist law formation even in a mandatory manner in the laws concerning bills of lading[5] and negotiable instruments, especially Eurobond and Euromarket practices, including

---

[5] See W. E. Haak, 'Internationalism above Freedom of Contract', in *Essays on International and Comparative Law in Honour of Judge Erades*, presented by the Board of the *Netherlands International Law Review* (Dordrecht and The Hague: Martinus Nijhoff and T.M.C. Asser Instituut, 1983), 69–78, 69.

clearing and settlement,[6] in international assignments, and in set-off and netting, which may all be considered connected to transnational custom supported by general principles wherever necessary, which may then even acquire a mandatory nature.

It is easy to discern here the infrastructure of the *international* market-place. In letters of credit (UCP) and trade terms (Incoterms),[7] we see further examples of transnational law, here merely directory (or default) rule. But, rightly or wrongly, as from the nineteenth century, the continued force of transnationalisation was increasingly considered out of the main stream and at best tolerated as an aberration. It is only the more recent rediscovery of the law merchant or transnational *lex mercatoria* that now works as a liberating force and provides the necessary framework for legal dynamism in our area.[8] Who are the actors in this process absent a legislator proper? Judges and arbitrators spring to mind, but no less the daily practitioners and participants in the process of the law's application. We see here law in action besides law in litigation, and there may well be important differences. What motivates or constrains these actors? This contribution will focus on the reaction of judges, arbitrators and also practitioners.

It may be observed in this connection that ever since Roman times in the praetorian law – or *ius honorarium* – an extra law formation facility beyond legislation and precedent proved to be a necessary institutional prerequisite for the adequate functioning of private law, precisely to prevent it from stultifying and to underpin private law's dynamic nature. Ordinary courts cannot easily take on this task, never mind how liberal they may become or have to be in their interpretation techniques. Also, legislators cannot adequately handle it – it would require a continuous process of updating which is beyond their purview, insights and interest.

In England this extra facility came about initially through the Lord Chancellor and later through separate courts of equity. Civil law missed this facility and suffered as a consequence in its evolution. Indeed, we may find here the most important differences between Civil and

---

[6] See P. Wood, *Law and Practice of International Finance* (London: Sweet & Maxwell, 1980), 184.

[7] The idea of the Uniform Customs and Practice for Documentary Credits (UCP) being transnational customary law is associated with the views of Frederic Eisemann (Austria), Director of the Legal Department of the International Chamber of Commerce (ICC) at the time, and was first proposed by him at a 1962 King's College London Colloquium. See F. Eisemann, *Le crédit documentaire dans le droit et dans la pratique* (Paris: Delmas, 1963), 4.

[8] See Dalhuisen, 'Legal Orders', *supra* n. 1.

Common law, as in the trust, conditional and temporary ownership rights, floating charges and tracing, the equitable assignment, much of the set-off and fiduciary duties. It may also be mentioned in this connection that the Swiss Civil Code in its Article 1 allows judges to act like legislators if the law is silent. This rule comes close to some similar facility, here institutionally given to the ordinary courts, but it has remained unique, misses the correcting facility and has not led to a generally more aggressive updating of private law in Switzerland.

The thesis of this chapter is that in international commerce and finance, this facility is now likely to come through international commercial arbitration, *institutionally* founded in the international public order itself or in what the French have come to call the 'international arbitral order'.[9]

Legal dynamism: liberal interpretation in Civil law and pragmatism in Common law – their limits

In the Civil law approach, through and after the codification, the system and its maintenance became all. Liberal interpretation was and is then needed to sustain the ideal of completeness. Judges move to the centre, much as in Common law that could only be known through them, even though in Civil law that was not the original idea. Rather, codification had been meant primarily to make the daily practice of the law easier and life better for all; it was not merely, or even mainly, a dispute resolution mechanism. But by the twentieth century, when codes became older and situations ever newer, attention shifted strongly toward the interpretation process and, therefore, to judges, in Civil law as well as in Common law. Hence also the greater role played by precedent in Civil law – but the ethos remained different and this activity was always confined by the system. In other words, the role of the judge is seen here, first and foremost, as perfecting the system, and not to step out of it or to find new ways. In this context, judges work primarily on the norm side, maintaining the logical completeness of the law as a system of rules. Even though there remained dissent, it became more muted.

---

[9] See notably *Ste PT Putrabali Adyamulia, Cour de Cassation Civile*, Judgment of 29 June 2007 www.courdecassation.fr/jurisprudence, and E. Gaillard, 'Aspects philosophiques du droit de l'arbitrage international', *RdC*, 329 (Leiden and Boston: Martinus Nijhoff, 2008), 49–216.

Thus, even where good faith notions now operate more freely in case-law, especially in contract behind which the other sources of private law may even revive, at least German academia tries to recapture it in system thinking.[10] The idea remains, therefore, palpable that the completion of the code and its system is all,[11] that it remains comprehensive and that it can or must in this way continue to cover all eventualities. The rest is legally irrelevant, never mind how intellectually prejudiced this system can be[12] and how much, in terms of relevant fact, might fall off its plate, as was the case earlier for pre-contractual disclosure and information duties, so that the whole idea of codification in this manner is increasingly questioned among its greatest scholars and practitioners.[13]

For Common law it was already noted that at the academic level, at least in England, there may be increasing closeness to codification thinking, in which connection it may also be noted that the Draft Common Frame of Reference (DCFR), which aims at codification of private law for all of the European Union (EU), including the United Kingdom, has received support in England especially in circles around the Law Commission. English courts remain pragmatic, however, and still move from case to case in the old Common law tradition, operate therefore first on the fact, not on the norm side, and interpret statutory law restrictively in order to leave as much room for law and equity as possible (unless clearly overruled). But even in this environment, other sources of law (besides case-law and statute) increasingly suffered, particularly custom

---

[10] Thus, German academics typically look for system everywhere, even in more open-textured provisions, and often talk in this connection of the inner system (*Innensystematik*) of the good faith notion (*Treu und Glauben*), referring in particular to the reliance notion, pre-contractual duties, normative interpretation, supplementation and correction techniques, the (continued) validity of the contract, the performance obligations and excuses of the parties and, in appropriate cases, to their re-negotiation duties, all originally developed on the basis of the good faith notion. See O. Palandt and H. Heinrichs, *Bürgerliches Gesetzbuch*, 66th edn. (2007), section 242, Nos. 2 and 13.

[11] See K. Larenz, *Methodenlehre der Rechtswissenschaft*, 6th edn. (Berlin: de Gruyter, 1991), 6, 437. There also remained academic currents in other directions, but they became more incidental and weaker – see, e.g., J. Koendgen, *Selbstbindung ohne Vertrag* (Tübingen: Mohr, 1981), and earlier J. Esser, *Vorverständnis und Methodenwahl* (Frankfurt/Main: Athenaeum, 1970).

[12] J. Vranken, *Exploring the Jurist's Frame of Mind* (Deventer: Kluwer Law International, 2006), 99 *et seq*. See also J. Tonnti, 'Law, Tradition and Interpretation', *International Journal for the Semiotics of Law*, 11 (1998), 25–38, 36.

[13] H. C. F. Schoordijk, 'Enkele opmerkingen over de bronnen van verbintenis en "European law in the making"', in H. C. F. Schoordijk, *Emeritaal Werk* (Nijmegen: Wolf Legal Publishers, 2006), 137.

and practices which soon were considered no more than implied contractual conditions[14] and in any event subject to the law of precedent, which deprived custom in particular of much of its dynamic force.

However, the Common law courts retained a number of tools that at least in contract may well exceed what the good faith notion contributes in flexibility in the Civil law.[15] This was achieved by the formulation of fiduciary duties in situations of dependency, of the notion of reliance, of implied conditions of reasonableness, or by cutting out excess through the remnants of the courts' original powers in equity. Above all, this was achieved through relationship thinking that clearly distinguishes between the type of parties, in private law foremost between consumer and professional dealings.

Nevertheless, domestic thinking, legal nationalism, mistrust of principle, a confining view of custom and a dislike of transnationalisation are particularly strong in England[16] – the latter much more so than in France, for instance, where one would have expected it sooner.[17] This is somewhat curious for a legal system like that of England, which finds its origin outside legislation and was as such never nationalistic *per se*,[18]

---

[14] On custom as an implied term in England generally, see 'Custom and Usage', in *Halsbury's Laws of England*, 4th edn., 56 vols. (1973), vol. 12(1), 601; but in commerce there may be more room for it, see *Product Brokers Co. Ltd* v. *Olympia Oil & Cake Co. Ltd* [1916] 1 AC 314, 324, cf. also *General Reinsurance Corp.* v. *Forsakringaktiebolaget Fennia Patria* [1983] QB 856.

[15] See Lord Bingham in *Interfoto Picture Library Ltd* v. *Stiletto Visual Pictures Ltd* [1989] 1QB 433, stating:

> In many civil law systems, and perhaps in most legal systems outside the common law world, the law of obligations recognizes and enforces an overriding principle that in making and carrying out contracts parties should act in good faith ... It is in essence a principle of fair and open dealing ... English law has, characteristically, committed itself to no such overriding principle but has developed piecemeal solutions in response to demonstrated problems of unfairness. Many examples could be given. Thus equity has intervened to strike down unconscionable bargains. Parliament has stepped in to strike down to regulate the imposition of exemption clauses and the form of certain hire-purchase agreements. The common law has also made its contribution by holding that certain contracts require the utmost good faith ... and in many other ways.

[16] In the United Kingdom, Lord Mustill used to be particularly critical of the *lex mercatoria* as a transnational legal system and wondered where this new law could come from. See L. J. Mustill, 'Contemporary Problems in International Commercial Arbitration. A Response', *International Business Lawyer*, 17 (1989), 161–4.

[17] Best summarised by E. Gaillard, 'Aspects philosophiques', *supra* n. 9.

[18] See also the comment to this effect by A. F. Lowenfeld, 'Lex Mercatoria. An Arbitrator's View', *Arbitration International*, 6 (1990), 133.

in a country whose legal environment and whose legal practitioners would benefit greatly from a more open and transnational perspective, especially in the commercial and financial sphere.

Legal dynamism: the Praetor and the praetorian law or *ius honorarium* in Rome and the equity judge in England

We often deem Civil law the successor of Roman law, but in Rome it had all been very different. In fact, there had been a special facility to constantly adapt and reform private law. We may look in this connection at the role of the Praetor, who by edict was meant and empowered to add to the available remedies. This became the *ius honorarium* that was crucial for the proper development of the *ius civile* (for Romans) and *ius gentium* (for foreigners), the latter having become the prevailing law in the Justinian compilation or *Corpus Iuris*, which, however, still allowed the Emperor in his praetorian role to interpret and add by rescript. Significantly, this force or facility did not continue to exist and develop on the continent of Europe after the Roman law reception, and the development of the *ius commune* was much hindered thereby, there not being a proper legislator either. The later Civil law also never developed a similar facility and was thus equally constrained in its development.

If we compare the praetorian law-creating facility to that of the Lord Chancellor in equity in England, it is clear that in both cases there developed an important vehicle to move the existing law forward. The Praetor had greater power, but as a jurist of repute and the bearer of high office (for one year only), he in practice became confined by the practices elaborated by his predecessors, by his training and by the views of his fellow jurists.

In Common law countries, we see the high point of this development in the eighteenth century, with the recognition of the trust and the concept of tracing, conditional and temporary ownership rights in movable assets, the equitable assignment, much of the set-off, and fiduciary duties. But eventually this equity law was deemed erratic and then gelled, primarily by being made subject to the rule of precedent, as custom also was at the same time.[19] However, equity is still important in

---

[19] In *Keppell* v. *Bailey* [1834] ER 1042, 1049, the Chancery Court famously held that 'incidents of a novel kind cannot be devised and attached to property at the fancy and caprice of any owner'; see also *Hill* v. *Tupper* [1863] 2 Hurlst. 7 C 121.

cases of abuse[20] and it was also able to complete the modern development of the law of assignment and of the floating charge,[21] even though notably in the United States it has been substantially superseded by legislation (namely, in Art. 9 of the Uniform Commercial Code, UCC). The current idea is mostly that rather than equity, legislation should lead the way in matters of reform of the Common law and it has largely taken over that role. Nevertheless, in business especially, the remaining original powers of the courts in equity must not be underestimated, if only because all of the law of trusts, companies, insolvency and taxation is equitable, even though now resting largely on a statutory basis.

Thus, the concept of equity judges and their powers may still be usefully explored. They were never clearly defined. It is easy to understand that at first, when the writs were limited, there was a need for relief in incidental cases of harshness or clear injustice. There was also a need for relief when juries were bribed or intimidated by powerful litigants. Hence the intervention of the Lord Chancellor – in the early days, always a high cleric – on the basis of reason, conscience or good faith. It mostly required some pressing *prima facie* case. Often the unconscionable use of Common law rights or abuse of power was the reason, especially in situations of dependency. In modern terminology, there was also concern with unintended effects of the legal rules and their strictness.[22] From early on, Roman and canon law sources were often cited in support of introducing greater objectivity. So was laudable custom and tradition. The situation was therefore *never* one of mere convenience or opinion about what was right.

Thus, equity was relevant, particularly in the area of fraud and breach of confidence, in more modern times equated with public order, in the development of the equity of redemption when forfeiture was threatened under a real estate mortgage, and later in the transformation of the old use into the modern trust. The development of specific performance and of the rescission remedies in contract law may also be mentioned. It should be noted in this connection that although equity would act *in personam* to give individual relief, there emerged nevertheless whole new legal structures that could also be proprietary or create rank and priority among creditors – namely, its coverage of assignment, temporary and conditional ownership rights, set-offs and liens.

---

[20] *Interfoto Picture* case, *supra* n. 15.
[21] See on the law of assignment, *Dearle* v. *Hall*, 3 Russ. 1 (1828) and *Rhodes* v. *Allied Dunbar Pension Services Ltd* [1987] 1 WLR 1703.
[22] See *Lord Dudley* v. *Lady Dudley*, (1705) Prec. Ch. 241, 244.

As has already been noted, since the nineteenth century the powers of the equity judges have been considered subject to the rule of precedent. This situation deprived equity of much of its dynamic character and suggests that the Common law's further development now chiefly depends on legislation. Beyond the already developed areas of equity law, it is not always clear what the true power of the equity judge still is and what distinguishes this power from that of the ordinary judicial function. It may indeed be asked how much law-formation power equity judges have retained beyond mere statutory, contractual or case-law interpretation in the areas in which they traditionally operated. It is clear, however, that important new vistas for original development still open on occasion. In England, that was the case early in the twentieth century through the development of the floating charge and, much later in the same century, the development of the *Mareva* injunction.[23] The substitution of reliance or estoppel notions for the consideration requirement in contract may also be mentioned. It is thus fair to say that the equity judge still assumes at times broad law-formation power and creates or develops new legal structures. In modern times in England, Lord Denning in particular proved an activist equity judge.[24]

It further is widely accepted that, especially in trust law but also in bankruptcy and company law administration, judges continue to exercise a somewhat different type of original power in equity. The key here is that they are not passive, only rendering a decision on disputed points of fact and law, while intervening to achieve or maintain order, even *ex parte*. This power is also clear in the way they administer injunctive relief or order (or refuse) specific performance. In this sense, they will exercise an auxiliary function in all litigation whilst ordering, for example, disclosure or testimony, preserve the status quo pending litigation or order other interim measures. In the rescission remedies in contract, which are equitable, they also retain great power as to the effect of any early termination of a contract because of mistake, misrepresentation, fraud and the like.

Legal dynamism: arbitrators as *amiables compositeurs* or acting *ex aequo et bono*

In more modern times, it may be asked to what extent arbitrators acting as *amiable compositeurs* may be compared to equity judges in a Common

---

[23] [1980] 1 All ER 213.
[24] Note his statement that '[e]quity is not beyond the age of childbearing', in *Eves* v. *Eves* [1975] 1 WLR 1338, 1341. Recent case-law may appear more cautious.

law sense. It is sometimes thought that this way of arbitrating refers implicitly to application of the modern *lex mercatoria*.[25] As it is clear that the powers of this type of arbitrator depend in the first place on party authorisation, it may be asked how much conferring powers parties have.

The concept of *amiables compositeurs* was never fully clear and arbitration clauses of this nature are relatively rare.[26] It was often said that the concept did not exist in England, it being an arbitration not based on the positive law, but it was always unclear how perceptive that was as settlement between parties was always allowed,[27] while in many trades dispute settlement by a member of a peer group did not require arbitration on the basis of law either. In any event, under the 1996 English Arbitration Act (section 46(1)(b)), there is nothing preventing parties from including such a clause in a contract under English law.

It is indeed clear that this kind of arbitration is not based on a formal concept of law. There remain, however, translation problems, and therefore questions about what is truly meant by the term. It could mean a reference to natural justice, often considered with suspicion in England, or to fairness, mostly seen as implicit in all judicial activity, or perhaps mainly to rationality, a strong recurrent theme in all (immanent) law formation and application, especially in professional dealings. To see here a fundamental *contradiction* between what is law and what is fair or makes sense would in any event appear somewhat perplexing.[28]

Even so, it is generally accepted that there are limits to the general inflow of notions of justice, social peace and efficiency into the law and its system of enforcement. In truth, this poses again the question of the true

---

[25] The opening statement is interesting here, see W. W. Park, 'Judicial Controls in the Arbitral Process', *Arbitration International*, 5 (1989), 230. Earlier, Berthold Goldman stated in this connection that *amiables compositeurs* must at least take account of the general principles of law and international commercial customs and that the clause could, therefore, be seen as introducing implicitly the *lex mercatoria* which, however, he admitted as being much more effective in arbitrations generally. See B. Goldman, 'La lex mercatoria dans les contracts et l'arbitrage international. Réalité et perspectives', *Journal du droit international*, 106 (1979), 475–505. See for a similar analysis, M. della Valle, *On Decisions ex aequo et bono in International Commercial Arbitration*, unpublished doctoral dissertation, University of Sao Paolo (2009), section 2.3.5.

[26] Stephen Bond reported in 1989 that fewer than 3 per cent of all arbitration clauses in the cases submitted to the ICC in 1988 included this concept. S. Bond, 'How to Draft an Arbitration Clause', *Journal of International Arbitration*, 6 (1989), 66, 73.

[27] Lord Steyn, 'Towards a New English Arbitration Act', *Arbitration International*, 7 (1991), 17–26, 23.

[28] A. W. Shilston, 'The Evolution of Modern Commercial Arbitration', *Journal of International Arbitration*, 4 (1987), 45–76, 54.

sources of private law, in international arbitrations especially at the transnational level. It impacts on all arbitration, but it is probably easier to deal within an *amiable composition*. At a minimum, the concept of *amiable composition* allows other sources beyond State law to operate freely. Hence also the close connection often seen with the modern *lex mercatoria* as the applicable law.

The concept of *amiable composition* and its confines has attracted more attention on the European continent. There are cases in France and Switzerland where the concept has been tested in some of its aspects.[29] This does not, however, completely resolve its status.[30] Literature also remains scarce.

In respect of *amiable composition*, there is broad agreement that this type of arbitration, although resulting in a binding award, is not strictly or necessarily based on law, or at least on a national law in the positivist tradition, which suggests, therefore, that this type of arbitration may proceed more directly on the basis of what arbitrators believe is reasonable or makes sense under the circumstances. As already mentioned, this also allows application of *lex mercatoria*, of principles of substantive transnational law therefore, and of other sources of private law, including of *sharia* law in appropriate cases – in other words, law that goes beyond a national legal system otherwise applicable if not also chosen by the parties. That gives *amiables compositeurs* a great deal of freedom, even when parties have chosen a national law to apply in matters at their free disposition (which law then becomes mere guidance), but even here *they are not free* and at a minimum must stay within the bounds of rationality and of what makes the most sense in the circumstances, and in respect of weaker parties also of what proves to be fair to them.

Amiables compositeurs must also respect domestic regulatory laws, which is no different from other arbitrators or judges,[31] although, as in all international cases, there must be sufficient contact with the case in the sense of Art. 9 of the EU Regulation of 2008 on the Law Applicable to

---

[29] See Court of Appeal Paris, judgment of 17 January 2008 (on file with the author).

[30] See also M. Rubino-Sammartano, 'Amiable Compositeur (Joint Mandate to Settle) and ex bono et aequo (Discretional Authority to Mitigate Strict Law). Apparent Synonyms Revisited', *Journal of International Arbitration*, 9 (1992), 1; E. Loquin, *L'amiable compositeur en droit comparé et international* (Paris: Librairies techniques, 1980), 13 *et seq.*; S. Saleh, *Commercial Arbitration in the Arab Middle East*, 2nd edn. (Oxford: Hart Publishing, 2006), 18.

[31] See, e.g., ICC Case No. 1677/1975, cited by W. L. Craig, W. W. Park and J. Paulsson, *International Chamber of Commerce Arbitration*, 3rd edn. (Oxford: Oceana, 2000), §5.07, 63, n. 54.

Contractual Obligations ('Rome I'), and in the United States of sections 402–403 of the *Restatement (Third) of the Foreign Relations Law of the United States*. The idea is, therefore, that like other arbitrators, *amiables compositeurs* can only ignore the positive law to the extent that it was at the free disposition of the parties, therefore, not mandatory. That is an important restriction, which Italian law expresses in section 822 of the Code of Civil Procedure. So all relevant public policy or public order requirements and other mandatory law, including in private law the law of property and the infrastructure of the law of contract, must be respected, at least in principle.

It should be repeated that, in Common law terms, equity judges have always had more original power. If transnationalisation or the *lex mercatoria*, which in commercial and financial matters are considered the same, is the proper province of *amiables compositeurs*, they might have similar powers even in areas of the mandatory law – for instance, to accept greater party autonomy in the creation of newer proprietary rights – always subject, however, to the protection of the international commercial and financial flows and issues of finality as a matter of overriding transnational public order.

In this connection, it should be considered that, for example in assignments, at least as between the parties to the assignment, *amiables compositeurs* may eliminate notification requirements or contractual assignment restrictions even if upheld under applicable domestic laws. This could go as far as affecting third parties, especially the debtors, or in a bankruptcy other interested parties, such as the creditors of the assignor who may still be considered the owner of a receivable if improperly assigned under applicable domestic law. This is so *if* indeed *amiables compositeurs* as equity judges could restate and develop the applicable objective property law at the transnational level. This may increasingly be so if they could cite in support evolving international custom and practices or general principles as other sources of law.

Legal dynamism: arbitrators in international commercial arbitrations

The question remains whether only *amiables compositeurs* or also ordinary international commercial arbitrators have similar powers to recognise, formulate and expand transnational law or the *lex mercatoria* in commerce and finance in this manner. It means first interpretating in a transnational context the laws that are at the free disposition of the parties, but subsequently also interpreting the applicable mandatory laws (a) of contract, notably those concerning the contractual infrastructure in terms of contractual validity, and (b) of movable property in a transnationalised manner or from a transnational perspective. If properly analysed, this may become an institutional issue, a question, therefore, of innate law-formation power, given especially the absence of a competent legislator at the transnational level. In fact, the question in this context is whether international arbitrators more generally have powers that transcend the more idiosyncratic and narrower *amiable composition* concept or concession and that are innate in or now derive from the international public order, or international comity, or the international commercial and financial legal order itself, or from the 'international arbitral order', as the French call it.

In this connection one may look more particularly at the evolution of the position of international commercial arbitrators in recent years. There are in fact a number of important recent progressions which may well go beyond what parties confer or could confer in their arbitration clause, therefore going beyond the confines of mere party autonomy. These progressions in modern international arbitration are then merely activated by the arbitration clause, but the impact derives from the international commercial and financial legal (or arbitral) order itself. We may think in particular of:

(a) The separability or severability of the arbitration clause, which finds its proper legal base in the transnational legal order or the transnational public order, as does the jurisdiction of arbitrators particularly in competition, securities and other public policy issues in terms of arbitrability;

(b) Procedural flexibility and discretion in procedural matters and in matters of admission of evidence and applicability of private international law;

(c) In matters of substantive law, direct acceptance of multiple sources of law and their hierarchy within the modern law merchant or *lex mercatoria*, unless parties have indicated otherwise especially by choosing a domestic law when, however, the meaning of such law still needs determination, particularly in view of any superior or mandatory rules emanating from the international commercial and financial legal order itself (e.g. established practices in movable property law, including the law of assignments, or in set-off);[32]

---

[32] See J. H. Dalhuisen, 'What Could the Selection by the Parties of English Law in a Civil Law Contract in Commerce and Finance Truly Mean?', in M. Andenas and D. Fairgrieve

(d) Consequential *limitation*, again as a matter of transnational public order, of the *lex arbitri* also in terms of any review by domestic courts, either when the awards are challenged in the country where they are rendered (of their seat) or in the context of their recognition and enforcement in other countries.

In this connection, Preamble 13 of Rome I makes it at least clear that parties may now opt for non-State law as the law applicable to their transaction. Absent such an election, the applicability of such law could remain in doubt. But international arbitration agreements and arbitrators are outside the scope of Rome I, and are not therefore subject to similar constraints and need not solely depend on the parties' choice of law, but may also rely in this connection on international public order notions directly.

This would also cover the autonomous applicability of the *lex mercatoria* in non-contractual matters, as in personal property or in contractual matters that are not at the free disposition of the parties, such as those concerning the contractual infrastructure and validity. Indeed, it may be posited that original powers are ceded to the modern international arbitrator to regain dynamism in modern contract and property law at the international business level. Sources of law other than mere domestic ones are thus likely to be re-activated, recognised and supported, including fundamental and general principles, custom and party autonomy, supplemented by powers to protect the ordinary commercial and financial flows and by notions of finality as further transnational public order requirements.

Thus, we see international arbitrators:

(a) break down nationalism, formalism and legal positivism, therefore, displaying a nationalistic black-letter law mentality;
(b) bridge the differences between Common and Civil law, although they are likely to move in the direction of the Common law technique of finding from case to case and refuting system thinking;
(c) use good faith language in contract (in a Civil law sense) and equitable notions in movable property (in a Common law sense), which both stand for dynamism, a variety of sources of law and transnationalisation, fostering the process to upgraded dynamic concepts of contract and movable property at the transnational level

(eds.), *Tom Bingham and the Transformation of the Law. A Liber Amicorum* (Oxford University Press, 2009), 619.

(d) avoid obvious excess or abuse, but
(e) respect domestic public policies or even public order notions sufficiently connected with the case, although they may increasingly be superseded by international minimum standards of protection, again under transnational public order notions more directly or in respect of international investments increasingly under bilateral investment treaties.

Creating a dynamic modern transnational contract law

In *contract*, the powers of international arbitrators identified in the previous section are indeed likely to be used to regain legal dynamism or momentum and a less static and statist approach. The modern notion of good faith may in particular be used to create flexibility, but then operate itself as a transnational concept. Even pressing moral, social and especially efficiency considerations may find readier acceptance in a more modern transnationalised liberal interpretation technique, although these considerations, except for efficiency, may not always be highly relevant in international trade, commerce and finance and in any event need not always give more protection. It could be less and may even lead to a literal contract interpretation, as we shall see.

But the pursuit of a dynamic concept of contract law[33] at the transnational level goes further. One may think here especially of the infrastructure of the modern contract, requiring a more dynamic approach to contract formation in which, depending on the phase of the negotiations, pre-contractual duties emerge and parties assume steadily increasing obligations. They do not, or no longer, depend on a ritual kind of mating dance in the offer and acceptance language resulting in a fixed moment of contract formation. It suggests a progression in commitment during the entire contract period in which disclosure duties, a beginning of performance and acceptance of risk of future developments also figure large.

This involves a process of *objectivation* of norms in which in a largely corporate modern environment traditional will theories, and an anthropomorphic attitude to private law and to contract in particular, are

---

[33] See, especially, M. A. Eisenberg, 'The Emergence of Dynamic Contract Law', *California Law Review*, 88, (2000), 1743–1814, 1747; S. Macaulay, 'Non-Contractual Relations in Business. A Preliminary Study', *American Sociology Review*, 28 (1963), 55; L. M. Friedman and S. Macaulay, 'Contract Law and Contract Teaching. Past, Present, and Future', *Wisconsin Law Review* (1967), 805–21; G. Gilmore, *The Death of Contract* (Ohio State University Press, 1974); P. S. Atiyah, *The Rise and Fall of Freedom of Contract* (Oxford: Clarendon, 1979); *idem., Essays on Contract* (Oxford: Clarendon, 1986).

abandoned and at least duration contracts may be seen as a form of partnership or a framework in which new obligations may emerge all the time in a continuous process of law formation – one that is not solely guided by the parties' will at a fixed moment in time, but rather by conduct, reliance and risk acceptance, especially of ever-changing circumstances. It may still give rise to post-contractual renegotiation duties on the basis of a change of circumstances, but in professional dealings only when the risk of new developments becomes manifestly unreasonable for one party to bear, while the overall effect on the debtor, not just the effect on the one contract, may also figure in order to determine whether it is such as to justify relief.

All of this should not distract from the fact that for professionals at the international level, the contract itself is likely to be foremost a *road map* and *prime risk management tool* which may require literal interpretation. The notion of party autonomy is recast here in that sense, therefore in terms of initiative and organisation. It is no longer psychological and is, therefore, more objective, supported especially by conduct and reliance notions and supplemented (and sometimes corrected) by other sources of law.

The modern notion of good faith supports this phenomenon and may thus extend *as well as limit* the protections of the parties, depending on the nature of their relationship (different in professional and consumer dealings) and on the type of their deal (different in duration contracts and the sale of goods). Good faith may indeed require that professional parties have fewer defenses or excuses, also in terms of rescission on the basis of mistake or suspension or termination of their compliance duty based on *force majeure* or a change of circumstances. These may become very limited excuses if the good faith notion is properly understood and applied in professional dealings.

Creating a modern transnational movable property law

In movable property, international commercial arbitrators may exert similar powers of transformation. The modern developments in this context mean a degree of party autonomy that may in particular do away with the Civil law notion of a limited number of proprietary rights (the idea of the *numerus clausus*) at the transnational level. It may seem extraordinary that parties may in this way expand their rights against third parties, who in the nature of all proprietary rights would have to respect them; but it is less objectionable where there is at the same time a strong protection of *bona fide* purchasers (as there always was in the Common law approach in equity which has this flexibility) or even of purchasers in the ordinary course of business of commoditised products, who need not then be *bona fide* and do not in any event have a search duty.

This may be seen as increasingly customary in professional circles and reflects the achievements and approach of the law of equity in a Common law sense. It means that not everything goes, and transnational public order restrictions may still impose themselves, but there is also the legitimisation through ever-evolving transnational practice. Public order in particular protects the *commercial flows* in the international marketplace against the effects thereon of greater freedom in the creation of proprietary rights, which then only operate among a group of professional insiders like banks and suppliers who are or become used to these newer techniques. This is closely connected to the notion of transactional finality.

These are, therefore, the limits of greater party autonomy in this area allowing movable property law nevertheless to become a *prime risk management tool*, which is especially clear in asset-backed funding, where floating charges and conditional or temporary ownership rights would then freely operate transnationally over whole portfolios of dispersed assets, which in this manner may be transferred or assigned in bulk, next to the operation of more traditional security interests. It is submitted that this is now emerging as a key facility in the concept of modern transnational movable property law, which needs support at the transnational level and is becoming the remit of international commercial arbitrators.

If one keeps in mind the autonomous development of negotiable instruments and documents of title in the older *lex mercatoria*, this more modern development relating to the operation of the international marketplace may be less surprising. It is now especially relevant in modern financial transactions and may then also affect them at the domestic level. In Civil law countries, this is mostly not yet identified and analysed as such, although even now sometimes spotted, as in the area of receivables and their transfer and in the interests that may be created in them.

For assets located in different countries, the technique is increasingly to locate them all at the place of the owner, often already favoured for receivables, suggesting the application of the domestic law of the assignor to the assignment. In a more advanced legal environment, in order to cover foreign assets more objectively, the owner's law could be considered transnationalised, again subject to proper protection of the commercial flows as a separate public order requirement. It is the supporting force of transnational practices and general principles operating in more advanced legal environments that make the difference here while imposing their own logic, ultimately also entering domestic legal regimes, even in bankruptcy when it especially matters. Again, the law concerning Eurobonds may serve as a powerful example in this context.

Thus, if we concentrate on transnational commercial and financial law, we may note that a more diverse and fractured system of proprietary rights is evolving at that level, therefore, with different proprietary notions for different areas of the law or for different (financial) products. This may eventually also be followed or recognised domestically in terms of transnational practice or custom. It assumes and confirms a greater degree of party autonomy even in proprietary matters, but it may also be more objective – i.e. fenced in by the practices evolving at that level and the protection of the commercial flows. It is posited that international commercial arbitrators are likely to show increasing sensitivity to these developments which the international commercial and financial practice needs and against which there are no clear public order requirements. Indeed, these structures have worked well in equity in Common law jurisdictions for a long time.

This may increasingly concern modern forms of (electronic) payment; securities entitlements and their transfer; the treatment of conditional and temporary ownership rights in finance leases and repurchase agreements; the (bulk) assignment of payment obligations, especially in the context of floating charges, receivables financing and securitisations; the development of security interests in the form of non-possessory floating charges; the notion of agency (and the transfer of ownership in indirect or undisclosed agency); the evolution of fiduciary duties and the important principle of segregation of assets in formal, resulting or constructive trusts; and the facility of tracing. No less important in this connection are the modern notions of set-off and netting and ultimately the notion of finality, as mentioned above.

Again, one recognises here transnationally the innovative pull and challenge of the *law of equity* in a Common law sense and the accompanying powers of the equity judge now to be assumed by international arbitrators.

The role of an International Commercial Court

Transnational commercial and financial law is likely to be responsive to practical needs and ultimately to become the leading law in international commerce and finance. International commercial arbitrators will facilitate this development and consider that they have powers to do so. Among professionals, it introduces in both contract and movable property law the *risk management perspective*, which connects the contractual and proprietary examples of legal dynamism mentioned above.

These powers may be reinforced by introducing an international facility for arbitrators to seek guidance from their peers through a preliminary question facility. It is in this context that the creation of an International Commercial Court (ICC) may usefully be considered,[34] which would offer the facility of issuing binding opinions in this regard, therefore, opinions on the application of the *lex mercatoria*, its various sources of law and its hierarchy of norms in international commercial and financial cases, including issues of modern contract and personal property law. A similar facility could be envisaged in matters of procedure and evidence, where any domestic *leges arbitrari* would thus be preceded by other rules, especially by the evolving practices and customs of international arbitration. This preliminary question facility follows in principle the EU model under Art. 234 EC Treaty, now in Art. 267 TFEU, which gives courts in the EU the facility to appeal to the European Court of Justice (ECJ) in connection with European law questions, and could even be stretched to questions concerning the reach of domestic mandatory (regulatory) laws or public policy in international transactions.

Such an ICC should have exclusive jurisdiction in the areas of its competence and be plainly empowered to base its decisions on transnational principles and practice, much as the ICJ does for public international law disputes under Art. 38(1) of its Statute. The decisions of this ICC should be accepted as final and be directly enforceable in all Contracting States. It follows that commercial judgments or arbitral awards ignoring such decisions would not be effective, or would be remedied accordingly.[35]

---

[34] See J. H. Dalhuisen, 'The Case for an International Commercial Court', in K. P. Berger (ed.), *Private and Commercial Law in a European and Global Context. Festschrift Norbert Horn* (Berlin: de Gruyter, 2006), 893. This Court could also usefully take over challenges of arbitral awards and their recognition and enforcement under domestic laws, or at least give preliminary opinions in these matters.

[35] See M. Rubino-Sammartano, *International Arbitration Law and Practice* (The Hague: Kluwer, 2001), 980. See further H. M. Holtzmann, 'A Task for the 21st Century. Creating a New International Court for Resolving Disputes on the Enforceability of Arbitral Awards', and S. M. Schwebel, 'The Creation and Operation of an International Court of Arbitral Awards', both in M. Hunter, A. Marriott and V. V. Veeder (eds.), *The Internationalisation of International Arbitration. The LCIA Centenary Conference* (London: Graham & Trotman, 1995), 109, 115.

Conclusion

The foregoing analysis is proffered here as the most realistic depiction of what is truly happening in international commercial arbitrations. It was posited that international arbitrators have substantial powers of transformation which for them are founded not in the arbitration clause but institutionally in the transnational commercial and financial legal order or in transnational public order itself. This power finds its limits in the evolving *lex mercatoria* which international arbitrators at the same time develop further in an autonomous manner. In fact, it was found that all private law, in order to remain living, needs that kind of facility. Hence the emergence of the equity judges in Common law countries and earlier the function of the Praetor in Roman law. There is no waiting here for legislators, which are in any event absent from the transnational commercial and financial legal order.

This development is perceived as positive and necessary in order to keep the private law in the professional sphere up to date and this facility is, therefore, seen as indispensable at the present moment especially to achieve the necessary transition from a domestic, statist and static perception of private law to a transnational dynamic and responsive law that is attuned to present-day business realities and the need for adequate legal support and rapid updating. The relevant perspectives in contract but also in movable property law were discussed in this connection and the contours of a dynamic modern law in these two vital areas of professional dealings were outlined as examples of where modern arbitrators are heading in the further development of the modern *lex mercatoria*.

While doing so, the *lex mercatoria* as substantive law may well develop beyond the hierarchy of sources of law described above as its present essence, and move to a more uniform legal environment. In finding structure in this process, it would appear that academia has a particular role of enlightenment to play in order to support this development and inform international arbitrators and practitioners alike.

26

Customary international law, Congress and the courts: origins of the later-in-time rule

WILLIAM S. DODGE

Introduction

Transnational law, in Philip Jessup's classic definition, is 'all law which regulates actions or events that transcend national frontiers'.[1] This means that transnational law includes not only international law but much domestic law, and since international and domestic law often bear on the same subjects, questions about their relationship frequently arise. In the United States today, the relationship between Federal statutes and international law is well settled. According to section 115 of the *Restatement (Third) of Foreign Relations Law of the United States*, 'An act of Congress supersedes an earlier rule of international law or a provision of an international agreement as law of the United States if the purpose of the act to supersede the earlier rule or provision is clear or if the act and the earlier rule or provision cannot be fairly reconciled'.[2] US courts will interpret Federal statutes to avoid such violations,[3] but in cases of clear conflict the later-in-time prevails.

It has not always been thus. At the time of the framing, the common understanding was that treaties were 'beyond the lawful reach of legislative acts'.[4] John Jay explained in *The Federalist* that as the consent of two nations was required to make treaties, 'so must it ever afterwards be to

---

[1] P. C. Jessup, *Transnational Law* (New Haven, CT: Yale University Press, 1956), p. 2.

[2] *Restatement (Third) of the Foreign Relations Law of the United States*, §115(1)(a) (1987) (hereafter, *Restatement (Third)*). Detlev Vagts served as an Associate Reporter for the *Restatement (Third)* but was not principally responsible for the provisions on the status of international law and agreements in US law, which fell to the Chief Reporter Louis Henkin.

[3] See *ibid.*, §114. This is often referred to as *The Charming Betsy* presumption, after an early case. See *infra* n. 14.

[4] *The Federalist*, No. 64, 394 (C. Rossiter ed., 1961).

alter or cancel them'.[5] In a 2001 article, Detlev Vagts traced the judicial origins of the later-in-time rule for treaties to the mid-nineteenth century.[6] Recent scholarship has shown its earlier emergence among members of Congress during the 1816 debates on the Commercial Convention with Great Britain.[7]

The origins of the later-in-time rule with respect to customary international law have been less well studied. In support of its rule, the *Restatement (Third)* cites two cases implying that the US President may violate international law if acting within his constitutional authority,[8] and two others stating that Congress may.[9] But the US Supreme Court seems never to have squarely held that a Federal statute supersedes customary international law as law of the United States.

Certainly one can find statements in the early cases suggesting that a statute may violate the law of nations. Take for example the seriatim opinions in *Ware* v. *Hylton*,[10] a case involving the validity of a 1777 Virginia statute confiscating debts owed to British creditors during the Revolutionary War.[11] 'It is admitted, that Virginia could not confiscate private debts without a violation of the modern law of nations', Justice Chase wrote, 'yet if in fact, she has so done, the law is obligatory on all the citizens of Virginia, and on her Courts of Justice; and, in my opinion, on all the Courts of the United States'.[12] Justice Iredell agreed: 'admitting that the Legislature had not strictly a right, agreeably to the law of nations, to confiscate the debt in question; yet, if they in fact did so, it would ... have been valid and obligatory within the limits of the State'.[13] A number of decisions from the Marshall Court seem to confirm that Congress could depart from the law of nations. The principle is at least implicit in Marshall's oft-quoted phrase from *The Charming Betsy* 'that

---

[5] *Ibid.*

[6] D. F. Vagts, 'The United States and its Treaties. Observance and Breach', *AJIL*, 95 (2001), 313–34, 313–23.

[7] J. T. Parry, 'Congress, The Supremacy Clause, and the Implementation of Treaties', *Fordham International Law Journal*, 32 (2009), 1209–1335, 1304–16.

[8] See *Restatement (Third)*, *supra* n. 2, §115, Reporters' Note 3 (citing *The Paquete Habana*, 175 US 677, 700 (1900), and *Brown* v. *United States*, 12 US 110, 128 (1814)).

[9] See *ibid.* (citing *Tag* v. *Rogers*, 267 F.2d 664 (DC Cir. 1959), and *The Over the Top*, 5 F.2d 838 (D. Conn. 1925)). Each of these cases is discussed below.

[10] 3 US 199 (1796).

[11] Because Virginia was an independent country in 1777, its status was analogous to that of the United States after ratification of the Constitution. For this reason *Ware* does not establish the authority of the States to violate the law of nations after 1789. That issue is beyond the scope of this chapter.

[12] 3 US 229 (Chase, J.).   [13] *Ibid.* 265 (Iredell, J.).

an act of Congress ought never to be construed to violate the law of nations if any other possible construction remains'.[14] In *Brown* v. *United States*, referring to practices concerning the confiscation of enemy property, Marshall wrote '[t]his usage is a guide which the sovereign follows or abandons at his will'.[15] And in *The Nereide*, he said that '[t]ill such an act [of Congress] be passed, the Court is bound by the law of nations which is a part of the law of the land'.[16]

On the other hand, one can also find statements in the early cases suggesting that a statute cannot violate the law of nations.[17] In 1781, the Federal Court of Appeals for Prize Cases established under the Articles of Confederation wrote that '[t]he municipal laws of a country cannot change the law of nations, so as to bind the subjects of another nation'.[18] In 1793, Chancellor George Wythe denied Virginia's authority to confiscate debts in violation of the law of nations, declaring that 'the legislature could not retract their consent to observe the preacepts of the law, and conform to the usages of nations'.[19] Indeed, as late as 1871, Justice Field would maintain that Congress' constitutional authority to make rules for captures during wartime was 'subject to the condition that they are within the law of nations'. The law of nations, Field wrote, 'was no less binding upon Congress than if the limitation were written in the Constitution'.[20]

To explain these apparently contradictory statements, and to understand how the later-in-time rule developed with respect to customary international law, we must look to the original understanding of the law of nations in the United States and to how that understanding changed during the nineteenth century. Today, we define customary international law in positivist terms. In the words of the *Restatement (Third)*, it 'results from a general and consistent practice of states followed by them from a sense of legal obligation'.[21] A State need not consent specifically to a rule of customary international law in order to be bound,[22] and once a State is bound it cannot disclaim the obligation.[23] Two or more States may

---

[14] *Murray* v. *The Schooner Charming Betsy*, 6 US 64, 118 (1804).
[15] *Brown* v. *United States, supra* n. 8.   [16] *The Nereide*, 13 US 388, 423 (1815).
[17] See, generally, J. Lobel, 'The Limits of Constitutional Power. Conflicts Between Foreign Policy and International Law', *Virginia Law Review*, 71 (1985), 1071–1180, 1076–95.
[18] *Miller* v. *The Ship Resolution*, 2 US 1, 4 (Fed. Ct App. 1781).
[19] *Page* v. *Pendleton*, Wythe's Rep. 211, 213 (Va. Ch. 1793).
[20] *Miller* v. *United States*, 78 US 268, 316 (1871) (Field, J., dissenting).
[21] *Restatement (Third), supra* n. 2, §102(2).   [22] *Ibid.*, §102, cmt. *b.*
[23] *Ibid.*, §102, cmt. *d.*

change a rule of customary international law between themselves by treaty, so long as the rule is not a *jus cogens* norm.[24] A group of States may also develop a 'special' customary international law for themselves through practice, although a State must have specifically accepted or acquiesced in such a custom in order to be bound.[25]

The understanding of the law of nations in the late eighteenth century was quite different. Emmerich de Vattel, the authority to whom the founding generation turned more frequently than any other, divided the law of nations into four categories: (1) the necessary; (2) the voluntary; (3) the conventional; and (4) the customary.[26] The 'conventional law of nations' consisted of treaties.[27] The other three categories were all unwritten law, but they varied significantly in their sources and in their obligatory force. What Vattel called the 'necessary law of nations' was based directly on the law of nature. It was immutable and absolutely binding, but only internally upon the conscience of the sovereign.[28] What Vattel called the 'voluntary law of nations' was also based on natural law (with certain adaptations to smooth relations between equal and independent sovereigns), but it was externally binding.[29] This 'voluntary law of nations' was not voluntary in the ordinary sense of the word. 'In this particular, nations have not the option of giving or withholding their consent at pleasure', Vattel wrote; they were 'bound to consent'.[30] Vattel's final category, the 'customary law of nations', was based on State practice. But unlike customary international law today, it required individual consent and a State could opt out of such a rule simply by declaring that it would no longer be bound.[31]

The differing statements in early cases about whether a statute could supersede the law of nations are largely explained by these different categories. Cases stating that the legislature could not violate the law of nations involved rules which were presumed to be 'voluntary' (whether or not Vattel would have classified them that way). Cases stating that the legislature could violate the law of nations involved rules which were presumed to be 'customary' (again, whether or not Vattel would have agreed). But Vattel's analytic framework did not stand the test of time.

---

[24] *Ibid.*, §102, cmt. *k*.   [25] *Ibid.*, §102, cmt. *e*.
[26] E. de Vattel, *The Law of Nations or the Principles of Natural Law Applied to the Conduct and to the Affairs of Nations and of Sovereigns* (1758) (J. Chitty trans., Philadelphia, PA: T. & J. W. Johnson & Co., 1883), Prelim., §§7–9, 21, 24–5.
[27] *Ibid.*, Prelim., §24.   [28] *Ibid.*, Prelim., §§7–9.
[29] *Ibid.*, Prelim., §§21, 28; Book III, §§188–92.   [30] *Ibid.*, Book III, §192.
[31] *Ibid.*, Prelim., §§25–6; Book IV, §106.

During the nineteenth century, courts and treatise writers began to misinterpret Vattel's 'voluntary' category, treating its rules as – well – voluntary. At the same time, the theoretical foundation for a 'voluntary law of nations' based on natural law was undermined as international law came to be seen in more positivist terms. Eventually, all international law was understood to be rooted in State practice, what Vattel would have called the 'customary law of nations'.

It did not have to follow, as it would have for Vattel, that nations were now free to violate customary international law. The shift from natural law to positivism could have been offset by another shift during the nineteenth century – the shift from individual consent to the idea that general practice could create universally binding rules. But that conclusion seems to have been blocked by a third change, the emergence of dualism in the US Supreme Court's jurisprudence. During the late nineteenth century, the Court began to see the international and the domestic as separate legal orders and to treat international law as part of the domestic order only to the extent it had been adopted by domestic law. If the United States was free not to adopt rules of customary international law in the first place, it followed that its legislature was free to supersede them as rules of domestic law.

All these developments were reflected at the turn of the twentieth century in the Supreme Court's famous *Paquete Habana* decision.[32] 'International law is part of our law, and must be ascertained and administered by the courts of justice of appropriate jurisdiction as often as questions of right depending upon it are duly presented for their determination', Justice Gray wrote. 'For this purpose, where there is no treaty and no controlling executive or legislative act or judicial decision, resort must be had to the customs and usages of civilized nations'.[33] Not only was Justice Gray's definition of customary international law thoroughly positivist ('customs and usages of civilized nations'), but he seemed to acknowledge the superiority of other sources of positive law ('where there is no treaty and no controlling executive or legislative act or judicial decision'). Twentieth-century courts would seize upon the 'controlling ... legislative act' language in particular to justify the later-in-time rule with respect to customary international law.

---

[32] 175 US 677 (1900). For another discussion of this decision which focuses on a few of these issues and some others as well, see W. S. Dodge, '*The Paquete Habana*. Customary International Law as Part of Our Law', in J. E. Noyes, L. A. Dickinson and M. W. Janis (eds.), *International Law Stories* (Westbury, NY: Foundation Press, 2007), 175.

[33] 175 US 700.

In telling this story, there is a danger of making it too neat. The shift from natural law to positivism did not occur all at once, and natural law ideas persisted even as positivism gained ground. The idea that statutes could violate customary international law and the idea that they could not both persisted for much of the nineteenth century, sometimes in stunning juxtaposition. And judges faced with a possible conflict between a statute and the law of nations usually tried to avoid the question by employing the *Charming Betsy* presumption and construing the statute so as not to violate the law of nations.

The early understanding

Two works above all others framed the founding generation's view of the law of nations and of that law's place in the American legal system: Emmerich de Vattel's *The Law of Nations* (1758) and William Blackstone's *Commentaries on the Laws of England* (1765–9).[34] Vattel, as we have already noted, divided the unwritten law of nations into three categories: (1) the necessary law of nations, which was based on natural law, immutable, but binding only internally upon the conscience; (2) the voluntary law of nations to which nations were 'bound to consent', which was also based on natural law and created external obligations; and (3) the customary law of nations, which was based on individual consent through State practice and from which nations were at liberty to withdraw their consent.

Blackstone's contribution was to explain how the law of nations fitted into England's legal system, and by extension into America's. '[T]he law of nations (wherever any question arises which is properly the object of it's [*sic*] jurisdiction) is here adopted in it's [*sic*] full extent by the common law, and is held to be a part of the law of the land.'[35] American lawyers and judges repeated this principle constantly, often in language nearly identical to Blackstone's.[36] But the law of nations' status as Common law raised a question about its relationship with

---

[34] Vattel, *The Law of Nations*, *supra* n. 26; W. Blackstone, *Commentaries on the Laws of England* (1765–9).

[35] Blackstone, *Commentaries*, vol. IV, *supra* n. 34, 67.

[36] See, e.g., James Iredell's Charge to the Grand Jury (May 12, 1794), reprinted in M. Marcus (ed.), *The Documentary History of the Supreme Court of the United States, 1789–1800*, 8 vols. (New York: Columbia University Press, 1985–2007), vol. 2, 454, 467; 1 Op. Att'y Gen. 26, 27 (1792); *Respublica* v. *De Longchamps*, 1 US 111, 116 (Pa. Ct. Oyer & Term. 1784).

legislative acts. Lord Coke had written controversially in *Dr. Bonham's Case* that 'when an Act of Parliament is against common right and reason, or repugnant, or impossible to be performed, the common law will controul it, and adjudge such an Act to be void'.[37] Blackstone expressly disagreed. He acknowledged that judges should construe ambiguous statutes to avoid unreasonable results, '[b]ut if the parliament will positively enact a thing to be done which is unreasonable, I know of no power that can control it'.[38] Both Blackstone's assertion of legislative supremacy and Vattel's categories would make repeated appearances as early American judges and writers struggled with the relationship between statutes and the law of nations.

The first American decision to address the question seems to have been *Miller* v. *The Ship Resolution*, decided by the Federal Court of Appeals for Prize Cases in 1781.[39] The question was whether a neutral Dutch ship, captured by a British privateer and then captured in turn by an American privateer, could be condemned by the American as prize. The American privateer claimed that under an ordinance of the Continental Congress the capture of a ship for twenty-four hours made it a prize. This meant the Dutch ship had become British property and was therefore liable to capture by the Americans. Employing what would come to be known as *The Charming Betsy* presumption, the Court read the ordinance as limited to legal captures – i.e. not captures of a neutral ship.[40] But the Court opined that even if the ordinance were intended to cover all captures, it would not affect this case. 'The municipal laws of a country cannot change the law of nations, so as to bind the subjects of another nation; and by the law of nations a neutral subject, whose property has been illegally captured, may pursue and recover that property in whatever country it is found, unless a competent jurisdiction has adjudged it prize.'[41] The law of nations concerning neutral rights, to which the Court referred, was part of the voluntary law of nations,[42] so it was those rules which the court in *Miller* was asserting could not be changed by a domestic statute.

The relationship between legislation and the law of nations arose again in *Rutgers* v. *Waddington*, a case decided by the Mayor's Court of New York, in which Alexander Hamilton acted as counsel for the

---

[37] 77 Eng. Rep. 646, 652 (1610).   [38] Blackstone, *Commentaries*, vol. I, *supra* n. 34, 91.
[39] 2 US 1 (Fed. Ct App. 1781).   [40] *Ibid.*, 3–6.   [41] *Ibid.*, 4.
[42] See Vattel, *The Law of Nations*, *supra* n. 26, Book III, §109.

defendants.[43] After the Revolutionary War, Rutgers brought a suit for trespass against British subjects who had taken over her brew house, invoking a New York statute which had been passed specifically to allow such suits. Hamilton opened his brief by recounting Vattel's division of the law of nations and noting that his arguments were based upon the voluntary law.[44] Under this law, he argued, captors were entitled to the proceeds of immovable property while they were in possession of it.[45] Relying on Vattel and on *Dr. Bonham's Case*, Hamilton asserted that the legislature could not 'alter the law of nations', and that if it tried to do so 'the *act is void*'.[46]

Writing for the court, Mayor James Duane rejected Hamilton's assertion that a legislature could not violate the law of nations.[47] Citing Vattel, he noted that the necessary law of nations consisted only of '*laws of moral obligation*', while consent to the customary law of nations could be withdrawn.[48] In a fine expression of the idea of individual consent, Duane wrote that 'if one nation must be subjected, at all events, to usages which she cannot approve, because others may have thought fit to adopt them, her liberty would no longer remain entire'.[49] As for the voluntary law of nations, on which Hamilton based his argument, Duane simply ignored it. In the end, Duane adopted Blackstone's position (and many of his words), stating that while the legislature *could* enact an unreasonable law, statutes should be construed to avoid such results.[50] 'The repeal of the law of nations, or any interference with it, could not have been in contemplation', Duane wrote, 'when the Legislature passed this statute; and we think ourselves bound to exempt that law from its operation'.[51] *Rutgers* nicely illustrates the ways in which early Americans thought about statutes and the law of nations. Coke, Blackstone and Vattel were all pressed into service on different sides. Hamilton argued that statutes could not violate certain rules of the law of nations based on their status as voluntary law, while Duane avoided that conclusion by pointing to the non-binding nature of the necessary and customary law. And in the end, the court construed the statute to avoid the conflict.

---

[43] Hamilton's papers relating to the case, as well as the opinion of the Court, are reprinted in J. Goebel, Jr. and J.H. Smith (eds.), *The Law Practice of Alexander Hamilton. Documents and Commentary*, 5 vols. (New York: Columbia University Press, 1964–80), vol. I, 282–419.
[44] See *ibid.*, 364. [45] See *ibid.*, 368–73. [46] *Ibid.*, 378, 382.
[47] He did suggest, however, that a State legislature could not. See *ibid.*, 405–6.
[48] See *ibid.*, 404–5. [49] *Ibid.* [50] See *ibid.*, 415. [51] *Ibid.*, 417.

A pair of cases involving Virginia's 1777 act confiscating debts owed to British creditors also illustrates the dominant influence of Vattel's categories on the thinking of the time. The more famous of the two is *Ware* v. *Hylton*,[52] which reached the US Supreme Court in 1796. The statute was alleged to violate both the law of nations and Art. 4 of the Treaty of Paris, now binding on the States under the Supremacy Clause of the US Constitution. The treaty alone was sufficient to invalidate the law, but on the point which interests us Justices Chase and Iredell each asserted that a legislative act was valid even if it violated the law of nations.[53] Vattel's influence is most apparent in Chase's opinion:

> The law of nations may be considered of three kinds, to wit, general, conventional, or customary. The first is universal, or established by the general consent of mankind, and binds all nations. The second is founded on express consent, and is not universal, and only binds those nations that have assented to it. The third is founded on tacit consent; and is only obligatory on those nations, who have adopted it.[54]

The rule against confiscating debts during wartime was a rule of customary law only, and that fact was critical for Chase. Having quoting Vattel,[55] Chase concluded that '[t]he relaxation or departure from the strict rights of war to confiscate private debts, by the commercial nations of Europe, was not binding on the State of Virginia, because founded on custom only; and she was at liberty to reject, or adopt the custom, as she pleased'.[56] His statements elsewhere in the opinion that Virginia's law was valid even if it violated the law of nations were founded on this premise.

---

[52] 3 US 199 (1796).
[53] See *ibid.*, 223–4, 229 (Chase, J.); *ibid.*, 265 (Iredell, J.).
[54] *Ibid.*, 227 (Chase, J.). Note Chase's substitution of 'general' for Vattel's 'voluntary'.
[55] The relevant passage reads:

> The sovereign has naturally the same right over what his subjects may owe to enemies, he may therefore confiscate debts of this nature, if the term of payment happen in the time of war; or at least he may prohibit his subjects from paying while the war continues. But, at present, a regard to the advantage and safety of commerce has induced all the sovereigns of Europe to act with less rigour in this point. And as the custom has been generally received, he who should act contrary to it would violate the public faith; for strangers trusted his subjects only from a firm persuasion that the general custom would be observed.

Vattel, *The Law of Nations, supra* n. 26, Book III, §77.
[56] 3 US 227.

The status of the rule against confiscating debts as part of the customary law of nations was also critical to Iredell. 'Whether this customary
law (admitting the principle to prevail by custom only) was binding on
the American States, during the late war, in respect to Great Britain at
least, may be a question of considerable doubt'.[57] Iredell's earlier writings
also show Vattel's influence on his thinking, although they seem to betray
some hostility to the idea of a binding voluntary law. In 1791 Iredell
prepared a memorandum on Attorney General Randolph's Report on the
Judiciary in which he stated that the law of nations was divided into three
kinds: (1) the 'necessary Law of Nations'; (2) the 'Conventional Law of
Nations'; and (3) the 'Customary Law of Nations'.[58] Iredell clearly had a
copy of Vattel at hand because he quoted Vattel's definition of the
customary law of nations. This makes it all the more remarkable that
Iredell omitted Vattel's voluntary law of nations from his list. Iredell did
assert in this memorandum that the necessary law of nations is binding
and 'unrepealable by the Legislative Authority'.[59] But he may not have
meant that the necessary law of nations was judicially enforceable. In
charging a South Carolina grand jury three years later, he would explain:
'Even the Legislature cannot rightfully controul [the principles of the
Law of Nations], but if it passes any law on such subjects is bound by the
dictates of moral duty to the rest of the world in no instance to transgress
them, although if it in fact doth so, it is entitled to actual obedience
within the sphere of its authority'.[60]

Justice Wilson did not reach the law of nations question in *Ware*,[61] but
the views he expressed elsewhere are notable for their differences from
both Iredell's and Vattel's. Like them, he viewed a part of the law of
nations as founded upon natural law, the obligations of which were
'[u]niversal, indispensible, and unchangeable'.[62] But Wilson thought
that natural law (presumably including this part of the law of nations)
could be enforced against the legislature. When Blackstone said there was
no power which could control Parliament, Wilson reasoned, he meant

---

[57] *Ibid.*, 263 (Iredell, J.). Iredell buttressed his assertion that a statute could violate the law of
       nations with a reference to Blackstone. See *ibid.*, 266.
[58] James Iredell's Memorandum on Attorney General Edmund Randolph's Report on the
       Judiciary, in Marcus (ed.), *The Documentary History of the Supreme Court, supra* n. 36,
       vol. IV, 541–2.
[59] *Ibid.*   [60] Iredell's Charge to the Grand Jury, *supra* n. 36, 467.
[61] See 3 US 281 (Wilson, J.).
[62] J. Wilson, 'Lectures on Law Delivered in the College of Philadelphia in the years 1790 and
       1791', in R. G. McCloskey (ed.), *The Works of James Wilson* , 2 vols. (Cambridge, MA:
       The Belknap Press, 1967), vol. I, 67, 151.

'that he knew no *human* power sufficient for this purpose. But the parliament may, unquestionably, be controlled by natural or revealed law, proceeding from *divine* authority'.[63] Judges had a 'duty to declare' statutes that violated the law of nature 'void, because contrary to an overruling law'.[64] Besides the law of nations based on natural law, there was another 'part of the law of nations, called their voluntary law, which is founded on the principle of consent: of this part, publick compacts and customs received and observed by civilized states form the most considerable articles'.[65] For Wilson, the voluntary law was not a separate category but characterisation of those rules based on consent, specifically treaties and customary law. Charging a grand jury in 1791, Wilson said that 'so far as the law of nations is *voluntary* or *positive*, it may be altered by the municipal legislature of any state, in cases affecting *only* its own citizens', and that 'by a treaty, the voluntary or positive law of nations may be altered so far as the alteration shall affect *only* the contracting parties'.[66] But he cautioned that 'no state or states can, by treaties or municipal laws, alter or abrogate the law of nations any farther'.[67]

The other case besides *Ware* to address the validity of Virginia's 1777 confiscation statute under the law of nations was *Page v. Pendleton*,[68] which came out the other way. Chancellor George Wythe wrote that 'the legislature could not retract their consent to observe the preacepts of the law, and conform to the usages of nations'.[69] Under the law of nations, 'the right to money due to an enemy cannot be confiscated'.[70] 'If this seem contrary to what is called authority', he added in a footnote, 'the publisher of the opinion will be against the authority, when, in a question depending, like the present, on the law of nature, the authority is against reason'.[71] Thus, Wythe dealt with the rule's status as part of the customary law of nations – so important to the justices in *Ware* – by denying that it had that status and assigning it to a category 'depending . . . on the law of nature'. This sort of manipulation of categories would later be seen in some of the decisions of the Marshall Court. The important point for now is that for Wythe – as for Chase, Iredell, Wilson and others at this time – it mattered into which category of the law of nations a particular rule fell.

---

[63] *Ibid.*, 329.   [64] *Ibid.*   [65] *Ibid.*, 165.

[66] James Wilson's Charge to the Grand Jury (May 23, 1791), reprinted in Marcus (ed.), *The Documentary History of the Supreme Court, supra* n. 36, vol. II, 166, 179.

[67] *Ibid.*   [68] Wythe's Rep. 211 (Va. Ch. 1793).   [69] *Ibid.*, 213.   [70] *Ibid.*, 212.

[71] *Ibid.*, 212 n.(b).

The Marshall Court's favourite technique for resolving conflicts between a statute and the law of nations was to construe the statute to avoid the conflict – a technique which came to be known as *The Charming Betsy* presumption. The presumption did not originate with that case. As we have seen, *Miller* and *Rutgers* had applied the same rule of interpretation two decades earlier. In fact, Marshall articulated and applied the presumption in his very first opinion as Chief Justice.[72] During his tenure, the US Supreme Court would apply this technique of avoidance again and again – to customs laws in *The Apollon*,[73] to the piracy statute in *United States* v. *Klintock*,[74] to jurisdictional statutes in *The Schooner Exchange* v. *McFaddon*[75] and even to the Declare War Clause of the US Constitution in *Brown* v. *United States*.[76]

Marshall's formulation of the presumption implied that Congress had the power to depart from the law of nations if it so chose. As he put it in *The Charming Betsy*, 'an act of Congress ought never to be construed to violate the law of nations *if any other possible construction remains*'.[77] But in several cases he went further and made the implication express. Perhaps the leading example is *Brown* v. *United States* – one of the cases cited by the *Restatement (Third)* to support the later-in-time rule. In *Brown*, Chief Justice Marshall construed the Declare War Clause of the Constitution and Congress' declaration of the War of 1812 not to authorise the immediate confiscation of enemy property in light of modern international practice.[78] But he went on to state: 'This usage is a guide which the sovereign follows or abandons at his will. The rule, like other precepts of morality, of humanity, and even of wisdom, is addressed to the judgment of the sovereign; and although it cannot be disregarded by him without obloquy, yet it may be disregarded'.[79] The usage to which Marshall referred, however, was at most a rule of the

---

[72] *Talbot* v. *Seeman*, 5 US 1, 44 (1801).   [73] 22 US 362, 370 (1824).

[74] 18 US 144, 151–2 (1820).   [75] 11 US 116, 146 (1812).   [76] 12 US 110, 125 (1814).

[77] *Murray* v. *The Schooner Charming Betsy*, 6 US 64, 118 (1804), *supra* n. 14 (emphasis added); see also *Talbot* v. *Seeman*, 5 US 1, 44 (1801), *supra* n. 72 ('the laws of the United States ought not, *if it be avoidable*, so to be construed as to infract the common principles and usages of nations') (emphasis added).

[78] 12 US 123–7.

[79] *Ibid.*, 128. The word 'sovereign' clearly referred to Congress not the President. Marshall made clear that the question whether to confiscate enemy property contrary to international usage was one of policy, which 'is proper for the consideration of the legislature, not of the executive or the judiciary'. *Ibid.*, 129. *Brown* thus does not support the notion that the President may violate customary international law.

customary law of nations.[80] 'That war gives to the sovereign full right to take the persons and confiscate the property of the enemy wherever found, is conceded', he wrote. 'The mitigation of this rigid rule, which the humane and wise policy of modern times has introduced into practice, will more or less affect the exercise of this right, but cannot impair the right itself.'[81] Thus, *Brown*, like *Ware* v. *Hylton*, stands for no more than the principle that Congress can supersede the customary law of nations.

A more difficult example is *The Schooner Exchange* v. *McFaddon*,[82] which involved a clash between two principles of the law of nations: the absolute jurisdiction of a nation within its own territory and the immunity of a foreign sovereign from suit. Chief Justice Marshall began with the propositions that '[t]he jurisdiction of the nation within its own territory is necessarily exclusive and absolute' and that any exceptions 'must be traced up to the consent of the nation itself'.[83] But consent could be implied from 'common usage' and Marshall found a practice of not exercising jurisdiction over a foreign sovereign's person, foreign ministers, foreign troops granted permission to pass through a nation's territory and friendly foreign warships entering a nation's ports.[84] He therefore construed the jurisdictional statutes not to grant jurisdiction over 'a case, in which the sovereign power has impliedly consented to wave [*sic*] its jurisdiction'.[85] But founding these exceptions to jurisdiction on consent implied that the consent could be withdrawn – a point the Chief Justice confirmed: 'Without doubt, the sovereign of the place is capable of destroying this implication [of immunity]. He may claim and exercise jurisdiction either by employing force, or by subjecting such vessels to the ordinary tribunals.'[86] *The Schooner Exchange* is a difficult case because Vattel clearly viewed the immunity of a foreign sovereign and his ministers as rules of the voluntary law of nations.[87] But by shifting the basis for the rule to tacit consent, Marshall effectively shifted

---

[80] Vattel wrote that after a declaration of war, a sovereign 'was bound to allow [enemy subjects] a reasonable time for withdrawing with their effects', but this was because the sovereign had 'tacitly promised them full liberty and security for their return'. Vattel, *The Law of Nations*, *supra* n. 26, Book III, §63. Rules based on tacit consent fell into the category of customary law.

[81] 12 US 122–3. Justice Story thought the alleged rule did not even amount to a custom because it had not been followed in practice. See *ibid.*, 144 (Story, J., dissenting).

[82] 11 US 116 (1812).   [83] *Ibid.*, 136.   [84] See *ibid.*, 136–46.   [85] *Ibid.*, 146.   [86] *Ibid.*

[87] See Vattel, *The Law of Nations*, *supra* n. 26, Book III, §92 (foreign ministers); *ibid.*, §108 (the sovereign himself). Vattel did not discuss the immunity of foreign warships.

sovereign immunity from the category of voluntary law to that of customary law.[88]

Vattel also viewed the rights of neutrals and belligerents as part of the voluntary law of nations,[89] but the Marshall Court seemed to acknowledge that Congress could alter the law of prize. *Talbot* and *The Charming Betsy* both involved prize law, and while they construed the statutes at issue to be consistent with the law of nations they also implied that Congress could violate that law. In *Thirty Hogsheads of Sugar* v. *Boyle*, Chief Justice Marshall wrote that British decisions construing the law of nations 'continued to be our prize law, so far as it was adapted to our circumstances *and was not varied by the power which was capable of changing it*'.[90] A week later, in *The Nereide*, he suggested that Congress could pass an act making all goods found on enemy ships subject to capture in retaliation against Spain, which had adopted such a rule.[91] 'Till such an act be passed, the Court is bound by the law of nations which is a part of the law of the land.'[92] None of these cases actually gave effect to a statute which violated the voluntary law of nations, but each of them suggested that Congress had the power to pass acts which departed from it. Moreover, in none of these cases was there any attempt to shift the rules from the voluntary law of nations to the customary. Although the Court looked to Vattel for the substance of the rules, it seemed to ignore his categorisations. That trend would continue in the nineteenth century as the rise of positivism undermined the basis for a binding law of nations based on natural law.

The nineteenth century

During the nineteenth century, ideas about customary international law changed in important ways. Vattel's categories, so important to the early understanding of our topic, became less influential. Indeed, important figures like Henry Wheaton and Chief Justice Taney would misconstrue

---

[88] The discretionary aspect of foreign sovereign immunity would lead Justice Story to characterise it as a doctrine based 'upon principles of public comity'. *The Santissima Trinidad*, 20 US 283, 353 (1822).

[89] See Vattel, *The Law of Nations*, *supra* n. 26, Book III, §109.

[90] 13 US 191, 198 (1815) (emphasis added).   [91] 13 US 388, 422–3 (1815).

[92] *Ibid.*, 423. Marshall's discussion is more ambiguous than it first appears. Although condemning neutral goods found on enemy ships would have been a departure from the law of nations, it might have been justified by the fact that Spain had acted first. Vattel recognised such a right of reprisal. See, generally, Vattel, *The Law of Nations*, *supra* n. 26, Book II, §§339–54.

Vattel's 'voluntary law of nations' as consisting of rules which nations could depart from at their pleasure. The very idea of a binding law of nations based on natural law became more problematic as scholars and judges looked increasingly to State practice as the foundation of international law. While the nineteenth-century shift to positivism has been much discussed, there was another (less noticed) change in thinking about consent. During the early nineteenth century rules based on State practice required individual consent, and a State was free to withdraw its consent, in which case it would not be bound. But by the late nineteenth century it was acknowledged that general practice could generate a legal rule binding on all. These changes can be tracked in the opinions of the US Supreme Court, but only rarely did those opinions discuss theoretical issues. To understand these, we must also look to the treatises of the day – principally to Wheaton, Phillimore, Halleck and Hall.[93] Finally, during the late nineteenth century, the Supreme Court began to articulate a theory of dualism with respect to international law. The international and the domestic were considered separate legal orders, and international law became part of the domestic legal order only insofar it was adopted by domestic law.

Although Vattel's categories formed an important part of the analytic framework early Americans used to understand the law of nations, we have already seen that some judges of that era ignored or misinterpreted the 'voluntary' category. The court in *Rutgers* ignored the voluntary law in considering whether a statute could violate the law of nations, while Justice Iredell omitted it from his 1791 list. Justice Wilson recognised a category of 'voluntary law' but conflated it with treaties and customs, which was not at all what Vattel meant. This misunderstanding continued in the nineteenth century. In *Bank of Augusta* v. *Earle*, the US Supreme Court held that by the 'comity of nations' a corporation chartered in one State was permitted to bring suit in another.[94] Comity was inherently discretionary, and a court would only give effect to foreign

---

[93] See H. Wheaton, *Elements of International Law* (Philadelphia, PA: Carey, Lea & Blanchard, 1836); R. Phillimore, *Commentaries upon International Law* (Philadelphia, PA: T. & J. W. Johnson, 1854); H. W. Halleck, *International Law; or Rules Regulating the Intercourse of States in Peace and War* (San Francisco, CA: H. H. Bancroft & Co., 1861); W. E. Hall, *International Law* (Oxford: Clarendon Press, 1880). Each of these treatises was repeatedly cited by the US Supreme Court. By my count, the Court has relied upon Wheaton sixty-two times (forty-three prior to 1900), Phillimore twenty-six times (twenty-one prior to 1900), Halleck thirty-four times (twenty-one prior to 1900) and Hall seventeen times (three prior to 1900).

[94] 38 US 519, 590 (1839).

laws when doing so was not 'contrary to its policy, or prejudicial to its interests'.[95] To emphasise the discretionary nature of the doctrine, Chief Justice Taney characterised it as 'part of the voluntary law of nations'.[96]

It is possible that Taney was not referring specifically to Vattel's 'voluntary law of nations', but Henry Wheaton clearly was. In the 3rd edition of his *Elements of International Law*, Wheaton recounted Vattel's categories of voluntary, conventional and customary law, describing the voluntary as 'derived from the presumed consent of nations arising out of their general usage and practice'.[97] He then commented:

> It is, perhaps, almost superfluous to point out, the confusion in this enumeration by *Vattel* of the different species of international law, which might easily have been avoided by reserving the expression, 'voluntary law of nations', to designate the *genus*, including all the rules of international law introduced by positive consent, and divided into the two *species* of conventional law and customary law.[98]

Wheaton, like Wilson, saw no difference between the voluntary law of nations on the one hand and the conventional and customary law of nations on the other. Not all nineteenth-century treatise writers made this mistake. Writing in 1861, Henry Halleck noted Wheaton's criticism but expressed his own view that 'the divisions of Vattel are not entirely without foundation, and, at least, as worthy of consideration'. Halleck added, however, that Vattel's terms 'are not well chosen'.[99]

The word 'voluntary' may well have contributed to the abandonment of Vattel's framework, but the nineteenth-century shift from natural law to positivism was probably the underlying cause, for this shift made it difficult to maintain that there were rules of international law which were

---

[95] *Ibid.*, 589; see also J. Story, *Commentaries on the Conflict of Laws*, 2nd edn. (Boston: Little & Brown, 1841), §38.

[96] 38 US 589. Apart from a later quotation of *Bank of Augusta* in another comity case, this is the only time the phrase 'voluntary law of nations' appears in an opinion of the US Supreme Court. When Justice Chase referred to this category in *Ware*, he used the word 'general' rather than 'voluntary'.

[97] H. Wheaton, *Elements of International Law*, 3rd edn. (Philadelphia, PA: Lea & Blanchard, 1846), §15.

[98] *Ibid.* This comment does not appear in Wheaton's 1st edn., which recites Vattel's categories with apparent approval. See Wheaton, *Elements*, *supra* n. 93, §13 (1836). The criticism first appears in H. Wheaton, *History of the Law of Nations in Europe and America from the Earliest Times to the Treaty of Washington* (New York: Gould, Banks & Co., 1845), 189, and was picked up in the 3rd edn. of *Elements* published the following year.

[99] Halleck, *International Law*, *supra* n. 93, ch. 2, §11.

binding without consent. The differences between natural law and positivism are often illustrated by comparing two cases involving the slave trade – Justice Story's circuit court decision in *United States* v. *The La Jeune Eugenie*,[100] and Chief Justice Marshall's opinion in *The Antelope*.[101] Story concluded that the slave trade violated the law of nations because it was contrary to natural law. Adopting a framework very much like Vattel's, Story wrote that:

> the law of nations may be deduced, first, from the general principles of right and justice, applied to the concerns of individuals, and thence to the relations and duties of nations; or, secondly, in things indifferent or questionable, from the customary observances and recognitions of civilized nations; or, lastly, from the conventional or positive law, that regulates the intercourse between states.[102]

Although the law of nations might be 'modified by practice', that was only on 'things indifferent or questionable' or, in other words, on issues not controlled by natural law, for 'no practice whatsoever can obliterate the fundamental distinction between right and wrong'.[103] In *The Antelope*, Chief Justice Marshall was willing to concede that the slave trade was 'contrary to the law of nature',[104] but he thought 'the test of international law' was different.[105] '[A] jurist must search for [the] legal solution, in those principles of action which are sanctioned by the usages, the national acts, and the general assent, of that portion of the world of which he considers himself as a part.'[106] The slave trade could not be considered contrary to the law of nations because it 'was authorized and protected by the laws of all commercial nations; the right to carry on which was claimed by each, and allowed by each'.[107]

The US Supreme Court did not suddenly convert from natural law to positivism between 1822 and 1825. In *The Prize Cases* decided in 1863, for example, the Court would state that '[t]he law of nations is also called the law of nature; it is founded on the common consent as well as the common sense of the world'.[108] But by 1872, the Supreme Court seems to have completed the shift to a positivist definition. 'Like all the laws of nations', Justice Strong wrote in *The Scotia*, the law of the sea 'rests upon the common consent of civilized communities. It is of force, not because it was prescribed by any superior power, but because it has been generally accepted as a rule of conduct.'[109] At the turn of the twentieth century,

---

[100] 26 F. Cas. 832 (CCC Mass. 1822).   [101] 23 US 66 (1825).   [102] 26 F. Cas. 846.
[103] *Ibid.*   [104] 23 US 120.   [105] *Ibid.*, 121.   [106] *Ibid.*   [107] *Ibid.*, 115.
[108] 67 US 635, 670 (1863).   [109] 81 US 170, 187 (1872).

Justice Gray followed this positivist approach in *The Paquete Habana*, looking 'to the customs and usages of civilized nations' to find 'the general consent of the civilized nations of the world'.[110]

The shift from natural law to positivism can also be tracked in the treatise writers. The first edition of Wheaton's *Elements of International Law* published in 1836 did not take a position on the theoretical foundations of the law of nations, though its general approach may fairly be characterised as positivist. 'The principle aim of the Author has been to glean from these sources [cabinets, courts and legislative assemblies] the general principles which may fairly be considered to have received the asset of most civilized and Christian nations.'[111] Among the sources of international law, the 1st edition listed '[t]he rules of conduct which ought to be observed between nations, as deduced by reason from the nature of the society existing among independent states' along with text writers, international tribunals, national ordinances, history and treaties.[112] The 3rd edition includes the same list, adding 'the written opinions of official jurists, given confidentially to their own governments'.[113] But two posthumous editions – the 6th by Lawrence in 1855 and the 8th by Dana in 1866, both supposedly based on final changes Wheaton made before his death – omit 'rules of conduct ... deduced by reason' from the list of sources.[114] Lawrence's *Wheaton* and Dana's *Wheaton* were the editions most widely used during the nineteenth century and most relied upon by the Supreme Court.

Wheaton's move towards positivism was not uniformly reflected in other writers of the age. Sir Robert Phillimore's *Commentaries upon International Law* were written in England, but an edition was published in Philadelphia in 1854 and was repeatedly cited by the US Supreme Court. According to Phillimore, international law was 'enacted by the will of God'.[115] Custom might 'outwardly express the consent of nations to things which are *naturally*, that is by the law of God, binding upon them', but in this case custom was 'the effect and not the cause'.[116] A rule could be based on custom alone only when natural law was 'indifferent'.[117] In his 1861 treatise *International Law*, the American

---

[110] 175 US 677, 700, 708 (1900).   [111] Wheaton, *Elements, supra* n. 93, iii (1836).

[112] *Ibid.*, §14.   [113] Wheaton, *Elements, supra* n. 97, §16 (1846).

[114] See H. Wheaton, *Elements of International Law*, 6th edn. (W. B. Lawrence (ed.), 1855), §12; H. Wheaton, *Elements of International Law*, 8th edn. (R. H. Dana (ed.), 1866), §15.

[115] Phillimore, *Commentaries, supra* n. 93, v.   [116] *Ibid.*

[117] *Ibid.* Phillimore repeatedly takes care to distinguish between custom and natural law, even when doing so is 'of not much practical importance'. *Ibid.*, vol. I, 274; see also *ibid.*, vol. II, 125.

writer Henry Halleck defined international law in a functional way – as *'The rules of conduct regulating the intercourse of states'* – trying to avoid the whole question of sources 'upon which there is very little prospect of agreement'.[118] But when he came to discuss the relationship between natural and positive law, he followed Phillimore, whom he quoted at length.[119]

Viewing the question from the perspective of 1880, the English writer William Hall observed in his treatise *International Law* that 'the majority of writers' believed international law to be founded on natural law or, as he put it, on 'an absolute right which is assumed to exist and to be capable of being discovered'.[120] Nevertheless, Hall noted, 'a considerable number' of these 'practically refer to positive law as the only evidence of what is right'.[121] Hall, however, was a positivist in theory as well as practice. He doubted there could be any agreement on the absolute standard of natural law,[122] and even if there could be, he felt that such moral obligations could not become legally binding unless 'received as positive law by the body of states'.[123] But it was Lassa Oppenheim's *International Law*, published just after the turn of the twentieth century, that gave the positivist theory its familiar, modern form.[124] Oppenheim flatly asserted that international law, like all law, was based on 'the common consent of the community'.[125]

The shift from natural law to positivism during the nineteenth century might well have undermined the idea that there could be any binding rules of customary international law at all. For Vattel, if a rule was based solely on consent, then a nation could free itself from the rule by withdrawing that consent; the most that was required was advance notice to other nations.[126] One can see the same idea at work in *The Schooner Exchange* v. *McFaddon*: because sovereign immunity was based on consent it could be withdrawn.[127] Wheaton, whose writings dominated American thinking around the middle of the nineteenth century, asserted that this was true of all the rules of the law of nations. In his

---

[118] Halleck, *International Law* , *supra* n. 93, ch. 2, §1.   [119] See *ibid.*, ch. 2, §6.

[120] Hall, *International Law*, *supra* n. 93, 1.   [121] *Ibid.*, 1–2.   [122] *Ibid.*, 2.   [123] *Ibid.*, 4.

[124] L. Oppenheim, *International Law. A Treatise* (New York: Longmans, Green & Co., 1905).

[125] *Ibid.*, §4; see also *ibid.*, §12 ('The customary rules of this law have grown up by common consent of the States – that is, the different States have acted in such a manner as includes their tacit consent to these rules').

[126] See Vattel, *The Law of Nations*, *supra* n. 26, Prelim. §§25–6.

[127] 11 US 116, 146 (1812).

1845 *History*, Wheaton observed that ambassadors were 'exempt from the local jurisdiction by the consent of that state', noting that such consent could be withdrawn only at the risk of retaliation.[128] 'The same thing may be affirmed of all the usages which constitute the law of nations', he continued. 'They may be disregarded by those who choose to declare themselves absolved from the obligation of that law, and to incur the risk of retaliation from the party specially injured by its violation, or of the general hostility of mankind.'[129] Though absent from the editions of Wheaton's *Elements* published during his lifetime, this passage was repeated in the introductions of both Lawrence's *Wheaton* and Dana's *Wheaton*, which were published (and widely relied upon) after his death.[130] One can see the hint of sanctions for the withdrawal of consent in Wheaton's mention of retaliation, but his statement that the law of nations 'may be disregarded by those who choose to declare themselves absolved from the obligation of that law' bears the stamp of early nineteenth-century thinking. Phillimore similarly recognised the right of nations to depart from those rules based only on customs and usages. '[I]n no instance are they to be lightly departed from by any single nation; never without due notice conveyed to other countries, and then only in those cases in which it may be competent to a nation so to act'.[131]

But beginning around the middle of the nineteenth century the idea began to develop that a general practice of States could give rise to a universally binding rule which individual States could not disclaim. Reflecting upon Vattel's customary law of nations in 1861, Halleck wrote:

> The foregoing remark of Vattel, that the customary law of nations may be varied or abandoned at pleasure, such variation or abandonment being previously notified, must be limited to the peculiar customs of particular states in their intercourse with other nations, and cannot be applied to general law, or what he calls the voluntary law of nations, which is founded on general usage or implied consent.[132]

Adapting Vattel to a more positivist age, Halleck identified 'the customary law of nations' with customs between particular States (what we would today call 'special custom'[133]) and 'the voluntary law of nations'

---

[128] Wheaton, *History*, *supra* n. 98, 96 (1845).   [129] *Ibid.*

[130] See Lawrence's *Wheaton*, *supra* n. 114, §5; Dana's *Wheaton*, *supra* n. 114, §5.

[131] Phillimore, *Commentaries*, *supra* n. 93, 70. Phillimore denied that nations could depart from natural or divine law, see *ibid.*, 62–3, which for him was the most important part of international law.

[132] Halleck, *International Law*, *supra* n. 93, ch. 2, §9.

[133] See *Restatement (Third)*, *supra* n. 2, §102, cmt. *e.*

with 'general usage'.[134] But the key move in the passage was that it explicitly denied the right of nations to depart from rules based on 'general usage'. Two decades later, Hall also took the position that general practice could create a rule binding even on nations which had not agreed to it. He observed that the provisions of the 1856 Declaration of Paris, which abolished privateering:

> cannot in strictness be said to be at present part of international law, because they have not received the adherence of the United States; but if the signataries [*sic*] to it continue to act upon those provisions, the United States will come under an obligation to conform its practice to them in a time which will depend upon the number and importance of the opportunities which other states may possess of manifesting their persistent opinions.[135]

For Oppenheim, writing in 1905, 'common consent' meant 'the express or tacit consent of . . . an overwhelming majority'.[136] 'It is therefore not necessary to prove for every single rule of International Law that every single member of the Family of Nations consented to it.'[137] Moreover:

> no State which is a member of the Family of Nations can at some time or another declare that it will in future no longer submit to a certain recognized rule of the Law of Nations. The body of the rules of this law can be altered by common consent only, not by a unilateral declaration on the part of one State.[138]

Thus, by the turn of the twentieth century, the customary law of nations was no longer optional, as it had been for Vattel, Wheaton and Phillimore. General practice could give rise to a universally binding rule.

As it moved from natural law to positivism, the US Supreme Court also seemed to adopt this shift in the definition of consent. 'Like all the laws of nations', Justice Strong wrote in *The Scotia*, the law of the sea

---

[134] Richard Wildman's 1849 treatise similarly identified Vattel's customary law with specific custom and his voluntary law with general custom, suggesting that only the former could be abandoned at pleasure. See R. Wildman, *Institutes of International Law* (London: William Benning & Co., 1849), 33. Wildman was little cited by the Supreme Court, however, and whatever impact he had in America on this particular point seems to have been through Halleck.

[135] Hall, *International Law*, *supra* n. 93, 12. At the start of the Spanish–American War, President McKinley proclaimed that the 'war should be conducted upon principles in harmony with the present views of nations and sanctioned by their recent practice', Proclamation No. 8, 30 Stat. 1770, 1770–1 (1898), and the United States did not engage in privateering.

[136] Oppenheim, *International Law*, *supra* n. 124, §11.   [137] *Ibid.*, §12.   [138] *Ibid.*

'rests upon the *common consent* of civilized communities. It is of force, not because it was prescribed by any superior power, but because it has been *generally accepted* as a rule of conduct.'[139] It was sufficient that the rules which the Court applied had been accepted by 'almost all' the nations that had commercial shipping on the Atlantic.[140] Such rules 'when generally accepted became of universal obligation'.[141] At the turn of the century, Justice Gray would quote this language in *The Paquete Habana*,[142] another opinion which makes repeated reference to 'the general consent of civilized nations'.[143]

At the start of the nineteenth century, then, there were two categories of unwritten international law which were externally binding: (1) the voluntary law of nations, based on natural law, from which States could not depart; and (2) the customary law of nations, based on usages, from which they could. By the end of the century, there was a single category of unwritten international law. It was based on general consent through State practice, and individual States were not at liberty to depart from it. The shift from individual to general consent could have led to the re-establishment of the idea that the legislature could not violate international law. Indeed, in *Miller* v. *United States*, decided in 1871, two justices declared that a statute could not violate the laws of war, which were 'no less binding upon Congress than if the limitation were written in the Constitution'.[144] But this idea did not take hold. Instead, the Court would adopt the position expressed in *The Paquete Habana* that customary international law was applicable 'where there is no treaty and no controlling executive or legislative act or judicial decision'.[145] Why the relationship between statutes and customary international law took this turn is not entirely clear, but it may be attributable to the emergence of dualism in the Supreme Court's jurisprudence during the second half of the nineteenth century. This dualism had two aspects. First, it viewed the international and the domestic as separate legal orders. Second, it

---

[139] 81 US 170, 187 (1872) (emphasis added). [140] *Ibid.*, 188. [141] *Ibid.*, 187.
[142] 175 US 677, 711 (1900). [143] *Ibid.*, at 701, 708, 711.
[144] 78 US 268, 316 (1871) (Field, J., dissenting). Justice Field's dissent made no reference to general consent as the basis for the law of nations. Rather, he explained that 'the rules and limitations prescribed by that law were in the contemplation of the parties who framed and the people who adopted the Constitution', *ibid*. This suggests that international law did not bind Congress *proprio vigore* but only by implicit incorporation in the Constitution. The majority did not reach any of these questions, since it found Congress' rules to be consistent with international law. *Ibid.*, at 305.
[145] 175 US at 700.

considered international law to be part of the domestic legal order only to the extent it had been adopted by domestic law.

The separation of the international and domestic legal orders can perhaps be seen most clearly in the Supreme Court's decisions adopting the later-in-time rule with respect to treaties.[146] In 1871, the Supreme Court held for the first time that '[a] treaty may supersede a prior act of Congress, and an act of Congress may supersede a prior treaty'.[147] In the *Head Money Cases*, the Court extended this holding to treaties with foreign nations and established it, at least in part, on the basis of dualism. 'A treaty is primarily a compact between independent nations. It depends for the enforcement of its provisions on the interest and the honor of the governments which are parties to it. If these fail, its infraction becomes the subject of international negotiations and reclamations.'[148] A treaty might contain provisions 'which partake of the nature of municipal law', but their domestic effect depended not on international law but on the US Constitution, which gives a treaty 'no superiority over an act of Congress'.[149] The Court repeated these observations in *Whitney* v. *Robertson*, adding that '[i]f the country with which the treaty is made is dissatisfied with the action of the legislative department, it may present its complaint to the executive head of the government ... The courts can afford no redress.'[150] And in the *Chinese Exclusion Case*, the Court noted that '[t]he question whether our government is justified in disregarding its engagements with another nation is not one for the determination of the courts'.[151] In each of these cases, the Supreme Court treated the international obligation and the domestic force of treaties as different things, the former being beyond judicial cognisance and the later being subject to the control of Congress. None of these cases spoke directly to Congress' authority to supersede customary international law, and there are reasons one might distinguish between treaties and customary international law and apply the later-in-time rule only to treaties.[152] Indeed Justice Field, who wrote the Court's decision in both *Whitney* and the *Chinese Exclusion Case*, also claimed that the law of nations was 'no less binding upon Congress than if the limitation were written in the

---

[146] On the development of this rule with respect to treaties, see Vagts, 'The United States and its Treaties', *supra* n. 6, 313–23.

[147] *The Cherokee Tobacco*, 78 US 616, 621 (1871).   [148] 112 US 580, 598 (1884).

[149] *Ibid.*   [150] 124 US 190, 194 (1888).   [151] 130 US 581, 602 (1889).

[152] See L. Henkin, 'The Constitution and United States Sovereignty. A Century of *Chinese Exclusion* and Its Progeny', *Harvard Law Review*, 100 (1987), 853–86, 874–5.

Constitution'.[153] But acknowledging that Congress had the power to depart from one kind of international law made it more difficult to assert that Congress could not depart from the other.

The second aspect of dualism – that international law was part of the domestic legal order only to the extent it was adopted by domestic law – first appeared in Justice Bradley's 1875 opinion for the US Supreme Court in *The Lottawanna*:

> [I]t is hardly necessary to argue that the maritime law is only so far operative as law in any country as it is adopted by the laws and usages of that country. In this respect it is like international law or the laws of war, which have the effect of law in no country any further than they are accepted and received as such . . . Each State adopts the maritime law, not as a code having any independent or inherent force, *proprio vigore*, but as its own law, with such modifications and qualifications as it sees fit.[154]

The Court repeated this adoption theory in a series of cases involving general maritime law.[155] It is not clear that *The Lottawanna* marked a major shift in practice. Bradley's opinion acknowledged the power of the courts as well as Congress to adopt international law,[156] and the Court had long recognised Congress' authority to alter the law of prize.[157] But *The Lottawanna* did mark a major shift in theory. In the early nineteenth century, the Supreme Court began with the assumption that international law was part of the domestic legal order unless Congress made an affirmative decision to the contrary. As Chief Justice Marshall wrote in *The Nereide*, '[t]ill such an act be passed, the Court is bound by the law of nations which is a part of the law of the land'.[158] *The Lottawanna* began

---

[153] *Miller* v. *United States*, 78 US 268, 316 (1871), *supra* n. 20 (Field, J., dissenting).

[154] 88 US 558, 572–3 (1875).

[155] See, e.g., *The John G. Stevens*, 170 US 113, 126–7 (1898); *Ralli* v. *Troop*, 157 US 386, 407 (1895); *Ex parte Garnett*, 141 US 1, 13 (1891); *Butler* v. *Boston & Savannah SS Co.*, 130 US 527, 556 (1889); *Liverpool & GW Steam Co.* v. *Phoenix Ins. Co.*, 129 US 397, 444 (1889); *The Scotland*, 105 US 24, 29 (1882). Bradley clearly thought his adoption theory applied to all customary international law, as the quotation from *The Lottawanna* (*supra* n. 154) shows. Indeed, he repeated it the following year in a dissent involving the laws of war. See *New York Life Ins. Co.* v. *Hendren*, 92 US 286, 287–8 (1876) (Bradley, J., dissenting).

[156] See *The Lottawanna*, 88 US 558 (1875), 571. Later decisions make this more explicit. See, e.g., *The John G. Stevens*, 170 US at 126–7, *supra* n. 155 ('the general maritime law is in force in this country, or in any other, so far only as administered in its courts or adopted by its own laws and usages').

[157] See, e.g., *Thirty Hogsheads of Sugar* v. *Boyle*, 13 US 191, 198 (1815); *The Hampton*, 72 US 372, 376 (1866).

[158] 13 US 388, 423 (1815).

with the opposite assumption – that international law was not part of the domestic legal order until it had been adopted by Congress or the courts. The adoption theory reinforced the idea that Congress could change international law as applied in American courts, for the greater power to adopt included the lesser power to make alterations.

All these changes during the nineteenth century – the shift from natural law to positivism; the shift from individual to general consent; and the dualism of international and domestic law – were reflected in the Supreme Court's *Paquete Habana* decision at the turn of the century. The question in that case was whether coastal fishing vessels captured during the Spanish–American War were subject to condemnation as prize. Justice Gray found the applicable rule of international law in 'the customs and usages of civilized nations'.[159] He looked to treatise writers not for deductions from natural law but for compilations of State practice – 'not for the speculations of their authors concerning what the law ought to be, but for trustworthy evidence of what the law really is'.[160] Justice Gray also adopted *The Scotia*'s rule that general practice can give rise to 'universal obligation'[161] and referred repeatedly to 'the general consent of civilized nations'.[162] And while *The Paquete Habana*'s famous paragraph begins with a seemingly monist declaration that '[i]nternational law is part of our law, and must be ascertained and administered by the courts of justice of appropriate jurisdiction as often as questions of right depending upon it are duly presented for their determination',[163] that declaration is quickly qualified. Courts look to customary international law, Gray explains, 'where there is no treaty and no controlling executive or legislative act or judicial decision'.[164]

The twentieth century

The stage was thus set for the adoption of the later-in-time rule in the twentieth century. Beginning in the 1920s, US courts began to rely on a combination of dualism generally, the Supreme Court's later-in-time

---

[159] 175 US 677, 700 (1900).   [160] *Ibid.*   [161] *Ibid.*, 711.   [162] *Ibid.*, 701, 708, 711.
[163] *Ibid.*, 700.
[164] *Ibid.* Justice Gray certainly did not dissent from the emerging dualism of the age. He had repeated *The Lottawanna*'s adoption theory with respect to general maritime law in three opinions for the Court, see *The John G. Stevens*, 170 US 126–7, *supra* n. 155 *Ralli* v. *Troop*, 157 US 407, *supra* n. 155; *Liverpool & GW Steam Co.*, 129 US 444, *supra* n. 155, and had joined the Court's decisions in the *Head Money Cases*, *Whitney* and the *Chinese Exclusion Case*.

treaty cases, and *The Paquete Habana*'s dictum to hold that an act of Congress could supersede a rule of customary international law.[165]

One of the leading authorities for the later-in-time rule is *The Over the Top*.[166] The United States sought the forfeiture of a British ship and its cargo on the grounds that the ship had sold whiskey to an Internal Revenue agent nineteen miles off the coast of the United States. The ship's owner argued that under international law the jurisdiction of the United States extended only three miles from shore, but according to the court this argument rested on 'a misconception . . . as to the status, in a federal forum of so-called international law when that law encounters a municipal enactment'.[167] The court cited no authority, but it based its position squarely on dualism. 'International practice is law only in so far as we adopt it, and like all common or statute law it bends to the will of the Congress.'[168]

The other case cited by the *Restatement (Third)* in support of the rule is *Tag* v. *Rogers*.[169] *Tag* involved the seizure of German property during the Second World War under the Trading with the Enemy Act, a seizure alleged to violate 'a practice amounting to an authoritative declaration of international law forbidding the seizure or confiscation of the property of enemy nationals during time of war'.[170] Sitting by designation, retired Supreme Court Justice Burton wrote that '[w]hatever force appellant's argument might have in a situation where there is no applicable treaty, statute, or constitutional provision, it has long been settled in the United States that the federal courts are bound to recognize any one of these sources of law as superior to canons of international law'.[171] If one hears

---

[165] After publication of the *Restatement (Third)* in 1987, *supra* n. 2, courts also began to cite section 115, see, e.g., *In re Agent Orange Product Liability Litigation*, 373 F.Supp. 2d 598 (2000) (EDNY 2005); *Taveras-Lopez* v. *Reno*, 127 F.Supp. 2d 598, 609 (MD Penn. 2000), although the rule was well established by then.

[166] 5 F.2d 838 (D. Conn. 1925).   [167] *Ibid.*, 842.

[168] *Ibid.* In the end, the court held for the ship owner by applying *The Charming Betsy* presumption. In another Prohibition era case, the Supreme Court rejected an argument based on 'the antiquity of the practice of carrying intoxicating liquors for beverage purposes as part of a ship's sea stores', *Cunard SS Co.* v. *Mellon*, 262 US 100, 129 (1923). The Court noted that 'the avowed and obvious purpose of both the [eighteenth] amendment and the [national prohibition] act was to put an end to prior practices respecting such liquors, even though the practices had the sanction of antiquity, generality and statutory recognition', *ibid.* Because the Court's decision was based in part on a constitutional provision, it does not provide clear authority for the later-in-time rule.

[169] 267 F.2d 664 (DC Cir. 1959).   [170] *Ibid.*, 666.   [171] *Ibid.*

an echo here of *The Paquete Habana*, it is confirmed by Burton's quotation of that case in the accompanying footnote.[172]

The most careful modern consideration of the issue is found in the *CUSCLIN* case,[173] where Judge Mikva relied on a combination of dualism, treaty cases and *The Paquete Habana* to reject the argument that Congress' funding of the Contras in Nicaragua should be enjoined because it violated customary international law. The Plaintiffs argued that the United States was bound by customary international law to obey the judgment of the International Court of Justice (ICJ) in the *Nicaragua* case.[174] But Judge Mikva reasoned that even on the assumption that Congress' decision to disregard an ICJ judgment was a violation of customary international law, that violation was not cognisable:

> Once again, the United States' rejection of a purely 'monist' view of the international and domestic legal orders shapes our analysis. Statutes inconsistent with principles of customary international law may well lead to international law violations. But within the domestic legal realm, that inconsistent statute simply modifies or supersedes customary international law to the extent of the inconsistency.[175]

The 'Once again' referred to the court's earlier discussion of statutes and treaties.[176] The Supreme Court's decision in the *Head Money Cases*, Judge Mikva wrote, 'reflects the United States' adoption of a partly "dualist" – rather than strictly "monist" – view of international and domestic law'.[177] Judge Mikva then turned to *The Paquete Habana*. He acknowledged that its statement about 'controlling legislative acts' was *dictum*, but he read it as having nevertheless 'laid down [the rule] that subsequently enacted statutes would preempt existing principles of customary international law – just as they displaced prior inconsistent treaties'.[178]

In only one line of cases during the twentieth century did American courts allow customary international law to trump Federal statutes. In 1885, Congress gave the Court of Claims jurisdiction to hear claims of American citizens for spoliation by the French reaching back to the

---

[172] *Ibid.*, 666 n. 8.
[173] *Committee of United States Citizens Living in Nicaragua [CUSCLIN] v. Reagan*, 859 F.2d 929 (DC Cir. 1988).
[174] *Case Concerning Military and Paramilitary Activities in and Against Nicaragua* (*Nicaragua v. United States of America*), 1986 ICJ Rep. 14. For the Supreme Court's latest statement on the force of ICJ judgments, see *Medellín v. Texas*, 552 U.S. 491 (2008).
[175] 859 F.2d 938.   [176] *Ibid.*, 936–8.   [177] *Ibid.*, 937.   [178] *Ibid.*, 939.

1790s.[179] In 1927, it similarly authorised the Court of Claims to hear foreign claims against the United States arising from the First World War.[180] In both contexts, the Court of Claims consistently rejected arguments that it should give effect to US statutes over customary international law.[181] What made these cases different was that Congress had authorised the court to decide them in accordance with international law. As the court explained, its position was 'not different than it would be if we sat as an arbitration tribunal, chosen by agreement of the nations involved, to decide the questions here presented upon the basis of the law of nations as applied to the facts in the case'.[182] In a sense, then, these cases also reflected the dualism of the age. The later-in-time rule operated only on the level of domestic law. On the international plane the United States was bound by customary international law notwithstanding domestic statutes to the contrary.

Conclusion

Like the later-in-time rule with respect to treaties, the notion that Federal statutes can supersede customary international law as a rule of decision does not reflect the original understanding. Early Americans understood that Congress could depart only from the 'customary law of nations' based on practice and not from the 'voluntary law of nations' based on natural law, even if they sometimes played fast and loose with which rules belonged in which categories. But a series of shifts during the nineteenth century obscured the original understanding and finally made it untenable. Judges and treatise writers lost faith in natural law as a basis for binding international rules and turned to a positivism based on State practice and consent. At the same time, the requirement of consent changed from individual to general. Nations could no longer declare, as they could throughout the first part of the nineteenth century, that they would not be bound by a rule of customary international law. Dualism was the final piece of the puzzle. The separation of the international and domestic legal orders and the theory of adoption reinforced the idea that Congress could reject customary international law. All of

---

[179] Act of January 20, 1885, ch. 25, §3, 23 Stat. 283.

[180] Act of March 3, 1927, ch. 463, 44 Stat. 1838.

[181] See *Royal Holland Lloyd* v. *United States*, 73 Ct Cl. 722, 736–7 (1931); *The Jane*, 37 Ct Cl. 24, 29 (1901); *The Rose*, 36 Ct Cl. 290, 301 (1901); *The Nancy*, 27 Ct Cl. 99, 109 (1892).

[182] *Royal Holland Lloyd*, 73 Ct Cl. at 736–7, *supra* n. 181.

these currents came together in *The Paquete Habana*. Its statement that customary international law could be superseded by 'controlling ... legislative acts' was pure *dictum*. But the decision accurately reflected nineteenth-century changes in thinking about international law and its place in the US legal system, changes which made adoption of the later-in-time rule with respect to customary international law all but inevitable.

27

Mediation and civil justice: a public–private partnership?

PETER L. MURRAY[*]

Introduction

For the last thirty years in the United States and for the last ten years in England, Germany, Italy and other continental systems, various forms of mediation have been increasingly incorporated into the processes of civil justice. Interparty mediation by neutral third parties to facilitate settlements of civil disputes has become more and more commonplace in all public processes of dispute resolution. This mediation can take several forms, ranging from informal efforts by the trial judge to encouraging parties to settle the pending dispute to highly formalised settlement proceedings conducted by private professional mediators retained by the parties or appointed by the court.

To date, court-annexed mediation has met with a generally enthusiastic reception by parties, courts, lawyers and academics. There is an abundant literature documenting the value of mediative techniques to facilitate case settlement, both anecdotally and statistically.[1] The predominant tone of academic literature to date praises mediation for its

---

[*] The author thanks Renée Flaherty, Harvard Law School Class of 2011, for her assistance in preparing this chapter for publication. Professor Vagts' wide-ranging interests have included all processes for dispute resolution on a national, as well as an international scale and the performance of these systems under stress. See, e.g., D. F. Vagts and P. L. Murray, 'Litigating the Nazi Labor Claims. The Path not Taken', *Harvard International Law Journal*, 43 (2002), 503–31. Vital to the consideration of any system of criminal adjudication or civil dispute resolution is the extent to which core values of neutrality, independence, transparency and systemic accountability are embodied and maintained.

[1] See, e.g., O. Chase, *Law Culture and Ritual. Disputing Systems in Cross-Cultural Context* (New York University Press, 2005), chapter 6; O. Fiss and Judith Resnik, *Adjudication and Its Alternatives* (Westbury, NY: Foundation Press, 2003); Th. Hitter, 'What is So Special About the Federal Circuit? A Recommendation for ADR Use in the Federal Circuit', *Federal Circuit Bar Journal*, 13 (2004), 441–74, 443; F. Neate, 'Mediation. A Constructive Approach

flexibility, maintenance of party autonomy, ability to save costs of contested proceedings and the value of termination of disputes by agreement.[2] Court decisions, on the other hand, are discounted as expensive, delayed and often not well adapted to the parties' real needs.[3]

The American civil justice system, with its high level of adversariality and expensive cost profile based on the jury trial model, has offered particularly fertile ground for the growth of alternative dispute resolution (ADR) and incorporation of ADR into public justice processes. Incorporation of ADR modalities in civil justice processes has proceeded more slowly in Europe. In some legal cultures, such as Germany, judges have traditionally exercised a mediative function to encourage settlements at various points during the course of litigation, thus reducing the need for additional settlement facilitative services.[4] In other countries it has taken time for an entrepreneurial ADR culture and industry to develop. However, as of the present time, various forms of ADR services, primarily mediation, are beginning to appear on a regular basis in civil litigation in many Civil law as well as Common law jurisdictions.[5]

As mediation has become more ubiquitous in American civil justice and more seriously considered in other countries, the initial unconditional enthusiasm with which it has been regarded has become tempered

---

to Dispute Resolution', in G. Aksen *et al. Global Reflections on International Law, Commerce and Dispute Resolution* (Paris: ICC Publishing, 2005), 557.

[2] See, e.g., L. L. Riskin, 'Mediation and Lawyers', 43 *Ohio State Law Journal*, 43 (1982), 29–60, 34 ('Mediation offers some clear advantages over adversary processing: it is cheaper, faster, and potentially more hospitable to unique solutions that take more fully into account nonmaterial interests of the disputants'); *idem.*, 'Understanding Mediators' Orientations, Strategies and Techniques. A Grid for the Perplexed', *Harvard Negotiation Law Review*, 1 (1996), 7 52, 18 (describing problem definition as '[t]he focus of a mediation – its subject matter and the problems or issues it seeks to address'); L. Rozdeiczer and F. E. A. Sander, 'Matching Cases and Dispute Resolution Procedures. Detailed Analysis Leading to a Mediation-Centred Approach', *Harvard Negotiation Law Review*, 11 (2006), 1–42, 33–4 (advocating mediation as a starting-point in resolving disputes because of its flexibility and likelihood to lead to settlement).

[3] See Hitter, 'What is So Special About the Federal Circuit?', *supra* n. 1, 111; Riskin, 'Mediation and Lawyers', *supra* n. 2, 34.

[4] See, e.g., P. L. Murray, 'ADR und die amerikanische Ziviljustiz', in P. Gottwald (ed.), *Aktuelle Entwicklungen des europäischen und internationalen Zivilverfahrensrechts* (Current Developments of European and International Civil Procedure Law) (Bielefeld: Gieseking, 2002), 25; J. M. von Bargen, *Gerichtsinterne Mediation* (Tübingen: Mohr Siebeck, 2008), 65–6.

[5] See, e.g., H. E. Chodosh, 'The Eighteenth Camel. Mediating Mediation Reform in India', *German Law Journal*, 9 (2008), 251–84, 255–6; S. Higgs, 'Mediating Sustainability. The Public Interest Mediator in the New Zealand Environment Court', *Environmental Lawyer*, 37 (2007), 61–104.

with expressed concerns based on both systemic considerations and observations of ADR functioning in practice.[6] Some of these have been based on the private entrepreneurial nature of the American ADR industry and its effect on institutions of public justice.[7] Others relate to the need to maintain accountability and transparency in institutions of public justice, while providing ADR practitioners with the conditions of confidentiality and flexibility needed to foster fruitful settlement activity.[8] The pooled perspectives of proceduralists from Common law and Civil law frames of reference may well be able to contribute to developing solutions to these problems as they appear in their respective legal contexts.

Public and private mediation services

The notion of third-party facilitation of consensual resolution of private disputes is as old as the hills and extends far beyond the purview of what is now considered as civil justice. Various forms of mediative activity can be found in many contexts of personal and economic interaction between members of every human society. The forms of such facilitation, as well as the sources and roles of the mediators and the parties, are almost infinite in variety. This chapter is not intended to address this broad concept of mediation as a social or economic phenomenon. The focus of this discussion will be mediation in the context of those civil disputes which have been or are being presented to a civil court having the power to render a decision with respect to the subject matter of the dispute.

---

[6] See, e.g., L. Kratky Doré, 'Public Courts Versus Private Justice. It's Time to Let Some Sun Shine in on Alternative Dispute Resolution', *Chicago–Kent Law Review*, 81 (2006), 463–520; D. R. Hensler, 'Suppose It's Not True. Challenging Mediation Ideology', *Journal of Dispute Resolution*, (2002), 81–99; C. Menkel-Meadow, 'Are There Systemic Ethics Issues in Dispute System Design? And What We Should [Not] Do About It. Lessons from International and Domestic Fronts', *Harvard Negotiation Law Review*, 14 (2009), 195–231; N. A. Welsh, 'The Thinning Vision of Self-Determination in Court-Connected Mediation. The Inevitable Price of Institutionalization?', *Harvard Negotiation Law Review*, 6 (2001), 1–96.

[7] P. L. Murray, 'The Privatization of Civil Justice', *Zeitschrift für Zivilprozess International*, 12 (2007), 283–303. An abbreviated version is available at *Judicature*, 91 (2007–8), 272–5.

[8] See, e.g., E. Brunet, 'Questioning the Quality of Alternative Dispute Resolution', *Tulane Law Review*, 62 (1987), 1–56; J. Resnik, 'Many Doors? Closing Doors? Alternative Dispute Resolution and Adjudication', *Ohio State Journal on Dispute Resolution*, 10 (1995), 211–65.

Mediation programmes associated with institutions of civil justice are of two types. In a few cases in the United States and more frequently abroad, mediation services are provided by functionaries in the court system who are paid by public funds and do not receive compensation, directly or indirectly, from any private party. For instance, in many US Courts of Appeals appellate cases are diverted to mandatory mediation provided by retired judges or other court appointees who do not perform mediation services on a private fee-for services basis.[9] In some jurisdictions domestic relations case managers provide mediation services to parties in pre-divorce matters.[10] Public mediation in labour disputes has also been around for a long time.

In Germany, the Civil Procedure Code has long required judges to attempt to facilitate settlement discussions among the parties in all civil cases. Many German judges have no compunction about discussing possible settlements of pending cases with the parties.[11] Most American judges have historically been reluctant to discuss concrete settlement terms of pending litigation with the parties and their counsel, for fear of showing partiality or pre-judging the case. German judges are required to communicate their tentative conclusions of fact and law to the parties before reaching a final decision so that the parties can focus their arguments in the most effective fashion.[12] Thus it may not be so remarkable for them to share potential settlement scenarios as well.

---

[9] E.g. the First Circuit Court of Appeals mandates mediation of all civil appeals in a settlement programme run by a judge or a person appointed by the court. See Federal Rules of Appellate Procedure and First Circuit Local Rules, Rule 33, www.ca1.uscourts.gov/files/rules/rules.pdf. The Second Circuit also utilises mandatory mediation. Each case is randomly assigned to a circuit mediator employed by the court. See Second Circuit Civil Appeals Management Plan, www.ca2.uscourts.gov/staffcounsel.htm#Assignment. For a comprehensive assessment of court-annexed mediation in the US Courts of Appeals, see S. P. Davisson, 'Privatization and Self-Determination in the Circuits. Utilizing the Private Sector within the Evolving Framework of Federal Appellate Mediation', *Ohio State Journal on Dispute Resolution*, 21 (2006), 953–1003.

[10] In the State of Maine, family law magistrates function in a mediative capacity in working out with the parties provisions for custody, support and living arrangements pending divorce. See Maine Rules of Civil Procedure 110A (a). In Delaware, divorce and child custody mediation is scheduled as a pre-trial conference with a court staff mediator primarily to 'attempt amicable settlement of all unresolved issues'. See Delaware Family Court Civil Rules 16(a).

[11] See P. L. Murray and R. Stürner, *German Civil Justice* (Durham, NC: Carolina Academic Press, 2004), 487–90 for a discussion of the case settlement function of German judges.

[12] ZPO §139(4); Murray and Stürner, *German Civil Justice*, *supra* n. 11, 166–77.

In very recent years, a number of German pilot projects have augmented the trial judge's role in encouraging settlement by providing for court-annexed mediation services provided by another judge of the court in which the case is pending.[13] This development recognises the fact that in some cases parties might not be completely frank and ready to make concessions when they are talking with the judge who will decide their case. Judges who provide mediation receive special training for this function.[14] Although there is some development of private mediation in Germany, it is significant that almost all court-annexed mediation is currently being provided by the judicial establishment.[15]

The great bulk of mediation in civil justice contexts in the United States, however, is provided by private professional mediators who generally function on a fee-for-services basis. For example, since 2002 mediation has been required in most civil actions in the Maine Superior Court.[16] The parties may choose whomever they wish to mediate their controversy, failure to agree on a mediator results in appointment of a mediator from a list. All mediators are private professionals who charge on a fee-for-services basis. The fee of the mediator, whether chosen by the parties or nominated by the court, is paid by the parties, usually equally. If the mediation results in agreement, the mediated disposition is accepted and incorporated into the court's final judgment without further examination by the trial judge. This pattern holds for the great bulk of court-annexed mediation programmes in the United States.

---

[13] See von Bargen, *Gerichtsinterne Mediation*, *supra* n. 4, 70–114 for a comprehensive description and discussion of the various pilot projects for court-annexed mediation in Germany.

[14] The nature and extent of mediation training provided to participating judges varies among the pilot projects. In all cases it is substantial, generally of the order of 80–100 hours of training in the classroom and in simulated mediation proceedings. See von Bargen, *Gerichtsinterne Mediation*, *supra* n. 4, 73, 75, 78, 80, 82, 87, 91 for descriptions of some of the training provided in some of the projects.

[15] See von Bargen, *Gerichtsinterne Mediation*, *supra* n. 4, 62, where the author notes that although mandatory reference to private mediation has been tried in several German States, it has not been met with enthusiasm, ostensibly because of additional cost and delay involved in scheduling and conducting the mediation and compensating the private mediator. See also Murray, 'ADR und die amerikanische Ziviljustiz', *supra* n. 4, where the author notes that the quasi-mediative role of German judges in encouraging settlement discussions in ordinary civil cases has impeded the growth of a private mediation industry.

[16] See Maine Rules of Civil Procedure, 16B *supra*, n. 10, (adopted effective 1 January 2002); see also S. Press, 'Institutionalization of Mediation in Florida. At the Crossroads', *Pennsylvania State Law Review*, 108 (2003), 43–66, 55, for a discussion of Florida's extensive mandatory court-ordered mediation programme, which utilises private, licensed mediators.

The past thirty years has seen the development of a vibrant mediation profession with a large and growing number of full- and part-time mediators vying to provide mediation services on a fee basis in every one of the American States.[17] Until now this profession has been relatively unregulated, although recently there has been some regulation of mediators' qualifications.[18] In many States, however, parties required to mediate their cases by court rule or statute are entirely free to pick their mediator regardless of objective qualifications or licence requirements.[19]

At the outset of the mediation movement in the 1970s, mediation was very much a part-time occupation of persons who relied on other activities as their primary source of income. In recent years, however, the number of professionals who make their living from mediation and other ADR services has grown. In addition, mediations are now frequently performed by lawyers in law firms which offer such services as part of their professional practice offerings.[20] It is fair to say that there now exists a robust alternative dispute services profession, if not an industry, in the United States. Although this development is not as far advanced in Europe and East Asia, the trend seems to be somewhat in the same direction.[21]

---

[17] See, e.g., E. Plapinger and D. Stienstra, *ADR and Settlement in the Federal District Courts. A Sourcebook for Judges and Lawyers* (New York: Federal Judicial Center and CPR Institute of Dispute Resolution, 1996), 4 (describing mediation as 'the primary ADR process in the federal district courts'); Press, 'Institutionalization', *supra* n. 16, 55 (observing that Florida's '"official" statistics only tell part of the story because court-supported mediators and mediation programs exist alongside a thriving private mediator sector').

[18] This has taken place under the auspices of private associations of mediators as well as by statutory or court rule regulation. For instance, the Massachusetts Council on Family Mediation has adopted Standards of Practice for its members as well as a procedure of certification of mediators in family law matters, see www.mcfm.org. See J. M. Nolan-Haley, 'Lawyers, Non-Lawyers and Mediation. Rethinking the Professional Monopoly from a Problem-Solving Perspective', *Harvard Negotiation Law Review*, 7 (2002), 235–99, for a discussion of the relationship of mediation to the regulated practice of law.

[19] As noted above, this is true in the State of Maine. See Maine Rules of Civil Procedure 16B(h), *supra* n. 10. In Florida, the parties may agree upon a certified mediator or 'a mediator who does not meet the certification requirements of these rules, but who, in the opinion of the parties and upon review by the presiding judge, is otherwise qualified by training or experience to mediate all or some of the issues in the particular case'. Florida Rules of Civil Procedure 1.720(f)(1)(B).

[20] See, generally, B. G. Picker, 'ADR. New Challenges, New Roles and New Opportunities', *ADR Dispute Resolution Journal*, 56 (2001), 20–3.

[21] In England, courts routinely encourage resort to mediation during litigation and enforce their recommendations with stays pending mediation. See N. Andrews, *The Modern Civil Process* (Tübingen: Mohr Siebeck, 2008), 212–44. See von Bargen, *Gerichtsinterne Mediation*, *supra* n. 4, 7–11 for a discussion of the growing importance of mediation in

Problems with the private model

Even as privately provided mediation services have come to play an increasingly important role in the processes of American public civil justice, the enthusiasm with which mediation has been received has become tempered by some concern that certain attributes of private mediation services may be compromising vital values of public justice.[22] Mediators perform important roles in facilitating settlements of cases which have been confided to public justice for resolution. The potential of economic influence on their function from repeat players (see below), whose good will can enhance mediation fee income is at serious odds with the ideal that public justice should be totally insulated from such considerations. Mediation processes are conducted in an atmosphere of confidentiality to foster frank interchange among the parties. However, shrouding these activities in secrecy compromises the transparency of public justice functions and runs a risk that potential abuses in mediation processes may not be easily brought to light. Mediated settlements are routinely incorporated into court dispositions and are given the force of *res adjudicata*, even though there is no judicial review of their procedural fairness or substantive quality. Is public justice rubber-stamping results which would not stand the test of justice at all? Without taking anything away from the value of mediative techniques to promote settlement of litigated disputes, these considerations may suggest that the ongoing incorporation of private mediation into public justice will require more care and thoughtfulness to make sure that 'justice' does not suffer in the process.

Economic influence and impartiality

A person who is acting as mediator with respect to a matter in civil litigation exercises significant neutral power to structure and facilitate negotiations between the parties in order to promote settlement. While many mediators maintain that their role is purely facilitative, it is also clear that mediators' reactions to the parties' respective presentations, whether express or implied, can exercise subtle but significant pressure

---

Germany. The European Commission has also embraced mediation and has proposed a Directive on the topic. COM(2004) 718 final, Brussels, 22 October 2004.

[22] See, e.g., Murray, 'Privatization', *supra* n. 7; Brunet, 'Questioning the Quality of Alternative Dispute Resolution', *supra* n. 8.

toward settlement on a particular basis.[23] Some mediators are more ready to give feedback and evaluations of party positions than others.[24] However, all mediators have a certain amount of power to guide the parties in a particular direction toward a resolution, whether they exercise this power consciously or not.

At the same time, it has become increasingly clear that mediators who rely on the provision of mediation services for a living or as part of a professional practice are potentially subject to economic influence by parties or interests who are 'repeat players'.[25] Litigating parties who are required to participate in court-annexed mediation are almost always given the right to choose their mediators. A party such as a large corporate player or an insurance company which is frequently involved in litigation can be expected to exercise its right of choice in favour of mediators who have tended to facilitate satisfactory results in previous cases. By the same token, in many cases a mediator who is economically dependent on a flow of business cannot help but be aware that one of the mediating parties is likely to be the source of much more future business than the other.[26] The results of this kind of subtle, but real, economic influence on private mediators are very hard to gauge. Recent studies

[23] See Riskin, 'Understanding Mediators' Orientations', *supra* n. 2, 27–8 (1996) (describing the mediator techniques associated with evaluative mediation as proposing a settlement, pushing parties to accept a settlement, predicting court or other outcomes and assessing the strengths and weaknesses of each side's case).

[24] See K. K. Kovach and L. P. Love, '"Evaluative" Mediation Is an Oxymoron', *Alternatives to High Cost Litigation*, 14 (1996), 31–2; L. P. Love, 'The Top Ten Reasons Why Mediators Should Not Evaluate', *Florida State University Law Review*, 24 (1997), 937–48; R. B. Moberly, 'Mediator Gag Rules. Is It Ethical for Mediators to Evaluate or Advise?', *Southern Texas Law Review*, 38 (1997), 669–79, 675 (theorising that 'mediator evaluation can assist the parties in their self-determination efforts').

[25] Marc Galanter famously summarised the advantages of repeat players in his article entitled 'Why the "Haves" Come Out Ahead. Speculations on the Limits of Legal Change', *Law & Society Review*, 9 (1974), 95–160, 98–103. They include: '(1) experience leading to changes in how the repeat player structures the next similar transaction; (2) expertise, economies of scale, and access to specialist advocates; (3) informal continuing relationships with institutional incumbents; (4) reputation and credibility in bargaining; (5) long-term strategies facilitating risk-taking in appropriate cases; (6) influence over rules through lobbying other use of resources; (7) playing for precedent and favorable future rules; (8) distinguishing symbolic and actual defeats; and (9) resources invested in getting rules favorable to them implemented.' See also L. B. Bingham, 'On Repeat Players, Adhesive Contracts, and the Use of Statistics in Judicial Review of Employment Arbitration Awards', *McGeorge Law Review*, 29 (1998), 223–59.

[26] This structural incentive in private arbitration has been evident to observers of judicial and quasi-judicial institutions for some time. See, e.g., P. G. Carrington, 'Self-Deregulation, A "National Policy" of the Supreme Court', *Nevada Law Journal*, 3

have demonstrated a very marked influence of repeat players on private arbitrators.[27] While the influence of a mediator on a case result is more subtle than the ability of an arbitrator to make an award, the notion that a mediator has a private economic interest in the outcomes of her mediation activity is inconsistent with the standards of absolute neutrality and impartiality associated with public justice. It has been observed that it is a little ironic to maintain a civil justice system which is fully insulated from economic influence, and then to permit the great bulk of cases to be resolved under the auspices of private neutrals who are subject to the same economic influences from which we so rigorously insulate our judges.[28]

Party choice is not an adequate safeguard against this kind of economic interest. Parties likely to be disadvantaged by repeat-player bias of ADR neutrals have very little ability to get information about the performance of mediators or previous matters which they have mediated that have involved the same parties or interests.[29] Only the repeat player can keep score on mediators and other professionals whose services it retains. In the absence of a comprehensive mediator disclosure regime, the one-shot player, typically the personal injury plaintiff, the consumer, or the small commercial party, is at the mercy of the repeat player in the selection of mediators who may be subject to subtle economic interests to favour the repeat player's interests.

Opacity and public justice

Transparency and publicity have long been considered as core elements of public justice and fundamental guarantees of its fairness and regularity. In the United States, court records and proceedings are generally open to the public. Courtrooms and court records are closed and sealed only in the exceptional case and for good cause, generally in order to

---

(2002), 259–88; W. M. C. Weidemaier, 'Arbitration and the Individuation Critique', *Arizona Law Review*, 49 (2007), 69–112.

[27] See 'The Arbitration Trap. How Credit Card Companies Ensnare Consumers', *Public Citizen* (September 2007) for a well-documented study of this phenomenon in the credit card industry. See also C. Menkel-Meadow, 'Do the "Haves" Come Out Ahead in Alternative Judicial Systems? Repeat Players in ADR', *Ohio State Journal on Dispute Resolution*, 15 (1999), 19–61; Murray, 'Privatization', *supra* n. 7.

[28] See Murray, 'Privatization', *supra* n. 7, 300–3.

[29] ADR professionals have resisted required disclosure of prior engagements and participants. See J. Folberg, 'Arbitration Ethics. Is California the Future?', *Ohio State Journal on Dispute Resolution*, 18 (2003), 343–89, 347.

protect some highly vulnerable person or information. It is hard for an American jurist to think of civil justice other than as public justice.

The widespread incorporation of mediation as a mandatory element of civil justice systems is beginning to create a serious tension with the 'public' aspect of public civil justice. Mediators insist that successful mediation requires an atmosphere of confidentiality to induce the parties to speak out and interact with the mediator and each other in a free and untrammelled manner.[30] Traditional rules of evidence which deny evidentiary admissibility to settlement offers as well as discussions and conduct in the course of settlement negotiation are seen as inadequate guarantees of the level of confidentiality that the mediators deem desirable. Mediators wish to be able to assure parties that nothing that happens in the mediation will ever come to light outside it, either in the case being mediated or otherwise.

The mediators' campaign for confidentiality of mediation proceedings has culminated in the US Uniform Mediation Act (UMA).[31] Despite the generality of its title, this uniform law regulates primarily mediation confidentiality.[32] The Act creates a privilege for all statements made by any party or mediator in a mediation session and protects mediators from being called as witnesses, subject in each case to a relatively narrow range of exceptions.[33] Putting aside the logical incongruity of grouping mediation discussions on the same plane as lawyer–client, physician–patient and priest–penitent confidences, the comprehensiveness of the UMA privilege raises real questions about the appropriateness of such a cloak of secrecy about a process that is a part of public civil justice.[34] To require a party who has sought public justice to participate in a

---

[30] See, e.g., Andrews *The Modern Civil Process*, *supra* n. 21, 232–40; P. A. Kentra, 'Hear No Evil, See No Evil, Speak No Evil. The Intolerable Conflict for Attorney–Mediators Between the Duty to Maintain Mediation Confidentiality and the Duty to Report Fellow Attorney Misconduct', *Brigham Young University Law Review* (1997), 715–75, 722 ('Confidentiality lies at the heart of the mediation process. Mediation would not be nearly as effective if the parties were not assured their discussions would remain private'); C. McEwen, 'The Rule Moves Maine Backward', *Maine Bar Journal*, 24 (2009), 44–9; von Bargen, *Gerichtsinterne Mediation*, *supra* n. 4, 342.

[31] The Uniform Mediation Act (UMA) was adopted by the National Conference of Commissioners on Uniform State Laws in 2001. To date, ten American States have adopted the Act in whole or substantial part: the District of Columbia, Illinois, Iowa, Nebraska, New Jersey, Ohio, South Dakota, Utah, Vermont and Washington.

[32] See UMA §§7–8.   [33] UMA §4.

[34] Professor Judith Resnik has written extensively about the significance of publicity and community presence of institutions of civil justice. See, e.g., J. Resnik, *The Processes of Law. Understanding Courts and Their Alternatives* (New Haven, CT: Yale University

proceeding which is conducted by a private neutral and which is subject to a privilege that prevents subsequent judicial access to what happened there can make the concept of public justice somewhat hollow.[35] Considering the relatively high success rate of mediation in reaching case settlements, this means that for many cases the crucial neutral intervention which results in a disposition of the case takes place behind closed doors outside the purview of the public and is protected from later public scrutiny by a comprehensive privilege.

The opacity problem is exacerbated by the fact that generally no record is made of what transpires in mediation. The statements of parties and mediator to each other are not recorded in any way. No detailed report or protocol is made. Court rules which require parties to engage in mediation do not require that any record be made of the process. On the contrary, typical mandatory mediation court rules provide that if the mediation fails to produce agreement, the only report which shall be made is that no agreement was reached and that a report of a successful mediation is limited to describing the agreement reached.[36] Mediators are not required to keep any notes of the proceedings and routinely destroy any notes which they make in order to frustrate efforts to make them witnesses.[37]

Acknowledging the importance to negotiating parties of some kind of guarantee that their offers and responses in negotiation will not be used against them in the court case being negotiated, one can ask whether the degree of secrecy sought by the mediation industry is really needed to make mediation work. Certainly the importance of maintaining confidence in the transparency of public justice should be given serious weight in considering mediators' requests for ever-greater mediation secrecy.

Accountability of mediators

Also fundamental to the theory and practice of mediation, even court-annexed mediation, is an almost total lack of judicial oversight over the mediation processes or the results obtained. A party who enters into an

---

Press, 2004); idem., 'Courts. In and Out of Site, Site and Cite', Villanova Law Review, 53 (2008), 771–810.

[35] See Kratky Doré, 'Public Courts Versus Private Justice', supra n. 6.

[36] See, e.g., Maine Rules of Civil Procedure 16B(h), supra n. 10, Florida Rules of Civil Procedure 1.730, supra n. 19.

[37] E.g. in the Second Circuit, '[t]he mediator's notes do not become part of the Court's file nor anything submitted by the attorneys or parties to Staff Counsel pertaining to the merits'. See Civil Appeals Management Plan: Pre-Argument Conference Guidelines, www.ca2.uscourts.gov/Docs/Forms/Preargument.pdf.

agreement in a mediation proceeding has very little recourse if she later concludes that either the process or the agreement was unfair.

The basic guarantee of the fairness of the process and the agreements reached is the fact that a party must agree in order to be bound by any mediation result. If a party thinks that the process is not fair or that the proposed agreement is not fair, that party can withhold her agreement and the mediation will have been for naught.

The problem with this justification is that we know that parties to mediation are of different levels of sophistication and economic power. In domestic relations mediation, at any rate, a high percentage of the parties are without counsel.[38] Under these circumstances, there is a certain risk that the results of the mediation may be something other than a fair negotiated reflection of the shadow of the law. Although a very high percentage of American civil cases settle, with and without mediation, this is no particular guarantee that all of these settlements are good settlements.[39] Such factors as delay, disparate bargaining power and financial exhaustion can play a big part.

All of this suggests that mediated proceedings and settlements could well use some level of judicial review. Parties claiming that the process was unfair, or that the 'agreement' was one sided or even fraudulent, should be able to petition a court to re-examine the process and the agreement. As a matter of constitutional law, matters delegated to administrative agencies receive both procedural and substantive judicial review. Is there a good reason why civil justice matters resolved through mediation should not?

Mediators recoil from the suggestion that there might be anything wrong with their process which would need review: 'We are good people. All we want to do is help the parties reach agreement. We do not do anything wrong.' Most judges are also good people who are doing their best to do justice. This does not mean that we do not need those judges to be accountable for their processes and results so that errors of good judges and misdeeds of not-so-good judges can be corrected.

The lack of transparency or any meaningful judicial oversight for mediation processes is entirely appropriate when mediation is being

---

[38] See S. K. Berenson, 'A Family Law Residency Program?. A Modest Proposal in Response to the Burdens Created by Self-Represented Litigants in Family Court', *Rutgers Law Journal*, 33 (2001), 105–64.

[39] See M. Galanter and M. Cahill, '"Most Cases Settle". Judicial Promotion and Regulation of Settlements', *Stanford Law Review*, 46 (1994), 1339–91 (summarising and critiquing available analysis of settlement quality).

employed by private parties in an effort to reach an agreement outside of court. The result of such a process is a simple contract. Court proceedings would be required for either party to obtain enforcement of the agreement. Most objections to the process by which the agreement was reached could be raised with the court at the time enforcement is sought. In many cases the court could also gauge the appropriateness of the result embodied in the agreement compared with the pre-existing positions of the parties. The mediation and its results would be subject to at least mediate judicial oversight.

Court-annexed mediation, however, results in most cases in an immediate court judgment which can be enforced without further judicial proceedings. The results of the mediation are proffered to the court for incorporation into a public judgment, whether of dismissal or of granting relief, which binds the parties and is immediately enforceable. There is neither time nor opportunity following the mediation for a party who has concerns about the process or second thoughts about the fairness of an agreement to raise these issues with any court. Unless some form of court scrutiny of mediated settlements is built into the process, court-annexed mediation is subject to less court oversight and judicial review than purely private mediated agreements outside the context of judicial proceedings.

A public model for court-annexed mediation

Some of the problems inherent in the private mediator model can be solved by making mediators public employees and subjecting them to the same kind of conflict of interest regulations which apply to judges. The German civil justice system offers models under which judges function in a mediative capacity when discussing settlement possibilities with counsel in cases which are before them for decision. In recent years Germany has been experimenting with programmes which refer civil cases to specially trained mediation judges for settlement facilitation.[40] This programme provides a good example of the possibilities and limitations of a public mediation model.

It has long been known that German judges routinely discuss settlement of cases before them with counsel for the parties and with the parties themselves. The German Civil Procedure Code requires the judge

---

[40] See von Bargen, *Gerichtsinterne Mediation, supra* n. 4, 70–114 for a comprehensive description of several pilot projects functioning as of 2008 in the various German States.

to 'be mindful at all stages of the proceedings of the potential for an agreed disposition of the legal dispute or individual issues thereof'.[41] The Code requires the judge to raise settlement in discussions with counsel *sua sponte* at a 'settlement conference' (*Gütertermin*) before the plenary hearing in the case[42] and authorises the judge to refer the parties to another judge for settlement discussions and even to propose that the parties engage in out-of-court settlement discussions with a mediator or other settlement facilitator.[43]

A German judge can be quite specific in discussing settlement options in her own case, even to the point of proposing specific settlement terms based on her appreciation of the case at the time. This facility complements the judge's duty to give the parties 'hints and feedback' (*Hinweise*) on the judge's appreciation of the issues in the case as it develops. On the other hand, the deciding judge must use a certain restraint in pushing for particular settlement profiles in order not to undermine the parties' belief in her impartiality.[44]

In recent years German judges have been making greater use of the authorisation in the Civil Procedure Code to refer civil cases to other judges for settlement facilitation in a number of model projects in various German States and Appeals Court regions.[45] The common element of these projects is a systematic referral of civil cases to specially trained mediation judges for settlement facilitation prior to the plenary hearing. Although there has been an extensive debate about the extent to which mediative judicial activity is a part of the core function of justice, a systematic evaluation of these programmes has reached a positive result.[46] 'Court-internal mediation' is a core function of justice which ought to be provided to all citizens who have civil controversies in the public courts. There remain concerns about the financing of this additional judicial function and ongoing problems about the training and assignments of mediation judges. It is significant that the impartiality and immunity to economic considerations of these judicial mediators is not an issue.

German court-internal mediation also provides parties with a higher degree of transparency and judicial oversight than is available to parties

---

[41] ZPO §278(2).   [42] *Ibid.*   [43] ZPO §278(3).

[44] See Murray and Stürner, *German Civil Justice*, supra n. 11, 489–91.

[45] For a comprehensive description of these programmes as of 2008, see von Bargen, *Gerichtsinterne Mediation*, supra n. 4, 70–114.

[46] See *ibid.*, 363–6.

in the United States. Although German court-internal mediations are not open to the public, the judge dictates or drafts minutes of the proceedings in the same manner as other judicial proceedings.[47] As a matter of practice, mediation judges exercise a degree of discretion in drafting or dictating the minutes. Sometimes they omit specific mention of statements which were made in an atmosphere of confidence.[48] By the same token, a party can file a miscellaneous appeal (*Beschwerde*) from any prejudicial action taken by the mediating judge to the same extent as if the judge were the deciding judge.[49] Mediating judges are liable for mistakes and misconduct to the same extent as other judges exercising judicial functions.[50]

Although the predominant model for court-annexed mediation in the United States involves the use of private mediators, there are a few examples of public mediators. The most well known is the use of public mediators in US Courts of Appeal. In several circuits retired judges serve as mediators in programmes of compulsory mediation of civil appeals.[51] Most, if not all, of these mediators are insulated from the economic considerations which affect mediators in private practice. Their prior judicial service and sense of fairness and due process may also serve as some guarantee of regularity of their processes, even though there is no built-in judicial oversight or transparency in the programme.

Making a public–private partnership work

One can say that permitting private professionals, paid by the parties, to exercise significant neutral roles, is theoretically irreconcilable with our basic concepts of public civil justice. Although the potential for economic influence upon mediated decisions may be less well defined than on private arbitral determinations, any mediator commencing a mediation is aware at some level that one of the parties may be more likely to bring her future cases than the other. The influence of this awareness, often not even consciously articulated, cannot be underestimated.

---

[47] See ZPO §159 for the requirement that judicial proceedings be minuted.
[48] See von Bargen, *Gerichtsinterne Mediation, supra* n. 4, 332–3.
[49] See ZPO §569; Murray and Stürner, *German Civil Justice, supra* n. 11, 403.
[50] See BGB §839; von Bargen, *Gerichtsinterne Mediation, supra* n. 4, 340–1.
[51] E.g. the First and Fourth Circuits utilise former State court judges as mediators. See R. Niemic, 'Mediation and Conference Programs in the Federal Courts of Appeal' (Washington, DC: Federal Judicial Center, 1997), 10, www.fjc.gov/public/pdf.nsf/lookup/mediconf.pdf/$File/mediconf.pdf.

A model similar to the German model which uses specially trained judicial personnel to perform mediation of cases in the public justice system is the only system which can really guarantee that economic considerations will not influence mediator function. It is not likely, however, that the American legal culture, notoriously stingy in its investment in public justice resources, will embrace such an investment in public neutrals. The question is thus whether there are measures which can address this issue and make the public–private partnership work better.

Here are some suggestions:

(a) All mediators who mediate cases already within the civil justice system should be registered with the court and subject to some court oversight and disciplinary authority. This will enable the court to keep track of their mediated outcomes, any complaints, and to prescribe standards of conduct, qualifications and continuing education.[52]

(b) Records of mediations, including names of parties, counsel, mediators and outcomes (settled or not settled) should be recorded with the court and available for parties to use in connection with choices of mediator.[53]

(c) Mediators should be required to disclose before the outset of mediation any prior cases mediated with either party and with counsel for either party.[54]

---

[52] Many States already provide lists of civil mediators who register with the court and meet certain qualifications. See, e.g., Indiana Rules of Court: Rules for Alternative Dispute Resolution, www.in.gov/judiciary/rules/adr/index.html#_Toc202589225. In Florida, the parties may agree upon a certified mediator or 'a mediator who does not meet the certification requirements of these rules, but who, in the opinion of the parties and upon review by the presiding judge, is otherwise qualified by training or experience to mediate all or some of the issues in the particular case'. Florida Rules of Civil Procedure 1.720(f)(1)(B), *supra* n. 19.

[53] California has sought to address the problem of repeat-player arbitration and its effect on impartiality of arbitrators by enacting a code of ethics for arbitrators under which they would be required to disclose not only their relationship to the parties, that have been traditionally disclosed, but also the number of cases previously handled involving either party to a present claim. See Folberg, 'Arbitration Ethics', *supra* n. 29; California Civil Procedure Code §1281.85 (West Supplement, 2002).

[54] Section 9 of the UMA requires mediators to disclose any 'facts that a reasonable individual would consider likely to affect the impartiality of the mediator, including a financial or personal interest in the outcome of the mediation and an existing or past relationship with a mediation party or foreseeable participant in the mediation'. This is a

(d) Mediators should be required to maintain a summary record of the mediation which should be filed with the court. The record could be sealed, but made available in appropriate cases where the results of the mediation or the conduct of parties or mediator is being challenged.

(e) Mediation proceedings should not be privileged. Statements in mediation should be barred from admissibility in any trial between the parties on the issue being mediated.[55]

(f) Mediated results should be subject to at least some level of judicial review at the time the mediated agreement is incorporated into a binding court judgment or final settlement of a court proceeding.[56]

(g) Mediators should be subject to discipline and liability for malfeasance and negligence in the performance of their mediation function to the same extent as other professionals.[57]

Although these measures may be greeted with hostility by private mediators, to the extent that they are fulfilling roles in the public justice system, such a regimen is the minimum that is consistent with the values of public justice as we understand them. Party agreement is too fallible to be relied on as the sole guarantee of regularity of mediation functions which are otherwise opaque, unaccountable and subject to economic considerations of private practitioners. Good policy demands something more rigorous if this partnership is to retain the character of public justice.

---

step in the right direction, but may not go far enough because it does not require mediators to disclose whether they have previously mediated for any of the parties.

[55] The debate about the nature and extent of mediation confidentiality, privilege and the non-admissibility of statements in mediation continues without any end in sight. Compare C. McEwen, 'The Rule Moves Maine Backward', *supra* n. 30, with P. L. Murray, 'No, It's Really Not So Bad', *Maine Bar Journal*, 24 (2009), 45–54, where the respective authors debate the necessity and policy wisdom of a partial privilege covering 'confidential communications' between a party and a mediator. See also J. Reitman, 'Bumps in the Road of Maine's New Rule of Evidence 514', *Maine Lawyers Review*, 16 (22) (2008), 16–19.

[56] See Brunet, 'Questioning the Quality of Alternative Dispute Resolution', *supra* n. 8, 53.

[57] See, e.g., A. Chaykin, 'Mediator Liability. A New Role for Fiduciary Duties?', *University of Cincinnati Law Review*, 53 (1984), 731–64 (proposing to use fiduciary obligations as a means of constraining mediators' behaviour); A. K. Esquibel, 'The Case of the Conflicted Mediator. An Argument for Liability and against Immunity', *Rutgers Law Journal*, 31 (1999), 131–72.

28

The borders of bias: rectitude in international arbitration

WILLIAM W. PARK

La raison et le jugement viennent lentement; mais les préjugés accourent en foule.

Jean-Jacques Rousseau*

Introduction

Detlev Vagts continually impresses us with the serious clarity by which he interweaves the precise details of a complicated fact pattern with a broader analysis of their legal and policy implications. The catalogue of his learning includes mainline concerns like corporations and taxation, innovative tools for teaching international business law and historical analysis on the wartime comportment of neutrals or the legal system of the Third Reich.[1]

Professional rectitude has also found its way into the scholarly territories where Detlev has left his intellectual footprint. His service as Chair of a Task Force on legal ethics led him to address several aspects of ethics for both adjudicators (judges and arbitrators) and lawyers (advocates and advisers). With characteristic insight, he sensed that small study groups and legal education programmes commended themselves as an

---

* 'Reason and judgment come slowly; but prejudices rush up in crowds', J. J. Rousseau, *Émile, ou de l'Éducation, Oeuvres Complètes de Jean-Jacques Rousseau*, 5 vols. (The Hague: J. Néaulme, 1762), Book III, 332.
[1] D. F. Vagts, 'Switzerland, International Law and World War II', *AJIL*, 91 (1997), 466–75; Foreword to H. R. Reginbogin, *Faces of Neutrality. A Comparative Analysis of the Neutrality of Switzerland and Other Neutral Nations During World War II* (Berlin: LIT Verlag , 2009), 1–6; Introduction to I. Müller, *Hitler's Justice. The Courts of the Third Reich* (Cambridge, MA: Harvard University Press, 1991), ix–xviii.

essential preamble to guidelines and codes, but only 'when the time is ripe'.[2]

In the spirit of that work on professional ethics, this brief contribution to the honour of Vagts' scholarship looks at some of the salient deontological problems that implicate international arbitration, particularly when individuals move between roles as arbitrators and advocates. The modest hope is not to fix standards (the time is not ripe), but to take the first step of identifying issues and perhaps signalling some wrong directions and problematic solutions.

Few topics carry more significance for the health of private dispute resolution. Integrity is to arbitration what location is to the price of real estate: without it, other things do not matter all that much. In this connection, two different paths might bring arbitration down. One route would allow service by biased arbitrators, thus tarnishing the neutrality of the arbitral process. An alternate course to shipwreck would establish unrealistic standards for comportment that permit spurious challenges to derail proceedings and abusive annulment motions aimed at vitiating the arbitrator's decision.

To reduce the risk of either pernicious or precarious arbitrators, ethical standards have been grafted on to the arbitral process through a multiple of avenues. Requirements of both independence and impartiality have been included, explicitly and implicitly, in treaties, statutes, judicial decisions, institutional rules, professional guidelines and the simple folklore of practice. Representing both 'hard' law and 'soft', these standards implicate a tightrope walk between the rival goals of avoiding unprincipled sabotage and enhancing prospects that arbitrators will exercise independent judgment. What to the untutored eye might appear as 'high standards' (particularly for what has been called 'apparent' or 'perceived' bias) may lead to abuses as bad or worse than codes that seem too relaxed. If accusations of apparent bias become too easy, destabilisation of arbitrations will become standard fare for those lawyers unhappy with the award, or even the way proceedings seem to be headed, resulting in a decrease in arbitration's aggregate social and economic benefits.[3]

---

[2] American Society of International Law, Report of the Task Force on International Professional Responsibility (December 2007). Proposed Action Item No. 6, 32. Other Task Force members included Pieter Bekker, Mary Daly, Jan Paulsson, Michael Riesman and Catherine Rogers.

[3] For two recent studies which examine the problem, see S. Luttrell, *Bias Challenges in International Commercial Arbitration* (The Hague, London and Boston: Kluwer Law International, 2009) and C. A. Matheus López, *La Independencia e Imparcialidad del Árbitro* (San Sebastián: Instituto Vasco de Derecho Procesal, 2009).

Issue conflict and role confusion

Most international arbitrators tend to avoid the grosser manifestations of bias. One rarely hears of an arbitrator who asserts that 'all Portuguese are liars'[4] or who has a romantic relationship with a litigant's counsel.[5]

The appearance of pre-judgment can take subtler forms, however. One emerging set of trouble spots relates to the confusion faced by some individuals who fill the roles, alternatively, of both arbitrator and advocate. Questionable predispositions might derive from the same individual's service as advocate in one case and arbitrator in another, when the two proceedings raise similar issues. Justifiable worries may also arise when two lawyers sharing a single professional affiliation appear as arbitrator and advocate in the same case.

The first problem, implicating individuals who serve alternatively as arbitrator and advocate, has often been addressed under the rubric of 'issue conflict' and its sibling, 'role confusion'. Each represents a special form of pre-judgment, in that an arbitrator might consider in one case the very same issue presented to her or her firm when representing a litigant in another matter.

The arbitrator could be tempted, subconsciously perhaps, to add a sentence to an award that could later be cited in another case. Such an *arrière pensée* might lead to awards disparaging or approving some legal authority or argument regularly presented in similar disputes, with the intent to serve as persuasive authority in a different context. The risk presents itself most acutely in fields such as expropriation or insurance, where similar issues routinely arise in nearly the same context but in different cases.[6]

The flip side of the coin might present itself if an arbitrator in one case is influenced by her position as counsel in another case. In one treaty-based investment case seated in The Netherlands, a well-known French jurist was sitting as arbitrator in a dispute implicating Ghana, while at the

---

[4] *In re The Owners of the Steamship Catalina & The Owners of the Motor Vessel Norma*, Lloyd's Rep., 61 (1938), 360.

[5] For a tale of room-sharing by a male arbitrator and one of the female lawyers appearing before him in a case, see R. B. Schmitt, 'Suite Sharing', *The Wall Street Journal*, February 14, 1990, A1.

[6] For example, investor–State cases often implicate a shareholder's right to bring derivative claims on behalf of corporations in which it owns stock. See *Case Concerning the Barcelona Traction, Light and Power Co. Ltd* (*Belgium* v. *Spain*), Second Phase, Judgment, 1970, ICJ Rep. 3. Likewise, insurance arbitration regularly requires interpretation of the same language in different policies, such as whether an insured 'expected or intended' the third-party injury which led to liability.

same time advising a company that sought to annul an earlier award rejecting similar claims against Morocco. A Dutch Court gave the jurist ten days to decide whether to resign as arbitrator or as counsel. The Court reasoned that the jurist in his role as advocate in the Moroccan case might come to doubt the reasoning of the award relied on by Ghana for its defence. The arbitrator was required to remain open-minded towards the validity of the earlier award.[7]

The judicial reasoning in the Dutch case rested on the specific facts at bar, and did not necessarily create an automatic presumption of bias simply because the same individual served as arbitrator in one case and counsel in another. Yet the appointing authority in another recent proceeding has reached a similar result, this time in an UNCITRAL arbitration where an arbitrator appointed by Canada was advising Mexico on similar issues.[8]

The concern for role confusion and issue conflict is not limited to arbitration, of course. Similar problems may arise in national court proceedings where a judge relies on precedent that she had a role in making years before as a young advocate.[9]

Other wrinkles on this theme come from the world of sports. The cyclist Floyd Landis challenged an arbitral award upholding a doping disqualification for use of synthetic testosterone in the 2006 Tour de France. The Lausanne-based Court of Arbitration for Sport/Tribunal Arbitral du Sport (CAS/TAS) had convened the Arbitral Tribunal to review a ban imposed by the US Anti-Doping Agency.[10] Landis moved to

---

[7] See A. Marriott, 'The Arbitrator is Counsel', *Transnational Dispute Management*, December 2006, describing a decision of 18 October 2004 in the *Telekom Malaysia* case, where the Hague District Court addressed the arbitrator's role as counsel in *RFCC* v. *Morocco*, ICSID Case No. ARB/00/6 (2003).

[8] See *Vito G. Gallo* v. *Government of Canada*, PCA/NAFTA, Decision on Challenge (14 October 2009) by the Deputy Secretary-General of ICSID acting as appointing authority in a NAFTA Chapter 11 case brought under the UNCITRAL Rules. An arbitrator appointed by Canada had been advising Mexico on interpreting the NAFTA and similar investment treaty provisions. The Decision gave him seven days to choose between continuing to advise Mexico and serving as arbitrator in that case.

[9] See, e.g., *John Doe VII* v. *Exxon Mobil*, US District Court for the District of Columbia (Civ. 07-1022, 30 September 2009), involving an allegation that Indonesian soldiers retained by Exxon Mobil committed various torts against local residents. In dismissing the action for lack of standing, Judge Royce Lamberth relied in part on a decision of more than thirty years earlier in *Berlin Democratic Club* v. *Rumsfeld*, 410 F.Supp. 144 (DDC 1976), which he had argued as an Assistant US Attorney.

[10] The panel comprised a tribunal including David Williams, Jan Paulsson and David Rivkin. *Landis* v. *US Anti-Doping Agency*, CAS 2007/A/1394 (Court of Arbitration for Sport, 2008).

challenge the decision in a US Federal court in California, contending that the Arbitral Tribunal had been tainted by conflicts of interest.[11] The gist of the argument seems to be that the arbitrators had been drawn from a limited pool that often filled rotating functions that made them prone to rule favourably for each other.[12]

At first blush it may be tempting to suggest that individuals should choose to serve as either arbitrator or advocate. Practical problems would arise with such an expectation, however. Most arbitrators learn the ropes by serving as counsel in some capacity. At what point would the duty arise to choose between the two paths? After the first appointment as arbitrator? The second? The third? While some individuals may gravitate to one function or the other, the membrane between the two functions will likely remain porous for the near future.

---

[11] Mr Landis filed a Motion to Vacate Arbitration Award in the US District Court for the Central District of California. Motion to Vacate Arbitration Award and Demand for Jury Trial, *Landis* v. *US Anti-Doping Agency*, No. CV 08-06330 (CD Cal., 25 September 2008). The motion alleges, '[T]hese arbitrators constantly find themselves changing hats, arbitrator one day, litigant the next', *ibid.*, 27. The case was ultimately settled with prejudice after Landis moved to vacate on the basis of the US Federal Arbitration Act, section 10(a)(2) (evidential partiality or corruption) and Art. V(1)(a) (invalid arbitration agreement), V(1)(d) (improper composition of the tribunal) and V(2)(b) (violation of public policy) of the 1958 Convention on the Recognition and Enforcement of Foreign Arbitral Awards (the 'New York Convention').

[12] The independence of the CAS/TAS itself has not always been free from doubt. In its early days, the body was challenged following an incident implicating a German equestrian whose horse had ingested a prohibited substance. A challenge to the ban was brought before Switzerland's highest court, the *Tribunal fédéral*, which had to determine whether the decision was in fact an arbitral award in the sense of the Swiss Federal and Cantonal statutory legal framework for arbitration. *Elmar Gundel* v. *Fédération internationale d'équitation, Recueil Officiel Tribunal fédéral Suisse*, 15 March 1993, *Recueil Officiel des Arrêts du Tribunal fédéral* [ATF], 119 (1993), vol. II, 271 (Switzerland), extract reprinted in M. Reeb (ed.), *Recueil des sentences du TAS Digest of CAS Awards 1986–1998* (The Hague, London and Boston: Kluwer Law International, 1998), 561. Although not denying the validity of the decision in the instant case, the *Tribunal fédéral* drew attention to the numerous then-existing links between the CAS/TAS and the International Olympic Committee (IOC). See A. Rigozzi, *L'arbitrage international en matière de sport* (Basel: Helbing & Lichtenhahn, 2005), §523, 274; J. Paulsson, 'The Swiss Federal Tribunal Recognises the Finality of Arbitral Awards Relating to Sports Disciplinary Sanctions Rendered by the IOC's Court of Arbitration for Sports', *International Arbitration Report*, October 1993, 12. In response to the hesitation expressed in this decision, a new supervisory body was created to insulate the CAS/TAS from the influence of the IOC. See, generally, G. Kaufmann-Kohler, *Arbitration at the Olympics. Issues of Fast-Track Dispute Resolution and Sports Law* (The Hague, Boston and London: Kluwer Law International, 2001).

On occasion, a terminology problem results in mixing discussion of the 'role confusion' and 'repeat player' rubrics. The two concerns remain distinct both conceptually and in practice. Role confusion relates to change of functions in the arbitral process, serving one day as advocate and another as arbitrator, thus arguably sitting in judgment of each other. Repeat players, by contrast, are individuals appointed on several occasions by the same company or industry group. For example, in an insurance matter the repeat player might be an underwriter, or a barrister with a long history of acting on behalf of insurers, who is regularly named by the same insurers. Although some professional guidelines address the matter, greater clarity might be in order.[13]

Nor should the notion of repeat players be confused with the professional arbitrator, an experienced individual who serves regularly in commercial and investment disputes, sometimes nominated by the claimant, sometimes by the respondent and sometimes as chair. Strong incentives exist to safeguard professional status in such cases. Individuals who serve as arbitrators care deeply, both personally and professionally, about the respect of their peers and colleagues. Few enticements to good behaviour are stronger than a colleague's appreciation of one's ability and integrity.[14]

One final word on pre-judgment relates to scholarship, which presents special challenges. If an arbitrator has written or lectured on the narrow and controverted point on which a case hangs, the party receiving the rough side of the analysis might feel uneasy. Yet it would be counterproductive to bar from service as arbitrators those scholars who shared expertise through teaching and writing. A professor might be challenged in a commercial case simply for having written a general treatise on contract law which addressed matters such as offer and acceptance, *force*

---

[13] The International Bar Association Guidelines on Conflicts of Interest in International Arbitration ('IBA Guidelines') include the 'Orange List' of situations that may, depending on the facts of the case, give rise to 'justifiable doubts' about an arbitrator's independence or impartiality. IBA Guidelines, Part II, §3.13. That provision describes an arbitrator who 'has within the past three years been appointed as arbitrator on two or more occasions by one of the parties or an affiliate of one of the parties'. See generally F.-Z. Slaoui, 'The Rising Issue of "Repeat Arbitrators". A Call for Clarification', *Arbitration International*, 25 (2009), 103–19.

[14] On the general comportment of who might be sometimes called 'elite arbitrators', see J. Paulsson, 'Ethics, Elitism, Eligibility', *Journal of International Arbitration*, 14 (1997), 13–21. On the profiles of those chosen to serve as arbitrators in international disputes, see Y. Dezalay and B. G. Garth, *Dealing in Virtue. International Commercial Arbitration and the Construction of a Transnational Legal Order* (Chicago: University of Chicago Press, 1996).

majeure, or the measure of damages. Such a policy would disenfranchise many of the most learned, and inhibit the free exchange of information on which intellectual progress depends.[15]

Barristers

In addition to their role as advocates, English barristers often serve as arbitrators, and rightly so in most cases. Traditionally, barristers cluster in 'chambers' (which they resist calling 'firm'), which take on a special significance for international arbitration. In at least one investor–State case, an Arbitral Tribunal held that a barrister should not appear as counsel before another member of his chambers.[16] Although free to select its lawyers prior to constitution of the Arbitral Tribunal, the respondent was not entitled to change the composition of its legal team in a way that might imperil the Tribunal's legitimacy.[17] The Tribunal found no absolute bar to barristers from the same chambers being involved as counsel and arbitrator in the same case, but found equally no absolute rule to the opposite effect. Consequently, the

---

[15] An arbitrator's speaking engagements can provide special challenges. In one recent ICSID case, an arbitrator was disqualified on the basis of statements made during an interview. See PCA Case No. IR-2009/1, decision of 8 December 2009, in which the Secretary-General of the Permanent Court of Arbitration ('PCA') in The Hague sustained Ecuador's challenge against Charles Brower in a case related to Ecuador's share of revenues under certain oil participation agreements. Judge Brower had given an interview in the August 2009 issue of *The Metropolitan Corporate Counsel* magazine which reported, *inter alia,* that Bolivia and Ecuador had been recalcitrant in their compliance with orders issued in investor–State arbitration. See, generally, *Perenco Ecuador Ltd* v. *Republic of Ecuador and Empresa Estatal Petróleos del Ecuador (Petroecuador)* (ICSID Case No. ARB/08/6, 2008). Both sides in the case had previously agreed that any arbitrator challenges in the case would be resolved by the Secretary-General of the PCA, applying the IBA Guidelines.

[16] *Hrvatska Elektroprivreda d.d.* [*HEP*] v. *The Republic of Slovenia,* ICSID Case No. ARB/05/24 (2008), (implicating claims by a Croatian entity before a Tribunal composed of David Williams (Chairman), Jan Paulsson and Charles N. Brower). It was determined that David Mildon (appointed co-counsel of the respondent) could not participate further in the case because Messrs. Mildon and Williams were both members of Essex Court Chambers.

[17] Art. 56 of the 1966 International Convention for the Settlement of Disputes between States and Nationals of other States (ICSID Convention) stresses the stability of properly constituted tribunals, providing that a tribunal's composition shall remain unchanged except for death, incapacity, or resignation. ICSID Convention, Art. 56. The continued appearance of Mr Mildon might have undermined the legitimacy of the Tribunal by giving an appearance of impropriety, or by requiring the resignation of Mr Williams, the Tribunal's Chairman.

justifiability of an apprehension of bias would depend upon 'all relevant circumstances'.[18]

Barristers' chambers bear both similarities and differences when compared with law firms in general. The chambers include shared office space and administrative assistants styled as clerks, as well as the normal accoutrements of law practice such as word processors, fax machines and photocopiers. The career development of younger barristers often depends on guidance, referrals and recommendations from senior members of their chambers.

Most barristers seem to reject application of the conflict-of-interest rules that would normally be relevant to practice within a law firm. Considering themselves independent and self-employed, sharing expenses but not revenues,[19] barristers see no reason why two members of the same chambers should refrain from acting for opposite sides of an arbitration, or why one should not sit as arbitrator in a case where another serves as advocate.

Not all are convinced, however, that the integrity of proceedings remains uncompromised when barristers from one set of chambers serve as arbitrator and counsel in the same arbitration. Shared profits are not the only type of professional relationships that can create potential conflicts. Senior barristers often have significant influence on the progress of junior colleagues' careers. Moreover, London chambers increasingly brand themselves as specialists in particular fields, with senior clerks taking marketing roles for the chambers, sometimes travelling to stimulate collective business. And of course, one barrister's success and resulting enhanced reputation would normally reflect well on the chambers as a whole.

In response to doubts about the ethics of their practice, some barristers suggest that outsiders just do not understand the system, characterising the critiques as naïve. Like a Paris waiter impugning a tourist's ability to speak French in order to distract him from insisting on the correct change, the critique aims to camouflage what is at stake. Often, however, outsiders do understand the mechanics of chambers. They simply evaluate the dangers differently.

---

[18] *Hrvatska Elektroprivreda d.d.* [*HEP*] v. *The Republic of Slovenia, supra* n. 16, Decision on Jurisdiction, para. 31 (2008).

[19] See, e.g., R. Pillai, 'Independence and Impartiality. The Situation of English Barristers Acting in Arbitrations', *Transnational Dispute Management*, July 2008, www.transnational-dispute-management.com; D. Branson, 'An ICSID Tribunal Applies Supranational Norms to Banish Counsel from Proceedings. *Note on Hrvatska Elektropriveda* v. *Republic of Slovenia*', *Arbitration International*, 25 (2009), 615–31.

The position under English law is what it is.[20] However, an indulgence by English courts does not prevent parties to international arbitration from raising justifiable doubts concerning independence as between two barristers of the same chambers in a single proceeding. Under the conflicts of interest Guidelines of the International Bar Association (IBA Guidelines), an 'Orange List' of potentially problematic situations includes relationships 'between an arbitrator and another arbitrator or counsel'.[21] This non-exhaustive iteration of various fact patterns covers common scenarios which, depending on the circumstances of each case, might give rise to justifiable doubts as to arbitrator impartiality or independence in the eyes of the parties. A special provision covers barristers when one arbitrator and another arbitrator, or the counsel for one of the parties, are members of the 'same barristers' chambers'.[22]

Of course, when barristers from the same chambers oppose each other as advocates, each wants to show special cleverness. Competitive juices may work against inappropriate behaviour, with incentives to deviate from duty outweighed by the goal of proving oneself the better gladiator.

---

[20] At least one English case has rejected a challenge to an arbitrator who shares chambers with a barrister serving as advocate in the same case. See *Laker Airways, Inc.* v. *FLS Aerospace Ltd*, Lloyd's Rep., 2 (1999), 45 (QB) (judgment of Mr Rix, as he then was). A more nuanced view, however, may be evolving. See, e.g., *Smith* v. *Kvaerner Cementation Foundations Ltd*, [2006] EWCA (Civ.) 242, [2006] 3 All ER 593 (CA) (involving litigation for personal injuries sustained in a road accident). Both sides' barristers and the 'Recorder' (a legal officer acting as magistrate within a given locality) were from the same chambers. On appeal from a judgment against the claimant Smith, the Court of Appeal expressed concern that the claimant's barrister had not properly explained to his client the complexity of the matter. The judgment was reversed, with Mr Smith's waiver found to be ineffective.

[21] IBA Guidelines, Part II, section 3.3. The broad category of relationships 'between an arbitrator and another arbitrator or counsel' is amplified by section 3.3.1, which includes a situation where 'the arbitrator and another arbitrator are lawyers in the same law firm', and supplemented in section 3.3.3 by a further enumeration of troublesome relationships, to include an arbitrator who was 'within the past three years a partner or colleague of, or otherwise affiliated with, another arbitrator or any of the counsel in the same arbitration'.

[22] IBA Guidelines, Part II, section 3.3., §3.3.2. The IBA Guidelines' inclusion of this category was not without debate or objection, and became the subject of a discussion in the 'Background' report issued by the IBA Working Group. O. L. O. de Witt Wijnen *et al.*, 'Background Information on the IBA Guidelines on Conflicts of Interest in International Arbitration', *Business Law International*, 5 (2004), 433–58, 455–6. The IBA Working Group notes the distinction between the operation of law firms and barristers' chambers (including differences among barristers in different jurisdictions) but then adds: '[I]n light of the content of the promotional material which many chambers now disseminate, there is an understandable perception that barristers' chambers should be treated the same way as law firms', *ibid.*, 455.

Furthermore, when one barrister serves as arbitrator while another from the same chambers acts as counsel, their interaction takes place in the open, for all to observe.

Different factors operate, however, when two barristers from the same chambers sit together as arbitrators and exclude meaningful participation by the third member of the tribunal. Their bilateral deliberations remain outside the reach of party scrutiny. The junior of the two barristers might draft the award for the senior to present as 'our award' to the third arbitrator, followed perhaps by a perfunctory conference call replacing genuine deliberations.

When a same-chambers relationship is apparent from the start, the litigants will have renounced any objection to the composition of the Tribunal as such. This does not mean, however, that they waive integrity and good faith in the Tribunal's internal communications, which form an essential part of due process. Parties who stipulate three arbitrators have a right to expect that all three of them will be allowed to participate in discussions.

Normally, exclusion of an arbitrator from deliberations derives not from any inherent wickedness in her colleagues, but from the moral hazard implicit in any 'in-group' complicity, facilitated by the confidential nature of deliberations. The undesirable effects remain the same, however, whether the behaviour is intentional or inadvertent. An enlightened barrister, sitting with a colleague from the same chambers, would normally take special pains to avoid injury to the fabric of the Tribunal by ignoring the third member.[23]

'Incentives' to bad behaviour

Institutional bias

Special considerations may arise with respect to treaty-based investor–State arbitration, designed to address claims of expropriation and

---

[23] On good practice in arbitral deliberations see, generally, Y. Derains, 'La pratique du délibéré arbitral', in G. Aksen *et al.* (eds.), *Global Reflections on International Law, Commerce & Dispute Resolution. Liber Amicorum in Honour of Robert Briner* (Paris: ICC Publishing, 2005), 221. Derains distinguishes between harmonious and pathological deliberations. In the latter situation he suggests that a first draft of the award is to be prepared by the chairman alone, and presented at a fixed meeting for deliberations, *ibid.*, 229, para. 12. Of course, a different practice may obtain when informal discussions among the Tribunal members lead to a consensus that the merits favour one side or the other, or when issues can easily be parcelled for drafting after general agreement has been reached. All three arbitrators may agree that no credible evidence supports the claim, or that one arbitrator has expertise that can be pressed into service in drafting an award along lines previously accepted by all.

discrimination. One theme fashionable in some circles posits that systemic 'incentives' push arbitrators to decide for investors. The argument seems to run that arbitrators seek to promote growth of investor–State proceedings in order to get future appointments, and efforts to promote arbitration translate into decisions that favour claimant-investors.[24] Neither evidence nor logic supports a conclusion that such incentives either exist or have any practical import.

As a preliminary matter, the role of any inducement to pro-investor decisions remains counterintuitive. Reputations tarnished by deviation from duty do not bring reappointment, at least when both host State and investor have a role in the process. In highly visible international cases, rational arbitrators seek to enhance their status by gaining a reputation for fairness and intelligence. Biased decision-making would be an odd way to do so, given that UNCITRAL awards would be subject to review by either national courts (for lack of due process or violation of public policy) or before an ad hoc committee convened in connection with an ICSID proceeding.[25] Thus if arbitrator incentives operate at all in large international cases, they work to promote accuracy and honesty.

Although teenage boys may hope to attract adolescent girls by showing themselves dangerous and daring, no similar rule works for judges or arbitrators. Rumours of prejudice and partiality do little to enhance the credibility of professional arbitrators who normally benefit from being known for reliability and accuracy. Bad arbitrators do exist. But lack of integrity does them no favours.

One author suggests that 'as merchants of adjudicative services, arbitrators have a financial stake in furthering [arbitration's] appeal to claimants', which results in an 'apprehension of bias in favour of allowing claims and awarding damages against governments'.[26] Of course, no one is immune from the temptations to greed and bias to which humanity has always been heir, and all of us should be conscious of the risk that we may fall prey to astigmatic perspectives. The beginning of wisdom lies in a healthy fear of latent bias.

---

[24] See G. Van Harten, *Investment Treaty Arbitration and Public Law* (Oxford University Press, 2007), 152–3, 167–75.

[25] ICSID Convention, Art. 52 provides for award annulment when there was, *inter alia*, 'corruption on the part of a member of the Tribunal' or 'a serious departure from a fundamental rule of procedure'. ICSID Convention, Art. 52(c). Challenge to an arbitrator will be allowed as to individuals who do not meet the standards for Art. 14, which requires that an arbitrator 'may be relied upon to exercise independent judgment'.

[26] Van Harten, *Investment Treaty Arbitration and Public Law*, *supra* n. 24, 152–3.

Nevertheless, no evidence supports the proposition that the arbitral system as it now exists provides incentives to produce inaccurate decisions that favour either claimants or respondents, or even that such incentives actually exist. Common sense tells us that the big losers would be none other than professional arbitrators themselves if the process did not inspire general confidence. Although concern may be justified against certain types of arbitration, broad theories of 'arbitrator incentives' remain difficult to support in logic or in practice, particularly for cross-border transactions where the principal motivation to arbitrate lies in apprehension about potential anti-foreign prejudice in national courts.[27]

Arbitral institutions will also want to obtain a reputation for evenhandedness. In a world where treaties and contracts are freely negotiated, and multiple institutions compete for arbitration business, it would be self-destructive if any organisation became known for systematically manufacturing awards on behalf of either claimant or respondent. The disfavoured side would simply insist on using another forum.

Even if a system of tenured international judges should be explored as a theoretically better system, as suggested by advocates of the 'public law' model,[28] finding an appointing authority that would command worldwide confidence remains problematic. The most realistic baseline against which to measure the present system is not a 'World Arbitrators' Corps' appointed by one universally admired body, but rather a diffuse set of national courts staffed by judges perceived as even more partial (toward their appointing governments) than arbitrators constituted by a joint decision of the parties. The present base line against which to evaluate arbitrator bias remains a judiciary beholden to a national government. While ideals are worth pursuing even if not fully realisable, the best would become the enemy of the good if a yen for perfect neutrality led to dismantling the current system, which suffers less bias than its alternatives. In the world as it exists, some party input into the arbitrator selection process remains a condition for the litigants to feel comfortable with the legitimacy of the tribunal, and perhaps for acceptance of the treaty commitments in the first place.

---

[27] One study found evidence that in Federal civil actions in the United States, foreigners actually fare better than domestic parties. The explanation for this counterintuitive finding may well lie in the fear of litigation bias that causes foreigners to continue to final judgment only if they have particularly strong cases. See K. Clermont and Th. Eisenberg, 'Xenophilia in American Courts', *Harvard Law Review*, 109 (1996), 1120–43.

[28] See Van Harten, *Investment Treaty Arbitration and Public* Law, *supra* n. 24, 175–84.

An even more compelling reason to doubt the plausibility of pro-investor incentives lies in the bilateral or multilateral nature of treaty negotiations. Without host State participation in investment treaties and free trade agreements (FTAs), investment arbitration would have little future. Just as it takes two to tango, so it takes at least two countries to conclude a treaty. Investor–State arbitration succeeds only if the process appears fair to both sides. Moreover, host States appoint as many arbitrators as investors, and a presiding arbitrator must be acceptable to both sides. Incentives to 'repeat-player' status can operate just as well for arbitrators known to be regularly appointed by host States as by investors.

Debates on the propriety of the current arbitrator selection system often touch on what is referred to as 'transparency', a notion that includes public pleadings and open hearings. On occasion, the more titillating term 'secrecy' is used to imply an aura of something untoward about arbitration, perhaps evoking the *omertà* or code of silence operating among criminal organisations in southern Italy. The assumption of such loaded language seems to be that secrecy is suspect, perhaps, because it breeds lack of accountability.[29] In any event, it is not clear who benefits from lack of publicity.[30] Host States themselves may resist the glare of publicity when an expropriation risks exposing political corruption or victimisation of ethnic groups through unfair spoliation.

Assertions of systemic bias can detract attention from consideration of more concrete measures to promote arbitrator integrity. Thoughtful dialogue should focus on how to articulate and implement ethical principles that avoid the two principal paths by which arbitration may come into disrepute: (i) lax ethical canons that tolerate arbitrator prejudgment and hidden links to parties, and (ii) unrealistic rules that

---

[29] See generally 'Behind Closed Doors', *The Economist*, 25 April 2009, 63 (reporting on the 'struggle' of an Indian lawyer named Ashok Sancheti who wished to receive publicity for his claim against the United Kingdom). For earlier debate on the subject, see also A. De Palma, 'NAFTA's Powerful Little Secret', *New York Times*, March 11, 2001, §3–1 (late edn.). In December 2001, an advertisement in *The Washington Post* attacked investment arbitration under the headline 'Secret Courts for Corporations'. Sponsored by Ralph Nader's 'Public Citizen's Global Trade Watch', the publication referred to arbitrators as judges whose 'identit[ies] can be kept secret indefinitely'. *The Washington Post*, December 5, 2001, A-5.

[30] See N. Rubins, 'Opening the Investment Arbitration Process. At What Cost, For Whose Benefit?', in Ch. Klausegger *et al.* (eds.), *Austrian Arbitration Yearbook* (Boston: Kluwer Law International, 2009), 483.

facilitate abusive arbitrator challenges designed to disrupt the arbitral process.[31]

In some instances, of course, incentives to arbitrator bias do exist, particularly when arbitrators are taken from one particular industry. A particular arbitral institution might be perceived as tending to appoint arbitrators likely to favour one category of litigants over others. For example, in a consumer debt action, arbitrators with long affiliations to banks and lending institutions might not inspire confidence in borrowers.[32] Or, in a dispute over mismanagement of an investment account, an arbitrator who worked for a large financial institution might create an understandable apprehension of being predisposed to favour the brokerage house.[33]

Where necessary, dispute resolution systems can implement mechanisms to promote the balanced composition of a Tribunal.[34] For example,

---

[31] Of course, smart people sometimes know how to mask their bias. This remains a fact of life no matter what the guiding principles on impartiality. Unless we establish a way to cut open an arbitrator's head to see what is really going on (and then put things back together again), the best clues to partiality lie in the things that have actually been said or written.

[32] Precisely such concerns arose with respect to the 'National Arbitration Forum', and have received considerable press. See C. Mollenkamp, D. Searcy and N. Koppel, 'Turmoil in Arbitration Empire Up-Ends Credit Card Disputes', *The Wall Street Journal*, October 14, 2009, 1 (October 15, 2009 for on-line version). The article speaks of the debt collection system allegedly organised by J. Michael Cline and his 'Accreditive Funds' which had interests in the Minnesota-based National Arbitration Forum as well as the 'Mann Bracken' law firm which played a role in the debt-collection process.

[33] Analogous issues arise in employment arbitration, although the ways to assuage the concern are not yet that clearly identified. See, e.g., *Cole* v. *Burns International Security Services*, 105 F.3d 1465 (DC Cir. 1997), in which Chief Judge Harry Edwards understandably held that an employee alleging discrimination cannot be subject to a *de facto* bar in the vindication of statutory rights by virtue of inability to pay the arbitrator's fee. Ironically, the rise of consumer and employment arbitration within the United States derives in some measure from a mirror-image concern over civil juries being predisposed toward the 'little guy' as represented by the customer or the worker. For expressions of concern from someone who questions the tradition of 'mandatory' arbitration in the United States, see J. R. Sternlight, 'Panacea or Corporate Tool? Debunking the Supreme Court's Preference for Binding Arbitration', *Washington University Law Quarterly*, 74 (1996), 637–712, and *idem.*, 'In Defense of Mandatory Binding Arbitration (If Imposed on the Company)', *Nevada Law Journal*, 8 (2007), 82–106.

[34] In response to a lawsuit brought by the Minnesota Attorney-General, at least one provider of arbitration services recently decided not to supervise consumer arbitration. See Press Release, 'Minnesota Attorney-General, National Arbitration Forum Barred from Credit Card and Consumer Arbitrations Under Agreement with Attorney-General Swanson' (July 20, 2009). The complaint asserted that the arbitral institution had impermissible links with debt-collection services.

American securities arbitration has understandably been concerned that the majority of a three-member Tribunal should not be drawn from the ranks of lawyers who make their living representing financial advisers. Consequently, it has long been the practice to identify 'public' as opposed to 'industry' arbitrators, and to make sure that the latter do not predominate in any Arbitral Tribunal.[35]

Analogies from domestic arbitration do not always transplant well, however. When disputes address a specific sector of the economy, arbitrators should not be closely identified with the relevant industry. By contrast, when the distinction lies between the two broad categories of host State and investors, few potential arbitrators of any experience or ability will be able to avoid association with one group or the other. Most will have links with both.

Moreover, when the alleged enticements to bad behaviour relate to the simple dichotomy between investor and host State, the domestic paradigm loses much of its force. Through sovereign wealth funds, host States such as China often invest in investor countries such as the United States. And an investor nation like the United States has often found the shoe on the other foot when respondent in arbitrations brought by Canadian investors.[36]

Four special issues

The mechanics of ICSID challenge

Challenges to arbitrators in investor–State disputes would normally be brought under either the ICSID Convention or the UNCITRAL

---

[35] The US Securities and Exchange Commission (SEC) has issued directives to limit the role of arbitrators with substantial connections to financial advisors. The directives mandate that arbitrators who decide consumer disputes involving brokerage houses should not be drawn unduly from the ranks of stock brokers or their lawyers. Many of these cases fall to be decided under the auspices of the Financial Industry Regulatory Authority (FINRA), a self-regulatory body that in 2007 consolidated the dispute resolution for both the National Association of Securities Dealers (NASD) and the New York Stock Exchange (NYSE). FINRA Rule 12402 provides in pertinent part that for a single-arbitrator case the arbitrator will be a 'public' arbitrator and for a panel of three arbitrators, only one may be a non-public arbitrator. On June 9, 2008, FINRA amended the definition of a 'public' arbitrator under NASD Rules 12100(u) and 13100(u), as set forth in the Code of Arbitration Procedure for Customer Disputes and the Code of Arbitration Procedure for Industry Disputes. The amendment adds an annual revenue limitation to the definition of 'public' arbitrator in order to exclude from that category individuals with a direct or indirect connection to the securities industry.

[36] See W. W. Park and G. Aguilar Alvarez, 'The New Face of Investment Arbitration', *YJIL*, 28 (2003), 365–407, reprinted in *International Arbitration Report*, 19 (2004), 39–76, *International Arbitration*, 5 (2004), 25–94.

Arbitration Rules (UNCITRAL Rules),[37] each of which provides the frame-work for private claims under BITs and FTAs.[38] Although these systems share some common elements, their treatment of challenges will diverge with respect to two key elements: the person who decides whether the challenge is justified, and the possibility of judicial review. On both matters, UNCITRAL arbitration falls toward the commercial arbitration model.[39]

In ICSID arbitration, the touchstone will be the words in Art. 14 of the ICSID Convention, which speak of the individual's ability to 'exercise independent judgment'.[40] This requirement is supplemented by a

---

[37] Under some investment treaties, investors and host States may have the option to choose other arbitration regimes. In addition, arbitration might arise under the terms of a concession agreement containing its own arbitration clause. In some instances, arbitration claims have been filed on the same set of facts under both ICSID and ICC Rules. See *S. Pac. Prop. Ltd* v. *Egypt*, Jurisdiction, ICSID Case No. ARB/84/3 (1988). The ICC award was subject to extensive discussion in the French judicial actions that led to its vacatur. See Cour d'appel de Paris, 12 July 1984, trans. in *ILM*, 23 (1984), 1048–61; Cour de Cassation, 6 January 1987, trans. in *ILM*, 26 (1987), 1004–7. For the ICSID award of 20 May 1992, see *ICSID Reports*, 3 (1995), 189, 241. See also W. L. Craig, 'The Final Chapter in the Pyramids Case. Discounting an ICSID Award for Annulment Risk', *ICSID Review – Foreign Investment Law Journal*, 8 (1993), 264–93.

[38] In theory at least, challenges might also arise under other institutional or ad hoc rules. For example, Art. 24(3) of the 2004 US Model Bilateral Investment Treaty (BIT) provides that a claimant may submit a request for arbitration under the rules of ICSID, the ICSID Additional Facility, UNCITRAL, or 'if the claimant and respondent agree, to any other arbitration institution or under any other arbitration rules'. US State Department, Treaty Between the Government of the United States of America and the Government of [Country] Concerning the Encouragement and Reciprocal Protection of Investment, Art. 24(3) (2004). The same language appears in FTAs, for example Art. 11.16 of the South Korea–United States FTA (pending ratification at the moment this chapter goes to print). Free Trade Agreement Between the United States and the Republic of Korea Art. 11.16, US–S. Korea, 30 June 2007, www.ustr.gov/trade-agreements/free-trade-agreements/korus-fta. By contrast, Art. 1120 of NAFTA limits itself to the ICSID, the ICSID Additional Facility and UNCITRAL. North American Free Trade Agreement, US–Canada–Mexico, Chapter 11, Art. 1120, 17 December 1992, *ILM*, 32 (1993), 289–456.

[39] The UNCITRAL Arbitration Rules are not to be confused with the UNCITRAL Model Law on International Commercial Arbitration (UNCITRAL Model Law). Although the former entails procedural rules for handling an arbitration arising from a governing instrument that warrants application of the UNCITRAL Rules, the latter constitutes a matrix of what UNCITRAL deems to be a 'model' national arbitration statute. Both the UNCITRAL Rules and Model Law address arbitrator challenge, and unsurprisingly, display vast similarities.

[40] The full text of Convention Art. 14(1) contains both ethical and professional components. The full text reads: 'Persons designated to serve on the Panels shall be persons of high moral character and recognized competence in the fields of law, commerce, industry or finance, who may be relied upon to exercise independent judgment. Competence in the field of law shall be of particular importance in the case of persons on the Panel of Arbitrators.'

certification of independence made by the arbitrator at the beginning of the proceedings.[41] A party to the arbitration may propose disqualification of an arbitrator on account of any fact indicating a 'manifest' inability to meet that standard.[42]

When a litigant contests an arbitrator's fitness in an ICSID proceeding, the remaining arbitrators normally determine whether the individual lacks the capacity to exercise independent judgment.[43] The challenged arbitrator would first be given the opportunity to furnish explanations. If the remaining two members are equally divided, or the challenge relates to a majority of the arbitrators, the disqualification decision will be made by the Chairman of the ICSID Administrative Council, a post filled *ex officio* by the President of the World Bank pursuant to Art. 5 of the ICSID Convention.[44] Any review of the resulting award would normally be made by an ICSID-appointed panel, rather than national judges who might conduct their own review of independence and impartiality.[45] By contrast, outside ICSID, challenges to arbitrators in commercial

---

[41] Rule 6(2) of the ICSID Arbitration Rules requires each arbitrator, prior or during the Tribunal's first session, to sign a declaration affirming, *inter alia*, that the individual will 'judge fairly as between the parties, according to the applicable law' and attach a statement of past and present professional, business and other relationships with the parties as well as any other circumstance that might cause the arbitrator's reliability for independent judgment to be questioned by a party. In signing the declaration, the arbitrator assumes a continuing obligation to promptly notify ICSID of any such relationship that subsequently arises during the proceedings.

[42] Art. 57, ICSID Convention provides as follows:

> A party may propose to a Commission or Tribunal the disqualification of any of its members on account of any fact indicating a manifest lack of the qualities required by paragraph (1) of Article 14. A party to arbitration proceedings may, in addition, propose the disqualification of an arbitrator on the ground that he was ineligible for appointment to the Tribunal under Section 2 of Chapter IV.

[43] See *ibid.*, Art. 58. See, generally, Ch. H. Schreuer, *The ICSID Convention. A Commentary* (Cambridge University Press, 2001), 1202–6. See also the procedure amplified in Rule 9 of the Arbitration Rules adopted by the ICSID Administrative Council pursuant to Art. 6 of the Convention itself.

[44] For one recent case in which the remaining arbitrators did not agree, see *PIP Sàrl v. République gabonaise* (Case No. ARB/08/17, 2009), decision communicated on 12 December 2009 by Meg Kinnear, ISCID Secretary-General, rejecting disqualification of Ibrahim Fadlallah following disagreement between Brigitte Stern and Jan Paulsson.

[45] Under ICSID Convention, Art. 52, the limited grounds for challenge do not include an arbitrator's lack of independent thinking. An award may be set aside for the following reasons: (1) improper constitution of the Tribunal; (2) Tribunal excess of authority; (3) corruption of a Tribunal member; (4) serious departure from a fundamental rule of procedure; or (5) failure of the award to state reasons. This challenge is made not to

arbitrations would initially be heard by the relevant supervisory institution and then again come before whatever national court is charged with considering motions to review awards.

Challenge under the UNCITRAL Rules differs in procedural mechanics, notwithstanding a basic similarity in the standards themselves. Art. 10 provides for challenge if circumstances give rise to 'justifiable doubts' about the arbitrator's impartiality or independence.[46] Unless the other side agrees or the arbitrator withdraws voluntarily, the challenge decision will be made by the appropriate 'appointing authority' that constituted (or would otherwise have constituted) the Tribunal itself.[47] In UNCITRAL arbitration, as in ordinary commercial cases, the ultimate validity of any appointing authority decision will be subject to review by national courts under the appropriate arbitration statute or within the framework of the New York Convention. At least one author has suggested that ICSID take a serious look at its practices with respect to arbitrator challenge. The proposed reforms include, *inter alia*, (i) a change in the grounds for challenge from 'manifest' lack of independence to 'justifiable doubts' as to independence and impartiality and (ii) decisions on challenge made by an independent ad hoc committee rather than the challenged arbitrator's colleagues on the tribunal.[48]

In some cases an arbitrator's challenge will take place under what might be seen as a hybrid process under the ICSID Additional Facility. In such instances, the arbitration will be supervised by ICSID, under procedures

national courts but pursuant to an internal ICSID process triggered by a letter to the ICSID Secretary-General. Review is conducted by an ad hoc committee of three persons with authority to annul the award in part or in total. If an award is annulled, either party may require that it be submitted to a new Tribunal.

[46] United Nations Commission on International Trade Law Arbitration Rules, G. A. Res. 31/98, Art. 10(1), UN Doc. A/31/17 (15 December 1976). A similar formulation exists in Art. 12 of the UNCITRAL Model Law on International Commercial Arbitration. UNCITRAL Model Law on International Commercial Arbitration, G. A. Res. 40/72, Art. 12, UN Doc. A/40/17/Annex I and A/61/17/Annex I (21 June 1985), modified in 2006 in ways not relevant to its standards for arbitrator bias.

[47] The wording in Art. 12 contains an unfortunate (albeit perhaps unavoidable) complexity with respect to who gets to decide arbitrator challenges, distinguishing between situations (i) 'when the initial appointment was made by an appointing authority' (situations in which *Kompetenz* to hear the challenge lies with the same appointing authority); (ii) 'when the initial appointment was not made by an appointing authority' (in which case the challenge will be heard by a previously designated authority); and (iii) 'all other cases', whereby 'the decision on the challenge will be made … [by the] appointing authority as provided for in Article 6' of the Rules, under which the Permanent Court of Arbitration serves by default as the entity to designate an appointing authority if the parties cannot agree.

[48] See, generally, A. Sheppard, 'Arbitrator Independence in ICSID Arbitration', in Ch. Binder, U. Kriebaum and A. Reinisch (eds.), *International Investment Law for the 21st Century. Essays in Honour of Christoph Schreuer* (Oxford University Press, 2009), 131, 147–8.

similar to those of conventional ICSID cases, but *outside* the framework of the Washington Convention. The rule for challenge remains the ability to 'exercise independent judgment',[49] and the decision will normally be made by the challenged arbitrator's remaining colleagues.[50] However, national courts might also have their say on the matter when asked to vacate an award pursuant to their own standards of arbitrator fitness.[51]

Trivial relationships

On a planet where butterflies flap wings in Africa so as to cause Canadian snowstorms, clever minds can present scenarios under which most individuals might be deemed less than virgin in attitude or predisposition. Healthy standards for arbitrator integrity require distinctions to be drawn between the material and the trivial in both relationships and predispositions. Some experiences may create distant but nevertheless worrisome relationships with litigants. Others do not. Some statements or writings raise the prospect of an arbitrator's troubling predilections about controverted issues in the arbitration. Others simply demonstrate expertise.

In a professionally and economically interdependent world, some principles of proportionality and reasonable nexus must operate to triage between genuine and spurious challenges.[52] Analysis does not end with

---

[49] Rules Governing the Additional Facility for the Administration of Proceedings by the Secretariat of ICSID.

[50] Art. 15(5) ('Disqualification of Arbitrators').

[51] The Additional Facility Rules might apply in disputes where ICSID jurisdiction would not otherwise exist because either the host State or the investor's State is not party to the Washington Convention. For example, in the *Metalclad* case an American company filed an Additional Facility Claim related to a hazardous waste disposal facility in Mexico. The arbitrators found that Mexican regulatory action had denied 'fair and equitable treatment' and constituted expropriation without adequate compensation. Mexico petitioned to have the award set aside by the British Columbia Supreme Court, which had jurisdiction by virtue of the arbitration's official *situs* fixed in Vancouver notwithstanding that for convenience hearings had been held in Washington. The Court found that some but not all of the arbitrators' conclusions exceeded their jurisdiction. *Metalclad Corp. v. United Mexican States*, ICSID Case No. ARB(AF)/97/1 (2000) (Award), reprinted in *International Arbitration Report*, 16 (2001), A-1-16.

[52] In this connection, one remembers the delightful tirade in Molière's *Don Juan* when the valet Sganarelle proves the inevitability of his master's damnation by invoking a series of causal links, each plausible on its own, but together reaching a conclusion in no way justified by the reasoning. The bird clinging to a branch reminded Sganarelle of the duty to cling to moral precepts, and then led him through sky, sea, ships, earth and beasts to the conclusion that his miscreant philandering boss was lost forever, which in any event was the place which the scandalised wanted to reach from the beginning. Molière, *Don Juan*, act 5, sc. 2.

the discovery of a link between arbitrator and dispute, but must proceed to assess the proximity or intensity of the troublesome relationship, having been called into service to evaluate an arbitrator's allegedly disqualifying links with one side.[53]

In this connection, the IBA Guidelines attempt to provide concrete criteria for judging arbitrator relationships and predispositions. General Standard 2 of the Guidelines obliges arbitrators to resign if they know of facts or circumstances which, from a reasonable person's point of view, give rise to 'justifiable doubts' about the arbitrators' impartiality or independence.[54] In defining justifiable doubts, Standard 2(d) speaks of a 'significant' economic or personal interest, not 'any' interest.[55]

Looking to national law for analogies, a *de minimis* standard can also be found in the American Bar Association 2007 Model Code of Judicial Conduct, which requires a judge to 'disqualify himself or herself in any proceeding in which the judge's impartiality might reasonably be questioned, including but not limited to the following circumstances: ... (2) The judge knows that [he/she] has more than a de minimis interest that could be substantially affected by the proceeding'.[56] The ABA Model Code of Judicial Conduct defines *de minimis* to mean 'an insignificant interest that could not raise a reasonable question regarding the judge's

---

[53] See the concurring opinion in *Commonwealth Coatings Corp.* v. *Continental Casualty Co.*, 393 US 145 (1968), where Justice White considered it enough that the challenged arbitrator had done 'more than trivial business' with one of the parties, *ibid.*, 152 (White, J., concurring). This test was adopted by the US Court of Appeals for the Second Circuit in *Applied Industrial Materials Corp.* v. *Ovalar Makine Ticaret Ve Sanayi, AS*, 492 F.3d 132 (2d Cir. 2007). See also decisions dismissing the challenges in ICSID Cases Nos. ARB/03/17 (*Suez, Aguas de Barcelona and Interagua Servicios* v. *Argentina*, 2006) and ARB/03/19 (*Suez, Vivendi and Aguas de Barcelona* v. *Argentina*, 2006). In their decision of 12 May 2008, the remaining arbitrators identified four criteria relevant to their colleague's links with the party that had nominated her: (i) proximity of the connections; (ii) intensity of interaction; (iii) dependence on the party by virtue of benefits said to have been conferred; and (iv) materiality of any benefits allegedly accruing to the arbitrator. The challenge was based on the arbitrator's position as a director of a Swiss bank which apparently held small amounts of portfolio investments in the claimant companies.

[54] Standard 2(a) speaks of the arbitrator's subjective 'doubts' while Standard 2(b) refers to an objective test based on a 'reasonable third person's point of view'. IBA Guidelines, General Standards 2(a), 2(b).

[55] A comment to General Standard 6 discussing troublesome relationships throws further light on the overlap of arbitrators' interests with those of their law firm. Explanation 6(a) States that 'the activities of the arbitrator's firm should not automatically constitute a conflict of interest'. Rather, each firm's activity must be considered in the individual case. IBA Guidelines, General Standard 6 cmt. (*a*).

[56] ABA Model Code of Judicial Conduct R. 2.11 (2007).

impartiality'. It also defines 'economic interest' to mean ownership 'of more than a de minimis legal or equitable interest'. In applying this principle, the ABA Model Code of Judicial Conduct states that an economic interest does not include an interest in 'a mutual or common investment fund'.

Other jurisdictions with developed arbitration laws take a similar perspective. In *AT&T Corp.* v. *Saudi Cable Co.*, the English Court of Appeal had to consider the effect of an arbitrator's ownership of shares in a telecommunications company in competition with one of the parties. Any benefit from the arbitration's outcome that could indirectly accrue to the company whose shares were owned by the arbitrator was deemed 'of such minimal benefit to [the arbitrator]' that the Court held it unreasonable to conclude that the arbitrator's share ownership would be a relevant influence.[57] An insignificant ownership interest in a company will not be cause for disqualification.

The costs of an absolutist perspective will usually outweigh any advantages. If ethical standards did not include some notion of triviality, it would be unduly easy to derail arbitration by asserting a tenuous connection between arbitrators and facts that might arguably have an effect on their decisions. A 'no-link-too small' theory would permit removal of arbitrators simply because they occasionally socialised with colleagues from the host State. The damage to the stability and efficiency of the arbitral process would affect all those who depend on it to provide relatively fair and neutral adjudication.

Pre-judgment in procedural orders

One of the most tricky types of challenge relates to alleged pre-judgment in a procedural order, which might express conclusions about a matter not yet the subject of evidentiary hearings. Interim orders preserving the status quo might make reference to contested property ownership that is yet to be established one way or the other. And jurisdictional rulings might draw tentative conclusions about agency as between different members of a corporate group.

Whether or not such expressions of opinion taint the arbitrator depends very much on the facts and circumstances of each case. The

---

[57] *AT&T Corp.* v. *Saudi Cable Co.*, Lloyd's Rep., 2 (2000), 127, §43(c) (CA) (Eng.), available at 2000 WL 571190. In Australia, a variant of the *de minimis* principle has been enacted by statute to provide that justifiable doubts on impartiality exist only if there is a 'real danger' of bias. See Sam Luttrell, 'Model Law Plus Lawmaking', *Arbitration International*, 26 (2010) (forthcoming).

context of the order might make clear that ownership was presumed merely for the sake of determining whether to grant interim relief to prevent assets from being diverted. The offending language might be tentative and *prima facie* with no intention of depriving either side of a full and fair hearing on the matter, and inserted in an order with qualifying language such as 'if so decided by the Tribunal' or 'on the assumption that Claimant is ultimately found to be the owner'.

Such potential pre-judgment causes problems under both the statutory provisions of developed legal systems and the rules of most arbitral institutions. The interaction of these rules might be illustrated by a hypothetical arbitration in London. The English Arbitration Act establishes mandatory norms that an arbitral tribunal shall 'act fairly and impartially as between the parties, giving each party a reasonable opportunity of putting his case and dealing with that of his opponent'.[58] A rich English case-law on 'apparent bias' makes clear that justice must not only be done, but must be seen to be done.[59] Among the tests proposed by judicial and scholarly pronouncements, one that commends itself looks to see whether the circumstances of the case would lead a fair-minded and informed observer to conclude that there was a real danger that the Tribunal was biased.

Institutional rules often applied in London follow similar lines. The London Court of International Arbitration (LCIA) Rules provide that an arbitrator may be considered unfit if she 'does not act fairly and impartially as between the parties', and that an arbitrator may be challenged if 'circumstances exist that give rise to justifiable doubts as to his impartiality or independence'.[60] 'Bias' under that text includes pre-judgment of an issue, in the sense of deciding without giving each side an opportunity to present its case.[61]

---

[58] Arbitration Act 1996, c. 23, §33(1) (Eng.).

[59] Cases include *R* v. *Sussex Justices*, [1924] 1 KB 256; *Locabail Ltd* v. *Bayfield Properties Ltd*, [2000] 1 All ER 65; *R* v. *Gough*, [1993] AC 646 (HL); *In re Medicaments & Related Classes of Goods (No. 2)*, [2001] 1 WLR 700 (CA); *Porter* v. *Magill*, [2002] 2 AC 357 (HL); *ASM Shipping Ltd* v. *TTMI Ltd*, [2005] EWHC (Comm.) 2238; *National Assembly for Wales* v. *Condron*, [2006] EWCA (Civ.) 1573; *Hagop Ardahalian* v. *Unifert International SA*, (The 'Elissar'), Lloyd's Rep., 1 (1984) (QB), 206; *AWG Group Ltd* v. *Morrison*, [2006] EWCA (Civ.) 6; *Modern Engineering (Bristol) Ltd* v. *C. Miskin & Son Ltd*, Lloyd's Rep., 1 (1981) (CA), 135; *R.* v. *Bow Street Metropolitan Stipendiary Magistrate, Pinochet No. 2*, [2000] 1 AC 199 (HL); *Gillies* v. *Secretary of State for Work & Pensions*, [2006] 1 WLR 781 (HL); and *Flaherty* v. *National Greyhound Racing Club*, [2005] EWCA (Civ.) 1117.

[60] LCIA Arbitration Rules, Arts. 10.2 and 10.3.

[61] Sometimes it is said that a party-nominated arbitrator should possess maximum pre-disposition and minimum bias. Although the value of this unduly cute saying remains doubtful, it is true that, for international arbitration, the party-nominee often plays a

Duty to investigate

Among the new frontiers being addressed by judicial decisions, few are more intellectually challenging than the matter of an arbitrator's duty to investigate. It has long been common coin of conflicts analysis that arbitrators must disclose significant relationships that might call into question their independence.

What happens, however, when the arbitrator knows of no relevant relationships? Must she go one step further and investigate possible conflicts? Must arbitrators actively look for trouble? The answer, perhaps unsatisfying to those who seek hard and fast rules, must be 'sometimes'.

In a US case in 2007, an appellate court stopped short of imposing a general duty to investigate, limiting its holding to situations in which the arbitrator had reason to believe that some conflict might exist.[62] The case confirmed vacatur of a commercial award for 'evident partiality' (the relevant standard under the US Federal Arbitration Act) because the challenged arbitrator had failed to investigate possible business transactions that might have affected his independence.

The facts of the case merit close scrutiny. A dispute between a Turkish company and an American corporation led to arbitration in which the presiding arbitrator learned of a potential conflict that was disclosed by e-mail, with no objection by either side. After the Arbitral Tribunal determined liability in favour of the American party, the proceedings continued into the damages phase. It was then discovered that the challenged arbitrator's company had been involved in a relatively small transaction (approximately $275,000) with the entity that acquired the American party. On the arbitrator's refusal to recuse himself, the Turkish side brought an action to vacate the award on liability. The tribunal chairman was President and CEO of what the reviewing court described as 'a multi-billion dollar company with 50 offices in 30 countries'.[63] An affiliate of that group apparently had a relatively small business transaction with a company related to the American side. The chairman had earlier informed the parties of the negotiations with that entity, but did not reveal that at a later time a contract had been actually concluded. The

---

special role in assisting the presiding arbitrator to understand arguments that may otherwise be less accessible, due to differences in legal culture.

[62] See *Applied Industrial Materials Corp.* v. *Ovalar Makine Ticaret Ve Sanayi, AS*, 492 F.3d 132 (2d Cir. 2007).

[63] *Ibid.*, 135.

court was not impressed by the arbitrator's explanation that a 'Chinese Wall' had been erected between himself and the potential conflict.

The appellate decision noted that the lower court had cited both the American Arbitration Association/American Bar Association Code of Ethics for Arbitrators in Commercial Disputes (AAA/ABA Code of Ethics) and the IBA Guidelines. To the thoughtful observer, this provides an illustration of the trend towards cross-pollination of ethical standards in international arbitration, with national courts looking to professional guidelines just as arbitral institutions look to judicial decisions.

Conclusion

Arbitrator integrity takes on significance not only for the direct participants in cross-border trade and investment, but also for the wider global community whose welfare is directly affected by the arbitral process. Arbitrators are individuals to whom business managers, investors and nations entrust their treasure and their welfare.

Even if universally accepted standards of conduct remain elusive, all communities implicated by cross-border arbitration must continue a dialogue on the subject which at the least will help to identify wrong directions and false solutions. While many of the recent attacks on arbitration remain transparently self-serving, and even silly, concerns related to arbitrator independence and impartiality must be taken with utmost seriousness in all their multi-faceted aspects.

Although traditional ethical models will serve as starting points for evaluating arbitrator fitness, they must be flexible enough to address novel professional temptations. In particular, vigilance commends itself when lawyers take on various professional roles, making arguments as advocates in one case about propositions that remain open in other cases where they sit as arbitrators. The constant movement in arbitrators' lives and activities requires regular adjustment in both formulation and application of contours for acceptable and unacceptable arbitrator behaviour. In evaluating these adjustments, those of us privileged to have worked with Detlev Vagts will continue to be inspired by his example of scholarly integrity and intellectual rigour.

29

Managing conflicts between rulings of the World Trade Organization and regional trade tribunals: reflections on the *Brazil – Tyres* case

JULIA YA QIN[*]

Introduction

The proliferation of international tribunals in recent decades has given rise to much concern about potential conflicts between judicial decisions and possible 'fragmentation' of international law.[1] Most of the discussions have focused on conflicts of jurisdictions and conflicts of norms that may result from competing or overlapping jurisdictions.[2] While some commentators believe that judicial competition can have a positive effect on the development of international law, others worry that different judicial interpretations may create inconsistent rights and

---

[*] I dedicate this chapter to Detlev Vagts, whose advice guided me to the field of international economic law, which has since evolved into one of the most dynamic areas of international legal studies.

[1] See generally, International Law Commission (ILC), Report of the Study Group, *Fragmentation of International Law. Difficulties Arising from the Diversification and Expansion of International Law*, UN Doc. A/CN.4/L.702 (18 July 2006); UN Doc. A/CN.4/L.682 (13 April 2006).

[2] See generally, e.g., Y. Shany, *The Competing Jurisdictions of International Courts and Tribunals* (Oxford University Press, 2003); J. Pauwelyn, *Conflict of Norms in Public International Law. How WTO Law Relates to Other Rules of International Law* (Cambridge University Press, 2003); G. Marceau, 'Conflicts of Norms and Conflicts of Jurisdictions. The Relationship between the WTO Agreement and MEAs and Other Treaties', *Journal of World Trade*, 35 (2001), 1081–1131. See also K. Kwak and G. Marceau, 'Overlaps and Conflicts of Jurisdiction Between the World Trade Organization and Regional Trade Agreements', in L. Bartels and F. Ortino (eds.), *Regional Trade Agreements and the WTO Legal System* (Oxford University Press, 2006), chapter. 20; N. Lavranos, 'Regulating Competing Jurisdictions among International Courts and Tribunals', *ZaöRV*, 68 (2008), 575–621.

obligations for the States.[3] The worst type of conflicts, however, is the conflict of obligations where a State cannot comply with the decisions of two tribunals at once because their separate decisions require the State to act in entirely opposite directions.

Unfortunately, such a direct conflict of obligations has occurred, for the first time to the author's knowledge, as a result of the decision of the World Trade Organization (WTO) in the *Brazil – Tyres* case.[4] The WTO Appellate Body held in this case that, by following the ruling of an Arbitral Tribunal of Mercosur – the regional trade agreement (RTA) between Brazil and several South American countries[5] – Brazil had acted inconsistently with WTO rules. Consequently, Brazil found itself in a legal bind in which it could not comply with its WTO obligations without breaching its obligations under Mercosur. Although as a regional free trade agreement (FTA) Mercosur needs to meet certain WTO requirements – in particular Art. XXIV of the General Agreement on Tariffs and Trade (GATT) – institutionally it is completely independent from the WTO, and there is no hierarchical relationship between the Mercosur tribunal and the WTO adjudicatory body.

Significantly, this direct conflict of obligations did not stem from competing or overlapping jurisdictions, or conflicts of norms arising from different treaty provisions. Instead, it arose entirely from the Appellate Body's interpretation of a WTO provision. This particular case, therefore, gives us pause. Is the Appellate Body's interpretation correct and, if so, is it the only correct interpretation possible? If there are alternative interpretations that could have been made to avoid giving rise to such a direct conflict of obligations, should the Appellate Body have chosen such an alternative? Does the Appellate Body have a duty to explore such alternatives? To what extent should avoiding conflicts be part of the judicial policy of international tribunals? Are there

---

[3] For different perspectives on the issue, see W. T. Worster, 'Competition and Comity in the Fragmentation of International Law', *Brooklyn Journal of International Law*, 34 (2008), 119–49. See also G. Hafner, 'Pros and Cons Ensuing from Fragmentation of International Law', *Michigan Journal of International Law*, 25 (2004), 849–63.

[4] Appellate Body Report, *Brazil – Measures Affecting Imports of Retreaded Tyres*, WT/DS332/AB/R, adopted 17 December 2007 (hereafter, Appellate Body Report).

[5] Mercosur (the Southern Common Market) was established by the Treaty Establishing a Common Market Between Argentina, Brazil, Paraguay and Uruguay (Treaty of Asuncion), done at Asuncion on 26 March 1991, entry into force 29 November 1991, 2140 UNTS 319. Bolivia, Chile, Columbia, Ecuador, Peru and Venezuela are currently associated members. Venezuela signed a membership agreement in 2006, but has yet to obtain full membership.

international legal principles and norms that provide guidance in this regard? This chapter seeks to explore these issues. Answers to these questions may shed light on how to prevent similar conflicts from reoccurring in the future.

The *Brazil – Tyres* Case

Background

The import ban on retreaded tyres

At issue in both the Mercosur and WTO litigations was the import ban Brazil imposed on retreaded tyres. Retreaded tyres are produced by reconditioning used tyres. They have a shorter lifespan than new tyres and are sold at a lower price. Pursuant to international standards, passenger car tyres may be retreaded only once, whereas commercial vehicle tyres may be retreaded more than once.

The import ban on retreaded tyres was formally introduced in 2000, but had its origin in Brazil's ban on used tyre imports as early as 1991. For historical reasons, there were millions of used tyres scattered throughout Brazil. In the tropical and subtropical climate, these uncollected used tyres became breeding grounds for mosquito-borne diseases, such as dengue fever, yellow fever and malaria. It is, however, very costly to collect discarded tyres so widely dispersed across the vast territory of Brazil, and technologically very difficult to dispose of tyre waste properly. As part of its effort to control the health hazards associated with used tyres, Brazil began to prohibit imports of used tyres in 1991 under regulation Portaria DECEX 8/1991.[6]

The main importers in Brazil of used tyres were domestic producers of retreaded tyres, who preferred imports because it was cheaper to import than to collect used tyres domestically. By prohibiting the importation of used tyres, Brazil effectively required its retreading industry to use domestically generated used tyres exclusively which, it was anticipated, would lead to a reduction in the accumulation of used tyres in the country. The ban on used tyre imports met, however, with strong opposition from the domestic retreading industry. Some producers succeeded in obtaining court injunctions against the ban. Consequently, importation of used tyres continued through court order despite the ban.

---

[6] See Panel Report, *Brazil – Measures Affecting Imports of Retreaded Tyres*, WT/DS332/R, 12 June 2007 (hereafter, Panel Report), paras. 7.24–7.28.

Although technically retreaded tyres are not used tyres, in practice Brazil treated retreaded tyres as used tyres and prohibited their imports under the 1991 ban. Despite this *de facto* prohibition, importation of retreaded tyres grew significantly after 1995, with a majority of the imports coming from the European Union (EU).[7] In 2000, Brazil issued regulation Portaria SECEX 8/2000, that expressly prohibited the importation of retreaded tyres. By 2002, the total imports of retreaded tyres had fallen to the pre-1995 level, and imports from the EU dropped to zero.[8]

It should be noted that imported retreaded tyres have essentially the same effect on the environment as imported used tyres. That is because each imported retread made from a foreign-sourced used tyre will introduce an additional used tyre to Brazil. All retreaded tyres utilising foreign-sourced used tyres, whether produced abroad and imported into Brazil or produced locally in Brazil, will eventually become tyre waste in Brazil, unless they can be re-exported to another country. As compared to new tyres, retreaded tyres become tyre waste faster because they have a shorter lifespan and in most cases cannot be retreaded again. Consequently, imports of retreaded tyres can be expected to result in a faster accumulation of waste tyres than imports of new tyres.

The Mercosur litigation

Brazil's 2000 ban on imports of retreaded tyres was challenged by Uruguay in an ad hoc Mercosur Arbitral Tribunal in 2001. At the time of the Uruguay-Brazil litigation, Mercosur members were obligated to submit their disputes to ad hoc arbitrary tribunals, whose decisions were final and binding upon the parties.[9]

---

[7] See F. Morosini, *The Mercosur and WTO Retreaded Tires Dispute. Rehabilitating Regulatory Competition in International Trade and Environmental Regulation*, SIEL Working Paper No. 42/08, www.ssrn.com/link/SIEL-Inaugural-Conference.html, chapter VI, graph 2: Brazil's Imports of Retreaded Tires (showing that the total imports of retreaded tyres grew from less than 5,000 tons in 1995 to more than 25,000 tons in 1998, then tapered off to less than 20,000 tons in 2000, and that imports from the EU during this period accounted for 60–80 per cent of the total imports).

[8] *Ibid.*

[9] Protocol of Brasilia for the Solution of Controversies (1991), www.sice.oas.org/Trade/ MRCSR/brasilia/pbrasilia_e.asp. The Mercosur dispute settlement mechanism has since changed to allow its members to have a choice of forum in either Mercosur or the WTO, and to provide the opportunity to appeal the arbitral decisions to a Permanent Review Body. Protocol of Olivos for the Settlement of Disputes in Mercosur (2004), http://untreaty.un.org/unts/144078_158780/5/7/13152.pdf.

Uruguay claimed that prior to the 2000 ban, it was able to export remoulded tyres (one type of retreaded tyres) to Brazil without obstruction, and that the 2000 ban introduced a new measure in violation of a Mercosur decision which required its members not to introduce new trade restrictions of any nature.[10] In defence, Brazil argued that its 2000 regulation prohibiting imports of retreaded tyres was not a new restriction, but merely a clarification of the scope of the 1991 ban on used tyre imports.

The Arbitral Tribunal disagreed with Brazil and found that the 2000 regulation was a new restriction, because it interrupted the previously continuous imports of remoulded tyres from Uruguay. Accordingly, the Tribunal ruled that the import ban was inconsistent with Mercosur law and ordered Brazil to amend its law to comply with the ruling.

In response to the Tribunal's ruling, Brazil adopted new regulations which exempted remoulded tyres originating in Mercosur countries from the import ban on retreaded tyres (the Mercosur exemption).[11]

The WTO dispute

In 2005, the European Communities (EC) brought a WTO complaint challenging Brazil's ban on the importation of retreaded tyres. As noted above, a majority of retreaded tyres imported by Brazil prior to the ban came from the EU, and as a result of the ban EU exports of retreaded tyres to Brazil had dropped to zero by 2002. The EC claimed that the ban violated GATT Art. XI which prohibits quantitative restrictions, and that the Mercosur exemption discriminated against the EC in violation of GATT Arts. I and XIII (most-favoured-nation, or MFN, requirements). Brazil defended its position by invoking GATT Art. XX(b), which excuses measures 'necessary to protect human, animal or plant life or health'. With respect to the Mercosur exemption, Brazil argued that it adopted the exemption out of its international legal obligations under Mercosur, and that differential treatment of its Mercosur partners was permitted under GATT Art. XXIV. The EC countered that the ban was not designed to protect health and the environment, but to protect Brazil's domestic retread industry, and that the Mercosur exemption could not be justified under Art. XXIV.[12]

---

[10] Decision of the Council of Common Market, 22/00.

[11] Portaria SECEX 2/2002, which was incorporated into Portaria SECEX 14/2004. See Panel Report, *supra* n. 6, para. 7.265.

[12] The EC pointed out that Art. XXIV:8 specifically excluded from the requirements of RTAs restrictions permitted under Art. XX.

The Panel's decision   The Panel found that Brazil's import ban violated GATT Art. XI and could not be justified by Art. XX(b), because it had not been applied in a manner consistent with the requirement of the chapeau of Art. XX. However, the Panel agreed with Brazil that its import ban on retreaded tyres was necessary to protect health and the environment, thus validating the legitimate purpose of the ban. The Panel's unfavourable decision was based on used tyre imports through court injunctions. The Panel found that permitting importation of used tyres directly contradicted the rationale of the ban on retreaded tyres, because it effectively allowed the very used tyres which were prevented from entering into Brazil after retreading to be imported before retreading, and that imports of used tyres had been taking place in such a large quantity that they had significantly undermined the objective of the ban.

The Panel also examined the Mercosur exemption under the chapeau of Art. XX, but found no violation thereof. The chapeau requires that measures taken under Art. XX 'are not applied in a manner which would constitute a means of arbitrary or unjustifiable discrimination between countries where the same conditions prevail, or a disguised restriction on international trade'. The Panel found that, although the Mercosur exemption had resulted in discrimination against non-Mercosur countries, such discrimination was not 'arbitrary' or 'unjustifiable' within the meaning of the chapeau. According to the Panel, the discrimination was not 'arbitrary' because Brazil had adopted the exemption pursuant to the ruling of a Mercosur tribunal, not out of its own capricious decision; and it was not 'unjustifiable' because the volume of retread tyres imported from Mercosur countries, at the time of the ruling, had not been significant enough to undermine Brazil's ability to fulfil the objective of the ban.

Having concluded that the import ban could not be justified by Art. XX(b), the Panel exercised judicial economy with respect to the EC's claim that the Mercosur exemption violated the MFN requirements. Consequently, it did not examine Brazil's defence under GATT Art. XXIV. It should be noted, however, that the Panel did not exclude the regional trade arrangement categorically from the application of Art. XX. Rather, its ruling suggested that, should the volume of imports from Mercosur countries increase significantly in the future, the Mercosur exemption might well become 'unjustifiable' within the meaning of the chapeau. Thus, while excusing the Mercosur exemption, the Panel's decision kept the door open for possible future challenges.

The Appellate Body's decision On appeal by the EC, the WTO Appellate Body upheld the Panel's main findings, but reversed its decision on the Mercosur exemption. The Appellate Body disagreed with the Panel's approach of focusing on the trade effect of the measure in the interpretation of the chapeau. According to the Appellate Body, the assessment of whether discrimination is arbitrary or unjustifiable should be made in the light of the objective of the measure at issue, and the reasons given for discrimination must bear a rational connection with the objective pursued by the measure.[13] The Appellate Body's reasoning regarding the Mercosur exemption was summarised in the following paragraph:

> In this case, the discrimination between Mercosur countries and other WTO Members in the application of the Import Ban was introduced as a consequence of a ruling by a Mercosur tribunal. The tribunal found against Brazil because the restriction on imports of remoulded tyres was inconsistent with the prohibition of new trade restrictions under Mercosur law. In our view, the ruling issued by the Mercosur arbitral tribunal is not an acceptable rationale for the discrimination, because it bears no relationship to the legitimate objective pursued by the Import Ban that falls within the purview of Article XX(b), and even goes against this objective, to however small a degree. Accordingly, we are of the view that the Mercosur exemption has resulted in the Import Ban being applied in a manner that constitutes arbitrary or unjustifiable discrimination.[14]

Thus, the Appellate Body concluded that the Mercosur exemption, as well as the used tyre imports through court injunctions, resulted in Brazil's import ban being applied in a manner inconsistent with the chapeau requirement. The WTO adopted the Appellate Body report on 17 December 2007, and ordered Brazil to bring its measures into compliance.

The arbitrator's decision Under WTO law, Brazil may have 'a reasonable period of time' to implement the WTO decision.[15] After Brazil and the EC failed to agree on the timeframe for implementation, the WTO appointed an arbitrator (a member of the Appellate Body) to determine what would constitute the reasonable period in this case.

---

[13] Appellate Body Report, *supra* n. 4, para. 227. [14] *Ibid.*, para. 228.
[15] Art. 21.3 of the Understanding on Rules and Procedures Governing the Settlement of Disputes (DSU).

In the arbitral proceedings, Brazil requested until September 2009 to achieve full compliance, explaining that it would take time for it to negotiate a solution with its Mercosur partners. The EC opposed, arguing that a Mercosur-wide arrangement would not lead to removal of the Mercosur exemption and Brazil should not be given any time for pursuing such negotiation.

The arbitrator issued his decision in August 2008.[16] While recognising that Brazil may choose to negotiate with other countries as a means of implementing a WTO ruling, the arbitrator found that such negotiation was a process 'external' to the law-making and regulatory system of Brazil, and was therefore not indispensable for Brazil's implementation of the WTO decision. Accordingly, the arbitrator decided not to factor into his determination any time needed for such negotiation. Based on the time necessary for Brazil to revise its domestic law concerning the importation of used tyres through court injunctions, the arbitrator set 17 December 2008 as the deadline for Brazil's compliance.

Current status

Brazil failed to meet the deadline set by the arbitrator. Consequently, Brazil has been in breach of its WTO obligations, which gives the EC the right to seek compensation or retaliation under WTO law. Fortunately for Brazil, the EC agreed in January 2009 to allow additional time to resolve the dispute.[17]

In June 2009, the Supreme Court of Brazil ruled that imports of used and retreaded tyres are unconstitutional, because they constitute 'environmental waste' and the Constitution guarantees the preservation of the environment.[18] The Supreme Court's ruling put an end to imports of used tyres through court injunctions. On 14 September 2009, Brazil notified the WTO that it had adopted a new regulation prohibiting issuance of new licences for the importation of used and retreaded

---

[16] Award of the Arbitrator, *Brazil – Measures Affecting Imports of Retreaded Tyres, Arbitration under Art. 21.3(c) of the Understanding on Rules and Procedures Governing the Settlement of Disputes*, WT/DS332/16, 29 August 2008 (hereafter, Arbitral Award).

[17] See WT/DS332/18, 9 January 2009 (Understanding between Brazil and the European Communities Regarding Procedures under Article 22 of the DSU). The EC nonetheless continued to express its dissatisfaction with Brazil's actions and called for Brazil to lift its import ban on retreaded tyres. See WTO Dispute Settlement Body, Minutes of Meeting on 20 April 2009, WT/DSB/M/267, 26 June 2009, para. 50.

[18] See BNA WTO Reporter, 'Brazilian Supreme Court Calls Used Tires "Environmental Waste", Bans Their Import', 9 July 2009.

tyres, irrespective of their origin.[19] Thus, Brazil claims that it has fully complied with the WTO ruling. The EC has the right to challenge Brazil's compliance claim under WTO rules.[20]

Analysis

The WTO ruling left Brazil in a legal quandary: Brazil could not honour its treaty obligation under the WTO without breaching its obligation under Mercosur – and vice versa – unless it agreed to lift the import ban altogether, which was not an option given its declared environmental objective. In the end, Brazil chose to honour its WTO obligation over its Mercosur obligation, consistent with its declared environmental objective. It is unclear whether Brazil has reached an agreement with its Mercosur partners so as to avoid the breach of its Mercosur obligation. But no matter what Brazil has managed to do within Mercosur, the fact remains that the WTO decision has given rise to a direct conflict of treaty obligations for Brazil.

It should be noted that the conflict arising in this case has its unique features. Formally speaking, since the WTO and Mercosur both ruled against Brazil's import ban, there is no apparent conflict between the two rulings. However, because the WTO decision upheld the legitimate purpose of the ban, and because its objection was solely to the inconsistency of the Mercosur exemption with such purpose, the decision can only be reasonably understood as a call for Brazil to remove the Mercosur exemption, rather than to lift the import ban altogether.[21] It is in this substantive sense that the WTO ruling has created a direct conflict of treaty obligations for Brazil.[22]

This conflict, however, is neither inherent nor inevitable. Instead, it arose purely as a result of the Appellate Body's interpretation of the chapeau of GATT Art. XX.

Conflict not inherent

The conflict of treaty obligations in this case did not stem from competing or overlapping jurisdictions. The WTO permits its members to enter

---

[19] See WT/DS332/19/Add.6, 15 September 2009 (Status Report by Brazil).

[20] Art. 21.5, DSU.

[21] As is typically the case, the WTO decision merely requires Brazil to bring its offending measures into conformity with its obligations under the WTO Agreement, without specifying how this should be achieved.

[22] To argue that the WTO ruling did not create a conflict because its text did not directly contradict the Mercosur ruling would be to rely on empty formalism in disregard of reality.

into agreements for closer economic integration and allows preferential treatment among parties to such agreements, provided that certain conditions are met.[23] Mercosur was designed to be such an agreement.[24] The dispute between Uruguay and Brazil involved claims for the breach of a Mercosur decision, over which the Mercosur dispute settlement system had the exclusive jurisdiction.[25] The EC–Brazil dispute, on the other hand, was between two WTO members concerning the application of GATT, over which the WTO dispute settlement system had the exclusive jurisdiction.[26]

The conflict in this case did not arise from inconsistent treaty norms, either. The WTO and Mercosur are both FTAs which share the same values and speak the same language of trade liberalisation. Although the controversies surrounding Brazil's import ban highlighted the tension between trade and the environment, there is no inherent conflict between the two norms under the applicable treaties. Like the WTO, Mercosur seeks to balance the need for liberal trade against the need to protect health and the environment. The Preamble of the Treaty of Asuncion (establishing Mercosur) states explicitly that the objective of economic integration and development must be achieved by 'making optimum use of available resources' and by 'preserving the environment'.[27] The Mercosur obligation to eliminate all restrictions on trade among its parties does not apply to 'measures taken in the situations envisaged in article 50 of the Treaty of Montevideo of 1980'.[28] And one of such situations envisaged in Art. 50 is the adoption of measures regarding 'protection of human, animal

---

[23] Art. XXIV of GATT; Article V of the General Agreement on Trade in Services (GATS); and para. 2(c) of the Decision on Differential and More Favourable Treatment, Reciprocity and Fuller Participation of Developing Countries (1979) (the Enabling Clause).

[24] Mercosur was notified under the Enabling Clause on 17 February 1991 and has been under review within the WTO as a customs union under both the Enabling Clause and GATT Art. XXIV.

[25] See *supra* n. 9 and accompanying text.

[26] This contrasts with an apparent conflict of jurisdictions between NAFTA and the WTO, arising from Mexico's resort to the WTO dispute settlement in *United States – Measures Concerning the Importation, Marketing and Sale of Tuna and Tuna Products*, WT/DS381/4 (10 March 2009), and the US invocation of NAFTA dispute settlement procedures to address the same dispute. See WTO Dispute Settlement Body, Minutes of Meeting on 20 April 2009, WT/DSB/M/267 (26 June 2009), paras. 77–80.

[27] Treaty of Asuncion, *supra* n. 5.   [28] *Ibid.* Art. 2(b).

and plant life and health'.[29] The language of this provision is remarkably similar to that of GATT Art. XX(b).

In the Mercosur litigation, Brazil did not invoke Art. 50 of the Treaty of Montevideo to justify its import ban. This fact significantly complicated its case in the WTO proceedings, as will be explained below.

Conflict not inevitable

The conflict in this case arose as a result of the Appellate Body's interpretation of the chapeau of Art. XX. Therefore, unless this interpretation is the only legally correct one, the conflict was not inevitable. The following analysis suggests that alternative interpretations not only exist, but may well be legally sounder than the one given by the Appellate Body.

The chapeau of Article XX provides a condition for invoking the general exceptions set out in paragraphs (a)–(j) of Art. XX. It requires that measures to be justified by these exceptions 'are not applied in a manner which would constitute a means of arbitrary or unjustifiable discrimination between countries where the same conditions prevail, or a disguised restriction on international trade'.

Conceptually, the kind of discrimination prohibited by the chapeau is to be distinguished from a violation of the MFN or national treatment provisions under GATT. The kind of discrimination prohibited by the chapeau is differential treatment of countries with the same prevailing 'conditions', and such discrimination further possesses the character of being 'arbitrary or unjustifiable'. A violation of the MFN or national treatment provisions, on the other hand, involves differential treatment of 'like products' originating from different countries.[30] As the Appellate Body indicated in *US – Shrimp*, 'the nature and quality of this discrimination [under the chapeau of Article XX] is different from the discrimination in the treatment of products which was already found to be inconsistent with one of the substantive obligations of the GATT 1994, such as Articles I, III or XI'.[31] The reasons for making such distinction were explained by the Appellate Body in *US – Gasoline*:

---

[29] Treaty of Montevideo, www.sice.oas.org/trade/Montev_tr/indexe.asp, was entered in 1980 among Argentina, Brazil, Columbia, Chile, Equator, Mexico, Paraguay, Peru, Uruguay and Venezuela, to promote the integration of the Latin American countries. Mercosur was designed to be part of the process of this integration.

[30] See GATT Arts. I and III.

[31] Appellate Body Report, *United States – Import Prohibition of Certain Shrimp and Shrimp Products*, WT/DS58/AB/R, adopted 6 November 1998 (hereafter, *US – Shrimp*), para. 150.

The provisions of the chapeau cannot logically refer to the same standard(s) by which a violation of a substantive rule has been determined to have occurred. To proceed down that path would be both to empty the chapeau of its contents and to deprive the exceptions in paragraphs (a) to (j) of meaning. Such recourse would also confuse the question of whether inconsistency with a substantive rule existed, with the further and separate question arising under the chapeau of Article XX as to whether that inconsistency was nevertheless justified.[32]

In *Brazil – Tyres*, however, neither the Panel nor the Appellate Body made the distinction between the product-based discrimination and the condition-based discrimination. In their examination of the Mercosur exemption under the chapeau, there was no discussion at all on whether 'the same conditions' prevailed between Mercosur countries on the one hand, and other WTO Members, on the other.[33] Instead, the discrimination found by the WTO adjudicators to be inconsistent with the chapeau was based solely on the likeness of retreaded tyres imported from Mercosur countries and other WTO Members. Recall that the Panel had exercised judicial economy on the EC's claim that the Mercosur exemption violated GATT MFN requirements, and consequently no violation of GATT Art. I was found. By examining the Mercosur exemption under the chapeau solely on the basis of treatment of like products, however, the Panel and the Appellate Body effectively dealt with the MFN claim under the chapeau of Art. XX.[34] It is beyond the scope of this chapter to assess the merit of this interpretive approach.[35] Suffice it to say that by neglecting to discuss whether 'the same conditions prevailed' between Mercosur and the EC, the WTO adjudicators were not exactly faithful to the chapeau language.[36]

---

[32] Appellate Body Report, *United States – Standards for Reformulated and Conventional Gasoline*, WT/DS2/AB/R, adopted 20 May 1996 (hereafter, *US – Gasoline*), 23.

[33] In examining used tyre imports under the chapeau, the Panel made a brief analysis on 'the same conditions prevail', but the analysis was based on the similarity between products rather than prevailing conditions. See Panel Report, *supra* n. 6, paras. 7.307–7.309.

[34] This is not the first time that the WTO judiciary effectively dealt with MFN claims under the chapeau. A similar approach was taken in *US – Shrimp*. See Panel Report, *United States – Import Prohibition of Certain Shrimp and Shrimp Products*, WT/DS58/R, paras. 7.18–7.23.

[35] For a thoughtful analysis of the approach, see A. Davies, 'Interpreting the Chapeau of GATT Article XX in Light of the "New" Approach in Brazil – Tyres', *Journal of World Trade*, 43 (2009), 507–39.

[36] This interpretive approach is, however, not surprising, given that the concept of condition-based discrimination is underdeveloped in WTO jurisprudence. For detailed discussion, see J. Y. Qin, 'Defining Non-Discrimination under the Law of the World Trade Organization', *Boston University International Law Journal*, 23 (2005), 215–97, 258–62.

Alternative interpretation based on different prevailing conditions Indeed, if we focus on the question of whether the same conditions prevailed between Mercosur and EC countries, we may reach the same conclusion as the Panel that the Mercosur exemption did not constitute a means of arbitrary or unjustifiable discrimination, albeit for a different reason. From the perspective of tyre waste management, a country's capacity for producing retreaded tyres for export should be a highly relevant factor. Compared to the Mercosur countries, the EC is by far the largest producer and exporter of retreads.[37] Given their income levels, the Europeans generally prefer new tyres to retreads, and as a result, the EC is a net exporter of retreaded (used) tyres. In comparison, Mercosur countries tend to consume more retreads due to their lower price, and their capacity to produce retreads for export is much more limited at their current stage of economic development. Hence, the prevailing socio-economic conditions which significantly impact the capacity to produce and export retreaded tyres are not the same between Mercosur and the EC. Put differently, the EC, with its large domestic capacity to produce retreads and its need to export most of its retread production, posed a much larger threat to Brazil's goal of waste tyre management than did Mercosur countries. Given the differences in these relevant conditions, the differential treatment between the EC and Mercosur countries may well be justifiable.

Going forward, the differences in prevailing domestic conditions may also justify a Mercosur-wide regime for importing retreaded tyres, which Brazil indicated was under negotiation as part of its effort to implement the WTO rulings. In addition to the socio-economic conditions, relevant ecological conditions – the tropical and subtropical climates which have made the accumulation of waste tyres a special health hazard – also differentiate Mercosur countries from the EC as well as most other WTO Members.

Alternative interpretation informed by Basel principles on waste transfers The justification for Brazil's import ban on retreaded tyres is ultimately based on the rationale of waste transfers. It is suggested here that the Mercosur exemption is consistent with the prevailing international principles governing such transfers.

At present, the most comprehensive international regime governing waste transfers is the Basel Convention on the Control of Transboundary

---

[37] See *supra* n. 7.

Movements of Hazardous Wastes and Their Disposal (1989), which has more than 170 parties, including all Mercosur countries, the EC and most other WTO Members.[38] The objective of the Convention is to protect human health and the environment against the adverse effects of hazardous wastes. A major concern underlying the adoption of the Convention is the disastrous consequences of uncontrolled disposal of hazardous wastes from industrialised nations to developing countries.[39] Accordingly, the Convention requires that waste generation be reduced to a minimum (the reduction principle), that waste be disposed locally to the extent possible (the proximity principle) and that the export of waste be made with prior written consent of the importing country (the consent principle).[40] Furthermore, the Convention prohibits the export of hazardous wastes to 'a State or group of States belonging to an economic and/or political integration organization that are Parties, particularly developing countries, which have prohibited by their legislation all imports' of such wastes.[41] Nonetheless, the Parties may enter into 'bilateral, multilateral, or regional agreements or arrangements' regarding transboundary movements of wastes, provided that such agreements or arrangements 'do not derogate from the environmentally sound management of hazardous wastes and other wastes as required by this Convention', taking into account in particular 'the interests of developing countries'.[42] Subsequently in 1994, the Parties decided to completely ban the export of hazardous wastes from OECD countries to non-OECD countries, which decision was incorporated into an amendment to the Convention.[43]

Thus, the Basel Convention recognises the special interests of developing countries in preventing waste transfers from developed nations, as well as their right to enter into regional agreements on waste

---

[38] Basel Convention, done at Basel on 22 March 1989, entry into force 5 May 1992, 1673 UNTS 125. For the ratification status, see www.basel.int/index.html.

[39] See K. Kummer, *Transboundary Movements of Hazardous Wastes at the Interface of Environment and Trade* (Geneva: United Nations Environment Programme, 1994), 3. For a summary introduction and a list of literature on the Basel regime, see P. Sands, *Principles of International Environmental Law*, 2nd edn. (Cambridge University Press, 2003), 690–5.

[40] Basel Convention, *supra* n. 38, preamble and Arts. 4 and 6.

[41] Basel Convention, *supra* n. 38, Art. 4(2)(e).

[42] Basel Convention, *supra* n. 38, Art. 11(1).

[43] The amendment was adopted by the Parties in 1995, but has yet to take effect as it awaits ratification by three-quarters of the Parties. For the status of the amendment, see www. basel.int/pub/baselban.html.

management. In short, the Convention restricts North–South waste transfers while encouraging South–South cooperation in waste management.

Although the Basel Convention applies only to hazardous wastes and
other wastes specifically defined therein,[44] which do not include tyre
waste, the Parties did recognise 'the serious health and environmental
problems' which may be caused by used tyres, and adopted the Basel
Technical Guidelines on the Identification and Management of Used
Tyres in 1999 (the Basel Guidelines).[45] The Basel Guidelines follow the
principles set out in the Basel Convention.

More importantly, the principles of the Basel Convention provide a
normative framework for cross-border waste transfers in general.
Technically, trade between WTO Members in all products, including
waste and used products, is subject to WTO law.[46] From an economic
standpoint, liberal trade in wastes conducted in a non-discriminatory
manner can lead to an optimal allocation of resources worldwide,
thereby maximising global economic welfare.[47] However, because wastes
and used products may have adverse effects on health and the environment, and because such effects tend to be felt disproportionately by the
communities in which waste products are stored and disposed, nations
may desire to impose restrictions on the import of waste and used
products. When it comes to movement of wastes, sovereign nations are
simply not ready to 'sink or swim together' as the communities within a
nation might be.[48] The Basel principles reflect this political reality. A
WTO Member who is also a party to the Basel Convention should be able
to justify its import restrictions on wastes covered by the Convention
through the health and environmental exceptions of GATT Art. XX.[49] As
for products not covered by the Convention, if a Member's restriction on

---

[44] Basel Convention, *supra* n. 38, Art. 1; Annexes I–III.
[45] www.basel.int/meetings/sbc/workdoc/old%20docs/tech-usedtyres.pdf.
[46] The term 'products' is not defined in WTO agreements. Many wastes have economic
values, and waste management and disposal are major businesses.
[47] See C. P. Brown and J. P. Trachtman, 'Brazil – Measures Affecting Imports of Retreaded
Tyres. A Balancing Act', *World Trade Review*, 8 (2009), 85–135.
[48] For example, the US Supreme Court has struck down State statutes that prohibited the
importation of waste generated outside its territory, despite the asserted purpose of the
statutes being to protect the State's environment and public welfare. An underlying
rationale for the Court's position is that '[o]ur Constitution was framed upon the theory
that the peoples of the several States must sink or swim together'. *American Trucking
Assns, Inc.* v. *Michigan Pub. Serv. Comm'n*, 545 US 429, 433 (2005).
[49] As between WTO members who are also Basel parties, the treaty interpreter is obliged to
interpret the two treaties consistently. See Art. 31(3)(c) VCLT, *infra* n. 58.

the import of such products is based on the rationale of waste transfer, as in *Brazil – Tyres*, a treaty interpreter may refer to Basel norms in evaluating whether such restriction can be justified by Art. XX. Hence, it is in the context of interpreting Art. XX standards that the Basel principles become normatively relevant.

In fact, in *Brazil – Tyres* we can easily observe the influence of the Basel Convention in both the Panel and the Appellate Body decisions. In response to the EC's comment that the Basel reduction principle applied to hazardous waste only, the Panel noted that the evidence presented to it was 'sufficient to support the conclusion that policies to address "waste" by non-generation of additional waste are a generally recognized means of addressing waste management issues'.[50] In the context of deciding whether the import ban was necessary within the meaning of Art. XX(b), the Panel made numerous references to the Basel Guidelines.[51] On appeal, the Appellate Body made it crystal clear that its reasoning under Art. XX(b) was based on the rationale of waste management. According to the Appellate Body, '[t]he issue [of whether the import ban is necessary within the meaning of Art. XX(b)] illustrates the tensions that may exist between, on the one hand, international trade and, on the other hand, public health and environmental concerns arising from *the handling of waste generated by a product at the end of its useful life*'.[52] It concluded that the import ban on retreaded tyres was necessary within the meaning of Art. XX(b), because it produced 'a material contribution' to the realisation of its objective of reducing the 'risks arising from the accumulation of waste tyres', and because none of the alternatives proposed by the EC were reasonably available alternatives to the import ban, which was 'a preventive non-generation measure'.[53] Thus, although the WTO adjudicators did not cite the Basel Convention directly – for the obvious reason that the Convention does not apply to retreaded tyres – they nonetheless applied the reduction principle of the Convention in interpreting the necessity test under Art. XX(b).

Regrettably, however, neither the Panel nor the Appellate Body considered Basel norms in their chapeau analysis, and therefore failed to

---

[50] Panel Report, *supra* n. 6, para. 7.100; n. 1170.
[51] See *ibid.*, paras. 7.61–7.208 (containing more than a dozen references to the Basel Guidelines).
[52] Appellate Body Report, *supra* n. 4, para. 210 (emphasis added).   [53] *Ibid.*, paras. 210–1.

carry through the rationale of waste transfer in the interpretation of Art. XX. The most relevant Basel norms in this case include the proximity principle, the consent principle, differential treatment between wastes generated by the developed and developing countries and regional arrangements on waste transfers. Obviously, the Mercosur members, all being developing countries, are geographically proximate to each other, whereas the EC is a group of developed nations on another continent. Under the Mercosur arrangements, Brazil has consented to the transfer of tyre waste from other Mercosur members, indicating its willingness to 'sink or swim together' with them in the disposal of tyre waste; but it has not given similar consent to others. The liberalisation of trade in used and retreaded tyres among Mercosur countries should enhance the efficiency and economic welfare on a regionwide basis. Viewed in this light, it should become clear that the Mercosur exemption is consistent with the relevant international principles (Basel and the WTO) governing waste trade.

Questions remain as to whether the Basel norms can and should be used to 'justify' the Mercosur exemption under the chapeau. As a logical matter, if Basel norms can be incorporated into the interpretation of the necessity test under Art. XX(b), there should be no reason to reject their incorporation into the interpretation of the chapeau of Art. XX. As a policy matter, it is important to recognise that paragraphs (a)–(j) of Art. XX do not list every legitimate ground for exceptions from GATT obligations. Major environmental treaties, such as the Basel Convention, came into being long after the GATT was formulated. Thus, it is up to the WTO treaty interpreters to integrate the contemporary treaty norms with the GATT provisions. The Appellate Body has famously done so with respect to some environmental treaties.[54] Unlike most environmental treaties, however, the Basel Convention endorses country-based discrimination, which is directly at odds with the non-discrimination provisions of the

---

[54] In *US – Shrimp*, the Appellate Body interpreted the term 'exhaustible natural resources' in Art. XX(g) by reference to several international conventions adopted subsequent to the GATT, *supra* n. 31, paras. 127–131. The Appellate Body States: 'where concepts embodied in a treaty are "by definition, evolutionary", their "interpretation cannot remain unaffected by the subsequent development of law . . . Moreover, an international instrument has to be interpreted and applied within the framework of the entire legal system prevailing at the time of the interpretation."' *Ibid.*, n. 109 (quoting the ICJ in *Legal Consequences for States of the Continued Presence of South Africa in Namibia (South West Africa) notwithstanding Security Council Resolution 276 (1970)*, Advisory Opinion, 1971 ICJ 16, 31).

GATT.[55] Whether such country-based discrimination can be reconciled with the GATT requirements will ultimately depend on how the chapeau standard of 'arbitrary or unjustifiable discrimination' is interpreted, since all environmental defences under Art. XX must pass muster with the chapeau. In other words, in order to incorporate the Basel principles into the WTO Agreement, it is necessary to allow the application of the Basel norms as a possible justification for country-based discrimination under the chapeau of Art. XX.[56]

In sum, if the Appellate Body had focused on comparing the prevailing conditions in Mercosur and EC countries, and/or had taken into account the Basel principles concerning waste transfers between developed and developing countries, it may well have come to a different conclusion on the chapeau consistency of the Mercosur exemption. Such alternative interpretations would have avoided the conflict with the Mercosur ruling.

Conflict management: lessons from the *Brazil* – *Tyres* case

Identifying the source of the problem

Treaty interpretation is more of an art than exact science.[57] In practising that art, the treaty interpreter is to follow the interpretive rules codified in the 1969 Vienna Convention on the Law of Treaties (VCLT),[58] but the application of those rules in particular circumstances requires skills and techniques that go well beyond their brief prescriptions.[59] And there is always room for creativity. Indeed, the Appellate Body is well known for its ability to develop new and exciting WTO jurisprudence, and for integrating the WTO agreements with other areas of public international law, especially multilateral environmental agreements.[60] As one member

---

[55] Non-discrimination between trading nations is inherently consistent with the objective of protecting health and the environment under most environmental treaties that deal with general polluting matters (e.g. air or water pollution) or conservation of natural resources (e.g. endangered species).

[56] Marceau also suggested that reference to a multilateral environmental agreement could be used as an element in establishing that discrimination in the application of the measure should not be characterised as 'unjustifiable' under the Art. XX chapeau. See Marceau, 'Conflicts of Norms', *supra* n. 2, 1099.

[57] See R. Gardiner, *Treaty Interpretation* (Oxford University Press, 2008), 5–7.

[58] Done at Vienna on 23 May 1969; entered into force on 27 January 1980. 1155 UNTS 331.

[59] Gardiner, *Treaty Interpretation, supra* n. 57, 6.

[60] See, e.g., Appellate Body Report, *US* – *Shrimp, supra* n. 54.

of the Appellate Body observed, by drawing on common principles and shared criteria embedded in legal reasoning, the diversity of specific rules and the different institutional settings are 'capable of being interpreted consistently'.[61]

Hence, if the Appellate Body in the *Brazil – Tyres* case had desired to avoid collision with the Mercosur ruling, it certainly could have found the way to do so. The question then is why the Appellate Body did not opt for an alternative interpretation to avoid the conflict. While we may never know the answer to that question, some observations can be made concerning the possible sources of the problem.

Is Brazil to blame?

It appears that the Appellate Body may have blamed Brazil, at least partially, for the rise of conflict. As noted above, in the Mercosur litigation, Brazil did not in its defence invoke Art. 50 of the Treaty of Montevideo, which contains similar language as GATT Art. XX(b).[62] As a result, the Mercosur tribunal did not examine the question of whether Brazil's import ban could be justified by the need to protect public health. The EC seized upon this fact and argued that Brazil was at least partially responsible for the obligation it incurred under the Mercosur ruling. Brazil explained that it did not invoke Art. 50 because of the way in which the legal issues were framed in the Mercosur litigation.[63]

Both the Panel and the Appellate Body took note of this fact, but showed very different understanding of its implications. According to the Panel, although Brazil's litigation strategy failed to persuade the Mercosur tribunal, 'it does not, in itself, seem unreasonable or absurd'.[64] Furthermore, the Panel indicated that 'it is not clear that a different strategy would necessarily have led to a different outcome', noting that in a similar case between Argentina and Uruguay, the Tribunal also reached the conclusion that the restriction was unjustified despite the invocation of the relevant exception by Argentina.[65] By contrast, the Appellate Body was much less forgiving:

---

[61] G. Sacerdoti, 'WTO Law and the "Fragmentation" of International Law. Specificity, Integration, Conflicts', in M. E. Janow, V. Donaldson and A. Yanovich (eds.), *The WTO. Governance, Dispute Settlement and Developing Countries* (Huntington, NY: Juris Publishing, 2008), 595–610, 600.

[62] See *supra* text at nn. 28–29.   [63] See Panel Report, *supra* n. 6, para. 7.275.

[64] *Ibid.*, para. 7.276.   [65] *Ibid.*, n. 1451.

[B]efore the arbitral tribunal established under Mercosur, Brazil could
have sought to justify the challenged Import Ban on the grounds of
human, animal, and plant health under Article 50(d) of the Treaty of
Montevideo. Brazil, however, decided not to do so. It is not appropriate
for us to second-guess Brazil's decision not to invoke Article 50(d), which
serves a function similar to that of Article XX(b) of the GATT 1994.
However, Article 50(d) of the Treaty of Montevideo, as well as the fact
that Brazil might have raised this defence in the Mercosur arbitral
proceedings, show, in our view, that the discrimination associated with
the Mercosur exemption does not necessarily result from a conflict
between provisions under Mercosur and the GATT 1994 [footnotes
omitted].[66]

By pointing out that there was no conflict between treaty provisions and
that Brazil could have raised a different defence, the Appellate Body
appears to have implicitly blamed Brazil for its predicament of being
caught in between the Mercosur and WTO rulings.

The Appellate Body's attitude was only amplified by the WTO arbitrator, a member of the Appellate Body presiding in the original case.
Quoting the above statement by the Appellate Body, the arbitrator
opined that Brazil would not 'necessarily be required to work towards
negotiating a Mercosur-wide tyre regime in order to comply with its
WTO obligations while, at the same time, respecting its commitments
under Mercosur'.[67] In the end, the fact that Brazil did not invoke Art. 50
of the Treaty of Montevideo in the Mercosur litigation was cited by the
arbitrator as one of the two reasons for his decision not to consider
Brazil's request for time to negotiate with its Mercosur partners.[68] By
refusing to give Brazil any time to negotiate, the arbitrator not only held
Brazil responsible for the conflict, but also forced Brazil to suffer the
consequences. Had the EC not agreed to allow Brazil extra time for
compliance, Brazil would have become the target of WTO-approved
trade sanctions.

Yet, is it appropriate for the WTO tribunals to blame Brazil for the
conflict, or even 'punish' it for failure to raise particular defences in
another forum? Unquestionably, the litigant's ability to frame the
issues can make a critical difference in the outcome of the litigation.
Certainly international lawyers would be well counselled to learn the
lessons from Brazil's experience. However, it is one thing to recognise

---

[66] Appellate Body Report, *supra* n. 4, para. 234.   [67] Arbitral Award, *supra* n. 16, para. 82.
[68] The other reason cited by the arbitrator was that Brazil had introduced modifications to
the Mercosur exemption by mere domestic measures. *Ibid.*, paras. 84–5.

the important role played by the litigators, and quite another for a tribunal to hold the litigant responsible for a conflict that arose merely as a result of the tribunal's interpretation of a treaty provision. It is inevitable that different tribunals may interpret the same legal language differently. In a domestic legal system, conflicts between different interpretations can be resolved by a higher authority. In the international setting, no such final authority exists. Although Art. 50(d) of the Treaty of Montevideo contains similar language to GATT Art. XX(b), the two treaties are separate international agreements. There is no hierarchical relationship between the WTO and Mercosur tribunals. Hence, it would seem rather presumptuous for the WTO adjudicators to assume that, had Brazil invoked Art. 50(d) of the Montevideo treaty, the Mercosur tribunal would have interpreted that provision in the same way as they would interpret GATT Art. XX(b) in this particular case.[69]

It was unfortunate that Brazil, in defending the Mercosur exemption under the chapeau, did not argue that different conditions prevailed between the EC and Mercosur, or invoke the Basel norms on South–South cooperation in waste management. Had it done so, it would have stood a good chance to succeed in its defence. In this sense, Brazil can be blamed for its loss in the WTO litigation. However, Brazil's failure to make particular legal arguments should not prevent the WTO adjudicators from making their own interpretations of the chapeau requirements.[70] After all, panels and the Appellate Body are obligated to ascertain and apply the relevant law independently in the given circumstances of the case.

---

[69] The *Argentina* case noted above proves this point. See *supra* text, n. 65. Note that the WTO arbitrator tried to distinguish the *Argentina* case on the grounds that the Mercosur decision in the *Argentina* case was not binding on Brazil, and that the tribunal rejected Argentina's defence for specific reasons. See Arbitral Award, *supra* n. 16, n. 141.

[70] As the party asserting defences under Art. XX, Brazil had the burden to establish such defences. However, the scope of burden of proof is in principle limited to the issue of facts. J. Pauwelyn, 'Evidence, Proof and Persuasion in WTO Dispute Settlement. Who Bears the Burden?', *Journal of International Economic Law*, 1 (1998), 227–58, 242 ('None of the parties can be required to "prove" the legal inconsistency or consistency of a measure with a WTO provision. Panels and the Appellate Body alike are presumed to know the law (*jura novit curia*)'). See also J. Waincymer, *WTO Litigation. Procedural Aspects of Formal Dispute Settlement* (London: Cameron May, 2002), 537 ('if each of the parties to a case argued for different interpretations of a WTO provision, and a Panel thought that a third interpretation was preferable, it is duty bound to adopt its own line of reasoning').

Need to balance the parties' interests?

The Appellate Body has viewed the chapeau as a place to 'maintain a balance' between the right of a Member to invoke the exceptions in Art. XX para. (a)–(j), and the right of the other Members under the GATT substantive provisions.[71] The two previous cases in which the Appellate Body interpreted the chapeau language both involved environmental measures – protection of clean air in *US – Gasoline*, and conservation of sea turtles in *US – Shrimp*. In both cases, the Appellate Body upheld the measure, defined as the broad legislation encompassing some offending aspects, as justifiable under the relevant paragraph of Art. XX, but struck down the offending aspects (as the means of applying the measure) under the chapeau. In so doing, the Appellate Body was able to integrate environmental values into the GATT provisions, and establish a balance between trade and the environment in those cases.

The same pattern holds in *Brazil – Tyres*: the Appellate Body found the import ban to be justifiable under Art. XX(b), but struck down the used tyre exception and the Mercosur exemption – as the way in which the ban was applied – under the chapeau. Because retreaded tyres contribute only indirectly to the health risks associated with the accumulation of waste tyres, the finding that the import ban on retreaded tyres is 'necessary' to protect health under Art. XX(b) was a major victory for Brazil.[72] Perhaps out of a desire to balance against that weighty decision, the Appellate Body held in favour of the EC on the Mercosur exemption, even at the expense of creating a conflict of treaty obligations for Brazil.

Lack of concern for conflicts: a mindset of WTO superiority?

Whatever the underlying reasons, it is apparent that the Appellate Body was largely unconcerned with the potential conflicts between its decision and that of the Mercosur tribunal. This attitude contrasted sharply with that of the Panel, which had designed the 'effect' test under the chapeau in order to avoid an immediate clash with the Mercosur ruling.

The lack of concern for conflicts on the part of the Appellate Body appears to be the main source of the problem. This mentality may have stemmed from a sense of WTO centrality or superiority. To the extent that WTO Members have obligations to ensure that their RTAs meet

---

[71] Appellate Body Report, *US – Shrimp*, *supra* n. 31, para. 156.

[72] For a scathing criticism of the Panel and Appellate Body decisions, see Brown and Trachtman, 'Brazil – Measures', *supra* n. 47.

certain conditions contained in the GATT and GATS,[73] the WTO may indeed be viewed as 'central' or 'superior' to the regional trade regimes. However, one must not forget that RTAs are treaties independent from the WTO and that there is no hierarchical relationship between the WTO and RTAs under international law. Hence, it would be legally unwarranted to assume the superiority of the WTO beyond the specific conditions set out in the GATT and GATS concerning RTAs. Moreover, it is important to recognise that the notion of WTO centrality is now passé. Today, nearly all WTO Members belong to one or more preferential trade arrangements.[74] Thanks to their proliferation and to the lack of progress in the WTO multilateral negotiations, RTAs have increasingly become the locus where further trade liberalisation is achieved and new trade norms created. Consequently, the global trading system has become multi-polar. The large number of preferential trade agreements have emerged as regimes parallel, rather than merely supplementary, to the WTO. Given this reality, a lack of concern on the part of the WTO judiciary for conflicts with RTA decisions can be detrimental to the proper functioning of the global trading system.

Duty to avoid conflicts: towards a judicial policy on conflicts

The Appellate Body's determination on the Mercosur exemption embodies a conscious decision to disregard the damaging consequences of conflicts between WTO and RTA rulings. This decision thus raises a broad question: to what extent, if any, do WTO judges have a duty to avoid creating conflicts with prior decisions of RTA tribunals? Given the lack of any formal relationship between the WTO and RTAs, it may be tempting simply to dismiss the existence of any such duty. Indeed, a WTO panel may be required to exercise jurisdiction, even when doing so may give rise to overlapping or conflicting jurisdiction with an RTA tribunal.[75] Besides, WTO judges are to apply WTO law, not RTA law. Hence, one might conclude that while the WTO judiciary should be

---

[73] *Supra* n. 23.

[74] According to one account, 'all but one WTO Member, Mongolia, are engaged in RTAs of one sort or another. For some WTO Members, preferential trade now represents more than 90 per cent of their total trade'. J. A. Crawford and R. V. Fiorentino, 'The Changing Landscape of Regional Trade Agreements', WTO Discussion Paper 8 (2005), n. 4.

[75] Art. 23, DSU (providing that when Member States seek the redress of a violation of obligations under the WTO agreements, 'they shall have recourse to' the WTO dispute settlement procedures).

urged to consider prior RTA decisions with a view to avoiding potential conflicts, they would not be under any legal obligation to do so.

It is submitted here that WTO judges do have a legal duty to avoid creating conflicts with prior RTA rulings through their interpretations of the WTO agreements. This duty can be seen as arising directly from Art. 3.2 of the Dispute Settlement Understanding (DSU), instructing WTO adjudicators to clarify the existing provisions of the covered agreements 'in accordance with the customary rules of interpretation of public international law'. One such rule is the presumption of good faith. This presumption stems from the principle of *pacta sunt servanda*, which is codified in Art. 26 of the VCLT, providing that '[e]very treaty in force is binding on the parties to it and must be performed by them in good faith'.[76] Under the 'pervasive' principle of good faith in international law,[77] a State is presumed to have negotiated and performed all its treaty obligations in good faith.[78] In this sense, the treaty obligations of the State are cumulative and should be read together.[79] A corollary of this rule is the presumption against conflicts. It is generally assumed in international law that, absent an explicit expression to the contrary, a State intends to perform all its international obligations consistently. Consequently, when faced with two possible interpretations, a treaty interpreter should give preference to the one that allows for harmonisation of different international obligations.[80]

---

[76] This principle 'underlies every international agreement for, in the absence of a certain minimum belief that States will perform their treaty obligations in good faith, there is no reason for countries to enter into such obligations with each other', M. N. Shaw, *International Law*, 5th edn. (Cambridge University Press, 2003), 811–12.

[77] Appellate Body Report, *United States – Transitional Safeguard Measure on Combed Cotton Yarn From Pakistan*, WT/DS192/AB/R, 8 October 2001, para 81. See also Appellate Body Report, *United States – Tax Treatment for 'Foreign Sales Corporations'*, WT/DS108/AB/R, 24 February 2000, para. 166 (considering good faith to be 'at once a general principle of law and a principle of general international law').

[78] WTO panels and the Appellate Body have accepted this presumption. See, e.g., Appellate Body Report, *EC – Trade Description on Sardines*, WT/DS231/AB/R, 26 September 2002, para. 278 ('We must assume that Members of the WTO will abide by their treaty obligations in good faith, as required by the principle of *pacta sunt servanda* articulated in Article 26 of the *Vienna Convention*'); Panel Report, *Canada – Continued Suspension of Obligations in the EC–Hormones Dispute*, WT/DS320/R, 31 March 2008, paras. 7.310–7.357 (elaborating and accepting a presumption of good faith compliance in the WTO context). See also R. Jennings and A. Watts, *Oppenheim's International Law*, 9th edn., 2 vols. (London and New York: Longman, 1996), vol. 1, 1206, 1249.

[79] Marceau, 'Conflicts of Norms', *supra* n. 2, 1089.

[80] See generally, Pauwelyn, *Conflict of Norms in Public International Law, supra* n. 2, 240–1. Art. 30 VCLT, which provides rules on the application of successive treaties relating to

The same presumption of legality exists with respect to acts of international organisations.[81] Although the decision of an international tribunal does not have the same status as a treaty provision under international law,[82] the validity and binding force of such decision derives from the treaty establishing the competence of the tribunal, and a party subject thereto has the treaty obligation of compliance. Thus, when WTO adjudicators are informed of a possible conflict with a prior decision of an RTA tribunal, they should, in accordance with the rule of presumption of good faith, proceed with the assumption that the WTO provisions at issue can and should be interpreted consistently with that RTA decision.

The presumption against conflicts, however, is rebuttable. It cannot reconcile truly irreconcilable obligations.[83] Thus, the presumption will remain only to the point when proof of a genuine conflict is provided. In WTO litigation, the burden to rebut the presumption should fall on the party opposing a harmonising interpretation of the WTO and RTA obligations.[84] But unless and until the rebuttal is made, WTO judges should not be free to choose an interpretation that will give rise to conflicts with a prior RTA decision when an alternative interpretation remains possible.

It is implicit in the presumption against conflicts that the treaty interpreter must make an effort to explore alternative interpretations of the provision at issue with a view to avoiding conflicts. In this context, the customary rule of interpretation codified in Art. 31(3)(c) VCLT becomes particularly relevant. Pursuant to Art. 31(3)(c), a treaty interpreter 'shall' take into account, together with the context of the treaty terms, 'any relevant rules of international law applicable in the relations between the parties'. This rule is an expression of the systemic nature of international law. It assumes that treaty obligations are accumulative and requires 'the integration into the process of legal reasoning – including reasoning by courts and tribunals – of a sense of coherence and meaningfulness' among various treaty

---

the same subject matter, also reflects the presumption against conflicts in treaty interpretation.

[81] Pauwelyn, *Conflict of Norms in Public International Law, supra* n. 2, 241 (citing for support the ICJ in the *Certain Expenses* case, *Certain Expenses of the United Nations (Article 17, paragraph 2, of the Charter)*, Advisory Opinion, 1962 ICJ 151, 168).

[82] ICJ Statute, Art. 38.

[83] See Pauwelyn, *Conflict of Norms in Public International Law, supra* n. 2, 243.

[84] *Ibid.* ('it is for the party relying on the conflict of norms to prove that there is such conflict').

provisions.[85] It is important to note that this rule is mandatory, not optional, which means that WTO judges are obligated to take into account any relevant rules of international law in interpreting a WTO provision. While what constitutes 'relevant rules of international law applicable in the relations between the parties' is subject to interpretation,[86] it seems reasonable to infer from the requirement of Art. 31 (3)(c) that the judges have a duty to identify what such other relevant rules might be, rather than relying solely on the parties to do so.

To summarise, it is submitted that under the interpretive principles of international law, WTO judges have a legal duty to avoid conflicts with a prior RTA decision to the following extent: (a) they must proceed with the presumption that there is no conflict between WTO and RTA obligations until proof is provided to the contrary; (b) they are obligated to explore alternative interpretations and give preference to the interpretation which can reconcile an apparent (but not genuine) conflict between the WTO and RTA obligations at issue; and (c) they need to identify what other international rules within the meaning of Art. 31(3)(c) must be taken into account in their interpretation of the WTO provision, with a view to avoiding conflicts between the WTO and RTA obligations.

If the above analysis is correct, then it is not difficult to see how the Appellate Body failed to fulfil its duty to avoid conflicts in *Brazil – Tyres*. Having made no presumption against conflicts, the Appellate Body proceeded to interpret the chapeau of Art. XX in a way that it knew would require Brazil to breach its treaty obligation under Mercosur. In contrast with the Panel, whose interpretation of the chapeau indicated an effort to avoid an immediate clash with the Mercosur ruling, the Appellate Body showed no interest in exploring alternative interpretations. Hence, despite the fact that Brazil's defence was based on the logic of waste transfer and that the EC and Brazil were both parties to the Basel Convention, the Appellate Body failed to identify the relevance of the Basel norms in interpreting the chapeau, arguably contrary to the requirement of Art. 31(3)(c) VCLT.[87]

---

[85] See ILC, Report of the Study Group, *supra* n. 1, UN Doc. A/CN.4/L.682, para. 419, and related parts in section F (Systemic Integration and Article 31(3)(c) VCLT).

[86] *Ibid.*, section F.

[87] On the scope of applicable law in WTO disputes, see J. Pauwelyn, 'The Role of Public International Law in the WTO. How Far Can We Go?', *AJIL*, 95 (2001), 535–78; *idem.*, 'Bridging Fragmentation and Unity. International Law as a Universe of Inter-Connected Islands', *Michigan Journal of International Law*, 25 (2004), 903–16.

In light of its legal duty, the WTO adjudicatory body should adopt a judicial policy on the avoidance of conflict. Such a policy is needed because *Brazil – Tyres* is unlikely to be the last case where RTA and WTO decisions clash. Given the proliferation of RTAs and increasing utilisation of RTA tribunals, situations of overlapping jurisdictions and inconsistent decisions are bound to occur, giving rise to the problem of conflicting obligations for the Member States.[88] Furthermore, a clear judicial policy on conflicts is necessary for 'providing security and predictability to the multilateral trading system'.[89] In today's multipolar global trading environment, the WTO must find a way to coexist with the growing number of regional and bilateral trading regimes in a harmonious fashion. The security and predictability of the WTO system cannot be ensured if its members do not have a clear sense whether or to what extent their regional undertakings will be respected in the WTO court.

At the systemic level, it is important for the WTO judiciary to acknowledge that RTA laws – including RTA treaties, internal decisions and tribunal rulings – are part of public international law,[90] from which the WTO agreements cannot be read in 'clinical isolation'.[91] Indeed, given their shared values and similar regulatory schemes, WTO and RTA laws should be capable of being interpreted in a consistent and coherent manner. The question of how WTO and RTA laws can be integrated through interpretations or otherwise raises complex and systemic issues that are beyond the scope of this chapter. However, a coherent approach towards conflict avoidance should be at the core of any systemic integration. Compared to RTA tribunals, the WTO judiciary is clearly in a superior position to influence the development of any systemic integration. Thus, it should be urged to take the first step in establishing a clear policy on conflict avoidance. While the detail of the policy may take time to develop, the need for such a policy is immediate.

---

[88] For a list of dispute settlement mechanisms of major RTAs and their compatibility with the WTO, see Kwak and Marceau, 'Overlaps and Conflicts of Jurisdiction', *supra* n. 2, table I.

[89] Art. 3.2, DSU.

[90] See I. Van Damme, 'What Role is there for Regional International Law in the Interpretation of the WTO Agreements?', in Bartels and Ortino (eds.), *Regional Trade Agreements and the WTO Legal System*, *supra* n. 2, 553–75.

[91] Appellate Body Report, *US – Gasoline*, *supra* n. 32, 17.

Conclusion

Brazil – Tyres may be the first case in which the decision of an international tribunal has given rise to a direct conflict of international obligations for a sovereign State. This conflict did not result from competing jurisdictions, or conflicting treaty norms. Instead, it occurred purely as a result of treaty interpretation. As demonstrated in this chapter, the conflict could have been avoided because alternative interpretations, arguably legally sounder ones, do exist.

It is regrettable that this unfortunate situation should occur in the WTO context as a result of the decision of the Appellate Body, which has been widely credited for integrating WTO law with general international law through its interpretation of the WTO agreements. While we may never know what motivated the Appellate Body in rendering this particular decision, it seems clear that its judges were not particularly concerned by the potential conflict and its damaging consequences.

This lack of concern on the part of Appellate Body judges is problematic, for at least three reasons. First of all, a WTO decision requiring a sovereign State to breach its legal obligation under another treaty – i.e. violating its international law obligation – is a grave matter, and should never be taken lightly. Next, the lack of concern shows disrespect for the RTA regime, which is at odds with the general practice of WTO members who have been actively building the RTA regime and have blessed its legitimacy as an alternative to the WTO. Finally, the lack of concern for causing conflicts between international rulings is not a responsible attitude to be displayed by WTO judges in an era when the proliferation of international tribunals threatens to 'fragment' international law. With its high profile and reputation, the Appellate Body is expected to be particularly sensitive to the issues of fragmentation and to make positive contributions to the development of a coherent system of international law, of which RTA laws constitute a part.

As a matter of treaty interpretation, it is submitted that there are indeed international legal principles and rules that require WTO adjudicators to avoid creating conflicts with prior RTA decisions through their interpretations of the WTO agreements. Specifically, the generally accepted rule on the presumption against conflicts, derived from the good faith principle, requires that the WTO treaty interpreter begin her interpretation with the presumption that there is no conflict between WTO and RTA obligations. Until proof to the contrary is provided, she is not free to choose an interpretation that will give rise to a conflict when an alternative interpretation remains available. In addition, Art. 31(3)(c) of the VCLT obliges the treaty interpreter to take into account all relevant rules of international law in her interpretation of the WTO agreements, with the objective of giving coherence to obligations arising from different sources of international law.

In light of its duty to avoid conflicts under the interpretive principles of international law, and considering the realities of today's multi-polar trading environment, it is recommended that the WTO adjudicatory body adopt a judicial policy on the avoidance of conflicts with RTA decisions. Such a policy will help to ensure that potential conflicts between decisions of WTO and RTA tribunals be managed in a systematic and consistent manner, thus providing the level of security and predictability desired by the global trading system.

30

Cross-border bankruptcy as a model for the regulation of international attorneys

CATHERINE A. ROGERS

Introduction

In 1951, the young Detlev Vagts began working as a lawyer in the Paris office of New York firm Cahill, Gordon & Reindel. Although an American lawyer in Paris would hardly be remarkable today, Vagts' position was extraordinary for its time. Back then, law practice was a predominantly local affair. There was no such thing as a global law firm, and even the largest US firms would be considered minuscule in comparison with today's behemoths. The firms of yesteryear ventured overseas only haltingly, and usually in response to a specific client need rather than as part of a larger mission to establish a global practice.[1] Cahill was one of the very few law firms that had a Paris outpost 'manned'[2] by a few lawyers.[3] The most obvious candidates for these overseas postings were lawyers like Vagts, whose personal background included links to foreign jurisdictions.[4]

---

[1] One of the earliest examples is when John Foster Dulles of the New York firm Sullivan & Cromwell played a key role in the negotiations of the Versailles Treaty at the end of the First World War and his firm went on to promote capital flows from North America to Europe. J. Flood and F. Sosa, 'Lawyers, Law Firms, and the Stabilization of Transnational Business', *Northwestern Journal of International Law & Business*, 28 (2008), 489–525, 502.

[2] Law practice was at that time also almost exclusively the province of male attorneys. See C. F. Epstein, *Women in Law*, 2nd edn. (Chicago, IL: University of Illinois, 1993), 4–5.

[3] Prior to the Second World War, only four US firms had offices abroad. C. Silver, 'Winners and Losers in the Globalization of Legal Services. Offshoring the Market for Legal Services', *Virginia Journal of International Law*, 45 (2005), 897–934, 916–17.

[4] Detlev Vagts was born in the United States to German parents while his father was conducting scholarly research in Washington, DC. In the 1930s, Vagts' father moved his family to the United States in political protest against the rise of the Third Reich in Germany.

As Vagts recalls, in the early days of his Paris practice there were no fax machines, let alone internet connections. Transnational phone calls often relied on unstable radio-based connections, and transatlantic flights still had a sense of adventure to them. These technological obstacles limited the internationalisation of law firms, but they also rendered law practice less frenzied and more genteel. Before the arrival of overnight services by FedEx and DHL, as Vagts recalls, an attorney could sigh with relief as he sent off a professional communication by 'special airmail', knowing that no response could possibly be received back for at least a week.[5]

Today, transnational law firms stand transformed. Foreign offices are no longer eccentric analogues to a firm's 'main practice', but essential credentials for any firm wishing to compete in the global market place. Six out of ten of 'the world's . . . highest-grossing firms had more than 50% of their lawyers working in countries outside of the firm's home country'.[6] Over the past twenty years, US (and UK) law firms have merged with many local firms in foreign States, resulting in nearly 400 foreign law offices spread out in over seventy-five foreign cities around the world that belong to US law firms.[7] As modern law firms have grown in size and complexity, they bear an uncanny resemblance to the monolithic multinational enterprises that they represent[8] and that were the focus of Vagts' earlier scholarship.

Vagts was first known for his work expanding traditional concepts of international law to include those decisional principles and procedures that had been developed to regulate problems involving a foreign element. His work, building on ideas originated by Philip Jessup,[9] extended

---

[5] These and other personal details derive from a presentation Detlev Vagts made at the conference 'Globalization of the Legal Profession', Harvard Law School, 21 November 2009, and in a telephone interview with this author in August 2009.

[6] L. S. Terry, 'A "How To" Guide for Incorporating Global and Comparative Perspectives into the Required Professional Responsibility Course', *St. Louis University Law Journal*, 51 (2007), 1135–60, 1138.

[7] Silver, 'Winners and Losers', *supra* n. 3, 916–17.

[8] Although not all firms have expanded to this gargantuan size, even smaller and medium-size law firms are increasingly delving into the global market for legal services. See C. Silver, 'Regulatory Mismatch in the Market for Legal Services', *Northwestern Journal of International Law & Business*, 23 (2003), 487–550, 495. This phenomenon is a logical counterpart of the increased participation of smaller and medium-sized companies in the global economy. See E.V. Helmer, 'International Commercial Arbitration. Americanized, "Civilized", or Harmonized?', *Ohio State Journal of Dispute Resolution*, 19 (2003), 35–68, 40 (noting the increase in the number of American law firms providing arbitration services).

[9] P. C. Jessup, *Transnational Law* (New Haven, CT: Yale University Press, 1956), 2.

study of transnational activities beyond treaty-makers and treaty-making processes, to include national courts, domestic legislators and other governmental instrumentalities, international officials and regional and international organisations.[10] Even in this early work, Vagts' analysis was laced with references to the attorneys whose daily work shaped this realm of activity. Instead of treating lawyers as silent spectators on the shadowed sidelines of an intellectual discourse,[11] Vagts consistently treated them as central players.[12] In numerous articles on various subjects, Vagts depicted attorneys as active participants, rather than as passive observers or incidental by-standers.[13] These references are more than a rhetorical flourish. They reveal Vagts' conviction that attorneys engaged in cross-border and international practice have

---

[10] See H. J. Steiner and D. F. Vagts, *Transnational Legal Problems*, 1st edn (Westbury, NY: Foundation Press, 1968).

[11] Modern legal scholarship is often criticised as having little practical impact because it ignores its potential effect on the real work of lawyers and judges. See A. Liptak, 'When Rendering Decisions, Judges Are Finding Law Reviews Irrelevant', *New York Times*, March 10, 2007 (describing statistics and comments by Second Circuit Judges that suggest that law review articles 'no longer had any impact on the courts' and positing that many law professors 'seem to think they are under no obligation to say anything useful or to say anything well').

[12] For example, Vagts states that '[c]orporate lawyers have become accustomed to having issues of domestic law, particularly in connection with important regulatory policies, decided on the basis of "control"'. D. F. Vagts, 'The Multinational Enterprise. A New Challenge for Transnational Law', *Harvard Law Review*, 83 (1970), 739–92, 778. Vagts also sees lawyers as primary consumers of comparative corporate governance, stating that the 'American corporation lawyers' will be the primary beneficiaries of 'a picture of the corporate responsibility question as seen from European perspectives'. D. F. Vagts, 'European Perspectives. A Foreword', *Hastings Law Journal*, 30 (1979), 1413–18.

[13] E.g. in discussing the challenges of regulating MNEs, Vagts reasons that '[a] lawyer would expect a host country confronted by a problem like that of the MNE to respond by regulation. This is particularly true of the American lawyer accustomed to a pattern of economic legislation that is developed by an administrative agency through supplementary rulemaking or adjudication subject to judicial review.' Vagts, 'The Multinational Enterprise', *supra* n. 12, 777. Vagts also expressly pondered what role lawyers will play in harmonising regulation of MNEs with national policies, suggesting that it may be 'their skill in bargaining out problems on a case by case basis and what ought to be [regulators'] sensitivity to the interests at stake', *Ibid.*, 792. In other words, he posited that lawyers and their lawyering skills might be pivotal in the development of global regulatory policy. See also A. Vagts and D. F. Vagts, 'The Balance of Power in International Law. A History of an Idea', *AJIL*, 73 (1979), 555–80, 557 (framing definitions of 'balance of power' in terms that 'international lawyers' think about); D. F. Vagts, 'Hegemonic International Law', *AJIL*, 95 (2001), 843–8, 846 (noting that 'German international lawyers paid special attention to [the] doctrine' of the *clausula rebus sic stantibus*).

unique insights and contributions to make to international law and transnational regulatory issues.

Having conspicuously located the lawyer at the hub of his investigations of various global regulatory issues, Vagts eventually turned his intellectual energies directly to the transnational regulation of lawyers themselves.[14] As others in this volume have pointed out, Vagts was among the first and most insistent about the need to regulate global legal practice.[15] In this chapter, I attempt to reconnect the identified need to regulate global law practice with some of Vagts' earlier interests in other areas of transnational regulation.

Attorneys are consistently identified as essential actors in the transnational networks that produce global regulation in other areas, and undoubtedly represent 'epistemic communities' comprised of 'professionals with recognized expertise and competence in a particular domain and an authoritative claim to policy-relevant knowledge within that domain or issue-area'.[16] To date, however, the well-developed conceptual frameworks used to analyse other areas of transnational regulation have not been directly employed in the quandaries underlying the regulation of attorneys engaged in transnational practice.

While insights may be drawn from a number of areas, in this chapter I argue that the regulatory challenges and pragmatic responses in the cross-border bankruptcy context provide a useful analogue for transnational regulation of attorneys. Specifically, I invoke the broad outlines of the UNCITRAL Model Law on Cross-Border Insolvency (the 'Model Law') as a template from which to delineate a model for regulation of attorneys engaged in transnational practice. The salient features of the Model Law are that it provides an internationally agreed-upon choice-of-forum and choice-of-law regime that also promotes procedural coordination across legal systems to ensure effective implementation of the applicable law. The success of the Model Law is measured both by its widespread support and its ability to resolve what had been regarded as an intractable debate on

---

[14] D. F. Vagts, 'The International Legal Profession. A Need for More Governance?', *AJIL*, 90 (1996), 250–62; D. F. Vagts, 'Professional Responsibility in Transborder Practice. Conflict and Resolution', *Georgetown Journal of Legal Ethics*, 13 (2000), 677–98; D. F. Vagts, 'International Legal Ethics and Professional Responsibility', *ASIL Proceedings*, 92 (1998), 378–9; see also ASIL, Report of the Task Force on International Professional Responsibility (December 2007) (D. F. Vagts, Chairperson).

[15] See C. N. Brower and S. W. Schill, 'Regulating Counsel Before International Tribunals', *supra* p. 488.

[16] P. M. Haas, 'Introduction. Epistemic Communities and International Policy Coordination', *International Organisation*, 46 (1992), 1–35, 2.

substantive standards. These features make it a useful paradigm for developing an effective regime for the distinct area of attorney regulation.

I provide first a brief overview of the challenges involved in developing an effective regime for transnational regulation of attorneys. I examine how attorney regulation both resembles other areas of transnational regulatory concern, and presents problems that are relatively unique in transnational regulation, but perhaps more closely related to cross-border bankruptcy than to other areas. I then recount the limited and largely unsuccessful efforts to develop an effective regime for transnational regulation of attorneys to date. Finally, I outline those features of the Model Law that can provide guidance for developing a model for global regulation of attorneys, and sketch the general features of such a regime.

Attorney regulation as archetype and counterexample

Three key features of cross-border regulation of attorneys provide instructional analogues and points of contrast to other areas of transnational regulation, including cross-border bankruptcy. These features, taken up in turn below, involve the nature of the underlying regulatory conflicts, the relative degree of interest among the regulators and the objects of regulation, and the competing frameworks proposed as solutions.

Regulatory overlap and conflict

The first key feature of cross-border legal ethics, which is similar to many other subjects of global regulation, is the multitude of rules that apply to the same conduct. Just as with other transnational activities, when legal services span multiple jurisdictions, the rules of more than one jurisdiction may govern the attorneys' conduct. In this regard, transnational attorney regulation appears to present problems common to all transnational regulatory issues. On closer examination, the essential regulatory challenge can be understood as relatively unique.

To take one example, when the activities of an economic actor span multiple jurisdictions, multiple national antitrust or competition laws may apply to its activity. Most likely, however, one country's laws will prohibit or limit activities that are permitted by the laws of other countries.[17] The laws may be inconsistent, but in general they do not

---

[17] R. Hardt, 'Kodak v. Fuji. A Test Case for the Extraterritorial Application of the Sherman Act', *Boston University International Law Journal*, 15 (1997), 309–42, 337 (noting that 'rarely, if ever, will a 'true conflict' [between national antitrust laws] be found').

directly conflict. Thus, while it may be inconvenient and inefficient for the economic actor to comply with all applicable national laws, it is generally not impossible. The same is not true of legal ethics.

With professional ethics, an attorney whose activities span multiple jurisdictions may be mandated to perform certain conduct expressly prohibited by the rules of another jurisdiction. For example, many jurisdictions, such as Germany, France and Switzerland, prohibit pre-testimonial contact with witnesses,[18] which is a practice often deemed to be ethically mandated as part of a US attorney's obligation of competency. The UK Proceeds of Crime Act of 2002 mandates that attorneys disclose certain information to law enforcement agencies (while withholding the disclosure from the client), even if such disclosure is forbidden under US ethical rules.[19] Meanwhile, the French doctrine of '*sous la foi du Palais*' may require that an attorney maintain as confidential from a client a communication conveyed by opposing counsel, even if such communication contains a proposed settlement that US ethical rules mandate that the attorney disclose to the client.[20]

These conflicts among national ethical rules create two distinct problems for regulation of transnational legal practice. The first is sometimes referred to by ethicists as the 'double deontology' problem. Viewed as a regulatory problem, it may also be regarded as a problem of direct conflict between, or 'mutual exclusivity' of, applicable regulations. When an attorney is either licensed in more than one jurisdiction or otherwise subject to the regulatory power of more than one jurisdiction, that attorney may be subject to conflicting obligations that are impossible to comply with simultaneously. The attorney is faced with the prospect of professional discipline regardless of what action she takes.[21]

---

[18] M. Damaska, 'Presentation of Evidence and Factfinding Precision', *University of Pennsylvania Law Review*, 123 (1975), 1083–1106, 1088–9; J. H. Langbein, 'The German Advantage in Civil Procedure', *University of Chicago Law Review*, 52 (1985), 823–66, 834.

[19] See G. F. Leckie and A. E. Woods, 'Developments in Ethics', *ALI-ABA* SJ027 (2003), 221–44 (describing the Proceeds of Crime Act as a 'troubling development' that erodes the relationship between lawyer and client and the duty of confidentiality).

[20] L. S. Terry, 'An Introduction to the European Community's Legal Ethics Part 1. An Analysis of the *CCBE Code of Conduct*', *Georgetown Journal of Legal Ethics*, 7 (1993), 1–88, 36–7.

[21] By obliging attorneys under UK law to disclose information that they are required by their home ethical or legal rules to maintain secret, this legislation can provide a potent trap for well-intentioned lawyers. See H. J. Hellwig, 'At the Intersection of Legal Ethics and Globalization. International Conflicts of Law in Lawyer Regulation', *Penn State International Law Review*, 27 (2008), 395–401, 399 (describing a German attorney

The second problem is that, when attorneys from different jurisdictions participate in a single international proceeding, if they abide by different ethical rules (from their home jurisdictions), the proceedings may be structurally unfair. As Miller recounts, lawyers from different jurisdictions working with the International Criminal Tribunal for the Former Yugoslavia (ICTY) in The Hague have starkly different opinions about pre-testimonial communication with witnesses:

> An Australian lawyer felt that from his perspective it would be unethical to prepare a witness; a Canadian lawyer said it would be illegal; and an American lawyer's view was that not to prepare a witness would be malpractice.[22]

Allowing them to each abide solely by their own ethical precepts will result in procedural pandemonium. On an increasingly regular basis, tribunals are being pressed into service to resolve such conflicts on an ad hoc basis, for example when one party seeks disclosure of documents from an in-house counsel that hales from a jurisdiction where such communications are not subject to confidentially protections, while the opposing party seeks similar documents from an in-house counsel whose communications are protected as confidential.[23] The much-noted 'proliferation' of international tribunals[24] has focused increasing attention on conflicts among national ethical obligations and emphasised the inescapable need for uniform rules in international adjudication. This problem, along with the double deontology problem described above, are the two most pressing problems underlying transnational ethical regulation. They are also the features that suggest that cross-border bankruptcy may be a helpful prototype for global regulation of attorneys.

In other transnational regulatory contexts, jurisdictions prescribe different limitations on particular conduct, which is primarily enforced through administrative bodies. Competition or coordination among regulators may either enhance or undermine the relative enforceability of different systems' limitations, but the very possibility of enforcement

---

imprisoned in London for refusing to disclose information deemed confidential under German law).

[22] K. L. K. Miller, 'Zip to Nil?: A Comparison of American and English Lawyers' standards of Professional Conduct', *ALI–ABA* CA32 (1995), 199–223, 204.

[23] J. T. Mackintosh and K. M. Angus, 'Conflict in Confidentiality. How EU Laws Leave In-House Counsel Outside the Privilege', *International Lawyer*, 38 (2004), 35–54.

[24] See, e.g., S. Spelliscy, 'The Proliferation of Transnational Tribunals. A Chink in the Armor', *Columbia Journal of Transnational Law*, 40 (2001), 143–76, 164–8; C. P. R. Romano, 'The Proliferation of International Judicial Bodies. The Pieces of the Puzzle', *New York University Journal of International Law and Politics*, 31 (1999), 709–52.

is not inherently threatened by the existence of conflicting national standards.

By contrast, cross-border insolvency does not aim to limit conduct, but instead to determine the disposition of assets. As a practical matter, in the absence of international coordination (and putting aside incidental overlap among national rules), application of one jurisdiction's insolvency rules to disposition of a particular asset necessarily precludes application of another jurisdiction's rules.[25] Just as an asset cannot be disposed of by two different national bankruptcy rules, certain attorney conduct cannot comply with the rules of two different jurisdictions. This double deontology or mutual exclusivity problem means that an attorney's compliance with the rules of one jurisdiction necessarily precludes compliance with another jurisdiction's rules. In both the cross-border bankruptcy and transnational ethical contexts, therefore, the operation of national rules is often mutually exclusive, as opposed to merely cumulative.[26]

This mutual exclusivity of the rules raises the stakes and may partially account for why cross-border bankruptcy reform efforts did not follow a path to substantive convergence. Substantive solutions, such as convergence around international norms as is occurring in transnational antitrust and anticorruption laws, is less feasible.

[25] The same would not be true, for example, of the application of antitrust law to invalidate a particular contract. While a court in the United States might apply US antitrust law to find that a merger is permissible, that decision would not preclude the European Commission from deciding that the same merger was prohibited under EU competition law. E. M. Fox, 'GE/Honeywell. The US Merger that Europe Stopped – A Story of the Politics of Convergence', in E. M. Fox and D. A. Crane (eds.), *Antitrust Stories* (Westbury, NY: Foundation Press, 2007), 331, 338.

[26] E.g. in other areas such as antitrust law, there is significant overlap among national rules, but only rarely if ever instances of direct conflict. See M. Bloom, 'The US and EU Move Towards Substantial Antitrust Convergence on Consumer Welfare Based Enforcement', *Antitrust*, 19 (2005), 18 ('Despite different histories, cultures, legal systems, and statutes, and notwithstanding occasional differences, the United States and Europe have largely converged toward consumer welfare based antitrust enforcement'); S. M. Biggers *et al.*, 'Intellectual Property and Antitrust. A Comparison of Evolution in the European Union and United States', *Hastings International & Comparative Law Review*, 22 (1999), 209–90, 215 (observing the 'unprecedented level of international cooperation between enforcement agencies, particularly those in the EU and the United States' such that 'there currently exists a greater degree of convergence ... than ever before'). As a result, global regulatory efforts are channelled into negotiated harmonisation efforts, though there remain areas of conflict between national regulators when one jurisdiction's application of its rules appears to thwart the policy interests of another.

The consequence of mutual exclusivity is compounded by what might be deemed the 'practical necessity' feature that adjudicatory contexts present in cross-border bankruptcy and ethics before international tribunals. Adjudicatory decision-making has a forced immediacy not present in conventional political and administrative decision-making. For example, regulators and policy-makers can defer the question of how a general category of assets should be treated in bankruptcy, but a bankruptcy court asked to dispose of a particular asset in a cross-border bankruptcy cannot.[27] Similarly, the promulgators of ethical rules can defer, for example, answering the question of whether in international contexts in-house attorney communications should be treated as confidential, but a court seized of a dispute with competing assertions about the discoverability of in-house communications cannot.

The practical necessity of adjudicatory decision-making undoubtedly contributed significantly to the informal, improvised solutions among national bankruptcy courts that were the precursors to the Model Law. Similarly, as discussed in more detail below, practical necessity in adjudicatory contexts has led to development of ad hoc ethical rules in international adjudication.

Harmonisation versus territorialism

Like most areas of transnational regulation, efforts at regulating cross-border legal services has coalesced around two competing alternatives: internationalisation and territorialism. In the context of professional regulation, some claim that the primary solution is a single international code of ethics, policed by a single transnational bar association.[28] Promoters of this approach tout the predictability and reassurance that comes with uniformity,[29] as well as the avoidance of conflicts and the need for reciprocity and coordination. Others contend that such

---

[27] Indeed, there is an entire school of thought that regards bankruptcy as primarily if not exclusively a matter of procedure. D. G. Baird, 'Bankruptcy's Uncontested Axioms', *Yale Law Journal*, 108 (1998), 573–600, 576–7; C. W. Mooney, Jr., 'A Normative Theory of Bankruptcy Law. Bankruptcy as (is) Civil Procedure', *Washington & Lee Law Review*, 61 (2004), 931–1062, 934.

[28] See, e.g., M. Majumdar, 'Ethics in the International Arena. The Need for Clarification', *Georgetown Journal of Legal Ethics*, 8 (1995), 439–54, 451–2; J. Toulmin, 'A Worldwide Common Code of Professional Ethics?', *Fordham International Law Journal*, 15 (1992), 673–98, 685.

[29] M. Walsh, 'The International Bar Association Proposal for a Code of Professional Conduct for Counsel Before the ICC', *Journal of International Criminal Justice*, 1 (2003), 490–501.

universalism is impossible,[30] and promote instead greater reciprocal respect for conflicting national rules and clearer choice-of-law rules to determine their application to particular conduct.[31] Proponents of this view identify the link between ethical rules and national legal culture and national policies,[32] as well as the inherent complexity in developing universally acceptable standards.

The nature of these proposed solutions is similar to those offered in the bankruptcy context, where reform efforts have similarly swirled around these two poles. At the one end, proponents of the universalist approach lauded it for its ability to reduce transactional costs and increase efficiency.[33] At the other end, advocates of the territorial approach staunchly defended the need to protect local interests embodied in local bankruptcy law.[34] Like many other areas of transnational regulation, ultimate solutions have grown out of 'flexible and adaptable' transborder relationships that 'foster experimentation and innovation' and are characterised by networks that produced reforms in cross-border bankruptcy (and other transnational regulatory contexts).[35] Transnational networks among policy-makers at a sub-State level have

---

[30] C. Menkel-Meadow, 'Are Cross-Cultural Ethics Standards Possible or Desirable in International Arbitration?', Georgetown Public Law Research Paper No. 1130922; University of California Irvine School of Law Research Paper No. 2008–2, 19, http://ssrn.com/abstract=1130922 (concluding that cultural differences make it impossible to develop universal ethical standards for international arbitration).

[31] K. Weisenberger, 'Peace is not the Absence of Conflict: A Response to Professor Rogers's Article "Fit and Function in Legal Ethics"', Wisconsin International Law Journal, 25 (2007), 89–128 (arguing that extant rules of conduct are adequate for the purpose of regulating international arbitrations, and a conflict-of-laws approach is the best option); see also C. J. Whelan, 'Ethics Beyond the Horizon. Why Regulate the Global Practice of Law?', Vanderbilt Journal of Transnational Law, 34 (2001), 931–52 (tentatively accepting the inevitability of global regulation, but questioning its desirability); R. L. Abel, 'Transnational Law Practice', Case Western Reserve Law Review, 44 (1994), 737–870, 762–3 (advocating deregulation of foreign and transnational legal practice, and proposing modest coordinating reforms to improve information asymmetries).

[32] Weisenberger, 'Peace is not the Absence of Conflict', supra n. 31, 99 (describing legal ethics as 'a historical contingency that operates in tandem with the procedural and other features of a legal system to express the lawyer's role within it').

[33] J. A. E. Pottow, 'Procedural Incrementalism. A Model for International Bankruptcy', Virginia Journal of International Law, 45 (2005), 935–1016, 944–7.

[34] Ibid., 947–9.

[35] K. Raustiala, 'The Architecture of International Cooperation. Transgovernmental Networks and the Future of International Law', Virginia Journal of International Law, 43 (2002), 1–92, 17–24 (exploring how 'traditional liberal internationalist organizations and treaties' are being displaced by the 'adaptable and decentralized network model' of transnational regulation).

been more effective at resolving complex problems than traditional international models.[36]

Although a common feature of transnational networks is decentralisation and depoliticisation of decision-making, this feature is heightened in the contexts of cross-border bankruptcy and transnational regulation of lawyers. The reason is that, in both contexts, primary enforcement resides principally with non-political actors, meaning courts in the bankruptcy context and bar regulatory authorities in the attorney context. Because lawyers are a self-regulating profession, ethical disciplinary authorities are not part of formal political structures and legal ethics are intentionally separate from conventional law-making mechanisms. Meanwhile, as described in more detail in the following section, efforts to resolve existing conflicts through international codes or ethical rules which are abstracted from actual practice often obscure the most essential problems.[37]

Regulators and objects of regulation

A second key feature of cross-border attorney regulation is the relative zeal of regulatory authorities and the objects of regulation. In other areas such as antitrust, securities and anticorruption, governmental authorities enthusiastically extend their regulatory reach to extraterritorial activities in order to protect national interests, while the objects of those regulations often seek to avoid such reach. Corporations, for example, outsource labour to avoid domestic employment laws, build manufacturing facilities abroad to bypass domestic environmental and safety regulations, incorporate subsidiaries in tax havens, etc. When regulatory authorities extend extraterritorially to reach such activities, corporate targets of such efforts often complain loudly.

The opposite dynamic has existed with attorney regulation. On the one hand, until recently local ethical rules were generally deemed not to extend beyond national borders. In the United States, although

---

[36] S. Picciotto, 'Networks in International Economic Integration. Fragmented States and the Dilemmas of Neo-Liberalism', *Northwestern Journal of International Law & Business*, 17 (1996–7), 1014–56; Raustiala, 'The Architecture of International Cooperation', *supra* n. 35; A. M. Slaughter, 'The Accountability of Government Networks', *Indiana Journal of Global Legal Studies*, 8 (2001), 347–68.

[37] C. A. Rogers, 'Fit and Function in Legal Ethics. Developing a Code of Attorney Conduct for International Arbitration', *Michigan Journal of International Law*, 23 (2002), 341–424, 372.

disciplinary authority purportedly extended to wherever attorney conduct occurred, bar associations showed an almost palpable ambivalence toward investigating or punishing alleged attorney misconduct abroad. Moreover, lawyers engaged in transnational legal practice were explicitly exempted from the choice-of-law provisions, which left such questions to non-existent 'agreements between jurisdictions or of appropriate international law'.[38] In most other jurisdictions, bar authorities simply do not extend their power to overseas activities,[39] and often demonstrate a similar reluctance to sanction foreign attorneys for ethical violations,[40] unless their conduct also violates local criminal law.[41]

[38] L.S. Terry, 'US Legal Ethics. The Coming of Age of Global and Comparative Perspectives', *Washington University Global Studies Law Review*, 4 (2005), 463–534, 525 (noting that before the revisions in 2002, 'US lawyers engaged in transnational legal practice had been explicitly exempted from the choice of law provisions in ABA Model Rule 8.5'). Comment 7 of ABA Model Rule 8.5 now states that '[t]he choice of law provision applies to lawyers engaged in transnational practice, unless international law, treaties or other agreements between competent regulatory authorities in the affected jurisdictions provide otherwise'.

[39] Even when flagrant and well publicised, misconduct abroad was not pursued by bar authorities. One of the most notable examples was when dozens of US attorneys descended on unsophisticated victims of the Union Carbide gas leak in Bhopal (India). In apparent violation of several US ethical rules, they directly solicited victims in the wake of the disaster to sign contingent fee retainer agreements for tort actions to be brought in the United States. See 'Bhopal is for Lawyers', *National Review*, January 11, 1985, 20; D.T. Austern, 'Is Lawyer Solicitation of Bhopal Clients Ethical?', *Legal Times*, January 21, 1985.

[40] Notably, the US attorneys' conduct in soliciting Bhopal victims was a fairly clear violation of Indian law. As one scholar explains, in India prohibitions are so strict that 'there is an absolute bar on attorney advertising that would preclude Indian attorneys from being listed on a referral website'. M.A. Gollin, 'Answering the Call. Public Interest Intellectual Advisors', *Washington University Journal of Law and Policy*, 17 (2005), 187–224, 209. Despite the clear violation, there were no reported efforts by Indian authorities to professionally sanction the US attorneys. This reluctance is perhaps best illustrated by the California Supreme Court decision that touched off the firestorm of concern about multi-jurisdictional practice within the United States. In concluding that New York lawyers in an arbitration in California were engaged in the unauthorised practice of law in violation of California ethical rules, the Court expressly exempted international arbitration from its analysis. See *Birbrower, Montalbano, Condon, and Frank, P C* v. *Superior Court*, 949 P.2d 1, 7 (Cal. 1998) (noting that the California Code of Civil Procedure permits parties to an international commercial dispute to either appear in person or be represented or assisted by any person of their choice, regardless of whether that person is licensed to practise law in California or any other jurisdiction).

[41] For example, in 2007, an American-licensed attorney who was a French national employed with a major US law firm was criminally convicted and ordered to pay a fine in France for interviewing a witness in France for the purposes of obtaining information for a proceeding in the United States in violation of French law. See Paris Court of

One likely explanation for this regulatory reluctance is that, unlike other areas, attorney regulation does not strictly speaking reside with national political apparatus, but instead with local bar associations and courts. These institutions traditionally regard themselves as having jurisdiction limited by the territorial boundaries of political sub-divisions because they compete for that jurisdiction with bars from other political sub-divisions.[42]

While these hypotheses might explain bar associations' reluctance to regulate international attorneys, they only serve to heighten two inherent, intertwined ironies. On the one hand, these unregulated or underregulated international attorneys are the same ones advising multinational enterprises (MNEs) how to engage in the regulatory arbitrage described above, and have even been charged with capturing some of the very regulatory agencies that might otherwise be policing such behaviour. Under one view, they seem to have effectively captured the American Bar Association (ABA) and hampered its ability to effectively regulate them. An earlier version of Rule 8.5, quoted, in above, was adopted explicitly at the behest of the ABA's section on International Law. At their urging, it exempted attorneys engaged in transnational practice from the purview of the 'choice-of-law' provisions. Instead, the rule purported to leave choice-of-law issues to 'agreements between jurisdictions or of appropriate international law'. In fact, no such agreements and international law existed.

Despite having successfully created this gaping loophole, however, international attorneys did a complete about-face to close the regulatory gap they themselves had created. In 2001, the Section of International Law again lobbied the ABA, this time to extend Rule 8.5 to US lawyers engaged in transnational activities to provide clearer guidance regarding which rules apply to their activities overseas.[43] Whatever the explanation for this change of heart,[44] it demonstrates a unique desire to close regulatory gaps by those who might otherwise seem poised to benefit from them. The basic starting-points for transnational attorney regulation are the impracticality of universal harmonisation, the sense of

---

Appeals, File n. 06/06272, Judgment of 28 March 2007 (unofficial translation on file with author).

[42] For related reasons, bar associations have been slow to respond to other shifts in the legal profession, including the rise of the mega-law firm and legal practice extending to several jurisdictions within national borders.

[43] Terry, 'US Legal Ethics', *supra* n. 38, 525.

[44] This episode may simply demonstrate that international lawyers know better than anyone that effective regulatory arbitrage requires a degree of certainty in the content and application of relevant regulations.

urgency created by the double deontology problem and the incompatibility of different national rules in international proceedings, and the inherent decentralisation of attorney regulation.

The inadequacy of existing efforts at transnational ethical regulation

Although the initial regulatory response was slow to start, today there seems to be a virtual explosion of efforts to respond to the perceived need for transnational attorney regulation. This section provides a brief overview of those efforts, which have been mostly focused on 'top-down' development of substantive rules.

Universalism in legal ethics

The overwhelming focus for proposals to regulate international attorneys has focused on the substantive rules and their divergences. Literally dozens of new international codes of ethics have been drafted. The earliest effort was the 1956 International Bar Association (IBA) International Code of Legal Ethics, which is probably most accurately described as a set of professional notions rather than rules that provide any meaningful guidance.[45] More recent efforts include the IBA 'Core Values' Resolution, which began in 1998, and the IBA General Principles of the Legal Profession of 2006, for which a new commentary is currently being drafted. The Bar Association Presidents' Meeting developed a Statement of Core Principles in 2005, which was adopted by 100 bar associations from around the world, and the Union Internationale des Avocats (UIA) developed the Turin Principles in 2002.[46] While laudable efforts, these efforts have largely been 'top-down' and operate at a level of abstraction which reveals the challenges in drafting a truly harmonised international code.[47]

---

[45] M.C. Daly, 'The Dichotomy Between Standards and Rules. A New Way of Understanding the Differences in Perceptions of Lawyer Codes of Conduct by US and Foreign Lawyers', *Vanderbilt Journal of Transnational Law*, 32 (1999), 1117–63, 1158.

[46] For a detailed survey of reform efforts to date, see Terry, 'A "How To" Guide', *supra* n. 6, 1140–6.

[47] For example, the Statement of Core Principles provides such broad admonitions as: 'An independent legal profession, without which there is no rule of law or freedom for the people.' While obviously an important principle, absent a meaningful definition of what constitutes 'independent' or 'rule of law', the general principle provides little meaningful guidance.

Other international efforts have had a more tailored focus. For example, the Council of the Bars and Law Societies of Europe (CCBE) developed the Code of Conduct in 1998 (later revised in 2006), which governs European lawyers. In addition to these efforts, some international tribunals, such as the International Criminal Tribunal for the Former Yugoslavia (ICTY) and the International Criminal Court (ICC) in The Hague, have developed codes of ethics for defence counsel. There has also been a virtual explosion of auxiliary regulation of attorneys through national legislation and international agreements aimed at regulating money laundering, corruption, terrorism, tax evasion and trade in legal services.[48] These various sources demonstrate increased recognition of the need to regulate attorneys, but they serve only to heighten the double deontology problems and the conflicts that can arise in adjudicatory settings.

Choice-of-law reforms

The flurry of reform activity resulting in the proliferation of new international codes and legal rules is a response to a perceived need for more substantive guidance. The increased number of sources, however, arguably has the opposite effect, particularly in the absence of shared understanding about the interrelationship of the various sources and coordinated mechanisms for ordering their application to specific conduct. Instead of resolving the tensions and conflicts in transnational legal practice, these new sources create additional conflicts, thereby heightening the need for clearer choice-of-law guidance and increased coordination among regulators.

To date, these latter goals have proven resistant to reform. For example, in developing a code of conduct for the ICC, the IBA was faced with specific precedents illustrating the need for primacy of tribunal ethical rules over home State rules[49] and it debated the issue extensively.[50] Despite these efforts, delegates were unable to reach agreement on 'strategies' for preventing conflicts between national and the newly

---

[48] For an overview of these developments, see L. S. Terry, C. Silver, E. Rosen and C. A. Needham, 'Transnational Legal Practice', *International Lawyer*, 42 (2008), 833–62.

[49] D. D. Ntanda Nsereko, 'Ethical Obligations of Counsel in Criminal Proceedings. Representing an Unwilling Client', *Criminal Law Forum*, 12 (2001), 487–507.

[50] M. Walsh, 'The International Bar Association Proposal for a Code of Professional Conduct for Counsel before the ICC', *Journal of International Criminal Justice*, 1 (2003), 490–501, 499.

proposed supranational ethical rules.[51] Similarly, the CCBE Code identifies the double deontology problem, but does not offer any real guidance other than to suggest that attorneys inform themselves.[52] Jonathan Goldsmith 'the Secretary-General of the CCBE' has raised, but expressed extreme hesitancy about, the prospects for an international choice-of-law rule.[53] Meanwhile, while Model Rule 8.5 attempts to resolve the double deontology problem for US lawyers, however imperfectly,[54] ultimately it is not a meaningful solution since other jurisdictions apply different choice-of-law rules.

Perhaps some of the most effective choice-of-law innovations are the limited carve-outs that a few bar associations have created to permit conduct in international arbitration that is otherwise prohibited in domestic practice. For example, both Swiss[55] and French ethical regimes have incorporated exceptions for international arbitration cases allowing local attorneys to engage in pre-testimonial communication with witnesses, which would otherwise be prohibited in domestic litigation or arbitration.[56] These pragmatic responses relieve attorneys from the perils of double deontology, but also fall short of the mark.[57] By removing an existing rule but failing to provide any meaningful guidance, these exemptions simply shift the nature of the conflict between different

---

[51] *Ibid.*

[52] Art. 2.4 of the CCBE Code provides: 'When practising cross-border, a lawyer from another Member State may be bound to comply with the professional rules of the Host Member State. Lawyers have a duty to inform themselves as to the rules which will affect them in the performance of any particular activity.' For a more comprehensive overview of recent developments, see Terry, 'US Legal Ethics', *supra* n. 38, 463, 494.

[53] *Ibid.*

[54] C. A. Rogers, 'Lawyers Without Borders', *University of Pennsylvania International Law Review*, 30 (2009), 1035–86.

[55] In Switzerland, while pre-testimonial contact with witnesses is generally prohibited, Article 7 of the *Code Suisse de Déontologie* provides with respect to *Contact avec les témoins* (contact with witnesses): '*L'avocat s'abstient d'influencer les témoins et experts. Demeurent reservée les règles particulières des procédures d'arbitrage et procédures devant les Tribunaux supranationaux*' (prohibiting attorneys from contacting witnesses, but suspending such prohibition in proceedings before arbitral or supranational tribunals).

[56] For a recent example of a criminal conviction and fine of a US-licensed attorney in France, see *supra* n. 41.

[57] While US attorneys are permitted to speak to witnesses, their ethical rules do impose some limitations, even if those limits can be 'permeated by ethical uncertainty'. J. S. Applegate, 'Witness Preparation', *Texas Law Review*, 68 (1989), 277–352, 281. There are no limitations whatsoever when, under Swiss and French rules, the initial prohibition is simply eliminated.

ethical regimes, without resolving it.[58] Existing choice-of-law rules all suffer from the same problem – they are enacted at the national level, which means that they only perpetuate the double deontology problem and the existence of conflicts in international tribunals.

Increased cooperation and communication

In addition to the need for clearer choice-of-law provisions, there is also a heightened need for effective coordinated cross-border enforcement mechanisms. Even more than choice-of-law reforms, this subject has been largely resistant to concrete reforms, as opposed to just dialogue. Transnational practice and existing national choice-of-law rules mean that the disciplinary authorities of one jurisdiction may be required to apply the ethical rules of another jurisdiction with respect to activities that took place in a foreign State, potentially in a foreign language and involving foreign clients.[59] This task, I contend, requires explicit multilateral coordination, not simply increased communication and dialogue. Within both the United States and Europe, regulators have acknowledged this need for coordination when discipline involves multiple sub-jurisdictions within a political unit.[60] At an international level (outside the EU), the need for interjurisdictional coordination is even more critical when the regulatory authorities of one country are called upon to impose discipline based on the ethical rules of another jurisdiction.

National disciplinary authorities exist and operate in domestic political and legal contexts. They are familiar with, and fundamentally oriented to, applying the language, concepts and policies embodied in

---

[58] See L. Reed and J. Sutcliffe, 'The "Americanization" of International Arbitration?', *Mealey's International Arbitration Report*, 4 (2001), 37–47, 42 (suggesting that while some consensus has emerged about the possibility of preliminary communication with witnesses, there remains conflict as to the extent permitted).

[59] See Rogers, 'Lawyers Without Borders', *supra* n. 54, 1040–7.

[60] E.g. in the United States Rule 22 of the ABA Model Rules for Lawyer Disciplinary Enforcement imposes notification obligations and requires, subject to certain conditions, that disciplinary authorities impose reciprocal penalties for violations committed in another (domestic) jurisdiction, and the US Conference of Chief Justices has proposed a resolution regarding cooperation in ethical discipline. See www.abanet.org/cpr/disenf/rule22.html; http://ccj.ncsc.dni.us/2-ProposedCCBEResolution1-6-09.pdf. In the EU, there have been similar efforts at coordination. See Resolution of the Council of the Bars and Law Societies of Europe (CCBE) Regarding Discipline Cooperation (February. 2009), www.ccbe.eu/fileadmin/user_upload/NTCdocument/Resolution_in_Suppor1_1 241602552.pdf.

their own local ethical rules. This orientation undermines their ability to apply foreign or international ethical rules, whose content may be both difficult to discern and contrary to regulatory authorities' own institutional sense of proper attorney conduct. For example, it is difficult to imagine that US disciplinary authorities would be inclined to punish a US attorney for 'improperly' preparing a witness when French ethical rules are deemed to apply to that conduct. It is similarly difficult to imagine that US authorities would condemn a US attorney for disclosing essential information even if a foreign system deems such information to be 'confidential' as against the client.[61] Alternatively, it seems far-fetched to assume that a French bar association would discipline a French attorney for unethically withholding discoverable documents when no such offence exists in France and France has a historical tradition of hostility to the very notion of discovery.[62]

Regulatory authorities are not all-purpose machines into which a set of ethical rules can be input at one end and a disinterested disciplinary decision applying those rules be produced at the other. Like the lawyers they administer, the individuals who staff bar disciplinary authorities are products of a local legal culture.[63] Their legal history, background and training necessarily colour their perceptions about the propriety of attorney conduct and their interpretation of rules applied to such conduct. When filtered through national regulatory authorities, international and foreign legal ethical rules will be refracted through these national perspectives. The ambiguities inherent in legal translation will increase the potential for distortion.[64]

---

[61] For an extended discussion of these issues, see Rogers, 'Lawyers Without Borders', *supra* n. 54, 1045–56.

[62] France, Germany, The Netherlands, Norway, Belgium, Sweden and Canada have all enacted blocking statutes forbidding their citizens from complying with certain US discovery requests. See W. S. Dodge, 'Extraterritoriality and Conflicts-of-Laws Theory. An Argument for Judicial Unilateralism', *Harvard International Law Journal*, 39 (1998), 101–70, 164, n. 357.

[63] In the United States, there are international sections to State regulatory authorities, but they play no role in discipline. Their functions are limited to organising research, networking opportunities and symposia on issues of international law and practice.

[64] A similar phenomenon has already been observed as substantive international and foreign law have been distorted when interpreted by national courts. See E. Benvenisti, 'Judicial Misgivings Regarding the Application of International Law. An Analysis of Attitudes of National Courts', *EJIL*, 4 (1993), 159–83, 160–75 (discussing reasons prompting most national courts to approach international norms apprehensively and limit their application within national legal systems).

A regulatory model borrowed from cross-border bankruptcy

This section develops a general analogy between the solution developed for cross-border bankruptcy and a proposed regime for coordinated regulation of lawyers engaged in transnational legal practice. Like proposals for transnational regulation of lawyers, proposed solutions for cross-border bankruptcy initially focused on substantive rules. The Model Law is successful, however, because it eventually adopted a predominantly procedural solution.[65] The Model Law skirts substantive international harmonisation and instead facilitates efficient procedural coordination by identifying criteria for selecting a forum, by ordering the relationship between that forum and other related fora, by articulating clear choice-of-law provisions and, most importantly for this discussion, by facilitating international cooperation and communication.[66] These various features, and an overall focus on procedural mechanisms, make the Model Law a useful paradigm for developing a regime for ethical regulation of transnational lawyers.

The form of the reform

One fundamental feature of the Model Law that led to its success is its form as a free-standing international model law, as opposed to a treaty. There had been numerous unsuccessful efforts at drafting an international bankruptcy treaty that would provide substantively harmonised provisions for cross-border bankruptcy.[67] The Model Law intentionally rejected this format and, at least according to Mooney, provided a superior means for attaining the desired ends:

> In many respects the process of harmonization through an international convention is much more cumbersome and unwieldy than the model law paradigm. An international convention normally would be sponsored by an inter-governmental organization, with all the usual formality and delay. The road from an idea, to a study, to successful meetings of governmental experts, and eventually to a diplomatic conference may be long, winding, and rocky. A model law, on the other hand, need not have explicit or unqualified approval of any governmental or intergovernmental organization, inasmuch as it is itself not a law at all but only a 'model'.[68]

---

[65] Pottow, 'Procedural Incrementalism', *supra* n. 33, 947–51.   [66] *Ibid.*, 961–2.

[67] *Ibid.*, 938 (noting the 'historic inability to craft an international agreement among nations, by treaty or other means').

[68] C. W. Mooney, 'Extraterritorial Impact of Choice-of-Law Rules for Non-United States Debtors Under Revised UCC Article 9 and a New Proposal for International Harmonization', in M. Bridge and R. Stevens (eds.), *Cross-Border Security and Insolvency*

The argument for a model law format in transnational attorney regulation may be more compelling than in the cross-border bankruptcy setting.

Attorneys generally regard themselves as self-regulating professionals, even if there is mounting evidence that this self-perception has outlived the reality.[69] While erosion of lawyers' self-regulation has been substantial, arguably it is neither complete[70] nor desirable as an absolute. For example, in arguing that government attorneys had an obligation to 'speak... law to power' in the war on terror and the torture debate, Vagts and others have relied on attorneys' ethical obligations and invoked independence arguments as something more than empty nostalgia for a bygone era.[71] Even more telling, while the response to the authors of the so-called 'Torture Memos' during the administration of US President George W. Bush has evaluated the full range of regulatory sanctions – from criminal law, to impeachment standards, to civil sanctions – the report by the Office of Professional Responsibility, an internal ethics unit within the US Department of Justice, appears poised instead to refer the issue to State bar associations for possible disciplinary action.[72] While many commentators are ready to declare the legal profession as simply another form of 'services', in this context the independent bar disciplinary authorities are perceived as having a unique role to play in matters which involve legal activities intertwined with the exercise of political power.

Bar associations continue to have some role to play in professional regulation, and if nothing else their resistance to undesirable regulatory

---

(Oxford University Press, 2001), 193 (quoted in Pottow, 'Procedural Incrementalism', *supra* n. 33, 985).

[69] See, e.g., F. Zacharias, 'The Myth of Self-Regulation', *Minnesota Law Review*, 93 (2009), 1147–90.

[70] T. Schneyer, 'An Interpretation of Recent Developments in the Regulation of Law Practice', *Oklahoma City University Law Review*, 30 (2005), 559–610, 569–70 (arguing that bar associations 'continue, often with ABA support, to resist federal "intrusions"' but conceding that 'they must increasingly content themselves with trying to influence, rather than staving off, federal initiatives').

[71] R. B. Bilder and D. F. Vagts, 'Speaking Law to Power. Lawyers and Torture', *AJIL*, 98 (2004), 689–95.

[72] D. Johnston and S. Shane, 'Interrogation Memos. Inquiry Suggests No Charges', *New York Times*, May 6, 2009, www.nytimes.com/2009/05/06/us/politics/06inquire.html. The final report by the US Department of Justice had now been released, see http://judiciary.house.gov/hearings/pdf/OPRFinalReport090729.pdf, Office of Professional Responsibility, Investigation into the Office of Legal Council's Memorandum Concerning Issues Relating to the Central Intelligence Agency's use of 'Enhanced Interrogation Techniques,' on Suspected Terrorists, July 29, 2009.

encroachments is well documented.[73] These observations suggest the potential benefits of a model law as the vehicle for introducing transnational legal reforms. A model law would be developed and endorsed by lawyers' own institutions and subject to modification on enactment, all of which may make its solutions more readily acceptable, as the Model Law did in cross-border bankruptcy.[74]

Procedural coordination over substantive harmonisation

Transnational attorney regulation reform can also draw from the Model Law's mechanisms for ordering the relationships among otherwise competing jurisdictions, its related determination of applicable law and its facilitation of cooperation and support between actors from the relevant jurisdictions. Specifically, the Model Law designates a 'main proceeding', which is the jurisdiction where a debtor's main interests are located.[75] The location of the main proceeding is what determines both the forum for the primary adjudication and the national law that will govern those bankruptcy proceedings. In addition, the Model Law provides for 'protocols' for coordination with 'ancillary proceedings' in other jurisdictions where a debtor's assets or foreign creditors are located in order to facilitate enforcement of the orders of the court of the main proceeding.[76] The precise distinction between main and ancillary bankruptcy proceedings, and the details of communication protocols, is not particularly important for regulating transnational legal practice. The helpful insight concerns the allocation of competences and coordination that these distinctions facilitate.

One of the historical problems for attorney regulation, described above, is the relative reluctance of regulatory authorities to impose

---

[73] See, e.g., L. S. Terry, 'The Future Regulation of the Legal Profession. The Impact of Treating the Legal Profession as "Service Providers"', *Professional Lawyer* (2008), 189–211 (describing ABA and other bar association responses to international treaty provisions regarding legal services and rules proposed by the intergovernmental Financial Action Task Force that pertain to attorney confidentiality, but were drafted by non-lawyers).

[74] Laurel Terry has proposed what is undoubtedly the most far-sighted solution to date: an international choice-of-law provision to be implemented through the 'additional commitments' provisions under GATS, drafted in cooperation with the IBA. See L. S. Terry, 'From GATS to APEC. The Impact of Trade Agreements on Legal Services', *Akron Law Review* (2010) (forthcoming) (draft on file with the author).

[75] J. A. E. Pottow, 'The Myth (and Realities) of Forum Shopping in Transnational Insolvency', *Brooklyn Journal of International Law*, 32 (2007), 785–818, 786.

[76] Pottow, 'Procedural Incrementalism', *supra* n. 33, 935, 948, 962.

professional sanctions for attorney conduct abroad or on foreign attorneys' local activities. In a similar vein, some international tribunals appear reticent to exercise any disciplinary role, while other tribunals, particularly international arbitration tribunals, seem to doubt their own power to do so (or face legal impediments to doing so). More recently, this reluctance is being overcome in the light of a pragmatic need to respond to professional issues that cannot be obviated or ignored. For example, as pointed out elsewhere in this volume, investment arbitration tribunals are increasingly being asked to rule on issues of professional conduct, and showing a greater willingness to do so.[77] Meanwhile, the ICTY has been even more directly engaged in issues of ethical conduct and regulation, with an established record of assessing alleged misconduct by attorneys and issuing sanctions for contempt of court and, in a presage of the proposal to come, referring incidents of misconduct to an attorney's home bar.[78]

While these are important developments, they also signal the increased importance of developing comprehensive international choice-of-law provisions, as opposed to substantive rules or national choice-of-law rules.[79] The ever-increasing number of sources purporting to govern attorney conduct signals the need for an international choice-of-law provision, and underscores the inadequacy of national choice-of-law rules to provide a meaningful response. Early on, Vagts appreciated this need and argued in favour of development of 'rules of private international law or conflicts of law to determine which countries' standards should apply'.[80]

---

[77] C. N. Brower and S. W. Schill, 'Regulating counsel conduct before international arbitral tribunals', see chapter 24 in this volume (arguing that 'treaty-based arbitral tribunals have the power to develop and enforce rules concerning counsel conduct in order to ensure the functioning, the fairness and the legitimacy of the arbitral proceedings before them').

[78] See Rule 46 of the Rules of Procedure and Evidence for the ICTY, UN Doc. IT/32/Rev.41, entered into force 14 March 1994, as amended 28 February 2008, www.un.org/icty/legaldoc-e/index-t.htm; International Criminal Tribunal for Rwanda, Rules of Procedure and Evidence, UN Doc. ITR/3/Rev.1, adopted 29 June 1995, as amended 14 March 2008, http://69.94.11.53/default.htm.

[79] Although the proposal here is a general regulatory framework that does not include substantive rules, I have argued elsewhere that it is essential that international tribunals develop their own codes of ethics. See C. A. Rogers, 'Fit and Function in Legal Ethics' *supra* n. 37, 341–424; *Idem*, 'Context and Institutional Structure in Attorney Regulation. Constructing an Enforcement Regime for International Arbitration', *Stanford Journal of International Law*, 39 (2003), 1–58; *Idem*, 'Lawyers Without Borders', *supra* n. 54.

[80] Vagts, 'The International Legal Profession', *supra* n. 14, 378.

Meanwhile, consistent with this effort and the cross-border bankruptcy example, reforms should construct a procedural framework that facilitates coordination among the various entities, as opposed to imagining a unitary regulatory authority or leaving disperse regulatory authorities to act wholly independently. Express coordination is distinct from increased communication among regulators. While it is beyond the scope of this chapter to map out each of these tasks in detail, I sketch below the outlines of such a reform, tying the specific proposals to analogous elements of the cross-border bankruptcy regime.

While cross-border bankruptcy has a 'main proceeding' based on a centre of interests test in bankruptcy, I propose that attorneys' home disciplinary authority operate as the fulcrum for transnational attorney discipline. This role is necessary since a home disciplinary authority may, as a practical matter, be the only entity capable of imposing professional sanctions affecting the attorney's status as a lawyer, such as suspension or disbarment. An attorney's home jurisdiction may also on occasion have an important role to play in rejecting alleged violations of foreign ethical rules.

Similar to how cross-border bankruptcy facilitates coordination with 'ancillary proceedings', a meaningful reform of transnational attorney regulation should facilitate communication between an attorney's home jurisdiction disciplinary authority and international adjudicatory tribunals, foreign disciplinary authorities or other regulatory bodies. Non-licensing tribunals or foreign disciplinary authorities could have two important functions to play, even if discipline is imposed by an attorney's home jurisdiction. First, they could receive complaints locally and, as appropriate, refer them to the disciplinary authority of an attorney's home jurisdiction. The express engagement of a local regulatory authority will presumably heighten the accountability of transnational attorneys to clients and third parties in foreign jurisdictions. If, for example, the attorneys improperly soliciting after the Bhopal disaster knew the local bar could refer a complaint to their home bar, they might at least have been motivated to look up local ethical rules, if not abide by them. Meanwhile, if local Indian regulatory authorities knew that a US disciplinary authority would pursue a complaint for the improper solicitation, they might have been less inclined to ignore the misconduct.[81]

---

[81] Notably, much improper foreign conduct by attorneys is already directly addressed by foreign regulators when such conduct constitutes violation of a generally applicable regulation or criminal law.

A second function of these 'ancillary' authorities would be to provide an attorney's home authority with assistance and support in pursuing complaints of alleged misconduct that are governed by their local rules. An international choice-of-law rule will occasionally require that a bar association apply foreign law or foreign ethical rules. Representatives of foreign bar associations would be the primary interpreters of their own national rules and, particularly in the case of international tribunals, in some instances fact-finders. This approach would permit interpretation, or at least guidance on interpretation, by the promulgator of the relevant rules and avoid the situation of having to rely on competing experts, as described above.

An equally important, and ultimately related, issue is that any adjudicatory tribunal must have the ability to sanction and control the behaviour of attorneys appearing before them. The ability to apply rules implies the ability to develop and refine their content. International tribunals and their rules of conduct cannot, as Daly has suggested, be held 'captive to out-of-State disciplinary authorities'.[82] As noted above, the ICTY is the international tribunal that has most directly engaged issues of ethical conduct and regulation. It has an established record of assessing alleged misconduct by attorneys and issuing sanctions for contempt of court. Some tribunals are more reticent in light of less clear sources of authority to exercise a similar disciplinary role. The power to resolve important international and transnational legal issues must be understood as being accompanied by a power to control and regulate the attorneys who participate in those proceedings. Given the real or perceived limitations on the authority of international adjudicatory bodies, this prescription requires the cooperation of national bar associations in receiving referrals and meting out appropriate sanctions.

Conclusion

Since Detlev Vagts' interest in regulation of the global legal profession grew out of the challenges posed by other topics of transnational regulation, it is fitting that those areas of transnational regulation be mined

---

[82] M. C. Daly, 'Resolving Ethical Conflicts in Multijurisdictional Practice – Is Model Rule 8.5 the Answer, an Answer, or No Answer at All?', *South Texas Law Review*, 36 (1995), 715–98, 778. Daly refers to domestic US courts being held captive by the regulatory authorities of a different State, but the problem she identifies is equally applicable in the international context.

now for insights and guidance about global ethical regulation. Many of the regulatory challenges – the multiplicity of rules, the impossibility of developing a unitary, harmonised body of rules, and the competing national interests – are similar. The Model Law, which achieves a unique and uniquely functional system of coordination, can provide meaningful guideposts in developing a model for attorney regulation.

One incidental benefit to the proposed model is that it will necessarily link international tribunals, courts, and bar associations in an ongoing dialogue that is contextualised in specific cases and with respect to individual incidents. To date, most efforts in the area of transnational attorney regulation involve discussion and debate at a relatively high level of abstraction in an effort to develop political solutions to the practical problems.

BIBLIOGRAPHY OF DETLEV VAGTS

Books

Transnational Legal Problems, 1st edn. 1968, 2nd edn. 1976, 3rd edn. 1986, 4th edn. 1994 (Westbury, NY: Foundation Press) (with Henry Steiner for 1st–3rd edn. and with Henry Steiner and Harold Hongju Ko for 4th edn.)

Basic Corporation Law, 1st edn. 1973, 2nd edn. 1979, 3rd edn. 1989 (Westbury, NY: Foundation Press)

Transnational Business Problems, 1st edn. 1986, 2nd edn. 1998, 3rd edn. 2003, 4th edn. 2008 (Westbury, NY: Foundation Press) (with William Dodge and Harold Hongju Koh)

Secured Transactions under the Uniform Commercial Code (Albany, NY: Matthew Bender & Co., 1963) (with Peter Coogan and William Hogan)

Demokratie, Marktwirtschaft und Recht/Democracy, Market Economy, and the Law (Heidelberg: Verlag Recht & Wirtschaft, 1995) (with Werner Ebke)

International Encyclopedia of Comparative Law, vol. XIII, Business and Private Organizations (Tübingen: Mohr Siebeck, 2006) (with Alfred Conard)

Articles

'Freedom of Speech in the Armed Forces', *Columbia Law Review*, 57 (1957), 187–218

'The Corporate Alien. Definitional Questions in Federal Restraints on Foreign Enterprise', *Harvard Law Review*, 74 (1961), 1489–1551

'The United States of America's Treatment of Foreign Investment', *Rutgers Law Review*, 17 (1963), 374–404

'The Accounting Principles Board and Differences and Inconsistencies in Accounting Practice. An Interim Appraisal', *Law and Contemporary Problems*, 30 (1965), 706–26 (with Robert Sprouse)

'The Impact of the Uniform Commercial Code on the Oil and Gas Mortgage', *Texas Law Review*, 43 (1965), 825–41

'The Logan Act. Paper Tiger or Sleeping Giant?', *AJIL*, 60 (1966), 268–302

'Reforming the "Modern" Corporation', *Harvard Law Review*, 80 (1966), 23–89

'The Multinational Enterprise. A New Challenge for Transnational Law', *Harvard Law Review*, 83 (1970), 739–92

'The Global Corporation and International Law', *Journal of International Law and the Economy*, 6 (1972), 247–62

'Law and Accounting in Business Associations and Private Organizations', *International Encyclopedia of Comparative Law*, XIII CL. 12A (Tübingen: Mohr Siebeck, 1972), 1–91

'The Host Country Faces the Multinational Enterprise', *Boston University Law Review*, 53 (1973), 261–77

'Formal and Structural Problems of International Organization for Control of Investment', in Don Wallace (ed.), *International Control of Investment. The Düsseldorf Conference on Multinational Corporations* (New York: Praeger, 1974), 235–83

'The Societas Europea. A Future Option for US Corporations?', *Business Lawyer*, 29 (1974), 823–33 (with Thomas Wälde)

'American Restraints on Foreign Banks', in Marcus Lutter (ed.), *Festschrift für Johannes Bärmann* (Munich: C. H. Beck, 1975), 981–94

'The Governance of the Corporation. The Options Available and the Power to Prescribe', *Business Lawyer*, 31 (1976), 929–38

'The "Other" Case Method. Education for Counting House and Court House Compared', *Journal of Legal Education*, 28 (1977), 403–22

'Coercion and Foreign Investment Rearrangements', *AJIL*, 72 (1978), 17–36

'Strict Equity, Law and the Corporation', in R. Newman (ed.), *The Unity of Strict Law. A Comparative Study* (Brussels: Bruylant, 1978), 35–54

'Why Directors Need to Keep Records', *Harvard Business Review*, (November–December 1978), 28

'The Balance of Power in International Law. A History of an Idea', *AJIL*, 73 (1979), 555–80 (with Alfred Vagts)

'European Perspectives. A Foreword', *Hastings Law Journal*, 30 (1979), 1413–18

'Legal Opinions in Quantitative Terms. The Lawyer as Haruspex or Bookie', *Business Lawyer*, 34 (1979), 421–8

'Railroads, Private Enterprise and Public Policy', in N. Horn and J. Kocka (eds.), *Law and the Formation of the Big Enterprises in the 19th and Early 20th Centuries* (Göttingen: Vandenhoeck & Ruprecht, 1979), 604–18

'A Reply to A Critical Evaluation of the Mexican–American Transfer of Penal Sanctions Treaty', *Iowa Law Review*, 64 (1979), 325–38

'Sovereign Immunity Decisions of the Department of State, May 1952 to January 1977', *1977 Digest of United States Practice in International Law* (Washington, DC: Government Printing office, 1979), 1017–82 (with Michael Sandler and Bruno Ristau)

'Trends in International Business Law. Towards a New Ethnocentricity?', *Northwestern Journal of International Law & Business*, 1 (1979), 11–21

'The United States and its Multinationals. Protection and Control', *Harvard Journal of International Law*, 20 (1979), 235–51

'Disclosure and the Multinational Enterprise. The Costs of Illumination', in N. Horn (ed.), *Legal Problems of codes of conduct for Multinational Enterprise*' (Deventer: Kluwer, 1980)

'Are There No International Lawyers Anymore?', *AJIL*, 75 (1981), 134–7

'Multinational Corporations and International Guidelines', *Common Market Law Review*, 18 (1981), 463–74

'Canada's Foreign Investment Policy. An International Perspective', *Boston University International Law Journal*, 1 (1982), 27–32

'A Turnabout in Extraterritoriality', *AJIL*, 76 (1982), 591–4

'Challenges to Executive Compensation. For the Markets or the Courts?', *Journal of Corporation Law*, 8 (1983), 231–76

'The Scope of Application and Enforcement of US Law', *Wirtschaft und Recht*, 35 (1983), 72–97

'International Law under Time Pressure. Grading the Grenada Take-Home Examination', *AJIL*, 78 (1984), 169–72

'An Introduction to International Civil Practice', *Vanderbilt Journal of Transnational Law*, 17 (1984), 1–10

'The Pipeline Controversy. An American Viewpoint', *GYIL*, 27 (1984), 38–53

'*The Question of a Reference to International Obligations in the United Nations Code of Conduct on Transnational Corporations. A Different View*' (New York: United Nations, 1986) (pamphlet)

'Dispute-Resolution Mechanisms in International Business', *Hague RdC*, 203 (1987), 1–94

'Foreign Investment Risk Reconsidered. The View from the 1980s', *ICSID Review*, 2 (1987) 1–18

'Konzernrecht in den Vereinigten Staaten', in J.-N. Druey (ed.), *Das St Galler Konzernrechtsgespräch* (Bern and Stuttgart: Paul Haupt, 1988), 31–41

'Going to Court, Internationally', *Michigan Law Review*, 87 (1989), 1712–17, 1717

'Risk Management in International Bank Financing and Payment', in N. Horn (ed.), *Law of International Trade Finance*, (Deventer: Kluwer, 1989), 23–37

'Senate Materials and Treaty Interpretation. Some Research Hints for the Supreme Court', *AJIL*, 83 (1989), 546–50

'International Law in the Third Reich', *AJIL*, 84 (1990), 661–704

'The Leveraged Buyout and Management's Share', *Lake Forest Law Review*, 25 (1990), 129–40

'Introduction', in I. Müller, *Hitler's Justice. The Courts of the Third Reich* (Cambridge, MA: Harvard University Press, 1991), 341–2

'Balance of Power' and 'Minimum Standard', in *Encyclopedia of Public International Law*, Rudolf Bernhardt (ed.), *EPIL*, resp. vol. I and vol. III (Amsterdam and New York: North-Holland, 1992), resp. 313–15 and 468–70

'Nationalism and International Lawyers. Centrifugal and Centripetal Forces in the International Legal System', *Thesaurus Acroasium*, 19 (1992), 7–44

'State Succession. The Codifiers' View', *Virginia Journal of International Law*, 33 (1993), 275–97

'Treaty Interpretation and the New American Ways of Law Reading', *EJIL*, 4 (1993), 472–505

'Repealing the Cold War', *AJIL*, 88 (1994), 506–11

'Wohin mit der beschränkten Haftung der Aktionäre', *Zeitschrift für Unternehmens- und Gesellschaftsrecht*, 23 (1994), 227–336

'The International Law Communications Network. Four Decades of Change', in U. Beyerlin (ed.), *Recht zwischen Umbruch und Bewahrung. Festschrift für Rudolph Bernhardt* (Berlin: Springer, 1995), 279–88

'The Proposed Expatriation Tax. A Human Rights Violation?', *AJIL*, 89 (1995), 578–80

'The International Legal Profession. A Need for More Governance?', *AJIL*, 90 (1996), 250–62

'Rethinking the Conceptual Framework of Extraterritoriality Issues and the Methods for Resolving Conflicts', in M. K. Young and Y. Iwasawa (eds.), *Trilateral Perspectives on International Legal Issues. Relevance of Domestic Law and Policy* (Irvington, NY: Transnational Publishers, 1996), 199–212

'Bär and Karrer. Connecting Two Legal Systems', in N. Vogt (ed.), *The International Practice of Law. Liber Amicorum for Thomas Bär and Robert Karrer* (Basel: Helbing & Lichtenhahn, 1997), 247–62

'Currency Translation Accounting', *Wirtschaftsprüfer Mitteilungen*, 36 (special Issue, June 1997), 61–7

'The Helms–Burton Act. Exercising the Presidential Option', *AJIL* 91 (1997), 83–4 (with Theodor Meron)

'Switzerland, International Law and World War II', *AJIL* 91 (1997), 466–75

'Editorial Comment. Taking Treaties Less Seriously', *AJIL*, 92 (1998), 458–62

'International Legal Ethics and Professional Responsibility', *ASIL* Proceedings, 92 (1998), 378–9

'Neutrality Law in World War II', *Cardozo Law Review*, 20 (1998), 459–82

'Restitution for Historic Wrongs. The American Courts and International Law', *AJIL*, 92 (1998), 232–5

'The Traditional Legal Concept of Neutrality in a Changing World', *American University International Law Review*, 14 (1998), 83–102

'Das Gefälle bei den Gehältern von Spitzenmanager – Amerika gegen den Rest der Welt', in U. Schneider *et al.* (eds.), *Festschrift für Marcus Lutter zum 70. Geburtstag* (Cologue: O. Schmidt, 2000), 767–77

'The Hague Peace Conference and Arms Control', *AJIL*, 94 (2000), 31–41

'The Impact of Globalization on the Legal Profession', *EJIL*, 2 (2000), 403–14

'Professional Responsibility in Transborder Practice. Conflict and Resolution', *Georgetown Journal of Legal Ethics*, 13 (2000), 677–98

'Securities Regulation – An Introduction', in D. F. Vagts (ed.), *Business and Private Organizations, vol. XIII, International Encyclopedia of Comparative Law* (Dordrecht: Mohr Siebeck and Martinus Nijhoff, 2000)

'Hegemonic International Law', *AJIL*, 95 (2001), 843–8

'The Impact of Globalization on the Legal Profession', *EJLR*, 2 (2000), 403–14, reprinted in J. Drolshammer and M. Pfeifer (eds.), *The Internationalization of the Practice of Law* (The Hague: Kluwer, 2001), 31–42

'Trial and Sentencing of Prisoners of War', *Financial Times*, 30 November 2001

'The United States and its Treaties. Observance and Breach', *AJIL*, 95 (2001), 313–34

'Carl Schmitt in Context. Reflections on a Symposium', *Cardozo Law Review*, 23 (2002), 2157–63

'Comparative Company Law – The New Wave', in R. J Schweizer, H. Burkert and U. Gasser (eds.), *Festschrift für Nicolas Druey zum 65. Geburtstag* (Zurich: Schulthess, 2002), 595–605

'Litigating the Nazi Labor Claims. The Path not Taken', *Harvard Journal of International Law*, 43 (2002), 503–31 (with Peter Murray), German trans., *Zeitschrift für Zivilprozessrecht International*, 7 (2002), 333–68

'Ajuri v. IDF Commander in West Bank. Case No. HCJ 7015/02', *AJIL*, 97 (2003), 173–5

'Extraterritoriality and the Corporate Governance Law', *AJIL*, 97 (2003), 289–94

'The Ideology and Politics of American Tort Litigation', *Bitburger Gespräche*, 61 (2003), 61–70

'The UN Norms for Transnational Corporations', *Leiden Journal of International Law*, 16 (2003), 795–802

'Which Courts Should Try Persons Accused of Terrorism?', *EJIL*, 14 (2003), 313–26

'International Relations Looks at Customary International Law. A Traditionalist's Defence', *EJIL*, 15 (2004), 1031–40

'Restricting Business in the Public Interest', *Europarecht*, 1 (2004) 51–60

'Sovereign Bankruptcy, In re Germany (1963), In re Iraq (2004)', *AJIL*, 98 (2004), 302–6

'Speaking Law to Power. Lawyers and Torture', *AJIL*, 98 (2004), 689–95 (with Richard Bilder)

'Essay in Honor of Oscar Schachter, Rebus Revisited. Changed Circumstances in Treaty Law', *Columbia Journal of Transnational Law*, 43 (2005), 459–76

'American International Law. A Sonderweg?', in K. Dicke, S. Hobe, K. O. Meyn, A. Peters, E. Riedel, H. J. Schütz and C. Tietje (eds.), *Weltinnenrecht. Liber Amicorum Jost Delbrück* (Berlin: Duncker & Humblot, 2005), 835–47

'The Governance of the Multinational', *Wisconsin International Law Journal*, 23 (2005), 525–40

'Military Commission Law', *The Army Lawyer*, 47 (December 2005), 47–53 (with Eugene Fidell and Dwight Sullivan)

'Transnational Litigation and Professional Ethics', in B. Legum (ed.), *International Litigation Strategies and Practice* (Chicago, IL: ABA Publishing, 2005), 25–31

'International Economic Law and the American Journal of International Law', *AJIL*, 100 (2006), 769–82

'"War" in the American Legal System', *ILSA Journal of International and Comparative Law*, 12 (2006), 541–6

'Balance of Powers', in R. Wolfrum (ed.), *Max Planck Encyclopedia of Public International Law*, 3rd edn. (Oxford University Press, 2007), www.mpepil.com.

'Military Commissions. A Concise History', *AJIL*, 101 (2007), 35–48

'Military Commissions. The Forgotten Reconstruction Chapter', *American University International Law Review*, 23 (2008), 231–74

'Political Threats to Overseas Scholars', *Fletcher Forum*, 32 (2008), 181–8

'The Financial Meltdown and its International Implications', *AJIL*, 103 (2009), 684–91

'Foreword to the Backlash against Investment Arbitration', in M. Waibel, A. Kaushal, K.-H. L. Chung and C. Balchin (eds.), *The Backlash against Investment Arbitration. Perceptions and Reality* (The Hague: Kluwer Law International, 2010), xxiii–xxvi.

Book reviews

'Heinrich Kronstein and Carsten Claussen, Publizität und Gewinnverteilung im neuen Akienrecht', *Harvard Law Review*, 75 (1962), 1046–51

'Robert Campbell, Accounting in Soviet Planning and Management', *Harvard Law Review*, 77 (1964), 590–5

'Erwin Smigel, The Wall Street Lawyer. Professional Organization Man?', *Harvard Law Review*, 78 (1964), 491–6

'Lawrence Ebb, Regulation and Protection of International Business', *AJIL*, 59 (1965), 184–6

'Günther Grassman, System des internationalen Gesellschaftsrechtes', *American Journal of Comparative Law*, 18 (1970), 863–4

'Hans-Georg Koppensteiner, Internationale Unternehmen in deutschen Aktienrecht', *AJIL*, 66 (1972), 683–5

'Christopher Stone, Where the Law Ends', *Southern California Law Review*, 49 (1976), 635–9

'Alfred Conard, Corporations in Perspective', *Business Lawyer*, 33 (1978), 2063–84

'Werner Feld, Multinational Corporations and UN Politics', *Harvard International Law Journal*, 22 (1981), 257–9

'M. Steinberg, Corporate Internal Affairs. A Corporate and Securities Law Perspective', *Journal of Corporate Law*, 10 (1985), 551–2

'Lori Damrosch (ed.), The International Court of Justice at a Crossroads', *Michigan Law Review*, 87 (1989), 1712–17

'Carsten Ebenroth and Joachim Heidelberg, Die Multilaterale Investitions-Garantie Agentur', *International Lawyer*, 24 (1990), 854–6

'Walter Weyrauch, Gestapo V-Leute', *Florida Law Review*, 42 (1990), 425–8

'Inga Markovits, Die Abwicklung. Ein Tagebuch Zum Ende der DDR-Justiz', *Texas International Law Journal*, 29 (1994), 511–18

'Arthur Eyffinger, The 1899 Hague Peace Conference. The Parliament of Man, The Federation of the World', *AJIL*, 94 (2000), 599–600

'Rudolf Bernhardt (ed.), Encyclopedia of Public International Law', *AJIL*, 95 (2001), 726–7

'Craig Scott (ed.), Torture as Tort. Comparative Perspectives on the Development of Human Rights Litigation', *AJIL*, 95 (2001), 1002–3

'Christian Joerges and Navraj Singh Ghalleigh (eds.), The Darker Legacies of Law in Europe. The Shadow of National Socialism and Fascism over Europe and Its Legal Traditions', *American Journal of Comparative Law*, 51 (2003), 959–62

'Michael Byers and Georg Nolte, United States Hegemony and the Foundations of International Law', *AJIL*, 98 (2004), 214–16

'Peter Judson Richards, Extraordinary Justice', *Law & History Review*, 26 (2007), 434

'Harold Berman, Soviet Law, From its Challenge to the West to Dissolution', *Emory Law Journal*, 57 (2008), 1451–3

'Bardo Fassbender, Studien zur auswärtigen Gewalt und zur Völkerrechtssubjektivität bundesstaatlicher Teilstaaten in Europa', *AJIL* 102 (2008), 211–12

'Susan Marks (ed.), International Law on the Left. Re-Examining Marxist Legacies', *AJIL*, 103 (2009), 178–80

Tributes

'Leo Gross (1903–90)', *AJIL*, 85 (1991), 149–50

'Louis Loss', *Harvard Law Review*, 111 (1998), 2144–6

'David Westfall', *Harvard Law Review*, 119 (2006), 956–8

'Louis Sohn', *Harvard Journal of International Law*, 48 (2007), 19–21